IMPORTANT:

HERE IS YOUR REGISTRATION CODE TO ACCESS
YOUR PREMIUM McGRAW-HILL ONLINE RESOURCES.

For key premium online resources you need THIS CODE to gain access. Once the code is entered, you will be able to use the Web resources for the length of your course.

If your course is using **WebCT** or **Blackboard**, you'll be able to use this code to access the McGraw-Hill content within your instructor's online course.

Access is provided if you have purchased a new book. If the registration code is missing from this book, the registration screen on our Website, and within your WebCT or Blackboard course, will tell you how to obtain your new code.

Registering for McGraw-Hill Online Resources

To gain access to your McGraw-Hill web resources simply follow the steps below:

1. USE YOUR WEB BROWSER TO GO TO: **www.mhhe.com/rothwell2**
2. CLICK ON **FIRST TIME USER**.
3. ENTER THE REGISTRATION CODE* PRINTED ON THE TEAR-OFF BOOKMARK ON THE RIGHT.
4. AFTER YOU HAVE ENTERED YOUR REGISTRATION CODE, CLICK **REGISTER**.
5. FOLLOW THE INSTRUCTIONS TO SET-UP YOUR PERSONAL UserID AND PASSWORD.
6. WRITE YOUR UserID AND PASSWORD DOWN FOR FUTURE REFERENCE. KEEP IT IN A SAFE PLACE.

TO GAIN ACCESS to the McGraw-Hill content in your instructor's **WebCT** or **Blackboard** course simply log in to the course with the UserID and Password provided by your instructor. Enter the registration code exactly as it appears in the box to the right when prompted by the system. You will only need to use the code the first time you click on McGraw-Hill content.

Thank you, and welcome to your McGraw-Hill online Resources!

eucaryotes-82575683

REGISTRATION CODE

Mc Graw Hill **Higher Education**

* YOUR REGISTRATION CODE CAN BE USED ONLY ONCE TO ESTABLISH ACCESS. IT IS NOT TRANSFERABLE.

0-07-293502-2 T/A ROTHWELL: IN THE COMPANY OF OTHERS, 2/E

IN THE COMPANY OF OTHERS

An Introduction to Communication

Second Edition

J. Dan Rothwell

Cabrillo College

Boston   Burr Ridge, IL   Dubuque, IA   Madison, WI   New York   San Francisco   St. Louis
Bangkok   Bogotá   Caracas   Kuala Lumpur   Lisbon   London   Madrid   Mexico City
Milan   Montreal   New Delhi   Santiago   Seoul   Singapore   Sydney   Taipei   Toronto

DEDICATION:
To my family,
Marcy, Hilary, Geoff, Barrett, and Clare

Higher Education

IN THE COMPANY OF OTHERS: AN INTRODUCTION TO COMMUNICATION
Published by McGraw-Hill, a business unit of The McGraw-Hill Companies, Inc.,
1221 Avenue of the Americas, New York, NY, 10020. Copyright (2004, 2000, by
The McGraw-Hill Companies, Inc. All rights reserved. No part of this publication may be
reproduced or distributed in any form or by any means, or stored in a database or retrieval
system, without the prior written consent of The McGraw-Hill Companies, Inc.,
including, but not limited to, in any network or other electronic storage or transmission,
or broadcast for distance learning.
Some ancillaries, including electronic and print components, may not be available to customers
outside the United States.
This book is printed on acid-free paper.

1 2 3 4 5 6 7 8 9 0 DOW/DOW 0 9 8 7 6 5 4 3

ISBN 0-7674-3009-3

Publisher: *Phillip A. Butcher*
Senior sponsoring editor: *Nanette Giles*
Developmental editor: *Pamela Gordon*
Marketing manager: *Leslie Oberhuber*
Producer, Media technology: *Jessica Bodie*
Project manager: *Ruth Smith*
Production supervisor: *Janean Utley*
Lead designer: *Jean M. Mailander*
Associate supplement producer: *Kathleen Boylan*
Manager, Photo research: *Brian J. Pecko*
Art manager: *Robin K. Mouat*
Art director: *Jeanne Schreiber*
Permissions: *Marty Granahan*
Cover design: *Joan Greenfield*
Cover photos: *Top: © BobDaemmrich/The Image Works;*
    Middle left: © Peter Beck/Corbis; Middle: © Mark Richards/PhotoEdit;
    Middle right: Cory Sorensen/Corbis; Bottom: © Bill Aron/PhotoEdit
Interior design: *Ellen Pettengell/Jean Mailander*
Typeface: *9.5/12 Palatino*
Compositor: *GAC Indianapolis*
Printer: *R.R. Donnelley and Sons Inc.*

Library of Congress Control Number: 2003107392

w.mhhe.com

BRIEF CONTENTS

CONTENTS

Part One *Fundamentals of Communication* 1

PREFACE

Second Edition Overview

A cosmetic face-lift of a successful textbook doesn't justify the considerable expenditure we ask our students to make when purchasing a revised edition. Consequently, although a glance at the Table of Contents might indicate that little has changed in this second edition, substantial revisions and improvements in fact have been made. These include:

1. A new chapter on communication climate (Chapter 2) was added to address more thoroughly the benefits of cooperative communication patterns and to provide relevant skills training earlier in the text.
2. All chapters have been refined, some significantly, to avoid overwhelming the student reader with too much information for a one-term course. (For instructors who are interested in a customized edition, with even fewer chapters, your local McGraw-Hill publishing representative is prepared to assist.)
3. Chapter 9, Technology and Communication Competence, has been substantially rewritten and updated to address the rapid changes in communication technologies over just the past few years. The chapter has been moved to Part One to reflect the profound influence of communication technologies on contemporary personal and social relationships. Additional references to technology appear throughout the book.
4. New *Sharper Focus* sidebars such as "Cell Phone Etiquette" and "Netiquette" and *Focus on Controversy* sidebars such as "The Monster Study: The Ethics and the Power of Mislabeling" and "Gender and Relationship Violence" have been developed, and previous ones have been updated.
5. Hundreds of new studies and research references have been added. This brings the book total to more than 1,300 references, of which the majority are recent.
6. Coverage of ethical communication has been expanded significantly. The NCA ethical guidelines are integrated into the communication competence model provided in Chapter 1 and are applied appropriately throughout the text.
7. Coverage of how to use the Internet to research speech topics has been expanded and updated (Chapter 15).
8. Gender and culture have been thoroughly integrated into the text even more substantially than in the first edition.
9. Hundreds of new examples, stories, jokes, and anecdotes have been added to make the content current and to engage the reader.
10. Keeping visual learners in mind, the visual program has been edited and expanded to include new photos, cartoons, and graphics.

11. I recognize that students rarely act on suggestions for additional reading material since perusing the textbook is a major undertaking. Thus, I have suggested credible readings from popular publications, which students might find enticing, and purposely have avoided recommending esoteric journal articles and academic tomes.

12. A new learning tool entitled *Film School* identifies carefully selected movies on video/DVD that illustrate key concepts for each chapter. Instead of doing the work for students by analyzing each film and applying it to chapter material, students are asked to answer critical thinking questions about each film.

13. Quizzes without Consequences (short practice tests) can be accessed by logging on to the Web site for this text: www.mhhe.com/rothwell2

For those who are unfamiliar with the first edition of *In the Company of Others*, the primary features that distinguish it from other human communication textbooks are provided in the next section.

Features

While covering all the standard topics in substantial detail, and remaining faithful to the core material almost all instructors agree is essential to the basic communication course, *In the Company of Others* also is unique in significant ways. Here are the main distinguishing features.

Cooperation: A Recurring Theme

One contribution of great potential for the communication discipline is that not only can we discuss cooperation theoretically, but we can also provide specific, concrete advice on how to structure human transactions so that cooperation can become a reality. Many textbooks, not only in the communication discipline, pay lip service to the need for human cooperation, but they are curiously devoid of informed suggestions about how to make it happen. This does little more than frustrate students who are looking for concrete ideas and specific advice to help them work together with others. *In the Company of Others* thoroughly addresses the issue of cooperation in interpersonal relationships, in group transactions, even in public speaking. This book is based on the assumption that cooperation should be embraced, nurtured, and cultivated. The addition of Chapter 2, Communication Climates, to the second edition expands on this theme. Material on defensive versus supportive communication has been moved from Chapter 10 and incorporated in this new early chapter so students can begin to develop the important supportive, cooperative communication skills early in the term. Chapter 2 also features a new discussion of connecting bids, a process that research shows can save relationships from deterioration or demise.

Communication Competence Model: A Foundation for Students

The communication competence model is one of our discipline's unique contributions to understanding and improving human behavior. One of the premises of this book is that communication competence, whether in the arena of interpersonal, small group, public speaking, or communication technology, is critical to student success and achievement. The five components of the model—knowledge, skill, sensitivity, commitment, and ethics—highlight the complexity of the communication process and provide direction and guidance for students. The communication competence model is fully and systematically integrated throughout the text, not merely discussed in the first chapter, then dropped entirely or given passing mention in later chapters. Most topics and issues in the text, including perception of self and others, intercultural communication, language use, listening, transacting power, managing conflict, and using communication technologies are analyzed from the model's perspective.

Integration of Gender and Culture

Gender and culture are important themes because we live in a world of increasing diversity. *In the Company of Others* treats gender and culture as integral parts of the overall discussion of communication. Gender receives special attention early in the text in Chapter 3, and culture is the subject of Chapter 4. These two chapters form the basis for gender and culture coverage in almost every chapter. Topics related to gender and culture include: cultural differences in perception and nonverbal meanings, the role of gender and culture in powerful/powerless language, cross-cultural friendships and romantic relationships, gender and cultural bias in the workplace, the effects of communication technologies on cultural transactions, and many others.

Emphasis on Power

Power is inherent in every human transaction, and the communication discipline has many valuable insights to offer on this important subject. This text is unique in how it treats power as a central variable within all communication. Chapter 8 gives special focus to the subject of power in relationships, and later chapters include additional discussions and applications. Such topics as the effects of power imbalances in relationships, sexual harassment in the workplace, sources of personal power, strategies for transacting power competently and cooperatively, and ways to empower ourselves and others are addressed.

Focus on Critical Thinking

Asking students to think critically and to determine which ideas and conclusions make more sense than others may strike some as promoting closed-mindedness. "Shouldn't all ideas be given an equal hearing?" Chapter 7 explores skepticism and the probability model like no other textbook, discussing the issue of open- and closed-mindedness in the process. The point is made that open-minded communication follows where evidence and reasoning leads us, and that closed-minded communication accepts or rejects an idea or conclusion despite the evidence and reasoning. The chapter provides criteria for evaluating evidence and reasoning to help students sort out the sensible from the not-so-sensible ideas and conclusions while they listen to the messages of others. Chapters 16, 17, and 18 offer further coverage of critical thinking, with a focus on using sound reasoning and concrete evidence to build both informative and persuasive speeches. Finally, the "Focus on Controversy" sidebars are designed specifically to encourage critical thinking about complex issues.

Focus on Controversy Boxes

Communication theory separated from the realities of a complex and troubling world can seem sadly irrelevant to students faced with vexing problems. Addressing important controversies directly can provide significant opportunities for student learning. The "Focus on Controversy" sidebars present current, controversial issues. The aim is to show students how to weigh evidence and draw conclusions supported by research. Examples include:

> The Ethics of Hypercompetitiveness,
> Excessive Self-Esteem,
> Gender and Relationship Violence,
> Verbal Obscenity,
> Crying in the Workplace,
> The Silencing of Female Public Speakers,
> The Ethics of Deleting Presidential Verbal Gaffes, and
> Plagiarism of Public Speeches.

Every controversy receives a balanced treatment, with conclusions drawn and thought-provoking questions posed. Treatment of relevant controversies are certain to spark interesting discussion in the classroom and, more importantly, trigger critical thinking.

A Fresh Look at Communication Technologies

No one can doubt the enormous impact communication technologies are having on our lives. How we cope with these technologies and the huge changes that they bring to our lives is a vital issue. Chapter 9 addresses the trends and issues associated with these changes. Students should learn not only how to evaluate the accuracy of information and the credibility of sources but also how to handle the sheer volume of information that technology makes available. The chapter gives students concrete suggestions for coping with information overload and balancing their real lives and face-to-face relationships with their time in the virtual worlds of the Internet and the World Wide Web. Advice is also provided on cell phone and e-mail etiquette.

Extensive Treatment of Speech Anxiety and Attention Strategies

In the Company of Others provides the most extensive treatment of speech anxiety of any human communication textbook. It is the most important concern on most students' minds when they are told that giving speeches will be a required activity in class. Also, no hybrid textbook on communication covers attention strategies as thoroughly as *In the Company of Others*. Let's face facts: no one wants to listen to boring speeches and no one wants to present a speech that induces audience catatonia. Attention strategies are a vital part of an effective speech.

Carefully Composed Model Speeches

A major concern I had with general communication textbooks before I wrote *In the Company of Others* was that models for informative and persuasive speeches only partially followed advice offered in the text I used. Often the model speech contradicted advice provided in the main text. Model informative and persuasive speeches have been carefully composed to illustrate the advice offered in the text.

Readability

Samuel Johnson's comment, "What is written without effort is in general read without pleasure" guided the writing of this textbook. Readability is a vital concern to me. Textbooks should not induce a coma, although it is understandable why some might cause eyelids to slam shut. Textbooks are not meant to read like the latest Stephen King novel, but they don't need to be a horror by reading like instructions for programming your VCR. Similarly, an overly dense, theoretical text written in technical language can impede clarity and understanding for students and create the kind of frustration many people experience when reading manuals for using the latest computer software. Consequently, obvious and not-so-obvious places have been searched to provide the precise example, the amusing illustration, the poignant event, and the dramatic instance to engage readers, enhance enjoyment, and improve clarity. Colorful language and lively metaphors have been sprinkled throughout the text to provide vividness. Additionally, a recurring segment called "Sharper Focus" uses extended examples to illustrate important points and ignite student interest. Sample topics include stereotyping of Asian students, cultural differences in perception of the "nanny trial," dealing with a Bill Gates temper tantrum, challenging the "glass ceiling" in the workplace, teamwork and the U.S. women's Olympic basketball team, stage fright among great speakers and performers, and China and the Internet. (Questions do not appear at the end of "Sharper Focus" sidebars as they do in FOC sidebars because the information presented is straightforward and offered to expand on a concept or idea, not to challenge a point of view or idea.)

Finally, the readability of *In the Company of Others* has been enhanced by extensive classroom testing of the book. Hundreds of students offered constructive comments, which were used to improve the readability of the final product. If this textbook is successful in gaining and maintaining the interest of readers, I owe a debt to those students who provided helpful advice.

Organization of the Text

In the Company of Others is divided into four parts. Part One, Fundamentals of Communication, lays the groundwork for the other three parts. Chapters 1 through 9 discuss the communication competence model, establishing a constructive communication climate, the role of perception in human transactions, intercultural communication, the use and misuse of language, nonverbal communication, the listening process, power in communication transactions, and the influence of communication technologies on human transactions. Each of these subjects crosses into every arena of communication. These arenas are treated in Parts Two through Four.

Part Two, Interpersonal Communication, discusses interpersonal dialectics, strategies for making relationships work, and conflict management techniques (Chapters 10–11). Part Three, Group Communication, explains the anatomy of small groups, teambuilding, and teamwork in groups and organizations (Chapters 12–13). Part Four, Public Speaking, addresses beginning the public speaking process, developing a speech, presenting the speech to an audience, and constructing an effective informative or persuasive speech (Chapters 14–18).

Supplements

In the Company of Others is accompanied by a comprehensive package of instructor resources that specifically address the challenges of teaching and managing the basic communication course. Please consult your local McGraw-Hill representative for more information on any of the supplements.

For the Student

The Student CD-ROM includes relevant videos, helpful practice quizzes, unique activities and more. Icons in the text margins indicate content that is supported by the CD-ROM. All new copies of *In the Company of Others* include the Student CD-ROM. However, it is available for purchase separately.

- *Video Clips*—Offer students over 60 minutes of footage that illustrates communication concepts and fundamentals. Sample student speeches help novice speakers visualize classroom presentations.
- *Communication Competence Activities*—Engage students in chapter-related activities that integrate the strategies of the Communication Competence Model presented throughout the text.
- *Quizzes Without Consequences*—Allow students to take practice tests for each chapter in the text and feature multiple choice and true/false questions.
- *Topic Helper*—Lists hundreds of sample topics for speeches.
- *Checklist for Preparing and Delivering a Speech*—Provides a handy list of steps to help students manage and prepare their speeches.
- *Outline Tutor*—Helps students organize their materials by providing a computerized form for creating conventional outlines.
- *Audio Flashcards*—Allow students to review key terms aurally and visually and improve comprehension of key chapter concepts.
- *PowerPoint Tutorial*—Explains basic steps for creating an effective PowerPoint-assisted presentation.
- *Bibliography Formats*—Illustrates how to cite a broad range of sources with examples from two of the most popular style guidelines: Modern Language Association (MLA) and American Psychological Association (APA).
- *Internet Primer*—Guides students on the basics of computer and Internet usage.
- *Guide to Electronic Research*—Offers an in-depth look at using a computer and the Internet as a research tool.

The Online Learning Center (www.mhhe.com/rothwell2)—This free, web-based, student supplement features helpful tools for class and exam preparation, interactive exercises related to communication competence, and links to relevant Internet Web sites. Designed specifically to complement each text chapter, the Online Learning Center offers:

- *Communication Competence Activities*—Designed to engage students in the strategies of the Communication Competence Model that is integrated throughout the text.

- *Chapter Objectives, Outlines, and Summaries*—Intended to give students sign-posts for understanding and recognizing key chapter content while participating in class and while studying on their own or in groups.
- *Quizzes Without Consequences*—Allow students to take practice multiple choice and true/false tests for each chapter.
- *Glossary*—Provides easy access to key terms while using the Online Learning Center.
- *Crossword Puzzles*—Allow students to test their recall of key concepts.
- *General Web links*—Offer relevant chapter-by-chapter links for further research.
- *Worksheets*—Offer activities and projects that are based on chapter content.

PowerWeb—This resource is offered free with the purchase of a new copy of the text. It is available by logging onto the Student's Online Learning Center and by using the registration code printed on the PowerWeb postcard bound directly into *In the Company of Others*. PowerWeb helps students conduct online research by providing access to high quality academic sources. PowerWeb is a password-protected site that provides students with three outlets for accessing primary source material: first, through a library of course-specific, peer-reviewed articles from the scholarly and popular press, structured according to the typical basic course syllabus; second, through weekly updates that reflect key concepts and themes in the basic course; and third, through Northern Lights, a search engine that filters the Internet for reliable source material. For further information about PowerWeb, visit www.dushkin.com/powerweb/pwwt1.mhtml.

For the Instructor

A wide range of useful instructor resources is available on the Instructor's Resource CD-ROM and via the Online Learning Center at www.mhhe.com/rothwell2. (Please note, for reasons of security, the test bank is not posted on the Online Learning Center)

- *Chapter Outlines*—Offer comprehensive reviews of chapter material for easy reference and course design.
- *Lecture Suggestions and Exercises*—Provide ideas and activities for classroom discussion, lectures, and group work.
- *Web sites For Further Information*—Offers addresses and descriptions of sites recommended for student research and instructor resources.
- *Recommended Films*—Provides an annotated list of helpful films for classroom use.
- *Transparency Masters*—Provide presentation materials for professors who want to focus on those sections in the text that deliver specific advice and skill building concerning communication competence.
- *A Complete Test Bank*—Offers numerous multiple choice and true/false questions along with suggestions on how to set up cooperative testing. The Test Bank is available on the Instructor's Resource CD-ROM as an easy-to-use computerized test bank program that is compatible to both Windows and Macintosh computers or as a basic Word document.
- *Resource Integrator*—Organizes all print and media resources by learning objective so that instructors can tailor the Rothwell learning system to their

courses and develop syllabi that indicate not only relevant content in the book but also across the whole *In The Company of Others* package: text, CD-ROM, and Online Learning Center.
- *PowerPoint Lecture Slides*—Provide professionally developed chapter-by-chapter presentation visual aids.

PageOut: The Course Web site Development Center—All online content for the text is supported by WebCT, Blackboard, eCollege.com, and other course management systems. Additionally, McGraw-Hill's PageOut service is available to get professors and their courses up and running online in a matter of hours, at no cost. PageOut was designed for instructors who are just beginning to explore Web options. Even a novice computer user can create a course Web site with a template provided by McGraw-Hill (no programming knowledge necessary). To learn more about PageOut, visit www.mhhe.com/pageout.

Acknowledgments

Since the initial publication of *In the Company of Others* much has changed, not the least of which is that Mayfield, publisher of the first edition, was acquired by McGraw-Hill. Executive editor Nanette Kauffman made the transition from Mayfield to McGraw-Hill an amazingly smooth one for me. She deserves my great gratitude for believing that *In the Company of Others* has the potential to be a market-leading textbook and then providing the resources to support this belief. She also proved to be a most pleasant and capable editor at every stage of this revision.

Pam Gordon, my developmental editor, was a joy to work with and a true professional. Through a convergence of unforeseen circumstances, I found myself simultaneously revising two different textbooks, each for a different publisher. Pam managed to keep me on track, gently pointed out to me when I had confused one book for another, and helped me keep my sanity throughout this challenging time. Her attention to detail was astounding.

Brian Pecko, photo researcher extraordinaire, devoted hours to finding elusive photographs from not always helpful sources. Although we were disappointed to find that some photographs were not available, Brian managed to locate alternatives that were as good, even better in some instances. I thank him for his commitment to this project and his considerable skill in translating my occasionally vague description of a photographic idea into a concrete image.

I owe a special debt to all reviewers for your very helpful critiques:

Carlos Galvan Aleman, James Madison University
Lori J.N. Charron, Concordia College
George Denger, Lake Superior State University
Lisa A. Flores, University of Utah
Trudy L. Hanson, West Texas A & M University
Tina M. Harris, University of Georgia
Stephen A. King, Delta State University
Gerianne Merrigan, San Francisco State University
Donna A. Oti, Bowie State University
Thomas E. Ruddick, Edison Community College
Patrick A. Sciarra, College of DuPage.

I was often impressed by your insights and the eloquence and passion with which you expressed your wisdom.

I also cannot resist commenting specifically on Carlos Aleman's more than 65-page final review. In addition to providing numerous useful ideas and trenchant comments, I was simply impressed by the sheer magnitude of the effort. I hope McGraw-Hill provided appropriate compensation. As appreciative as I am for Professor Aleman's massive critique, I am thankful that the other reviewers didn't decide to do likewise. It would have been similar to reading *War and Peace*.

To all the production staff who worked on this revision—Jessica Bodie, Media Producer; Ruth Smith, Project Manager; Janean Utley, Production Supervisor; Jean Mailander, Designer; Kathleen Boylan, Supplement Producer; Robin Mouat, Art Editor; and Marty Granahan, Permissions Editor—I offer a heartfelt thank you.

Finally, to my wife, Marcy, a special thanks is due. She was unflagging in her support of me throughout this revision. Her support, love, and understanding during the hundreds of hours I spent isolated in my home office sustained me through many moments of frustration.

A VISUAL PREVIEW OF
In the Company of Others, SECOND EDITION

Designed to provide an overview of the field of human communication, *In the Company of Others* develops cooperation and competence as recurring themes and offers strategies for communicating with others in more effective ways. This new edition includes expanded coverage of the communication climate, the rapid changes in technological communication, organizational communication, ethics, gender, and culture.

Icons throughout the book prompt readers to use corresponding features on the exciting student CD-ROM where students will find a variety of learning tools that can be used both in and outside of the classroom. With the CD-ROM, students can view video clips, take practice quizzes, and engage in unique communication competence activities developed by Dan Rothwell and Charlotte Morrison. Other components of the CD-ROM include outlining software, a PowerPoint tutorial, a topic helper, bibliography formats, and more.

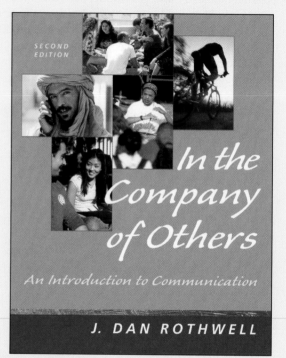

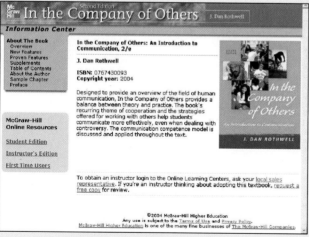

To support and extend the content of the text, the Online Learning Center, a text-specific Web site, offers students and instructors an array of useful resources such as chapter quizzes, Web links, interactive activities, vocabulary-enhancing crossword puzzles, and PowerPoint slides at www.mhhe.com/rothwell2. All of these resources were designed to provide students with opportunities to practice and to help them excel in the course.

PowerWeb, a password-protected, course-specific Website is set up for *In the Company of Others.* Accessible from a link on the Rothwell Online Learning Center, PowerWeb helps students with online research by directing them to more than 6,000 high-quality academic sources. An access card with information about setting up a password to PowerWeb is bound into the text.

TEACHING STUDENTS THE FUNDAMENTALS OF
COMMUNICATING COMPETENTLY

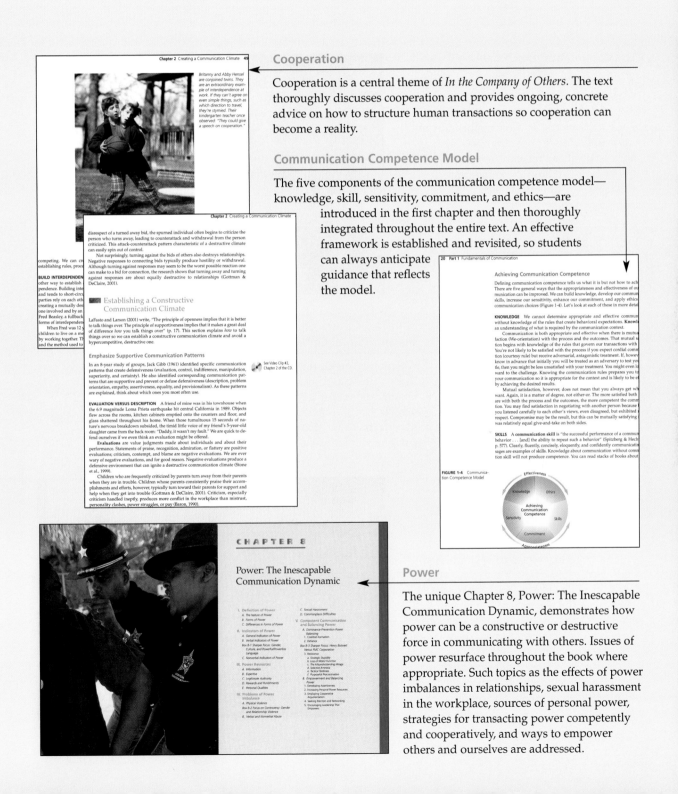

Cooperation

Cooperation is a central theme of *In the Company of Others*. The text thoroughly discusses cooperation and provides ongoing, concrete advice on how to structure human transactions so cooperation can become a reality.

Communication Competence Model

The five components of the communication competence model—knowledge, skill, sensitivity, commitment, and ethics—are introduced in the first chapter and then thoroughly integrated throughout the entire text. An effective framework is established and revisited, so students can always anticipate guidance that reflects the model.

Power

The unique Chapter 8, Power: The Inescapable Communication Dynamic, demonstrates how power can be a constructive or destructive force in communicating with others. Issues of power resurface throughout the book where appropriate. Such topics as the effects of power imbalances in relationships, sexual harassment in the workplace, sources of personal power, strategies for transacting power competently and cooperatively, and ways to empower others and ourselves are addressed.

OFFERING IMPORTANT, UNIQUE CONTENT AND
WAYS OF SEEING

The Communication Climate

A new Chapter 2, Creating a Communication Climate, offers useful insights and advice on skill building early in the text. This chapter gives students the time and opportunity to learn and practice important skills, such as how to solicit and respond to connecting bids from others and how to communicate supportively rather than defensively.

Chapter 13 Teambuilding and Teamwork in Small Groups and

Third, the team can assign the devil's advocate role to a specific member. This can combat the excessive concurrence seeking typical of groups that slide into groupthink. The devil's advocate challenges any decision the group is likely to make to test the ideas. Fourth, the team can set up a "second chance" meeting in which members can reconsider a preliminary decision. This allows team members to reflect on any proposal and avoid making impulsive decisions.

Teams in Organizations

Organizations in the United States have changed markedly in the last decade or so. The trend has moved from "hierarchical, function-based structures to horizontal, integrated workplaces organized around empowered individuals and self-directed work teams" (Graham & LeBaron, 1994, p. xi). This trend is discussed in this section. To understand the trend, you must know some basics about traditional organizational structure in the United States. Then the move toward "flattening the hierarchy" with self-managed teams will be explained.

Traditional Structure of Organizations

What began as a very small business in 1937 with a half-dozen employees grew into 30,000 establishments worldwide employing about 1 million workers, exceeding any other American organization, public or private. One of every eight workers in America has at some time been employed by this organization (Schlosser, 2002). Can you guess what it is? If you guessed McDonald's you are correct.

Small groups sometimes grow into large organizations, and with the transition come changes in structure. Small groups typically operate with an informal structure. A meeting of a three-person group certainly doesn't require formal communication rules such as Robert's Rules of Order. Communication is usually conducted informally as conversation rather than formally as public presentations. Procedures for managing conflict also remain informal. There is little need for formal grievance procedures. The three group members can usually handle their differences through discussion and a meeting. They also can easily share power.

As groups increase in size, complexity increases. Thus, when small groups become large groups and eventually organizations, structure typically becomes more formal to cope with increased complexity. Individuals receive formal titles with written job descriptions. Power is distributed unevenly. Those with the most prestigious titles typically are accorded the most status and decision-making power. The larger the organization, the more likely it is that the structure will become **hierarchical**, meaning that members of the organization will be rank ordered. This pyramid of power has those at the top—the CEOs, presidents, and vice-presidents—wielding the most power, with middle managers coming next, followed by the "worker bees" or low-level employees.

Organizational Communication

A section on organizational communication appears in the Teambuilding and Teamwork in Small Groups and Organizations chapter (Chapter 13). The coverage of organizational communication naturally extends from the material on teams since organizations are a primary environment for teams.

Technology

Chapter 9, Technology and Communication Competence, provides a fresh, comprehensive look at the influence of rapidly changing communication technologies on human relationships and transactions. The chapter gives students important advice on cell phone and e-mail etiquette. It also makes suggestions for coping with information overload and balancing students' face-to-face relationships with their mediated communication transactions.

PROVIDING THOROUGH COVERAGE OF GENDER, CULTURE, AND ETHICS

Gender and Culture

Gender and culture are integrated in the text substantially and are framed so the content can directly help students cope with their diverse worlds. The text treats gender and culture as natural, integral parts of the overall discussion of communication. The subjects are given special early attention in Chapter 3, Perception of Self and Others, and Chapter 4, Intercultural Communication. With these two chapters as a foundation for considerations of gender and culture, further coverage appears in almost every other chapter in the text.

Part 1 Fundamentals of Communication

liban man in hanistan beats women a steel whip for a or infraction of rules for ring the burka. Avoid- ethnocentrism does not n that we have to pt brutal treatment omen.

world, however, that are condoned within the culture but contradict universal human rights. Female genital mutilation (female circumcision), foot binding of women, suttee (the practice of widows joining their dead husbands on the funeral pyre even if they protest), denial of education and political participation to women, the selling of children, slavery, and myriad other practices are behaviors that some cultures condone.

The United Nation's Universal Declaration of Human Rights declares that every human being has certain basic rights that include the right to life, liberty, security, freedom of speech and belief, equal protection under the law, participation in the political process, a decent standard of living, necessary social services, and education. Harrison (2000) notes, "The vast majority of the planet's people would agree with the following assertions:

Life is better than death.
Health is better than sickness.
Liberty is better than slavery.
Prosperity is better than poverty.
Education is better than ignorance.
Justice is better than injustice (p. xxvi).

Customs, practices, and communication behaviors that do not dehumanize people should not be rejected as inferior simply because they are different from our own cultural ways of operating. Sexism, racism, homophobia, and all the "isms"

Chapter 4 Interc

cultural groups be treated with respect and as equals" (p. 609). Multiculturalism assumes universal human rights. As Moghaddam (1998) explains,

> In order for multiculturalism to work, there must be certain universal rules to allow communication and understanding to take place. For example, without mutual respect and orderly turn taking, there can be no meaningful dialogue. Furthermore, in a situation in which universal rules of justice are not accepted, the weak will necessarily suffer because they cannot use the law to protect their interests (p. 506).

Multiculturalism incorporates the five ethical standards discussed in Chapter 1—respect, honesty, fairness, choice, and responsibility. To be a competent intercultural communicator, you must accept cultural diversity and eschew ethnocentrism, but always you must be guided by the ethical standards of the competent communicator. Inhumane behavior that degrades and diminishes others cannot be accepted with the justification, "That's just the way they do things in their culture." Diversity is part of the colorful tapestry of humankind, but inhumanity is a blight on any culture's fabric.

Misattribution

Attribution, or the causes assigned to people's behavior, and problems associated with attribution were discussed in Chapter 3. Similar attribution problems occur during intercultural communication. What is appropriate and expected communication in your own culture may be perceived as rude, arrogant, or uncivilized by individuals from other cultures. This is called **misattribution,** or "an attribution about the reason for an event given by a foreigner which differs from that typically given by a member of the host culture" (Smith & Bond, 1994, p. 177).

Intercultural communication is fraught with uncertainty and anxiety. When communicating with individuals from distinctly different cultures, we search for causes of their behavior, especially if the behavior is unexpected or seems odd by our culture's standards. We do this to reduce the uncertainty in intercultural encounters. Unfortunately, we often do not sufficiently understand the rules, norms, customs, and common practices of other cultures, so our attributions are made based on what makes sense and is expected in our culture. Individuals are too late for appointments or too early, are too talkative or too quiet, express their anger too openly or hide their anger too much, stand too close or too far apart when conversing, look too directly at the other person or look down or away too often. Each of these communication behaviors can receive a positive or negative attribution. The principal factor influencing the attribution is the culture of the observer. For instance, looking down when conversing with another person could be interpreted as a sign of weakness or intimidation (negative personal attribution) in American culture. The same behavior, however, when viewed by a member of an Asian culture, might be interpreted as an indication of respect and politeness (positive personal attribution). Conversely, looking directly at a speaker will likely be interpreted as a sign of confidence in the tates but an indicator of rudeness in Asian cultures.
ibutions in individualist and collectivist cultures are likely to be markedly , making misattribution commonplace. Individualist cultures typically are to characteristics of a person (trait causes) that explain behavior. Collec tures are typically sensitive to the context (situational causes). A conversa veen two people, one from an individualist and the other from a collectivist

Chapter 3 Perception of Self and

Mars and Venus, or do we live in more neighborly, closely associated worlds akin to "South Dakota and North Dakota" (Dindia, 1997)? The "truth is out there," and we're going to pursue it here.

Before beginning this discussion of gender and perception, let's first differentiate sex from gender (Talbot, 1998). **Sex** is biology (female-male); it is genes, gonads, and hormones. One sex difference is that a male can impregnate a female, and a female can become pregnant. It doesn't work in the reverse. **Gender** is socially constructed (feminine-masculine); it is learned role characteristics and behavior derived from communicating with others. There are norms and rules established in every culture that define what it is to be feminine or masculine.

Gender Differences in Communication

"Why does it take 1 million sperm to fertilize one egg? The sperm won't stop to ask for directions." "When do women stop advocating equality? When they have to kill large, hairy spiders." "How do you impress a woman? Compliment her, cuddle her, caress her, love her, listen to her, support her, and spend money on her. How do you impress a man? Show up naked. Bring beer."

What is your reaction to these "jokes" found on several Internet sites? Do you find them funny? Offensive? (These are tame examples compared to the truly crude and tasteless jokes on several Web sites.) Do you agree with the assumption expressed in these jokes that men and women act and communicate very differently? Let's look at the evidence.

SMALL DIFFERENCES Some researchers don't think gender differences in communication are significant. One review of a large number of studies found, in aggregate, that men and women are 99% similar in their communication and only 1% different (Canary and Hause, 1993). Other researchers disagree (Mulac, 1998; Wood in Wood & Dindia, 1998).

Assuming for the moment that gender differences in communication are small, please note that *even small differences can produce large effects* (Eagley, 1995). Chimpanzees and humans, for example, are almost 99% similar in chromosomes; yet consider the enormous differences in performance and behavior (not even counting looks). Differences in competitiveness between men and women are small overall, but there are more than twice as many hypercompetitive men (Gayle et al., 1994). Extreme competitive behavior seen so much more often in men can create the stereotype that men are far more competitive as a group than women (Allen, 1998). One computer simulation study of organizational hiring practices found that, when gender accounted for a mere 1% difference in performance ratings that favored men over women, 65% of the highest-level positions in the organization were filled by men (Martell et al., 1996, p. 158).

LARGE DIFFERENCES Although most gender differences in communication are small, there are many large differences. For example, women rely more on conversation to build and maintain intimacy with friends and romantic partners, while men rely more on shared activities and doing things for others; women are better at inferring accurate meanings from face, body, and vocal nonverbal channels; women are more inclined to talk about their relationships than men; and women are greater caregivers than men (Wood & Dindia, 1998). In addition, women smile much more

BOX 5-6 Focus on Controversy

The "Monster Study": Ethics and the Power of Mislabeling

In 1939, Wendell Johnson, a speech pathology professor at Iowa State University, embarked on a controversial experiment to determine the cause of stuttering (Dyer, 2001). A severe stutterer himself, Johnson theorized that labeling young children as stutterers when they stumble over words will not only worsen the affliction, but also could induce stuttering in normal speakers. This was a revolutionary idea that contradicted the prevailing

deteriorate after the experiment ceased. Tudor re
to the orphanage three times to try to reverse the
of the mislabeling and negative therapy but with
success. An investigative report by the *San Jose M*
News (Dyer, 2001) brought the experiment to the
nation's attention.
Defenders of the experiment argue that Johns
theory and the clear benefits of using positive no
ative therapy with stutterers helped millions of c
with this terrible problem. Detractors argue that
experiment was unethical. Children who had be
induced to stutter by the mislabeling and negati
apy were never told about the experiment, nor w
normal speakers in the study, until the *Mercury N*
began its investigation more than 60 years later.
the children never recovered. They were torment
other children, their school grades plummeted, t
esteem shriveled, and a few became withdrawn
even reclusive adults.
This mislabeling experiment fails all five ethic
ria: respect, honesty, fairness, choice, and respon
It treated these children with disrespect. Not eno
concern for their future welfare was demonstrate
though years later Mary Tudor lamented her par
tion in the study (Dyer, 2001). This was a dishon
with tragic consequences. Individuals' lives were
in some instances. The irresponsible lies told to t
children, their teachers, and the administrators o
orphanage were perpetuated for more than 60 ye
The children were never given a choice to partici
in the experiment. They didn't even know they w
being treated like lab rats. Following a three-part
in the *Mercury News*, Iowa State University apolo
calling the experiment "regrettable" and indefen
John Bernthal (2001), President of the American S
Language-Hearing Association, wrote to the pap
"The research described in this article cannot be
on theoretical, moral, or ethical grounds and rep
a serious error in judgment by the researcher" (p

Questions for Thought

1. The intentions of the experimenters were nobl help children with stuttering problems becom communicators. What effect does this have on assessment of the ethics of this study?
2. The power of mislabeling is clearly shown in study. Should this be a consideration in your ment of the ethics of this experiment?

Chapter 1 Communication Competence **23**

> channels, and media. Moreover, ethical communication enhances human worth and dignity by fostering truthfulness, fairness, responsibility, personal integrity, and respect for self and others. We believe that unethical communication threatens the quality of all communication and consequently the well-being of individuals and the society in which we live.

Ethics is a set of standards for judging the moral correctness of communication behavior. In its entirety, the NCA credo identifies five ethical standards to guide our communication with others:

1. *Respect*. "Some form of the Golden Rule is embraced by virtually all of the major religious and moral systems" (Jaksa & Pritchard, 1994, p. 101). Treating others as you would want to be treated is a central guiding ethical standard. Respect shows concern for others (We-orientation) not just concern for self (Me-orientation).
2. *Honesty*. Ethically responsible communicators try to avoid intentionally deceptive messages. Honesty is a cultural expectation. There is a "presumption against lying" (Bok, 1978, p. 32). All ethical systems condemn lying ("Lying Is Part," 1996). One poll found that honesty was the most prized attribute in a friend ("Lying in America," 1987).
3. *Fairness*. Prejudice has no place in the communication arena. Racism, sexism, homophobia, ageism, and all the other "isms" that plague the human spirit and divide nations and peoples would diminish if we applied the standard of fairness in our communication with diverse groups. Permitting some people to express their points of view but stifling others' expression of dissent is unfair. Fairness requires equal treatment.
4. *Choice*. Our communication should strive to allow people to make their own choices, free of coercion (Jaksa & Pritchard, 1994). Persuasion allows free choice among available options. Coercion forces choice without permitting individuals to think or act for themselves. "Choice must be intentional and voluntary. . . . A communicator's intention is a prime consideration in ethical judgment" (Jensen, 1997, p. 4). When a person is forced to lie or mistreat others, the actions are unintentional. In such a circumstance the person performing the unethical behavior is not culpable.
5. *Responsibility*. "People constantly struggle with the tension between rights and responsibilities, and conscientious people seek to balance the tensions in meaningful and fair ways. Individuals demand the right of free expression, but society demands that individual freedom not harm the larger community" (Jensen, 1997, p. 10). Responsibility means that ethical communication requires a We-orientation. Competent communicators must concern themselves with more than merely what works to achieve personal or group goals. A person may be quite effective at accomplishing individual goals (Me-orientation), but if these goals produce bad outcomes for others, their appropriateness must be questioned. We have a responsibility to consider the consequences of our communication on others.

www.mhhe.com/rothwell2

Go to the Online Learning Center for an "ETHICS Questionnaire"

In the abstract, these standards may seem straightforward and noncontroversial, but almost nothing in human communication is absolute and clear-cut. Human communication behavior is so complex that any list of standards for judging the ethics of communication, applied without exceptions, is bound to run into difficulty. In some cases two or more ethical standards may collide. Free choice, for example, collides with parents' responsibility when they insist that their children behave in

Ethics

Coverage of ethical communication has been expanded significantly in this edition. The NCA ethical guidelines are introduced in Chapter 1 and applied throughout the text.

FOSTERING CRITICAL THINKING
AND DISCOVERY

Critical Thinking

Students are asked to think critically throughout the text. Most notably Chapter 7, Listening to Others, provides criteria for evaluating the messages of others. Chapters 16, 17, and 18 also focus on using sound reasoning and concrete evidence to build both informative and persuasive speeches.

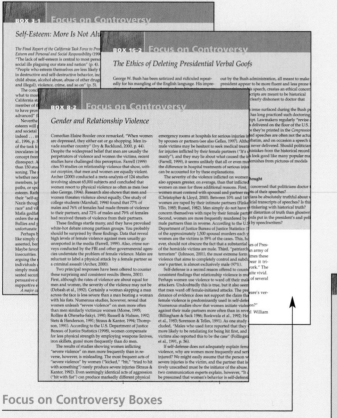

Focus on Controversy Boxes

Focus on Controversy boxes present current, controversial issues related to human communication and include questions for thought to show students how to think critically about evidence and draw conclusions supported by research.

Sharper Focus Boxes

Sharper Focus boxes provide students with the opportunity to explore in-depth examples that illustrate key concepts in the chapter.

FEATURING OUTSTANDING COVERAGE
OF PUBLIC SPEAKING

Speech Anxiety and Attention Strategies

The text provides extensive coverage of speech anxiety and attention strategies—two key areas of utmost concern to students.

Model Speeches

Carefully composed model speeches illustrate the guidelines suggested in the text.

Using the Internet

Coverage of how to use the Internet to conduct academically sound research and to generate reliable sources during the speech-making process is substantial and up to date.

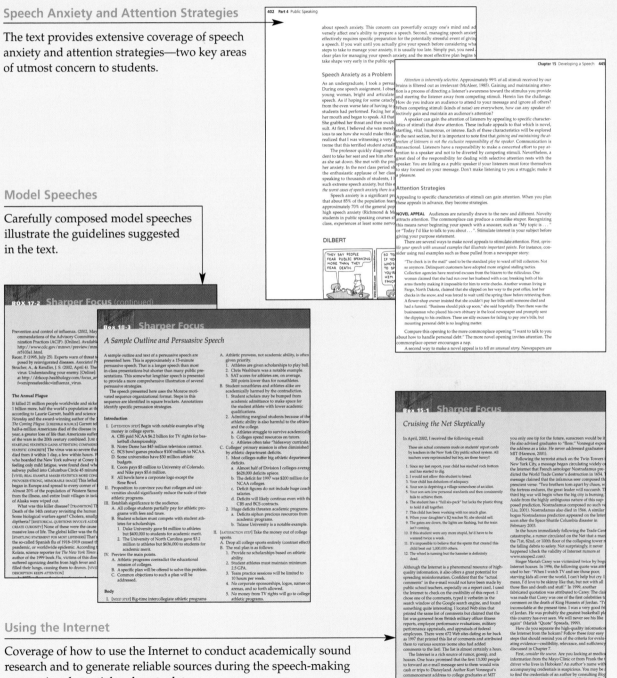

HELPING VARIOUS STYLES OF LEARNERS
SUCCEED WITH USEFUL STUDY TOOLS

Supporting Pedagogy

Chapter opening outlines, objectives, and purpose statements, along with chapter ending summaries, quizzes without consequences, and key terms help students master chapter content.

Additional Readings and Film School

Suggestions for additional reading offer selections from popular mass-market publications that students might find enticing and purposely avoid more esoteric journal articles and academic texts. A new end-of-chapter "Film School" feature identifies carefully selected movies on video/DVD that illustrate key concepts for each chapter and asks students to answer critical thinking questions about each film.

CHAPTER 7

Listening to Others

I. The Listening Process
   A. Comprehending
      Box 7-1 Sharper Focus: Mondegreens
   B. Retaining
   C. Responding
II. Specific Listening Problems
   A. Shift Response
   B. Competitive Interrupting
   C. Glazing Over
   D. Pseudolistening
      Box 7-2 Sharper Focus: Focused Attention
   E. Ambushing
   F. Content-Only Response
III. Competent Informational Listening
   A. Confirmation Bias
      Box 7-3 Focus on Controversy: Reliability of Children's Testimony Child Abuse Cases: Confirmation Bias in Action
   B. The Vividness Effect
IV. Competent Critical Listening
   A. Skepticism
   B. Probability Model
      Box 7-4 Focus on Controversy:

C. Criteria for Evaluating Reasoning and Evidence
   1. Credibility
      a. Questionable Statistic
      b. Biased Source
      c. Expert Quoted Out of Field of Expertise
   2. Relevance
      a. Irrelevant Statistic

In this regard, there are four objectives:
1. to define and explain the listening process,
2. to discuss several listening problems that impede competent communication,
3. to explore different kinds of listening and problems unique to each kind, and
4. to identify specific ways that you can become a competent listener.

The general thrust of this chapter can be summed up in the slogan of the Sperry Corporation: "Nothing new ever entered the mind through an open mouth."

The Listening Process

The International Listening Association adopted an official definition of listening. With slight modification, it defines **listening** as "the process of receiving, constructing [and reconstructing] meaning from, and responding to spoken and/or nonverbal messages" (Emmert, 1996, p. 2). This definition implicitly highlights listening as a dynamic, active process, not a passive activity. In the next several sections, we'll primary elements of listening: comprehend-

180 Part 1 Fundamentals of Communication

Summary

Nonverbal communication affects our communication with others in powerful ways, yet nonverbal communication is often ambiguous and difficult to interpret. Much of the advice on nonverbal communication offered in the popular media is incorrect or overstated because a single nonverbal cue is given too much emphasis. Specific advice on communicating competently has been offered for each of the numerous types of nonverbal communication (physical appearance, facial communication, gestures, touch, voice, space, and environment), but general...

Chapter 6 Nonverbal Communication: Sharing Meaning Without Words

Montagu, A. (1986). *Touching: The human significance of the skin.* New York: Harper & Row. This is the classic work on touch communication by an internationally renowned anthropologist.

Quizzes Without Consequences

Go to
www.mhhe
@ com/
/rothwell2

Film School

The Birdcage (1996). Comedy; R ★★★ ✓
A very amusing remake of *La Cage Aux Folles* about a gay couple "acting straight" to fool a conservative U.S. Senator. Analyze the main characters' nonverbal behavior, especially when Robin Williams attempts to teach Nathan Lane to act like a straight male. Are these merely stereotypic male behaviors or is there truth in the depiction?

Mrs. Doubtfire (1993). Comedy; PG-13 ★★★★
Robin Williams assumes the role of an Irish nanny to be near his children when he and his wife (Sally Field) split up. Does Williams get the "feminine" behaviors correct? Analyze the different types of nonverbal behavior exhibited by Mrs. Doubtfire. Are these merely stereotype feminine behaviors?

Quest for Fire (1982). Drama; R ★★★★✓
A very original film about humankind's initial attempts to make fire. Concentrate on the importance of nonverbal communication, especially since the "language" depicted in the movie is very limited. What are the limitations on nonverbal cues for communication?

Tootsie (1982). Comedy; PG ★★★★★
This is the classic "cross-dressing" film. Dustin Hoffman's portrayal of Dorothy Michaels, who is actually the out-of-work actor Michael Dorsey, was Oscar worthy. Why does Hoffman's portrayal seem genuine? Did he make any mistakes in his nonverbal portrayal of a middle-aged woman?

Key Terms

See Audio Flashcards study aid.

www.mhhe
@ com/
/rothwell2

See Crossword Puzzle study aid.

Suggested Readings

Chapter 9 Technology and Communication Competence 265

Doonesbury
G. B. TRUDEAU

© 19XX insert source line here.

Internet chat rooms to lure victims into face-to-face meetings. D... child abusers using online chat rooms to entice kids to meet face... 4,000 in the year 2001 (Camp-Flores, 2002). About 12% of t... strangers online follow up with offline in-person encounter... Christina Long met a 25-year-old man at a mall in Danbury, C... 2002. She was strangled to death by her chat-room partner.

COMBATING MISINFORMATION So what can you do about th... formation? What you can't do reasonably is slow the down the tr... mation, censor the Internet, or reduce competition in the prod... Those are structural changes that bump against constitutional... smarter choice. The answer lies in becoming a more competent... of information.

Seek Credible Sources of Information Ignore Web sites from c... and obvious hate groups. Follow advice provided in Chapter... Net Skeptically." Pay no attention to tabloid stories (except pe... unless they have been verified by more reputable news sources...

Question the Reliability of Any Unidentified Sources Repu... ingly use such dubious sources as "administrative sources"...

FIGURE 8-1 Power Struggle Dynamic
FIGURE 8-2 Empowerment—and Enhancing Capabilities

ABSOLUTELY NOTHING
NEXT 22 MILES

Illustrations

Many photos, cartoons, and graphics provide an outstanding visual program that contributes to understanding and invites reader interest.

ENGAGING READERS WITH AN INTERESTING, ACCESSIBLE, AND CONTEMPORARY NARRATIVE

Readable Narrative

All chapters include contemporary examples, stories, jokes, and anecdotes to make the text material current and to entice the reader.

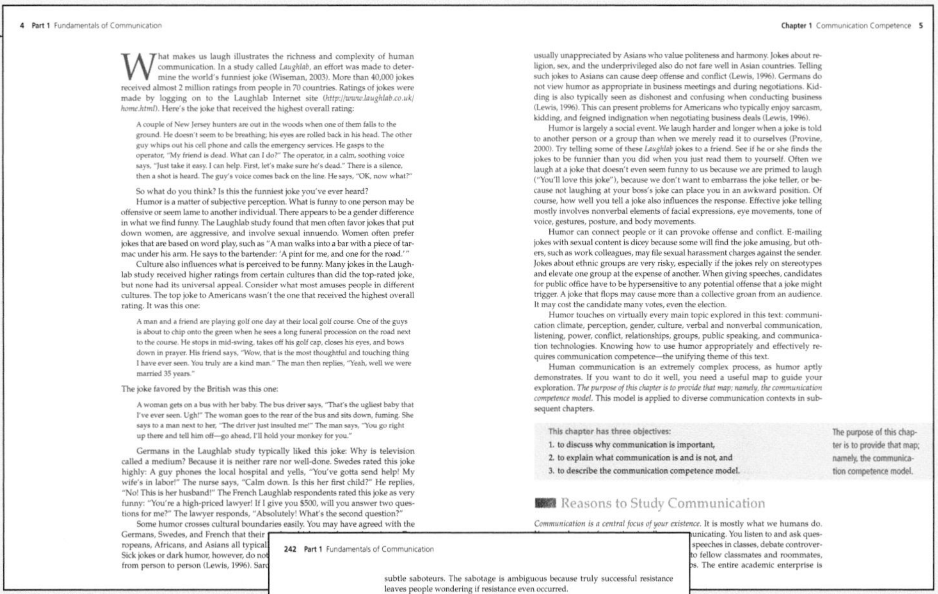

4 Part 1 Fundamentals of Communication

What makes us laugh illustrates the richness and complexity of human communication. In a study called *Laughlab*, an effort was made to determine the world's funniest joke (Wiseman, 2003). More than 40,000 jokes received almost 2 million ratings from people in 70 countries. Ratings of jokes were made by logging on to the Laughlab Internet site (*http://www.laughlab.co.uk/home.html*). Here's the joke that received the highest overall rating:

> A couple of New Jersey hunters are out in the woods when one of them falls to the ground. He doesn't seem to be breathing; his eyes are rolled back in his head. The other guy whips out his cell phone and calls the emergency services. He gasps to the operator, "My friend is dead. What can I do?" The operator, in a calm, soothing voice says, "Just take it easy. I can help. First, let's make sure he's dead." There is a silence, then a shot is heard. The guy's voice comes back on the line. He says, "OK, now what?"

So what do you think? Is this the funniest joke you've ever heard?

Humor is a matter of subjective perception. What is funny to one person may be offensive or seem lame to another individual. There appears to be a gender difference in what we find funny. The Laughlab study found that men often favor jokes that put down women, are aggressive, and involve sexual innuendo. Women often prefer jokes that are based on word play, such as "A man walks into a bar with a piece of tarmac under his arm. He says to the bartender: 'A pint for me, and one for the road.'"

Culture also influences what is perceived to be funny. Many jokes in the Laughlab study received higher ratings from certain cultures than did the top-rated joke, but none had its universal appeal. Consider what most amuses people in different cultures. The top joke to Americans wasn't the one that received the highest overall rating. It was this one:

> A man and a friend are playing golf one day at their local golf course. One of the guys is about to chip onto the green when he sees a long funeral procession on the road next to the course. He stops in mid-swing, takes off his golf cap, closes his eyes, and bows down in prayer. His friend says, "Wow, that is the most thoughtful and touching thing I have ever seen. You truly are a kind man." The man then replies, "Yeah, well we were married 35 years."

The joke favored by the British was this one:

> A woman gets on a bus with her baby. The bus driver says, "That's the ugliest baby that I've ever seen. Ugh!" The woman goes to the rear of the bus and sits down, fuming. She says to a man next to her, "The driver just insulted me!" The man says, "You go right up there and tell him off—go ahead, I'll hold your monkey for you."

Germans in the Laughlab study typically liked this joke: Why is television called a medium? Because it is neither rare nor well-done. Swedes rated this joke highly: A guy phones the local hospital and yells, "You've gotta send help! My wife's in labor!" The nurse says, "Calm down. Is this her first child?" He replies, "No! This is her husband!" The French Laughlab respondents rated this joke as very funny: "You're a high-priced lawyer! If I give you $500, will you answer two questions for me?" The lawyer responds, "Absolutely! What's the second question?"

Some humor crosses cultural boundaries easily. You may have agreed with the Germans, Swedes, and French that their ... ropeans, Africans, and Asians all typical... Sick jokes or dark humor, however, do not ... from person to person (Lewis, 1996). Sarc...

Chapter 1 Communication Competence 5

usually unappreciated by Asians who value politeness and harmony. Jokes about religion, sex, and the underprivileged also do not fare well in Asian countries. Telling such jokes to Asians can cause deep offense and conflict (Lewis, 1996). Germans do not view humor as appropriate in business meetings and during negotiations. Kidding is also typically seen as dishonest and confusing when conducting business (Lewis, 1996). This can present problems for Americans who typically enjoy sarcasm, kidding, and feigned indignation when negotiating business deals (Lewis, 1996).

Humor is largely a social event. We laugh harder and longer when a joke is told to another person or a group than when we merely read it to ourselves (Provine, 2000). Try telling some of these *Laughlab* jokes to a friend. See if he or she finds the jokes to be funnier than you did when you just read them to yourself. Often we laugh at a joke that doesn't even seem funny to us because we are primed to laugh ("You'll love this joke"), because we don't want to embarrass the joke teller, or because not laughing at your boss's joke can place you in an awkward position. Of course, how well you tell a joke also influences the response. Effective joke telling mostly involves nonverbal elements of facial expressions, eye movements, tone of voice, gestures, posture, and body movements.

Humor can connect people or it can provoke offense and conflict. E-mailing jokes with sexual content is dicey because some will find the joke amusing, but others, such as work colleagues, may file sexual harassment charges against the sender. Jokes about ethnic groups are very risky, especially if the jokes rely on stereotypes and elevate one group at the expense of another. When giving speeches, candidates for public office have to be hypersensitive to any potential offense that a joke might trigger. A joke that flops may cause more than a collective groan from an audience. It may cost the candidate many votes, even the election.

Humor touches on virtually every main topic explored in this text: communication climate, perception, gender, culture, verbal and nonverbal communication, listening, power, conflict, relationships, groups, public speaking, and communication technologies. Knowing how to use humor appropriately and effectively requires communication competence—the unifying theme of this text.

Human communication is an extremely complex process, as humor aptly demonstrates. If you want to do it well, you need a useful map to guide your exploration. *The purpose of this chapter is to provide that map; namely, the communication competence model.* This model is applied to diverse communication contexts in subsequent chapters.

This chapter has three objectives:

1. to discuss why communication is important,
2. to explain what communication is and is not, and
3. to describe the communication competence model.

The purpose of this chapter is to provide that map; namely, the communication competence model.

Reasons to Study Communication

Communication is a central focus of your existence. It is mostly what we humans do. ... unicating. You listen to and ask ques... speeches in classes, debate controver... to fellow classmates and roommates, ...s. The entire academic enterprise is

242 Part 1 Fundamentals of Communication

subtle saboteurs. The sabotage is ambiguous because truly successful resistance leaves people wondering if resistance even occurred.

Resistance, like defiance, is usually the choice of the less powerful. Resistance has an advantage over defiance. It is often safer to use indirect means of noncompliance than direct confrontation when faced with a more powerful person or group. Those who are defiant dig in their heels and openly cause trouble, but those who resist merely drag their feet.

There are several resistance strategies (Rothwell, 2001). Resistance strategies are sometimes referred to as *passive aggression*.

Strategic Stupidity This is the playing stupid strategy. When children don't want to do what their parents tell them to, they sometimes act stupid when they know better. "But mom, I don't know how to fold the laundry" may simply be an effort to frustrate the parent who may give up in disgust and fold the laundry rather than show the child for the "bizillionth" time what should be plainly obvious.

Strategic stupidity works exceedingly well when the low-power person claims stupidity, is forced to attempt the task anyway, and then performs it ineptly. In one study of 555 married adults (Home chores, 1993), 14% of the men admitted purposely botching house chores to get out of doing them again. The poor performance becomes "proof" that the stupidity is real. The passive aggressor can assert, "I told you I didn't know how to do laundry."

Loss of Motor Function This resistance strategy is an effective companion to strategic stupidity. The resister doesn't act stupid, just incredibly clumsy, often resulting in costly damage. There is a mixed message here of resistance on one hand but apparent effort on the other. "I tried really hard not to let dishes slip out of my hands; I'm sorry I broke two plates" may be an honest apology from your housemate for accidental behavior. If it becomes repetitive, however, it may be an effort to avoid doing dishes.

The Misunderstanding Mirage This is the "I thought you meant" or the "I could have sworn you said" strategy. The resistance is expressed "behind a cloak of great sincerity" (Bach & Goldberg, 1972, p. 110). Students sometimes excuse late assignments by using this strategy. "You said it was due Wednesday, not today, didn't you?" they'll say hopefully. The implied message is that, since this is a simple misunderstanding, penalizing the student for a late paper would be unfair.

Selective Amnesia Have you ever noticed that some people are particularly forgetful about those things that they clearly do not want to do? This temporary amnesia is highly selective when used as a resistance strategy. Selective amnesiacs rarely forget what is most important to them. No outward signs of resistance are manifested. Resisters agree to perform the task—but conveniently let it slip their minds.

In a sophisticated version of this strategy the individual remembers all but one or two important items. A person shops for groceries and purchases all but two key items. Hey, no one's perfect. He or she remembered almost everything. The dinner menu, however, will have to be altered because the main course wasn't purchased.

Tactical Tardiness When you really don't want to attend a meeting, a class, a lecture, or a party, you can show contempt by arriving late. Tactical tardiness irritates and frustrates those who value the event. It can hold an entire group hostage while

Box 9-2 Focus on Controversy

Cyberaddiction

On June 27, 1999, Kelli Michetti became enraged with her husband Robert for his excessive use of the Internet, especially his chats with women until 4 a.m. several days in a row. Kelli seized a meat cleaver and began whacking power cords on the computer and then she started hacking at the computer terminal as her husband struggled with her. Kelli was arrested and charged with domestic violence (Women angry, 1999).

The case of Sandra Hacker stirred national outrage when she was discovered neglecting her children so she could spend up to 12 hours a day online. She apparently would lock her children in a filthy room while she obsessively used the Internet (Bricking, 1997).

Cyberaddiction has become an issue of popular interest recently. Some evidence suggests that as many as 10% of Internet users in the United States are cyberaddicts. They average 38 hours a week online and about 4 hours of sleep a night (Baran, 1999). A large study claimed that the figure of cyberaddicts is closer to 6%, a smaller figure but still significant (Donn, 1999).

The University of Maryland in College Park began a counseling service for cyberaddicted students called "Caught in the Net." One study at the University of Glasgow in Scotland revealed that 16% of participants admitted they were irritable, restless, depressed, or tense if prevented from going online; 27% felt guilty about the time they spent online; 10% confessed that they neglected a partner, child, or a project at work because of their addiction (cited in Locke, 1998). Kraut and his associates (1998) found that, like television viewing, the Internet displaces time that could have been spent with family members and friends in conversation and social activities. This time displacement is particularly serious when Internet use becomes excessive. The Stanford Institute for the Quantitative Study of Society reported that, of the respondents who spent 5 or more hours per week on the Internet, 13% spent less time with family and friends, 26% talked less often with them on the telephone, and 8% attended fewer social events because of excessive Internet use (Stanford, 2000).

Some surveys, however, challenge whether Internet addiction even exists, and if it does whether it is a significant problem. The UCLA Internet study (Chmielewski, 2003) found that Internet use sacrifices time in front of the television, not social contact with friends and family members. Internet users reported that they watch 30% less television than nonusers. A 2000 Pew Internet survey of 3,500 adults found that 72% of Internet users had visited a friend or relative the previous day compared to 61% of non-Internet subscribers.

Whether Internet addiction is a real psychological disorder is open to question, even though the American Psychological Association has recognized it (Wood & Smith, 2001). The APA issued a press release in 1996 entitled "Internet Can Be as Addicting as Alcohol, Drugs, and Gambling, Says New Research." Dr. Kimberly Young (1996) conducted this new research. She studied 496 heavy users of the Internet. When she compared these subjects' Internet use to clinical criteria used to classify pathological gambling, she assessed 396 of the 496 subjects as Internet dependent.

Are there individuals who spend excessive time on the Internet at the expense of their interpersonal relationships? Undoubtedly there are (Barnes, 2001). Even those who spend less time watching television when they use the Internet may still ignore interpersonal relationships because of excessive Internet usage. The Stanford Institute study (Stanford, 2000) found that 59% of Internet users spend less time watching television, but 13% also spend less time with family and friends. Heavy Internet usage may bite into both time spent watching television and contact with friends and family. The Pew Internet survey also measured visits to friends and relatives as an operational indicator of social contact, but it merely compared Internet users and nonusers. It did not separate respondents according to degree of Internet usage. Heavy users may be much more prone to diminished social contact with family members and friends than are light users. The pervasiveness of Internet addiction is debatable, but "it is clear that there are negative effects associated with people who use the Internet disproportionately" (Wood & Smith, 2001, p. 104).

Questions for Thought

1. Do you think that Internet addiction is a serious problem? Have you ever spent excessive amounts of time on the Internet at the expense of your interpersonal relationships?
2. Is it likely that some Internet addicts spend large amounts of time developing interpersonal relationships online, not ignoring important relationships?

268

Citations

Every chapter is current, reflecting hundreds of new studies and research references. *In The Company of Others* cites over 1,300 references in total.

ABOUT THE AUTHOR

J. Dan Rothwell is chair of the Communication Studies department at Cabrillo College. He has a BA in American history from the University of Portland (Oregon), an MA in rhetoric and public address, and a PhD in communication theory and practice. His MA and PhD are both from the University of Oregon. He has authored three other books: *In Mixed Company: Communication in Small Groups and Teams, Telling It Like It Isn't: Language Misuse and Malpractice,* and (with James Costigan) *Interpersonal Communication: Influences and Alternatives.* He is currently co-authoring a general psychology text with Terry Fetterman and David Douglass, psychology professors at Cabrillo College. During his extensive teaching career, Dr. Rothwell has received eight teaching awards.

Professor Rothwell appreciates feedback and correspondence from both students and instructors regarding *In the Company of Others.* Anyone so inclined may e-mail him at darothwe@cabrillo.edu or send correspondence care of the Communication Studies department, Cabrillo College, Aptos, CA 95003. Dr. Rothwell may also be reached by phone at 1-831-479-6511.

PART ONE

Fundamentals of Communication

CHAPTER 1

Communication Competence

What makes us laugh illustrates the richness and complexity of human communication. In a study called *LaughLab,* an effort was made to determine the world's funniest joke (Wiseman, 2003). More than 40,000 jokes received almost 2 million ratings from people in 70 countries. Ratings of jokes were made by logging on to the LaughLab Internet site (*http://www.laughlab.co.uk/home.html*). Here's the joke that received the highest overall rating:

> A couple of New Jersey hunters are out in the woods when one of them falls to the ground. He doesn't seem to be breathing; his eyes are rolled back in his head. The other guy whips out his cell phone and calls the emergency services. He gasps to the operator, "My friend is dead. What can I do?" The operator, in a calm, soothing voice says, "Just take it easy. I can help. First, let's make sure he's dead." There is a silence, then a shot is heard. The guy's voice comes back on the line. He says, "OK, now what?"

So what do you think? Is this the funniest joke you've ever heard?

Humor is a matter of subjective perception. What is funny to one person may be offensive or seem lame to another individual. There appears to be a gender difference in what we find funny. The LaughLab study found that men often favor jokes that put down women, are aggressive, and involve sexual innuendo. Women often prefer jokes that are based on word play, such as "A man walks into a bar with a piece of tarmac under his arm. He says to the bartender: 'A pint for me, and one for the road.'"

Culture also influences what is perceived to be funny. Many jokes in the LaughLab study received higher ratings from certain cultures than did the top-rated joke, but none had its universal appeal. Consider what most amuses people in different cultures. The top joke to Americans wasn't the one that received the highest overall rating. It was this one:

> A man and a friend are playing golf one day at their local golf course. One of the guys is about to chip onto the green when he sees a long funeral procession on the road next to the course. He stops in mid-swing, takes off his golf cap, closes his eyes, and bows down in prayer. His friend says, "Wow, that is the most thoughtful and touching thing I have ever seen. You truly are a kind man." The man then replies, "Yeah, well we were married 35 years."

The joke favored by the British was this one:

> A woman gets on a bus with her baby. The bus driver says, "That's the ugliest baby that I've ever seen. Ugh!" The woman goes to the rear of the bus and sits down, fuming. She says to a man next to her, "The driver just insulted me!" The man says, "You go right up there and tell him off—go ahead. I'll hold your monkey for you."

Germans in the LaughLab study typically liked this joke: Why is television called a medium? Because it is neither rare nor well-done. Swedes rated this joke highly: A guy phones the local hospital and yells, "You've gotta send help! My wife's in labor!" The nurse says, "Calm down. Is this her first child?" He replies, "No! This is her husband!" The French LaughLab respondents rated this joke as very funny: "You're a high-priced lawyer! If I give you $500, will you answer two questions for me?" The lawyer responds, "Absolutely! What's the second question?"

Some humor crosses cultural boundaries easily. You may have agreed with the Germans, Swedes, and French that their preferred jokes are funny. Americans, Europeans, Africans, and Asians all typically find slapstick amusing, even hilarious. Sick jokes or dark humor, however, do not travel well from culture to culture or even from person to person (Lewis, 1996). Sarcasm, exaggeration, satire, and parody are usually unappreciated by Asians who value politeness and harmony. Jokes about religion, sex, and the underprivileged also do not fare well in Asian countries. Telling such jokes to Asians can cause deep offense and conflict (Lewis, 1996). Germans do not view humor as appropriate in business meetings and during negotiations. Kidding is also typically seen as dishonest and confusing when conducting business (Lewis, 1996). This can present problems for Americans who typically enjoy sarcasm, kidding, and feigned indignation when negotiating business deals (Lewis, 1996).

Humor is largely a social event. We laugh harder and longer when a joke is told to another person or a group than when we merely read it to ourselves (Provine, 2000). Try telling some of the LaughLab jokes to a friend. See if he or she finds the jokes to be funnier than you did when you just read them to yourself. Often we laugh at a joke that doesn't even seem funny to us because we are primed to laugh ("You'll love this joke"), because we don't want to embarrass the joke teller, or because not laughing at your boss's joke can place you in an awkward position. Of course, how well you tell a joke also influences the response. Effective joke telling mostly involves nonverbal elements of facial expressions, eye movements, tone of voice, gestures, posture, and body movements.

Humor can connect people or it can provoke offense and conflict. E-mailing jokes with sexual content is dicey because some will find the joke amusing, but others, such as work colleagues, may file sexual harassment charges against the sender. Jokes about ethnic groups are very risky, especially if the jokes rely on stereotypes and elevate one group at the expense of another. When giving speeches, candidates for public office have to be hypersensitive to any potential offense that a joke might trigger. A joke that flops may cause more than a collective groan from an audience. It may cost the candidate many votes, even the election.

Humor touches on virtually every main topic explored in this text: communication climate, perception, gender, culture, verbal and nonverbal communication, listening, power, conflict, relationships, groups, public speaking, and communication technologies. Knowing how to use humor appropriately and effectively requires communication competence—the unifying theme of this text.

Human communication is an extremely complex process, as humor aptly demonstrates. If you want to do it well, you need a useful map to guide your exploration. *The purpose of this chapter is to provide that map; namely, the communication competence model.* This model is applied to diverse communication contexts in subsequent chapters.

There are three chapter objectives:

1. to discuss why communication is important,
2. to explain what communication is and is not, and
3. to describe the communication competence model.

The purpose of this chapter is to provide that map; namely, the communication competence model.

Reasons to Study Communication

Communication is a central focus of your existence. It is mostly what we humans do. You spend most of your time in college communicating. You listen to and ask questions of your professors, give oral reports and speeches in classes, debate controversial issues, engage in class discussions, talk to fellow classmates and roommates, and quiz each other in student study groups. The entire academic enterprise is

Box 1-1   Sharper Focus

The Story of Genie

Genie was 13 years old when she was discovered in a suburb of Los Angeles in 1970. From the time she was 2 years old, Genie had been confined in a bare room with the curtains drawn. She was strapped naked to a potty chair and sometimes tied in a makeshift straitjacket by her abusive father. Genie had minimal human contact. If she made noise, her father literally barked or growled or beat her with a stick. Genie's mother, almost blind, finally escaped from the house with Genie (Rymer, 1993).

When Genie was discovered, she could not walk, talk, stand erect, chew solid food, or control her bodily functions. Despite years of intensive training, Genie

never lost her unnatural voice quality, and she never learned to master more than an immature, pidgin-like language. She constructed sentences such as these:

"Mike paint."

"I like elephant eat peanut."

"Genie have Momma have baby grow up."

Genie was incapable of mastering the full grammar of the English language (Pinker, 1994). Her ability to communicate—a vital link to other human beings—had been profoundly impaired by her early isolation.

largely a communication event. Anything that occupies so much of your time is certainly worth serious attention. This section presents a brief discussion of two general reasons to study communication: (1) the benefits of communicating competently and (2) the need to improve our communication with others.

Benefits of Competent Communication

We humans are "the social animal" (Aronson, 1999). This is an observation made by Aristotle almost 2,500 years ago and confirmed by many others since. Communication is the means by which we establish social connection and build relationships. Kids "talk friendships into existence" (Yingling, 1994). A primary distinction between relationships that endure and thrive and those that do not is effective communication (Gottman, 1994; Gottman & Silver, 1999).

Imagine if your cell phone, pager, e-mail, and postal access were unavailable to you for even a day. Consider what your life would be like if you did not interact with another human being for a week, a month, or even a year. Ironically, we need to communicate with others to establish social connection and build relationships, but lack of social connection retards our ability to communicate. Stories of feral or "wild" children growing up without any apparent human contact and horrific instances of children imprisoned in closets or basements demonstrate this point. Despite intensive training, these unfortunate children do not learn to communicate normally unless their plight is discovered within the first 6 years of life. After age 6, language learning is very difficult, and shortly after puberty the capacity to learn language virtually disappears (Pinker, 1994). Obviously, this does not mean that a "foreign" language can't be learned after puberty, although it is more difficult than at an earlier age. If the capacity for language, *any language*, is not activated by social interaction and communication with others by puberty, however, it is unlikely that it ever will be after puberty (see Box 1-1).

Communicating competently also produces specific, practical benefits. *Communication skills are critical to landing a job, receiving a promotion, and performing effectively in the workplace.* In one study, *all* 253 personnel interviewers at businesses large and small reported that oral communication skills had a major impact on hiring decisions (Peterson, 1997). A survey of more than 400 employers identified "communication skills" as the *most important qualification* a candidate for employment can possess; it is more important than academic background, technical expertise, or work experience (Job Outlook, 1999). Moreover, once people are hired, skillful communication is the determining factor in how well they perform on the job ("Making the Grade," 2001; Schmidt, 1991).

Competent communication is also linked to our personal well-being. The recurrent "toxic talk" that usually accompanies bad relationships can literally talk us into heart disease, strokes, and even cancer (Lynch, 1999).

Need for Communication Improvement

Most Americans believe they are better communicators than the people on the receiving end think. A national Roper poll of more than 1,000 Americans reported that 91% of the respondents saw themselves as very or somewhat effective when communicating with other people ("How Americans Communicate," 1998). Numerous studies, however, question these self-assessments. Many national reports emphasize the need for college students to upgrade their oral communication skills (see Berko & Brooks, 1994). Only about 1 in 8 people (15%) believe college students are adequately prepared to speak up at a meeting or give an oral presentation, and only about 1 in 5 (21%) believe students are adequately trained for successful face-to-face communication ("How Americans Communicate," 1998). Most Americans believe that a "lack of effective communication between partners" is the most frequent cause of marriage and relationship breakups ("How Americans Communicate," 1998).

A huge long-term study conducted in a wide variety of organizations found that the self-assessments of 600 team leaders were wildly more generous than those of the 6,000 team members who had to endure their inappropriate and ineffective communication (LaFasto & Larson, 2001). In fact, team members' assessments of leaders were a whopping *50% lower* than the team leaders' self-assessments. These same team members also noted the inadequacy of the entire team's communication. Another study of 144 managers found that 94% rated themselves "good" or "very good" listeners, and none rated themselves as "poor." More than half of their employees, however, rated these managers' listening skills as "poor," and few managers were given high marks (Brownell, 1990). A study of 402 companies found that 80% of their employees *at all levels* needed improvement in public speaking, listening, and interpersonal communication ("Workers Lack," 1992). An overwhelming 91% of personnel interviewers at established businesses agree that applicants' communication skills are inadequate (Peterson, 1997).

No one is a perfect communicator, so studying communication can benefit everyone. This is why more than 1,000 faculty members surveyed from a wide variety of academic disciplines and colleges identified these *essential skills* for every college graduate: speaking, listening, problem solving, interpersonal skills, working in groups, and leading groups (R. Diamond, 1997).

■■ Communication Myths

American humorist Will Rogers once remarked, "It isn't what we don't know that gives us trouble, it's what we know that ain't so" (Fitzhenry, 1993, p. 243). As used in this text, a **myth** is a belief that is contradicted by fact. Communication myths disrupt our ability to improve our communication knowledge and skills. If what we know about communication "ain't so" then what chance do we have to improve our communication competence? Because common misconceptions interfere with our understanding of what communication is, let's first discuss what communication is not.

Myth 1: Communication Is a Cure-All

Gurus, pop psychologists, and self-appointed experts fill the shelves of bookstores with their writings and offer advice on talk shows. They offer communication as the magic elixir that will solve all relationship problems, but communication is not a cure-all. Relationships can't always be fixed by better communication. Sometimes communicating clearly reveals just how far apart individuals in a relationship have grown. Skillful communication may ease the pain of breaking up, but it may not sufficiently heal the wounds of a bruising relationship. Similarly, despite its importance to your employment future, improving your interviewing skills may not be sufficient to land a job. If the most challenging aspect of any job you've held involved asking, "Would you like fries with that?" then your chances of landing a high-skills, managerial, or technical position are about the same as a snail's safe passage across a freeway.

Recent research also reveals that some problems that occur between individuals are not solvable (Gottman & Silver, 1999). Your partner may never learn to enjoy events attended by large crowds. Your coworker may never develop a sunny disposition and a less cynical view of his or her job. Your boss may never exhibit a warm, friendly demeanor. Your roommate may never become a tidy person. Competent communication can help us cope with our recurring disagreements, but it may not change people.

Communication is a very important tool. When employed skillfully, communication can help solve numerous problems. Communication, however, is a means to an end, not an end in itself. It is not the basis of all human problems. Thus, not all problems can be solved even by textbook-perfect communication.

Myth 2: Communicating Is Just Common Sense

For an example of the Hindsight Bias Test, see CD Chapter 1 activity.

"Hindsight is 20-20" goes the adage. Once the victor is known, people often claim that they "knew" in advance who would win the election. When tested in advance of an election, however, most aren't very accurate (Powell, 1988). This tendency to look back after a fact or outcome has been revealed and say to yourself, "I knew that all along," is called the **hindsight bias** (Fischhoff, 1975).

Because all of us have communicated all of our lives, it is seductively simple to get snared in the hindsight bias trap by thinking as you read this text, "Oh, that's just common sense" or "I already knew that." The proof for such claims, of course, is the ability to provide the accurate information *before* you are told what the research says is true. I regularly quiz my students at the beginning of each term on their general knowledge of communication. I do not ask them technical definitions of concepts or query them about remote facts. I keep the questions within the realm of the average college student's communication experience (e.g., "Is venting or 'blowing off steam' an effective way to manage one's anger?" "Should our society attempt to increase everyone's self-esteem?"). Consistently, students do very poorly on this test. Such results, naturally, make sense. I don't expect my students to do well when the class has barely begun. One of the primary purposes for taking a communication course is to learn new information and to gain new insights.

The "common sense" notion of communication is contradicted by our all too common experience. If communication consists mostly of "common sense" with no requirement for studying or training, then why do so many people exhibit inadequate communication knowledge and skills? Why are most teams unsuccessful in achieving their desired goals (Ju & Cushman, 1995)? Why is the divorce rate so persistently high and breakups so often nasty, uncivilized battles? Why does it seem that public speaking is almost a lost art as politicians anesthetize us with bland, ghost-written speeches (Shachtman, 1995)? As you read this text, note that what passes for knowledge and insight about communication in the popular press and what may seem like common sense are often pure myth.

Myth 3: Communication Quantity Equals Quality

Legendary actors Jimmy Stewart and Henry Fonda had opposing viewpoints on politics. Stewart was a strong conservative, Fonda a steadfast liberal. In their early acting days they roomed together in New York. One day a political argument between them turned into a fistfight in the street. "Thank God it was snowing," recalled Stewart. "I went down on my face more than he did." They subsequently agreed never to discuss politics, and they never did throughout their close, 30-year friendship (Ansen, 1997).

More communication isn't always better communication. If you have a disagreement with your professor about a grade, repeatedly approaching your teacher in the hope that persistence will produce a favorable grade change will likely fail. It may even harden your professor's resolve to stop listening to you. According to long-term studies of couple communication (Gottman & DeClaire, 2001), 69% of all marital conflicts never go away, and arguments about such conflicts recur year after year. Couples who argue sometimes try to resolve recurring disagreements by engaging in communication marathons. They keep resurrecting points of contention, and, like someone picking a scab, they reopen old wounds again and again. Occasionally, as Stewart and Fonda discovered, agreeing to disagree and not discussing an issue at all may be the best choice.

▉▉▉ Communication Defined

The *Oxford English Dictionary (OED)* includes a 1,200-word definition of *communication*. Communication scholars and researchers have contributed more than 100 different definitions of their own. There is no ideal, or sacred, definition of *communication*. Authors, scholars, and students of human communication offer definitions suitable to their perspectives on the subject.

The definition that best fits the perspective presented in this textbook is as follows: **Communication** *is a transactional process of sharing meaning with others* (Rothwell, 2001). This seemingly simple 10-word definition requires explanation. Be thankful that you won't be asked to memorize or explain the *OED*'s definition.

Communication Is Transactional

Many communication models have been developed over the years, and each attempts to describe communication in concrete terms. In this section, three communication models are described: linear, interactive, and transactional. Each of these models provides insights that explain how the communication process works.

LINEAR MODEL   The communication process has been described as a linear, one-way phenomenon (Figure 1-1). Communication, from this perspective, involves a **sender** (initiator and encoder) who sends a **message** (stimulus that produces meaning)

FIGURE 1-1 Linear Model of Communication

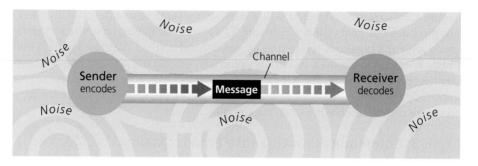

through a **channel** (medium through which a message travels, such as oral or written) to a **receiver** (decoder of a message) in an atmosphere of **noise** (interference with effective transmission and reception of a message).

When the President of the United States addresses the nation on television, all the components of the linear model are present. The president is the sender who encodes the message (puts ideas into a spoken language). The message is composed of the ideas the president wishes to express (for example, what this country should do about terrorism). The channel is the medium of television and is oral, aural (hearing), and visual. The receivers are members of the television audience who tune into the address and decode the message (translate the president's spoken ideas). Noise might be the static in the television transmission or, perhaps, family members fighting over the remote control.

The linear model provides insight into the communication process, especially by highlighting the concepts of channel and noise. The choice of channel can make an enormous difference in the way a message is received. Do you ask your partner to marry you, for example, by sending an e-mail message? By having a banner pulled across the sky by an airplane? Face to face on bended knee? By having your best friend do it because you're too chicken? By registered mail with a prenuptial agreement attached?

John Robinson learned that he had been fired from his position as football coach at the University of Southern California when USC athletic director Mike Garrett left a message on Robinson's answering machine. Robinson was not pleased with the impersonal channel choice ("At the Beep," 1997). Actor Daniel Day-Lewis actually chose both the answering machine and the fax to deliver bad news. He notified Isabelle Adjani, the mother of their child who was pregnant with their second child, that their relationship was over. He communicated this devastating news by fax machine. Then he informed Adjani on her answering machine that he had gotten married. Later he felt remorse for his thoughtlessness, so he apologized to Adjani—on her answering machine (Locke, 1998). Teenagers have recently taken to using computer instant messaging to break up with their girlfriends and boyfriends (e-dumping). A study of 754 teenagers by Pew Internet and American Life Project found that 13% had used instant messaging for this purpose (Ostrom & Seipel, 2001). Communicating a personal message via an impersonal channel makes the choice of channel as much an issue as the message itself. How would you feel if you were e-dumped?

Changes in channel can improve communication. New McDonald's restaurants have switched from taking orders over an intercom to taking food requests face to face at the drive-through window. The channel change has improved the accuracy of the orders ("McDonald's Listens," 1998). We are more likely to be abusive, insulting, offensive, and intemperate in our communication with others when using

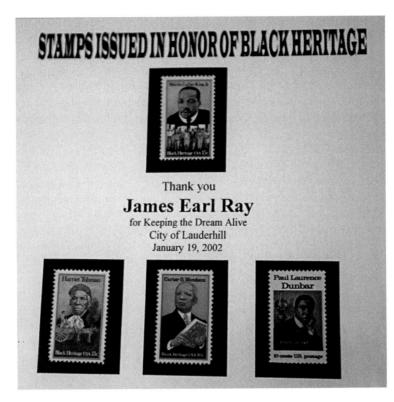

This plaque to honor actor James Earl Jones at a 2002 celebration of civil rights legend Rev. Martin Luther King, Jr. in Lauderhill, Florida mistakenly honors James Earl Ray, the man who assassinated King in Memphis in 1968. This is a startling example of semantic noise—interference with the intended meaning of a message by word choice (wrong name). Local Commissioner Margaret Bates called it "an outrage."

e-mail than we are in face-to-face conversation (Wallace, 1999). When it is especially important to remain civil in our communication with others, switching from e-mail to face-to-face communication can prove to be a more productive channel choice.

Broadening the definition of noise to include interference that goes beyond mere loud or irritating sounds is another important contribution of the linear model. **Physical noise**, or external, environmental distractions, such as startling sounds, the discomfort of poorly heated rooms, or the unfortunate periodic reappearance of bellbottom pants and paisley ties, can divert our attention from the message sent by a source. **Physiological noise**, or biological influences, such as sweaty palms, pounding heart, and butterflies in the stomach induced by speech anxiety, or feeling sick or exhausted at work, can have a dramatic effect on both senders and receivers of messages. **Psychological noise**, in the form of preconceptions, biases, and assumptions, also interferes with effective message transmission and reception. For example, one poll found that 40% of African Americans and Latinos questioned and 27% of White Americans agreed with the statement, "Asian Americans are unscrupulous, crafty, and devious in business" (Goldberg, 1994). Such preconceived, dangerous biases make effective transmission and reception of messages between different ethnic groups extremely difficult. **Semantic noise** in the form of word choice that is confusing or distracting also creates interference. Racist, sexist, and homophobic labels and descriptions, even if unintended, easily derail productive conversation.

Despite its insights, the linear model is quite limited in its application. Its most glaring weakness is the absence of **feedback,** the receiver's verbal and nonverbal responses to a message. The linear model assumes that communication consists of the transmission of a message from a sender to a receiver with no receiver response; listeners are merely passive targets for information. Without feedback, senders of messages are relatively independent from receivers. You can't even determine if comprehension of the message sent has occurred without feedback. The absence of feedback is a serious flaw because all of us constantly adjust our communication with others based on the feedback we receive. The inability to read feedback accurately and to make appropriate adjustments is a serious communication competence issue.

INTERACTIVE MODEL   The interactive model of communication has added feedback (Figure 1-2). The addition of feedback clearly indicates that communication is not a one-way but a two-way process. Receivers are actively involved in the process; they are not static targets. Receivers become senders, and senders become receivers of messages.

The importance of feedback to the communication process cannot be overestimated. Of the 35,000 assessments gathered from 6,000 team members in a long-term study (LaFasto & Larson, 2001), *two consistent problems emerged: giving feedback and receiving feedback*. As noted in the study, the ability to give and receive feedback effectively is key to any constructive self-correction that can occur in teams. The huge disparity previously identified between an individual's self-assessment of his or her communication skills and the assessments made by others exists primarily because too often we insulate ourselves from feedback. How else could managers deem themselves highly effective listeners when their employees view the managers' listening skills as woefully substandard?

A second component of the interactive model missing from the linear version is fields of experience. **Fields of experience** include our cultural background, ethnicity, geographic location, extent of travel, and general personal experiences accumulated over the course of a lifetime. Fields of experience between individuals may be poorly matched and consequently produce misunderstanding. Parents, who know how important education was to their own attainment of important goals, want the same for their children. Their kids, however, don't yet have equivalent experience that might give them that same perspective. Languishing in a math or chemistry class may seem more like torment to teenagers than a pursuit of life goals. The more experiences we have in common, the more likely it is that misunderstandings can be avoided.

FIGURE 1-2   Interactive Model of Communication

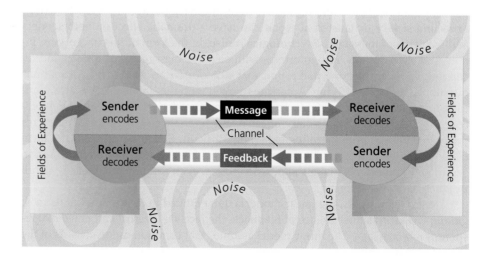

TRANSACTIONAL MODEL   The transactional model, by definition, assumes that people are connected through communication; they engage in a transaction. Viewing communication as transactional (Figure 1-3) provides two insights.

First, it recognizes that *each of us is a sender-receiver, not merely a sender or a receiver*. You may be the speaker in a conversation, but you are receiving feedback from your listeners constantly, mostly nonverbally. This feedback may encourage you to speak as you've been speaking or to make adjustments.

Second, the transactional perspective recognizes that *communication has an impact on all parties involved*. We are defined in relation to each other as we send and receive messages, not as individuals separate from others. A teacher requires students. Parents must have children or they can't be defined as parents. An interviewer cannot exist without an interviewee. A leader must have followers. The roles we play in life result from how we are defined in relation to others. Thus, transactional communication is not merely two-way interaction. Something more than movement of information back and forth occurs when humans communicate. We continuously influence each other and develop a relationship one to the other as we communicate (Anderson & Ross, 1994).

We can more clearly see the influence we have on each other during communication by examining the two dimensions of every message: content and relationship (Watzlawick et al., 1967). The **content dimension** refers to what is actually said and done. The **relationship dimension** refers to how that message defines or redefines the association between individuals.

A college student might say, "Professor Tillson, I didn't like your test" or "Hey Tillson, your test sucks." Both messages have the same essential content (unhappiness with the test), but the relationship dimension is different. The first statement exhibits respect. The second statement, by contrast, is disrespectful, even abrasive. Of course, nonverbal cues can change the relationship. If a student jabbed an index finger in the professor's face while making the first statement in an aggressive tone of voice, then the relationship would clearly change. Likewise, if a student made the second statement with a big, knowing grin that signaled lighthearted playfulness, the nature of the relationship might be the opposite of what the words themselves indicated. This highlights the vast potential for misunderstanding that exists in e-mail messages, which restrict nonverbal cues.

FIGURE 1-3 Transactional Model of Communication

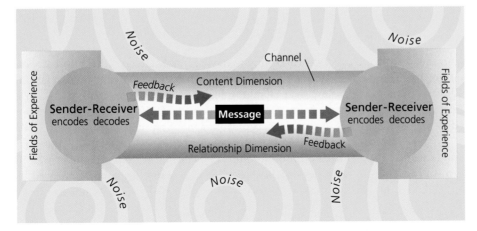

Message content can also differ while the relationship dimension stays the same. "Will you please lend me 50 bucks?" and "Would you please help me study for my math final?" are messages that display different content but essentially the same relationship. Although the specific requests differ, respect is shown to the person receiving the request in both instances.

These illustrations show the content and relationship dimensions of messages, but they are not transactional. We don't see the reaction to the message and the impact it has on each party. Here is an example that shows transactional communication:

STUDENT: "Hey Tillson, your test sucks."

PROFESSOR TILLSON: "Did you actually study for the exam?"

STUDENT: "No. I figured you'd give an easy test, so I didn't need to study. Besides, I had to party last night."

PROFESSOR TILLSON: "Perhaps you should take this class *more* seriously?"

STUDENT: "Perhaps you should take me *less* seriously. I'M KIDDING. I studied hard for your test, but I was confused on several questions. I want to go over the exam with you."

PROFESSOR TILLSON: "Fine, but that'll cost you a 5-point deduction on your exam score."

STUDENT: "WHAT?"

PROFESSOR: "Just kidding!"

The professor and the student are sparring with each other, defining their relationship as they converse. Will this be a formal relationship between teacher and student or will this be an informal relationship between relative equals? The nature of the conversation and their relationship shifts once the professor realizes that the student is being glib but has a serious concern. The professor then makes an attempt at the end to match the informality of the student but also to reassert status.

This conversation, of course, could have progressed in many different ways. The professor could have chastised the student for the "test sucks" remark. This would have defined their relationship as a formal one of unequal power. The professor also could have chosen to end the conversation with an abrupt "Try studying next time" retort while walking away. This would likely produce an unfriendly, distant relationship between teacher and student. In each case, both parties are affected not only by what is said (content) but also by how it is presented (relationship).

Communication Is a Process

Communicating is a process of adapting to the inevitable changes that affect any relationship. The process view of communication recognizes "events and relationships as dynamic, ongoing, ever-changing, continuous" (Berlo, 1960, p. 24). In a relationship, "nothing never happens" (Johnson et al., 1974) or, as the bumper sticker says, "Change is inevitable, except from a vending machine."

If you wanted to understand the ocean, you wouldn't just take a picture of a single wave or scoop up a cupful of water. The ocean can be understood only in terms of its entirety—the tides and currents, waves, plant and animal life, and so forth. Likewise, to understand communication, you have to focus not on single words, sentences, or gestures but on how currents of thought and feeling are expressed by both verbal and nonverbal means in the context of change.

Relationships can't be frozen in time, even though our memories of the "way we were" sometimes have this effect. Every conversation is a foothold on our next conversation, and we bring our accumulated experiences to each new conversation. Communication is an ongoing process, and each new experience influences future transactions.

Communication Is Sharing Meaning with Others

Meaning is "the conscious pattern humans create out of their interpretation of experience" (Anderson & Ross, 1994, p. 73). We construct meaning by making connections and patterns in our minds that "make sense" of our world. When we seek help from friends or counselors about problems we are experiencing in our romantic relationships, we are trying to make sense of what may be too confusing for us to sort out by ourselves. When we "make sense" of our experience, it takes on significance (Anderson & Ross, 1994). Realizing that an argumentative pattern of conversation with your coworker triggers friction may produce a strong desire to alter the pattern to improve the relationship.

We say something is "meaningless" when it makes no sense (someone speaking Chinese to us when we speak only English), but it is "meaningful" when it makes sense and has an impact on us in some way. A college education may be meaningful to you because it helps you make sense of your world and because it opens doors of opportunity (significance) that wouldn't exist without the experience.

Meaning doesn't occur in a vacuum. It is socially constructed. Words, for example, have no meaning until we construct their meanings from social agreement (see Chapter 5). There is never a perfect "meeting of the minds" regarding meaning. The meaning I have for an experience, idea, relationship, concept, or symbol is an approximation of the meaning you have for the same things. *Meaning is shared when there are overlapping interpretations between individuals.* When you view a relationship as a friendship and the other person sees it likewise, there is an overlap and meaning is shared. The depth of that friendship or even what constitutes friendship, however, is not identical between two people. There are always subtle differences.

Communicating is sharing meaning with others. We share meaning verbally and nonverbally. Sometimes meaning doesn't get shared verbally even though words are transmitted from one person to another in a common language. For example, there is a story of a Catholic nun teaching religion to her third graders and conducting standard catechism drills. She repeatedly asked her students, "Who is God?" Her students were to respond in unison, "God is a supreme being." Finally, she decided to test the fruits of her patient labor and called on one of the boys in the class. When asked, "Who is God?" he promptly and proudly replied, "God is a string bean." Words were transmitted, but meaning was not shared. *Supreme being* was meaningless to the third grader. *String bean* at least could be grasped, even if applying it to the divinity was a tad abstruse.

Sharing meaning cross-culturally poses its own unique problems. Electrolux, a Scandinavian manufacturer, discovered this when it tried selling its vacuum cleaners in the United States with the slogan, "Nothing sucks like an Electrolux." As Ray Gordon, a sociologist and expert on Latin America, puts it, "If you know the language but not the culture in a country you visit, you will be able to make a fluent fool of yourself" (Brembeck & Howell, 1976, p. 205).

Sharing meaning nonverbally can be equally problematic. Nodding the head up and down means "yes" in the United States, and shaking it side to side means "no."

The "thumbs up" sign translates as an offensive message in some cultures, making an international sporting event a potential source of embarrassment.

In Bulgaria, Turkey, Iran, the former Yugoslavia, and Bengal, however, it is the reverse. In Greece, tipping the head back abruptly while raising the eyebrows means "no," and dropping the chin several times means "yes." Nodding the head backwards while simultaneously clicking one's tongue means "no" in Saudi Arabia and some other parts of the Middle East (Axtell, 1998). (Nod your head if you understand all of this.)

Communication is a transactional process of sharing meaning with others. We are sender-receivers trying to make sense of our dynamic, ever-changing relationships with others. These relationships define who we are and what roles we play in life.

Communication Competence Model

Defining communication does not tell us how to communicate in a competent manner. For that we need a map, or a theoretical model, to guide us. This section explains what competent communication is and is not. It also presents the communication competence model, which offers general ways to improve our communication with others. These strategies will be applied specifically as subsequent chapters unfold.

Communication Competence Defined

Communication competence *is communicating effectively and appropriately in a given context* (Spitzberg & Cupach, 1989). What this means is explained by discussing communication competence as a matter of degree of proficiency within a specific context, as We-oriented, as partly dependent on effectiveness, and as guided by rules of appropriateness.

DEGREE OF PROFICIENCY Some people are proficient at establishing intimate relationships with a few individuals but feel awkward and ill at ease in large gatherings of strangers. Others would rather body surf a tidal wave or eat a disease-carrying roach than give a public speech. Our competence varies by degrees from highly proficient to severely deficient depending on our current set of circumstances. Thus, you may see yourself as "highly proficient" in social gatherings, "moderately skillful" in leadership positions in groups, and "woefully inadequate" in public-speaking situations. We are more to less effective, not merely competent or incompetent. Labeling someone a "competent communicator" makes a judgment of that individual's degree of proficiency *in a particular context*, but it does not identify an immutable characteristic of that person. Being a competent communicator is also not an idyllic state of perfection. Even the best communicators occasionally err.

WE- NOT ME-ORIENTED Because communication is transactional, competence comes from focusing on "We" (what makes the *relationship* successful), not "Me" (what makes *me* successful). When you enter into an intimate relationship, for example, interdependence (a We-orientation) is primary, and independence (a Me-orientation) is secondary. A 20-year study of why marriages succeed and fail found that the more that marriage partners, especially husbands, viewed their marriage as a joint undertaking, the more likely the marriage would succeed (Gottman & Silver, 1994). Problems for either partner are viewed as difficulties that impact both individuals together.

The "me-first" attitude also destroys teamwork in groups (LaFasto & Larson, 2001). In fact, a collection of individuals doesn't function as a group at all if the members are more interested in individual accomplishment than group achievement (Zander, 1982). In organizations, the Me-orientation is called **politics** (LaFasto

& Larson, 2001). Individual agendas become more important than organizational goals. "Politics must be avoided at all costs. It [creates] winners and losers. When that happens, the organization is always shortchanged" (LaFasto & Larson, 2001, p. 172).

Not all individual goals clash with relationship or group goals, and some individual goals (intimacy) can only be accomplished in a context of interdependence. Nevertheless, trying to achieve individual goals at the expense of relationship, group, or organizational goals usually produces unsatisfactory outcomes for both you and others.

EFFECTIVENESS   How well you progress toward the achievement of your goals defines the **effectiveness** of your communication (Spitzberg & Cupach, 1989). If your cynical humor provokes hostility from your roommate, you may need to modify your humor if your goal is to remain roommates.

In the context of communication competence, effectiveness is relational, not individualistic. Individual effectiveness may be deemed deficient if such effectiveness prevents others from accomplishing their own goals and if a more cooperative, We-orientation could have been chosen (Spitzberg & Cupach, 1989).

Effectiveness is not the sole determinant of communication competence, however. Sometimes, despite your best efforts and highly proficient communication, you may not achieve your goals. Your lack of effectiveness may be due to forces beyond your control, not the quality of your communication. A person can exhibit exemplary communication and still have relationships with family, friends, spouses, and coworkers fail. A public speech can be beautifully constructed and delivered, but listeners may still be unmoved because they don't share the values and beliefs of the speaker.

APPROPRIATENESS   Spitzberg and Cupach (1989) define **appropriateness** as "the avoidance of violating social or interpersonal norms, rules, or expectations" (p. 7). Appropriateness can be determined only within a specific context. **Context** is the environment in which communication occurs: *who* (sender-receiver) communicates *what* (message) to *whom* (receiver-sender), *why* a message is sent (purpose), *where* (setting) it is sent, and *when* (timing) and *how* (channel) it is transmitted. We determine the appropriateness of our communication by analyzing all of these elements.

Every communication context is guided by rules. A **rule** "is a followable prescription that indicates what behavior is obligated, preferred, or prohibited in certain contexts" (Shimanoff, 1980, p. 57). A family, for example, has many rules (Yerby & Buerkel-Rothfuss, 1982). Rules stipulate who takes out the trash, who cooks the meals, who pays the bills, and so forth. There are also rules constraining and structuring communication transactions within the family unit, such as "We never go to bed angry," "Children will address a parent or stepparent in a respectful way at all times," and "Don't interrupt someone during dinner conversation."

Rules create expectations regarding appropriate behavior. Some rules are explicitly stated (directly expressed) such as "no shoes, no shirt, no service" and "no smoking." Most rules, however, are merely implied (indirectly indicated) by patterns of behavior. We don't have to be told directly what to do or not do. For example, it is unlikely that you will find signs in a grocery store that read, "Don't have cart races in the aisles," "Don't eat cookies and put the half-empty bag back on the shelf," "Don't crash into other customers with your cart," "Don't steal food from another person's cart," and "Be nice to the clerks." When we encounter a coworker or stranger who asks, "How ya doing?" we know better than to respond with a long-winded appraisal of our current state of affairs. Normally, we just say, "I'm fine. How are you?" Cultural greeting rules dictate that the question not be interpreted literally. Consequently, the greeting becomes ritualistic, even mindless, which is why I've caught myself on more than one occasion asking, "How are you?" receiving the response from the other person, "I'm fine—how are you?" whereupon I give the slightly embarrassing response, "I'm fine—how are you?" (Oops, already asked that—trapped in a feedback loop).

When we do encounter explicit rules that seem to underestimate our grasp of the implicit rules guiding social conventions, it causes a start. Wallace (1999), for example, tells of a tavern in rural Texas that conspicuously displays signs that read, "No spitting" and "No fighting." There is even a sign in the men's restroom, meant to be amusing I assume, that advises, "Do not eat the urinal cakes."

A violation of an implicit rule often leads to an explicit statement of the rule. College instructors take for granted that students won't interrupt the flow of a lecture or class discussion by talking inappropriately with fellow students. On occasion, however, this implicit rule has to be made explicit to students whose enthusiasm for casual conversation outweighs their ardor for the classroom task.

Although appropriateness of communication is determined by context, which is rules-oriented, rules are not sacred. Some rules may need to be modified. When students share a dorm room or an apartment, rule modification is almost inevitable if communication is to remain competent. Difficulties living together will occur if one person expects a spotlessly clean, orderly environment, and the other person expects a more casual environment. When rules clash, a modification of the rules will have to be negotiated unless one person is willing to accept the other's rules completely.

No matter how bizarre a rule may seem to outsiders, the appropriateness of our communication is maintained as long as those most affected abide by the rule. Two guys that I knew, for instance, lived in an apartment together, and both agreed never to do any dishes (explicit rule). This may sound like a health hazard in the making, but they concocted a unique idea for avoiding dishes without turning their apartment into a roach motel. They threw away their dishes after using them and purchased cheap replacement dishes from Goodwill. Most people would find this rule oddball to say the least, but it worked for them. They negotiated the rule when they first moved into the apartment, and both were happy with the result. Their communication was appropriate because they both abided by the rule that they had negotiated.

Communication becomes inappropriate if it violates rules when such violations could be averted without sacrificing a goal by choosing alternative communication behaviors (Getter & Nowinski, 1981). If one of the guys in the previous example began violating the dishes rule by refusing to pay for replacement dishes, this would be inappropriate communication. The violation is premature when no effort to renegotiate the rule is made. Renegotiation might produce a mutually satisfactory alternative (paper plates). Renegotiation of the rule would ask questions such as "Is the rule still mutually accepted?" "Is the rule violation an unusual, one-time infraction?" and "What would be an acceptable alternative rule if one is desired?" Recognizing which rules thwart communication effectiveness and learning ways to change these rules appropriately are important tasks if you hope to maintain or improve your relationships with others.

Achieving Communication Competence

Defining communication competence tells us what it is but not how to achieve it. There are five general ways that the appropriateness and effectiveness of our communication can be improved. We can build knowledge, develop our communication skills, increase our sensitivity, enhance our commitment, and apply ethics to our communication choices (Figure 1-4). Let's look at each of these in more detail.

KNOWLEDGE   We cannot determine appropriate and effective communication without knowledge of the rules that create behavioral expectations. **Knowledge** is an understanding of what is required by the communication context.

Communication is both appropriate and effective when there is mutual satisfaction (We-orientation) with the process and the outcomes. That mutual satisfaction begins with knowledge of the rules that govern our transactions with others. You're not likely to be satisfied with the process if you expect cordial communication (courtesy rule) but receive adversarial, antagonistic treatment. If, however, you know in advance that initially you will be treated as an adversary to test your mettle, then you might be less unsatisfied with your treatment. You might even look forward to the challenge. Knowing the communication rules prepares you to adapt your communication so it is appropriate for the context and is likely to be effective by achieving the desired results.

Mutual satisfaction, however, does not mean that you always get what you want. Again, it is a matter of degree, not either-or. The more satisfied both parties are with both the process and the outcomes, the more competent the communication. You may find satisfaction in negotiating with another person because both of you listened carefully to each other's views, even disagreed, but exhibited mutual respect. Compromise may be the result, but this can be mutually satisfying if there was relatively equal give-and-take on both sides.

SKILLS   A **communication skill** is "the successful performance of a communication behavior . . . [and] the ability to repeat such a behavior" (Spitzberg & Hecht, 1984, p. 577). Clearly, fluently, concisely, eloquently, and confidently communicating messages are examples of skills. Knowledge about communication without communication skill will not produce competence. You can read stacks of books about public

FIGURE 1-4   Communication Competence Model

speaking, but there is no substitute for skill gained by practice and experience speaking in front of an audience.

Conversely, skill without knowledge is equally unproductive. Learning to "express your feelings honestly" can be an important communication skill in many situations. Expressing your honest feelings indiscriminately, however, no matter what the likely consequences, mimics the act of an innocent child, not a mature adult.

One key to achieving communication competence is using a mixture of both knowledge and skills. Lack of knowledge constrains your understanding of the skills required in a given situation. Limited skills constrain your ability to respond appropriately even if you know what is required. Having a variety of skills allows you to make choices appropriate to the specific context. For example, the ability to communicate a message concisely and precisely is an important skill. Lacking fluency—speaking with long pauses and vocal fillers (uhms and ahs)—can nullify an individual's effectiveness despite an otherwise concise and precise message.

SENSITIVITY Can you accurately perceive the difference between a look of disgust, anger, playfulness, frustration, or contempt from a friend, stranger, or relative? Can you detect a shift in someone's mood? Can you determine when a power struggle occurs by listening to a conversation? Do you recognize when an individual wants to enter a conversation but hasn't? Do you realize when a group task is cooperative, not competitive? Can you identify when a person has subtly violated a social convention (rule)? Can you detect flirtation? Deceit? Confusion? Discomfort? Can you sense when your audience doesn't like or is hostile to something you've said during a speech? Do you know when a joke has made others feel embarrassed? Knowing what constitutes appropriate communication in a specific context (understanding the rules) and having the skill to communicate appropriately are essential, but what if you don't have your antenna extended to pick up signals coming from others? How will you know which rules apply and how you should communicate? What if you simply aren't attentive to signals from others that indicate tension, disharmony, anger, irritation, and a host of other feelings?

Sensitivity is receptive accuracy whereby we can detect, decode, and comprehend signals in our social environment (Bernieri, 2001). Sensitivity can help us adapt our messages to a particular context in an appropriate and effective manner. Failure to recognize and to comprehend signals can severely retard our social effectiveness (Hall & Bernieri, 2001). If you are obviously angry but your partner doesn't have a clue that this is how you feel, you will easily perceive this cluelessness as insensitivity to your needs, and an argument will likely ensue. Competent communicators develop sensitivity to nuances and subtleties of communication transactions and respond to them.

Sensitivity can be learned (Hall & Bernieri, 2001). One of the functions of this text is to help you become more sensitive to your social environment by identifying patterns of communication that cause problems in relationships and by learning how to analyze an audience before giving a speech.

A major aspect of sensitivity is being mindful, not mindless, about your communication and that of others. We're **mindful** when "we think about our communication and continually work at changing what we do in order to become more effective" (Griffin, 1994, p. 406). For instance, we notice when friends or loved ones reach out to us for support and affection, and we respond. We're **mindless** when we're not cognizant of our communication with others and we put little or no effort into improving it.

Gottman tells a story of a neurosurgeon he had as a client who exhibited mindlessness, not from any desire to be mean but from emotional distance that served him well in his profession (Gottman & DeClaire, 2001). As a successful neurosurgeon, he practiced giving objective, clinical analyses of patients' afflictions. When he came home, he communicated with his wife in the same manner. His wife once asked him, "How do you think we're doing—as a couple?" He provided a long-winded, accurate analysis. His wife burst into tears and ran from the room, leaving him flummoxed. He hadn't been mindful of what her question was actually seeking from him. She desired reassurance, support, and affection. Had he thought about why his wife would ask in a serious manner about the state of their relationship, surely he would have realized that she was not seeking an emotionally detached analysis? If you don't attend to the signals that indicate other people's emotional needs because you aren't looking, then you can't connect with those who can make life a joyful experience. This doesn't mean that we are obliged to connect with everyone we encounter daily, but we surely must connect with those individuals who are important influences on our lives.

As computers are increasingly used to communicate with others, nonverbal cues that we use to detect signals in our social environment are minimized. Feedback processes used in face-to-face transactions are interrupted. Consequently, our sensitivity is disrupted. Think of the number of times that you've read an e-mail and mistaken the tone for irritation or hostility when no such feeling was intended by the sender. Technological advances in communication pose new challenges to our sensitivity.

COMMITMENT   Knowledge, skills, and sensitivity are important ways to improve our communication competence. The We-orientation also requires commitment. **Commitment** is a conscious decision to invest time and energy in improving our communication with others. We must be resolved to monitor our communication. We do this by identifying weaknesses, by learning constructive communication patterns, by dedicating considerable effort toward changing from bad habits to good patterns, and by practicing our skills.

Attitude is as important as aptitude. No one can force you to be a proficient communicator. You have to want to be proficient. In sports, athletes develop a high-level of skills when they commit themselves to hard work, study, and practice. Academic success also does not come from lackluster effort. You have to want to do well and then invest time and effort to make it happen. The same holds true for communication competence. You have to want to improve, to change, and to make an investment in your personal improvement.

ETHICS   A few years ago a national poll ("Amoral Majority," 1991) asked 5,500 Americans whether they would kill a stranger for $10 million; 7% said they would. Applied to the total adult population of the United States, this response means that about 15 million people would be willing assassins for a big chunk of cash. How do we decide whether behavior is right or wrong? Should personal gain (Me-orientation) serve as the primary criterion?

In 1999, the National Communication Association adopted a "Credo for Ethical Communication." The opening statement of this credo establishes the significance of and justification for ethics being included in any communication competence model. The statement reads as follows:

> Questions of right and wrong arise whenever people communicate. Ethical
> communication is fundamental to responsible thinking, decision making, and the
> development of relationships and communities within and across contexts, cultures,

channels, and media. Moreover, ethical communication enhances human worth and dignity by fostering truthfulness, fairness, responsibility, personal integrity, and respect for self and others. We believe that unethical communication threatens the quality of all communication and consequently the well-being of individuals and the society in which we live.

Ethics is a set of standards for judging the moral correctness of communication behavior. In its entirety, the NCA credo identifies five ethical standards to guide our communication with others:

www.mhhe
com/ rothwell2

Go to the Online Learning Center for an "ETHICS Questionnaire"

1. *Respect.* "Some form of the Golden Rule is embraced by virtually all of the major religious and moral systems" (Jaksa & Pritchard, 1994, p. 101). Treating others as you would want to be treated is a central guiding ethical standard. Respect shows concern for others (We-orientation) not just concern for self (Me-orientation).
2. *Honesty.* Ethically responsible communicators try to avoid intentionally deceptive messages. Honesty is a cultural expectation. There is a "presumption against lying" (Bok, 1978, p. 32). All ethical systems condemn lying ("Lying Is Part," 1996). One poll found that honesty was the most prized attribute in a friend ("Lying in America," 1987).
3. *Fairness.* Prejudice has no place in the communication arena. Racism, sexism, homophobia, ageism, and all the other "isms" that plague the human spirit and divide nations and peoples would diminish if we applied the standard of fairness in our communication with diverse groups. Permitting some people to express their points of view but stifling others' expression of dissent is unfair. Fairness requires equal treatment.
4. *Choice.* Our communication should strive to allow people to make their own choices, free of coercion (Jaksa & Pritchard, 1994). Persuasion allows free choice among available options. Coercion forces choice without permitting individuals to think or act for themselves. "Choice must be intentional and voluntary. . . . A communicator's intention is a prime consideration in ethical judgment" (Jensen, 1997, p. 4). When a person is forced to lie or mistreat others, the actions are unintentional. In such a circumstance the person performing the unethical behavior is not culpable.
5. *Responsibility.* "People constantly struggle with the tension between rights and responsibilities, and conscientious people seek to balance the tensions in meaningful and fair ways. Individuals demand the right of free expression, but society demands that individual freedom not harm the larger community" (Jensen, 1997, p. 10). Responsibility means that ethical communication requires a We-orientation. Competent communicators must concern themselves with more than merely what works to achieve personal or group goals. A person may be quite effective at accomplishing individual goals (Me-orientation), but if these goals produce bad outcomes for others, their appropriateness must be questioned. We have a responsibility to consider the consequences of our communication on others.

In the abstract, these standards may seem straightforward and noncontroversial, but almost nothing in human communication is absolute and clear-cut. Human communication behavior is so complex that any list of standards for judging the ethics of communication, applied without exceptions, is bound to run into difficulty. In some cases two or more ethical standards may collide. Free choice, for example, collides with parents' responsibility when they insist that their children behave in

Corporate ethics was a central issue during Congressional hearings following the collapse of Enron. Here members of the Enron Board of Directors swear to tell the truth before being grilled by members of Congress.

certain ways and they use coercion (the threat of punishment) to get their children to make certain choices. Also, what if being honest shows disrespect and lack of concern for another person's feelings ("Yes, you are fat and unattractive")? Despite these difficulties, all five of these ethical standards are strong values in our culture, and they serve as important guidelines for our communication behavior.

Summary

Communication is the transactional process of sharing meaning with others. The communication competence model acts as a map that can guide your transactions with others. Studying the human communication process increases your knowledge of how to behave appropriately and effectively in a specific context. Communication skill development allows you to use your knowledge of communication in useful ways. Knowledge and skills, however, don't automatically improve relationships. Being sensitive to your social environment by detecting, decoding, and comprehending signals increases effective communication. Sensitivity means monitoring your communication so you can improve. Being committed to improving your communication by investing time, energy, feelings, thoughts, and effort is also necessary. The communication competence model of knowledge, skills, sensitivity, commitment, and ethics will serve as a map directing your journey into a variety of communication environments that will be explored in subsequent chapters.

Quizzes Without Consequences

Go to *Quizzes Without Consequences* at the book's Online Learning Center at **www.mhhe.com/rothwell2** or access the CD-ROM for *In the Company of Others.*

www.mhhe
●com/
/rothwell2

Key Terms

appropriateness
channel
commitment
communication
communication
  competence
communication skill
content dimension
context
effectiveness
ethics

feedback
fields of experience
hindsight bias
knowledge
meaning
message
mindful
mindless
myth
noise
physical noise

physiological noise
politics
psychological noise
receiver
relationship dimension
rule
semantic noise
sender
sensitivity

Key Terms

See Audio Flashcards
Study Aid.

www.mhhe
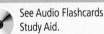 com/ **rothwell2**

See Crossword Puzzle
Study Aid.

Suggested Readings

Aronson, E. (1999). *The social animal*. New York: Worth. A highly readable work on
  the complexities of human behavior.

Bok, S. (1979). *Lying: Moral choice in public and private life*. New York: Vintage Books.
  This is the classic and highly respected work on dishonesty.

Film School

This activity section found in every chapter presents select films for you to analyze. A movie rating (PG-13, R, etc.) and critics' rating (★ for "turkey" to ★★★★★
for "excellent") provided by Martin and Porter (2002) are included to assist you in
deciding which films to view. A plot summary can be found in Martin and Porter
or any other video guide. This is a critical thinking activity. A specific question or
issue is raised that is relevant to each film listed. You are asked to explore this
question or issue, using chapter material for your analysis.

French Kiss (1995). Comedy; PG-13 ★★★↲
This is a very amusing "relationship" movie, with Kevin Kline and Meg Ryan
turning in wonderful comic performances. Notice the influence of culture on communication transactions. What examples do you see of all four types of noise
(physical, physiological, psychological, and semantic)?

The Insider (1999). Drama; R ★★★★↲
Russell Crowe plays a tobacco-industry scientist who has secrets to tell. Analyze
the issue of communication ethics.

Nell (1994). Drama; PG-13 ★★★★
This is the story of a socially isolated individual. Identify the powerful effects social isolation has on a person, especially in the main character's ability to communicate and establish connection with others.

Return to Paradise (1998). Drama; R ★★★↲
Under-rated film about a harrowing moral dilemma. You'll be contemplating what
you would do in the same circumstances. Analyze the film for communication
ethics. You'll find much material to chew over.

CHAPTER 2

Creating a Communication Climate

You're reading from the Sunday comics section of the newspaper, trying to share with your romantic partner, in between convulsive laughter, what strikes you as the funniest cartoon you've ever seen. How would you react if your partner began laughing at you for "finding such adolescent humor entertaining?" Would you accuse your partner of having no sense of humor? What if your partner ignored you and continued reading from another section of the paper? Would you place the comic section on top of your partner's "serious reading material" and encourage a moment's attention?

You've been served dinner by a friend who has spent considerable time preparing the meal, but the steak is undercooked for your taste, appearing to wiggle it is so raw. Would you criticize your friend for "never quite finishing the job?" Wink playfully and stab the steak with a knife so it "won't get up and walk away?" Eat the underprepared meat in silence, stifling your gag reflex? Compliment the meal but offer to cook the steak a bit more because you prefer your meat "more dead than alive?"

You're sitting in an auditorium listening to a speaker rant against "spoiled, emasculating women who want all the benefits of equality but none of the responsibilities." Are you offended, and if so, how do you respond? Do you walk out? Do you heckle the speaker with pig noises? Do you challenge the speaker during a question-and-answer period? Do you sit quietly and endure the sexist remarks?

In each of these instances, the messages sent and the responses they provoke contribute to a communication climate. A **communication climate** is the emotional atmosphere, the pervading or enveloping tone that we create by the way we communicate with others.

A constructive communication climate is composed of two general elements: a pattern of **openness**, or a willingness to communicate, and a pattern of **supportiveness**, or a confirmation of the worth and value of others and a willingness to help others be successful (LaFasto & Larson, 2001). At its core, openness and supportiveness are We-oriented in that our individual agendas are secondary to the relationship, group, or organizational agenda.

A destructive communication climate is composed of two general elements: a pattern of **closedness**, or an unwillingness to communicate with others, and a pattern of **defensiveness**, or a protective reaction to a perceived attack on our self-esteem and self-concept.

The protective reaction usually takes two forms (LaFasto & Larson, 2001). First, we *counterattack* the person whose communication diminishes our self-perception. When Margaret Thatcher was prime minister of Great Britain, she was often called the "Iron Maiden" for her aggressive style and tactics that are stereotypically associated with men, not women. When she received the backhanded "compliment" from a male opposition Labour Party official, "May I congratulate you on being the only man on your team," she shot back, "That's one more than you've got on yours" (Barreca, 1991, p. 84).

Withdrawal is a second way we respond protectively to a perceived attack on our self-esteem. We psychologically and/or physically remove ourselves from a threatening arena.

Climates are the result of sustained transactions. *Individual instances of openness and supportiveness or closedness and defensiveness do not constitute constructive or destructive communication climates.* This is analogous to weather climates. We say that a part of the country has a "temperate climate." We don't base this on a single 70-degree, sunny day. One critical comment is an *episode* that might provoke an immediate defensive response, but it doesn't create a destructive climate. A *pattern* of criticism (several episodes), however, can create a destructive climate. Although examples offered in this chapter to illustrate communication climates are by necessity just episodes, keep in mind that it is repetitive episodes of the same kind of communication that create climates.

The communication climate we create has significant consequences. A careful examination of 98 studies conducted during a 20-year period revealed that the constructive climate of openness and supportiveness is "critical to the success of any relationship" (LaFasto & Larson, 2001, p. 42). This includes relationships at home, at work, and at play. By contrast, the destructive climate of closedness and defensiveness corrodes relationships like sea spray eats away the paint on your car. It corrodes a little bit at a time until irreparable damage transforms what once was a glistening source of pride into a cause of dejection or embarrassment.

For more than two decades, John Gottman has conducted the most extensive scientific investigation of marriage and divorce ever attempted. He has interviewed more than 2,000 couples. He also has videotaped them engaged in day-to-day conversation, and measured their heart rates, blood flow, sweat output, blood pressure, and immune function as they converse. Based on this remarkable research, Gottman concludes that if one partner in a marriage "feels judged, misunderstood, or rejected by the other, you will not be able to manage the problems in your marriage. This holds for big problems and small ones" (Gottman & Silver, 1999, p. 149). Quite likely it also holds true for gay and lesbian couples, although the research was confined to married couples. It definitely holds true for relationships within small groups, teams, and organizations (LaFasto & Larson, 2001).

The communication climate is critical to relationship effectiveness, team achievement, and organizational success. Even in the public speaking arena, the effectiveness of a speech is largely dependent on the communication climate that exists between speaker and listeners. Repeatedly attacking your audience's beliefs or values, for example, will likely provoke a counterattack in the form of heckling or withdrawal as demonstrated by audience members leaving the speech in disgust.

The purpose of this chapter is to explore the communication patterns that produce constructive and destructive communication climates.

This chapter has three objectives:

1. to explain how competitive and cooperative communication transactions influence communication climates,
2. to describe connecting bids and the key role they play in establishing communication climates, and
3. to discuss what a competent communicator can do to build a constructive climate and prevent a destructive one.

The purpose of this chapter is to explore the communication patterns that produce constructive and destructive communication climates.

Competition and Cooperation

Challenging the wisdom of competing can be difficult because the uncritical acceptance of the benefits of competition and the passion with which this view is often held are so widespread in the United States. *My intention is not to trash all competitiveness as evil and offer some fairy-tale notion of total cooperation in a world of perfect harmony.* In fact, the knowledge and skills discussed in this text will give you distinct advantages over rivals when competition is unavoidable. Nevertheless, a sober examination of the research will show that there are significant differences between competitive and cooperative communication climates, and we ignore this evidence at the expense of our relationships with others and our ability to achieve many of our goals in life. This section will provide that sober examination.

Definitions

Although the terms *competition, cooperation,* and *individual achievement* seem straightforward, there can be some confusion regarding their differences. To provide conceptual clarity and to avoid confusion, these key terms are defined, and the term *hypercompetitiveness* is introduced.

COMPETITION   The single inescapable fact that defines *competition* is that the system of rewards inherently benefits the victorious. Thus, **competition** is a process of mutually exclusive goal attainment (MEGA); for you to win, others must lose (Kohn, 1992). Recently, the city of San Francisco advertised 50 new firefighter positions and received more than 10,000 applications. The city had 200 disappointed candidates for each successful applicant.

Examples of competitive communication include engaging in public debates; waging battles to win arguments with friends, spouses, or partners; arguing over material possessions and child custody during a divorce; interrupting a conversation to seize the floor and the attention of listeners; insisting that your opinion is correct and another person's is incorrect; demanding obedience from employees who have less power in an organization; trying to win recognition at work as the best performer; and criticizing and diminishing others to look superior to rivals at work. In all of these acts, communication is a vehicle to defeat others and to establish oneself as best at others' expense.

COOPERATION   Unlike competition, **cooperation** is a process of mutually inclusive goal attainment (MIGA); for me to achieve my goal, you must also achieve your goal. We sink or swim together. Examples of cooperative communication include negotiating problems to the mutual satisfaction of all parties in a conflict; engaging in teamwork to solve problems and make decisions; encouraging participation from those who have not had a chance to be heard in a group discussion; teaching those with inadequate skills to improve and become more capable team members; and expressing support to those who are discouraged. The essence of cooperation is to raise everyone to a high standard for the benefit of all, not to drag anyone down to defeat for the sake of individual glory.

Competitive communication can be tumultuous, but cooperative communication also can be difficult and at times contentious, even frustrating. *Cooperative communication is a process, not an outcome.* Parties in a conflict, for example, may communicate cooperatively yet still not reach an agreement because they seek very different outcomes.

The cooperative communication process also doesn't mean yielding to others. Management guru W. Edwards Deming relates a story to make the point: "I was stuck in an airplane waiting for several hours to disembark. When we finally were able to get off, the stewardess said, 'Thank you for your cooperation.' That's not cooperation. What choice do prisoners have?" (Aguayo, 1990, p. 230).

INDIVIDUAL ACHIEVEMENT   When 1,030 females from ages 11 to 49 were asked with whom they competed, 75% of the respondents chose "with myself; my own standards

Hypercompetitiveness knows no bounds. A hot dog eating contest celebrates eating to excess. Who won? Not the big guy. The small fellow in the middle downed a record 50 hot dogs in 12 minutes. Remarked a spokesman for the International Federation of Competitive Eating, "He [the winner] has truly redefined the sport."

and goals" (Nelson, 1998). Although we sometimes refer to setting increasingly higher standards for ourselves and to striving for a previously unrealized goal as "competing with ourselves," no loser is required or desired. Thus, no competition occurs. *Competition is not a solitary undertaking; it is interactive* (Kohn, 1992). Saying that you compete with yourself makes as much conceptual sense as saying you wrestled or lost a tennis match with yourself. What we often call competing with ourselves is more accurately termed *individual achievement*. **Individual achievement** is the realization of personal goals without having to defeat an opponent. Giving a speech better the second time you perform it is an individual achievement. It becomes competitive when you try to outperform someone else, as in a speech contest or debate tournament, not when you attempt to improve on your own previous performance.

HYPERCOMPETITIVENESS   The excessive emphasis on beating others to achieve one's goals is called **hypercompetitiveness**. Americans "manifest a staggering cultural obsession with victory" (Aronson, 1999, p. 263). Kevin Daugherty, youth sports specialist for the American Sport Education Program, says, "Our culture bombards us with messages that winning is everything" (Krucoff, 1998, p. D3). Nathan Miller writes "conversation in the United States is a competitive exercise in which the first person to draw a breath is declared the listener"(Bolton, 1979, p. 4). No discussion of human communication can ignore competition without being woefully incomplete. Competition saturates our society and influences our relationships with others. It is "the common denominator of American life" (Kohn, 1992, p. 1).

Hypercompetitiveness and Communication Competence

My students were assigned a group symposium presentation. Although I had not indicated that groups had to choose different topics, the students assumed this without checking with me. When two groups discovered they had chosen the same topic, their communication became openly hostile. One group tried to preempt the

cathy®   **by Cathy Guisewite**

© 1994 Cathy Guisewite. Distributed by Universal Press Syndicate. www.ucomics.com.

other by negotiating with me to present its symposium first, thereby stealing the thunder of the other group. The group left out of this negotiation cried foul. Tempers flared. I tried to resolve the conflict by instituting a random drawing to designate the order of presentation. I assured both groups that they could work on the same topic because grades were determined on specific criteria, not by a comparison between groups. The groups were not mollified.

Outside of class, the competitive communication persisted. Members of the two groups engaged in a nasty verbal confrontation during lunch in the cafeteria. Voices were raised, threats were made, and menacing gestures were exchanged. Two individuals almost came to blows, so I was told later. Members of one group swarmed the library and checked out every source they could locate on the topic. They hoarded these resources, giving themselves an advantage while handicapping the opposing group.

The competition between these two groups was fierce, completely unnecessary, and counterproductive. Thus, they exhibited hypercompetitiveness. Neither group did the assignment well. Each was busy trying to hurt the other instead of focusing on doing a high-quality presentation. These groups could have used cooperative communication by coordinating their efforts, agreeing to share resources, pooling information, and negotiating a way to minimize repetition in their presentations. Instead, they chose to compete ruthlessly, blind to the destructive communication climate they were creating and the conflict spiral that it produced.

These two groups took a Me-oriented, competitive approach to their perceived problem. This raises an important question. Is Me-oriented, competitive communication always incompetent communication? Not necessarily.

First, communication competence is a matter of degree. *It is excessive competition, not competition itself, that produces incompetent communication.* Psychological, spiritual, or emotional benefits can be derived from competing and knowing that you tried your best, even though you lost. Some individuals, usually those who are victorious, thrive in a competitive environment. The emphasis is what matters, not the mere presence of occasional competitive communication patterns. The We-orientation of competent communication implies primary, not exclusive, focus. My two warring groups were exclusively Me-oriented. They never made any attempt to communicate cooperatively. Trying to win an argument with your relationship partner, however, can be challenging and fun as long as this verbal jousting is playful or entertaining and doesn't wound.

Because we live in a hypercompetitive society does not mean we must resign ourselves to the inevitability of competing at almost every turn when little attempt to transform competitive climates into cooperative ones has occurred. *Encouraging greater cooperation in our communication with others merely calls for a better balance in a society awash in competition, not the impractical abolition of all competition.*

Second, a cooperative option doesn't always exist. Interviewing for a job is unavoidably competitive whenever more than one applicant is vying for a single position. Encouraging individuals to hone their oral communication skills so that they might compete more effectively in such situations should be applauded. Also, a constructive communication climate isn't always possible. Individuals may be so hypercompetitive that, despite your best efforts, they simply refuse to cooperate even in small ways. In these instances, competent communication is determined by your degree of effectiveness and appropriateness in the competitive arena. *The guiding principle should be to look for ways to establish a cooperative climate when possible and to engage in competitive communication when you must.*

Effects of Competition and Cooperation

Competing and cooperating are wholly different processes and they create very different communication climates. When we compete, we try to prevent others from achieving their goals so we can achieve our goals. *The more competitive our transactions with others become, the more we encourage closedness and defensiveness, the two components of a destructive communication climate.* Openness and supportiveness, the two components of a constructive communication climate, are discouraged by competitiveness because they give an advantage to your opponent. A sports team, for example, that reveals its strategy and weaknesses openly and encourages players on the opposing team diminishes its chance of victory. You want your opponent guessing about your strategy and feeling demoralized when losing to you because it increases your chances of victory.

See Video Clip #1 on the CD, Chapter 2.

Cooperation, unlike competition, requires the attainment of our goals by working with, not against others. Thus, openness and supportiveness are encouraged because mutual goal attainment is more likely in such an atmosphere. As discussed in this section, substantial research reveals the clear advantages of a cooperative communication climate.

EFFECTS ON INTERPERSONAL RELATIONSHIPS   Competition is not structured to enhance interpersonal relationships. Trying to win an argument with your housemate about who does the most cleaning and who is most responsible for making repairs has "victory" as the goal. "Losing" an argument doesn't usually foster friendliness toward your antagonist.

Competition can reduce empathy (Kohn, 1993). **Empathy** is "thinking and feeling what you perceive another to be thinking and feeling" (Howell, 1982, p. 108). Empathy is the We-orientation of communication competence. When you have empathy, you experience another person's perspective. Trying to win at someone else's expense clouds your ability to empathize. Your focus is on yourself, not on the other person or on what damage winning might produce. The more empathy you feel, the more difficult it becomes to view another person as a rival to be vanquished.

Competition can also incite hostile communication (Van Oostrum & Rabbie, 1995). In a survey of 60 high school athletic associations, 76% of the respondents said increased verbal and nonverbal hostility are causing many officials of high school sporting events to quit (Dahlberg, 2001). Parents have brawled at T-ball games in Florida, coaches across the nation have been threatened and physically harmed by

We've probably all experienced the thrill of victory and the agony of defeat.

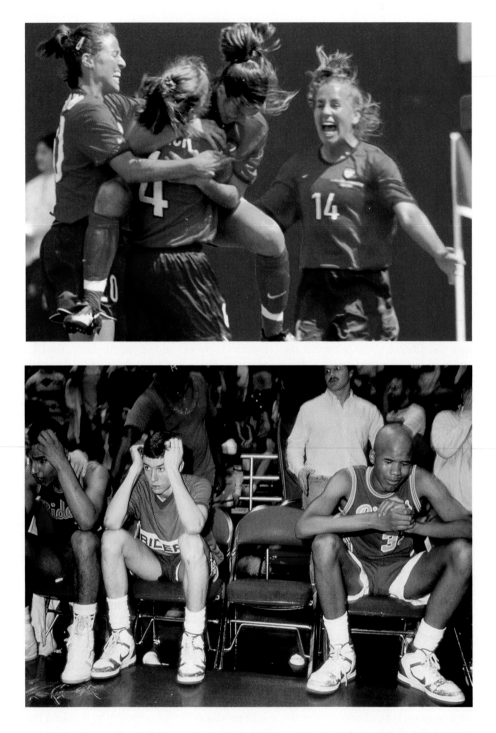

parents and opposing coaches, and kids are regularly yelled at by parents during and after sporting events (Dahlberg, 2001). A Little League district in Albuquerque, New Mexico, for example, cancelled an entire baseball season for 500 kids because of open hostility among parents, coaches, and league officials. In Whitehall, North Carolina, one coach slashed the throat of a rival coach, spattering blood on one of the Little

Box 2-1 | Focus on Controversy

Ethics and Hypercompetitiveness

Competent communication involves ethical considerations, and hypercompetitiveness raises serious ethical concerns. Lying and deception clearly violate the ethical criterion of honesty, and hypercompetitiveness encourages dishonesty. As Sissela Bok (1978), in her widely acclaimed book, *Lying*, explains, "The very stress on individualism, on competition, on achieving material success which so marks our society also generates intense pressures to cut corners. . . . [S]uch motives impel many to participate in forms of duplicity they might otherwise resist" (p. 258).

Cheating, in addition to being dishonest, violates the ethical criterion of fairness because it gives an unfair advantage to the cheater. Cheating has become widespread in the United States, and hypercompetitiveness is the driving force behind it. On February 18, 1999, NBC News reported that 70% of college students cheat on tests, and 84% cheat on term papers, usually by buying them off the Internet. Intense competition for grades was cited as a primary reason students cheat.

Another ethical standard, respect for others, is communicated through sportsmanship, empathy, and compassion. Hypercompetitiveness, which glorifies the victors and is indifferent to or even contemptuous of losers in a contest, teaches none of these elements of respect. As Alice Walker so eloquently notes, we live in a culture where "the only way I can bloom is if I step on your flower, the only way I can shine is if I put out your light" (cited in Lanka, 1989, p. 24). Respect, not in the sense of being impressed by a potential rival's talent but of valuing someone as a person, doesn't blossom in a hypercompetitive climate.

This is all well and good, you may be saying, but we live in a hypercompetitive society. Our children will have to face the disappointment of losing throughout their lives, and so will we. They'll lose jobs because others gave better interviews; they'll lose arguments with parents and teachers; they may even lose in divorce proceedings. Is it not the responsibility of parents to teach children how to lose?

Teaching a child how to lose with grace and dignity is an important communication lesson, but just as important is teaching them how to communicate cooperatively with others. Our children will be afforded many opportunities to practice losing without any encouragement from us. Does it not make more sense to offer cooperative experiences for our children to counterbalance the competitive exposure they most surely will face without our assistance?

Questions for Thought

1. Are the ethical questions raised here merely misplaced idealism that ignores the unavoidable realities of American society? Don't we have to deal with what is, not with what we might like our society to be?
2. Are the ethical questions raised here an indictment only of hypercompetitiveness, or can the same questions be raised about competition in general?

is a central part of establishing a constructive communication climate. This next section explores types of connecting bids, responses made to our connecting bids, and the consequences of those responses on the communication climate.

Types of Connecting Bids

Connecting bids come in all sizes and shapes (Gottman & DeClaire, 2001). There are the hugely significant ones such as "Let's move in together" or "Do you want to start a business with me?" or "Mom and Dad, I'm pregnant" or even "I finally passed a math class; isn't that great?"

Bids also can be seemingly insignificant requests or comments characteristic of day-to-day communication. "Honey, will you get me a beer?" or "Mommy, will you help me tie my shoe?" or "Did you read the e-mail I sent to you?" typify these kinds of bids.

Some bids are subtle. For example, "You look very nice today," "Good morning," or "How was your vacation?" may be overlooked as bids to connect, yet each attempts connection with another person.

Connecting bids also can be very direct. "Let's have sex," "Do you still love me?" and "Do you think of me as a good friend?" are typical examples because they are point-blank attempts to connect or to determine the degree of connection with another person.

Some bids disguise the emotions. A young boy might say to his busy dad, "Look, there's Jeff's dad playing catch with him." What the boy really wants to say is, "I wish you'd spend time with me doing fun stuff."

Sometimes bids are purposely vague. Asking a person for a date, for example, can be an emotionally risky bid. To protect our vulnerable self-esteem, we may choose to hint at a dating possibility instead of asking a person directly. For example, instead of asking, "Do you want to see a movie with me on Saturday?" you might ask, "What's your favorite kind of movie?" followed by "Maybe some time we could check out one of those classic movies you love?" The vague bid doesn't usually risk outright rejection as a more direct bid might.

Responses to Connecting Bids

Making a bid is only the initial step of a conversational dance of connection. Every bid provokes one of three responses: turning toward, turning away from, or turning against the bid (Gottman & DeClaire, 2001).

TURNING TOWARD RESPONSE The **turning toward response** to a bid for connection means we react positively to the bid. Your partner tells a joke, and you laugh. A parent calls to invite you for dinner, and you accept enthusiastically. A friend wants to talk, and you join in conversation. A coworker seeks your advice concerning how to handle a difficult individual in your work team, and you make some suggestions. A stranger stops you on the street and asks for directions, and you provide clear, detailed instructions. In each instance, your response establishes a connection because you have turned toward the bid by responding positively. The response validates the other person.

Sometimes a response may appear to be negative, unless you recognize an understanding that exists between two people. For example, a good male friend and I regularly engage in verbal jousting for fun. We ridicule each other, sometimes with seemingly brutal put-downs. To outsiders it may appear that we do not like each other until they observe the typical laughter and amusement such verbal sparring elicits from both of us. We perceive this feigned fighting as friendly banter, and it connects us in friendship. Even though on the surface our put-downs appear to be turning against the other person, we understand that this is merely a friendly verbal game, and our participation is actually a turning toward response. Such verbal jousting may seem odd, even repellent to some people, especially women who do not engage in such banter nearly as much as men (Tannen, 1994). Nevertheless, it is a reminder that communication is not always what it seems on the surface.

TURNING AWAY RESPONSE The **turning away response** occurs when we ignore a bid to connect or act preoccupied when a bid is offered. You ask your partner if she wants her wash put in the dryer and she waves dismissively as she focuses intently on her computer screen. You ask your supervisor at work for advice on a project and, without looking up from reading a report, she tells you to figure out what to do. You're driving with a friend when you exclaim, "Look at that sports car." Your friend

A turning away response can be as destructive to a relationship as a turning against response. Which is this?

never looks and continues to fiddle with the CD player. A panhandler on the street approaches you for "spare change." You walk by without responding. You ask your audience during your speech, "How many of you own a DVD player?" Nobody raises a hand even though several individuals have DVD players. These turning away responses are rarely malicious. They simply may be mindless and inattentive because of stress, overwork, or fascination with the task of the moment. Nevertheless, they are disconnecting. In essence, the turning away response communicates the message, "You're not very important to me right now; I choose to ignore you."

TURNING AGAINST RESPONSE The **turning against response** is an overtly negative rejection of a connecting bid. You ask your partner, "Do you want to watch some TV?" and your partner responds, "All we ever do is watch that lobotomy box. Can't you come up with something more original?" A child approaches her parent and complains, "I don't understand this stupid English assignment." The parent responds, "Maybe you'd understand it if you paid more attention in class." You offer to help your roommate clean up clutter in your apartment. Your roommate remarks, "Don't get your tights in a twist. I know how psycho you can get about a little mess." You approach a coworker and ask for assistance figuring out how to use a new software program. The coworker responds, "I don't have time to help you out. Try reading the manual for a change." Unlike the turning away response, these turning against responses seem mean, even malicious. In essence, the turning against response says, "Get lost" or "I'm angry with you."

Consequences of Bidding Process

Establishing a constructive communication climate prevents many of the emotional upheavals and troubling conflicts that can jeopardize our transactions with others. The number of bids offered and the type of response made to connecting bids determine the likely consequences.

cathy®   **by Cathy Guisewite**

© 2002 Cathy Guisewite. Distributed by Universal Press Syndicate. www.ucomics.com.

NUMBER OF BIDS MATTERS   The very act of bidding to connect has significant effects on our relations with others. Long-term studies of couple communication found that, during a typical conversation over dinner, happy couples offered bids as often as 100 times in a 10-minute period. Those couples headed for a breakup offered one-third fewer bids (Gottman & DeClaire, 2001). Fewer bids mean fewer opportunities to connect and nurture an important relationship.

Even when the goal is merely to maintain cordial transactions with coworkers or individuals we've just met, the number of bids can markedly affect these relations. When first introduced to a stranger at a party or a new coworker or a friend of a friend, for example, we generally ask about what they do for a living, whether they have children, and so forth. We ask these types of questions, not because we desire a close, lasting relationship, but because it can make our transactions with others pleasant. We may appear socially retarded when we are introduced to others and we make little or no effort to connect with them even superficially. The initial impression may taint later transactions with these same individuals in the future.

TYPE OF RESPONSE MATTERS   The responses to bids are even more telling (Gottman & DeClaire, 2001). Husbands heading for divorce turn away from their wives' bids 82% of the time. Wives in similar unhappy circumstances turn away from their husbands' bids 50% of the time. Husbands in strong relationships, however, turn away from only 19% of their wives' bids, and wives in strong relationships turn away from only 14% of their husbands' bids. When we turn away from the connecting bids of others, we dampen further attempts to connect. The bidder easily loses heart when a bid is ignored. In fact, attempts to **rebid**, to try again after an initial bid has been ignored or rejected, are *near zero*. This is a classic withdrawal reaction typical of a destructive communication climate. The more that bids are turned away the more the spurned individual loses confidence in and enthusiasm for the relationship.

Ignoring bids produces hostility and defensiveness. We can easily become hypervigilant, overly sensitized to the insult of a turned-away bid, even when the offender is not an important person in our life. Repeatedly dealing with a salesperson who ignores your questions about a product can ignite hostility and defensiveness quickly. We start looking for bad treatment and magnifying each episode of disregard. No one can turn toward every connecting bid offered, so it is easy to find examples of disregarded bids even in close relationships. Stung by the apparent disrespect of a turned away bid, the spurned individual often begins to criticize the person who turns away, leading to counterattack and withdrawal from the person criticized. This attack-counterattack pattern characteristic of a destructive climate can easily spin out of control.

Not surprisingly, turning against the bids of others also destroys relationships. Negative responses to connecting bids typically produce hostility or withdrawal. Although turning against responses may seem to be the worst possible reaction one can make to a bid for connection, the research shows that turning away and turning against responses are about equally destructive to relationships (Gottman & DeClaire, 2001).

Establishing a Constructive Communication Climate

LaFasto and Larson (2001) write, "The principle of openness implies that it is better to talk things over. The principle of supportiveness implies that it makes a great deal of difference *how* you talk things over" (p. 17). This section explains *how* to talk things over so we can establish a constructive communication climate and avoid a hypercompetitive, destructive one.

Emphasize Supportive Communication Patterns

In an 8-year study of groups, Jack Gibb (1961) identified specific communication patterns that create defensiveness (evaluation, control, indifference, manipulation, superiority, and certainty). He also identified corresponding communication patterns that are supportive and prevent or defuse defensiveness (description, problem orientation, empathy, assertiveness, equality, and provisionalism). As these patterns are explained, think about which ones you most often use.

See Video Clip #2, Chapter 2 of the CD.

EVALUATION VERSUS DESCRIPTION A friend of mine was in his townhouse when the 6.9 magnitude Loma Prieta earthquake hit central California in 1989. Objects flew across the rooms, kitchen cabinets emptied onto the counters and floor, and glass shattered throughout his home. When those tumultuous 15 seconds of nature's nervous breakdown subsided, the timid little voice of my friend's 5-year-old daughter came from the back room: "Daddy, it wasn't my fault." We are quick to defend ourselves if we even think an evaluation might be offered.

Evaluations are value judgments made about individuals and about their performance. Statements of praise, recognition, admiration, or flattery are positive evaluations; criticism, contempt, and blame are negative evaluations. We are ever wary of negative evaluations, and for good reason. Negative evaluations produce a defensive environment that can ignite a destructive communication climate (Stone et al., 1999).

Children who are frequently criticized by parents turn away from their parents when they are in trouble. Children whose parents consistently praise their accomplishments and efforts, however, typically turn toward their parents for support and help when they get into trouble (Gottman & DeClaire, 2001). Criticism, especially criticism handled ineptly, produces more conflict in the workplace than mistrust, personality clashes, power struggles, or pay (Baron, 1990).

Blame, a close cousin of criticism, is no better. Blame seeks to pin responsibility for a perceived failure on an individual. Focusing on blame makes what *has* occurred more important than what *should* occur to solve problems. Blame impedes understanding of a problem, thwarts problem solving, and often "serves as a bad proxy for talking directly about hurt feelings" (Stone, Patton, and Heen, 1999, p. 59).

Relationships, even casual associations with coworkers, supervisors, or distant relatives, are strained by even moderate amounts of criticism, contempt, and blame. Gottman's research found that maintaining a constructive climate requires a disproportionate emphasis on positive communication (Gottman & Silver, 1994, 1999). It takes at least five positive communication acts to counterbalance every negative one. Criticism often can eat at us more than praise can sustain us.

Any evaluation, even praise and recognition, has the potential to create a defensive climate. Although praise tends to connect people, it can in some circumstances be disconnecting. Praising one individual in a group, for example, may trigger jealousy or hostility from other group members not likewise praised, especially if members are hypercompetitive. That's why praising team accomplishment, not individual success, is often more effective.

Nevertheless, disavowing all evaluative communication is too simplistic. A study of the 1,000 largest companies in the United States found that lack of recognition and praise was the number-one reason employees left their companies ("Praise Thy Employees," 1994). Praise and recognition for significant accomplishments and commendable performance play an important part in constructing supportive communication climates. Inflated accolades for trivial accomplishments and indiscriminate praise for both good and mediocre performance, however, devalue praise.

We counter evaluative communication patterns, especially criticism, contempt, and blame, with descriptive communication. A description is a first-person report of how we feel, what behaviors we observe, or what we perceive to be true in specific situations. Three primary steps can help you become more descriptive:

1. *Use "first-person singular" statements* (Narcisco & Burkett, 1975). Begin by identifying your feelings; use the "I" form and then describe behavior linked to the feeling. "I feel alone and unconnected to you when I share my concerns with you and receive no response" is an example. It is a descriptive, first-person singular statement related to a turning away response to a bid for connection. Unlike an "I" statement, a "you" statement places the focus on the other person. "You make me feel stupid and uninformed" is an accusation that assigns blame and is likely to provoke a denial or a counterattack (Stone et al., 1999).
2. *Make your descriptions specific, not vague.* "I feel sort of weird when you act inappropriately around my boss" is an inexact description. "Sort of weird" and "inappropriately" require more specific description. "I feel awkward and embarrassed when you tell jokes to my boss that ridicule gays and women" makes the description much more concrete.
3. *Eliminate editorial comments from descriptive statements.* "I get annoyed when you waste my time by talking about silly side issues" uses the first-person singular form without the supportive intent or phrasing. "Waste time" and "silly side issues" are editorial, opinionated language. Instead, say, "I get annoyed when you introduce side issues." Then provide specific examples of side issues.

Textbook-perfect first-person singular statements produce no supportive response, of course, if the tone of voice used is sarcastic or condescending, eye contact is threatening or leering, facial expressions and body language are contemptuous or intimidating, and gestures are abusive. Place the spotlight on your own feelings and on the specific behaviors you find objectionable without sending mixed messages composed of verbal descriptions and nonverbal evaluations.

CONTROL VERSUS PROBLEM ORIENTATION   "He who agrees against his will, is of the same opinion still" observed the English poet Samuel Butler (Brussell, 1988). Most people dislike being controlled by others. **Control** is communication that seeks to regulate or direct a person's behavior.

Control can easily lead to a contest of wills brought about by psychological reactance (Brehm, 1972). **Psychological reactance** is the tendency to resist efforts to control our behavior and restrict our choices, especially if we feel entitled to choose. For example, if upon returning to your parked car you see another car waiting for your space, are you inclined to leave faster or slower? What if the waiting driver honks at you to encourage a faster exit? One study (Ruback & Jweng, 1997) found that most people slow their exit, especially if the waiting driver honks at them.

If the pressure to restrict becomes intense, we may be strongly attracted to what is prohibited. This phenomenon is well known to parents. As advice columnist Ann Landers (1995) observed, "There are three ways to make sure something gets done: Do it yourself, hire someone to do it, or forbid your kids to do it" (p. D5). When parents oppose romantic relationships, such as a teenage daughter dating an older boy, it often intensifies feelings of romantic love (Driscoll et al., 1972). The more strongly parents admonish their children not to take drugs, smoke, or get their tongues pierced, the more likely the kids are to do those very behaviors in order to restore their sense of personal freedom (Dowd et al., 1988; Graybar et al., 1989). Parents step into the psychological reactance quicksand when they insist that their children obey them. Nevertheless, parents want to protect children from foolish or dangerous behavior. All controlling communication can't be eliminated, but it can be kept to a minimum and used only when other choices are not practical.

"And just who the hell are you to tell me I'm entitled to my opinion?"

We can prevent defensiveness from occurring when we collaborate on a problem and seek solutions cooperatively instead of demanding obedience. Try working on the problem and how to solve it, not on how best to control other people's behavior or "win" a power struggle. Parents and children can work together, brainstorming possible solutions to troublesome conflicts.

The problem-orientation approach also works well in the work setting. One study (McNutt, 1997) of strategic decision-making at 356 U.S. companies found that 58% of plans were turned down when the executives overseeing the plans tried to impose their ideas on colleagues. When executives sought participation and counsel from colleagues, however, 96% of the plans were adopted.

Consider some examples differentiating controlling and problem-solving communication:

Controlling	Problem Orientation
Pick up your room—now!	I've asked you repeatedly to clean your room. You haven't done it. I have a problem with the fact that the chores I expect you to perform are not getting done. How do you see our situation?
Stop talking on the phone.	I need to make an important call. Please let me know when you're finished.
If you don't start pulling your weight, I'll fire you.	We need to talk about how to improve your performance.

MANIPULATION VERSUS ASSERTIVENESS   Imagine that you have just met an interesting person at a party. This person seems very open, honest, and attentive. You are complimented by the attention this person pays you. Then imagine that you hear later from a friend that this same person was using you to gain favor with your older sibling. You were a pawn in a chess game. How would you feel being manipulated in such a callous and deceptive way?

Manipulative communication (Gibb calls it "strategic") is an attempt by one person to maneuver another toward the manipulator's goal. Most people resent manipulation, especially if it is based on deception. As noted in the previous chapter, politics in organizations, a particularly cutthroat form of manipulative communication, can destroy teamwork and team effectiveness (LaFasto & Larson, 2001). Even knowing that someone will attempt to manipulate us can make us defensive. Political candidates face this challenge when they give speeches in election bids. Phone solicitors face a similar difficulty. The 1998 Roper poll found that telemarketers and slick salespeople make 46% of respondents uncomfortable ("How Americans Communicate, 1998). Only 18% of respondents feel "very comfortable" dealing with salespeople, and only 30% feel "very effective" dealing with them.

Gibb (1961) suggests spontaneity is the answer to manipulative communication. Spontaneity is communication by impulse. The term *spontaneity* suggests off-the-top-of-your-head, ill-conceived communication. Knowledgeable, skillful communication used appropriately and effectively requires careful thought and consideration, not impulsiveness. A better term is *assertiveness*, a skill discussed at length in Chapter 8. Impulsive communication is often aggressive. Assertiveness requires thought, skill, and concern for others. Assertive communication says, "No games are being played. This is how I feel and this is what I need from you." It is honest and direct, unlike manipulative communication.

INDIFFERENCE VERSUS EMPATHY   Playwright George Bernard Shaw observed, "The worst sin towards our fellow creatures is not to hate them, but to be indifferent to them; that's the essence of inhumanity" (Brussell, p. 281). The Fatherhood Project at the Families and Work Institute in New York concluded, "It is presence, not absence, that often lies at the heart of troubled families. It is common for family members to be in the same room and be oblivious to each other's thoughts and feelings" (Coontz, 1997, p. 160). This neutrality, as Gibb terms it, or indifference toward others, is a sign of a disintegrating family. It also encourages further family deterioration and conflict.

The turning away response is a form of indifference to others. Such indifference can produce defensiveness. A father's turning away responses to his children attack their self-esteem. The lowest self-esteem among teenagers occurs in two-parent families in which the father shows little interest in his children (Clark & Barber, 1994). Children often grow resentful of an indifferent or absent parent. This resentment can turn into outright hostility, making future reconciliation between parent and child difficult.

Pretending to listen or not listening at all also exhibits indifference, whether it occurs in the home, school, work environment, or public speaking arena. Students want their professors to hear what they have to say. Employees feel snubbed when fellow workers or supervisors pay no attention to them when they speak. Speakers feel irritated or even angry when audience members sleep through their speeches. Romantic partners want to be listened to, not ignored. Hite's (1987) survey results from 4,500 female respondents, most of whom were very unhappy with their partners, found this: When asked, "What does your partner do that makes you the maddest?" 77% responded, "He doesn't listen."

You counter indifference with empathy. Empathy is built on sensitivity to others, a necessary quality of a competent communicator. Parents who are indifferent to their children might try putting themselves in their children's shoes. What would it have been like if their parents had shown no interest in them? Would they have felt abandoned, worthless, or hostile? What does it mean to a child when a father refuses to pay child support? What message does that send to the child? Think and feel as the child might think and feel. Take the child's perspective. That's empathy.

Rosenfeld (1983) found that when an instructor exhibited empathic behaviors, students liked the class and the teacher. These empathic behaviors included showing interest in the problems students face, exhibiting a perception of subject matter as students see it, and making students feel that the instructor understands them.

SUPERIORITY VERSUS EQUALITY   The line "No matter what this guy does, he thinks that no one can hold a candle to him, although a lot of people would like to" (Perret, 1994, p. 92) expresses the typical feeling most people have to expressed egotism. Expressing one's personal superiority over others is Me-oriented.

Projecting one's superiority tarnishes others as inferior. Treat anyone as an inferior and there is likely to be a defensive reaction. The history of the women's movement, the battle for civil rights, and the fight for the rights of the disabled all reveal that labeling and treating people as inferior will produce a strong defensive reaction. In fact, the dispute over substituting the term "differently abled" for "disabled" spotlights the defensiveness caused when some individuals are perceived as being less able than others.

The superiority attitude invites defensiveness because it says, "You're less than I am. You're a loser. Stay in your place." Few like to be viewed as inferior in anyone's eyes. The NBC-TV program "The Weakest Link" made sport of host Anne Robinson's acerbic put-downs of contestants. As this British emcee hectored contestants and questioned their mental capacity with "Who is allergic to intelligence?" and "Who is the poster child for incompetence?" the studio audience laughed uncomfortably. Anova, a British online news service, conducted a poll and found that 40% of Americans considered Robinson "too rude" even for a game show that celebrates the put-down of contestants ("Game Show," 2001).

Research on boastfulness, bragging about our superiority to others, reveals that braggarts are generally disliked (Holtgraves & Dulin, 1994). Research in the classroom reveals that teachers who communicate an air of superiority are generally disliked. "My teacher treats us as equals with him/her" was a common response from students who liked their classes (Rosenfeld, 1983).

Whatever the differences in our abilities, talents, and intellect, treating people with respect and politeness, as equals on a human level, is supportive and encourages harmony and cooperation. Treating people like gum on the bottom of your shoe will invite defensiveness, even retaliation.

Note the difference between these examples of expressed superiority and equality:

Superiority	**Equality**
That's incorrect!	Can you think of why that might be incorrect?
When you get to be a parent then you'll know I'm right!	Can you see why I might not agree with you on this?
I'm the boss and I know what's best.	Let's discuss this and see if we can find common agreement.

CERTAINTY VERSUS PROVISIONALISM　Few things in this world are certain. Death, taxes, and that your toast will always fall buttered side down are a few that come to mind. Because most things are not certain, there is room for discussion and disagreement. When someone makes absolute, unqualified statements of certainty, however, he or she closes off discussion and disagreement. Withdrawing from the conversation, leaving the auditorium where the speech is being presented, or counterattacking with an attempt to prove the know-it-all wrong is often the result.

Dogmatism, a common form of the certainty communication pattern, is a "belief in the self-evident truth of one's opinion. The dogma, or declaration of truth, warrants no debate in the mind of the dogmatist" (Rothwell, 2001, p. 106). A dogmatic person shows closed-mindedness, rigid thinking, and an unwillingness to consider alternative ideas. Spell the word dogma backward and you get *am-god*, an easy way to remember what a dogmatist is. Dogmatists act godlike in their certainty of the rightness of their own opinions.

In one study (Leathers, 1970), five typical dogmatic statements were introduced into conversations:

1. That's a ridiculous statement. I disagree.
2. Are you serious in taking such an absurd position?
3. You are wrong. Dead wrong!
4. I don't understand why I ever agreed with you.
5. That's downright foolish.

Study participants reacted to these dogmatic statements with heightened tension (rubbing their hands together nervously and squirming in their seats). These statements also provoked opinionated statements in response.

Provisionalism is an effective substitute for dogmatism, or the certainty attitude. **Provisionalism** is the qualifying of our statements, avoiding absolutes. Problems and issues are approached as questions to be investigated. Options not yet explored are viewed as possibilities worthy of discussion. "Let's discuss it," "That's an interesting idea," or "I hadn't thought of that" exhibit provisional communication.

Those who communicate certainty easily slip into using terms such as *always, never, must, can't,* and *won't.* Conversely, provisionalism is communicated by using terms such as *possibly, probably, perhaps, may, maybe, might,* and *could be.* Consider these examples:

Certainty	**Provisionalism**
You're never on time.	You're often late.
You always ignore me.	Sometimes you ignore me.
You seriously can't be considering him for the position.	He probably isn't right for the job.
That's total nonsense!	That probably isn't true.

Perhaps you are thinking that this discussion of defensive and supportive communication patterns appears useful in the abstract but not very useful when you are in the middle of a heated argument with your partner, friend, coworker, or boss. Consider several responses to this question of real-life application. First, supportive communication is primarily preventive in nature. The more you learn to use supportive communication patterns, the less likely heated arguments will unfold. Defensive patterns provoke counterattacks. Supportive patterns can dampen anger and aggression and create connection. Second, don't attempt to learn all six supportive patterns simultaneously. Pick the one that seems best suited to your current circumstances, and practice it first. You want to learn supportive patterns so well that they become virtually automatic. When you've learned one pattern, go on to another. When a heated argument does surface, your new skills may help to turn down the heat. Instead of escalating the battle with defensive communication, your supportive responses may turn the conflict into a problem to be solved together.

See Defensive vs. Supportive activity on CD.

Defuse Defensiveness and Hypercompetitiveness

Supportive communication patterns can prevent defensive, hypercompetitive responses from occurring, but what if your partner, relative, friend, or coworker becomes highly defensive despite your best efforts to create a cooperative environment? You're trying to resolve a difference of viewpoint, for example, but the other person becomes defensive the moment the subject is introduced. What do you do? There are several ways to short-circuit the defensiveness of others.

AVOID DEFENSIVE SPIRALS Lady Astor, the first female member of the British Parliament, was exasperated by Winston Churchill's opposition to several of the causes she espoused. Frustrated, she acerbically commented, "Winston, if I were married to you, I'd put poison in your coffee." Churchill shot back, "And if you were my wife, I'd drink it" (Fadiman, 1985, p. 122). An attack produces a counterattack that can easily spiral out of control. Refuse to be drawn into a hypercompetitive defensive spiral in which you begin sounding like two kids arguing: "You did so." "You did not." "Did so." "Did not." This means that you speak and listen nondefensively, even if your partner, friend, relative, or coworker exhibits defensive, hypercompetitive communication patterns. This takes discipline and patience. You have control over your communication. Try using that control to create a constructive dialogue, not a malignant spiral of defensiveness.

FOCUS ON THE PROBLEM, NOT THE PERSON   Unless the problem is the other person, stick to the agenda for discussion. Do not make turning against responses even if the connecting bid seems provocative. For example, this kind of diverting response is not advisable:

> SHASHA: We need to go out more.

> MIKE: Do you have to tap your fingers on the table all the time? It drives me nuts. Maybe we'd go out more if you didn't irritate me so much.

When serious issues get detoured by irrelevant remarks about the person, not the problem, and turning against responses are made to connecting bids, defensiveness is encouraged (Fisher & Brown, 1988). Mike's response diverts attention from the issue raised and centers the discussion on irritating mannerisms. That shifts the agenda and will likely induce a counterattack. Shasha could respond to the criticism of her finger tapping this way: "We can talk about my finger tapping another time. Let's discuss going out more often, and let's do it without insulting each other." Staying focused on the problem and being constructive can defuse defensiveness.

BE EMPATHIC   During "difficult conversations," each party tends to see the disagreement from his or her point of view (Stone, Patton, and Heen, 1999). Consequently, we usually think that the other person is the problem, not us. Not surprisingly, the other person thinks we are the problem. From each of our viewpoints, our interpretation of events seems reasonable. Telling the other person to change his or her viewpoint will likely ignite psychological reactance and a quick retort: "Why don't *you* change?" You don't defuse defensiveness by attacking or by assuming that all rationality and truth resides with you. Try to view the other person's defensiveness from his or her perspective. Strive for understanding, not retaliation. Ask to get the other person's story of events.

MAKE FREQUENT TURNING TOWARD RESPONSES   When you make turning toward responses to connecting bids from a defensive individual, you create an "emotional bank account" in which the positive, supportive goodwill from subsequent exchanges will be saved (Gottman & Silver, 1999). Eventually, the defensive person will be so rich in emotional resources that the defensiveness toward you can diminish. You build goodwill between you.

Create Cooperative Structures

We've discussed ways to talk to others that can promote a constructive communication climate. There also need to be structures for cooperation to thrive. Cooperation typically occurs when all parties perceive benefits from cooperating instead of

Britanny and Abby Hensel are conjoined twins. They are an extraordinary example of interdependence at work. If they can't agree on even simple things, such as which direction to travel, they're stymied. Their kindergarten teacher once observed: "They could give a speech on cooperation."

competing. We can create those benefits by creating cooperative structures—establishing rules, procedures, or interrelationships that foster cooperation.

BUILD INTERDEPENDENCE   Besides emphasizing supportive communication, another way to establish a constructive communication climate is to build interdependence. Building interdependence enhances cooperation in human relationships and tends to short-circuit hypercompetitiveness. **Interdependence** means that all parties rely on each other to achieve goals. Interdependence can be established by creating a mutually desirable goal that can only be achieved by the effort of everyone involved and by an interdependent division of labor and resources. The story of Fred Beasley, a fullback for the San Francisco 49ers, and his family illustrates both forms of interdependence.

When Fred was 12 years old, his father died suddenly, leaving his wife and nine children to live on a meager Social Security income. The family survived the crisis by working together. The interdependent goal was for the family to survive intact, and the method used to accomplish this interdependent goal was to share labor and resources interdependently. Alma Beasley, Fred's mom, worked cleaning houses. All of the kids found odd jobs. Whatever they earned they pooled to meet family, not individual, needs. Four boys slept in a single room. Dresser drawers were divided among the children, and household chores were everybody's responsibility. As Alma Beasley explains, "It was tough on all of us. . . . I just did the best I could. I think we all pulled together" (Judge, 1998). Fred says this about his mom, "She almost took food out of her mouth to give to us. She did what a mother has to. She raised nine kids on her own. . . . There is no way to pay her back for what she did. I just want to give her love, help her out financially, and give her the things she always wanted." Fred's mom displays her obvious pride in her son: "I thank God all the time for the way he turned out. He turned out to be a great young man."

PROMOTE EQUALITY   Another important way to establish a constructive communication climate is to promote equality. Equality doesn't mean treating everyone as though there are no differences in degrees of talent, skill, ability, and the like. Equality means giving everyone the same opportunity to succeed and expecting that each will shoulder his or her fair share of responsibility. Equality means sharing power in relationships, not establishing a hierarchy in which one person dominates the decision-making. Long-term research by Gottman found that women typically attempt to share decision-making power in relationships, but men are less inclined to do this. *When a man is unwilling to share power, to treat his female partner as an equal, there is an 81% chance that the relationship will self-destruct* (Gottman & Silver, 1999). High levels of marital satisfaction are found most frequently among power-sharing couples (Giblin, 1994).

Equality can be structured into relationships in two ways. First, *labor and responsibilities can be shared equally whenever possible.* This, of course, must be negotiated between the parties involved through supportive communication patterns. The failure by some men to share household and child-care chores and responsibilities equally is a primary cause of relationship conflict (Coontz, 1997). One study comparing six different living situations found that men do far less housework than their female partners, and married men do the least housework (Adelmann, 1995). A more recent study, however, shows the disparity between men and women narrowing, with women averaging 27 hours of housework a week (*down* from 40 hours in 1965) and men performing 16 hours per week (*up* from 12 hours in 1965)/(cited in Johnson, 2002).

Lesbian couples typically negotiate domestic chores in a more equal way than do heterosexual couples or gay male partners (Huston & Schwartz, 1995). Lesbians are more inclined to communicate cooperatively when making decisions about division of household labor. Gay men, however, follow the pattern of heterosexual males. The man with the greater income usually exercises greater dominance. With greater power comes the privilege of avoiding domestic chores (Huston & Schwartz, 1995).

When coworkers do not accept their fair share of labor and responsibility on a team project, for example, the inequality can produce friction. When friends do not share equally in the planning and workload for a ski trip, hard feelings and hostility can result. Cooperative communication is unlikely in such an atmosphere. Bickering will likely ensue. An equal sharing of labor and responsibilities can create harmony.

A second way to structure equality, and thereby defuse hypercompetitiveness, is to *distribute rewards, if any, among everyone involved in achieving a mutually desirable goal.*

Most pay raises in the workplace are distributed equally. This avoids the nasty communication fostered by competitive merit pay (only the best receive the reward) and equity pay (those who did the most get the most) schemes (Schuster, 1984). Merit pay and equity pay typically pit worker against worker in a battle for limited resources. The final report of the Merit Pay Task Force of the California State University Academic Senate (Charnofsky et al., 1998) notes that of the 3,000 studies of merit pay, only 100 (3%) claim any positive outcomes. The report concludes that most merit pay systems fail to motivate workers to improve performance, and they often produce hostile and devisive communication among employees and supervisors.

Establishing equality can occur only if it is a key agenda item during any negotiation between individuals. Roommates, housemates, married couples, family members, and coworkers must agree that equality is essential in their relationships.

Some people believe an equal distribution of rewards encourages unequal labor on the part of all but the most committed individuals. Admittedly, there are those who would take advantage of a reward system of equal distribution if there were no individual accountability— the topic addressed in the next section.

ESTABLISH INDIVIDUAL ACCOUNTABILITY Establishing individual accountability is also an important way to establish a constructive communication climate. Individual accountability provides consequences for performance, ensuring that everyone honors his or her agreements and commitments in relationships and groups. If there is no individual accountability for lackluster performance, then some will hitchhike on the effort of others. Working with others is not truly cooperative if some individuals let others do most or all of the work.

You can establish individual accountability by negotiating minimum standards of performance with every individual affected. Spouses, roommates, and cohabiting partners, for example, have to agree on what constitutes a fair division of labor and the level of quality expected when the tasks are performed. All parties should embrace the minimum standards. Those who fail to honor the agreement once all parties have accepted it are held accountable by confronting their lack of commitment to the agreement. Picking up the slack of those who fail to honor a division of labor agreement by performing their tasks for them merely encourages persistent loafing.

Individual accountability is often more straightforward in work situations than it is in personal relationships. In the workplace, pay sometimes can be withheld for inadequate performance. Work teams can set specific standards, such as no more than two absences from meetings, arrival on time for all work sessions, and so forth. Persistent slackers can ultimately be booted out of the group or, in some cases, fired from the job, often with little personal consequence to other team members.

Accountability is more difficult in close relationships because connection is desired. (Love and affection can be withheld from a loafing partner, but that uses emotional blackmail as a weapon.) Accountability, however, is certainly necessary and achievable even in close relationships. The chief way to hold partners, friends, and family members accountable is to confront them when they have failed to abide by agreements and commitments.

A system of individual accountability does not interject a competitive structure into human transactions. The term *accountability,* as used here, is not intended to mean that we watch, wait for a mistake, and then lower the boom in righteous indignation. Cooperation, working together, is the goal, not working against others to claim a victory. Minimum standards set a level that all can reach, and they allow everyone to share the results (e.g., a clean house) equally. The emphasis is on raising everyone to at least a minimum level of performance and effort, not on looking for a way to designate who did best, second best, or worst. *Minimum standards establish a floor below which no one should sink, not a ceiling that only a very few can reach.*

DEVELOP MEANINGFUL PARTICIPATION Making sure all involved have a meaningful say in decision-making is a final way to structure cooperation. Few people in our culture like others to make decisions that affect their lives without participating in the decision-making. If the father in a family decides to accept a promotion and move everyone from the West Coast to the East Coast without even consulting family members and seeking their feedback, he should not be surprised when his spouse and children do not nominate him for Husband or Father of the Year awards.

Participative decision-making is essential to cooperation in human relationships in our culture, and it cannot occur without dialogue. When everyone has a say in the decision, communication is the primary vehicle by which choices are explored and decided. A review of 47 studies showed that meaningful participation in decision-making worked well in groups and organizations (Miller & Monge, 1986). Worker productivity and job satisfaction were enhanced.

For participation to be meaningful, several conditions must be part of the normal procedure for decision-making:

1. *Participation must have a significant effect on the outcome.* Asking for input after the decision has been made doesn't encourage cooperation. Rubber-stamping is not meaningful participation.
2. *All affected parties should be involved in the decisions.* Some individuals' participation, however, may have more weight than others (e.g., parents more than children).
3. *Decisions made by participants should be consequential.* Asking for participation only when the decisions are trivial will not promote cooperation.
4. *Messages communicated from all parties must be given serious consideration.* If your input is always ignored, soon you will decide that participation is a charade.

Summary

Communication climate control is critical to the likelihood of effective communication in all arenas. A constructive climate is composed of a pattern of openness and supportiveness. A destructive climate is composed of a pattern of closedness and defensiveness. Although a competitive communication climate is not always destructive, it easily can become so. Hypercompetitiveness mostly strains interpersonal relations, thwarts the creation of teamwork and cohesiveness, reduces achievement and performance, and encourages cheating.

Another key element of communication climates is connecting bids. The turning toward response to connecting bids helps develop a constructive climate, while the turning away and the turning against responses lead to a destructive climate. Not all connecting bids can receive a turning toward response, and in some instances we may not want to connect with another person for very good reasons. When we do want to connect, however, the principal ways to establish a constructive communication climate include emphasizing supportive communication patterns, defusing defensiveness, building interdependence, promoting equality, establishing individual accountability, and developing meaningful participation.

Go to *Quizzes Without Consequences* at the book's Online Learning Center at **www.mhhe.com/rothwell2** or access the CD-ROM for *In the Company of Others*.

Quizzes Without Consequences

www.mhhe
● com/ rothwell2

Key Terms

closedness
cohesiveness
communication climate
competition
connecting bid
control
cooperation
defensiveness
dogmatism

empathy
evaluations
hypercompetitiveness
individual achievement
interdependence
manipulative
 communication
openness
provisionalism

psychological reactance
rebid
supportiveness
turning against
 response
turning away response
turning toward
 response

See Audio Flashcards
Study Aid.

www.mhhe
● com/ rothwell2
See Crossword Puzzle
Study Aid.

Suggested Readings

Butler, S. (1986). *Everyone's a winner: Non-competitive games for all ages*. Minneapolis, MN: Bethany House. Butler provides a wonderful compendium of games that require no winners and losers—just fun for everyone.

Etzioni, A. (1993). *The spirit of community*. New York: Crown. The author makes a strong case for cooperation.

Frank, R., & Cook, P. (1995). *The winner-take-all society*. New York: The Free Press. Two economists offer an excellent discussion of the economic disadvantages of hypercompetitiveness.

Gottman, J. M., & DeClaire, J. (2001). *The relationship cure: A 5-step guide for building better connections with family, friends, and lovers*. New York: Brown. Gottman's research on emotional bids is exceptional. This is the book to begin any attempt to improve your relationships.

Kohn, A. (1992). *No contest: The case against competition*. New York: Houghton Mifflin. This is the best single source of research on competition and cooperation. Kohn is a hard-core critic of competition.

Nelson, M. (1998). *Embracing victory: Life lessons in competition and compassion*. New York: William Morrow. A former star athlete presents the positive effects of competition, especially for women, with some cautionary notes on excessive competitiveness.

Film School

Dinner with Friends (2001). Drama; Not Rated
This is a powerful relationship movie. Identify the numerous connecting bids presented in the film and the types of responses made to these bids. Which responses are appropriate and effective and which are not? Explain.

October Sky (1999). Drama; PG ★★★★
This fact-based story about Homer Hickam, a West Virginia coalminer's son who becomes a rocket scientist, is a film of great sensitivity, passion, and compassion. Analyze the relationship between Homer and his father by focusing on the number of connecting bids and the responses to these bids.

Who's Afraid of Virginia Woolf? (1966). Drama; R ★★★★★
This is an Oscar-winning, powerful, intense, and often witty drama about relationships in turmoil. Analyze the film for defensive communication patterns and responses.

CHAPTER 3

Perception of Self and Others

The Scottish dish called *haggis* is a mixture of sheep innards blended with chunks of sheep fat, seasonings, and oatmeal, all cooked in the animal's stomach. It has little appeal to most Americans. The thought of eating beetle grubs, which have the appearance of plump white worms, makes most Americans gag, but they are a delicacy to the Asmat of New Guinea. The Inuit eat raw fish eyes like candy, and several East African tribes enjoy a tall drink of fresh cow's blood. "Survivor," "Fear Factor," and other "reality television" shows have grossed out American audiences by having contestants ingest grubs, worms, and beetles or drink cow's blood as a challenge. To Americans, insects and raw animal blood don't qualify as food. Other cultures, however, find some of our food choices equally revolting (Archer, 2000). Many South Americans perceive our common peanut butter sandwich to be disgusting in taste, texture, and smell, and most people from India find our common practice of eating meat offensive. Imagine the revulsion many Indians must experience walking down the aisles of our grocery stores seeing packaged meats displayed. Perhaps you can appreciate the perceptual difference better if you imagine seeing an entire grocery counter of packaged dog meat (beagle burger). Dog is a common food in some cultures.

Our culture teaches us what is food and what is inedible. This is largely a matter of learned expectation, not objective taste. If you are not told what you are eating, it may taste good or at least palatable until you are informed that it is lizard or fish innards, at which point you may feel compelled to chuck *your* innards. Food preferences of all sorts can present communication challenges at mealtime when you don't want to cause offense by declining to eat the meal presented, but what is offered as food may be stomach churning.

Competent communication with others is a complicated process, partly because we can have the "same" experience as someone else but perceive it quite differently. There is no "immaculate perception" that can objectively convince everyone of the single correct view of our world. For example, unlike in some cultures, speaking is highly valued in the United States. Oral communication skills are considered essential to success in the business world. Silence, conversely, is not prized. Quiet individuals do not become leaders in groups (Bormann, 1990). Americans interpret silence in mostly negative ways, as indicating sorrow, criticism, obligation, regret, or embarrassment (Wayne, 1974).

Some cultures, however, value silence, and they devalue speaking. There is a Chinese proverb that says, "Those who know do not speak; those who speak do not know." Inagaki (1985) surveyed 3,600 Japanese regarding their attitude toward speaking. He found that 82% agreed with the saying, "Out of the mouth comes all evil." Of 504 Japanese proverbs analyzed, such as "A flower does not speak" and "The mouth is to eat with, not to speak with," 320, or 63%, were found to express negative values regarding speech (Katayama, 1982). Japanese, Chinese, and Koreans typically are more comfortable with long pauses or silence during business negotiations than are most American businesspeople (Lewis, 1996). Chinese negotiators usually do not like to engage in small talk (Hellweg et al., 1994).

Communication in the classroom exhibits these differences in the perceived value of speech in the United States and other cultures. Class participation is often encouraged, even required, as part of the grade in U.S. schools. Japanese students, however, initiate and maintain fewer conversations and are less apt to talk in class discussions (Ishii et al., 1984). One study found that in 76% of the small groups studied in the United States, the member who talked the least during discussions was Asian (Kirchmeyer & Cohen, 1992). Students whose cultures place little value on speaking are at a substantial disadvantage in U.S. classrooms where open and frequent participation is often expected. When you've been taught to value silence, speaking up is difficult to do, especially in a public forum. Yet communication effectiveness in the American classroom is often associated with verbal skills. When the larger mainstream culture dictates rules of appropriate communication that clash with a particular cultural group's rules, adaptation to the larger cultural context becomes necessary for communication to be competent.

Disagreements and conflicts are bound to emerge over perceptual differences, not just between diverse cultures but also within one's own ethnicity, family, group of friends, and intimates. A memorable scene from Woody Allen's Oscar-winning movie *Annie Hall* illustrates this point. When Annie is asked by her therapist how often she and Alvie have sex, she replies, "Constantly. Three times a week." When Alvie's therapist asks him the same question, he responds, "Never. Three times a week." Both characters have the same physical experience, but they have a markedly different perception of that experience. Imagine the difficulty two individuals like Annie and Alvie would have conversing about this issue. You can almost hear the argument, "You demand too much." "You want too little." "Too much." "Too little."

Returning for a moment to perceptions of food, some of my family members have tried countless times to convince me that it is merely my stubbornness and bias that prevents me from enjoying shrimp, crab, or any other shellfish. I assure them that I haven't grown to love shellfish since the last time the topic surfaced, and, yes, I have indeed tried all shellfish and found them wanting. "How can you not love shellfish?" I hear them cry. "Perception is a subjective experience," I retort. They groan. "One person's ambrosia is another person's poison," I add hopefully. They groan more loudly. I anticipate future exchanges on the virtues of shellfish.

Perception is not an unbiased process. Consequently, *the primary purpose of this chapter is to address how to communicate competently when perceptions are inherently subjective and often markedly at odds with the perceptions of others.*

This chapter has four objectives:

1. to describe the perceptual process in general,
2. to discuss the perception of self and others and its impact on our communication,
3. to explore gender differences in communication, and
4. to offer specific ways to improve our communication effectiveness and appropriateness, given perceptual differences with others.

> The primary purpose of this chapter is to address how to communicate competently when perceptions are inherently subjective and often markedly at odds with the perceptions of others.

We all behave as we do largely because of our perceptions of the world. Understanding the perceptual process is an important step toward improving our communication with others.

The Perceptual Process

Perception *is the process of selecting, organizing, and interpreting data from our senses.* It is an active process, not a passive one, whereby we make sense of the world and give meaning to our experience. The eye is not a camera, nor the ear a tape recorder.

Some people "see" an image of Satan in the smoke billowing from the Twin Towers resulting from the terrorist attack on September 11, 2001. Do you see Satan? Do you think that a culture that doesn't believe in Satan would see the same Image?

Sight, sound, touch, taste, and smell are sensations, but *sensation and perception, although related, are not the same.* Our sense organs (eyes, ears, nose, skin, and tongue) contain sense receptors that change physical energy (light, sound waves, and so forth) into neural impulses. Perception is the processing of these neural impulses so we go beyond merely sensing, and we begin to *make sense* of the impulses; we build meaningful patterns from them. "We sense the presence of a stimulus, but we perceive what it is" (Levine & Shefner, 1991, p. 1). Sound waves, for instance, are the raw materials of hearing, but they are not actual hearing.

This section briefly explains the perceptual process. The three elements of perception—selecting, organizing, and interpreting—do not occur in isolation from each other. Perception is a process, so all three elements interact. Nevertheless, understanding the perceptual process requires that each element first be discussed separately.

Selecting

The world is teeming with stimuli. Selecting which stimuli to notice begins the perceptual process. Selecting is determined by sensory limitations and selective attention.

Table 3-1 The Threshold of Human Senses

Sense	Stimulus	Receptors	Threshold
Vision	Electromagnetic energy	Rods and cones in the retina	A candle flame viewed from a distance of about 30 miles on a clear night
Hearing	Sound pressure waves	Hair cells on the basilar membrane of the inner ear	The ticking of a watch from about 20 feet away in a quiet room
Touch	Mechanical displacement or pressure on the skin	Nerve endings located in the skin	The wing of a bee falling on a cheek from one-half inch
Smell	Chemical substances in the air	Receptor cells in the upper part of the nasal cavity	One perfume drop diffused throughout a small apartment
Taste	Chemical substances	Taste buds on the tongue	About one teaspoon of sugar dissolved in 2 gallons of water

Source: Adapted from Galanter (1962).

SENSORY LIMITATIONS   What sensory data we select and how it is organized and interpreted are influenced greatly by the capacity of our sensory receptors to be stimulated in the first place. "We experience everything in the world not as it is—but only as the world comes to us through our sensory receptors" (Singer, 1987, p. 9).

As sensitive as these receptors are, they have a limited capacity to receive stimuli. Table 3-1 indicates the average threshold, or minimal amount of energy, that triggers a sensation for each human sensory system.

The sensitivity of our five sense organs is impressive but limited. Vision is our primary sense organ, but we do not see ultraviolet rays, X rays, gamma rays, or cosmic rays, nor do we see heat waves, radar, or long radio waves. If we could see light energy of slightly longer wavelengths than we do, we would see warmblooded animals glowing in the dark (Rathus, 1990).

Human hearing, likewise, is sensitive yet limited. The human ear registers sound from about 20 cycles per second up to about 20,000 cycles per second. This may seem impressive, but it is not when compared to a dog that can hear up to 50,000 cycles per second, a mouse that can hear up to 90,000 cycles per second, or a bat that can hear up to 100,000 cycles per second (Roediger et al., 1991). This tells us that we cannot sense a huge amount of stimuli that envelops us each moment.

Perception is inherently subjective and selective. We perceive what we can sense. Much of our world is hidden from us by the limitations of our senses. Individual differences in **sensory acuity**, which is the level of sensitivity of our senses, add another element to the subjective perception of our world. The tongue may have as many as 10,000 taste buds or as few as 500 (Plotnik, 1996). About 25% of the population have more abundant taste buds and are "supertasters." If you are a supertaster, sugar (don't even mention shellfish) seems twice as sweet to you as it does to average tasters. Arguments about something being "too sweet" or "not sweet enough" are wasted effort. Sensory acuity is an individual subjective difference.

Individual differences in tasting ability are also greatly affected by sense of smell. Flavor is the combination of taste and smell. Your sense of smell is about 10,000 times more sensitive than your sense of taste (Reyneri, 1984). Recently, the issue of smell perception has become a source of interpersonal communication conflict. I have observed some rather nasty verbal exchanges between people in movie

See Perception Activity on CD; very weird.

theatres, on elevators, and in other public places that were triggered by one person wearing "offensive" perfume. Signs have even begun appearing in some public facilities asking people not to wear strong smelling perfumes or colognes that might provoke allergic reactions. Some people with a clearly diminished sense of smell do not realize that marinating themselves in potent perfume, aftershave, or cologne and leaving a vapor trail as they walk can be troublesome for others.

SELECTIVE ATTENTION   The limitation of our senses is an inherently selective system. We don't process what we don't see, hear, taste, touch, or smell. What is available to our senses, however, is too voluminous for our brains to process. Even within the normal range of human sensory ability, up to 10,000 bits of "minimally discernible" sensory data are available to an individual *each second* (Birdwhistell, 1970). Our senses have the potential to receive a wide range of data, but the channel capacity of our senses is limited. Consequently, we must selectively attend to stimuli.

Selectively attending to stimuli involves two processes: (1) focusing on specific stimuli and (2) screening out other data (van der Heijden, 1991). You do both when you're talking intently to your date at a restaurant. You focus on that person and what he or she says and does, and you screen out conversations occurring all around you. These two processes working at the same time can produce some interesting results. For example, in one study a young man approaches a passerby on a college campus, asks for directions, and then points to a campus map. The passerby looks at the map and begins directing the man when two individuals carrying a wooden door step between the two conversing, blocking their view of each other momentarily. One of the men carrying the door changes places with the young man who asked directions. Once the door no longer obstructs the passerby's view, the "original" conversation continues except with a different person seeking directions. Half of the individuals who were stopped and asked directions did not notice that they were talking to a different young man who was dressed differently and was significantly taller (Simons & Levin, 1998). (Check out the http://viscog.beckman.uiuc.edu/djs_lab/demos.html website for this and additional fascinating demonstrations of "inattentional blindness.") We can become so focused on selectively attending that even seemingly obvious changes go unnoticed.

What we attend to at any given moment is influenced by the nature of the stimulus (Passer & Smith, 2001). The *intensity* of the stimulus draws our attention without conscious effort on our part. For example, someone shrieking can snap our head around before we have a chance to think what it means. It may be a child excitedly playing with a sibling or it might be a person in serious trouble. *Novelty* invites attention. Perhaps that is why some individuals channel surf, looking for anything different to watch on TV. *Movement* also draws attention. If a friend approaches you and feigns a punch to your stomach, you'll notice and reflexively protect yourself with your arms. *Repetition*, if it is irritating or annoying, triggers attention. If you're talking with someone at a party and they keep snorting when they laugh, you'll probably notice it if you find the noise bothersome. The constant repetition of sounds from other party-goers talking, however, likely fades into the background unnoticed. Finally, *contrast* invites attention. When conversation at that same party suddenly stops, you'll notice the contrast. You may even feel anxious or concerned.

What we attend to is also influenced by internal factors particular to each individual. *Hunger* can make you notice a friend eating a large pepperoni pizza. *Fatigue* can screen out important stimuli such as your partner's new hairdo or your teacher's announcement of an assignment due date. If your *interest* is riding horses, you will likely notice two people conversing about dressage. If you're fearful walking down a dark street at night because you've had an *experience* with a mugger, you'll likely notice strangers or anyone who might appear menacing.

Organizing

Perception does not operate apart from meaning, and we must organize selected stimuli to create meaning. Schemas organize perceptual stimuli. **Schemas** are mental frameworks that create meaningful patterns from stimuli. The three types of schemas discussed here are prototypes, stereotypes, and scripts (Wood, 1997).

PROTOTYPES Humans categorize persons, places, events, objects, phenomena, ideas, and so forth. Categorizing helps us make sense of our world. One way we categorize is by forming prototypes in our minds. A **prototype** is the most representative or "best" example of something. You have prototypes of "a boss from hell," a "best friend," an "ideal relationship," a "great movie," and a "perfect date." One study found that the prototype of a "competent communicator" is an individual who is intelligent, confident, articulate, outgoing, a good listener, and well-dressed (Pavitt & Haight, 1985).

Poorly matched prototypes can be problematic. If one person's prototype of an "ideal date" is attending a ball game and munching on hotdogs but the other person's prototype is dressing elegantly and eating at a five-star restaurant, then a second date may not be in the offing. A problem may also develop even if both parties share a similar prototype. The "made-in-Hollywood" prototype of a "perfect romance" may set an unreachable standard and inevitably lead to disappointment when your own relationship doesn't measure up to the prototype.

STEREOTYPES Which professional sport is women's favorite? Figure skating? Gymnastics? Baseball? Ice hockey? Basketball? Would you believe professional football? What percentage of National Football League fans are women? 10%? 15%? 20%? Would you believe 43%? That's what NFL Properties, the marketing and licensing arm of the National Football League determined (Killion, 1999). Seem difficult to believe? Sara Levinson, president of NFL Properties notes, "We had some disbelievers. When there's a stereotype out there, it's hard to remove it" (Killion, 1999, p. A22).

A **stereotype** is a generalization about a group or category of people. Stereotypes organize individuals according to categories such as ethnic origin, socioeconomic status, gender, sexual orientation, religious affiliation, and even body type, and they attribute common traits to all individuals in that group. For example, a Gallup poll (Lewin, 1996) conducted in 1995 that surveyed 1,000 adults in 22 countries found that women were consistently described as more "talkative," "emotional," and "affectionate" than men. In the same poll, men were consistently perceived as more "aggressive," "courageous," and "ambitious" than women. Some stereotypes are positive ("Artists are creative, interesting people"), and some are negative ("College professors are stuffy and arrogant").

Stereotyping isn't always bad. Positive stereotypes of others—such as "Most Hispanics are good-hearted or hard-working people"—can lead to cooperative transactions. Stereotypes are not necessarily completely incorrect either (Lee et al., 1995). Sometimes they are mostly true and accurate, such as "College professors are avid readers." Nevertheless, stereotypes organize cookie-cutter images of sameness that discount individual differences within a group.

SCRIPTS   A **script** is a predictable sequence of events that indicates what we are expected to do in a given situation. When you are sitting at a table in a restaurant and the server hands you a menu, you don't ask, "What's this?" You already know that you're expected to choose a meal from the menu. You have a "restaurant script." The more predictable the sequence of events is, the more scripted it is. A mental script operates the way a movie script works. The movie script tells us what to say and do. The script organizes our behavior into a sequence of activities. Your mental script does the same. We have scripts for greeting people, for expected behavior in classes, for asking someone for a date, and so on.

Scripts allow us to behave without having to think carefully. This can be positive and negative. When partners begin finishing each other's sentences, the script is well-known to both individuals. Finishing your partner's sentences may be appreciated as "really knowing me." It also may be annoying because you are "too predictable." Partners may act out "conflict scripts" that repeat the same destructive behaviors. Without deviation from the script, the same ineffective "arguing patterns" get repeated seemingly without end.

Interpreting

We select stimuli and organize them, but we also interpret what they mean. We try to make sense of the stimuli that we've organized. Principally, we make sense of our own behavior and our transactions with others by assigning causes to behavior. Assigning causes to people's behavior is called **attribution**. We attribute two primary causes to behavior: the situation, or environment, and the personal characteristics, or traits, of the individual.

Deciding the causes of our own behavior is a highly subjective process. Did we fail the exam because we didn't care enough, or was the exam "too difficult" for a lower-division class? Some individuals assign personal reasons for their failure ("I'm not smart enough") and others attribute situational causes ("There wasn't enough time to do my best on the exam").

Accurately attributing causes to the behavior of others is particularly difficult because we usually do not have enough information to make valid conclusions. This doesn't stop us, however. Usually, we consider two types of information to make attributions about others: consistency and distinctiveness (Seibold & Spitzberg, 1982). For example, you're walking across campus and a classmate, Felicia, passes you without acknowledging your existence. Why were you ignored? You notice during the week that she acknowledges other classmates when she passes them, but she does not acknowledge you on several occasions. Her behavior toward you is consistent and distinctive (she does it only to you). Perhaps you said something that offended her (situational cause). Felicia may be ignoring you because she is upset with what you said, not because she is unfriendly (trait). If, however, she ignores everyone she passes, perhaps she is shy (trait cause). Her behavior is consistent but not distinctive (she ignores everyone).

Person perception is not simply a linear, one-way process beginning with selecting, then organizing, and finally ending with interpreting stimuli. Our interpretations of self and others often double back and influence what data we continue to select and organize that influence our self-perceptions and our view of others.

Perception of Self

From the moment you are welcomed into the world, you begin the process of becoming who you are, a person separate from others but defined in relation to others. This section examines the perception of self and the role it plays in human communication. We'll look at self-concept, self-esteem, the self-serving bias, perceptual set, and self-disclosure.

Self-Concept

Each one of you has a sense of who you are and what makes you a person distinct from other persons. This **self-concept** is the sum total of everything that encompasses the self-referential term "me." It is your identity or self-perception. It is "a conviction of self-sameness—a bridge over the discontinuities which invariably creep or crash into our lives. It is the link between the child of seven and that same person at seventeen; between the seventeen-year-old and the seventy-year-old" (Kilpatrick, 1975, p. 31).

Your self-concept is not formed in isolation. *Self-concept is a social construction, a product of interpersonal communication.* "You find out who you are by meeting who you aren't" (Anderson & Ross, 1994, p. 116). Infants haven't formed a self-concept. Their self-concept gradually develops through communication with significant people over a long period of time. Parents, teachers, friends, relatives, coworkers, bosses, and even strangers are instrumental in shaping our concept of self. We learn to think of ourselves as humorous if others laugh at our jokes. We see ourselves as leaders if we notice that others follow us. We see ourselves as quiet if others seem much more talkative in social circumstances.

Our self-concepts are relatively stable. They don't change easily even in the face of contradictory evidence (Adler & Towne, 1996). We may see ourselves as shy because, when we were children, our parents, relatives, and teachers told us so. In later life this may no longer be as true, yet we may still cling to an outdated view of self. I once attended a workshop composed of faculty, staff, and administrators from Cabrillo College on the topic of "interest-based bargaining." The federal mediator who conducted the workshop began the first meeting with this instruction: "Each of you tell your group one thing about yourself that would surprise them. Identify a trait, not a behavior." When it came time for my revelation, I told my group of about a dozen individuals with whom I had interacted many times on and off campus for years that I see myself as a shy person. The entire group burst into raucous laughter. I was a little stunned by their reaction. As a child I was painfully shy and was described as such by relatives and teachers. I still see myself as somewhat shy, even though this is definitely not my persona on campus.

Self-Esteem

Self-concept is the descriptive element of self-perception. **Self-esteem** is the evaluative element of self-perception (Hamachek, 1992). It is self-appraisal: your perception of self-worth, attractiveness, and social competence. "I am a quiet person" describes your perception of self without attaching an evaluation to the perception. "I'm *too* quiet," however, attaches an evaluation to the perception.

Feedback from significant people in our lives strongly influences our self-esteem. It is difficult for us to perceive ourselves as smart, for example, if every

College of Positive Self-Image 7,
University of Low Self-Esteem 0.

important person to us is saying that we are slow-witted or just average. Our self-esteem is also a product of social comparison. When we are in the presence of someone we perceive to be impressive, even our superior, our self-esteem tends to diminish. When we are in the presence of someone we perceive to be unimpressive, however, our self-esteem tends to inflate (Morse & Gergen, 1970). Comparing ourselves to others influences our self-esteem.

Two dimensions of social comparison are relevant to self-esteem: One dimension asks how inferior or superior you are, and the second dimension asks how similar to or different from others you are (Adler & Towne, 1999). Images of beautiful, successful people presented in the mass media can reduce the self-esteem of those who feel inferior and very different from models and celebrities.

If people think well of themselves, they are likely to think well of others (but see Box 3-1 for an exception). Conversely, if individuals have a negative view of themselves, they are likely to disapprove of others (Hamachek, 1992). We see in others what we see in ourselves. We interpret the world through the lens of self-esteem.

The publicity given to self-esteem as an issue in our culture suggests that as a rule we suffer from inadequate self-esteem. Research, however, reveals otherwise. One study (Kamprath, 1997) found that most sixth and eighth graders rated themselves as having moderately high self-esteem. Another study found that almost 90% of both male and female high school seniors were "pretty happy" or "very happy" (Johnston et al., 1992), an indicator that self-esteem is not an issue.

Most of us feel quite accomplished, even more so than statistically makes sense. When male participants in a study were asked to rank themselves on their ability to get along with others, *all* of them ranked themselves in the top half of the population. Sixty percent ranked themselves in the top 10% of the population, and 25% were convinced they qualified for the top 1% (Gilovich, 1991). The same study found that 70% of the participants ranked their leadership abilities in the top 25% of the population, and only 2% thought they had below-average leadership abilities. Ninety-four percent of university professors believe that they outperform their

Box 3-1 | **Focus on Controversy**

Self-Esteem: More Is Not Always Better

The Final Report of the California Task Force to Promote Self-Esteem and Personal and Social Responsibility (1990) asserts, "The lack of self-esteem is central to most personal and social ills plaguing our state and nation" (p. 4). It claims, "People who esteem themselves are less likely to engage in destructive and self-destructive behavior, including child abuse, alcohol abuse, abuse of other drugs (legal and illegal), violence, crime, and so on" (p. 5).

The conclusions of the task force report were based on what to most people may seem to be self-evident truths. California state assemblyman John Vasconcellos, a member of the task force, had to admit, "We didn't claim to have proven it all. The science was not very far advanced" (Bauer, 1996, p. A20).

Nevertheless, "the hope that raising everyone's self-esteem will prove to be a panacea for both individual and societal problems continues unabated today, and indeed . . . may even be gaining in force" (Baumeister et al., 1996, p. 30). High self-esteem, so goes the reasoning of the task force, should provide a "social vaccine" that inoculates individuals against attacks on their self-concept from criticism, insults, and demonstrations of disrespect. A review (Baumeister et al., 1996) of more than 150 studies on self-esteem contradicts this reasoning. The most aggressively violent individuals, whether neo-Nazi skinheads, terrorists, Ku Klux Klan members, juvenile delinquents, gang members, psychopaths, or spouse abusers, do not suffer from low self-esteem. Rather, they exhibit superiority complexes, and their "self-appraisal is unrealistically positive" (p. 28). Nazis thought of themselves as members of the "master race" and vilified Jews as "vermin." The image of a Mafia godfather suffering from low self-esteem as he orders the assassinations of rivals is difficult to visualize. Bullies and psychopaths seem contemptuous of the unfortunate victims they torment.

Perhaps bullies, godfathers, gang members, and the like simply camouflage their low self-esteem, as is often asserted, beneath the veneer of bluster and self-assertion. Maybe favorable self-appraisals mask deep-seated insecurities. If this sounds reasonable to you, then try arguing the reverse proposition: that timid, reticent individuals don't suffer from low self-esteem. They simply mask their enormous self-confidence and deep-seated security. Both claims require us to ignore persuasive evidence to the contrary without providing supportive evidence for the validity of the assertions.

A major cause of aggression in human relations seems to be not low self-esteem, masked or otherwise, but "high self-esteem combined with an ego threat" (Baumeister et al., 1996, p. 8; see also Bushman & Baumeister, 1998; Rodkin et al., 2000). In other words, aggression, with its emphasis on competitive, adversarial communication, results from a discrepancy between two views of self: favorable self-appraisal but an unfavorable appraisal from others. When others do not communicate "proper respect" worthy of a "superior person"—and instead criticize, insult, or show disrespect—an aggressive response is likely. "The higher . . . the self-esteem, the greater the vulnerability to ego threats. Viewed in this light, the societal pursuit of high self-esteem for everyone may literally end up doing considerable harm" (Baumeister et al., 1996, p. 30).

Is the emphasis on bolstering self-esteem completely misguided? If we are looking for a cure-all in raised self-esteem, the answer is "yes." *Raising self-esteem is not always a desirable goal, especially if it is indiscriminate.* When children's self-esteem is inflated by effusive praise for relatively trivial accomplishments ("Nice breathing"), the potential for later disillusionment and deflated egos increases. As psychologist Robert Brooks of Harvard explains, "There are well-meaning parents who have seen self-esteem as 'every little thing your kid does, praise them to the sky.' [But] if [teaching self-esteem] is done wrong, you can raise a generation of kids who cannot tolerate frustration" (Begley, 1998, p. 69). Conversely, ignoring low self-esteem of our children and even adults is not desirable either. What good can possibly come from people feeling bad about themselves?

The answer lies in moderation. Modesty and humility should be part of the mix. When we see professional athletes strutting and posturing before their fans, insisting that they receive thunderous applause and accolades for relatively insignificant athletic accomplishments, modesty and humility are missing. *Constructive self-esteem comes from accomplishing significant things without expecting a coronation* (Kohn, 1994).

Questions for Thought

1. In your estimation, how much should improving self-esteem be emphasized in our schools?
2. Do you agree with the conclusion that overemphasizing self-esteem can lead to egomaniacal self-centeredness?
3. Is it ethical to indiscriminately praise children or adults for completion of commonplace tasks knowing that this might lead to egomaniacal self-centeredness in some individuals?

colleagues (cited in Gilovich, 1991). One survey even found that 79% of respondents thought Mother Teresa was at least "somewhat likely" to go to heaven, but 87% of respondents believed they themselves would make it to heaven ("Oprah," 1997). (O. J. Simpson was only 19% likely, Bill Clinton 52%, and Michael Jordan 65%.)

Self-Serving Bias

Assigning causes (attribution) to our own behavior is not an objective process. We protect our self-concept and our self-esteem by exercising a self-serving bias. The **self-serving bias** is the tendency to attribute our successful behavior to ourselves (personal traits) but to assign external circumstances (situations) to our unsuccessful behavior. Gilovich (1991) summarizes a large body of research on this phenomenon. Athletes tend to attribute their victories to personal prowess but blame their losses on bad officiating or cheating by their opponents. Students who perform well on tests usually view exams as valid indicators of knowledge, whereas students who perform poorly on exams may see them as arbitrary, unfair measures of knowledge. Teachers may take credit for the success of their students but blame lack of motivation, effort, or ability for student failures.

Our tendency to emphasize our accomplishments and downplay or deflect our shortcomings and failures is common. We accentuate the positive and diminish the power of the negative. This is self-serving (Hamachek, 1992). Unless we are mindful of this tendency, we are unlikely to learn new skills and gain knowledge. Why seek to improve our communication skills if we believe communication difficulties are usually someone else's fault?

The self-serving bias can also create problems in our transactions with others. Relationships run into trouble when the self-serving bias emerges. Blaming others for difficulties in relationships can provoke "fights between friends, breakups between spouses, and, on a larger scale, wars between nations" (Hamachek, 1992, p. 38).

Perceptual Set

A **perceptual set** is a mental predisposition to perceive a stimulus in a fixed way as the result of an expectation. We perceive the world the way we are prepared to perceive it. Try this demonstration of a perceptual set on your unsuspecting friends to see how easily they fall victim to it. Have a friend spell the word *shop* out loud. Now ask that person to respond immediately to the question, "What do you do when you come to a green light?" Almost everyone will automatically reply, "stop." Why? Spelling the word *shop* establishes an expectation that the answer will rhyme, even though the correct answer does not. Our perception is fixed on a single type of answer. You may be surprised by the power of perceptual sets. Follow the shop/stop demonstration with this version of the same illustration: Have people spell *joke* out loud. Then ask, "What do you call the white of an egg?" A surprising number of people, although usually far fewer than the first demonstration, will be victimized a second time and answer "yolk."

The perceptual set phenomenon is quite common and often allows us to maneuver through life without much thought. Nevertheless, it is often the source of perceptual distortion, which can produce serious consequences. An airline pilot, beginning the takeoff down the runway glances at his copilot who looks glum. The pilot encourages the copilot to "Cheer up." The copilot, set to hear "Gear up," promptly raises the plane's wheels—before they've left the runway (Reason & Mycielska, 1982).

cathy® **by Cathy Guisewite**

© 1986 Cathy Guisewite. Distributed by Universal Press Syndicate. www.ucomics.com.

Perceptual sets can seriously distort our perceptions of self. Consider our body image. It is "the foundation of our self-image. . . . Our body image does not constitute the whole of the self, but it is a highly significant aspect of it" (Hamachek, 1992, p. 159). Body image is largely influenced by society's conception of an ideal body. So consumed are we by body image that, in one study, 11% of the participants claimed they would abort a fetus if they thought the fetus had a tendency toward obesity (cited in Pipher, 1994).

The case of Samantha illustrates the distorting potential of perceptual set on body image. Samantha is 5 ft 6 in. tall and is wafer thin at 99 lb. Her eyes are sunken, and her light brown hair is brittle. Diagnosed by her doctor as anorexic, 16-year-old Samantha is terrified of gaining weight. When asked to comment on her mother's description of her eating habits, she replies, "I eat plenty. Just last night I had pizza and ice cream" (Pipher, 1994, p. 176). Her mother explains that Samantha consumed a mere teaspoon of ice cream and less than a slice of pizza with the cheese removed. A typical meal consists of lettuce and a few grapes.

Anorexics have a perceptual set that they are fat despite the objective evidence. They are mentally predisposed to see a "fat person" so concerned are they with their weight. So when they look in the mirror they expect to see a fat person, and even as their body continues to shrink alarmingly, they still view their body in a fixed way—as fat. Some anorexic girls (only about 10% of anorexics are boys) can be full height yet weigh as little as 60 lb. Bruch (1978) cites one case of a young woman who thought she was gorging herself when she ate more than one cracker with peanut butter. She even avoided licking postage stamps because she thought the sweet tasting glue on the stamps contained calories.

Despite exaggerated reports in the popular press, anorexia nervosa is a relatively rare disorder, occurring in less than 1% of the population (Walters & Kendler, 1995). Nevertheless, anorexics illustrate the strong perceptual distortion that can occur when a certain expectation is created. Anorexics tend to come from families guided by very rigid rules (Bruch, 1980). Desperate to stop their child's suicidal starvation, parents may adopt controlling communication when trying to force their child to eat. Showering their troubled child with supportive communication, however, may be a far more effective approach.

Anorexia is the extreme example of a wider perceptual set permeating our society; namely, that for women "thin is in." Social standards dictating what constitutes "overweight" and "thin" have changed drastically in the last few decades. Miss

Most people see a skinny young woman on the left and a massively muscled young man on the right. Anorexics, however, perceive a fat woman and muscle dysmorphs perceive an embarrassingly scrawny man. Perception is inherently subjective.

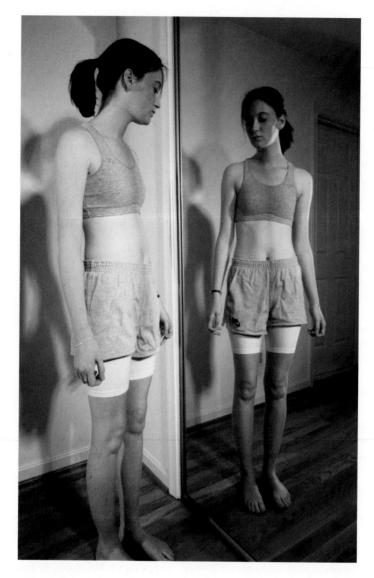

Sweden of 1951 was 5 ft 7 in. tall and weighed 151 lb, hefty by today's beauty pageant standards. By 1983 Miss Sweden had slimmed down considerably, weighing in at a scant 109 lb on a 5 ft 9 in. frame. Since 1979, the majority of Miss America contestants have been at least 15% below recommended body weight for their height, coming alarmingly close to a medical definition of anorexia (Schneider et al., 1996). In the past 30 years, the voluptuous size-12 Marilyn Monroe image of beauty has been downsized to the size-2 Teri Hatcher of *Lois & Clark* and Radio Shack advertising fame. The average size of a professional model is 5 ft 9 in. and 110 lb. An average woman in the United States is 5 ft 4 in. and 142 lb. Ironically, men actually prefer a woman who is heavier and more curvaceous than what women believe is men's perception of the ideal female figure (Fallon & Rozin, 1985).

What is the result of this disparity between fantasy and reality? Eighty percent of women diet at some time, and 50% are on a diet at any specific time (Schneider et al., 1996). Almost half of all female college students describe themselves as

overweight (Drewnowski & Yee, 1987). More than 95% of women who have no eating disorder *overestimate* their actual body size, on average by 25% (Thompson, 1986). They expect to see a "fat person" and that is what they see.

Body image distortion is also a problem for men. In one study, 28% of college men described themselves as overweight, and 40% reported that they wanted to gain muscle (Drewnowski & Yee, 1987). For men the perceptual set is often that they are too skinny (Pope et al., 2000). Up to 11% of high school boys use anabolic steroids to increase muscle size (Schneider et al., 1996). In a cross-cultural study of male college students in the United States, Austria, and France, respondents on average chose an "ideal body" image with *28 lb more muscle* than they themselves possessed (Pope, Gruber et al., 2000). When these same college men were asked to choose the body image they thought women prefer in a man, they chose a body with *30 lb more muscle* than their own. Do women have the same "ideal body" image for men that males expect them to have? When American and Austrian college women were given the same Body Image Test as the male college students, they chose a male body image with *15 to 20 lb less muscle* than what the men thought women preferred (Pope et al., 2000).

www.mhhe
 com/**rothwell2**

See Body Image Activity on the Online Learning Center, Chapter 3.

A study by Harrison Pope, chief of the Biological Psychiatry Laboratory at McLean Hospital, and his colleagues found that, of 276 bodybuilders, 33 men and 32 women had muscle dysmorphia ("Body Builders," 1998). **Muscle dysmorphia** is a preoccupation with one's body size and a perception that, though very muscular, one actually looks puny. It is the opposite of the anorexic perceptual set. Muscle dysmorphs are set to see puniness when they look at themselves in a mirror, and this is what they see, even when other people see massiveness. One individual studied by Pope and his associates was 6 ft 3 in. tall, weighed 270 lb, and had a 52-in. chest and 20-in. biceps. Despite his huge, massively muscular physique, he confessed, "When I look in the mirror, I sometimes think that I look really small. . . . You'd be amazed at how hard it is, sometimes, for me to actually convince myself that I'm big" (Pope et al., 2000, p. 83). These researchers estimate that more than 1 million men have this disorder (Pope et al., 2000). Muscle dysmorphs give up jobs, careers, and social engagements so they can spend hours every day lifting weights to "bulk up." They may refuse to appear in public in a bathing suit, turn down dates, or refuse to go to social gatherings fearing that people will see their bodies as tiny and out of shape. Muscle dysmorphs report checking themselves in the mirror an average of 9.2 times a day. They also average *325 min*, more than 5 hr per day, worrying about their muscularity and body size (Pope et al., 2000).

Self-Disclosure

We reveal our self-concept and self-esteem to others through self-disclosure. **Self-disclosure** is the process of purposely revealing to others information about ourselves that they otherwise would not know. Self-disclosure is purposeful, not accidental communication. You may demonstrate without meaning to that you're clumsy at sports, but this is not self-disclosure. If you tell a friend that you are afraid to give public speeches, however, and it is news to your friend, that is self-disclosure.

There are gender and cultural differences in self-disclosure. Women disclose more than men (Dindia & Allen, 1992). Female-to-female self-disclosure is the most frequent, and male-to-male self-disclosure is the least frequent. Men typically make emotional revelations to women, especially girlfriends or spouses, but not to other males, even male friends (Doyle, 1995). This may be more a cultural influence than a gender difference, however. Although U.S. culture suppresses intimate self-disclosure among men, cultures such as Jordan and Hong Kong encourage male-to-male disclosure (Reis & Wheeler, 1991). For U.S. couples, higher satisfaction with their relationship is associated with greater verbal disclosure. Couples from India in love-based marriages also were more satisfied with greater self-disclosure, but in arranged marriages satisfaction was not related to levels of disclosure (Yelsma & Athappilly, 1988).

CONSTRUCTIVE GOALS FOR SELF-DISCLOSURE   There are many possible goals for self-disclosing to others. Five primary constructive goals are addressed here.

Developing Relationships with Others   Self-disclosure encourages disclosure from others. This reciprocal sharing of information about self allows you to connect with others. Self-disclosure can be an important gateway to intimacy. The more you limit your self-disclosure to another person, the more you remain a stranger to that person. If you know little about someone, you have little that connects you to that person. Self-disclosure is critical to the development of close personal relationships.

Whether you and another person perceive each other as strangers, acquaintances, friends, or intimate partners depends largely on the breadth and depth of self-disclosure that takes place between the two of you (Altman & Taylor, 1973). **Breadth** refers to the range of subjects discussed. There may be several topics that you don't discuss with an acquaintance, but almost any topic is open for discussion with loved ones. **Depth** refers to how personal you become when discussing a particular subject. Intimate relationships usually have both breadth and depth, whereas impersonal, casual relationships usually have little of either. Breadth and depth of self-disclosure are critical factors in connecting with others.

Gaining Self-Knowledge   Sharing information about yourself with others helps you gain perspective. If you disclose to another person that you lack self-confidence, that person may point out several instances when you appeared very self-confident in front of others. That may cause you to revise your perception of self in this regard.

Correcting Misperceptions   Others may have misperceptions about you. They may perceive you to be unfriendly, for example. Revealing to them that you are shy and explaining that engaging in conversation has always been challenging and anxiety producing for you can open them to a different perception of you, one that is more accurate.

Eliciting Reassurance   When we have doubts about our body image, communication abilities, or other capabilities, disclosing these doubts often produces reassurance from others. Students frequently come to me with doubts about their public speaking abilities. I reassure them that they are fully capable of mastering the fundamentals of speaking in front of an audience. It is helpful to hear from others that we are capable.

Creating Impressions   We usually want others to like who we are. That's difficult to do if the other person knows little about you—your likes and dislikes, passions, goals, fears, and concerns. Self-disclosure is part of the process of creating favorable impressions with others. We let others know what makes us tick.

COUNTERPRODUCTIVE GOALS FOR SELF-DISCLOSURE   Two principal goals for self-disclosure—manipulation and catharsis—are Me-oriented, not We-oriented. Both encourage incompetent communication.

Manipulation   Research clearly shows that self-disclosure by one person induces self-disclosure by another (Dindia, 2000). Pretending to reveal important personal information about oneself merely to coax knowledge from another person that can be used against him or her is inappropriate and unethical communication. It may provide a competitive advantage—"So, Marissa doesn't like confrontation; how interesting"—but it is dishonest.

Using self-disclosure to deceive others is also an ethical issue. Glenn Souther was a student at Virginia's Old Dominion University. He also was a Soviet spy. He successfully deceived students and professors alike. Virginia Cooper (1994), a communication professor at the university, knew Souther well, or so she thought. Souther was a student of hers, her research assistant, and a frequent guest in her home. Curious how Souther could have deceived her so totally, she examined four hours of audiotape she had of Souther working with a group on a project. She discovered that

Souther "was skilled in relationship deception due, in part, to his strategic disclosures that projected a plausible false image." Souther manipulated people into believing that he was trustworthy by disclosing large amounts of personal information. He disclosed more personal information than any other group member. He seemed so "transparent" that no one suspected he was hiding an awful truth.

Catharsis   Spur-of-the-moment purging of personal information to "get it off your chest" or to relieve guilt is a poor reason to self-disclose. This is especially true if it is likely to damage the relationship you have with another person. Getting it off your chest may put it on the other person's chest.

GUIDELINES FOR APPROPRIATE SELF-DISCLOSURE   Here are five characteristics that act as guidelines for appropriate self-disclosure:

Trust   When you self-disclose to another person, you risk being hurt or damaged by that person. Some of the risks involved with self-disclosure are indifference, rejection, loss of control, and betrayal (Derlega, 1984). Disclosures we make to others may be used against us. Sometimes people betray our trust and reveal our secrets disclosed in confidence. Trusting another person to honor your feelings and to refrain from divulging the disclosure to anyone unless given permission says, "I value our relationship, and I trust that you will not hurt me."

Reciprocity   Reciprocal, or mutual, self-disclosure demonstrates that trust and risk taking are shared. If you disclose but the other person does not, you should be wary of further disclosures until reasons for the one-way self-disclosure become apparent. Perhaps the other person is merely reticent and needs encouragement. One-way self-disclosure leaves you vulnerable and the other person protected. That asymmetry can spell trouble. Therapy, of course, is one exception. Counselors need to hear about you; they don't need to self-disclose in return. Individuals also reveal intimate details about their sex lives to doctors who monitor sexually transmitted diseases, but they don't expect their doctors to reciprocate. If a counselor or doctor did disclose intimate information to clients and patients, charges of unethical behavior could be made and his or her license to practice jeopardized.

Cultural Appropriateness   Not all cultures value self-disclosure. Compared to North Americans, Japanese students disclose very little about their personal lives. During initial interactions, North American students will discuss gossip, politics, marriage, life goals, friends, and after-graduation plans, topics that Japanese students usually will not discuss (Nishida, 1991). Japanese students discuss universities, ages, and club activities more than North American students during initial conversations. Both North American and Japanese students discuss neutral topics such as the weather, recent movies, music, and college life. Appropriate self-disclosure in one culture may not be appropriate in another culture.

Situational Appropriateness   Public settings and private information are a poor fit. A public speech before a large audience is an awkward, uncomfortable setting for self-disclosure, as several political campaigns have demonstrated. The classroom also doesn't usually lend itself well to intimate self-disclosure.

A colleague of mine told of a surprising incident in her public speaking class that illustrates the importance of situational appropriateness. Students were assigned a 4-min speech in which they were to describe to the class some event that had altered their lives in an important way. My colleague expected to hear speeches about trips taken abroad, geographic relocations, the college experience, and so forth. She did hear this—and more. A female student in her 30s began her speech by informing the class that she had never achieved sexual fulfillment in her life until the previous weekend. She then proceeded to explain to her astonished classmates what it was like to experience her first orgasm. Such revelations might be appropriate in a professional counselor-client relationship whose purpose is to explore intimate issues in a comfortable setting. Such intimate self-disclosure might even be appropriate with certain close friends, but not in front of relative strangers in a classroom where the main purpose is to hone public speaking skills. She needed to consider her audience and the obvious embarrassment she caused her listeners.

Incremental Disclosure   Overly zealous self-disclosure in which, for instance, you blurt out your whole life story in one sitting may overwhelm your listener and send him or her running to the nearest exit. Test the waters. Gradually disclose personal information to another person and see whether it is reciprocated. There is no urgency required. A person usually needs to get to know someone before having a proper perspective on intimate revelations about self. "I've always hated guys like you" or "Women make me nervous" probably aren't very good openers. Once you get to know the person, these disclosures may seem funny. Initially, they might end the conversation and any potential for a relationship.

   Most conversations concentrate on commonplace topics. Self-disclosure is important, especially during initial stages of a relationship, but it isn't the principal focus of people's lives. There is only so much to disclose, and then your partner has heard it all. Even couples in intimate relationships spend relatively little time divulging personal information to each other (Duck, 1991).

▨▨ Perception of Others

Perceptions of self influence our communication, but so do our perceptions of others. In this section we'll explore the impact our perceptions of others can have on our communication by discussing impressions of others, attribution error, and stereotyping.

Impressions of Others

Consider these descriptions of a man named Phil:

(**A**) *Phil enters a hardware store and stands at the counter waiting to be helped. The store is crowded. Phil mutters to himself. When a clerk waits on him, Phil explains that a cell phone he purchased a few days ago is defective. The clerk asks to see a receipt. Phil explains that he lost the receipt but points to the price tag with the store's name clearly marked on it. The clerk is hesitant to give Phil a refund. Phil asks to see a manager. After a short discussion with the manager, Phil receives his refund. On the way out of the store, Phil spots a young woman he knows from a class he is taking at the local college. He turns and walks away from her.*

(**B**) *Phil is due to meet a friend for lunch. He hurries down the street and arrives at a small cafe where his friend is sitting at a table sipping a drink. Phil greets his friend. They converse for a while before Phil looks at the menu. A waiter comes to take Phil's*

See video clip #3, Chapter 3 of CD.

What's your first impression of this man with tattoos?

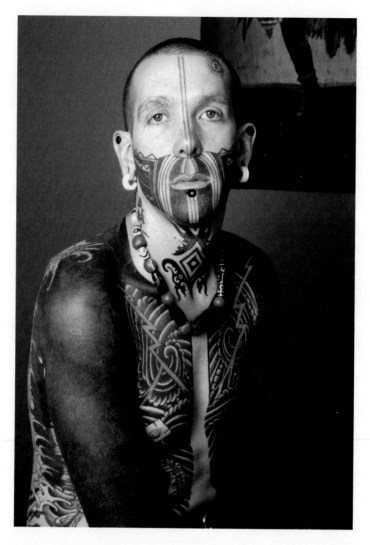

order. Phil gives his order and then continues his conversation with his friend. After lunch, Phil walks for a few blocks until he runs into an acquaintance from work. He talks to her for a few minutes and then continues on his way up the street.

What is your impression of Phil? On a scale from 1 (unfriendly) to 10 (very friendly), how would you rate Phil? Now read these two paragraphs about Phil to a friend, but read paragraph A *after* you read paragraph B. How does your friend rate Phil on friendliness? Is this different from your rating? Typically, the first paragraph we read has more influence on our impression of Phil than the second. In a classic study, only 18% of the participants who read a two-paragraph story similar to this one labeled the person in the story as "friendly" when the "unfriendly" paragraph appeared first, but 78% labeled the person in the story "friendly" when the "friendly" paragraph appeared first (Luchins, 1957). This is called the **primacy effect**, or the tendency to perceive information presented first as more important than later information. The primacy effect accounts for the power of first impressions.

A first impression can encourage further transactions with others when it is positive, and it can prevent any further contact with a person when it is negative. Once you've begun an interpersonal transaction, you never get to make another first impression, so you want to begin on a positive note.

Add to the primacy effect our strong tendency to weigh negative information more heavily than positive information, which is called **negativity bias,** and you can see how perceptions of others can become quite distorted. One study found a negativity bias when participants were asked to rate a person (Anderson, 1981). The person described as "kind" received a highly positive rating. The person described as "dishonest" received a very poor rating, but the person described as both "kind" and "dishonest" also received a fairly unfavorable rating. In other words, a positive and a negative quality are not equivalent. The negative quality is given more weight than the positive quality.

The negativity bias can be particularly strong during job interviews (Webster, 1964). In fact, negative information, especially if it is received early in the interview, is likely to lead to a candidate's rejection even when the total quantity of information about the candidate is overwhelmingly positive. In a hypercompetitive job market where differences in quality between candidates can be hard to discern, one poorly chosen phrase or inappropriate remark during an interview can negate a dozen very positive letters of recommendation.

If I described a person to you as "outgoing, casual, fun-loving, articulate, and manipulative," would you want to be friends with that person? Would the single negative quality cause you to pause despite the four very positive qualities? Conversely, if I described a person as "abrasive, rude, domineering, closed-minded, and fun-loving," would the one positive quality even make a dent in the negative impression created by the first four qualities? Would you even want to meet such a person?

Sometimes the negative information should outweigh the positive. Medical doctor Harold Shipman is England's worst serial killer. An official investigation determined that he murdered 215 of his patients by injecting them with a lethal dose of painkiller. Described by his patients as trustworthy, persuasive, and attentive, he conducted his killing spree over a 23-year period. He was finally caught in 1998 and is serving a life sentence in prison (Hoge, 2002). A heart surgeon who has a great sense of humor and a warm personality but is an alcoholic shouldn't inspire confidence as you're about to go under the knife. A potential date who is attractive, personable, articulate, and intelligent but occasionally loses his self-control and abuses women is a bad prospect. Not all qualities of a person are created equal. Some negative characteristics supersede even a host of positive traits.

When we formulate perceptions of others, initial information and negative information influence us more than later information and positive information. Sometimes this is appropriate. Often it is not.

Attribution Error

Research shows that we have a strong tendency to commit the **fundamental attribution error,** which is to overemphasize personal characteristics and underemphasize situational causes of other people's behavior (Kassin, 1998). Even when we know a person is required to communicate in a certain way, we still tend to perceive personal characteristics as the cause of behavior rather than situational factors

(Jones, 1979). In one study (Napolitan & Goethals, 1979) students conversed with a confederate of the experimenter who was either friendly or unfriendly. Even when the students knew that the confederate had been told to communicate in a friendly manner, they still perceived the confederate as "truly friendly." Knowing that the confederate was told to communicate in an unfriendly manner did not elicit a situational attribution from student participants. They perceived the confederate who was told to act unfriendly as "truly unfriendly."

Once again recall the self-serving bias. Notice how kindly we interpret our own behavior but how harshly we interpret the behavior of others. Our tendency is to believe that positive character traits cause our own successes and that situational forces beyond our control cause our failures. Conversely, we are inclined to believe that personal character flaws cause the failures of others and fortunate situational forces are responsible for their successes. As comedian George Carlin once observed, the slow driver blocking our progress is a "moron" and the fast driver attempting to pass us is a "maniac." Typically, we do not think of ourselves as either a moron or a maniac no matter what our driving speed. This is probably because we have much more information about our own situation that might affect our driving speed, such as trying to follow confusing or complicated directions or responding to an emergency, than we do about situations faced by other drivers.

Marriage partners can experience difficulties because of attribution error. Partners are inclined to attribute relationship problems to personal traits rather than to situational forces, often discounting the power of difficult circumstances (Bradbury & Fincham, 1990; Kelley, 1979, 1984). A wife might complain that her husband does not help out sufficiently with the housework, leaves his clothes on the floor to be picked up by her, and doesn't listen or pay attention to her. The tendency is for the wife to claim that her husband is lazy, sloppy, and uncaring, which are all personal traits. The husband, however, is likely to assign situational causes. He will interpret his behavior as caused by stress at work, exhaustion, or other factors beyond his control. If his wife is unmoved by such interpretations, the husband is likely to attribute her anger and frustration to "moodiness" or "irritability," also dispositional causes.

Attribution patterns of communication can indicate whether couples have happy or unhappy relationships (Fletcher & Fincham, 1991). Individuals in happy relationships, for instance, typically explain the nice behaviors of their partners as personal traits: "She did the grocery shopping after work because she is a caring, giving person." Negative behaviors are explained in situational terms: "He snapped at me because he's under a great deal of stress."

Individuals in unhappy relationships typically exhibit the reverse attribution pattern. Positive behavior is explained in situational terms: "She picked up my clothes at the laundry because she had nothing better to do with her time." Negative behaviors are explained in dispositional terms: "He was irritable with me because he is a very impatient person."

Attribution patterns of communication do not necessarily produce happy or unhappy relationships. Such patterns may be a reflection of individuals blissfully pleased with their partners or a signal of relationships already in deep trouble. Nevertheless, "the evidence supports the existence of a causal link between attributions . . . and relationship satisfaction" (Fletcher & Fincham, 1991, p. 14).

Explaining your partner's positive behavior as situationally caused and his or her negative behavior as the result of character flaws creates a destructive communication climate from which there is little chance of escape. Attribution error can kill a relationship. Conversely, preferring to see your partner's negative behavior as caused by bad situations and his or her positive behavior as a reflection of strength of character can reinforce a sense of happiness in a relationship.

It's not that traits are never the cause of bad behavior. Sometimes individuals just seem mean and disagreeable no matter what the circumstances (consistent and nondistinctive). Attribution error, however, denies a person reasonable doubt. We begin by assuming that character flaws explain antisocial communication patterns without adequately considering the influence of situational forces.

Stereotyped Distortion of Others

Stereotypes distort our perceptions of others in four ways (Hamachek, 1992; Wade & Tavris, 1990). First, stereotypes overgeneralize by underestimating the differences among individuals in a group (See Box 3-2). Acclaimed African American poet Maya Angelou tells a story about a White friend of hers who mentioned a Black woman they both had met some time ago. Angelou couldn't remember who this woman was, so she asked, "What color is she?" Her White friend responded, "I already told you she is Black." Angelou replied, "Yes, but what color of black?" (cited in Matlin, 1992). No shades of difference are perceived when we stereotype. All Black people are perceived to be the same color.

See video clip #4, Chapter 3 of CD.

People tend to generalize about all members of a group based on the behavior of a single member (Quattrone & Jones, 1980). A loud, abrasive individual from the United States traveling abroad creates an impression that all people in the United States deserve the tag "ugly Americans." One rude French person might stereotype all French people as rude in the minds of some people. We don't perceive individual members of our own group, however, as necessarily indicative of the entire group; we just do this with members of outside groups.

Second, stereotypes distort our perceptions of others by creating a selective memory bias. **Selective memory bias** occurs when we tend to remember information that supports our stereotypes but forget information that contradicts them. In one study (Snyder & Uranowitz, 1978), student participants read a fictitious biography of a woman that included stereotypical behaviors for both lesbians and heterosexuals. Those who were led to believe the woman was a lesbian remembered that she had never had a steady boyfriend in high school. Most forgot that she had dated several men in college. Those who were led to believe that the woman was heterosexual, however, remembered that the woman had developed a steady relationship with a man in college. They usually forgot that this relationship was more a friendship than a romance. Our stereotypes produce a selective memory bias and, in turn, our memory bias nurtures and hardens our stereotypes of others.

Third, stereotypes can magnify differences among groups while exaggerating commonalities within a group. This can create intergroup rivalry. Stereotypes emphasize what is different about others, not what we have in common. We exaggerate how odd, dangerous, or unlike us others are. In this way, stereotypes erect communication barriers between people rather than build bridges.

Fourth, negative stereotypes can influence our perceptions of self and produce poor performance. Jacobs (1999a) summarizes several studies on "stereotype vulnerability." Asian American women posted high scores on a standardized math test when reminded of their ethnicity before taking the test, but they scored much lower when reminded of their gender identity. When told that Asian students typically do better than Whites on a test, White students bombed the test. Female students

Box 3-2   Sharper Focus

Stereotyping Asian Students

Based on academic record, one of every three Asian public high school graduates in California is eligible for admission to the University of California (UC) system of higher education, the most competitive in the state. Only one in eight White students is similarly eligible (Lubman, 1998a). The stereotype of the academically excellent Asian student is largely true, but even with seemingly positive stereotyping, problems exist. The stereotype applies to Asian students in general, but many Asian students do not fit the stereotype. Some Asian students complain that they cannot get academic help as easily as other students because of the stereotype, despite the fact that almost half the remedial math students at the University of California, Riverside, are Asian (Lubman, 1998b).

The studious Asian student stereotype has also produced ugly bigotry from non-Asian students at many UC campuses. Asians comprise about 10% of California's population but they make up more than a third of the UC undergraduate population (Lubman, 1998a). The ability of Asian students to compete effectively in a highly competitive educational system has produced a backlash. As Stephen Nakashima, a Japanese-American UC regent, explains, "Every Asian that's accepted means another person gets left out" (Lubman, 1998a, p. A21). As a result of this competitiveness, Asian students have been the target of vicious anti-Asian phone calls, e-mails, and graffiti. Ombudsman Ron Wilson, who handles student complaints at the Irvine campus, notes that an increasing number of non-Asian students use "tough competition with Asian students" as a reason to drop a

class. He also notes that non-Asian parents complain that their children receive lower grades because there are "too many Asians" in the classes (Lubman, 1998a).

Asian students have become scapegoats, but the real culprit may be hypercompetitiveness. The more competitive the educational system becomes, the more stereotypes will feed the backlash against Asian students who are perceived as rivals standing in the way of non-Asian students' achievement of academic goals.

The stereotype of the studious Asian may be mostly accurate, but it allows for no individual differences.

scored as well as male students on a rigorous math exam when told beforehand that the exam didn't measure gender differences. They scored far lower, however, if made to think gender differences would be measured. Subtle reminders of stereotypes can have a negative effect on performance.

Gender and Perception

Gender is probably the most publicized of our perceptual differences in communication. This is in large part due to the popularity of John Gray's books, seminars, audiotapes, CD-ROMs, and even franchised counseling centers (Marano, 1997). They all assert his major premise that "Men are from Mars and women are from Venus." (See Wood [2002] for a critique of Gray's premise.) Close behind Gray in popularity is Deborah Tannen's book, *You Just Don't Understand: Women and Men in Conversation.* Are men's and women's perceptions and resulting communication patterns so different that men and women seem to exist in separate worlds metaphorically akin to

Mars and Venus, or do we live in more neighborly, closely associated worlds akin to "South Dakota and North Dakota" (Dindia, 1997)? The "truth is out there," and we're going to pursue it here.

Before beginning this discussion of gender and perception, let's first differentiate sex from gender (Talbot, 1998). **Sex** is biology (female-male); it is genes, gonads, and hormones. One sex difference is that a male can impregnate a female, and a female can become pregnant. It doesn't work in the reverse. **Gender** is socially constructed (feminine-masculine); it is learned role characteristics and behavior derived from communicating with others. There are norms and rules established in every culture that define what it is to be feminine or masculine.

Gender Differences in Communication

"Why does it take 1 million sperm to fertilize one egg? The sperm won't stop to ask for directions." "When do women stop advocating equality? When they have to kill large, hairy spiders." "How do you impress a woman? Compliment her, cuddle her, caress her, love her, listen to her, support her, and spend money on her. How do you impress a man? Show up naked. Bring beer."

What is your reaction to these "jokes" found on several Internet sites? Do you find them funny? Offensive? (These are tame examples compared to the truly crude and tasteless jokes on several Web sites.) Do you agree with the assumption expressed in these jokes that men and women act and communicate very differently? Let's look at the evidence.

SMALL DIFFERENCES Some researchers don't think gender differences in communication are significant. One review of a large number of studies found, in aggregate, that men and women are 99% similar in their communication and only 1% different (Canary and Hause, 1993). Other researchers disagree (Mulac, 1998; Wood in Wood & Dindia, 1998).

Assuming for the moment that gender differences in communication are small, please note that *even small differences can produce large effects* (Eagley, 1995). Chimpanzees and humans, for example, are almost 99% similar in chromosomes; yet consider the enormous differences in performance and behavior (not even counting looks). Differences in competitiveness between men and women are small overall, but there are more than twice as many hypercompetitive men (Gayle et al., 1994). Extreme competitive behavior seen so much more often in men can create the stereotype that men are far more competitive as a group than women (Allen, 1998). One computer simulation study of organizational hiring practices found that, when gender accounted for a mere 1% difference in performance ratings that favored men over women, 65% of the highest-level positions in the organization were filled by men (Martell et al., 1996, p. 158).

LARGE DIFFERENCES Although most gender differences in communication are small, there are many large differences. For example, women rely more on conversation to build and maintain intimacy with friends and romantic partners, while men rely more on shared activities and doing things for others; women are better at inferring accurate meanings from face, body, and vocal nonverbal channels; women are more inclined to talk about their relationships than men; and women are greater caregivers than men (Wood & Dindia, 1998). In addition, women smile much more

© Luann reprinted by permission of United Feature Syndicate, Inc.

than men (Hall, 1998). Women also laugh more than men, regardless of who's conversing with them (Provine, 2000).

Although women and men share very similar lists of preferred characteristics in a partner, they veer markedly from each other on the willingness to accept an offer of casual sex. One study (Clark & Hatfield, 1989) had attractive confederates of the experimenters approach individuals of the opposite sex and make three invitations: go out on a date that night, visit their apartment, or have sex with them. About half of the women accepted a date, but only 3% would visit the man's apartment, and *none* would have casual sex. About half of the men accepted a date, but *70%* were willing to visit the woman's apartment or have casual sex. Men want and do have more sex partners, a revelation only to someone new to the planet (Buss & Schmitt, 1993).

There are many additional significant gender differences in communication. Several of them will be discussed in later chapters. Why do the differences exist?

Reasons for Gender Differences

Not only is there disagreement regarding the magnitude of gender differences in communication, there is also a controversy concerning why gender differences, large and small, occur. Let's briefly discuss three main perspectives: difference, dominance, and deficiency.

DIFFERENCES IN COMMUNICATION STYLES   Tannen (1990) argues that "boys and girls grow up in what are essentially different cultures, so talk between women and men is cross-cultural communication" (p. 18). Consequently, males and females learn different communication styles (Noller, 1993; Wood, 2000; Bruess & Pearson, 1996).

Every conversation has two dimensions: *status* and *connection*. Status is hierarchical, and conversation perceived from this dimension is a "negotiation in which people try to achieve and maintain the upper hand if they can" (p. 24). When status is the focus, an individual asks, "Am I one up or one down?" Connection is non-hierarchical, and conversations perceived from the standpoint of connection view talk between self and others as a "negotiation for closeness" (p. 25). When connection is the focus, an individual asks, "Are we closer or farther apart?" Men and women are concerned with both status and connection, but *men typically give more*

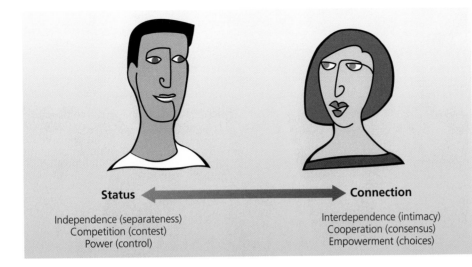

FIGURE 3-1 The Status-Connection Dimensions of Conversation

focus and weight to status, and women typically give more focus and weight to connection (see also Coates, 1993; Wood, 1996). (See Figure 3-1 for additional comparisons.)

According to Tannen, men usually see conversation as a contest, a competitive opportunity to increase status (see also Coates, 1993; Wood, 1996). Thus, men typically display their knowledge and expertise on a subject for all to appreciate. They offer solutions to problems because this spotlights their expertise (status enhancing). This explains the male propensity for cruising the globe rather than stopping to ask for directions when lost. Asking for directions diminishes status. Conversely, women typically make references to personal experiences, share feelings, and listen intently to establish cooperative rapport with others. This explains the female propensity to talk on the phone for long periods of time. Conversation, regardless of topic, connects the parties conversing.

Perceptual misunderstandings between genders often result from style differences in communication (Tannen, 1990). Women interpret men's refusal to ask for directions as pig-headed, exasperating stubbornness (a personal trait attribution), and men interpret women's long phone conversations as gossipy (also a personal trait attribution). Both interpretations are usually misperceptions based on differing communication styles.

Consider another example. Does inviting someone into a conversation in a group show sensitivity? When interpreted from the standpoint of connection, it certainly appears to do so. When interpreting this act from the standpoint of status, however, inviting a man into a conversation when he has been steadfastly quiet could be judged as very insensitive. It spotlights the man's nonparticipation, and it also may require the man to reveal that he knows nothing about the topic of conversation (both status diminishing and potentially embarrassing).

If men and women often approach simple conversation from conflicting perspectives, then conversation is often a negotiation between individuals with two different perceptions. This negotiation can be a competitive, adversarial contest of wills, or it can be a cooperative effort to find areas of agreement and to work out areas of disagreement.

DOMINANCE OF MEN Tannen's style difference explanation for gender communication has been criticized for seriously underemphasizing the dominance of men

According to Tannen, for females conversation is primarily "rapport talk," but for males it is "report talk." Women typically seek to connect; men seek to display knowledge during conversation.

(see Freed, 1992; Talbot, 1998; Tavris, 1992). "The fact that women are the outsiders, not that they have some universal conversational style, is what creates differences between the sexes," argues Tavris (1992, p. 300). Women communicate in ways typical of most people who are in a relatively powerless position, and men communicate in ways typical of those with more power (Tavris, 1992).

There is evidence to support this dominance perspective. Because women have historically been in subordinate positions to men, they have been forced to use a communication style that is relatively noncompetitive, friendly, accommodating, and unassertive (Cleveland et al., 2000). When you have little status and authority, adopting the "male style," which emphasizes status, would be self-defeating. Bosses can order employees to perform certain tasks. Employees would be foolish to try the same with their bosses. When women have been in positions of relatively equal power to men, however, they are likely to communicate in ways strikingly similar to men (Rosenthal & Hautaluoma, 1988; Sagrestano, 1992).

Tannen (1990) does not ignore the obvious power differences between men and women: "No one could deny that men as a class are dominant in our society, and that many individual men seek to dominate women in their lives" (p. 18). She simply offers the difference perspective as an additional view, not as a substitute for the dominance perspective. She explains, "Male dominance is not the whole story. It is not sufficient to account for everything that happens to women and men in conversations—especially in conversations in which both are genuinely trying to relate to each other with attention and respect" (p. 18).

Her point of view is supported by research (Mulac & Bradac, 1995). Distinctly different male and female linguistic styles emerge but they cannot be explained by looking at unequal power distribution. The "men-are-dominant" perspective is also complicated by research on conflict. When one partner in a male-female relationship is dominant during a conflict, women are about twice as likely to be the dominant partner (Gottman, 1994).

The dominance perspective on male-female communication emphasizes power imbalances, with men in the dominant position. The difference perspective emphasizes conversational styles. Both perspectives provide insights, but neither explains the whole story. They can be complementary perspectives because each explains a different aspect of gender differences.

DEFICIENCY IN SKILLS   Some communication experts argue that skill deficiencies can better explain some gender differences (Kunkel and Burleson, 1998). They argue that if men and women have distinctly different communication styles, then men should prefer the "masculine style" and women should prefer the "feminine style." One's own gender style should be more familiar, more comfortable, and make better sense. Both men and women, however, prefer the female communication modes of providing comfort and emotional support. Thus, women are more often sought for comfort and emotional support by *both* men and women because women have been socialized to develop these skills; men have not. In contexts in which persuasive skills are highly valued, however, such as in organizational meetings and legal proceedings, the female style might prove to be deficient. "Members of each sex tend to specialize in some skills while having comparative deficits in other skills" (Kunkel & Burleson, 1998, p. 118). Thus, accepting two distinct gender styles of communicating as "equally valid" ignores the perception of both sexes that *some* aspects of each style may be skill deficient. The appropriate advice, then, would not be to accommodate gender style differences uncritically, but to encourage skill development in areas where deficiencies exist.

In summary, most gender differences in communication are small, but there are some large, important differences. Even the small differences can produce large effects in the "real world." There are three primary explanations for gender differences, large and small: different communication styles, dominance of men, and deficiency in communication skills. Picking any one of the three as the correct explanation ignores the insights each perspective provides. When power disparities exist between men and women, communication differences will emerge. Diminishing the power imbalances, a subject for later discussion, will diminish gender communication differences. It will not eradicate such differences, however. Many such differences can be accurately explained as legitimate variation in styles. If, however, a clear skills deficiency exists (e.g., poor listening), then this may be the reason for communication differences. Skills training to diminish the gender differences will then be appropriate. So look to create power balance and correct skill deficiencies and then accommodate any style differences that still exist.

▰ Strategies for Communicating Competently

In this final section, we'll look at competent communication strategies that overlap more than one perceptual problem or issue. These strategies will help you connect the discussion of perception of both self and others to an interrelated whole.

Monitor Perceptual Biases

Self-serving bias and attribution errors need to be monitored carefully. If you see yourself rationalizing your mistakes and taking credit for successes that may be more attributable to luck and good fortune than to personal achievement, recognize your self-serving bias.

Resist attributing personal characteristics to the negative behaviors of others and situational causes to the positive behaviors of others. Practice the reverse. Try explaining the communication behaviors of your partner, coworker, friend, or relative that irritate or anger you with a situational attribution. Try explaining communication behaviors that please you with a personal characteristic attribution. In other words, be experimental. Test new ways of communicating with others and see what happens. If the results are constructive, continue. If the results are not constructive, modify your communication.

Recognize Cultural Differences

There is a cultural component to our self-appraisals. We live in a hypercompetitive culture that encourages self-promotion. A common question at most job interviews in the United States is "Why should we hire you?" You are asked to promote yourself for the position. You are, after all, competing against other candidates, and the hiring committee is presumably looking for the best person. In contrast, Asian cultures encourage the denial of self-importance. Reticence, not self-assertion, is valued. Promoting yourself is thought to be boastful. Your possible contribution to the group is important, as well as your likely conformity to the norms of the group or organization (Brislin, 1993). Consequently, the self-serving bias is found far more among Americans than Asian cultures (Anderson, 1999).

Attribution error also occurs more often in U.S. culture than in some other cultures. In one study, participants from India made primarily situational attributions for behavior, and Americans made primarily personal trait attributions (Miller, 1984). Similar results were found when comparing American and British students with Korean and Nigerian students. American and British students attributed criminal behavior to personal traits of offenders more than did the Korean and Nigerian students (Na-Eun-Yeong & Loftus, 1998; Pfeiffer et al., 1998).

Avoid Snap Judgments

The primacy effect characteristic of first impressions can be countered effectively by reminding yourself to avoid snap judgments. Luchins (1957) found that simply telling participants to avoid snap judgments about others countered the primacy effect and produced a recency effect. **Recency effect** is the tendency to evaluate others on the basis of the most recent information or evidence available (Rathus, 1990). Giving more weight to recent information can keep perceptions of others current. In this way individuals do not become prisoners of their own history, trapped by the perceptual sets of others that may be timeworn and no longer accurate. People change. Our perceptions of them should likewise change.

Manage Impressions

It is not enough to know that perceptual biases occur frequently in the human communication arena. Try taking an active approach, not a reactive one. Attempt to prevent perceptual biases before they occur. Create the impression you wish others to perceive. Of the many aspects of self, consider which you want to emphasize in a given situation. In a job interview, would you display your articulateness, friendliness, sense of humor, and dynamism, or would you display your irritability, cynicism, sarcasm, and interpersonal remoteness? These all may be aspects of your self-concept, but you can choose to display some aspects in a given situation and keep private other aspects of your self. This is especially important given the power of the negativity bias.

This is not meant to encourage phoniness or dishonesty, only communication flexibility. When you are interviewed for a job, you make choices regarding which aspects of your self-image you wish to display. You put forward your best self to create a positive impression. This is not dishonest. It is adapting to the expectations of your audience. Communication is situational. We don't show the same self to strangers as we do to intimate partners—at least we don't if we know what's good for us.

Practice Empathy

You can counter attribution errors by practicing empathy. Empathy has three dimensions (Stiff et al., 1988). The first is *perspective taking*. Here you try to see as others see, perceive as they perceive. You try on the viewpoint of another to gain understanding of their perspective. You don't have to accept the viewpoint of another to be empathic; you just have to understand it. A second dimension is *emotional understanding*. You participate in the feelings of others, experiencing their joy, anxiety, frustration, irritation, and so forth. The last dimension of empathy is *concern for others*. You care what happens to them.

One study (Regan & Totten, 1975) found that attribution errors were countered by empathy. College students were instructed to list their impressions of individuals either shown in a videotape or described in a short story. Those who were instructed to empathize with the person as deeply as possible and attempt to picture how that person was feeling were prone to attribute situational causes to behavior. Participants given no instructions to be empathic were inclined to choose personal traits as causes of behavior. Not all behavior is situationally caused, of course, but the fundamental attribution error predisposes us to assign personal characteristics as causes of the behavior, almost to the complete exclusion of situational causes. Empathy can provide attribution balance.

Check Perceptions

Perhaps the most obvious yet most often ignored method for dealing with perceptual biases and distortions is perception checking. That is, we should not assume our perceptions of others are accurate without checking to see whether this is so. The perceptual process of selecting, organizing, and interpreting is inherently subjective and prone to biases.

Assuming another person is angry, for example, can lead to misunderstanding. Statements such as "You're so irritable" and "I know you're bored but try to look interested" may assume facts not in evidence.

An effective perception check usually has three steps:

1. a behavior description,
2. an interpretation of the behavior, and
3. a request for verification of the interpretation.

Consider this example: "I noticed that you left the room before I was finished speaking (behavior description). You seemed offended by what I said (interpretation).

Were you offended (request for verification)?" All three steps are present in this perception check. Sometimes an effective perception check is more abbreviated: "You looked very angry. Were you?" Here, the behavior description is implied along with the interpretation, and the verification request follows.

Perception checking is a cooperative communication strategy. The goal is mutual understanding, a We-orientation. If you assume your perceptions are accurate without checking with the other person, you may elicit a defensive, competitive response.

Summary

Perception is the process of selecting, organizing, and interpreting data from our senses. This is an inherently subjective process with much potential for error, both in the perception of self and in the perception of others. Our self-concept and self-esteem are protected by the self-serving bias. Our perception of others is biased by the primacy effect, negativity bias, attribution error, and stereotyping. Our perception of self and others is a fundamental starting point of human communication. We reveal who we are to others by self-disclosing. To be a competent communicator, monitor your perceptual biases, avoid snap judgments, recognize cultural differences, manage the impressions you make with others, practice empathy, and check your perceptions of others with them.

Quizzes Without Consequences

www.mhhe
● com/
/ **rothwell2**

Go to *Quizzes Without Consequences* at the book's Online Learning Center at **www.mhhe.com/rothwell2** or access the CD-ROM for *In the Company of Others*.

Key Terms

See Audio Flashcards Study Aid.

www.mhhe
● com/
/ **rothwell2**

See Crossword Puzzle Study Aid.

attribution
breadth
depth
fundamental
 attribution error
gender
muscle dysmorphia
negativity bias

perception
perceptual set
primacy effect
prototype
recency effect
schemas
script
selective memory bias

self-concept
self-disclosure
self-esteem
self-serving bias
sensory acuity
sex
stereotype

Suggested Readings

Cytowic, R. (1993). *The man who tasted shapes.* New York: Warner Books. This is a highly recommended account of clinical cases of synesthesia. Cytowic speculates on the meaning of such remarkable case studies.

Pope et al. (2000). *The Adonis Complex*. This is an excellent book on male body image problems.

Sacks, O. (1990). *The man who mistook his wife for a hat and other clinical tales*. New York: Harper Perennial. Sacks provides some very interesting clinical cases of individuals with bizarre perceptual experiences.

Sacks, O. (1995). *An anthropologist on Mars: Seven paradoxical tales*. New York: Knopf. Sacks was depicted by Robin Williams in the popular movie *The Awakening*. Here he provides a fascinating account of seven unusual individuals whose perception of the world is wildly different from the norm.

Sommers, C. H. (2000). *The war against boys: How misguided feminism is harming our young men*. New York: Simon & Schuster. This very provocative book on the cultural bias against boys should trigger interesting discussion.

Tannen, D. (1990). *You just don't understand: Women and men in conversation*. New York: Ballantine. Begin with this book if you want to explore gender differences in communication. This is far superior to John Gray's Mars-Venus series of books.

Watzlavich, P. (1984). *The invented reality: How do we know what we believe we know?* New York: W. W. Norton. This is a mind-bending book on perception and reality.

Film School

The Color Purple (1986). Drama; PG-13 ★★★★★
This is Steven Spielberg's sensitive depiction of Alice Walker's Pulitzer Prize–winning novel. Analyze this movie for the relationship between self-esteem and communication competence, concentrating especially on the Whoopi Goldberg character.

For Love of the Game (1999). Drama; PG-13 ★★★★
This charming film ostensibly about baseball and a pitcher's swan song is much more complex and multitextured than most baseball movies. Identify gender differences in communication, especially between the Kevin Costner and Kelly Preston characters.

Thelma and Louise (1991). Drama; R ★★★★
This provocative movie raises more issues than it answers about gender differences in communication and behavior. Are the main characters merely stereotypes of gender communication differences?

CHAPTER 4

Intercultural Communication

Intercultural communication is important in our society because the United States has become increasingly multicultural. Two thirds of all immigrants in the world migrate to the United States (Ryan, 1991). There are almost 300 different ethnic groups in the United States (Klopf, 1998). In many schools, students speak more than 100 different languages. According to the 2000 U.S. Census, 31% of the nation is non-White, and 53% of its largest state, California, is non-White (Martinez & Garcia, 2001). Within 50 years, about half of the U.S. population will be non-White, composed mostly of Latinos, African Americans, and Asian Americans (Holmes, 1997). "Minority majorities," populations of non-Whites that outnumber Whites (European Americans), already exist in 48 of the largest cities in the United States. Cities such as Atlanta, Baltimore, Birmingham, Chicago, Cleveland, Dallas, Houston, Los Angeles, Memphis, New York, San Francisco, and Washington, D.C., all have non-White majorities (U.S. Bureau of the Census, 1998). In fact, Whites compose only 44% of the total population of America's 100 largest urban centers (Schmitt, 2001).

Where once Americans—generally those individuals who share and are influenced by mainstream U.S. culture—could mostly avoid contact with other cultures merely by staying within the borders of their states, this is no longer possible. Individuals with different cultural backgrounds carry their culture with them; they don't discard it while living in the United States. This means that we all are exposed to diverse cultures without stepping outside the boundaries of our cities and counties. Almost 60% of students in one survey said that they had dated someone from a different culture (Martin & Nakayama, 2000). Interracial marriages doubled between the 1990 and 2000 census to 2 million. Understanding how culture plays an increasingly important part in our communication with others is imperative if we are to meet the challenge of a rapidly changing society and world.

Intercultural communication offers opportunities to witness and appreciate the rich diversity of humankind. It also presents daunting communication challenges. As noted in the previous chapter, our perceptions are influenced by culture. Perceptual differences among cultures can affect communication enormously. For example, the hypercompetitive U.S. culture encourages verbal combat. We are expected to defend our rights even if it means openly confronting others. Our television talk shows often assume the character of verbal food fights in which individuals fling insults at each other, and occasionally the insults erupt into physical violence. In politics, attacking your opponent for even minor human failings has become commonplace. Americans can be blunt, critical, aggressive, abrasive, and argumentative. This is often the way we are viewed by other cultures (Samovar & Porter, 2001).

Imagine how American directness and in-your-face communication is perceived by cultures that value harmony between people. A Chinese proverb states, "The first man to raise his voice loses the argument." Chinese culture promotes "a conflict-free and group-oriented system of human relationships" (Chen, 1993, p. 6). Filipinos see bluntness and frankness as uncivilized. In a meeting, they will often agree outwardly, even if they have objections, in order to preserve smooth interpersonal relations and show respect for the feelings of others (Samovar & Porter, 2001). The Japanese are similarly inclined. This can be very frustrating to Americans who expect that everyone will speak openly and straightforwardly and who tend to view public agreement with private disagreement as phony or manipulative.

How can we be both effective and appropriate when communicating with individuals from cultures whose perceptions differ so radically from our own? *The principal purpose of this chapter is to explain how to communicate competently across cultures and co-cultures.*

There are three primary chapter objectives:

1. to show the underlying value differences that distinguish one culture from another,
2. to examine some of the common intercultural miscommunication that results from these value differences, and
3. to provide some ways to improve our communication competence across cultures.

The principal purpose of this chapter is to explain how to communicate competently across cultures and co-cultures.

Before beginning this discussion, let's define **culture** as "a learned set of shared interpretations about beliefs, values, and norms, which affects the behaviors of a relatively large group of people" (Lustig & Koester, 2003, p. 27). Culture is not a genetically inherited trait of human beings. Culture is learned. The shared interpretations are the product of sharing meaning with others; namely, communicating. A **co-culture** is a group of people who live in a dominant culture yet remain connected to another cultural heritage that typically exhibits significant differences in communication patterns, perceptions, values, beliefs, and rituals from the dominant culture. African Americans, Asian Americans, Native Americans, and Mexican Americans are some examples of co-cultures within the United States. Although these co-cultures share many communication patterns, values, perceptions, beliefs, and rituals of the mainstream, dominant culture because they live in the United States, there are important differences that are readily identifiable.

Anthropologist Edward Hall (1959) long ago observed that communication and culture are intertwined. Our communication reflects our culture, and our culture influences our communication. In this chapter, the myriad ways that culture affects the communication behaviors of "a relatively large group of people" will be explored.

Cultural Value Differences

Cultures vary widely in core values. Cultural **values** are the most deeply felt, generally shared views of what is deemed good, right, or worthwhile behavior or thinking. **Beliefs** are what we think is true or probable. Two cultures may both value human life, but one culture might believe that capital punishment preserves life and another culture might believe the opposite. The interconnection between values and beliefs can be seen when comparing religions. Every religion has a set of beliefs, but cultural conflicts have often been centered on which set of beliefs, which specific religion, is best. A value system is not a report of actual beliefs; it is the set of criteria used to judge beliefs and behavior and to impose sanctions for offensive beliefs and behavior (Samovar & Porter, 2001).

Hofstede (1991) has derived a number of core value dimensions from his research. These value dimensions help explain why intercultural communication is such a daunting challenge. Cultures can perceive the world in dramatically different ways, making communication between cultures difficult and frustrating, yet interesting and rewarding.

One note of caution must be considered before Hofstede's value dimensions are introduced. Hofstede identifies *cultural* values; these values may not always reflect *individual* values. *It would be a mistake to assume that every individual blindly conforms to his or her culture's values.* Nevertheless, until we get to know someone from another culture, the best we can do is make guesses regarding his or her values and preferred communication patterns. One daunting task that faces us when examining cultural differences in communication is the enormous number of specific differences that emerge as we shift our focus from one culture to another. Unless we make it our life's work, we cannot be expected to learn and remember the thousands of culturally unique practices that separate the hundreds of cultures and co-cultures on this planet. Hofstede's value dimensions allow us to make reasonably reliable predictions about communication differences and preferences without having to memorize an encyclopedia of cultural details.

Individualism-Collectivism Dimension

All cultures vary in the emphasis they place on individualism and collectivism. The individualism-collectivism dimension is thought by most scholars to be, by far, the most important of all value dimensions that distinguish one culture from another (Hui & Triandis, 1986).

GENERAL DESCRIPTION An **individualist culture** has an "I" consciousness. Individuals see themselves as loosely linked to each other and largely independent of group identification (Triandis, 1995). They are chiefly motivated by their own preferences, needs, and goals. Personal achievement and initiative are stressed (Samovar & Porter, 2001). The self assumes special importance in an individualist culture. Emphasis is placed on self-help, self-sufficiency, self-actualization, and personal growth. Relationships are mostly viewed as interpersonal, not intergroup. People communicate as individuals and pay little heed to an individual's group memberships. Competition, not cooperation, is encouraged. Decision-making is based on what is best for the individual, sometimes even if this sacrifices the group welfare. The saying "The squeaky wheel gets the grease" reflects the individualist perception. Words such as *independence, self, privacy*, and *rights* permeate cultural conversations.

A **collectivist culture** has a "we" consciousness. Individuals see themselves as being closely linked to one or more groups and are primarily motivated by the norms and duties imposed by these groups (Triandis, 1995). Relationships are seen as mostly intergroup, not interpersonal. People communicate with each other as members of groups, and they take notice of a person's place in the hierarchy of a group. In collectivist cultures, commitment to valued groups (family, organization) is paramount. Cooperation within valued groups is emphasized, although in-groups can be highly competitive with out-groups. Individuals often downplay personal goals in favor of advancing the goals of a valued group (Samovar & Porter, 2001). The Chinese proverb "No need to know the person, only the family" and the African adages "The child has no owner" and "It takes a village to raise a child" express the collectivist perception. Words such as *loyalty, responsibility,* and *community* permeate collectivist cultural conversations.

No culture is entirely individualist or collectivist. All cultures are a mix of both, but one or the other tends to predominate in each culture (Gudykunst, 1991). In a worldwide study of 50 countries and 3 geographic regions (Hofstede, 1991), the United States ranked number one in individualism, followed by other Western countries such as Australia, Great Britain, Canada, the Netherlands, and New Zealand. Asian and Latin American countries ranked high on collectivism. Guatemala was the most collectivist, followed by Ecuador, Panama, and Venezuela, with Pakistan,

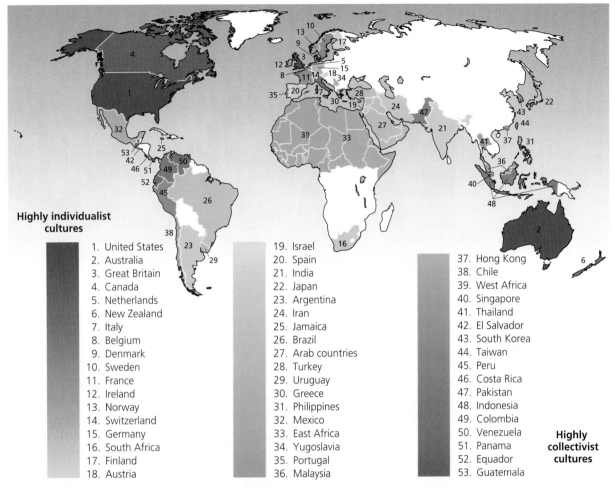

Highly individualist cultures

1. United States
2. Australia
3. Great Britain
4. Canada
5. Netherlands
6. New Zealand
7. Italy
8. Belgium
9. Denmark
10. Sweden
11. France
12. Ireland
13. Norway
14. Switzerland
15. Germany
16. South Africa
17. Finland
18. Austria

19. Israel
20. Spain
21. India
22. Japan
23. Argentina
24. Iran
25. Jamaica
26. Brazil
27. Arab countries
28. Turkey
29. Uruguay
30. Greece
31. Philippines
32. Mexico
33. East Africa
34. Yugoslavia
35. Portugal
36. Malaysia

37. Hong Kong
38. Chile
39. West Africa
40. Singapore
41. Thailand
42. El Salvador
43. South Korea
44. Taiwan
45. Peru
46. Costa Rica
47. Pakistan
48. Indonesia
49. Colombia
50. Venezuela
51. Panama
52. Equador
53. Guatemala

Highly collectivist cultures

FIGURE 4-1   Individualism-Collectivism Rankings for 50 Countries and 3 Regions. (Source: Hofstede, 1991)

Taiwan, Thailand, and Singapore following close behind (see Figure 4-1). About 70% of the world's population lives in collectivist cultures (Triandis, 1990).

The individualism-collectivism dimension also applies to co-cultures. The Mexican American co-culture, for example, expresses its collectivism in several proverbs (Zormeier & Samovar, 2000). "Better to be a fool with the crowd than wise by oneself," "A solitary soul neither sings nor cries," "He who divides and shares is left with the best share," and "Bewail your poverty, and not alone" all express the prominent value given to collectivism in Mexican American communities.

A poll of 131 businesspeople, scholars, government officials, and professionals in eight East Asian countries and the United States shows vast differences between individualist and collectivist cultural values (Simons & Zielenziger, 1996, p. A22). Respondents were asked the question, "Which of the following are critically important to your people?" The results were as follows:

	Asians	Americans
1. An orderly society	70%	11%
2. Personal freedom	32%	82%
3. Individual rights	29%	73%

Children from collectivist cultures (pictured on the top) are typically taught that "the nail that sticks up gets hammered down." Children from individualist cultures (below) typically are taught that "the squeaky wheel gets the grease." Asian children are taught to blend into the group; American children are taught to stand out from the group by being overtly expressive.

Clearly, people from individualist and collectivist cultures and co-cultures perceive the world in markedly different ways (see Box 4-1).

See Video Clip #5, Chapter 4 on the CD.

COMMUNICATION DIFFERENCES   Differences in emphasis on individualism and collectivism create differences in communication. Individualist cultures expect a person to initiate a job search and engage in personal promotion. Useful social skills in an individualist culture include getting to know people quickly, engaging easily in conversation on a wide variety of subjects, being interesting enough to make an impression on others, and employing public speaking skills in meetings (Brislin, 1993). You're largely on your own in social interactions, and dating, flirting, and small talk play an important part in self-promotion. In fact, receiving help from friends or family can make you appear somewhat desperate and ineffectual, such as getting set up with a blind date. Selection of a mate is considered a personal choice. Parental approval is desirable but not necessary, and marriage will occur even in the face of parental disapproval. During conflict, individuals tend to be direct, competitive, and more concerned with protecting their own self-esteem than worrying about the self-esteem of others (Ting-Toomey et al., 1991).

Box 4-1 Focus on Controversy

Culture and Competition

In a hypercompetitive society such as the United States, it is easy for us to assume that competition is a natural part of being human. It is not until we see another culture responding to competition in a dramatically different way from our own that we understand the powerful role culture plays in our view of competition. Here is a story that makes this point powerfully.

> A newly trained teacher named Mary went to teach at a Navajo Indian reservation. Every day, she would ask five of the young Navajo students to go to the chalkboard and complete a simple math problem from their homework. They would stand there, silently, unwilling to complete the task. Mary couldn't figure it out. Nothing she had studied in her educational curriculum helped, and she certainly hadn't seen anything like it in her student-teaching days back in Phoenix.
>
> "What am I doing wrong? Could I have chosen five students who can't do the problem?" Mary would wonder. "No, it couldn't be that." Finally, she asked the students what was wrong. And in their answer, she learned a surprising lesson from her young Indian pupils about self-image and a sense of self-worth.
>
> It seemed that the students respected each other's individuality and knew that not all of them were capable of doing the problems. . . . They believed no one would win if any students were shown up or embarrassed at the chalkboard. So they refused to compete with each other in public.
>
> Once she understood, Mary changed the system so that she could check each child's math problem individually but not at any child's expense in front of classmates. They all wanted to learn—but not at someone else's expense (Canfield et al., 1997, pp. 175–176).

There is plentiful evidence demonstrating that American hypercompetitiveness is primarily a product of an individualist value system, not a biological imperative common to all humans (Chatman & Barsade, 1995). Research shows marked differences in competitiveness and cooperativeness of subjects, depending on their cultural roots. Two studies (Parks & Vu, 1994) compared people from cultures that vary widely on the individualism-collectivism dimension: Americans (extremely individualist) and Vietnamese (extremely collectivist). The first study showed that the Vietnamese "cooperated at an extraordinarily high rate." The Americans were inclined to be competitive. In the second study, Vietnamese subjects exhibited high rates of cooperation even when faced with competitive strategies from other subjects. Americans showed far less cooperation and more competitiveness. The authors of these studies conclude that "The difference between the extremely individualistic and extremely collectivistic cultures was very large and consistent with cultural norms" (p. 712).

Co-cultures can exhibit a similar relationship between degrees of individualism or collectivism and competitiveness. One study (Cox et al., 1991) found that groups composed of African Americans, Asian Americans, and Latino Americans displayed far more cooperative behavior than groups composed of subjects from an individualist cultural tradition (European Americans). In a study of women conducted by Mariah Nelson (1998)

Reflecting a collectivist viewpoint, 7 ft 6 in Chinese basketball star, Yao Ming, viewed slam dunking as an exhibition of bad sportsmanship when he first joined the NBA. American NBA players are from the "layups are for whimps" school.

Box 4-1 | Focus on Controversy (continued)

and reported in *Embracing Victory*, African American women are the group most likely to support the statement that "friends should not compete with each other." Ruth L. Hall, psychology professor at the College of New Jersey, explains that many African American women are hesitant to compete with friends because they have been raised with the co-cultural value of cooperation and collectivism (cited in Nelson, 1998). African American women are thus pulled in two directions—the competitive direction by a dominant individualist culture and a cooperative direction by a co-cultural collectivist value system.

The collectivist value is exhibited during Kwanzaa, a weeklong African American celebration that starts on December 26. There are seven guiding principles of Kwanzaa, and none of them includes competitiveness. Three of them emphasize cooperativeness: umoja (unity), ujima (collective work and responsibility), and ujamaa (cooperative economics).

Cultural diversity makes enhancing cooperation an urgent goal. It is far too easy for us to perceive cultural differences and to make those differences an excuse to be enemies. We live in a "global village," where cultures rub against each other every day, but as Hall (1981) observes, "It is impossible to cooperate . . . unless we know each other's ways of thinking" (p. 3). As an individualist nation, the United States will find it challenging to become more cooperative.

Questions for Thought

1. Is competition in the classroom always a negative experience? Do some children thrive in a competitive environment? How might competitive and cooperative classrooms differ in teaching and learning styles?
2. Can you imagine a culture entirely free from competition? Would that be a desirable society? Could you avoid mass conformity in such a culture?

Collectivist cultures do not require the same social skills as individualist cultures. Self-promotion is discouraged because it can incite envy, jealousy, and friction within groups, and self-promotion is thought to divert energies away from the welfare of the group. In exchange for loyalty to the group and contributions to the group's effectiveness, members of collectivist cultures receive help from influential members of the group or organization in finding jobs and making social contacts (Brislin, 1993). Mate selection is often arranged by parents since family approval is important.

Hall (1981) was the first to identify a specific difference in communication styles between individualist and collectivist cultures. Individualist cultures typically use a low-context style and collectivist cultures typically use a high-context style (Griffin, 2003).

The chief difference between the two styles is in verbal expression. A **low-context communication style** is verbally precise, direct, and explicit. There is little assumption that others will be able to discern what you mean without precise verbal explanation. Self-expression and speaking ability are highly valued. Points of view are openly expressed and persuasion is an accepted goal of speech (Chen & Starosta, 1998b). Using a computer provides a technological example of low-context communication. Nothing can be left out of an e-mail or Internet address. Every space, period, number, and letter must be exact or the computer will exhibit how truly dumb it can be. Instructions given to computers must be precise and explicit; close doesn't count. Low-context human communication is similarly precise and explicit. "Say what you mean," "Tell me what you want," and "What's your point?" are statements that reflect a low-context communication style in individualist cultures.

In collectivist cultures, context is paramount, not the explicit message. A **high-context communication style** uses indirect verbal expression. You are expected to "read between the lines." Significant information must be derived from contextual cues, such as the relationship, situation, setting, and time. Harmony is highly regarded in collectivist cultures, and verbal messages tend to be vague so no offense will be caused. When a Japanese person says *Kangae sasete kudasai* ("Let me think about it") or *Zensho shimasu* ("I will do my best"), Americans are likely to translate these statements literally. This person, however, has actually said "no" in a polite way without saying it directly.

When cultural populations are quite similar, there is less need to be verbally explicit because there is historical understanding of the rules, roles, norms, and customary practices of the culture. Thus, *a high-context, implicit communication style is appropriate in collectivist cultures because they tend to have more homogeneous (similar) populations* (Hofstede, 1991; Samovar & Porter, 2001). Individualist cultures tend to have more heterogeneous (dissimilar) populations. With culturally diverse populations comes uncertainty. The rules, roles, norms, and customary practices are not immediately known by individuals from co-cultural backgrounds. There is a compelling need to be verbally explicit in individualist cultures to prevent misunderstanding and miscommunication. Thus, *a low-context, explicit communication style is appropriate in individualist cultures*.

Power-Distance Dimension

In the United States power imbalances are often the catalyst for aggressive behavior. The perceptions of power imbalances in some cultures, however, are strikingly different from those in the United States.

GENERAL DESCRIPTION   Cultures vary widely in their attitudes concerning the appropriateness of power imbalances (Figure 4-2). Hofstede (1991) calls these variations in the acceptability of unequal distribution of power in relationships, institutions, and organizations the **power-distance dimension** (hereafter referred to as PD).

Low-PD cultures have a relatively weak emphasis on maintaining power differences. Low-PD countries such as the United States, Great Britain, Sweden, Denmark, Austria, Israel, and New Zealand are guided by norms and institutional regulations that minimize power distinctions. These cultures challenge authority, flatten organizational hierarchies to reduce status differences between management and employees, and use power legitimately. Low-PD cultures, however, do not advocate eliminating power disparities entirely, and in a country such as the United States, power differences obviously exist. "In every society a social hierarchy exists that privileges some groups over others. Those groups that function at the top of the social hierarchy determine to a great extent the communication system of the entire society" (Orbe, 1998, p. 8). Maintaining hierarchical boundaries between the relatively powerful and the powerless nevertheless is deemphasized in low-PD cultures.

High-PD cultures place a relatively strong emphasis on maintaining power differences. Malaysia, Guatemala, the Philippines, Mexico, India, Singapore, and Hong Kong, among others, are guided by norms and institutional regulations that accept, and even cultivate, power distinctions. The actions of authorities are rarely challenged, the powerful are thought to have a legitimate right to use their power, and organizational and social hierarchies are encouraged (Lustig & Koester, 2003). In Japan, for example, seeking a second opinion on a health issue is taboo; it is an affront to the primary care physician's expertise and power position (Ricks, 2000). In India, a massive 7.7 magnitude earthquake struck parts of the country on January 26, 2001, killing almost 20,000 people, injuring more than 60,000, and leaving about

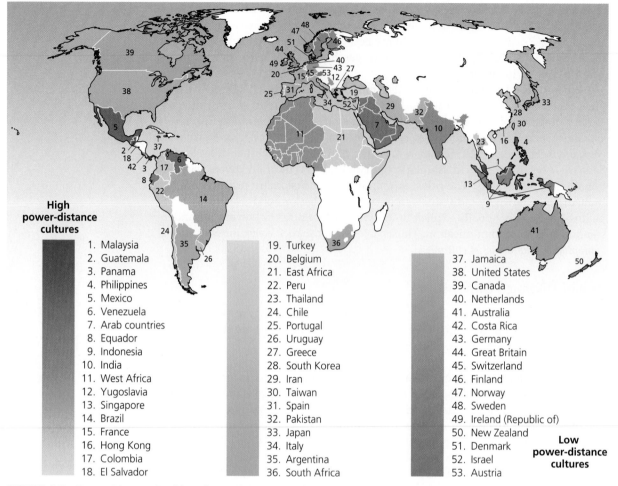

High power-distance cultures

1. Malaysia
2. Guatemala
3. Panama
4. Philippines
5. Mexico
6. Venezuela
7. Arab countries
8. Equador
9. Indonesia
10. India
11. West Africa
12. Yugoslavia
13. Singapore
14. Brazil
15. France
16. Hong Kong
17. Colombia
18. El Salvador

19. Turkey
20. Belgium
21. East Africa
22. Peru
23. Thailand
24. Chile
25. Portugal
26. Uruguay
27. Greece
28. South Korea
29. Iran
30. Taiwan
31. Spain
32. Pakistan
33. Japan
34. Italy
35. Argentina
36. South Africa

37. Jamaica
38. United States
39. Canada
40. Netherlands
41. Australia
42. Costa Rica
43. Germany
44. Great Britain
45. Switzerland
46. Finland
47. Norway
48. Sweden
49. Ireland (Republic of)
50. New Zealand
51. Denmark
52. Israel
53. Austria

Low power-distance cultures

FIGURE 4-2 Power-Distance Rankings for 50 Countries and 3 Regions. (Source: Hofstede, 1991)

a million individuals homeless (Coleman, 2001). The biggest impediment to the distribution of desperately needed aid to those afflicted was India's traditional caste system—a social hierarchy, outlawed long ago but still strong in practice, with Brahmans at the top and the "untouchables" at the bottom. As Catholic Relief Services worker Mayuri Mistry explained, "Whatever the distribution of aid, it first goes to the upper castes" (Coleman, 2001, p. 7A).

COMMUNICATION DIFFERENCES Communication in low-PD cultures reflects the minimization of power disparities. Workers may disagree with their supervisors; in fact, disagreement may be encouraged by some bosses. Socializing outside the work environment and communication on a first-name basis between workers and bosses is not unusual (Brislin, 1993). Students can question and disagree with their teachers. Some professors even encourage students to address them by their first names.

When I taught at Western Washington University in Bellingham, Washington, one of the hottest issues was a proposal to establish a pub on campus. Three quarters of the students favored the proposal. The most common argument used to support

This arranged marriage between two young adults from India highlights the power-distance dimension of cultures. A high power-distance country such as India values the right of parents to arrange their children's marriages. A low power-distance country such as the United States accords no such right to parents.

the proposal was that students and professors would have an informal place to meet, relax, sip a brew, and discuss philosophy, politics, or the state of the world. The pub would diminish power disparities between professors and students. Not surprisingly, the administration was not enthusiastic about the proposed pub—but for mostly legal and liability reasons, not out of any desire to maintain power disparities. The pub was never established. In a high-PD culture the issue would never be raised.

Communication in high-PD cultures reflects the desire to maintain power disparities. Children raised in high-PD cultures are expected to obey their parents without question. Students do not question or disagree with their teachers. Workers normally do not feel comfortable disagreeing with their bosses, and friendships and socializing between bosses and employees are rare.

The reactions to power imbalances are likely to reflect where a culture falls on the power-distance dimension. One study (Bond et al., 1985) compared people's reactions to insults in a high-PD (Hong Kong) and a low-PD culture (United States). Subjects from Hong Kong were less upset than those from the United States when they were insulted, as long as the initiator of the insult was a high-status person. Brislin (1993) explains, "When people accept status distinctions as normal, they accept the fact that the powerful are different than the less powerful. The powerful can engage in behaviors that the less powerful cannot, in this case insult people and have the insult accepted as part of their rights" (p. 255).

Box 4-2   Sharper Focus

Teaching South Koreans to Smile

"Whiskey, whiskey, whiskey" they chant, much as we say "cheese" when a photograph is being shot of us. Bank tellers and accountants are learning to smile. This is part of the training at the Korean Air Service Academy, a school in Seoul, South Korea, that specializes in making Korean businesses more globally effective by teaching "international manners" (Jelinek, 1998). Smiling, especially to high-status individuals, does not come easily to these employees. Years of authoritarian military governments influenced Korean citizens to show deference to authorities. The Confucian value of respecting elders and superiors also contributes to the difficulty of learning how to smile.

South Korea is an interesting example of a culture that has a high-PD history but is gradually moving toward becoming a moderate-PD culture. Smiling seems like such a simple nonverbal expression of warmth and friendliness. Most Americans find little difficulty smiling. South Koreans, however, must overcome years of social training that predispose them to reserved, formal communication, especially with high-status individuals. Smiling communicates informality and equal stature. A simple smile can exhibit a fundamental value difference between cultures.

Differences in the power-distance dimension do not mean that high-PD cultures never experience conflict and aggression arising from power imbalances. Members of low-PD cultures, however, are more likely to respond with frustration, outrage, and hostility to power imbalances than are members of high-PD cultures. This occurs because low-PD cultures value power balance even though the experience of everyday life in such cultures may reflect a somewhat different reality. African Americans, Mexican Americans, and Native Americans in particular recognize this disparity between the "ideal" of power balance and the reality of socioeconomic disadvantage in the United States. In a low-PD culture, the struggle to achieve the ideal of balanced power is more compelling, and the denial of power is likely to be perceived as more unjust, even intolerable, than in a high-PD culture where power balance is viewed differently (Box 4-2).

There is a strong correlation between the individualism-collectivism and the power-distance dimensions (Hofstede, 1991). *High-PD cultures are likely to be collectivist, and low-PD cultures are likely to be individualist.* Duane Alwin, a sociologist at the University of Michigan, studied parental values in the United States. Increasingly, parents in the United States encourage their children to become independent and autonomous (individualist). Alwin's study found that parents placed the highest value on "thinking for oneself" as the quality that will best prepare children for life. Questioning authority (low-PD) also emerged as an important parental value. As Alwin notes, "People are willing to question authority, to not necessarily believe that the parental generation is right or the church is right or some institutional authority is right" (cited in Frerking, 1995). This exhibits an individualistic, low-PD value system.

Masculinity-Femininity Dimension

Hofstede (1991) discovered that cultures differ along a masculine-feminine dimension. Although not as extensively researched by other scholars, the dimension does seem to hold up fairly well.

GENERAL DESCRIPTION   A **masculine culture** exhibits stereotypic masculine traits such as male dominance, ambitiousness, assertiveness, competitiveness, and drive for achievement (Hofstede, 1996). Using Tannen's (1990) term, a masculine culture

Box 4-3 Sharper Focus

The Falsetto Voice of Japanese Women

"The Voice is as fawning as her demeanor, as sweet as syrup, and as high as a dog whistle. Any higher, and it would shatter the crystal on the seventh floor" (Kristof, 1995, p. A27). "The Voice," described by *New York Times* reporter Nicholas Kristof, refers to the falsetto pitch used by Japanese women in formal settings, on the phone, or when interacting with business customers. (The falsetto is usually abandoned in normal conversation with family and friends.)

This unnaturally high-pitched voice historically has been viewed as a sign of politeness, much as a person in the United States would raise his or her voice at the end of a sentence to sound tentative or questioning (Kristof, 1995). This corresponds to a masculine culture's stereotype for "feminine" behavior, and Japan is at the top of Hofstede's (1991) list of masculine cultures.

Females in a masculine culture are expected to be deferential, polite, and nonaggressive—to conform to rigid gender stereotypes. "The Voice" shows such traits. Julie Saito, a reporter at *Asahi Shimbun*, explains, "A lower voice sounds too bullying, too aggressive, too manly. . . . A high voice sounds more cute, more like a girlish image of women" (Kristof, 1995, p. A27). Hideki Kasuya, professor of speech science at Utsunomiya University, did studies of TV announcers in the United States and Japan. He discovered that female announcers in the United States speak in a markedly lower pitch than female announcers from Japan (Kristof, 1995).

Not all Japanese women accept speaking in falsetto as appropriate. Mari Shimakura, a teenager in Tokyo, expresses the changing viewpoint about the female falsetto voice: "When girls speak in really high voices, I just want to kick them in the head. It's totally fake and really annoying. It gives me a headache. Mom tells me I speak in too low a voice, and that I should raise it. But I can't change it" (Kristof, 1995, p. A27). This attitude seems to be spreading despite the feminine stereotypes historically prominent in Japan. More recent studies by Kasuya reveal that female Japanese announcers have dropped the pitch of their voices significantly. Similarly, studies of taped announcements on subway platforms and recordings of female singers from the past and present reveal a lowering of the female pitch (Kristof, 1995).

Cultures that score high on masculinity do not necessarily communicate rigid gender stereotypes in the same ways. The United States is a fairly masculine culture, yet use of the female falsetto voice in formal situations would startle most of us. What "The Voice" demonstrates is that cultures that are similar on the masculinity-femininity dimension can communicate this similarity in surprisingly varied ways.

has a strong need for status. *Gender roles are rigid in masculine cultures*. Women are expected to "act feminine" (Box 4-3). In Japan, for instance, women comprise a scant 0.1% of the board members of Japan's top companies, and those who do work in the corporate world are mostly confined to clerical or ceremonial jobs (French, 2001). Women occupy only about 5% of legislative offices (Women in the House, 1997). Sexual harassment wasn't a punishable offense in Japan until 1999. Women also couldn't work the graveyard shift until the Equal Opportunity Law was amended in April 2000 (Lev, 2000).

Cultures ranking high on masculinity include Japan, Austria, Venezuela, Italy, Switzerland, and Mexico. The United States ranks relatively high on masculinity (Figure 4-3).

A **feminine culture** exhibits stereotypic feminine traits such as affection, nurturance, sensitivity, compassion, and emotional expressiveness (Hofstede, 1996). Using Tannen's term, a feminine culture has a strong need for connection. *In feminine cultures, however, gender roles are less rigid*, equality between the sexes is more typical, and individual achievement and competitiveness are deemphasized for both men and women. In Sweden, for example, equality between the sexes is highly valued. Almost half of the nation's legislature is comprised of women (Women in the House, 1997). Sweden has a well-entrenched social support system of pregnancy leave, lengthy paid vacations, and time off to tend to sick children since a very high proportion of

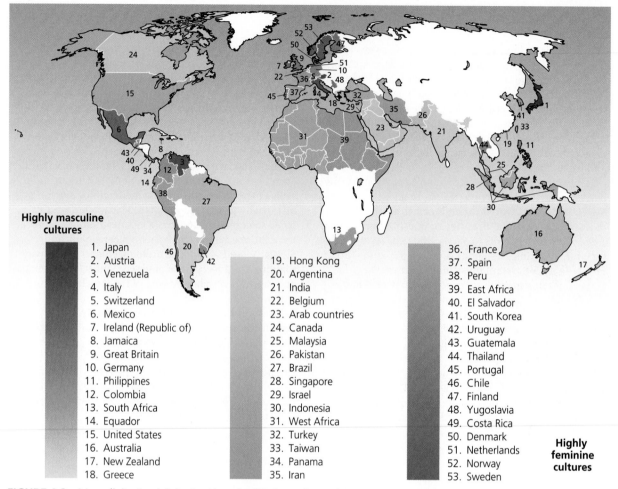

Highly masculine cultures

1. Japan	19. Hong Kong	36. France
2. Austria	20. Argentina	37. Spain
3. Venezuela	21. India	38. Peru
4. Italy	22. Belgium	39. East Africa
5. Switzerland	23. Arab countries	40. El Salvador
6. Mexico	24. Canada	41. South Korea
7. Ireland (Republic of)	25. Malaysia	42. Uruguay
8. Jamaica	26. Pakistan	43. Guatemala
9. Great Britain	27. Brazil	44. Thailand
10. Germany	28. Singapore	45. Portugal
11. Philippines	29. Israel	46. Chile
12. Colombia	30. Indonesia	47. Finland
13. South Africa	31. West Africa	48. Yugoslavia
14. Equador	32. Turkey	49. Costa Rica
15. United States	33. Taiwan	50. Denmark
16. Australia	34. Panama	51. Netherlands
17. New Zealand	35. Iran	52. Norway
18. Greece		53. Sweden

Highly feminine cultures

FIGURE 4-3 Masculinity-Femininity Rankings for 50 Countries and 3 Regions. (Source: Hofstede, 1991)

the workforce is comprised of women. Cultures ranking high on femininity include Sweden, Norway, the Netherlands, Denmark, Costa Rica, Finland, and Chile.

COMMUNICATION DIFFERENCES In masculine cultures men typically communicate in ways that will enhance their esteem (e.g., speak often, control the floor, interrupt). Women in masculine cultures typically communicate in ways that will enhance relationships (e.g., express support, encourage, listen well). In feminine cultures, both men and women communicate in ways that emphasize relationships over power. In Sweden, for example, management in organizations is democratic. Managers don't give orders to employees; they make suggestions or offer guidelines (Lewis, 1996). Nurturance and the creation of a caring society are paramount concerns.

Intercultural communication between members of masculine and feminine cultures poses challenges similar to the difficulties men and women in the dominant U.S. culture have communicating with each other. The potential for misunderstandings and miscommunication is enormous, as already discussed at length in the previous chapter.

Box 4-4 | Focus on Controversy

Critique of Hofstede's Cultural Dimensions

Although Hofstede's (1980, 1991) monumental study of cultural value differences provides useful insights into underlying causes of intercultural communication difficulties and challenges, Hofstede's work is not without its critics. The first criticism is that, although the data from Hofstede's original study are impressive, the dimensions he identifies from these data have not all received the same level of support from additional studies. The individualism-collectivism dimension has received the greatest support and has been validated in numerous studies (see especially Kim et al., 1994; Triandis, 1995). The power-distance dimension has been studied far less than individualism-collectivism, but some additional studies support this dimension as well (Bochner & Hesketh, 1994; Merritt, 1998). The masculinity-femininity dimension has received limited additional support beyond Hofstede's original study (Hofstede, 1996; Leung et al., 1990). Hofstede (1980, 1991) identifies a fourth dimension, *uncertainty avoidance*, in his original study. This dimension has not been discussed here, however, because several studies have been unable to validate it (Merritt, 1998; Schwartz, 1995; Smith et al., 1996), making the dimension suspect.

A second criticism of Hofstede's cultural dimensions is that his original research was conducted in the 1960s and 1970s. His data and the rankings of cultures on each dimension derived from his data may no longer be accurate. This would be an important criticism if it weren't for the fact that deep-seated cultural values are highly resistant to change, even over long periods of time (Samovar & Porter, 2001). There may be minor changes in rankings on each of his dimensions, but there is little reason to believe that general descriptions of cultures (e.g., individualist, high-PD) are any less valid now than when the data were gathered.

A third criticism of Hofstede's dimensions is that they were derived from data extracted from a detailed questionnaire with a Western bias. This criticism does not invalidate the three dimensions already discussed, but it does raise the question of whether other dimensions are missing from Hofstede's research. Hofstede (1991) accepts this criticism as valid, arguing that another more Eastern dimension, called Confucian dynamism, has some support. The degree of research support for this dimension is still slight, however, so it will not be explained here.

Questions for Thought

1. Can you think of additional value dimensions that distinguish cultures not included in Hofstede's work?
2. Why do you think deep-seated cultural values are highly resistant to change? Can you imagine American culture becoming collectivist, high power-distance, and feminine?

It is important to note here that the rankings of cultures on the masculinity-femininity dimension are relative, not absolute. A high ranking on femininity doesn't mean that a culture treats women as well as men. It simply means that feminine cultures have less rigid gender roles than do masculine cultures with their distinctly different behaviors for males and females. As the 1993 United Nations Human Development Report concludes, "No country treats its women as well as it treats its men" (Wright, 1993, p. A10).

Remembering all the details on value dimensions that distinguish cultures can seem daunting. When trying to condense all this material on cultural value differences, concentrate less on the details and more on three primary points.

First, recognize that individualism-collectivism is clearly "the crucial dimension of cultural variability" (Griffin, 1994, p. 401). Be particularly familiar with this dimension because it has the greatest support in cross-cultural research.

Second, remember that individualism-collectivism and power-distance are strongly correlated. This means that individualist cultures also tend to be low-PD cultures, and collectivist cultures tend to be high-PD cultures. If you know where a culture falls on one value dimension, you know where it will probably fall on the other dimension as well.

 See "Proverbs and Culture" activity on CD.

Third, the masculinity-femininity dimension is similar to Tannen's (1990) status-connection model of gender communication already discussed. Masculine cultures typically expect men to be concerned with status, expect women to be concerned with connection, and have communication patterns that conform to these expectations. Feminine cultures expect a less rigid distinction in gender behaviors and more overlapping of status and connection for both men and women.

Intercultural Miscommunication

Cultures can vary dramatically in how their members perceive the world. With differences in core values come numerous opportunities for miscommunication among members of differing cultures. In this section, basic intercultural miscommunication will be discussed.

Ethnocentrism

Imagine two different approaches to eating dinner. In the first version, the family believes dinner is a ritual that allows family members to put aside diversions and distractions of the day. The focus is on the family and what each person did that day—exciting things, happy experiences, problems, troubling issues, and the like.

The family begins by saying grace before eating, thanking God for the bounty. Each person seated at the table formally requests that food be passed to him or her. They also say, "Thank you" after the food is passed. No one reaches across the table and grabs anything. That is considered rude. Conversation is encouraged. Silence is noticed and discouraged. No one leaves the table without first asking to be excused. When dinner is over, everyone busses their dishes and pitches in on cleanup.

In the second version, the family does everything differently. Dinner is rarely eaten at the dinner table. It is usually consumed in front of the TV. When dinner is eaten together at the table, everyone grabs for the food as quickly as they can. No one asks for anything. No one thanks anyone for passing food. No grace is said. When dinner is over, the women take care of the dishes, and the men go about their business of relaxation or television watching.

Here we have two distinctly different ways of carrying out commonplace dinner activities. Do you deem superior the version that is closest to the way you were raised and the other version inferior? If so, you have captured the fundamental essence of ethnocentrism—the way we do things is good, and the way others do things differently from us is not so good.

ETHNOCENTRISM DEFINED   The term *ethnocentrism* is derived from two Greek words: *ethnos,* meaning "nation," and *kentron,* meaning "center" (Klopf, 1998). Literally, it means, "Our nation is the center of all things." **Ethnocentrism** "is the notion that one's own culture is superior to any other. It is the idea that other cultures should be measured by the degree to which they live up to our cultural standards" (Nanda & Warms, 1998, p. 9). The degree of difference between your own and other cultures determines ratings on a superiority-inferiority scale. The bigger the difference found in a culture distinct from your own, the greater is the perceived inferiority of that culture.

All cultures, to greater or lesser extent, are ethnocentric. Ethnocentrism usually involves "invidious comparisons that ennoble one's culture while degrading those of others" (Stewart & Bennett, 1991, p. 161). This ethnocentric bias is often shocking, even brutal in its judgment of other cultures. Names of various tribes and groups sometimes reflect this bias. *Kiowa* means "real or principal people." *Laplander* means "human being." Jews are the "chosen people," and gentiles are everyone else. Historically, among Christians *gentile* meant "heathen" or "pagan." Greeks and Romans referred to outsiders as "barbarians" (Klopf, 1998). Immigrants to the United States are referred to as "aliens," legal or otherwise. Common definitions of *alien* include "strange," "unnatural," "repugnant," "outsider," and, of course, "visitor from another galaxy."

Ethnocentrism is a learned belief. It is difficult to resist the temptation to devalue another culture simply because we are comfortable with how things are done in our own culture. Experiencing another culture's customs, practices, and beliefs that are different from what we are accustomed to may seem weird and wrong.

Consider differences in teaching and learning in schools (Samovar & Porter, 2001). In Russia, China, Japan, Korea, Vietnam, and Cambodia, learning is passive. Teachers read to their students. Students are mostly silent unless called on to answer questions or recite. Rote memorization is common. In Mexico, students are more active. They talk and learn through group work. In Germany, southern Italy, and the West Indies, students rise in unison when the teacher enters the classroom. In an Israeli kibbutz, students wander around the classroom, talk to each other, sharpen pencils, or get a drink without formal permission. They talk during lessons, even hum to themselves while working on an assignment. American classrooms are a mix of many of these practices, and they are less formal and more active places of learning than classrooms in most other cultures.

So which cultural communication practices are correct? Every culture believes the way it operates is preferable; otherwise the practices would change (unless enforced by an authoritarian regime). Ethnocentrism is judgment on a global scale.

CULTURAL RELATIVISM   In an effort to combat ethnocentrism, anthropologists have offered the cultural relativism viewpoint (Harrison & Huntington, 2000). **Cultural relativism** views cultures as merely different, not deficient. From this viewpoint "all phenomena can be assessed only from the perspective of the culture in which they exist" (Moghaddam, 1998, p. 506). We must respect all cultures and their inherent right to engage in practices, rituals, and communication behaviors that may appear strange, even repugnant. The "West is best" ethnocentrism should not be imposed on cultures that depart from the West's values. In several high-PD cultures, for example, women and children are expected to walk several paces behind the husband and father as deference to his authority. In Japan, individuals are greeted with a bow, and those of lower status are expected to bow lower than those of higher status. Men and women communicate openly with each other in Western cultures; they are far more restricted in most Arab cultures. Americans usually expect to speak without interruption and are often irritated when not accorded this privilege. Arabs have no such expectation and will exuberantly join a conversation that will appear to most Americans to be a chaotic shouting match (Lewis, 1996). Cultural relativism dictates that we respect these different cultural practices, despite personal misgivings.

In the abstract, cultural relativism appears egalitarian and unprejudiced. The ethical and moral correctness of an act can only be judged within the value system of the culture in which the practice takes place. Confusion, however, can arise from the use of the term "relativism." It seems to imply that there are no universal standards for judging cultural practices. There are practices in cultures around the

A Taliban man in Afghanistan beats women with a steel whip for a minor infraction of rules for wearing the burka. Avoiding ethnocentrism does not mean that we have to accept brutal treatment of women.

world, however, that are condoned within the culture but contradict universal human rights. Female genital mutilation (female circumcision), foot binding of women, suttee (the practice of widows joining their dead husbands on the funeral pyre even if they protest), denial of education and political participation to women, the selling of children, slavery, and myriad other practices are behaviors that some cultures condone.

The United Nation's Universal Declaration of Human Rights declares that every human being has certain basic rights that include the right to life, liberty, security, freedom of speech and belief, equal protection under the law, participation in the political process, a decent standard of living, necessary social services, and education. Harrison (2000) notes, "The vast majority of the planet's people would agree with the following assertions:

Life is better than death.
Health is better than sickness.
Liberty is better than slavery.
Prosperity is better than poverty.
Education is better than ignorance.
Justice is better than injustice (p. xxvi).

Customs, practices, and communication behaviors that do not dehumanize people should not be rejected as inferior simply because they are different from our own cultural ways of operating. Sexism, racism, homophobia, and all the "isms" that breed "ethnic cleansings" and genocidal wars, however, deserve no defense. Cultural relativists typically condemn these inhumane practices, which makes the term *cultural relativism* more confusing than clarifying.

MULTICULTURALISM An alternative to *cultural relativism* is *multiculturalism*. Flowers and Richardson (1996) define **multiculturalism** as a "social-intellectual movement that promotes the value of diversity as a core principle and insists that all cultural groups be treated with respect and as equals" (p. 609). Multiculturalism assumes universal human rights. As Moghaddam (1998) explains,

> In order for multiculturalism to work, there must be certain universal rules to allow communication and understanding to take place. For example, without mutual respect and orderly turn taking, there can be no meaningful dialogue. Furthermore, in a situation in which universal rules of justice are not accepted, the weak will necessarily suffer because they cannot use the law to protect their interests (p. 506).

Multiculturalism incorporates the five ethical standards discussed in Chapter 1—respect, honesty, fairness, choice, and responsibility. To be a competent intercultural communicator, you must accept cultural diversity and eschew ethnocentrism, but always you must be guided by the ethical standards of the competent communicator. Inhumane behavior that degrades and diminishes others cannot be accepted with the justification, "That's just the way they do things in their culture." Diversity is part of the colorful tapestry of humankind, but inhumanity is a blight on any culture's fabric.

Misattribution

Attribution, or the causes assigned to people's behavior, and problems associated with attribution were discussed in Chapter 3. Similar attribution problems occur during intercultural communication. What is appropriate and expected communication in your own culture may be perceived as rude, arrogant, or uncivilized by individuals from other cultures. This is called **misattribution,** or "an attribution about the reason for an event given by a foreigner which differs from that typically given by a member of the host culture" (Smith & Bond, 1994, p. 177).

Intercultural communication is fraught with uncertainty and anxiety. When communicating with individuals from distinctly different cultures, we search for causes of their behavior, especially if the behavior is unexpected or seems odd by our culture's standards. We do this to reduce the uncertainty in intercultural encounters. Unfortunately, we often do not sufficiently understand the rules, norms, customs, and common practices of other cultures, so our attributions are made based on what makes sense and is expected in our culture. Individuals are too late for appointments or too early, are too talkative or too quiet, express their anger too openly or hide their anger too much, stand too close or too far apart when conversing, look too directly at the other person or look down or away too often. Each of these communication behaviors can receive a positive or negative attribution. The principal factor influencing the attribution is the culture of the observer. For instance, looking down when conversing with another person could be interpreted as a sign of weakness or intimidation (negative personal attribution) in American culture. The same behavior, however, when viewed by a member of an Asian culture, might be interpreted as an indication of respect and politeness (positive personal attribution). Conversely, looking directly at a speaker will likely be interpreted as a sign of confidence in the United States but an indicator of rudeness in Asian cultures.

Attributions in individualist and collectivist cultures are likely to be markedly different, making misattribution commonplace. Individualist cultures typically are sensitive to characteristics of a person (trait causes) that explain behavior. Collectivist cultures are typically sensitive to the context (situational causes). A conversation between two people, one from an individualist and the other from a collectivist culture, invites misattribution and the friction that accompanies it (Box 4-5).

Box 4-5   Sharper Focus

Intercultural Misattribution

Triandis (1975) presents a dialogue between an American supervisor and a Greek subordinate to show the problem of misattributions during intercultural communication. The Greek employee, coming from a relatively moderate power-distance culture, expects to be told what to do. Since Greece is a collectivist culture with a high-context communication style, he also assumes that his supervisor will interpret his behavior as he would himself. His American supervisor, however, coming from a low power-distance, individualist culture, expects participation, initiative, and responsibility from an employee. He also expects a direct, explicit communication style. In this conversation the clash of cultures can be seen readily by the misattributions that emerge due to cultural value differences.

Message	Attribution
AMERICAN: "How long will it take you to finish this report?	AMERICAN: I asked him to participate.
	GREEK: His behavior makes no sense. He is the boss. Why doesn't he tell me?
GREEK: I do not know. How long should it take?	AMERICAN: He refuses to take responsibility.
	GREEK: I asked him for an order.
AMERICAN: You are in the best position to analyze time requirements.	AMERICAN: I press him to take responsibility for his actions.
	GREEK: What nonsense! I better give him an answer.
GREEK: 10 days.	AMERICAN: He lacks the ability to estimate time; this estimate is totally inadequate.
AMERICAN: Take 15. Is it agreed you will do it in 15 days?	AMERICAN: I offer a contract.
	GREEK: These are my orders, 15 days.

In fact the report needed 30 days of regular work. So the Greek worked day and night, but at the end of the 15th day, he still needed one more day's work.

AMERICAN: Where is my report?	AMERICAN: I am making sure he fulfills his contract.
	GREEK: He is asking for the report.
GREEK: It will be ready tomorrow.	(Both attribute that it is not ready.)
AMERICAN: But we agreed that it would be ready today	AMERICAN: I must teach him to fulfill a contract.
	GREEK: The stupid, incompetent boss! Not only did he give me wrong orders, but he does not appreciate that I did a 30-day job in 16 days.

The Greek hands in his resignation. The American is surprised.

	GREEK: I can't work for such a man.

Interpersonal Miscommunication

Lustig and Koester (2003) provide a prime example of interpersonal miscommunication that can easily occur between members of distinctly different cultures:

Brian Holtz is a U.S. businessperson assigned by his company to manage its office in Thailand. Mr. Thani, a valued assistant manager in the Bangkok office, has recently been arriving late for work. Holtz has to decide what to do about this problem. After carefully thinking about his options, he decides there are four possible strategies:

1. Go privately to Mr. Thani, ask him why he has been arriving late, and tell him that he needs to come to work on time.
2. Ignore the problem.
3. Publicly reprimand Mr. Thani the next time he is late.
4. In a private discussion, suggest that he is seeking Mr. Thani's assistance in dealing with employees in the company who regularly arrive late for work, and solicit his suggestions about what should be done (p. 65).

　　If you were Holtz, what choice would you make? Which one is likely to be both appropriate and effective? The first choice is a typical American solution. It is a low-context communication style (direct), and it fits a masculine culture that values assertiveness from men. It would probably be effective in curbing Mr. Thani's tardiness. In Thai culture, however, an individual does not directly criticize another person. This causes a loss of face and threatens harmony (collectivist value). The first choice would be very inappropriate, even embarrassing.

　　The second choice, ignoring the problem, would be appropriate but ineffective since Mr. Thani would likely continue arriving late to work. Mr. Holtz would view this as intolerable. Ignoring a problem is not direct and assertive.

　　The third choice, public reprimand, would be neither appropriate nor effective. Mr. Thani, a valuable employee, would likely resign in shame. Thai culture is strongly feminine, and tenderness and compassion are highly prized. Public rebuke is neither tender nor compassionate. It is aggressive and domineering.

　　Thus, the first three options, if chosen, would be examples of miscommunication. Such communication would likely aggravate the problem. The fourth choice, a problem-solving approach, is preferred because it is likely to be both appropriate and effective (Lustig & Koester, 2003). Mr. Thani can receive the message indirectly that he must arrive at work on time without losing "face." Mr. Holtz can comment to Mr. Thani that he needs his help solving a problem. "Tardiness has recently increased in the office." No specific person is identified. "I would be very pleased if you would help solve this problem." Mr. Thani can recognize that his tardiness is a

Doonesbury

BY GARRY TRUDEAU

problem without any public acknowledgment or humiliation. He can "solve" the problem by changing his own behavior in the context of assisting his boss.

Ethnocentrism and misattributions that flow from deep-seated cultural value differences provide abundant opportunities for interpersonal miscommunication between individuals from diverse cultures. Frequent interaction between supervisors and subordinates in work situations may be highly appreciated by members of some cultures but resented by others. In Japan, it is typically perceived as caring, but in the United States it is often perceived as micromanaging or "spying" on workers to evaluate their performance. Close supervision of teenagers by parents is usually perceived by teens as showing love in collectivist cultures but as interference in individualist cultures (Triandis, 1995).

Confusion and conflict spring from such contradictory perceptions. Appropriate communication could address these opposing perceptions effectively, except we tend to be wedded to communication styles that intensify conflict. Just as men and women have difficulty communicating with each other in American culture, individuals from diverse cultural backgrounds will find that their typical communication styles often clash. Tannen (1979) notes that "in seeking to clarify, each speaker continues to use the very strategy which confused the other in the first place" (p. 5). Individuals using low-context styles try to clarify issues and misunderstandings by being increasingly direct and explicit. Individuals using high-context styles, however, continue to be vague and indirect, as is their habit. This further frustrates both parties as the clash of poorly matched communication styles continues and misattributions abound.

The warm, friendly, say-whatever-you-feel communication style familiar to Americans that typifies an individualist, low power-distance culture can produce awkward confusion when it clashes with communication styles more typical of collectivist cultures. Brislin (1993) cites an apt example of poorly matched communication styles:

> [I]f a young man from an Asian culture interacts with an American woman who employs the warm and exuberant style . . . the man may attribute the style to a romantic interest in him, personally. For example, assume that an American woman helps an Asian male on a class assignment. The Asian (following norms in his culture) offers a small gift to show his appreciation. The American woman responds, "I just love it! It's great! How thoughtful of you!" The Asian may conclude that the comment about "loving it" extends to him, personally (p. 225).

Confusion over romantic intentions can be embarrassing and potentially nasty. Toning down her response would, of course, be the simple solution to this clash of communication styles. The woman would have to know there was a stylistic clash in the first place, however, as would the man if he were to draw a different interpretation of her response. This again underlines the importance of knowledge in the communication competence model.

Intercultural Communication Competence

Later chapters will delve into specific ways intercultural communication competence can be enhanced. In this section, three general ways to develop appropriate and effective communication between cultures will be discussed: mindfulness, uncertainty reduction, and convergence.

Become Mindful

Cultural values are so deep-seated, and communication that flows from these values is so automatic, we often take no notice. We see differences in the content of messages and the outcomes, but we often fail to see the communication process that separates members of diverse cultures.

One general way to take notice is to be mindful. As discussed in Chapter 1, **mindfulness** is thinking about our communication with others and persistently working to improve it. When we are mindful, we recognize our ethnocentrism and our tendency to stereotype and misattribute behavior, and we resolve to recognize our biases and correct our misperceptions.

We exhibit mindfulness in three ways (Langer, 1989). First, we make more careful distinctions. We aren't as prone to stereotype. We look for a wider variety of attributions for unfamiliar or unexpected behavior. Second, we are open to new information, especially that which focuses on the process, not the content, of communication. It is easy to identify disagreements over the content of messages—"You've asked for more office space, but we have none to spare." The disagreement on content of messages is usually so apparent that we often fail to examine the communication process that is essential to resolving differences. When individuals from diverse cultures communicate, a content-only focus can trigger ethnocentrism and misattributions. Third, we recognize different perspectives. This is the essence of empathy, and it is critical to competent intercultural communication. Members of differing cultures perceive the world from their own cultural perspectives, and each person believes his or her perspective is reasonable and comfortable. When we lock into our own cultural perspective, we respond to cultural differences in an unthinking, "mindless" way.

Mindless communication is a universe away from competent communication. Remember, sensitivity is recognizing signals that can alert us to potential difficulties or possible solutions to problems. You have to extend your antenna. Mindfulness raises your antenna. Mindlessness keeps your antenna lowered.

Reduce Uncertainty

Uncertainty Reduction Theory (URT) posits that, when strangers first meet, their principal goal is to reduce uncertainty and to increase predictability (Berger & Calabrese, 1975). We are so motivated because uncertainty produces anxiety. This is particularly true of intercultural communication (Neuliep & Ryan, 1998). Managing uncertainty and its attendant anxiety is an important part of competent intercultural communication (Gudykunst, 1995). You can see this most apparently when you reside in a culture that is distinctly different from your own. Initially, you will likely experience **culture shock,** the anxiety that comes from the unfamiliarity of new cultural surroundings, rules, norms, and practices (Oberg, 1960). You may feel helpless, isolated, even depressed because so much is different from what you are used to seeing and experiencing.

The primary way to reduce uncertainty in intercultural transactions is through verbal and nonverbal communication (Berger & Calabrese, 1975). Assertiveness and responsiveness reduce intercultural uncertainty and anxiety that accompanies uncertainty (Neuliep & Ryan, 1998). *Assertiveness* allows us to make requests, actively disagree, and initiate conversation (Chapter 8 explores this more fully). *Responsiveness* involves sensitivity to the communication of others, effective listening, and supportive responses.

Engaging others in conversation and contact is an important aspect of uncertainty reduction. If our anxiety and culture shock prod us into withdrawing from communication transactions with members of the unfamiliar culture, we will not reduce uncertainty. Merely spending time in another culture, however, is not sufficient to counter culture shock and reduce uncertainty. Making friends with indigenous members of a culture is an effective way to reduce uncertainty. Making friends with expatriates from your own culture who reside in the new culture is insufficient (Torbiorn, 1982).

Recognize, however, that a low-context communication style will likely increase frustration and anxiety when a high-context communication style is the cultural norm. Adapt to the values of the culture. Proceed cautiously, gently, and respectfully when interacting with individuals from other cultures. A wondrous curiosity about the unfamiliar culture can serve as a tonic for the inevitable ill-conceived but best-intentioned foray into the uncertainties of intercultural communication.

Promote Convergence

www.mhhe
● com/
  /rothwell2

Go to the Online Learning Center for the "Ask a Question" activity.

DeVito (1990) offers an apt example of the difficulties we face when trying to determine what is appropriate communication in an intercultural event:

> An American college student, while having a dinner party with a group of foreigners, learns that her favorite cousin has just died. She bites her lip, pulls herself up, and politely excuses herself from the group. The interpretation given to this behavior will vary with the culture of the observer. The Italian student thinks, "How insincere; she doesn't even cry." The Russian student thinks, "How unfriendly; she didn't care enough to share her grief with her friends." The fellow American student thinks, "How brave; she wanted to bear her burden by herself" (p. 218).

Here we see divergent interpretations of a single event. **Divergence** refers to differences that separate people. The American college student is either insincere, unfriendly, or brave, depending on your cultural perspective. Ethnocentrism nourishes divergence. It makes difference a reason to dislike, hate, avoid, or feel contempt for individuals from other cultures.

Communication is at the core of divergence. When we communicate with individuals from other cultures, we immediately notice differences in language, rate of speech, tone of voice; markedly "odd" sounding accents even when English is the common language; unusual customs for greeting people such as bowing, embracing, and kissing on the cheek; and a host of other verbal and nonverbal practices. All of these accentuate divergence. We seem so terribly separate from those who speak and behave differently from us. The contrast may magnify the differences beyond what they actually are.

Divergence widens the gap between cultures. Convergence closes the gap. **Convergence** refers to similarities that connect us to others. Convergence doesn't erase or attempt to change, core differences between cultures. Convergence is different from assimilation. **Assimilation** is the absorption of one group's culture into the dominant culture. The original idea of the United States as a "melting pot" encouraged immigrants to give up any customs and practices different from those of Americans; to blend, not to stand apart. Recently, the idea of assimilation has been criticized as a way of eradicating cultures and destroying the unique heritages of diverse peoples.

The Reverend Jesse Jackson has suggested the family quilt as a more appropriate metaphor. The quilt is composed of unique squares of material stitched together to form a whole. The unique squares of material in the quilt represent multicultural differences. Convergence is the stitching that binds unique people from diverse cultures. Convergence merely accentuates similarities that already exist and calls for minor adjustments in our communication to link people. Convergence says, "Celebrate our differences but find commonalities that allow us to connect."

Initial encounters with individuals from very different cultures will likely accentuate divergence. Differences leap out at us because these differences create uncertainty and anxiety. Once the initial divergence comes into focus, however, a mindful communicator looks for ways to create convergence.

There are two primary ways to create convergence in intercultural transactions. First, *adjust your style of speaking*. Minor adjustments can promote convergence. More closely align your speaking rate, pitch, vocal intensity, and frequency of pauses and silences with those of the other person. If an individual from another culture seems bothered by the typically rapid speaking rate of "majority" Americans, slow down your speech. Likewise, individuals from cultures that are accustomed to slower speech patterns can increase their speaking rate slightly. If your vocal intensity seems to overwhelm your listener, tone it down. Such minor adjustments can help create convergence. This is similar to advice offered to public speakers—adjust your speaking style to your audience so listeners can identify with you.

The issue of speaking style can be controversial. Historically, relatively powerless groups (African Americans, Latinos) have been expected by the mainstream U.S. culture to shift their style of speaking to the mainstream speech style (Hecht et al., 1993). Weber (1994) cites an example. During a class lecture, a vocal Black student began a "call and response," offering encouraging "all right," "make it plain," and "teach" responses to the lecture. Soon a few more Black students joined. Startled White students, quizzed afterward, found the vocal responses disruptive, annoying, and rude. Speaking style in mainstream American culture does not endorse "call and response" in college classrooms.

People take their speaking style very seriously. Minor adjustments in speaking style may be more immediately practical and less controversial than significant adjustments. Instituting a "call and response" in a college classroom is a rather large style shift, not to be taken lightly. Controversial adjustments may promote divergence between cultural groups when some people resent accommodating individuals and groups from other cultural backgrounds. Nevertheless, convergence requires effort from all parties, not just members of the mainstream culture or individuals from co-cultures. Expecting one-sided adjustments in communication, even minor ones, creates a competitive power struggle that promotes divergence. You may have to take the first step, however, to encourage others to do the same.

Second, work together; *cooperate to find common ground*. Interest in sports, religion, politics, history, and the like may offer an opportunity to find commonalities. You are not trying to change people's interests; rather, you are attempting to share interests. A note of caution is advisable here. Some research on communication patterns revealed that European Americans negatively stereotype African Americans by introducing sports and music as initial topics of conversation. African American participants sometimes view with disdain this attempt to communicate on "African American topics" (Ribeau et al., 2000). African Americans can feel patronized by White participants even when such an attempt to find common interests is genuine.

Introducing topics of a broader range might have been more effective. One participant in a study felt satisfied with her conversation with a White female because she was spoken to as a person, not a representative "for the whole of the black race" (p. 131).

Summary

Intercultural communication is a fact of life. Where once intercultural communication could mostly be avoided by never leaving the borders of our state, this is no longer possible. The United States is thoroughly multicultural. With cultural diversity comes new challenges. We tend to misunderstand individuals from other cultures and co-cultures because deep-seated cultural values differ. The main value dimensions identified by Hofstede are individualism-collectivism, power-distance, and masculinity-femininity. Cultures vary widely on these dimensions. These value differences and the communication patterns and styles that emerge from them can result in ethnocentrism, or the attitude that your own culture is the measure of all things, and that cultures that differ from your own culture are deficient. This ethnocentric attitude can produce misattributions and miscommunication. Finding ways to reduce uncertainty and create convergence while deemphasizing divergence can help produce competent intercultural communication.

Quizzes Without Consequences

www.mhhe
● com/
　/**rothwell2**

Go to *Quizzes Without Consequences* at the book's Online Learning Center at **www.mhhe.com/rothwell2** or access the CD-ROM for *In the Company of Others.*

Key Terms

See Audio Flashcards
Study Aid.

www.mhhe
● com/
　/**rothwell2**
See Crossword Puzzle
Study Aid.

assimilation
attribution
beliefs
co-culture
collectivist culture
convergence
cultural relativism
culture
culture shock

divergence
ethnocentrism
feminine culture
high-context
　communication style
high-PD cultures
individualist culture
low-context
　communication style

low-PD cultures
masculine culture
mindfulness
misattribution
multiculturalism
power-distance
　dimension
values

Suggested Readings

Derber, C. (1996). *The wilding of America: How greed and violence are eroding our nation's character.* New York: St. Martin's Press. Derber critiques the excessive individualism of U.S. culture.

Hall, E. (1981). *Beyond culture*. New York: Doubleday. This excellent discussion of the role culture plays in our lives was written by a recognized authority on the subject.

Hughes, R. (1993). *Culture of complaint: A passionate look into the ailing heart of America*. New York: Warner Books. An Australian who has lived in the United States for more than two decades offers a cultural criticism of U.S. life that is witty and provocative.

Wolfe, T. (1987). *The bonfire of the vanities*. New York: Bantam. Wolfe is a Pulitzer Prize–winning author who has written a powerful novel that exposes the many difficulties of multiculturalism in the United States.

Film School

Do the Right Thing (1989). Drama; R ★★★★★
This is Spike Lee's powerful urban drama about race and culture. Identify instances of misattribution depicted in the movie.

The Joy Luck Club (1993). Drama; R ★★★★★
This film version of Amy Tan's critically acclaimed novel is a wonderful depiction of intercultural communication. See if you can identify all of the instances of difficulties caused by the individualism-collectivism, power-distance, and masculine-feminine dimensions of cultures.

The Wedding Banquet (1993). Comedy; Not rated ★★★★
What happens when a New York real estate agent agrees to marry one of his tenants so she can get a green card and he can stop his parent's attempt to find him the "perfect Chinese wife," all with the knowledge of the agent's male lover? Check out this very amusing film and identify examples of convergence and divergence depicted in the movie.

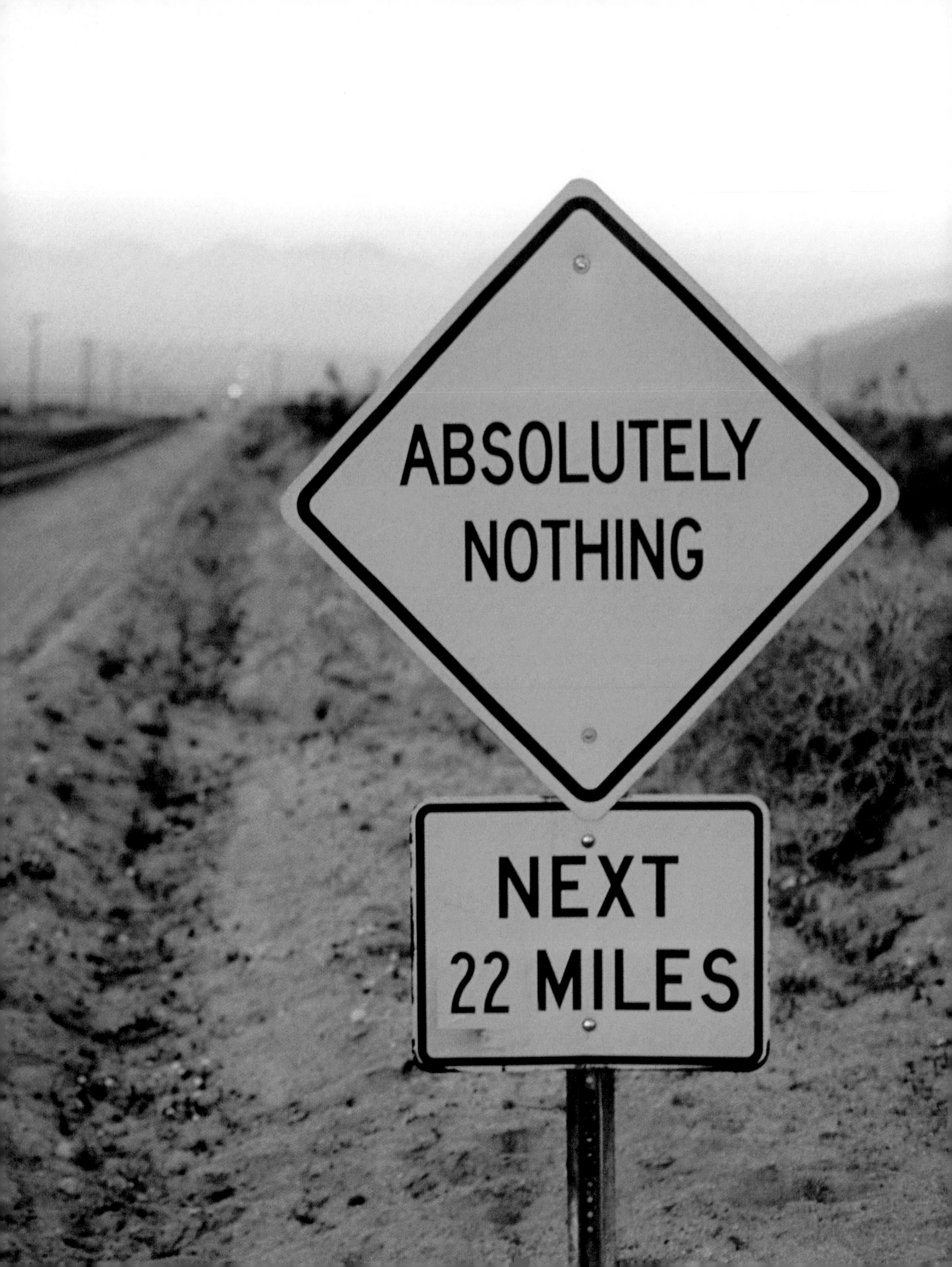
ABSOLUTELY NOTHING
NEXT 22 MILES

CHAPTER 5

Language: Sharing Meaning with Words

"There is no more awesome testimony to the power of language than the fact that there have been so many people ready to die, if their demands for linguistic recognition were not met" (Crystal, 1997, p. 34). People everywhere care very deeply about the language they speak. A language can mark an individual or group's ethnic and cultural identity, educational level, and socioeconomic class. "More than anything else, language shows we 'belong,' providing the most natural badge, or symbol, of public and private identity" (Crystal, 1997, p. 17).

Language and nationalism have been closely intertwined for centuries. When India won its independence from Great Britain in 1947, an attempt was made to impose the Hindi language on the entire country as a symbol of and an aid to national unity. Riots ensued and many thousands were killed in years of conflict. Almost 200 languages are spoken in India. Many people perceived that imposing a single language on the entire country was an act of linguistic, and by association, cultural genocide. In 1956, southern India was divided into language-based states, and 19 official languages for the entire country were recognized to quell the linguistic war.

A more benign language war has raged in Canada. In 1980 and again in 1995, Quebec province held an election on secession from Canada (the most recent attempt falling short of a majority vote by a mere 1%). In French-speaking Quebec, many people find it difficult to identify with the rest of English-speaking Canada (other issues are also involved in secession attempts). Quebec has passed numerous laws making French the principal language of the province, restricting the use of English. "Language police" enforce the laws. One year kosher products for the celebration of Jewish Passover were kept off store shelves because the packages were not properly labeled in French, and 15,000 Dunkin' Donuts bags were seized for the same reason (Crystal, 1997).

America has not escaped the language wars. The Bureau of Indian Affairs in the 19th century implemented a policy that prohibited children from speaking their native languages in reservation schools. Native American children were harshly punished for speaking their "barbarous dialects." Around the same time, the California legislature passed so-called "greaser laws" to penalize Spanish speakers (Crawford, 1996).

Following World War I, a wave of prejudice against immigrants produced laws in 35 states mandating English-only instruction in public schools (Crawford, 1996). Efforts continue to make English the official language of the United States, most notably the "English Language Empowerment Act of 1996," which passed in the U.S. House but failed in the Senate. For some individuals the English-only movement is a genuine attempt to unify an increasingly multicultural nation, but for others it seems to camouflage underlying, poisonous ethnic prejudice. In any case, it is a dubious effort. Designating English as the official language is a little like passing a law that designates wood as the official building material for American homes. The predominance of English in the United States seems secure without legislation.

We battle over language because at least vaguely we recognize its power to create meaning and influence our lives. Recent battles over "hate speech," "politically correct" speech, and "Ebonics" are testaments to the fact that a language is more than a neutral vehicle of information transmission. When George W. Bush used the word *crusade* to describe our "war on terrorism" following the destruction of the World Trade Center, he ignited an immediate controversy. Although he meant "a vigorous action in pursuit of a cause," *crusade* is a loaded term in the Arab world. It conjures recollections of the 11th century Crusades, the "holy war" waged by Christians against Muslims. President Bush did not want to frame our war on terrorism as a holy war on Muslims for obvious reasons. Similarly, when the Pentagon proposed labeling the campaign against terrorism "Operation Infinite Justice," a representative for the Council on American-Islamic Relations noted that eternal retribution is "the prerogative of God" only (Safire, 2001). The label was quickly changed to "Operation Enduring Freedom."

Language can influence thought, shape perceptions, and provoke a wide range of behaviors. Language can help us improve the human condition by promoting tolerance and cooperation, or it can fan the embers of prejudice, ignite aggression, and fuel the flames of violence.

With the power of language comes the responsibility to use it competently. Consequently, *the primary purpose of this chapter is to discuss how to use language competently.*

This chapter has four objectives:

1. to describe the basic anatomy of language,
2. to identify specifically how language influences thought, perception, and human behavior,
3. to identify common problems of language misuse and malpractice, and
4. to discuss specific ways to communicate competently with language.

The primary purpose of this chapter is to discuss how to use language competently.

The Anatomy of Language

Knowing how to use language competently begins with an understanding of what language is and how it works. In this section the basic anatomy of language is discussed. Language is defined, the essential characteristics of language are described, and the abstracting process is explained.

Definition of Language

Language *is a structured system of symbols for communicating meaning.* Meaning is derived from interpreting symbols. **Symbols** are arbitrary representations of frequently ambiguous referents. The symbols relevant to this discussion are words. **Referents** are the objects, events, ideas, or relationships referred to by the words. The referent for "table" is the physical object upon which we place lamps or the evening meal. Symbols have three primary characteristics: arbitrariness, representativeness, and ambiguity.

ARBITRARINESS   A basic rule of all languages is that *word origin is arbitrary.* This means that, within certain limits, what we choose to call something initially is up for grabs. A *house* could be called a *bumrester* or a *fadoydlehoffer.* Shakespeare invented more than 1,700 words (Bryson, 1990). *Barefaced, critical, leapfrog, monumental, excellent, summit, obscene, countless,* and *submerged* are just a few of his creations.

Although *word origin is arbitrary, word usage is conventional.* There must be common agreement (conventionality) among users that a particular invented word has a specific meaning and will be used accordingly (see Box 5-1). Otherwise there would be no shared meaning and words would be mere noise. Many of Shakespeare's

Box 5-1   Sharper Focus

Boontling

One particularly interesting example of word origin and conventionality rules in actual practice is the artificial "language" called Boontling (Adams, 1990). In the late 1800s, male residents of Boonville, California, who obviously had lots of time on their hands, invented a **lexicon,** or total vocabulary, of more than 1,300 words. All that individuals who *harp Boont* (speak Boontling) required was common agreement among Boonters (residents of Boonville) that the concocted words would mean specific referents. Some of the more colorful Boont vocabulary includes *burlapping* (having sexual intercourse), *fence-* *jumpy* (given to adultery), *grey-matter kimmie* (college professor), *mink* (a female of easy morals), *log-lifter* (heavy rainstorm), *trashmover* (heavy winter storm), *tongue-cuppy* (nauseated), *wheeler* (lie), *cott* (a curse), *shoveltooth* (medical doctor), *cotty* (heavy eater), and *high-split* (very tall, slender man). Knowing just these few Boont words gives you the ability to translate this sentence: "The high-split grey-matter kimmie told a wheeler to cover up his burlapping with a mink, daughter of the local shoveltooth." There are still a few speakers of Boontling, but most have *piked to the dusties* (died).

© 1992 Watterson. Distributed by Universal Press Syndicate.

www.mhhe
● com/
/ rothwell2

Go to the Online Learning Center for "SNIGLETS" activity

invented words did not catch hold with the English-speaking populace. *Barky, brisky, vastidity,* and *tortive* are some of the words that did not survive because they never caught on with users of English (Bryson, 1990).

The *TwistedHumor.com* Web site has offered a list of "words that don't exist but should" and would exist if commonly accepted and used by speakers. Some examples include *elbonics* ("the actions of two people maneuvering for one armrest in a movie theatre"), *phonesia* ("the affliction of dialing a phone number and forgetting whom you were calling just as they answer"), *pupkus* ("the moist residue left on a window after a dog presses its nose to it"), *telecrastination* ("the act of always letting the phone ring at least twice before you pick it up, even when you're only 6 inches away"), and *lactomangulation* ("manhandling the 'open end' spout on a milk container so badly that one has to resort to the 'illegal side'").

REPRESENTATIVENESS   Korzybski (1958) provides a useful analogy to clarify how words are representative. A word is to a referent as a map is to a territory. A map of San Francisco is obviously not the city of San Francisco, only a representation of it. You would be viewed as more than just a little odd if you spread a map of San Francisco in front of your car and then drove your car onto the map and happily

Word meaning can be ambiguous.

pronounced your arrival in "the city by the bay." Similarly, the word *sandwich* won't take the edge off anyone's hunger.

Nature does not assign meaning to words. We do. If words were naturally connected to referents and not simply verbal maps representing territories, *white* would not be printed in black type, nor would the word *big* contain fewer letters than the word *small*. *Invisible* would be impossible to read, and *oral* could not be written.

Even **onomatopoeic words**—those words that imitate sounds—are mere representations, not the actual sounds themselves. To Americans the sound of a gunshot is *bang*, but to Germans it's *peng*, to the Spanish it's *pum*, to the French it's *pan*, and to Basques it's *dzast* (Trask, 1999). A duck goes *quack-quack* in America, *rap-rap* in Denmark, and *ga-ga* in China (DeZutter & MacDonald, 1993).

AMBIGUITY   Words are often ambiguous because they have more than a single meaning, and you are presented with the challenge of determining which meaning is intended. Word ambiguity is made apparent by famous Groucho Marx statements: "Time *flies* like an arrow; fruit *flies* like a banana" and "Outside of a dog, a book is a man's best friend. Inside of a dog, it's too dark to read." There's a big difference between a movie *buff* and seeing a movie in the *buff*. The word *set* has almost 200 meanings, more than any other word in English, and it requires 60,000 words of explanation in the *Oxford English Dictionary* (Bryson, 1990). Some words are especially challenging because they can have contradictory definitions. *Sanction*, for example, can mean either "permit" or "forbid." *Fast* might denote "move quickly" or "stick firmly." Actual newspaper headlines reported in several issues of the *Columbia Journalism Review* illustrate the problem of ambiguity: "Kids Make Nutritious Snacks"; "Panda Mating Fails—Veterinarian Takes Over"; and "Prostitutes Appeal to Pope."

In brief review, the three characteristics of symbols (words) are arbitrariness, representativeness, and ambiguity. Words are the raw materials of language. Words alone, however, do not constitute language.

Essential Elements of Human Language

According to Worldwatch Institute (Superville, 2001), there are about 6,800 languages in the world. On the surface, they seem distinctly different from each other. The top five languages ranked in order according to the number of native speakers of each are Mandarin Chinese, Spanish, English, Arabic, and Bengali. As a speaker of English, it would be difficult for you to mimic closely even the sounds of Chinese, Arabic, or Bengali without practice, much less understand what is being said. From the standpoint of an extraterrestrial, however, all humans appear to speak a common tongue. That is because all languages share three essential elements: structure, productivity, and displacement.

STRUCTURE Language is a structured system of symbols. A language has to have a fairly predictable form, or structure, to communicate meaning. Every language follows a set of linguistic rules, or grammar, that provides this structure, although all languages do not necessarily follow the same rules.

For example, the most basic rules stipulate how **phonemes,** or the individual sounds that compose a specific spoken language, can be combined into a morpheme. A **morpheme** is the smallest unit of meaning in a language. A morpheme may be a word, prefix, or suffix. *Bat* is a word composed of three phonemes (the *b*, *a*, and *t* sounds), but it is a single morpheme because the three phonemes make a single word. Add an *s*, making *bats*, and there are now two morphemes because the *s* means "more than one." *Dropcloth* is one word but two morphemes: *drop* and *cloth*. *Rewind* also has two morphemes: *re* and *wind*.

Phonemes cannot be strung together in helter-skelter fashion to form morphemes. *Quagmire* is a recognizable English word. *Qgmruaie* is not, yet the exact same letters appear in both examples. No English word contains the *qgmr* phoneme combination. That's because English has approximately 40 phonemes that correspond to consonants (e.g., *b, c, d*), vowels (*a, e, i, o, u*), and consonant combinations (e.g., *ch, th*). There is no *qgmr* consonant combination in English. There may be in some other language but not the Hawaiian language, which has only 13 phonemes. Perhaps one of a number of African languages might have such a phoneme because several such languages have more than 100 phonemes (Trask, 1999).

We combine sounds into meaningful words, and then we combine words into phrases and sentences. The rules that govern appropriate combinations of words into sentences are called **syntax.** "Hoisted girders workers iron the" is not a meaningful sentence. "Workers hoisted the iron girders," however, uses the same words and is a meaningful sentence. The article (the) and adjective (iron) come before the noun (girders), a standard rule in English, and the verb (hoisted) comes after the subject (workers), a typical though not an absolute pattern in English.

Subject-verb-object is, syntactically, the typical English word order. That is why the speech of Yoda, the Jedi Master in the *Star Wars* films, seems so strange. "Strong am I with the Force" and "Your father he is" both have an object-subject-verb order that is very unusual for English. Yodaspeak (OSV word order), in fact, is an unusual construction in all but a few rare languages (Crystal, 1997). (See Box 5-2 for a discussion of the appropriateness of nonstandard grammatical constructions.)

PRODUCTIVITY "There are hundreds of millions of trillions of thinkable thoughts" (Pinker, 1997, p. 118). There are only a few phonemes in any language to communicate

Box 5-2   Sharper Focus

Linguistic Diversity: Telling It Like It Isn't

"Woe is I." "Whom shall I say is calling?" "Pahk the cah in Haavaad Yahd." What is your perception of a person who would use such sentence construction and pronunciation? Does this person sound like you? Now consider these sentences: "I be fine." "He don't look so good." "Mistah Cottah has a paynut bidness." Again, what is your perception of a person speaking in this way? Several studies reveal that both Northerners and Southerners in the United States rate the use of language in southern states, New York City, and New Jersey as the least "correct" form of English (for a summary, see Bauer & Trudgill, 1998).

In 1996, the Oakland, California, school board triggered a national controversy when it recognized Ebonics (African American English Vernacular) as the "primary language" of many students in the school district. The board recommended the use of Ebonics as a bridge to learning Standard English. The controversy centered on whether Ebonics—a term Robert Williams coined in 1973, combining "ebony" and "phonics"—is a language, a dialect of English, or merely street slang spoken by some African Americans.

Stigma is often attached to the way a person uses language. The dominant language variety in a culture normally becomes the standard by which all other varieties are judged. **Standardization** means that a language has a set of formal rules governing how we ought to speak and write it. Typically, the language version taught in schools, used in published books, and spoken or written by members of the educated middle class becomes the standard (Wolfram & Fasold, 1974). National news anchors on television speak Standard English. How well or poorly we use language is gauged by determining how closely we conform to the standardized grammar.

Linguists take a dim view of this **prescriptivism**—the perspective that tells us we have no business using language the way it is typically spoken. The prescriptivists are an informal group of English teachers, columnists, copy editors, and style manual and dictionary writers. Many of the rules they espouse are outdated, even silly (Trask, 1999). "They are bits of folklore that originated for screwball reasons several hundred years ago and have perpetuated themselves since" (Pinker, 1995, p. 373).

Robert Lowth, an 18th-century clergyman, is responsible for several of our most notable prescriptive rules (Bryson, 1990). For example, his influential book *A Short Introduction to English Grammar* prohibited the use of double or multiple negatives. According to Lowth's 18th-century "logic," two negatives make a positive (much like algebra). So if you were to ask a friend for a Coke and your friend replied, "I ain't got no Coke," you should logically ask, "So where is it?" Only an extraordinarily dense individual, however, would make such an interpretation.

Another irritant for the prescriptivists is the failure to obey the *like/as* rule. "Telling it *like* it is" should be "Telling it *as* it is," so decree the prescriptivists. As long ago as the 16th century, however, some cultured people used *like* and others used *as*. It wasn't until about the middle of the 19th century that the *like-as* distinction became "correct grammar."

Descriptivists—linguists who describe how language is used and identify rules for using a language as a tool of communication—decry the prescriptivists' stuffy elitism. "The social acceptability of a particular language variety is totally unrelated to its adequacy as a communication code" (Wolfram & Fasold, 1974, p. 7). Perceptions of the "inferiority" or "superiority" of any language variety reflect class prejudice, stereotyping of disadvantaged groups, and parochial comfort with the sound of a language as spoken in one's own speech community. *Ebonics is not an incorrect or inferior version of Standard English.* It is an English dialect. Some of its rules of grammar (how it *is* used, not how it *should* be used) are different from Standard English. "He sick" in Ebonics, for instance, means "He is sick today." "He be sick," however, describes a continuing or permanent condition. Standard English allows only the less precise "He is sick." Double, even multiple, negatives are grammatical in Ebonics. They are meant to stress increasing negative emphasis.

Descriptivists denounce linguistic prejudice, but they do not advocate an "anything goes" perspective. When George W. Bush ran for the 2000 Republican presidential nomination, he produced these linguistic hairballs: "Families is where wings take dream" and "Is our children learning?" (Ivins, 2000, p. 6B). These statements don't correspond to Standard English. Following rules of Standard English matters if you want to communicate intelligibly and avoid questions about your intellectual heft.

Standard English should be used on job applications and during job interviews because that is what is expected in these formal situations. English classes teach students the formal version of the language so students can use it in more than the most casual way. This textbook is written in Standard English. If it were written in African American English Vernacular or in the Appalachian dialect, readers would be able to decipher it with some effort, but the book would not be perceived as professional and competently written.

Box 5-2 **Sharper Focus** (continued)

Style shifting, sometimes referred to as code switching, is using language flexibly to suit the context. *Style shifting is what we should strive for in our use of language.* Formal occasions require formal language usage. Informal occasions allow us to use *like* instead of *as*, to use double negatives, to interject slang, or to shift into a nonstandard dialect. Some individuals so steadfastly adhere to rules of Standard English, however, that they make everyone feel self-conscious about their language usage. These grammarphobes cannot relax their speech and mingle with the "peons." Correcting someone's grammar when friends are gathered informally invites derision. Using language flexibly and appropriately for the situation is a mark of an effective communicator.

these thoughts. English transforms a few dozen phonemes into more than 600,000 words, the total vocabulary listed in the *Oxford English Dictionary* (the largest lexicon of any language), and the lexicon is expanding all the time. New words in English sprout up like mushrooms in loamy soil to name and describe new technologies, products, scientific discoveries, and abstract concepts. In fact, more than 65,000 new words have been added to the English lexicon since the 1960s (Davidson, 1996). This capacity of language to transform a small number of phonemes into whatever words, phrases, and sentences we require to communicate our abundance of thoughts, ideas, and feelings is called **productivity.**

By combining a handful of phonemes into a rich lexicon and then combining these words into sentences, we can express an infinite number of thoughts and feelings in an amazing variety of ways. There are approximately 100,000 5-word grammatically correct sentences possible in English, 1 million 6-word sentences, and an astounding 100 million trillion 20-word sentences possible (Pinker, 1999). It is very likely that any sentence of average length that you produce has never been spoken or written before, and it probably will never be reproduced by anyone in the future. *Language productivity permits maximum communication creativity.*

For a communication instructor, it is frustrating to hear student speeches and conversation in which words such as *like*, *absolutely*, and *totally* (and new variants sure to be added) appear to be the extent of the creative experiment with language. When you have Shakespeare as the measure of human language potential, why settle for so much less?

DISPLACEMENT   Language as a structured system of symbols allows us to communicate about "the not here and the not now." Since there is no natural connection between symbol and referent, we are not constrained to communicate only about the immediate and the physically present.

The human ability to use language to talk about objects, ideas, events, and relations that don't just exist in the here and now is called **displacement.** We can talk about things that don't exist, such as unicorns, fairies, and corporate responsibility. We can discuss past events ("How could you cheat on me with that woman? She's got the I.Q. of a beer can."). We can discuss possible future events ("Would you ever cheat on me again?"). We can ask questions about impossible things ("If I were 10 feet tall and weighed 450 pounds, would you consider me fat?" and "Would you still love me if I were?"). We can also receive answers to such odd questions. We can ponder abstract ideas. ("If you are in a spaceship that is traveling at the speed of light, and you turn on the headlights, does anything happen?" or "So what's the speed of dark?" [Stephen Wright, 2002]).

Koko is the most famous, and controversial, example of an animal using sign language. Francine Patterson, Koko's trainer, claims that Koko has command of almost 1,000 signs.

SELF-REFLEXIVENESS   Language has the capacity to reflect upon itself. **Self-reflexiveness** is the ability to use language to talk about language (Anderson & Ross, 1994; DeVito, 1986). "My last sentence was ungrammatical" is an example of self-reflexiveness. Because we can formulate abstract rules that describe how language works, we can describe nonconformity to language rules in sentence structure. We can devise ways to improve our use of language when communicating with others. This chapter is a detailed example of self-reflexiveness. A lexicon (phonemes, morphemes, etc.) has been created to identify the nature of language. We use our language to reflect on how we might explain its nature and how it works. We use this knowledge to improve its function in communicating.

The four essential elements of any language—structure, productivity, displacement, and self-reflexiveness—allow us to communicate in ways not available to other animal species (see Box 5-3). A communication code does not qualify as a language unless it has all four essential elements.

The Abstracting Process

All words are symbols, but all words do not reflect the same level of abstraction. **Abstracting** is the process of selective perception whereby we formulate increasingly vague conceptions of our world by leaving out details associated with objects,

Box 5-3 | Focus on Controversy

Signing Simians: The Debate over Animals' Linguistic Abilities

There can be no doubt that almost every creature on the planet communicates in some form. Chimpanzees make a "chutter" sound to warn of snakes, a "rraup" noise to sound an alarm about an approaching eagle, and a "chirp" sound to warn of a nearby leopard. Dolphins use clicks and whistles. Birds sing and screech; dogs snarl, bark, and howl; squirrels make "chuk, chuk" sounds; and every cat owner claims that Fluffy, Pumpkin, or Maytag has a special purr or yowl that signals a desire to be fed, to be let outdoors, or to share in the glory of the latest rodent kill. These signaling devices, however, are not languages. They have no grammatical structure. The signals never get more numerous or elaborate so they lack productivity. They communicate about immediate threats or desires and physically present objects so they lack displacement, and the signals are never used to improve or alter the communication so they are not self-reflexive. Although language develops in humans naturally, there is no convincing evidence that any other species has a communication system even remotely approaching a human language (Trask, 1999).

An intriguing question remains, however. Could other species acquire a language even though no such language appears to develop naturally for them? An inability to speak is a major impediment to teaching other species a language, but is the ability to speak a necessary precondition for using and understanding a language? If it were, then sign language would be disqualified.

Yet sign language meets all four of the principal language characteristics (Pinker, 1995; Trask, 1999). Sign languages have a structured system of gestural symbols that can be expanded to accommodate any thought or feeling, concrete or abstract, immediate or far away, real or imaginary, and sign languages can use signs to discuss signs. Since American Sign Language (ASL) clearly qualifies as a language yet doesn't require speech, it has become the most popular means of researching whether species such as apes can acquire a language.

The first notable effort to teach ASL to apes was undertaken by Allen and Beatrice Gardner in the 1960s (Gardner & Gardner, 1969). They began teaching signs to a female chimpanzee named Washoe. The Gardners claimed that, by age 12, Washoe had learned more than 180 signs, that she had mastered rudimentary syntax, and that she could combine signs in meaningful ways.

More impressive results, however, were claimed by Francine Patterson (Patterson & Linden, 1981). Working with a female gorilla named Koko, Patterson has claimed on various television programs that Koko has acquired about 1,000 signs, has made new signs when necessary, and has developed syntax.

Are these efforts to teach apes ASL merely simian antics with semantics, or can we conclude that chimps and gorillas are capable of learning a meaningful language? Some claims drawn from this research have provoked strong criticism. First, some critics challenge the assertion that any ape has learned ASL (Pinker, 1995). The only deaf signer on the team training Washoe, for instance, claimed, "I just wasn't seeing any signs. The hearing people were logging every movement the chimp made as a sign. . . . When the chimp scratched itself, they'd record it as the sign for scratch" (Neisser, 1983, pp. 214, 216). Patterson, by her own admission, has never made a verifiable list of each sign that Koko has mastered. We have only her say-so that Koko has a lexicon of about 1,000 signs.

A second criticism is that the lexicon of even the most capable apes, even if the authenticity of the signs credited to them is granted, is rudimentary when compared to that of the average child. Patterson has worked with Koko for more than 30 years teaching her 1,000 signs. The average 3-year-old child understands more than 1,000 words; a 6-year-old understands as many as 14,000 words (Carey, 1977). A high school graduate knows about 60,000 words; a college-educated adult may have a lexicon twice that size (Pinker, 1999).

A third criticism is that the signing apes exhibit virtually no ability to create grammatically coherent sentences. Pinker (1995) claims that "a three-year-old is a grammatical genius" (p. 19), but typical ape "sentences" such as "Me eat me eat" and "Give orange me give eat orange me eat orange give me eat orange give me you" are notably repetitious and bear little resemblance to the sentence structure of children.

Finally, none of the research with signing chimps or gorillas shows an aptitude for the self-reflexive nature of language. There is no evidence that apes use signs to comment on other signs so communication can be improved.

More recently, research with apes has taken a new twist. Using 256 symbols on a keyboard, each of which represents a word, the ape can point to or punch the symbols with a finger. This method has produced more interesting results (Savage-Rumbaugh & Lewin, 1994). Kanzi, a bonobo or pygmy chimp, has exhibited a grasp of almost 200 symbols and some basic grammar (Savage-Rumbaugh, 1993). By the most generous interpretation, however, at 17-years-old Kanzi exhibited the language ability of a 2-year-old child (Begley, 1998).

Box 5-3 | **Focus on Controversy** (continued)

The point in comparing animal and human linguistic abilities is not to ridicule our ape cousins and elevate ourselves, despite Mark Twain's comment, "Our Heavenly Father invented man because he was disappointed in the monkey." Humans would find it very difficult to learn the shrieks and hoots of ape signal communication, a project that would be an amusing parallel to imposing an unnatural sign language on apes. Linguist Noam Chomsky argues that "attempting to teach linguistic skills to animals is irrational—like trying to teach people to flap their arms and fly. Humans can fly about 30 feet—that's what they do in the Olympics. Is that flying? The question is totally meaningless." He continues, "If you want to find out about an organism you study what it's good at. If you want to study humans you study language. If you want to study pigeons you study their homing instinct" (Johnson, 1995, p. 1C). Language is the unique ability of our species. It is what we are "good at." No group of people, no matter how isolated, is without language. Learning about language is learning in part about what it is to be human.

Questions for Thought

1. Do you agree with the critics that research on ape linguistic abilities reveals commonplace results?
2. Do you think the research results with Kanzi clearly prove that some apes can be taught a true language? Explain by applying your answer to the four characteristics of language.
3. Can you imagine being limited to a 256-word vocabulary (Kanzi) or even a 1,000-word lexicon (Koko)? What problems would occur?

events, and ideas (Littlejohn, 1999). To clarify this definition, we need to explain the four levels of abstraction: sense experience, description, inference, and judgment.

SENSE EXPERIENCE   Figure 5-1 illustrates the abstracting process. The parabola represents the world we live in, the territory (a reference to Korzybski's map-territory analogy). The first level of abstracting occurs nonverbally when our sensory receptors are stimulated. As discussed in Chapter 3, our sense experience with the physical world is inherently selective. We are limited by the acuity of our senses and the neuronal wiring of our brains. In our day-to-day existence we do not perceive molecules, atoms, electrons, neutrons, protons, and quarks. Most of what comprises our physical world is not sensed. These details are left out. Without language, our experiences would remain essentially private ones. With language, however, we are able to share our perceptions of the world with others.

DESCRIPTION   The second level of the abstracting process is a description of our sense experience. **Descriptions** are verbal reports that sketch what we perceive from our senses. They are verbal maps for territories. These verbal maps—labels, classifications—are representations of reality, not reality itself. *Whenever we describe reality, we unavoidably distort it.* We leave important parts out, and we impose our own perceptual biases on the world around us. Your description of the world is an approximation of the world as you perceive it, not an exact duplicate. Something is always lost in the translation because you are describing what is in your head, not reality itself.

When your descriptions go from "I am in a committed, long-term relationship with Fran" to "I am in a committed relationship" and finally to "I am living with someone," you have become increasingly abstract. The more general your description is, and the more details that you leave out, the more abstract you are. *The potential for confusion and misunderstanding increases as we become more abstract in our use of language.*

FIGURE 5-1 The Abstracting Process

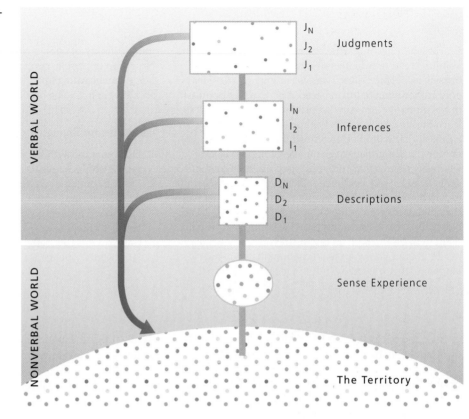

INFERENCE   The third level of the abstracting process is the inferential stage. **Inferences** are conclusions about the unknown based on the known. They are guesses, educated or otherwise. Some inferences are more educated than others because their probability of accuracy is higher. You can infer that a neighbor is not home (the unknown) because newspapers have accumulated on the front porch, the mailbox is crammed, and repeated phone calls connect with a message machine (the known). This is a relatively safe inference, probably true, but it is an inference and not a fact. Your neighbor may be sick in bed, unable to attend to the newspapers, mail, and phone calls.

Inferring from the same information that your neighbor is away on vacation is not as solid as the first inference, because a greater range of possibilities exists to explain the newspapers, mail, and unanswered phone calls. Your neighbor may be away on business, visiting relatives, attending a funeral, searching for a new house, or hiding from the law.

JUDGMENT   The fourth level of abstraction is making judgments. **Judgments** are subjective evaluations of objects, events, or ideas. We attach a subjective positive or negative value such as right or wrong, good or bad, and beautiful or ugly. "My partner is a generous person" is a judgment. It appears to be a description, but it is a subjective evaluation, not a factual report. Generosity is in the mind of the beholder.

The statement is also more than just an inference because it does more than draw an indifferent or neutral conclusion from what is known.

Let's illustrate the difference between a description, an inference, and a judgment.

1. The woman is wearing a navy blue suit.
2. The woman wearing the navy blue suit wants to look professional.
3. The woman wearing the navy blue suit is a good employee.

The first statement is descriptive because it merely reports a simple observation. The second is inferential because it makes a guess based on the woman wearing a navy blue suit. The third statement is judgmental because it expresses a positive opinion. It is more than just a guess (inference), and it's not a mere report (description). It's an evaluation.

The Power of Language

You view a videotape of an automobile accident. You are then asked to estimate how fast the cars were traveling when they *hit*. Do you think your estimate would be different if instead of *hit*, the experimenter used *smashed, collided, bumped,* or *contacted*? A study found that when the cars *smashed* into each other, average estimated speed by subjects was 40.4 mph. It was 39.3 mph when the cars *collided*, 38.1 mph when they *bumped*, 34.0 when they *hit*, and 31.8 when they *contacted* each other (Loftus & Palmer, 1974). Even small changes in word choice can influence our thinking.

In this section the power of language is discussed by addressing the relationship between language and thinking. Then signal reactions, framing, and labeling are explored.

Language and Thinking

Edward Sapir, an anthropologist, asserted in 1929 that human beings "are very much at the mercy of the particular language which has become the medium of expression for their society" (Mandelbaum, 1949, p. 162). Sapir ignited a debate that would last for decades concerning the power of language to affect thought and perception.

SAPIR-WHORF HYPOTHESIS   It was left to Sapir's student Benjamin Whorf to be the principal advocate for what became known as the **Sapir-Whorf hypothesis.** There are actually two versions of this perspective on the power of language: **linguistic determinism** claims we are the prisoners of our native language, unable to think certain thoughts or perceive in certain ways because of the grammatical structure and lexicon of our language; **linguistic relativity** claims the grammar and lexicon of our native language powerfully influences but does not imprison our thinking and perception. Whorf was not always clear in his writings which version he believed to be true (Schultz, 1990). Let's discuss linguistic determinism first.

There are significant grammatical differences among languages. In English, time distinctions are indicated not only by word choices, such as *last week, long ago,* or *75 days before,* but also by verb forms called *tenses.* Present becomes past by changing the verb: *like* to *liked, go* to *went, do* to *did.* Chinese has no tenses.

Appropriate time words must be added to make time distinctions, such as *I go now*, *I go yesterday*, *I go tomorrow*, *I go in an hour* (Trask, 1999). At the other extreme is the West African language Bamileke-Dschang that reportedly has eleven tenses (five degrees of remoteness in the past, five degrees of remoteness in the future, and a present tense). Do these differences in tense determine our capacity to think in terms of time? No! As Trask (1999) notes, "Whether a language has eleven tenses, three tenses, two tenses, or no tenses at all, its speakers have not the slightest difficulty in talking about any desired point in time, past, present, or future" (p. 62).

There are also significant differences in the lexicons of various languages. The Masai of Africa have 17 words for cattle. The Zulu language has 39 words for green. Italian has more than 500 words related to types of pasta, some of which have unappetizing literal translations (e.g., *vermicelli* means "little worms," and *strozzapreti* means "strangled priests"). Arabic reportedly has more than 6,000 terms for what, to most English speakers, is simply your basic ill-tempered camel, its parts, and equipment (Bryson, 1990). A more elaborate lexicon for an object would presumably allow us to perceive subtle differences in color, shape, size, substance, and so forth that would remain invisible to those with a less elaborate lexicon for that object.

Does the size of a language's vocabulary for an object or phenomenon determine our ability to perceive finer and subtler distinctions? It hardly seems so. In the United States we have an extensive lexicon for the makes and models of automobiles and for colors and types of cosmetics. An elaborate lexicon may allow us to perceive subtle distinctions between models of cars and types of cosmetics more easily, but surely anyone is capable of perceiving such distinctions if pressed to do so. The Dani tribe in New Guinea, for example, have only two color terms *mili* (black) and *mola* (white), yet they can perceive distinctions among a variety of colors (Rosch, 1973). A large vocabulary for an object merely reflects a culture's interest in that object. If a more extensive vocabulary becomes necessary, one will be created.

A principal problem with linguistic determinism is that it assumes thought is dependent on language, yet *we can think without language*. All of us have had the experience of not being able to express a thought in words, yet the thought exists. If thinking were dependent on language, did humans not begin thinking until language was created? Does a child's thinking remain in a dormant stage until a first word is uttered and then BAM, the child's brain suddenly kicks into gear and thinking is activated? The answer, of course, is no (Damasio & Damasio, 1999).

GENDER-BIASED LANGUAGE   *Although linguistic determinism has no merit, there is some support for linguistic relativity*. The term *sexism* wasn't introduced into the English lexicon until the late 1960s, and *sexual harassment* came even later. The fact that these two terms didn't exist until relatively recently didn't mean we couldn't recognize unequal treatment of women. The interjection of these terms, however, helped draw greater attention to the subordination of women (Lakoff, 2000). The parallels to *racism* (a term that didn't even appear in the 1933 *Oxford English Dictionary*) made sexism a subject of national debate.

Research on **masculine-generic gender references** in English, the use of masculine nouns and pronouns to include both women and men (*man, mankind, he, him,* and *his*), supports linguistic relativity. Sentences such as "*Man* is the master of *his*

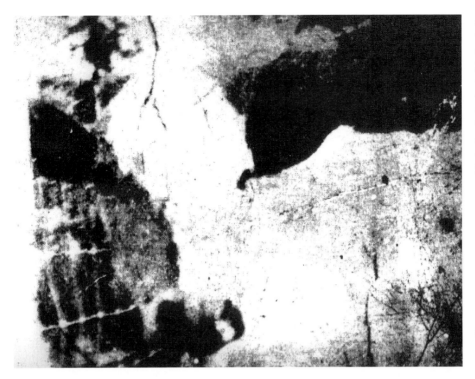

Look closely at this picture. Can you discern what it is? If you are like most people, you will have great difficulty until told what is pictured. If you can't identify the image (it is unmistakable once you see it) ask a classmate or your instructor. Now can you see it? Language labels help us see what may remain hidden without the label.

See "Identify the Photo" activity on CD for photo identification and discussion.

own destiny" and "A doctor should treat *his* patients compassionately" use masculine generic language. Research shows that the masculine-generic terms in these sentences are far more likely than gender-neutral terms (*humankind, they*) to produce mental images of men to the exclusion of women (Foertsch & Gernsbacher, 1997; Gastil, 1990; Hardin & Banaji, 1993). Similarly, terms ending with the *man* suffix (chairman, businessman, fireman) promote gender-biased stereotyping (McConnell & Fazio, 1996).

Gender-biased language makes women virtually invisible, and it tacitly brands them as less powerful and less important than men. Statements that use gender-biased language leave women guessing whether they are ever really included. Women may not apply for jobs advertised with gender-biased language (Bem & Bem, 1973). This raises an ethical issue besides the practical disadvantages affecting women. Gender-biased language shows disrespect for women, limits their choices, and is inherently unfair because it gives an advantage to men based not on merit or compassion, but merely on the basis of the sex of the person. It is irresponsible to do nothing about language bias that hurts women. Consequently, our society's recognition of the power of gender-biased language on thought, perception, and even behavior has led to a concerted effort in recent years to de-sex the English language (see Table 5-1).

Research clearly shows that, although we are able to form images of women when gender-biased language is used (invalidating linguistic determinism), it is far more difficult (supporting linguistic relativity). Some subjects in the masculine-generic gender reference studies did form mental images of both men and women, but most did not. Language may not create a mental straitjacket from which there is

Table 5-1 De-Sexing the English Language

Generic References	Gender-Neutral References
Man, mankind	Human, humankind, people
He, him, his	They, them, theirs or he and she, him and her, his and hers
Chairman	Chair, chairperson
Businessman	Businessperson, executive
Policeman	Police officer
Postman, mailman	Letter carrier, postal worker, mail carrier
Fireman	Firefighter
Nonparallel Usage	**Parallel Usage**
Men and girls	Men and women
Man and wife	Husband and wife
Sex Stereotypes	**Alternatives**
Housewife	Homemaker
Best man for the job	Best person for the job
Manhole cover	Sewer lid
Men at work	Workers' zone, men and women at work
Workman's compensation	Worker's compensation
Trivializing Forms	**Alternative Forms**
Lady lawyer	Lawyer
Male nurse	Nurse
Career girl	Career woman

no escape, but it certainly can narrow our thinking, making more expansive views of the world difficult to contemplate.

Signal Reactions

A **signal reaction** is an automatic, conditioned response to a symbol (Rothwell, 1982). It is the result of pleasant or unpleasant experiences associated with a word. Strong emotional reactions to verbal obscenity, vulgar language, ethnic slurs, pledges, oaths, slogans, ritualized greetings, chants, and buzz words in advertising and politics are a few instances of signal reactions to words. The political arena is saturated with signal reactions. The term *liberal* has become poison. *Feminazis, welfare queens, right wingers, bureaucrats, socialists,* and similar labels are used to discredit opponents during rhetorical food fights that pass for political debates.

Sometimes the mere combination of phonemes forming a word can trigger a signal reaction because of certain unpleasant associations in our past. In January 1999, David Howard, a staff member for Washington, D.C. Mayor Anthony Williams, resigned his position because he used the word *niggardly* in a press conference. Mayor Williams, an African American, explained, "Mr. Howard's resignation was prompted by reports that he made an inappropriate racial comment" (Misunderstood word, 1999, p. A2). *Niggardly,* however, means "miserly" or "stingy with money" even though it sounds very similar to the explosive term *nigger.* As Mayor Williams

The inscription on T-shirts sold by Abercrombie & Fitch provoked a strong signal reaction from those offended by the stereotype and racist implication. As one Chinese American remarked: "It is really disappointing because the T-shirts make fun of nearly everything about our culture—our language, our religious beliefs, our occupations." The company pulled the shirts from store shelves a day after complaints poured in.

admitted, "He (Howard) didn't say anything that was in itself racist" (p. A2). (Given the obscure "logic" of this incident, we can only speculate what the reaction from the mayor and others might be to *dicker, titular,* or *cockpit* which, like niggardly, should be inoffensive words.) Nevertheless, Howard, a white man, resigned his public advocacy position in the Mayor's office. A national debate ensued. Following a 3-week outcry, Mayor Williams agreed to reinstate Howard to his former position. Howard requested a different city government position instead.

Reacting signally to words is not always inappropriate, however. If I see that you are about to step in front of a speeding car, I'll shout, "Look out!" If you ponder what I have said instead of reacting reflexively, you'll become roadkill. Nevertheless, signal reactions to words are usually inappropriate because they suspend thinking.

Framing

Two Irish Catholic priests, Father O'Leary and Father Kelly, strongly disagreed with each other on the question of whether smoking and prayer are compatible behaviors. Unable to agree, they each decided to write the Pope, plead their own case, and ask for his wisdom. When they received the Pope's reply, both priests were triumphant. Puzzled that the Pope could agree with both of them when only two contradictory choices seemed available, Father O'Leary asked Father Kelly, "What question did you ask the Pope?" Father Kelly responded, "I asked the Pope if it was permissible to pray while smoking. The Pope said that praying should always be encouraged no matter what you are doing." Father O'Leary chuckled to himself. "Well, I asked the Pope whether it is permissible to smoke while praying, and the Pope said that I should take praying very seriously and not trivialize it by smoking." The way each question was framed by the priests dictated the answer they received from the Pope.

Framing is the influence wording has on our perception of choices (see Box 5-4). Much the way a photographer frames a picture to communicate a point of view, language frames choices. When a photographer changes the frame from a person as the center of interest to a mere bystander, our thoughts and perception of the picture change. Likewise, changing language that describes or identifies our choices can

Box 5-4 | Focus on Controversy

The Native American Name Frame

In 1995 the state of Minnesota enacted a law ordering counties to rename any natural geographic place with "squaw" in its name. Most of the places with the offending word (Squaw Pond, Squaw Lake, Squaw Creek) were so designated in the 19th century when Whites commonly referred to Native American women as squaws. Originally a corruption by the French of the Algonquin word for "woman," Native American linguists claim that it later became an obscenity describing female genitals (Schmitt, 1996).

Every county in Minnesota met the legal deadline and replaced the offending word with a suitable alternative—except Lake County in the northern part of the state. "The term 'squaw' is in common use throughout North America, far beyond its Algonquin origin," argued Sharon Hahn, head of the Lake County Board of Commissioners (Schmitt, 1996). Claiming that it would cost tens of thousands of dollars to replace maps and signs, county officials offered to rename Squaw Creek and Squaw Bay, only if they could call them Politically Correct Creek and Politically Correct Bay.

Glen Yakel, geographic name keeper of the Minnesota Department of Natural Resources, saw it differently. "They're trying to bill this as political correctness, but it's a matter of civility" (Schmitt, 1996). According to the United States Geological Survey's Board on Geographic Names, there are over a thousand geographical places in the United States whose names include the word *squaw*, including a former site of the winter Olympics, Squaw Valley, California.

Changing the name of a place to eliminate an offending term is not a new idea. In 1967 the Board on Geographic Names ordered 143 places with "Nigger" in their name (I know this is difficult to believe) to replace the term with "Negro" and 26 places with "Jap" to replace it with "Japanese."

In Utah the battle is over the term *Redskin* used on personalized license plates. Attorney Brian Barnard, on behalf of two Native Americans, Michael McBride and Jay Brummett, filed a formal complaint with the Utah Tax Commission, demanding that personalized plates bearing the word *Redskin* be revoked and removed from use in Utah. Brummett claimed that the word *Redskin* is

the "N-word" applied to Native Americans. Attorney Barnard (1994), commenting on the name of the National Football League's Washington Redskins, framed his argument this way: "Could you cheer for the Denver Darkies? Would you paint your face and go to a football stadium in freezing weather to scream for the Spokane Spics? Could you support the Kansas City Kikes? Would you watch the World Series as the Georgia Crackers took on the Nashville Niggers" (p. A9)?

Barnard's complaint was rejected in a split vote of the commission. Speaking for the majority, commissioners Val Oveson and Alice Shearer concluded, "In light of the fact that the term 'Redskin' is used pervasively throughout our society in reference to sports teams, it is the opinion of commissioners Oveson and Shearer that the term 'Redskin' is not 'offensive' and does not express 'contempt, ridicule, or superiority'" (p. A9). This view was later contradicted by a 1999 survey that showed 46% of the general public found Redskin to be "offensive to me" (Masters, 1999).

Notice in each case how the antagonists framed their positions. In the first case, the debate was framed between political correctness and civility and sensitivity. In the second case, the debate was framed between ethnic slurs and pervasiveness of usage. How would you have decided in each of these cases?

Language is a powerful shaper of thoughts, perceptions, and behavior. Do we have an obligation to respect the desires of those who are offended by the labels we use? Clearly, some individuals can be inordinately offended by seemingly harmless terms. Nevertheless, the cases cited here might not be so harmless.

Questions for Thought

1. Can other ethnic groups make a similar case against offensive terms used to describe them?
2. Does the ethical requirement for respect mean that we must recognize that labels might cause offense? Should we continue to use objectionable terms for groups if asked to stop? Would this be irresponsible?
3. Where do we draw the line? When does sensitivity become hypersensitivity? How do we decide?

change how we perceive those choices. As Fairhurst and Sarr (1996) explain, our "frames determine whether people notice problems, how they understand and remember problems, and how they evaluate and act upon them" (p. 4).

Studies abound showing the power of wording to shape our perception of choices. When subjects were presented with the option of treating lung cancer with surgery, 84% chose surgery when it was framed in terms of the odds of *living*, but 56% chose surgery when this option was worded in terms of *dying* (McNeil et al., 1982). Most subjects thought condoms were an effective method of preventing AIDS when they were told that condoms have a "95% success rate," but a majority did not view condoms as effective prevention when told that they had a "5% failure rate" (Linville et al., 1992). When business students and managers were told that a specific corporate strategy had a 70% chance of *success*, most favored the strategy. When it was framed as having a 30% chance of *failure*, however, the majority opposed it (Wolkomir & Wolkomir, 1990). In all instances the two choices compared have identical outcomes, but they are perceived differently because of how the wording frames them.

Labeling

Advertisers and producers of myriad products know the importance of labels. Chinese gooseberries didn't sell well until renamed kiwi. Opium perfume by Yves St. Laurent was banned in China in December 1999 because of its association with the narcotic. The California Prune Board (yes, there really is such a group) approved a move to call prunes *dried plums* to escape negative images attached to this wrinkled fruit. Blind taste tests repeatedly show that consumers are influenced by the labels attached to products. For example, when subjects are asked to choose unlabeled bottled waters based on their taste, *Perrier, Evian, Crystal Springs*, or other popular varieties are often not selected. Tap water is often the preferred choice. Perhaps the producers of *Evian* recognize this. *Evian* spelled backwards is, after all, *naive*.

Labels clearly matter, and research shows that they do. For example, in one study children were told that they were *kind* and *helpful*. These prosocial labels encouraged children to give prizes they received in the experiment to other children (Grusec et al., 1978). Even 3 weeks later, children labeled kind and helpful were more willing to aid others than were children not so labeled (Grusec & Redler, 1980). Prosocial labels influence adults as well. New Haven, Connecticut residents were more likely to give a donation to the National Multiple Sclerosis Society when they were described as *generous* and *charitable* 1 to 2 weeks prior to the donation request (Kraut, 1973).

The power of labels can also produce significant problems. In one study (Langer & Abelson, 1974) researchers showed therapists a videotape of an ordinary-looking man being interviewed. Half of the therapists were told in advance that the man was a "job applicant," and half were told he was a "psychiatric patient." Those therapists who thought they were watching a job interview described the man using terms such as *ingenious, open, straightforward, ordinary, candid*, and *upstanding*. Those therapists who thought they were observing a psychiatric patient described the man as *rigid, dependent, passive aggressive, impulsive*, and "frightened of his own aggressive impulses." Labels can have a powerful biasing effect. Both groups of therapists saw exactly the same videotaped interview, but each group perceived a different reality.

Labels can stigmatize and diminish people. The Reuters news agency reported that Germans with unflattering surnames such as Kotz (vomit), Dreckman (filth man), Dumm (stupid), Schwein (pig), and Moerder (murder) admitted having problems as children because of their easily ridiculed last names. Imagine introducing Mr. Pig (Schwein) to Ms. Vomit (Kotz). Now there's an awkward social moment.

Labels are a common source of debate because they have the power to define. Teachers may define students with labels such as *smart* or *underachiever*; physicians may define patients with the labels *hypochondriac* or *complainer*; supervisors may define employees with *dependable, goof-off,* or *hard worker* labels; parents may define children as *incorrigible, cooperative,* or *sweet*. Do we label individuals with alcoholism as *sick* with a *disease* or do we label them *drunks* who are *weak* and *undisciplined*? The choice of labels matters a great deal. The former leads to treatment; the latter leads to ostracism and possible punishment.

We have seen that language has the power to influence thought, perception, and behavior. Language can trigger signal reactions. Our wording can bias our preference for certain choices. Labels have the power to define. They can produce prosocial behavior, but they can also stigmatize individuals and diminish self-perceptions.

Competent Language Use: Problems and Solutions

In this section, we will discuss six problems of language use: denotative and connotative meaning, false dichotomies, mislabeling, dead-level abstracting, inferential errors, and language that confuses and conceals.

Denotation and Connotation

Language has two main types of meaning: denotation and connotation. **Denotation** is the socially agreed upon meaning of words; it is meaning shared by members of a speech community. Dictionary definitions are denotations. Words that are not included in a dictionary (slang, many technical terms, newly created words, etc.), however, also have denotative meaning. In short, denotation is shared meaning, not just dictionary definitions.

Connotation is the volatile, personal, subjective meaning of words. Connotations have three dimensions (Osgood, 1969): *evaluation* (good/bad), *potency* (strong/weak), and *activity* (active/passive). Connotation is personal meaning, so it changes from individual to individual, sometimes in barely perceptible shades of difference and sometimes in spectacular ways.

To compare denotation and connotation, consider the word *bulimia*. The typical denotative meaning found in a dictionary or psychology textbook is "an eating disorder characterized by instances of eating binges followed by induced vomiting." This denotation is straightforward, descriptive, objective, and impersonal. If you have experienced bulimia, however, what registers most is the connotative meaning. Your connotation might be *negative and bad* (evaluation), *frightening and life-changing* (potency), and *an inability to control the need to feed and the urge to purge* (activity). Connotations can vary widely. Individuals with bulimia may even see their behavior as positive (Crandall, 1988).

PROBLEMS OF DENOTATION   Denotation is shared meaning, but we sometimes assume the meaning of a word is shared when it is not. Consider the cross-cultural problems Americans and the British experience with their versions of the English language. *Private school* to Americans is *public school* to the British. An American *undershirt* is a British *vest*. Our *sweater* is their *jumper*, and our *jumper* is their *pinafore* *dress*. Got that? A British person asking for a *rubber* in an American drugstore would be sent to the *condom* display, not to school supplies for an *eraser*. There are more than 4,000 common words in English that have distinctly different meanings in America and Great Britain (Bryson, 1990). It is small wonder that playwright George Bernard Shaw reputedly remarked, "England and America are two countries separated by the same language" (Brussell, 1988).

The use of English by Australians can also pose problems for Americans and vice versa. The NBC "Today" show reported during the opening baseball game at the 2000 Olympics in Sydney, Australia, that 15,000 fans, many Australians, giggled during a rendition of "Take Me out to the Ball Game." The lyric "root, root, root for the home team" made for an interesting cross-cultural lesson. *Root* to the Aussies is equivalent to *shagging* (having sex) in England. Asking fans to "root, root, root" for their team in Australia would be taking fan support a bit far.

Translating from one language into a distinctly different language creates even greater problems of denotation. Without the shared experience of a culture, sharing meaning is problematic. A popular Mexican restaurant in Tucson, Arizona, includes a note on its menu: "The manager has personally passed all the water served here." A Chinese restaurant in Santa Cruz, California, serves a "rolling lettuce chicken salad." A Parisian-style dress shop in Los Angeles displays a sign: "Dresses for street walking." Multinational corporations struggle with cross-cultural translations. Chevy Nova doesn't translate well in Latin America. In Spanish *no va* means "it doesn't go." Clairol corporation introduced its "Mist Stick" curling iron in Germany before it learned that *mist* is a German slang term meaning "manure." A manure stick isn't likely to be a real hot seller.

PROBLEMS OF CONNOTATION   During the 1968 presidential campaign, a television commercial for Richard Nixon was aired depicting U.S. soldiers fighting and dying in the jungles of Vietnam. Clearly visible on the helmet of one of the soldiers in the final scene of the commercial was the scrawled word *love*. The commercial ended with Nixon's voice-over: "I pledge to you, we will have an honorable end to the war in Vietnam." Nixon and his advisors were very surprised that this political commercial sparked strong protest, especially from the Midwest. There was fierce objection to the word *love* printed on the soldier's helmet. Love wasn't the sort of thing a combat soldier should be scrawling on his helmet, the upset viewers complained. It connoted "lack of patriotism" and "radical protest against the war," they asserted. The soldier with the objectionable word on his helmet was excised from the commercial for future airings. Soon after, the agency that created the commercial received a letter from the mother of the soldier whose helmet had provoked the protest. She wrote how thrilled she was to see her son in a Nixon commercial and thanked the agency for including him. She signed her letter "Mrs. William *Love*" (Smith, 1982).

A connotation is often presumed to be a shared meaning, but it is a personal meaning acquired from individuals' unique experiences and associations with a word. Would you have thought the word *love* could invite such a strong negative reaction? The denotative meaning for love certainly wouldn't give you a clue.

Because connotations can be volatile and are often emotionally charged, they are the source of most signal reactions (see Box 5-5). Signal reactions can provoke aggression and violence. The U.S. Supreme Court recognized this decades ago in their famous decision, *Chaplinsky v. New Hampshire*, which ruled that "fighting words" are not protected speech. More recently, "speech codes" on college campuses banning "fighting

Box 5-5 | Focus on Controversy

Verbal Taboos

When he told this story, my colleague's daughter, Janie, was 4 years old. While playing with a neighbor boy about her same age, Janie became very angry in response to something the boy did to her. Janie turned to the little boy and yelled, "I'm going to shit on your head." Janie's mom heard this outburst and sternly admonished her daughter, "Janie, we don't talk like that." Janie paused, then turned to the neighbor boy and said, "I'm going to shit on your arm."

Janie's mom clearly had a signal reaction to Janie's use of an offensive word. The denotative meaning doesn't appear to be the real problem. Do you think Janie's mom would have been so alarmed and stern if Janie had said "I'm going to toidee on your head" instead? If denotative meaning is what is producing the signal reaction, why is it that a doctor can ask you for a *feces* or *stool* sample without inviting reproach (even though mild embarrassment might accompany the request) but not a *shit* sample? The denotation of all three terms is identical, yet the connotative meaning is not. It is the word itself that offends quite apart from its denotative meaning, and it offends because we have been conditioned to respond to such taboo words as though they are nasty, obscene, or dirty.

When we consider English words from Great Britain that incite similar signal reactions, it is even more apparent that denotation is not the source of the response. In England, *bloody* is an objectionable word, yet it has no denotation at all. There is no literal translation, despite an unsupported theory linking it to menstruation (Bryson, 1990). It simply became associated with swearing and therefore taboo. Americans find the word *bloody* quaint, not offensive. It has no potency for us; it sparks no negative evaluation. We don't have the cultural associations that condition us to react negatively.

The prohibition on taboo words has relaxed in recent years, but, despite the widespread and frequent use of taboo words among adults and especially college students (Jay, 1992), such language is still widely viewed as objectionable. Andre Agassi was forced to default a tennis match at the Sybase Open tournament in San Jose, California, in February 1999 when he violated the professional tennis players' code by using obscene words on three occasions during the match. During the 2000 presi-

dential election, George W. Bush referred to a reporter as a "major-league asshole." It became at least a minor-league news story. When counselors swear during a therapy session, clients are less likely to return to them (Kottke & MacLeod, 1989), and they are less compliant (Kurklen & Kassinove, 1991; Sazer & Kassinove, 1991). An August 1999 Gallup poll found that 24% of respondents thought frequent use of profane and obscene language in movies was extremely offensive, and another 52% thought it was very or somewhat offensive (Movie Content, 1999). Taboo words can also incite aggression and violence, as many historical incidences attest (Rothwell, 1982).

Individuals, however, respond to taboo words in various ways. Some individuals find even relatively mild epithets completely objectionable—fighting words. Other individuals are not bothered in the least even by the most outrageous obscenities. If you listen to some adolescents' conversations, the participants seem not to notice the use of "foul language." They might as well be saying *like* or *you know*. A poll by Teenage Research Unlimited found that 52% of the 2,000 teen respondents thought cursing was cool (Steelman, 1999). A poll conducted by the Shorenstein Center at Harvard's Kennedy School of Government found that only 18% of those who were aware of George W. Bush's vulgar expletive reported that it had affected their opinion of the candidate, while 7% of those affected said it had *improved* their estimation of him. Again, this underlines the connotative, personal meaning of taboo words.

Questions for Thought

1. Is it ever appropriate to use obscene language? Explain.
2. Which taboo words have recently had their ban on television lifted? Why has this happened? Relate your answer to denotative versus connotative meaning.
3. Are there ethical reasons to ban certain terms? Which words would you ban? Why? Under what circumstances? Should children be forbidden to use obscene and profane language? Explain.
4. Do you think there will ever come a time when there are no taboo words in the English language? Explain.

words"—derogatory references to "race, sex, sexual orientation, or disability"—have emerged, leading to court challenges and national debate over free speech.

Here are three suggestions for addressing problems of denotative and connotative meaning:

1. *Clarify denotative meaning.* Remember that a word can have many denotative meanings. If you sense any misunderstanding about the meaning of a word, clarify the meaning. This is especially important when cross-cultural communication takes place.

2. *Learn to substitute semantic reactions for signal reactions.* A **semantic reaction** is a delayed, thoughtful response to language that seeks to decipher the users' intended meaning of a word. It is the opposite of the hair-trigger signal reaction. Because a signal reaction is a learned behavior, it can be unlearned and replaced with a more appropriate semantic reaction. A helpful way to delay your response until meaning has been confirmed is to ask the question, "What do you mean?" This gives you time to collect your thoughts. This can help to short-circuit a potentially explosive confrontation.

   Recall the "niggardly" incident in Washington, D.C.? A simple question, "What does *niggardly* mean?" from anyone at the press conference at which David Howard used the term would have prevented the silliness that resulted. A semantic reaction is a thoughtful response. Those who heard Howard use *niggardly* should have asked themselves a few obvious questions: "Why would an advocate for an African American mayor use a racist epithet?" "Has David Howard ever exhibited racist behavior in the past?" "Is there a possibility that I misheard what he said or that he is using a word unfamiliar to me?" Signal reactions don't occur when this much thought takes place.

3. *Refrain from using words that will likely trigger signal reactions.* Verbal obscenity or "fighting words" may cause no signal reaction within certain groups and their use may even act as a mark of identification with the group (you speak the group lingo). Offensive language, however, will likely trigger signal reactions in many contexts. Consequently, it is advisable to shift your style. Adapt your language use to the context, avoiding words that will likely provoke aggression and violence with certain individuals and groups. Speakers should be mindful not to provoke unnecessary signal reactions, and listeners should resist being baited into such reactions.

False Dichotomies

Advice columnist Ann Landers raised a fuss a few years ago when she asked her female readers to answer the question, "Would you be content to be held close and treated tenderly and forget about 'the act?'" Landers was swamped with more than 90,000 responses. A stunning 72% of the respondents said that they would prefer hugs to sexual intercourse. The talk show circuit went crazy. Experts, self-appointed and otherwise, all wanted to comment on the results. Landers' survey results were largely interpreted as proof that men are jerks. Women are starved for affection from their insensitive lovers, so went the "analysis," and they are willing to forego sexual consummation for tender caresses from their partners.

If you recognized that Landers asked a question that presented two choices as mutually exclusive alternatives (sex or hugs) when a third choice exists, congratulations, you recognized a false dichotomy. A **false dichotomy** is using either-or

"Next question: I believe that life is a constant striving for balance, requiring frequent tradeoffs between morality and necessity, within a cyclic pattern of joy and sadness, forging a trail of bittersweet memories until one slips, inevitably, into the jaws of death. Agree or disagree?"

language to frame a choice as though only two opposing possibilities exist when at least a third option is clearly available. Do you think the "men are jerks" debate would have been stimulated by an Ann Landers survey that offered a third choice? How many women do you think would have answered "hugs only" if offered "hugs and sexual intercourse" as a third choice?

If a thousand people were randomly chosen and plotted on a graph according to height, weight, or age, most of them would bunch in the middle (average height, weight, etc.), and only a few would fit the extremes (very tall or extremely short). This result is called a bell-shaped curve or normal distribution. A dichotomy becomes false when our thinking and perception are focused on the extremes of the distribution while we ignore the vast middle.

Most people can't be described accurately as short or tall, fat or thin, smart or dumb, young or old, strong or weak. We fall somewhere in between. Consider, for example, Tiger Woods. He has been dubbed the greatest *Black* golfer in history. Did you know that his heritage is a combination of Caucasian (White), African American (Black), American Indian, and Asian in almost equal proportions (White, 1997)? As a young boy, Woods concocted the term "Cablinasian" to describe his mixed heritage. It would seem that the answer to the question, "Is Tiger Woods black or white?" should be "Neither."

False dichotomies can have a significant impact on how we think and act (Huspek, 2000). Previously, several studies were cited that showed the power of framing on choices people make. If presented with only two extreme opposing choices, it is quite likely that this false framing will conceal other, more accurate options.

In some instances, a dichotomy is not false because there are only two opposing choices possible. Being "sort of pregnant," "almost a virgin," or "slightly dead" aren't realistic third options. Most dichotomous framing, however, inappropriately implies that the only possibilities are the two extreme choices.

There are two steps you can take to avoid false dichotomies:

1. *Think pluralistically.* When presented with a dichotomous choice, search for additional options. Ask the questions, "Are these our only two choices?" and "Can't we think of other options?" These questions reframe our thinking from dichotomous to pluralistic, from considering only two extreme opposing choices to looking for other possibilities.
2. *Recognize degrees of difference when using language.* Although it is true that some individuals are fat (obese) or skinny (anorexic), it is simply inaccurate to describe most people with such extreme language. Our language should attempt to approximate reality, but false dichotomies allow for only gross approximations. Strive to use language more precisely. This means using terms such as *slightly, moderately, occasionally, rarely, sometimes, often,* and *usually.* This is not the language of the wishy-washy fence straddler, but the language of precision.

Mislabeling

Eight individuals, none with any real psychiatric problems, gained admission to 12 psychiatric hospitals in 1972 (some did it twice). This was the initial stage of a controversial study conducted by David Rosenhan (1973). These 8 "pseudopatients" gained admittance under slightly false pretenses. They were instructed to complain to the admissions staff at each hospital that they heard voices that said, "Empty," "Hollow," and "Thud." Once admitted, none of the pseudopatients was to complain of these symptoms again. Eleven of the pseudopatients were diagnosed (labeled) as *schizophrenic,* and one was said to have *manic-depressive psychosis.* The pseudopatients had to remain in the hospital until the staff recognized the mistaken diagnosis or until they were simply freed. The stays in the hospital ranged from 7 to 52 days, and the average was 19 days. Ironically, 35 of the 118 actual patients in the hospital recognized the ruse of the pseudopatients and said so openly, but none of the staff ever questioned the initial diagnosis. Even when the pseudopatients were released, hospital records showed that their psychiatric disorder was merely "in remission," not cured or a mistaken diagnosis. Rosenhan replicated these disturbing findings in later studies (Greenberg, 1981).

Earlier it was argued that labeling could have a significant effect on thought, perception, and behavior. When labels are misapplied, their significance becomes troubling (see Box 5-6). The stigma attached to these labels can linger even after full recovery from a mental disorder. People so labeled often become social lepers. Mislabeling mentally healthy individuals has the potential to ruin their lives.

No one wants to be mislabeled, especially if the labels can stigmatize. At one time the deaf were mislabeled as *imbeciles* (Sacks, 1990). Imagine how traumatic it would be if you were mislabeled as a *child abuser, spouse abuser, rapist,* or *murderer.*

Box 5-6   Focus on Controversy

The "Monster Study": Ethics and the Power of Mislabeling

In 1939, Wendell Johnson, a speech pathology professor at Iowa State University, embarked on a controversial experiment to determine the cause of stuttering (Dyer, 2001). A severe stutterer himself, Johnson theorized that labeling young children as stutterers when they stumble over words will not only worsen the affliction, but also could induce stuttering in normal speakers. This was a revolutionary idea that contradicted the prevailing viewpoint of the time that stuttering had a genetic or organic cause.

To prove his thesis, Johnson devised an experiment that was later dubbed "The Monster Study" by critics. He received permission from the state-run Iowa Soldiers' Orphans' Home to use 22 young orphans as experimental subjects. His graduate student, Mary Tudor, performed the experiment under Johnson's direction. The 22 orphans were divided into two groups: one composed of stutterers and the other of normal speakers. Half the children from each group were labeled "normal speakers" and given positive encouragement, and half were labeled stutterers and given negative "therapy." The therapy consisted of informing the children what stuttering was and then lecturing each of the children whenever they repeated a word so they would become more self-conscious about their stuttering. "Don't speak unless you can speak correctly. Watch your speech all the time. Do anything to keep from stuttering," Tudor instructed her unsuspecting subjects. Teachers and administrators at the orphanage were told that the children in the negative therapy group were stutterers even though half were not at the start of the study. Teachers reinforced the stuttering label, unaware that they were participating in a deceptive experiment.

Results of this experiment were dramatic. Of the 6 normal speaking children, 5 exhibited stuttering after being mislabeled and given negative therapy. The speech of 3 of the 5 stutterers deteriorated after they were labeled stutterers and received the negative therapy (Dyer, 2001). Only one child in the positive encouragement group developed greater speech problems.

Wendell Johnson never published the results of this experiment, and he was convinced by colleagues to keep it secret from the world because it would be likened to the Nazi experiments during World War II. His theory, supported only with anecdotal evidence, not the more direct and convincing evidence of his Monster Study, became the most widely accepted theory on the cause of stuttering. Johnson became a famous and revered academic figure. Mary Tudor became a speech pathologist in Wisconsin. The children, however, continued to

deteriorate after the experiment ceased. Tudor returned to the orphanage three times to try to reverse the effects of the mislabeling and negative therapy but without success. An investigative report by the *San Jose Mercury News* (Dyer, 2001) brought the experiment to the nation's attention.

Defenders of the experiment argue that Johnson's theory and the clear benefits of using positive not negative therapy with stutterers helped millions of children with this terrible problem. Detractors argue that the experiment was unethical. Children who had been induced to stutter by the mislabeling and negative therapy were never told about the experiment, nor were the normal speakers in the study, until the *Mercury News* began its investigation more than 60 years later. Some of the children never recovered. They were tormented by other children, their school grades plummeted, their self-esteem shriveled, and a few became withdrawn and even reclusive adults.

This mislabeling experiment fails all five ethical criteria: respect, honesty, fairness, choice, and responsibility. It treated these children with disrespect. Not enough concern for their future welfare was demonstrated, even though years later Mary Tudor lamented her participation in the study (Dyer, 2001). This was a dishonest study with tragic consequences. Individuals' lives were ruined in some instances. The irresponsible lies told to the children, their teachers, and the administrators of the orphanage were perpetuated for more than 60 years. The children were never given a choice to participate in the experiment. They didn't even know they were being treated like lab rats. Following a three-part story in the *Mercury News*, Iowa State University apologized, calling the experiment "regrettable" and indefensible. John Bernthal (2001), President of the American Speech-Language-Hearing Association, wrote to the paper: "The research described in this article cannot be justified on theoretical, moral, or ethical grounds and represented a serious error in judgment by the researcher" (p. 11B).

Questions for Thought

1. The intentions of the experimenters were noble—to help children with stuttering problems become better communicators. What effect does this have on your assessment of the ethics of this study?
2. The power of mislabeling is clearly shown in this study. Should this be a consideration in your assessment of the ethics of this experiment?

So how do you prevent the problem of mislabeling? There are two steps that you can take:

1. *Operationally define significant labels.* An **operational definition** grounds a label by specifying which measurable behaviors or experiences are subsumed under the label and which are ruled out. When you ask individuals to "be specific" or to "provide an example," you are asking them to operationalize their language.

   Operational definitions say, "For our purposes an 'A' student is anyone who scores 90% or above in the class." The Harvard School of Public Health operationally defines "binge drinking," a problem that afflicts almost half of the college students in the United States, as "consuming five or more drinks at one sitting for men, and four or more drinks for women" (Kalb & McCormick, 1998).

   Operational definitions may produce some surprises. A poll of Virginia mental health and legal professionals revealed that the "child abuse" label could be loosely applied. Twenty percent of those sampled believed frequent hugging of a 10-year-old constitutes child abuse and justifies intervention by state authorities. More than half defined "sexual abuse" as including a parent giving a child a brief good-night kiss on the lips (cited in Pendergrast, 1995).

   Remember, word usage is conventional. Thus, the accuracy of any label depends on common agreement. We should not be labeling someone a child abuser if we have no common agreement on which behaviors constitute child abuse. Legal definitions attempt to define illegal behaviors clearly.

2. *Apply the labels accurately once they have been operationalized.* Don't apply a label more broadly than the operational definition stipulates. Labeling older people *senile* simply because they have slowed down mentally or have minor memory problems is inaccurate and inappropriate.

Dead-Level Abstracting

Wendell Johnson (1946) coined the term **dead-level abstracting** for the practice of freezing on one level of abstraction. As previously explained, words can operate at different levels of abstraction, from very concrete or precise to very vague. Dead-level abstraction occurs when we stick rigidly either to vague words or when we get frozen in the detail of concrete words. When politicians use vague terms such as *family values* or *the people versus the powerful*, voters can be forgiven for not knowing precisely what is meant.

Research found that the degree of concreteness or vagueness of words could be the most important determinant of how easy or difficult it is to form mental images (Paivio, 1969). Forming a clear image of a *horse*, a *clown*, or a *baseball* is easy. Forming a clear image of *truth*, *justice*, and the *American way* is difficult (although these terms may produce signal reactions). Concrete words produce concrete images; vague words can remain imprecise in our minds, resulting in confusion and misunderstanding.

The answer to dead-level abstracting, however, does not lie in always speaking in concrete terminology. *Never rising above the level of the concrete and precise is also dead-level abstracting.* A professor who tells many jokes and stories may keep interest for a while, but eventually students will ask the question, "What does this have to do with the class?" The details need to be tied to a higher-level abstraction. All the jokes and stories need to be connected to concepts, principles, and generalizations.

Otherwise, the professor is teaching trivia—unconnected factoids. Combining both the concepts and generalizations to the jokes and stories can produce learning.

Here are two suggestions for avoiding dead-level abstraction:

1. *Operationally define abstract terms.* The operational definition of "having sex" or "sexual relations" was at the center of one of the two articles of impeachment filed against Bill Clinton in 1999. Clinton assured the American people that he did not "have sexual relations with that woman—Miss Lewinsky." He repeated this in sworn testimony before a grand jury. Independent Counsel Kenneth Starr charged President Clinton with perjury for this "deception." Clinton, however, claimed later that he viewed "sexual relations" as meaning sexual intercourse. Many people thought Clinton was merely parsing words to avoid impeachment and criminal prosecution (a reasonable conclusion). Surely everyone knows what *sexual relations* or *having sex* means, right? In a study of college students conducted by the Kinsey Institute, however, 59% apparently agreed with Clinton's operational definition (Brown, 1999). Students did not view oral sex as "sexual relations" or "having sex." A 1999 survey found that almost a third of health educators in schools view oral sex as "abstinence" (Wronge & Fernandez, 2000). "Sexual relations" or "having sex" are more abstract than they may have appeared to be. An operational definition would have prevented any parsing or misunderstanding from occurring.

   When a couple seeks help from a therapist, operational definitions likely will be requested frequently from the couple. If the husband says, "My wife and I are experiencing a problem," the therapist undoubtedly will ask, "What specific problem are you experiencing?" If the husband then responds, "We argue all the time," the therapist will pursue this abstraction by requesting, "What do you argue about?" "We argue about money," might be the response, whereupon the therapist might continue to ground the husband's language by further requesting, "Can you give me an example of a recent argument you had about money?" Each time the therapist will attempt to move the language from vague and abstract to precise and concrete.

2. *Use language flexibly.* Do not get stuck using either concrete or vague terms alone. Use both fluidly. When others get stuck at one level of abstraction, help them become more flexible by asking for examples or clearly identifiable behaviors that might clarify vague terms. When people remain frozen at the level of excessive detail, ask them to clarify the significance or relevance of the detail.

Inferential Errors

A story is told about two women from the United States (a grandmother and her granddaughter), a Romanian officer, and a Nazi officer seated together in a train compartment. As the train passes through a dark tunnel, the sounds of a loud kiss and a vigorous slap shatter the silence. When the train emerges from the tunnel, no words are spoken but a noticeable welt forms on the face of the Nazi officer. The grandmother muses to herself, "What a fine granddaughter I have raised. I have no need to worry. She can handle herself admirably." The granddaughter thinks to herself, "Grandmother packs a powerful wallop for a woman of her years. She sure is spunky." The Nazi officer, none too pleased by the course of events, ruminates to himself, "How clever is this Romanian. He steals a kiss and gets me slapped in the process." The Romanian chuckles to himself, "I am indeed clever. I kissed my hand and slapped a Nazi."

This story illustrates **inferential error**—a mistaken conclusion that results from the assumption that inferences are factual descriptions of reality instead of interpretations of varying accuracy made by individuals. The facts reported are that the four characters in the story heard what sounded like a kiss followed by a slap. The Nazi officer had a welt on his face. Any conclusion drawn from these facts is an inference (a conclusion about the unknown based on the known). It was completely dark in the tunnel, and inferences were made that the sounds heard were that of a kiss and a slap. These are reliable inferences because we've all heard the sounds of a kiss and a slap many times, but they are still inferences, not descriptions of fact. The visible welt on the face of the Nazi officer is further evidence of the reliability of the slap inference. Each person made an inferential error, however, because each leaped to a conclusion regarding who kissed and slapped whom based on superficial information. Only the Romanian knew the truth.

The seriousness of inferential errors is demonstrated by racial profiling. This is the unfortunate practice by some law enforcement agencies in the United States of disproportionately stopping African American males for suspected crimes based primarily on race. Racial profiling (race of the suspect) produces many more inferential errors than valid inferences (Lamberth 1998). This is because the information upon which the inferences are based is extremely limited. Elmo Randolph, a New Jersey dentist, was stopped more than 100 times during a 4-year period while driving his BMW from his home to his office. Dr. Randolph, guilty only of "driving while black," finally sold his automobile.

There are two ways to avoid inferential errors:

1. *Base inferences on a substantial quantity of information.*
2. *Base inferences on high-quality information.*

You don't have to check every inference you make, but you should check important ones, especially if the quantity and quality of information on which the inference is based are limited or questionable.

Words That Confuse and Conceal

Language can promote clear thinking, or it can confuse and conceal. Sometimes the confusion is unintentional, and occasionally concealment is warranted. Nevertheless, using words to confuse or conceal can be troublesome. Jargon and euphemism can make effective communication difficult.

JARGON   Every profession, trade, or group has its specialized language called **jargon**. Jargon is not inherently a poor use of language. One study (Bross et al., 1972) found that medical jargon allowed surgeons to communicate important factual information briefly and clearly. Jargon is a kind of verbal shorthand. When lawyers use terms such as *prima facie case* and *habeus corpus,* they communicate to other attorneys and officers of the court very specific information without tedious, verbose explanation. "To the initiated, jargon is efficient, economical, and even crucial in that it can capture distinctions not made in the ordinary language" (Allan & Burridge, 1991, p. 201). *Signal reactions, false dichotomies, dead-level abstracting,* and *inferential error* are apt examples of jargon used in this chapter.

Racial profiling often leads to inferential error. Someone who looks like Martin Luther King would more likely be stopped by police than someone who looks like mass murderer Charles Manson.

Jargon, however, can pose problems for those who do not understand the verbal shorthand. When doctors use terms such as *bilateral periorbital hematoma* (black eye), *tinnitus* (ear ringing), *agrypnia* (sleeplessness), *cephalalgia* (headache), and *emesis* (vomiting), they communicate very specific conditions to medical staff, but they more than likely mystify patients. The message is concealed when it should be revealed to those who most need to know.

Edspeak, the sometimes bewildering jargon of educators, can intimidate parents who may be loathe to reveal their unfamiliarity with the jargon. Parents can be forgiven if they are flummoxed by jargon used to "explain" their child's strengths and shortcomings: *phonemic sequencing errors, phonological process delays, normed modality processing, morphosyntactic skills, word attack skills, psychometrics, deficit model,* and *additive model,* to name just a few (Helfand, 2001). To most parents this bushel of buzzwords probably sounds closer to Klingon than any language they speak. Parents become the "outsiders," disconnected from teachers and administrators who "speak the language."

Competent use of jargon has two guidelines:

1. *Reduce or eliminate the use of jargon when conversing with someone unfamiliar with the jargon.*
2. *If jargon is necessary, operationalize terms unfamiliar to the receiver.* Some school districts offer free jargon handbooks to parents.

EUPHEMISM   Businesses and corporations don't lay off workers anymore; they engage in "force management programs" and "duplication reduction," or they give employees a "career-change opportunity." These are euphemisms. *Euphemism* is derived from the Greek *euphemismos*, meaning "to speak well of." It substitutes kinder and gentler terms for words that hurt, cause offense, or create problems for us. **Euphemism** is a form of linguistic novocaine whereby word choices numb us to or camouflage unpleasant or offensive realities.

Not all euphemisms qualify as language misuse and malpractice. Using *passed away* instead of *dead* is unlikely to cause harm to anyone, and it may cushion an ugly reality for grieving relatives and friends. Nevertheless, euphemisms can create mischief. When the nuclear power industry refers to out-of-control nuclear reactors as simply going on "power excursions" or experiencing "rapid oxidation" (a major fire), the public is left in a fog. When "unplanned hypercriticality" (approaching a meltdown of the reactor core) can result in "spontaneous energetic disassembly" (a catastrophic explosion), the potential danger is hidden from us. When our government calls killing enemy soldiers "servicing the target," which results in "decommissioned aggressor quantum" (dead bodies), who can guess what's really occurring? When doctors refer to "therapeutic misadventures" (operations that kill patients), we have a clear case of language misuse and malpractice.

Official-sounding medicalese used by hospitals and HMOs across the country has contributed to the U.S. Government Accounting Office's estimate of $10 billion a year in overpayments by patients (Palmer, 2000). With increasing out-of-pocket payments, patients are baffled by charges of $57.50 for "cough-support devices" (a teddy bear for pressing against one's chest to ease the pain of coughing after surgery), $10 for "mucus-recovery systems" (a box of tissues), and $18 for a "gauze collection bag" (an ordinary trash bag). Pat Palmer, author of *The Medical Bill Survival Guide*, provides this suggestion for frustrated patients who suspect medical fleecing camouflaged by euphemisms: "Pop open a mucus-recovery system, give your cough-support device a big hug, then get on the phone and give the billing office a piece of your cerebral control center" (Palmer, 2000, p. 82).

Here are two suggestions for dealing competently with euphemisms:

1. *Use euphemisms cautiously and wisely.*   This is a judgment call. Substituting euphemisms for profanities and obscenities should cause few, if any, problems. Using euphemisms to confuse, however, can be more problematic. Normally your communication goal should be clarity, not confusion. Confusing with language isn't always evil, but you wouldn't want to make it standard practice.
2. *Expunge dangerous euphemisms.*   Euphemisms that simply lie to us to hide ugly, dangerous truths should be eliminated from our communication in all but the rarest instances.

Summary

Language is a structured system of symbols for communicating meaning. All languages have rules that allow us to share meaning with others. Language influences thought, perception, and behavior by framing how we see the world, by labeling bits of that world, and by provoking strong, sometimes hair-trigger reactions to the words chosen to describe our world.

The power of language can produce several problems. We can have serious misunderstandings regarding the denotative meaning of words. Connotative meanings can ignite signal reactions. False dichotomies can frame our perceptions into two extreme opposing choices, leaving no room for flexible responses and negotiation. Mislabeling can stigmatize and scar those who are incorrectly labeled. Dead-level abstracting can confuse us or trivialize what might be important learning. Inferential errors can produce unequal treatment, and jargon and euphemisms can confuse and conceal the truth. We need to resist signal reactions to words by adopting semantic or delayed reactions. When presented with a false dichotomy, we should seek other options. We should identify and correct mislabeling. We should use our language flexibly to avoid dead-level abstractions. We should check for the accuracy of important inferences by relying on plentiful and high-quality information. We should use jargon only sparingly and define it clearly for those unfamiliar with the terminology. Finally, we should use euphemisms infrequently and cautiously.

Quizzes Without Consequences

www.mhhe
com/ **rothwell2**

Go to *Quizzes Without Consequences* at the book's Online Learning Center at **www.mhhe.com/rothwell2** or access the CD-ROM for *In the Company of Others.*

Key Terms

See Audio Flashcards Study Aid.

www.mhhe
com/ **rothwell2**

See Crossword Puzzle Study Aid.

abstracting	jargon	presciptivism
connotation	judgments	productivity
dead-level abstracting	language	referents
denotation	lexicon	Sapir-Whorf
descriptions	linguistic determinism	hypothesis
descriptivists	linguistic relativity	self-reflexiveness
displacement	masculine-generic	semantic reaction
euphemism	gender references	signal reaction
false dichotomy	morpheme	standardization
framing	onomatopoeic words	style shifting
inferences	operational definition	symbols
inferential error	phonemes	syntax

Suggested Readings

Bryson, B. (1990). *The mother tongue: English and how it got that way*. New York: Avon. Bryson provides an excellent history of the English language with its many peculiarities.

Bryson, B. (1994). *Made in America: An informal history of the English language in the United States*. New York: Avon. This is a very entertaining and unique view of U.S. history from the perspective of the English language.

Orwell, G. (1949). *Nineteen eighty-four*. New York: New American Library. This is the classic novel that explores the role language plays in furthering repression.

Pinker, S. (1994). *The language instinct: How the mind creates language*. New York: Harper Perennial. Few academics have the writing skills of Steven Pinker. This book is a superb treatment of linguistics for a lay audience. It is loaded with interesting information and written with wit and enthusiasm for the subject.

Sacks, O. (1990). *Seeing voices: A journey into the world of the deaf*. New York: Random House. This is a marvelous book on the evolution of sign language for the deaf.

Film School

My Fair Lady (1964). Musical; PG ★★★★✔
If you like musicals, you'll love this one that's all about language (okay, there is a love story too). Analyze the movie for the power of language and prescriptive versus descriptive grammar issues.

The Miracle Worker (1962). Drama. Not rated ★★★★✔
This is the story of Annie Sullivan, Helen Keller's tutor, and her work with Helen. What kind of a life would we have without a language? Here an adapted sign language provides Helen with the ability to communicate. Explore the issue of life without language.

CHAPTER 6

Nonverbal Communication:
Sharing Meaning Without Words

Katherine Harris, Florida's controversial Secretary of State, certified George Bush as the winner of the 2000 presidential election in Florida. This gave Bush the required electoral votes necessary to become President of the United States. Attention to this highly controversial act, however, was often overshadowed by unflattering and sexist focus on Harris's appearance. She received "as much attention for the way she handles her lipstick and mascara as her politics" (Sulek, 2000, p. 17A). Sulek (2000) gives examples of the blistering attack on her appearance during the contested Florida election battle. Robin Givhan of the *Washington Post* said that Harris "appeared to have applied her makeup with a trowel" and questioned how she could ever be taken seriously when her eyelashes looked like caterpillars. "One wonders how this Republican woman, who can't use restraint when she's wielding a mascara wand, will manage to use it and make sound decisions in this game of partisan one-upmanship." Margery Eagan of the *Boston Herald* declared that Harris was "Dustin Hoffman as Tootsie." University of Florida political science professor Richard Scher commented that "with the look she has adopted for herself, it hasn't presented an image of weight or gravity or seriousness of purpose." Deborah Rhode, a Stanford law professor and former director of the university's Institute for Research on Women and Gender claims that a "double standard exists" when it comes to female appearance. "Men aren't held to the same standard of youth and beauty" (Sulek, 2000, p. 17A).

Our appearance and a host of other nonverbal cues impact our lives every day; so much of what we perceive about ourselves and others is wrapped up in nonverbal communication. Sarah Collins (2001) conducted an interesting study on female perceptions of the male deep voice. She asked 34 males to pronounce vowel sounds. She then asked female participants to guess what the males looked like based only on their voices. Almost without exception, the men with the deepest voices were perceived to be more attractive, older, heavier, and more likely to have well-developed muscles and a hairy chest. In fact, Collins found no such correspondence between deep male voices and any physical attributes except weight (the deeper-voiced men were heavier). The quality of one's voice seems to matter to us even if the facts don't necessarily support our perceptions. The voice of David Prowse, the 6 ft 7 in. actor who played Darth Vader in *Star Wars,* was replaced with the deep, rumbling voice of James Earl Jones. Reportedly, Prowse's voice was too high pitched to communicate power and stature (Adam, 2001).

The power of nonverbal communication is also exemplified by its potential for miscommunication. Consider one example. A young photographer was flown to a remote area of Alaska one summer. When the weather turned bad, the photographer's father became concerned and sent a plane to look for his son. The pilot spotted the young man's camp and soon saw him waving a red jacket liner, which to a pilot is a signal to leave. The young photographer then made a thumbs-up gesture as the plane flew over. The pilot kept on flying, concluding that the thumbs-up gesture meant everything was fine. Weeks later the frozen body of the young man was found. He had left a diary. In it he wrote that he had been ecstatic to see the plane and had waved the red jacket liner to flag down the pilot. He had made the thumbs-up gesture to communicate his happiness at being rescued. He was dumbfounded to see the plane fly away. When he finally ran out of firewood, he used the last bullet in his gun to end his misery (Burgoon et al., 1996).

Despite the significance of language to human discourse, nonverbal communication also plays an important role in sharing meaning with others. Many communication texts, misinterpreting research by Mehrabian and Ferris (1967), assert that

93% of communication is nonverbal (see Lapakko, 1997, for a critique). Some claim communication is 65% nonverbal, based on limited research by Birdwhistell (1970). The exact percentage is unimportant, but nonverbal communication often has a greater impact on receivers than does verbal communication (Burgoon et al., 1996). This is a remarkable conclusion considering the power of language to shape thought, perception, and behavior.

The principal purpose of this chapter is to show how we might improve our nonverbal communication with others.

There are three chapter objectives:

1. to compare and contrast nonverbal and verbal communication;
2. to develop an appreciation for the power of various types of nonverbal communication, necessitating a keen regard for its competent use; and
3. to suggest ways to communicate competently with nonverbal codes.

The principal purpose of this chapter is to show how we might improve our nonverbal communication with others.

Verbal and Nonverbal Communication Distinctions

Communication is a lot more than just words. "Actions speak louder than words" is a cultural cliché. **Nonverbal communication** is sharing meaning with others non-linguistically. Let's explore this definition in more depth by drawing distinctions between nonverbal and verbal communication.

Nonlinguistic

The previous chapter identified four essential characteristics of language: structure, displacement, productivity, and self-reflexiveness. Nonverbal communication doesn't possess these four essential linguistic characteristics (Hickson & Stacks, 1989). Nonverbal communication is not structured for meaning. It possesses no explicit set of rules, grammar, or syntax. Nonverbal communication does not exhibit displacement because it communicates only about the here and now. Nonverbal communication also can show only minimal productivity. For example, new gestures for insults, affection, solidarity with others, and the like are created from time to time, but such nonverbal productivity is rare. Finally, nonverbal communication is not self-reflexive. We can't communicate indefinitely about nonverbal codes by using nonverbal codes.

Number of Channels

Verbal communication is single-channeled, but nonverbal communication is multichanneled (Burgoon, 1985). You can express enthusiasm verbally by saying, "I can't wait to get started on our project," or you can say, "Wow! Hold me back, I'm ready to burst with excitement." The statements change, but they all are expressed through the single channel of words.

The same enthusiasm can be expressed nonverbally through multiple channels: jumping up and down, making flailing gestures, widening your eyes, smiling, using an expressive tone of voice, making rapid utterances, hugging, screaming. The multichannel nature of nonverbal communication can add impact and believability to a message. It isn't difficult to lie with words, for instance, but it is extremely difficult to lie convincingly in a half-dozen nonverbal channels. If the nonverbal channels reveal inconsistent messages, credibility is questioned.

When you say, "I'm telling the truth," but your nonverbal communication says, "I'm lying," we tend to believe the nonverbal message. Because nonverbal communication is more spontaneous, is physiologically based, and has to be consistent across multiple channels, it seems more believable and genuine, even though it may not be.

The adult pattern of relying on nonverbal messages when verbal and nonverbal messages conflict is not typical of children. Infants begin life depending solely on nonverbal communication. Once language develops, however, children rely primarily on verbal communication (Burgoon, 1985). Young children take verbal comments literally. Sarcasm, which is indicated by tone of voice and facial expressions, belies the verbal message. One study found that children only gradually learn to understand sarcastic messages. A mere 14% of kindergartners understood a teacher's sarcasm, but this gradually increased to 39% of 3rd graders, 52% of 9th graders, and 66% of 12th graders (Andersen et al., 1985).

Degree of Ambiguity

Nonverbal communication is at least as ambiguous as language, probably more so. This point was made abundantly clear by rock musician Frank Zappa when he appeared on a television talk show hosted by an obnoxious individual named Joe Pine. This incident occurred in the 1960s, when a person's physical appearance, especially hair length for men, communicated nonconformity, rebelliousness, and antiwar sentiments. The most distinctive aspect of the show was Pine's shabby treatment of his guests, whom he tried to make look foolish. Pine had an amputated leg, but this was unremarkable until Zappa appeared on the show. When Zappa, sporting shoulder-length hair, was introduced to the audience, the following exchange took place:

PINE: I guess your long hair makes you a girl.

ZAPPA: I guess your wooden leg makes you a table (cited in Cialdini, 1993a, p. 224).

Zappa's laser-quick ad lib exposed the absurdity of treating a nonverbal cue (e.g., hair length) as if only a single meaning could be attached to it. Meaning isn't embedded in the nonverbal *cue* (whatever triggers meaning). Hair length has no meaning apart from those who observe it anymore than a wooden leg has an inherent meaning. We have to interpret nonverbal cues. With interpretation comes ambiguity.

Can you "read a person like a book," as is so often asserted in the popular media (see Box 6-1)? Consider the fact that even "experts" in lie detection do poorly when trying to determine truth tellers from liars. This is primarily because "There is no sign of deceit itself—no gesture, facial expression, or muscle twitch that in and of itself means that a person is lying" (Ekman, 1992, p. 80).

One study focused on individuals who administer lie-detector tests for the CIA, FBI, and the military; psychiatrists; court judges; police detectives; and Secret Service agents. The 509 participants were asked to detect deception. All of these people worked in professions in which deception is a common occurrence and an important issue. Nevertheless, only the Secret Service agents did better than chance (guessing) in detecting deception from nonverbal cues, and they were wrong more than a third of the time (Ekman & O'Sullivan, 1991). College students also participated in the study. They did the worst of any group. In another study, highly educated, well-trained child abuse experts, confident that their intuition and experience would enable them to discern true from false allegations, actually performed *worse*

Box 6-1 | Focus on Controversy

Nonverbal Courtship Cues: Mass-Market Misinformation

David Givens (1983), in his once-popular book *Love Signals*, offered this advice to men courting women:

> Men might try the following signals: Face to face with a woman, speak slowly. Tilt your head to one side and nod as she makes her points, to show you're listening. Lean forward, align your shoulders with hers, hold your face tipped down slightly toward the floor . . . and gaze upward into her eyes from under your eyebrows. Look for three seconds at a time, then drop your gaze to the table for three seconds before meeting her eyes again. Don't turn your head away to the side; keep it still as you listen (pp. 207–208).

Givens claims that this courtship-by-the-numbers is powerful. He offers abundant specific advice on how to manipulate people into liking and falling in love with you by both accurately reading and displaying precise nonverbal signals.

As I write this, I'm looking at an advertisement I received in the mail from *Men's Health* magazine. "Inside: 10 female flirting signals that secretly say 'I want you!'" reads the envelope, urging me to investigate further. On the inside (I opened the envelope out of purely academic interest) I'm told "how to know what a woman's body language is really telling you." Simply by purchasing this book I can discover the "seven secrets of seduction" and signals of "mating magic."

The mistake both Givens and *Men's Health* make is that their advice is based on a false premise. Both assume that nonverbal communication can be decoded with precise accuracy simply by carefully and knowledgeably observing the signals transmitted by others. This is not the case. Givens established a Web site on nonverbal communication in which he touts his nonverbal dictionary. In it, he identifies specific nonverbal cues and provides a definition for each cue. This is a pointless venture because, aside from a small number of emblems (to be discussed later), most nonverbal cues can't be accurately defined out of context. Most gestures, touches, physical greetings, adornments, emotional displays, use of space, and concerns about territoriality depend for meaning on a vast and complex array of individual and cultural variables. As anthropologist Edward Hall explains, "Because of its complexity, efforts to isolate out 'bits' of nonverbal communication and generalize from them in isolation are doomed to failure. Book titles such as *How to Read a Person Like a Book* are thoroughly misleading, doubly so because they are designed to satisfy the public's need for highly specific answers to complex questions for which there are no simple answers" (Trippett, 1981, p. 72).

Nevertheless, mass-market publications continue to offer erroneous advice on courtship behavior and mating rituals. "How to use body signals a woman can't resist" trumpets the *National Enquirer*. These "irresistible signals" include copying the woman's gestures, flexing muscles, touching her arm as you talk, eyeing her body up and down, moving into her "privacy bubble," preening, and physically guiding her into a private place. This nonverbal communication may work with some women, but in more cases than not such behavior will likely produce some very unpleasant, possibly even legal, repercussions.

Questions for Thought

1. Should we ever try to use nonverbal cues to convince others to like us? Why or why not? Is it ethical to do this since it is manipulative?
2. Is there any truth in the *National Enquirer* list of "irresistible signals" that "women can't resist"? How do you think a woman would likely respond to such nonverbal communication? Why?

than chance. They concluded that the children who gave the greatest amount of misinformation were most credible (Horner et al., 1993).

If the experts have trouble accurately reading nonverbal communication, how do the rest of us do? Despite our tendency toward overconfidence, most of us don't do all that well. Women, however, tend to be more accurate decoders of nonverbal messages than are men, and middle-aged people tend to be better at reading nonverbal communication than are younger individuals (Rosenthal, 1979). *Knowing the individual well markedly aids the accurate perception of nonverbal cues.*

The ambiguity of nonverbal communication is a source of significant misunderstanding between cultures (see Box 6-2). In the United States the "thumbs-up" gesture means "all right!" or "way to go." In Australia, however, it means the

See "Truth or Lie" Video Test on CD.

Box 6-2 Sharper Focus

The Nanny Trial

In 1997 Louise Woodward, a British teenager who was employed as a nanny by an American couple living in Newton, Massachusetts, was found guilty of manslaughter in the death of an infant under her care. Jonathon Raban (1997), also British and living in America, had an interesting take on this highly controversial trial. Regarding the truthfulness of Woodward's testimony claiming that the infant's death was an accident, Raban says, "My English eyes saw one thing; my American-resident eyes saw something else altogether" (p. 55).

Raban's "English eyes" observed a Louise Woodward with "shoulders hunched submissively forward, eyes lowered, voice a humble whisper. Woodward made a good impression as an English church mouse. Her posture announced that she knew her place; that she

acknowledged the superior authority of the court; that she was a nobody." He concluded, "I thought she was telling the truth" (p. 55).

Raban's "American-resident eyes" saw something quite different. "My second pair of eyes saw Ms. Woodward as sullen, masked, affectless, dissembling. Her evasive body language clearly bespoke the fact that she was keeping something of major importance hidden from the court." He concluded, "I thought she was telling lies" (p. 55).

Raban's dual-culture perspective of this widely publicized event emphasizes the ambiguity that results from having to interpret nonverbal cues. Different cultures may interpret the same nonverbal cues in strikingly different ways.

Halle Berry appears distraught and profoundly sad if you concentrate on her nonverbal communication. She is, in fact, thrilled by the honor of receiving an Oscar, the first ever given to an African American female for best actress. Nonverbal cues alone can be ambiguous.

disdainful "up yours!"(Axtell, 1998). An upraised palm with fingers moving back and forth signals "come here" in the United States, but in Italy, China, and Columbia it means "good-bye" (Jandt, 1995).

Discrete Versus Continuous

Verbal communication has discrete beginnings and endings. We begin it when we start talking, and we end it when we stop talking. Nonverbal communication, however, has no discrete beginning and end. We continuously send messages for others to perceive, even when we may wish not to do so. Robert Noel was convicted of

Nonverbal communication can send messages continuously, although we may prefer otherwise. Despite his attempt to communicate "nothing" to the jury in his dog mauling trial, do you form an impression about him from this picture?

involuntary manslaughter as the owner of a presa canario (a breed of dog) that viciously mauled and killed Diane Whipple. Noel seemed oblivious to the continuous nature of nonverbal communication. After the trial, jurors in the case offered their impressions of Noel. They saw him as a man who seemed unremorseful and generally unpleasant in his demeanor. Staring stoically into space for most of the trial, Noel gave this assessment of the jurors' characterization of him: "I made up my mind not to react one way or another. I'm sitting there just watching what was going on, making notes for the attorneys. . . . And it's just amazing that I could just sit there doing nothing and that gets twisted into, 'Oh, he's a cold-hearted son of a bitch'" (May, 2002, p. 18A).

Noel apparently believed that sitting expressionless and "doing nothing" would communicate nothing to a jury. Unfortunately for him it communicated volumes. We can't communicate "nothing" as long as others are observing us. Consider facial expressions, for example. Try not to display any facial expressions at all while another person looks at you. It can't be done. Even a blank stare is a facial expression that communicates a message. Others may perceive your blank stare to mean that you're introspective and are thinking deeply or that you don't want to be bothered by anyone or that you're inattentive, sullen, or disdainful.

Gestures and eye contact may seem to be discrete, not continuous, because a specific gesture begins and ends, and eye contact also begins and ends. Not gesturing and no eye contact, however, continue to send messages. Lack of gestures can indicate boredom, relaxation, or awkwardness, and lack of eye contact can indicate disinterest, intimidation, distraction, or a host of other messages.

Nonverbal communication is sometimes unintentional. We blush, blink our eyes rapidly, and shuffle our feet without necessarily intending to do so. We are sharing meaning with others without necessarily wanting to share. People standing before an audience giving speeches may want desperately to hide their nervousness. Nevertheless, their hands may shake, their voices may quaver, and perspiration may form on their brows. The nonverbal message that is likely received by their audience is that they are experiencing speech anxiety. Audience members, in turn, may want to hide their recognition of the anxiety to ease the tension, but averting eye contact with speakers or moving restlessly in their seats may, on the contrary, indicate such recognition.

Interconnectedness of Verbal and Nonverbal Communication

Verbal and nonverbal communication are interconnected. We don't speak without embellishing the words with gestures, facial expressions, tone of voice, eye contact, and so forth. In this section, several ways verbal and nonverbal codes interconnect will be discussed (Ekman & Friesen, 1969).

Repetition

We say, "Yes," and then nod our heads. We give verbal directions and then point in the appropriate direction. We profess our love for individuals and then hug them. We curse at another driver and then shake our fist for emphasis. All of these nonverbal cues repeat the verbal message. This repetition diminishes ambiguity and enhances accuracy of message perception. *Consistency of verbal and nonverbal communication increases the clarity and credibility of the message.*

Accentuation

When we use vocal emphasis such as *"Please* don't touch anything in the store," this accents the message. It adds emphasis where it is desired. "Don't you *ever* say that word" accents the unqualified nature of the verbal message. Pounding your fist on a table as you express your anger nonverbally repeats the message but also accents the depth of your emotion. Accenting enhances the power and seriousness of verbal messages.

Substitution

Sometimes nonverbal cues substitute for verbal messages. A yawn can substitute for the verbal "I'm bored" or "I'm tired." A wave can substitute for a "good-bye." Shaking your head "no" doesn't require a verbalized "no." We signal interest in courting another person without actually having to express this message in words. Eye contact, smiling, forward leans, room-encompassing glances, close distance, frequent nodding, and hair smoothing are just some nonverbal flirting cues (Muehlenhard et al., 1986). A later stage of courtship, sexual initiation, is usually accepted nonverbally but rejected verbally (Metts et al., 1992).

Regulation

Conversation is regulated by nonverbal cues. Turn taking is signaled by long pauses at the end of sentences and eye contact in the direction of the person expected to speak next, especially if the conversation occurs in a group. Interruptions may be prevented by speeding up the rate of speech, raising one's voice over the attempted interruption, or holding up one's hand to signal unwillingness to relinquish the floor. A teacher can recognize a student's desire to speak by pointing to the person. This means "Your turn."

Contradiction

"Sure, I love you," when said with eyes cast sideways and flat vocal tone doesn't exactly inspire believability. Sometimes we contradict verbal messages with nonverbal cues. These are **mixed messages**—inconsistencies between verbal and nonverbal messages. The words say one thing, but gestures, facial expressions, eye contact, posture, tone of voice, and physical proximity leak contradictory information. Leathers (1979) found that mixed messages had a highly disruptive impact on problem-solving groups. Mixed messages produced tension and anxiety, and group members found it difficult to respond to mixed messages in socially appropriate ways (Leathers, 1986).

See Video Clip #6, Chapter 6 on the CD.

Types of Nonverbal Communication

Distinctions between and interconnectedness of verbal and nonverbal communication have been discussed. Let's now explore the main types of nonverbal communication used during transactions with others. Let's begin with nonverbal types that exhibit the vast potential of our bodies and their accoutrements to communicate (physical appearance, face, gestures, touch, and voice). Let's end by discussing space and environment. In each instance, note the power of nonverbal communication and the potential for misunderstandings and miscommunication.

Physical Appearance

How we physically look to others often is the first nonverbal message communicated. Our physical appearance is strongly related to perceptions of physical attractiveness. In this section, body adornments, body shape and size, clothing, and hair will be explored.

BODY ADORNMENTS   He got his first tattoo—a rosary with a cross—etched on the back of his right hand when he was 11 years old. At 13 he had Chinese characters that translate to "Trust no man" tattooed on his left shoulder. At 16 an ornate cross that memorialized his dead older brother was added to his right hand. All of these tattoos were rites of passage into gang life in Watsonville, California for Mando (no last name given). "I had found a way of life," he explains simply (Barnett, 1996). After his brother's death, however, he began questioning his way of life and looking for alternatives. When he searched for a job, though, he found that potential employers would eye his gang tattoos and say, "Sorry, we don't have any openings."

Mando is only one of over 2,000 youths in Santa Cruz County who want to remove their gang-related tattoos and make a fresh start. The county's Youth Resource Bank began a tattoo removal program to help these youths find employment and turn their lives around. Mando was 18 when he had his tattoos removed. Other counties in California, Illinois, and Arizona have started similar tattoo-removal programs. Santa Clara County Superior Court Judge LaDoris Cordell states, "It's certainly an excellent thing to do. From my talking to kids it's a liberating experience to be rid of the mark on them because these kids get stereotyped very quickly, even if they decided to cut their gang affiliation" (Garcia, 1996).

Tattooing, body piercing, and scarification, however, are more popular than ever, especially with teens and young adults. A study by the Mayo Clinic found that of the 454 college students surveyed at Pace University, almost a quarter had body piercings other than ear lobes. Slightly less than a quarter of the students reported having tattoos (O'Neil, 2002). Such body adornment can signify individuality, rebelliousness, and autonomy (Martin, 1997). It can also produce negative reactions from the unadorned. Frequent complaints from customers at restaurants and coffee houses have caused some chains to set restrictions on piercings. The Chili's restaurant chain allows waitstaff to display pierced ears but no other visible body part. Starbucks permits two piercings of the ear only ("Business Bulletin," 1996).

Physical appearance, from adornments we put on our bodies to physical features we accentuate or camouflage, is of no small concern to us. Morris (1985) claims, "Nothing fascinates us quite as much as the human body. Whether we realize it or not, we are all obsessed with physical appearances. Even when we are engaged in a lively conversation and seem to be engrossed in purely verbal communication, we remain ardent body watchers" (p. 7).

BODY SHAPE AND SIZE   Are there any universal standards of physical attractiveness, or do culture and individual taste determine what is attractive and therefore desirable? Certainly culture has an influence. Ubangi women insert wooden disks into their mouths to stretch their lips up to 10 inches in diameter. Unlike the United States, some cultures prefer plump over skinny. In Niger and other countries in West Africa, fat is the female beauty ideal (Onishi, 2001). At one festival in Niger called *Hangandi*, women compete for a prize given to the heaviest contestant. Women train for this beauty contest by gorging themselves and drinking lots of water on the day of the contest. Women also take steroids to bulk up, and some even ingest animal feed advertised as a means to increase body weight. In Mali, the ultimate trophy wife is a fat spouse (McGirk, 1998). The wife's size signifies wealth. In Fiji, body weight indicates how well one's community takes care of its women. The worst insult for a Fijian woman is to say that she has thin legs (McGirk, 1998). In Nigeria, the Warirke people build Fattening Rooms to help young women pile on the pounds to improve their marriage prospects (McGirk, 1998). For 4 weeks the women gorge themselves, doing little else but eating.

The "ideal" voluptuous female figure of the 1950s in the United States is considered fat by today's American beauty standards. There are also individual differences in what is considered physically attractive. Some women find the male body builder physique extremely attractive, and other women think it is repulsive.

Despite cultural differences, some standards of physical attractiveness related to body shape and size seem to be universal. First, symmetry seems to be a universal attractiveness characteristic (Springen, 1997). Diverse cultures favor **bilateral symmetry**—that is, the right and left sides match. Lopsided features of the face (one eye slightly lower than the other, a crooked mouth or nose, uneven ears) are perceived to be less attractive than more symmetrical features.

Second, the waist-to-hip ratio in women was found to be a more important characteristic than facial features, height, body weight, and other physical attributes

(Singh, 1993). Generally, the lower the waist-to-hip ratio—the smaller the waist is compared to the hips—the greater is the perception of attractiveness. This held true whether those judging the female shape were 8 or 80 years old or were from any one of many different cultures and backgrounds (Springen, 1997). The "ideal" shape was a .70 waist-to-hip ratio (the waist is 70% the size of the hips). The range of perceived attractiveness, however, ranged rather broadly from .60 to .80.

Despite the marked change in preferred weight of women reflected in the Rubenesque female of the Renaissance era to the current waiflike body types, the waist-to-hip ratio preference still applies. Singh (1993) found that *Playboy* centerfolds and Miss America winners from 1923 to 1990 stayed within the narrow waist-to-hip ratio of .68 to .72 even though height and total weight varied significantly. Despite the "thin is in" images presented in the American mass media and some cultures' fascination with heavy women, the size of the female body seems to be less important than the body shape.

Some research suggests that an attractive physique for men is relatively broad shoulders and narrow waist and hips (the wedge shape). One study (Lavrakas, 1975) found that this broad at the shoulder and narrow at the hip male body shape is preferred by women, especially when compared to the pear-shaped body (large hips and narrow shoulders). Thus far, however, no ratio similar to the waist-to-hip ratio in women has been documented for male attractiveness across cultures.

Finally, average facial features are considered more attractive than extreme features (Langlois et al., 1994). Very large noses, thin lips, and so forth are less attractive as a rule than average noses, lips, and eyes. This is more true for females, however, than males (Grammer & Thornhill, 1994). Harrison Ford has a rather large nose, but you don't hear many women complaining about his looks.

Despite these universal standards of physical attractiveness, other nonphysical attributes influence perceptions of physical attractiveness. Women, for instance, rated men as more physically and sexually attractive if they were considerate of others and showed sensitivity (Jensen-Campbell et al., 1995). Chalk up another advantage for the competent communicator.

CLOTHING   Physical appearance can be enhanced or diminished in a variety of ways. Clothing expresses a person's identity. "It is impossible to wear clothes without transmitting social signals. Every costume tells a story, often a very subtle one, about its wearer" (Morris, 1977, p. 213). One study of dress in an international airport reported Tongans wearing ceremonial gowns, Sikhs in white turbans, Africans in white dashikis, Hasidic Jews in blue yarmulkes, and Californians in running shorts and halter tops (McDaniel & Andersen, 1995). The variety of clothing choices is astonishing.

Clothing matters. In Afghanistan, the traditional burkas worn by women became a symbol of subjugation in the eyes of most Americans during our war with the Taliban. The burkas covered women from head to toe, making them unrecognizable. Dress communicates social position, economic status, level of sophistication, social background, educational level, personal identity, and even moral character (Thourlby, 1978). Just observe the reactions to dress codes. School uniforms have become increasingly popular in elementary and high schools around the nation—not popular with students but with administrators and parents. Parents and school boards opt for uniforms to combat gang violence provoked by gang colors and attire and to instill a stronger focus on schoolwork over wardrobe. Strict

© Zits Partnership. Reprinted with special permission of King Features Syndicate.

dress codes often substitute for actual uniforms in many schools. Again, students object to the restriction of their "freedom of expression" and to the conformity that rigid dress codes require.

Ironically, as dress codes become more restrictive in schools, they are becoming looser in work environments almost everywhere in the United States. The business suit for men and the power suit for women are losing their popularity. Casual attire—jeans, athletic shoes, shirts/blouses—is the dress of choice. One survey of 505 personnel managers in a wide range of businesses shows that 9 of 10 companies nationwide let inside office staffers dress casually all or part of their work week (The Dress-Down, 1996). Casual dress has become a serious issue in job negotiations. The new dress-down policies help businesses attract top talent, say the managers surveyed. There's a simple reason for this—people prefer comfort to discomfort.

Even casual attire, however, has rules of appropriateness. Clothing choices communicate messages (Gottschalk, 1996). Casual dress at work does not include tight-fitting clothes (too provocative), cutoffs and bare midriffs (too sloppy and unkempt looking), tank tops (too recreational looking), sleeveless muscle shirts (too self-absorbed looking), or running shorts, sweatpants, and sweatbands (gym attire). Clothes that are neat, clean, unwrinkled, loose fitting, and undamaged (no rips or holes) are usually more appropriate for most workplaces.

Appropriate dress is an issue for teachers. One study (Morris et al., 1996) found that formal professional attire received the highest instructor competence ratings from students, with casual professional dress a close second. Casual dress, however, produced the highest sociability ratings (e.g., sociable, cheerful, good natured) from students. Interesting presentation of material was also associated with casual instructor dress. Casual professional dress seems to make instructors more approachable for discussions and more interesting from the student vantage point.

HAIR   Another significant element of physical appearance is hair. In the late 1800s, American Indians were forced to attend federal boarding schools. Upon their arrival, their long hair, a tie to their spiritual heritage, was shorn to "civilize" them. It was a traumatic introduction to White society (Arrillanga, 2001).

Hair style expresses self-concept. The Taliban brutally enforced a law in Afghanistan mandating that all men wear the traditional beard. When the Taliban were driven from power by the United States military, many Afghan men shaved off their beards as a symbolic act of freedom from oppressive rule (Filkins, 2001).

Hair has enormous communicative potential. Following Al Gore's disputed loss to George W. Bush in the 2000 presidential election, "Gore-the-Bore" grew a beard and sent the mass media into a frenzy of speculation and assessment. Gore was repeatedly asked about his new look, but he merely deflected the questions. Suddenly, Gore was his "own man," free from the stiff image he portrayed during the campaign. When actress Keri Russell cut her hair short, changing the look of her character Felicity, executives at the WB network almost had seizures. The new hairstyle was blamed for the sudden drop in ratings of the TV show (WB Lays Down Law, 2000). She was "encouraged" to grow her hair to its previous length.

The short-cropped hairstyle became a national issue in 1994 when Shannon Faulkner attempted to become the first woman to enter The Citadel, a military college in South Carolina. The issue was whether she should receive the same "knob" haircut all the male cadets receive on entering the school. The doorknob-shaped haircut has a communicative purpose. "The whole point is the subjugation of the individual to the interests of the group," explained Dawes Cooke, attorney for the school. "Many cadets have described that haircut as the most humiliating moment of their lives" (Goodman, 1996). "Shave Shannon" bumper stickers emerged all over South Carolina. The issue went to court. The same judge who forced the college to accept Shannon Faulkner ruled, "The Citadel is perfectly at liberty to treat the hair on her head the same way it treats the hair of every other cadet" (Goodman, 1996). This decision was not well received by women's groups. They argued that Shannon Faulkner was being targeted for harassment because she dared to enter an all-male bastion of power. The buzz cut hairstyle is far more humiliating, they claimed, on a woman than on a man. The military hairstyle is a rule made by men with no female input or influence.

Facial Communication

Your eyes and face are the most immediate cues people use to form first impressions of you. In this section, how eyes and face influence communication with others will be discussed.

EYES   Boston College neuropsychology professor Joe Tecce claims stress can be measured by how often someone blinks. Tecce examined the 1996 presidential and vice-presidential debates and found some interesting results. The normal blink rate of someone speaking on television, according to Tecce, is between 31 and 50 blinks per minute. Republican presidential contender Bob Dole averaged 147 blinks per minute. His highest blink rate was 163—nearly 3 blinks per second—when asked the question, "Is the country better off than it was 4 years ago?" President Clinton, who averaged a mere 43 blinks per minute in the 1992 presidential debates with George Bush and Ross Perot, averaged a surprising 99 in the 1996 debate. Clinton spiked to 117 blinks when asked about increases in teenage drug use. Vice-presidential candidates were apparently less stressed. Gore registered a mere 42 and Jack Kemp averaged a sleepy 31. According to Tecce, the faster blinker has lost every presidential election since 1980 (In the Blink, 1996). This may have been true until the 2000 presidential election when Gore averaged 36 blinks per minute to Bush's 48, and we all know how that election turned out (Eyes Wide Open, 2000). Of course, Gore did win the popular vote.

The Tecce blink-rate-equals-stress-level hypothesis is interesting and may have validity, but generalizing from a single-channel nonverbal code requires caution.

The blink rate of Jack Kemp in the 1996 debate was exceedingly low, yet anyone observing Kemp during the debate would have noticed the sheen of perspiration on his face and his stiff posture as well as several verbal miscues. Perspiration, rigid posture, and verbal mistakes suggest stress and nervousness. Gore also manifested greater stress than his eye blinks appeared to indicate. His stiff posture, downward glances, and head movements were those of a person feeling ill at ease. Nonverbal communication is multichanneled. Thus, one nonverbal cue may suggest relaxed demeanor while other nonverbal cues may contradict this observation. Concluding that Kemp and Gore were relaxed from blink rate alone is shaky.

Eye contact is an important aspect of nonverbal communication. Eye contact regulates conversational turn taking, communicates involvement and interest, manifests warmth, and establishes connections with others. It can also command attention, be flirtatious, or seem cold and intimidating (Andersen, 1999).

Interpersonal communication is quite dependent on eye contact, especially in the United States. Eye contact invites conversation. Lack of eye contact is usually perceived to be rude or inattentive. One study (Burgoon et al., 1985) found that of individuals interviewing for a job, those who averted eye contact were less successful than those who maintained eye contact with the interviewer. As you will see in later chapters, eye contact is a critical element of effective public speaking.

Cultures differ regarding the appropriateness of direct eye contact (Samovar & Porter, 1995). In Korea "direct eye contact among unequals connotes competition, constituting an inappropriate form of behavior" (p. 323). Indonesians, Chinese, Japanese, and many Latin Americans will show deference to others by lowering their eyes. This is a sign of respect. It is easy for Americans to misread this nonverbal cue and assume that Asians and Latin Americans lack self-confidence and can be manipulated easily.

Co-cultures within the United States also show different preferences regarding eye contact. Hopi dislike direct eye contact. Navajos have a creation story about a "terrible monster called He-Who-Kills-With-His-Eyes." This story teaches Navajo children that "a stare is literally an evil eye and implies a sexual and aggressive assault" (Understanding Culture, 1974).

Our eyes are highly communicative whether we want them to be or not. Pupil dilation (i.e., pupil opening) offers a subtle but significant cue of arousal or attraction. Experienced gem buyers wear sunglasses to hide pupil dilation that might reveal how much they want to buy a particular gem. In an amazing study (Hess & Goodwin, 1974), students were shown two photos of a mother holding her baby. The photos were identical in all respects, except one photo was retouched to show constricted pupils and the other retouched to show dilated pupils. The students were asked, "Which mother loves her baby more?" Every student chose the mother with the dilated pupils. Most student participants gave reasons other than the dilated pupils, even though pupil dilation was the only difference between the two photos. "She's holding her baby closer," "She has a warmer smile," and "Her face is more pleasant" were some of the explanations offered.

Not surprisingly, heterosexual men display more pupil dilation when viewing photos of women, and gay men display greater pupil dilation when viewing photos of other men (Hess et al., 1965). Pupil dilation is subconsciously perceived during interpersonal interactions and actually may increase the observer's attraction for the person with dilated pupils (Andersen et al., 1980). The soft light of candlelight dinners, moonlight walks, and conversations by firelight produces wider pupils.

This is probably part of the reason such experiences increase romantic attraction (Andersen, 1999). Again, be careful not to read too much into the single nonverbal cue of pupil dilation. A dimly lit restaurant can dilate your pupils even as you're thinking of ways to gracefully end the evening with your date.

FACIAL EXPRESSIONS   "The face is your personal billboard," says Dane Archer. "It never gets totally hidden" (Townsend, 1996). There has been extensive research on facial expressions. Several conclusions can be drawn from this research.

First, the face signals specific emotional states: A smile signals happiness, and a frown signals sadness. Research on facial expressions in 20 Western cultures and 11 nonliterate and isolated cultures shows that members of all of these cultures recognized the same basic emotions from photographs of specific facial expressions. These universal emotions identified by all cultures from specific facial expressions are fear, anger, surprise, contempt, disgust, happiness, and sadness (Ekman, 1994; Matsumoto, 1994).

Second, members of diverse cultures recognize the same emotions from specific facial expressions, but they don't necessarily perceive the same intensity of emotion (e.g., from annoyance to rage) communicated by facial expressions. One study asked

www.mhhe
com/ **rothwell2**

See Online "Face Emotion" test.

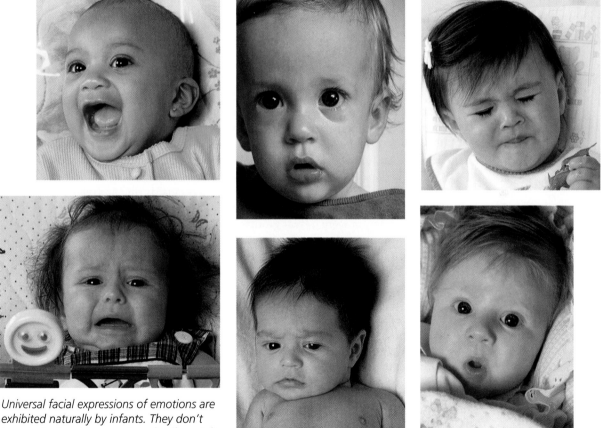

Universal facial expressions of emotions are exhibited naturally by infants. They don't have to be taught expressions for (from left to right) happiness, sadness, disgust, fear, anger, and surprise.

Box 6-3 Sharper Focus

The Girl with No Smile

Smiling is a primary cue that exhibits friendliness and warmth. A smile makes a person approachable. A person who doesn't smile at us can seem distant, even mean. Teachers who rarely if ever smile during class lectures and activities make it difficult for students to ask questions, disagree, or participate in discussions.

Seven-year-old Chelsea Thomas underwent facial surgery on December 16, 1995, to correct her perpetually grumpy facial expression. Chelsea suffered from an unusual condition called Moebius syndrome. She couldn't smile because the nerves that trigger the facial muscles that control smiling were missing. Chelsea's mother described how the inability to smile affected her daughter: "It's been hard for her because people think she's unfriendly or ignoring them or bored. . . . Kids stare at her. Adults are pretty understanding, but she has a worse time with kids" (Girl Undergoes, 1995).

Surgery grafted muscles and nerves from Chelsea's leg to her facial muscles used for chewing, and Chelsea now has a smile. Imagine what it would be like to be unable to smile when we feel joy or perceive humor. Imagine how others would respond to you if you always seemed to be frowning and you had no way of changing the sour expression on your face. Think of what that would do to your self-esteem and to your ability to communicate with others.

Chelsea's inability to smile may have affected even her emotional experience of happiness. Emotions clearly influence facial expressions, but according to the **facial feedback hypothesis** (Adelmann & Zajonc, 1989), the reverse is also true; facial expressions can influence emotions. In one study (Strack et al., 1988), those individuals who held a pen between their teeth parallel to their mouth rated cartoons as funnier than did those individuals who held a pen perpendicular to their mouth with their lips. Why? Because holding a pen between your teeth forces you to smile, but holding a pen with your lips forces you to frown. Try it. Do you seem happier when biting the pen than when holding it in your lips?

---

members in 10 different cultures to rate the intensity of the perceived emotions exhibited by facial expressions. Significant differences were found. Non-Asian cultures rated the emotions as more intense than did Asian cultures (Ekman et al., 1987).

Third, there are also differences in display rules for facial expressions. **Display rules** are culture-specific prescriptions for appropriateness of behaviors (Ekman, 1993). The Japanese would be more likely than Americans to suppress a negative emotion (e.g., anger, contempt) if the emotion occurs during a private conversation and the target of the emotion is an in-group member. If, however, the target of the negative emotion were a rival group or individual, Japanese would be more likely than Americans to display the emotion. Showing contempt or anger toward one of your own group members creates disharmony and may hurt the group. Showing anger or contempt to a competitive rival, however, may create in-group cohesion (Matsumoto, 1990).

Facial expressions influence our self-esteem and color the reactions others have to us (Box 6-3). They usually occur when we interact with others, not when we are alone. Smiling, for instance, is primarily transactional. Smiling occurs with much greater frequency and to a greater degree in the presence of other highly involved individuals than it does when a person is alone (Andersen, 1999). This is true of most facial expressions.

Gestural Communication

Gestures are everywhere. When we communicate with others, gestures accompany our verbal messages, even when we aren't aware that we're using them. Individuals who talk on the telephone usually gesture while they are talking even though the person on the other end cannot see the gestures. When we communicate with others, we often are wiggling, fidgeting, finger-tapping, hand-waving, toe-tapping, arm-flailing bodies in motion. There are three main categories of gestures: manipulators, illustrators, and emblems (Ekman, 1992).

Manipulators are gestures made by one part of the body, usually the hands, that rub, pick, squeeze, clean, or groom another part of the body. They have no specific meaning, although people observing such manipulators may perceive nervousness, discomfort, or deceit. Manipulators, however, also occur when a person is relaxed and feeling energized and when no deceit is occurring. Nevertheless, studies show that people will mistakenly judge deceitfulness when a person exhibits many manipulators (Ekman, 1992). The important point is not to jump to conclusions concerning what manipulators mean.

Illustrators are gestures that help explain what a person says to another person. They have no independent meaning of their own. Telling a person to go to the left and then pointing in the appropriate direction is an example of an illustrator. Describing how to zig-zag, while drawing the movement in the air, is another example. Many of the unconscious gestures we make that emphasize what we are saying are illustrators.

Emblems are gestures that have precise meanings separate from verbal communication. The hand wave communicates "good-bye" in the United States. There are fewer than 60 emblems used in the United States. Israel, however, uses more than 250 (Ekman, 1992).

No emblems are unique to the United States. The French, however, have a unique gesture for "He's drunk." The gesture is a fist placed around the nose and twisted. Germans have a unique "good luck" emblem that consists of two fists with the thumbs inside pounding an imaginary table (Ekman et al., 1984).

Many common emblems, especially obscene or vulgar ones, have spread to other cultures around the world. The extended middle finger is recognized almost everywhere as an obscene gesture and is used widely beyond the borders of the United States. Some Latin American cultures add to the gesture by extending the middle finger while raising the arm abruptly and grabbing the arm with the other hand.

The competent communicator needs to be mindful of the vast potential for misunderstanding inherent in the gestural code (see Box 6-4). Very few gestures are emblems with precise meanings in all contexts. Most gestures are far more ambiguous and require sophisticated interpretation tied specifically to the transactions and contexts in which they occur. Folding your arms across your chest, for example, may mean that you are closing yourself off to others in a defensive gesture, or it may simply be a comfortable way for you to rest your arms. Be cautious when interpreting the meaning of gestures. When you do interpret the meaning of gestures, match them with other nonverbal codes and look for consistency of meaning.

Touch Communication

There are approximately 5 million touch receptors in our skin, about 3,000 in a single fingertip, all sending messages through our spinal cord to our brain. Skin is the largest organ in the human body, covering about 19 sq ft on the average-sized human (Colt, 1997). Touching skin is an enormously powerful and important communication code, as you will see in this section.

Box 6-4   Sharper Focus

Cultural Diversity and Gestural Confusion

As cultures increasingly mix and countries become multicultural, misunderstanding can occur when the meaning of a specific emblem differs across cultures. The thumb inserted between the index and middle fingers is an old American gesture commonly used playfully with children that typically means, "I've got your nose!" This same gesture is a nonverbal invitation to have sex in Germany, Holland, and Denmark, but in Portugal and Brazil it wishes a person good luck or protection. The palm-up index finger waggle is the beckoning gesture used in the United States, but in Japan, Indonesia, Hong Kong, and Australia this gesture is restricted to beckoning animals. Using it to beckon people would be perceived as an insult (Axtell, 1998).

Shared gestures don't always produce shared meaning, especially across cultures. One large study of 40 different cultures isolated 20 common hand gestures,
all of which had different meanings in each culture (Morris et al., 1979). Pointing to objects with the index finger in parts of Central Africa is deemed vulgar and crude. The "A-OK" gesture in the United States that forms a circle with the index finger and the thumb is an obscenity in some Latin American countries and an insult in France (meaning worthless or zero) but a symbol for money in Japan (Axtell, 1998). If an American businessperson were to signal A-OK at the end of a deal to a Japanese businessperson, it could easily be perceived as a request for a bribe. In Texas, the "hook-'em horns" rallying gesture in which the thumb and little finger are extended and the remaining three fingers are curled, is the *cornuto* gesture in Italy. The cornuto is an insulting gesture that accuses one's spouse of unfaithfulness. In Brazil and Venezuela, however, the same gesture is a sign of good luck (Axtell, 1998).

SIGNIFICANCE OF TOUCH   American playwright Tennessee Williams testified to the power of touch when he wrote, "Devils can be driven out of the heart by the touch of a hand on a hand, or a mouth on a mouth" (Colt, 1997). Premature babies studied at Miami's Touch Research Institute show the remarkable benefits of touch to human well-being. With just three 10-min gentle massages each day, premature babies will become more alert, responsive, and active than infants of the same size and condition who are not massaged. Premature infants who are massaged will tolerate noise, sleep more soundly, gain weight 47% faster, and leave the hospital an average of 6 days sooner than will premature babies who are not massaged (Colt, 1997). With 430,000 premature babies born in the United States each year, the 6-day earlier hospital departure would translate into a $4 billion annual savings if gentle baby massage were practiced in all hospitals.

Voluminous research on infant and child development reveals that touch is not only beneficial, but also even critical for life itself. Infants in orphanages who do not receive much, if any, touch from other humans are usually maladjusted and quiet and show difficulty learning and maturing normally (Andersen, 1999). During Romania's strife in the early 1990s, thousands of infants were warehoused in orphanages, virtually alone in their cribs for 2 years. They were found to be severely impaired by the lack of physical contact, and some even died.

Touch has an impact on emotional health and well-being. Massage is a stress reducer. Approximately 25 million Americans visit massage therapists each year (Colt, 1997). A growing number of businesses and institutions offer massage in the workplace. Volunteer therapists gave massages to exhausted rescue workers, traumatized survivors, and medical pathologists to help them cope with the bombing of a federal building in Oklahoma City in 1996 (Colt, 1997).

Touch is essential to the expression of love, warmth, intimacy, and concern for others. Misuse of touch can repel, frighten, or anger others. Touch communicates power. Sexual harassment is often an issue of inappropriate, unwanted touch communication. Those with greater power typically feel less constraint in touching those with less power. Touch can also be quite influential. When teachers touched students on the arm at the beginning and at the end of a conference, there was a 25% increase in positive evaluations of the teacher-student conference (Steward & Lupfer, 1987). Waitresses receive bigger tips, on average, when they touch patrons subtly (Crusco & Wetzel, 1984). Psychologists gain greater compliance from their clients when they touch them appropriately (Patterson et al., 1986). Even shoppers purchase more merchandise when they are unobtrusively touched (Smith et al., 1982).

Despite the clear benefits of touch communication, Americans are "touchy about touch." Psychologist Tiffany Field, director of the Touch Research Institute, worries that Americans are becoming touch phobic (Colt, 1997). The growing concern about sexual harassment and child abuse has created a "touching is taboo" atmosphere. The National Education Association, the voice of 2 million teachers in the United States, uses the slogan "Teach, don't touch."

Compared with other cultures, Americans are a "nontactile society." Field found that French parents and children touch each other three times as often as do American parents and children, a pattern that doesn't vary with age. Field compared French and American teenagers in Paris and Miami McDonald's restaurants. French adolescents engaged in significantly more casual touch (leaning on a friend, putting an arm around another person's shoulder) than American teens. Field also concluded that "French parents and teachers alike are more physically affectionate and the kids are less aggressive" (cited in Colt, 1997, p. 62). The French, however, are not the "touchiest" culture. One study found that Italian and Greek dyads (pairs) touched more than French, English, and Dutch dyads (Remland et al., 1995).

TYPES OF TOUCH   There are several types of touching. Knowing which type of touch is appropriate for which context is a vital concern to the competent communicator. Heslin (1974) identified five types of touching based on their function, usage, and intensity.

The **functional-professional touch** is the least intense form of touching. The touch is instrumental communication that takes place between doctors and patients, coaches and athletes, and the like. Lately, teacher-student touch communication is limited to this type, if engaged in at all. Functional-professional touching is businesslike and limited to the requirements of the situation. A nurse helping a patient sit up in bed or a football coach demonstrating the "bump-and-run" are examples.

The **social-polite touch** occurs during initial introductions, business relationships, and formal occasions. The handshake is the standard form of social-polite touch in American culture. Many European cultures greet strangers with a hug and a perfunctory kiss on each cheek.

The **friendship-warmth touch** is the most ambiguous type of touch and leads to the most misunderstandings between people. The amount of touch has to be negotiated when showing friendship and warmth toward others. Too little touch may communicate unfriendliness, indifference, and coldness. Too much touch that seems too intimate communicates sexual interest when such interest may not be wanted. Friendly touches, especially those taking place in private, can mistakenly be perceived as sexual, especially by males (Andersen, 1999).

The **love and intimacy touch** is reserved only for a very few, special individuals—close friends, family members, spouses, and lovers. This is not sexual touch, although it may blend with sexual touch. Tenderly holding a friend's hand, softly touching the cheek of a spouse, and hugging are examples of this type of touch.

This is "The Kiss." Al Gore plants a wet one on his wife, Tipper, at the 2000 Democratic national convention just before he delivers his acceptance speech as his party's nominee for President of the United States. According to columnist, Molly Ivins, there were 138 stories in the media about this event, most speculating that maybe Al Gore wasn't a stiff, boring, "policy wonk" after all. Perhaps he was a man capable of great passion. A kiss isn't "just a kiss."

The **sexual touch** is the most personal, intimate touch and the most restricted. Mutual consent regarding this type of touch is the most important consideration to the competent communicator. Engaging in this type of touch when it is unwanted will produce serious repercussions.

Appropriateness of touch largely depends on understanding which type of touch is acceptable and desirable in which situation. *Types of touch help define relationships between people.* If one person initiates a friendship touch but the other person recoils because no real friendship has been established, then clearly this type of touch is inappropriate. Both parties must define their relationship similarly or problems will occur. Ignoring the social-polite touch during introductions can provoke a negative response from the party shown such indifference and disrespect. Choosing to engage in too much or too little touch communication in a particular situation can send a powerful message.

TOUCH TABOOS   There are many touch taboos both within our own culture and in other cultures. According to research conducted in the United States (Jones, 1994), about 15% of all touches on a daily basis are unwanted and rejected. A manual published by the University of California at San Francisco instructs nurses not to touch

Cambodians on the head. That is where they believe their soul resides. Greeting a Muslim by shaking his or her left hand is an insult because the left hand is reserved for toilet functions. In Korea, young people are forbidden to touch the shoulders of their elders. Kim (1992) notes, "Southeast Asians do not ordinarily touch during a conversation, especially one between opposite sexes, because many Asian cultures adhere to norms that forbid displays of affection and intimacy" (p. 321).

There are several forms of taboo touching in the United States. The competent communicator manifests sensitivity by recognizing these forbidden forms of touch and adopting more appropriate communication behavior (Jones, 1994). These touch taboos are as follows:

1. *Avoid touching strangers.* Nonfunctional touch is usually perceived as too intimate and personal. Inevitable jostling and bumping take place in crowded elevators, buses, stores, and the like. The American norm is to apologize when we bump or otherwise touch a stranger. Sexual touch by a stranger is highly inappropriate, even cause for arrest.

2. *Avoid harmful touches.* Children have to learn early that hurting someone by hitting, biting, or scratching is forbidden. Even if the person who inflicts the hurt is a spouse or partner and the hurt is accidental, the recipient of the painful touch will cry out in protest.

3. *Avoid startling touches.* Sneaking up on people and tapping them on the shoulder when they think they are alone will likely startle them and produce a strong negative response. There is no equivalent immediate countermove a person can use. You can't startle the person who just tapped you on the shoulder. Even though the startling touch is sometimes done playfully, most people resent being startled.

4. *Avoid the interruption touch.* Touches should not interfere with principal activities. Throwing your arms around your partner and hugging him or her tightly while your partner desperately tries to mix ingredients for dinner interrupts the primary activity. It will likely produce rejection of the touch. Trying to kiss your partner on the lips when he or she is trying to watch an engrossing movie will also likely produce rejection.

5. *Don't move others.* This is especially important advice when dealing with strangers. Ushering people from one place to another without warning or permission is usually seen as an aggressive act. Warning people that they need to move and offering a quick explanation, however, can nullify the negative reaction to being moved by someone. "Excuse me, I need to get through" or "Watch out, this coffee is very hot," followed by a touch gently moving a person out of the way likely will not produce the negative response that touch alone will produce.

6. *Avoid "rub-it-in" touches.* Don't intensify a negative remark with a touch. A husband pinching the thigh of his wife and remarking, "That's pretty fattening," as she orders a dessert, inappropriately rubs in the nasty dig. A woman who slaps her male partner's arm as she tells him, "Walk your mother to her car" intensifies the rebuke.

Dealing with those who violate touch taboos is fairly straightforward (Jones, 1994). Determining how accidental or purposeful the violation is will guide you in your response. Unintentional lapses of touch protocol are easily forgiven. Intentional violations usually require a stronger response.

Here are some suggestions for dealing competently with touch violations:

1. *Begin by assuming the violation is accidental.* Your nonverbal rejection—pulling away, frowning, and so forth—may be all that's required to convey the message that the touch is unwanted and inappropriate.

2. *Use descriptive statements* to identify your reaction and the behavior that ignited it. "I don't like to be moved out of the way like that. It seems aggressive, so please don't do it" is an example.

3. *Use intense nonverbal cues when faced with a purposeful violator.* Hard core touch violators are fond of putting the person who is upset on the defensive with statements such as "Don't be so touchy" or "Lighten up, I didn't mean anything by it." No need to engage in a tit-for-tat verbal competition. A prolonged glower, a disgusted look held for a bit longer than usual, or a penetrating stare without comment can make the violator very uncomfortable and communicate the appropriate message.

4. *Give repeat offenders strong nonverbal signs of rejection plus a direct, firm command.* "Don't ever touch me that way again" or "Don't ever grab my shoulder" are examples.

5. *Offer a brief apology after your own touch violation.* If you inadvertently violate a touch taboo, simply apologize. "Oh, I'm sorry. I didn't mean to bump you."

Voice Communication

Our voice is second only to our face in communicating our emotions. Our voice communicates information about our age, sex, socioeconomic status, ethnicity, and regional background. Vocal cues, or paralanguage, are usually divided into three classifications (Samovar & Porter, 1995): *vocal characterizers* (laughing, yelling, moaning, crying, whining, belching, yawning), *vocal qualifiers* (volume, tone, pitch, resonance, rhythm, rate), and *vocal segregates* ("uh-huh," "uh," "mm-hmm," "oooh," "shh"). A whispering soft voice may indicate speech anxiety when it is used in front of a large audience. A flat, monotone voice can induce sleep in listeners. Speaking at hyperspeed may communicate nervousness and excitement. Typically, listeners prefer a speaking rate that approximates their own speech pattern (Buller & Aune, 1992).

There are cultural differences regarding vocal communication. Arabs speak very loudly because it connotes strength and sincerity. Israelis view high volume as a sign of strong beliefs on an issue. Germans assume a "commanding tone that projects authority and self-confidence" (Ruch, 1989, p. 191). People from Thailand, Japan, and the Philippines tend to speak very softly, almost in a whisper. This communicates good manners and education. Laughing signals joy in Japan, but laughing often camouflages displeasure, anger, embarrassment, and sorrow (McDaniel, 2000).

Space Communication

Space communicates in very powerful and significant ways. Much of human history is a narration about wars fought over who controls what space. In this section, the influence that distance and territoriality have on our communication with others is discussed.

DISTANCE   Anthropologist Edward Hall (1969) has identified four types of spatial relationships based on distances between individuals communicating. These four types are intimate, personal, social, and public distances. The actual distances in

Table 6-1 Four Types of Spatial Relationships and Their Characteristics in Mainstream U.S. Culture			
Type	**Distance**	**Usage of Nonverbal Cues**	**Overlapping Nonverbal Cues**
Intimate	0–18 in.	Loving; showing tenderness	Limited eye contact; touch; smell
Personal	18 in.–4 ft	Conversing with intimates, friends	Eye contact; some touching; gestures
Social	4 ft–12 ft	Business talk; social conversing	Formal vocal tone; gestures; eye contact
Public	12 ft or more	Lectures; speeches	Eye contact; gestures; vocal tones

each category vary according to culture. The distances, their usages, and overlapping nonverbal cues for each distance for the mainstream culture of the United States are shown in Table 6-1.

The distance zones identified by Hall are averages. Individual preferences vary within a culture. Typically, strangers stepping into an intimate zone will produce great discomfort, even hostility. This is usually perceived as an aggressive act. An intimate partner, however, who avoids the intimate zone signals a distancing in the relationship. Counselors look for such cues to signal trouble or disagreement between relationship partners even when couples verbally insist that a problem doesn't exist. We signal that we are "far apart" in negotiations by moving away literally from our adversaries in the bargaining process.

Sometimes we are forced into intimate zones with strangers. A crowded elevator is an example. Being forced to rub elbows with individuals we've never met before is uncomfortable. Usually, when the intimacy zone is violated through nobody's fault, we try to establish a psychic distance from others. That is why occupants of crowded elevators often stare at the numbers indicating what floor is coming up next. This act distances us mentally from strangers and allows us to cope with an uncomfortable situation.

The personal space of short people is more often violated than that of tall people. In one observational study (Caplan & Goldman, 1981), short males (5 ft 5 in.) had their personal space invaded more than twice as often (69% to 31%) as tall males (6 ft 2 in.). Men also claim a larger personal spatial bubble around themselves than do women (Mercer & Benjamin, 1980).

In a multicultural country such as the United States, opportunities for misunderstanding associated with spatial zones are plentiful. Comfortable social distance for an Arab may violate personal or even intimate zones of Americans. Arabs typically move very close when conversing. Part of the reason for this is that Arabs perceive a person's smell to be an extension of the person and, thus, important. Hall (1969) describes the importance of smells to Arabs during conversation:

> Not only is it [smell] one of the distance-setting mechanisms, but it is a vital part of the complex system of behavior. Arabs consistently breathe on people when they talk. However, this habit is more than a matter of different manners. To the Arab good smells are pleasing and a way of being involved with each other. To smell one's friends is desirable, for to deny him your breath is to act ashamed. Americans, on the other hand, trained as they are not to breathe in people's faces, automatically communicate shame in trying to be polite (p. 149).

Not recognizing the cultural differences associated with distance can make an individual seem pushy and aggressive or distant and standoffish.

Rick Lazio moves away from his podium toward Hillary Clinton in their U.S. Senate debate in New York. In a New York Times/CBS News poll immediately following the debate, 53% of men and 56% of women thought Lazio was "too aggressive." Only 4% of men and 5% of women thought Clinton was too aggressive. Lazio's invasion of Hillary's space, at one point standing beside her, certainly didn't help him in this regard. Some women interviewed said Lazio acted like "a bully."

TERRITORIALITY   "To have a territory is one of the essential components of life; to lack one is one of the most precarious of all conditions" (Hall, 1973, p. 45). **Territoriality** is a predisposition to defend a fixed geographic area, or territory, as one's exclusive domain (Burgoon et al., 1996).

We stake out our territory in a variety of ways (Burgoon et al., 1996). We use *markers* such as hedges, small fences, and signs saying, "Keep Out." A coat left on the back of a chair marks temporary possession of that specific seat. Resting a lunch tray on a table in a cafeteria signals, "That's my eating area." We also claim a territory by erecting *barriers to entry*, using walls, locked doors, security guards, and snarling dogs (see Box 6-5). When office space is limited, we erect partitions that make our environment look like a rabbit warren. A third way that we stake out our territory is by *occupancy*. Students who sit in the same chair every class period quickly assume the chair is their recognized place. Homeless people often establish their spot on the street by consistently occupying that small territory.

Invasions of territories (homes, offices) by others are usually met with physical and verbal aggression. One notable form of such territorial invasion is loud, obnoxious noise from neighbors. Walls prevent outsiders from physically intruding into one's home. Loud noise from megadecibel stereos, however, penetrates the walls. You can't move your home like you can your automobile to escape the intrusion. Such territorial invasions have become a serious social problem in Great Britain where people live much closer together than they do typically in the United States. A survey in 1995 conducted by Britain's Chartered Institute of Environmental Health reported 162,000 prosecutions for noise offenses in the preceding year, most from late-night loud music (English Find, 1996). Prosecution of these offenses became necessary because of the high number of violent confrontations between neighbors triggered by excessive noise. In most other social situations, however, individuals are reluctant to use even verbal means to ward off intruders. Most individuals prefer

Box 6-5 | Focus on Controversy

Gated Communities

There are approximately 20,000 gated communities in the United States (Blakely & Snyder, 1997). One poll showed that 65% of respondents would like to live in a gated community (The Gate Debate, 1997). Gated communities come in many varieties. Some are housing projects that require using a keypad code to open a metal gate blocking access to the community. Other gated communities have erected much more elaborate barriers to entrance. Gates may be accompanied by fences surrounding the community, armed guards, security patrols, and tire-piercing devices that are triggered by improper entrance. The Hidden Valley community in Santa Clarita, California (a gated neighborhood of 400 homes), discourages intruders with a military-style antiterrorist device that launches a 3-ft metal cylinder from ground level into the bottom of any car trying to sneak past the gate. This device disables and seriously damages the intruder's car.

Protection of personal property and security against crimes of violence are the primary motivators for gating a community. Proponents claim they feel safer and that gated neighborhoods promote a sense of community where everybody knows everybody else. Opponents see it differently. Edward Blakely, dean of the School of Urban Planning and Development at the University of Southern California, warns, "Gated communities will accelerate the economic and social fragmentation of the nation" (D. Diamond, 1997, p. 4).

The desire to be safe in person and property cannot be taken lightly. Do gated communities afford real security or merely the illusion of safety? Ed Cross, member of the San Antonio planning commission and a real estate broker, claims, "People are living with a false sense of security. It's a marketing gimmick; it's a fad" (D. Diamond, 1997, p. 5). Blakely and Mary Gail Snyder (1997), authors of *Fortress America*, note that crime rates typically drop in the first year or two after a neighborhood becomes gated, but thereafter crime rates rise to levels equivalent to outside areas. In 1984, the 4,800 residents of Sudden Valley, a gated community in Bellingham, Washington, voted to tear down their five gates. Most residents felt that the gates enticed burglars instead of deterring them. When the gates were removed, crime rates went down (D. Diamond, 1997).

Regardless of who's right in this debate, gated communities manifest an adversarial, competitive territoriality (Blakely & Snyder, 1997). They signal to the outside world, "Keep Out!" Gated communities segregate in-groups and out-groups. Dividing America into thousands of enclaves homogenizes neighborhoods and very likely promotes divisiveness and conflict among groups. We see ourselves as adversaries competing for space. Out-group members resent the restriction on their freedom of travel.

Typically, gated communities are affordable only to the well off or the rich. A poor family's gated community consists of a locked apartment building. Finding common ground among ethnic groups and socioeconomic classes, developing opportunities for cooperation, working together as teams to make decisions and to solve personal and societal problems are probably more difficult when we wall ourselves in against those who look different and act differently from us. As Blakely puts it, "The nation's dream was equality and mutual assistance and the melting pot. . . . Take that away and we're just people who live on a piece of territory" (D. Diamond, 1997, p. 5).

Questions for Thought

1. Do you like the idea of gated communities? Would you like to live in a gated community? Is it ethical to create these enclaves that keep out mostly minorities and the poor?
2. Can you think of alternatives to gated communities that might produce the benefits proponents occur without closing off communication with groups who can't afford to live in such neighborhoods?

to avoid interaction or eventually to depart (for a summary of this research see Burgoon et al., 1996).

Environment

Winston Churchill once said, "We shape our buildings, then our buildings shape us." The design of our environment shapes communication. Airports and fast-food restaurants are designed with brightly lit buildings and uncomfortable plastic furniture to hurry people along and limit communication transactions. Such spaces are not meant for loitering, intimate communication, or relaxation. The environment communicates, "Do your business and leave."

Recently jails and prisons have been designed with communication in mind. The traditional prison environment provides little privacy and personal space, separates prisoners from guards, and restricts inmates' mingling. The Federal Bureau of Prisons began building prisons with a different design to encourage direct supervision of inmates. Prisons were built with open areas for inmate interactions. Guards mingle directly with prisoners, enabling them to develop ongoing relationships with the inmates and spot trouble before it explodes. There are no enclosed booths for officers. Inmates have small rooms, not cells with bars. Inmates control the lights in their rooms. There are more televisions available to reduce conflicts over which programs to watch. Furniture is "soft" (cushy and comfortable) not institutional "hard" (plastic and resistant), and floors are carpeted. These new prisons, despite their innovativeness, actually cost less to build than traditional jails (Wener et al., 1987).

Violent incidents are reduced 30% to 90% in the new prisons compared to traditional prisons. Inmate rape is virtually nonexistent, and vandalism and graffiti drop precipitously. Guards, hesitant at first, feel safer, and tension among inmates is reduced (Wener et al., 1987). Inmates still perceive direct-supervision jails as prisons, but the communication outcomes are dramatically different from those of traditional jails.

Communicating Competently with Nonverbal Codes

Knowledge of the myriad ways nonverbal codes influence our communication with others is the first step toward competent nonverbal communication. As indicated repeatedly throughout this chapter, appropriateness and effectiveness of nonverbal communication are key parts of the competence equation. Suggestions have been offered already on how you might improve your understanding and skill in nonverbal communication. This section will tie together common threads, linking all the nonverbal codes to communication competence.

Monitor Nonverbal Communication

Knowledge is not useful if it isn't applied. Use your knowledge of nonverbal codes to monitor your own communication and the communication of others. Observe nonverbal communication in action. Become sensitive to the subtleties of these codes. Try experimenting. Maintain eye contact during interviews or in conversations with others. Observe how this affects the outcome of the communication. Try appropriate touching to see if it produces greater closeness and more positive responses from others. If you tend toward a monotone voice, enliven it on purpose. If your facial expressions tend to be constrained, try to communicate your emotions with more dramatic facial expressions.

Resist Jumping to Conclusions

By now you should be aware that nonverbal communication can be highly ambiguous. Don't make the mistake that others have made. Don't assume that you can "read a person like a book," especially if you don't know that person well. Knowing the person well reduces the ambiguity of nonverbal cues. Nonverbal cues suggest certain messages, but you must consider them in their appropriate context. The easiest way to determine if you have interpreted nonverbal cues correctly is to ask. Check your perceptions with others. "I noticed you tapping your fingers and tugging at your ear. Are you nervous or upset about something?" is a quick way to determine if your nonverbal read is accurate.

Observe Multiple Nonverbal Cues

Relying on a single nonverbal cue will often produce a false perception. Blinking rate may suggest relaxed demeanor, but observe other nonverbal cues as well (e.g., posture, gestures). Silence may indicate disagreement, but do other nonverbal cues contradict this assessment? Be careful not to make a broad generalization based on a single nonverbal cue. Look for nonverbal clusters to determine more accurately what is being communicated.

Recognize Cultural Differences

The vast differences in cultural use of nonverbal codes have been stressed repeatedly. When you communicate with individuals from another culture or co-culture in the United States, recognize the nonverbal communication differences. If you come across a nonverbal cue that puzzles you, don't assume anything. Observe members of other cultures to determine what is appropriate behavior. If you still feel doubtful about your interpretation, check your perception by asking someone who would know.

Strive for Consistency

Try to match verbal and nonverbal communication. Mixed messages confuse those who communicate with us. Exhibiting nonverbal behavior that contradicts what we are saying will produce a negative reaction from others.

Get in Sync with Others

Fast talkers need to slow down when they are conversing with slow talkers. Getting "out of sync" with another person means that you aren't matching his or her nonverbal communication. "Dress for success" means adopting a style of clothing and attire that matches what other people wear within a specific context. Yelling when another person is talking softly, gesturing when another person is using almost no gestures, touching when the other person does not return the touching, and slouching in a chair with feet propped on a coffee table when other people are sitting straight in their chairs with feet firmly planted on the ground can produce awkward, counterproductive communication. Try practicing more synchronous communication. Match more closely what other people do and see what happens. This doesn't require blind conformity. Determine when synchrony is most important and when you desire productive outcomes. Knowing when matching is critical and when it doesn't much matter puts you in charge.

Summary

Nonverbal communication affects our communication with others in powerful ways, yet nonverbal communication is often ambiguous and difficult to read. Much of the advice on nonverbal communication offered in the popular media is incorrect or overstated because a single nonverbal cue is given too much emphasis. Specific advice on communicating competently has been offered for each of the numerous types of nonverbal communication (physical appearance, facial communication, gestures, touch, voice, space, and environment), but general, overlapping advice also has been offered: Monitor your nonverbal communication, resist jumping to conclusions based on a single nonverbal cue, observe multiple nonverbal cues before drawing conclusions about others, recognize vast cultural differences in nonverbal communication, strive for consistency in your verbal and nonverbal communication to avoid mixed messages, and get in sync with others to improve connection.

Quizzes Without Consequences

www.mhhe
com/**rothwell2**

Go to *Quizzes Without Consequences* at the book's Online Learning Center at **www.mhhe.com/rothwell2** or access the CD-ROM for *In the Company of Others.*

Key Terms

See Audio Flashcards Study Aid.

www.mhhe
com/**rothwell2**

See Crossword Puzzle Study Aid.

bilateral symmetry
display rules
emblems
facial feedback
  hypothesis
friendship-warmth
  touch

functional-professional
  touch
illustrators
love and intimacy
  touch
manipulators

mixed messages
nonverbal
  communication
sexual touch
social-polite touch
territoriality

Suggested Readings

Axtel, R. E. (1998). *Gestures: The do's and taboos of body language around the world.* New York: John Wiley & Sons. This is a very entertaining presentation of intercultural variations in gestures.

Ekman, P. (1992). *Telling lies: Clues to deceit in the marketplace, politics, and marriage.* New York: W. W. Norton. This is a fine treatment of nonverbal communication that focuses on deceit.

Hall, E. (1959, 1973). *The silent language.* New York: Doubleday. This book popularized the subject of nonverbal communication. It is far superior to most other mass-market books on the subject.

Montagu, A. (1986). *Touching: The human significance of the skin*. New York: Harper & Row. This is the classic work on touch communication by an internationally renowned anthropologist.

Film School

The Birdcage (1996). Comedy; R ★★★⭒
A very amusing remake of *La Cage Aux Folles* about a gay couple "acting straight" to fool a conservative U.S. Senator. Analyze the main characters' nonverbal behavior, especially when Robin Williams attempts to teach Nathan Lane to act like a straight male. Are these merely stereotypic male behaviors or is there truth in the depiction?

Mrs. Doubtfire (1993). Comedy; PG-13 ★★★★
Robin Williams assumes the role of an Irish nanny to be near his children when he and his wife (Sally Field) split up. Does Williams get the "feminine" behaviors correct? Analyze the different types of nonverbal behavior exhibited by Mrs. Doubtfire. Are these merely stereotypic feminine behaviors?

Quest for Fire (1982). Drama; R ★★★★⭒
A very original film about humankind's initial attempts to make fire. Concentrate on the importance of nonverbal communication, especially since the "language" depicted in the movie is very limited. What are the limitations on nonverbal cues for communication?

Tootsie (1982). Comedy; PG ★★★★★
This is the classic "cross-dressing" film. Dustin Hoffman's portrayal of Dorothy Michaels, who is actually the out-of-work actor Michael Dorsey, was Oscar worthy. Why does Hoffman's portrayal seem genuine? Did he make any mistakes in his nonverbal portrayal of a middle-aged woman?

CHAPTER 7

Listening to Others

We have speech contests but no listening contests. We give awards to great speakers but not to great listeners. A list of the 100 greatest speakers of all time doesn't seem ludicrous, but a list of the 100 greatest listeners of all time seems odd at best. Until recently, listening has been an underappreciated part of communication in our hypercompetitive society. Speaking, not listening, earns us power and status. The necessity to train people to be effective listeners is a relatively recent revelation. Twenty-five years ago, finding a college course on listening would have been a challenge. Today, many colleges offer such a course. Colleges that do not will usually offer a listening unit in a communication course.

Abundant research testifies to the importance of competent listening. Listening consumes more of a college student's time than any other communication activity. College students devote 53% of their communication time to listening, on average, but only 14% to writing, 16% to speaking, and 17% to reading (Barker et al., 1981). Poor listening in college produces poor academic performance. Sleeping or daydreaming your way through classes thwarts the learning process.

In the workplace, we spend an abundant amount of time listening. The average worker spends 55% of his or her time at work listening, 23% speaking, slightly more than 13% reading, and a little more than 8% writing (U.S. Department of Labor, 1991). Numerous studies identify listening as the most important communication skill necessary to obtain a job and earn a promotion (Wolvin & Coakley, 1996).

Interpersonally, listening is extremely important. When college students listened to taped conversations, the people who talked substantially more than they listened were the least liked (Wolvin & Coakley, 1996). In another study, adults said that listening was the most important communication skill in family and social situations (Wolvin, 1984).

Listening is a vitally important communication activity, but most of us receive little training in listening. We all have extensive experience listening to others. Experience alone, however, may be a very poor teacher. Without proper training, experience may simply reinforce bad habits. As Mortimer Adler (1983) observes, "How utterly amazing is the general assumption that the ability to listen well is a natural gift for which no training is required" (p. 5).

Experience without training produces many lousy listeners. Elgin (1989) observes that some individuals have had "nonlistening habits for so long that they are almost incapable of listening—if they had a listening gland, it would be atrophied from disuse" (p. 90). Poor listening is a key element in unhappy relationships (Hite, 1987). Speech professor Wayne Cameron (cited in Adler & Towne, 1999) confirmed the worst fear of college instructors delivering lectures to a room full of students. A gun was fired (not their worst fear) at random intervals during a lecture. Students were asked immediately to record their thoughts. Only 20% were mildly attentive to the lecture, and a mere 12% were actively listening. The rest were pursuing erotic thoughts (20%); reminiscing (20%); or worrying, daydreaming, or thinking about lunch or religion (8%).

Listening is important. We don't do it very well, and we receive scant instruction regarding how to improve it. *The principal purpose of this chapter is to learn how to listen competently.*

There are four chapter objectives:

1. to define and explain the listening process,
2. to discuss several listening problems that impede competent communication,
3. to explore different kinds of listening and problems unique to each kind, and
4. to identify specific ways that you can become a competent listener.

The principal purpose of this chapter is to learn how to listen competently.

The general thrust of this chapter can be summed up in the slogan of the Sperry Corporation: "Nothing new ever entered the mind through an open mouth."

The Listening Process

The International Listening Association adopted an official definition of listening. With slight modification, it defines **listening** as "the process of receiving, constructing [and reconstructing] meaning from, and responding to spoken and/or nonverbal messages" (Emmert, 1996, p. 2). This definition implicitly highlights listening as a dynamic, active process, not a passive activity. In the next several sections, we'll explore this process by looking at three primary elements of listening: comprehending, retaining, and responding.

Comprehending

Constructing meaning from the messages of others is, in reality, more a process of reconstruction. The speaker constructs the original message. A competent listener reconstructs that message to match the original as closely as possible, which produces **comprehension,** or shared meaning between or among parties in a transaction.

The first challenge facing the listener, which operates at the most basic level, is accurately discriminating speech sounds. This may seem ludicrously simple, but it isn't because *hearing and listening are different processes* (see Box 7-1). **Hearing** is the physiological process of registering sound waves as they hit the eardrum. The particular sounds have no meaning until we construct meaning for them. Listening is the active effort to construct meaning from verbal and nonverbal messages. It can be very difficult to stop hearing but quite easy to stop listening. We may wish not to hear barking dogs, but short of using earplugs or moving to a soundproof room, we will hear the barking.

Discriminating speech sounds and interpreting meaning from phonemes is more difficult than you might expect. For years, in hundreds of speech classes, my colleagues and I have played a tape I obtained from Dr. John Lilly at a conference in Portland, Oregon. The tape repeats a single word with no variation (the word was recorded once, then rerecorded hundreds of times from a loop). In every instance of playing it for a 10-minute period, students report hearing 50 to 75 words and phrases, frequently in several languages. Most believe there is more than one word on the tape. Ninety to 100% of the students can't give the correct word on the tape. Many give an incorrect word and insist that it is the correct word. In his lecture at the conference,

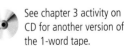

See chapter 3 activity on CD for another version of the 1-word tape.

Box 7-1 **Sharper Focus**

Mondegreens

Many of us have difficulty deciphering song lyrics, famous quotations, and aphorisms. Sometimes we mishear the phonemes and construct odd phrases and sentences. These mishearings are called *mondegreens*. (The obscure term *mondegreens* was coined by Sylvia Wright in an article in *Atlantic* in 1954. She had misheard the line in a folk song "and laid him on the green" as "and Lady Mondegreen.") We try to make sense of a seeming jumble of phonemes. Gavin Edwards (1995) compiled a list of commonly misheard song lyrics. Here are a few samples:

Mondegreen: "Excuse me while I kiss this guy."
Correct lyric: "Excuse me while I kiss the sky." (Jimi Hendrix)
Mondegreen: "The girl with colitis goes by."
Correct lyric: "The girl with kaleidoscope eyes." (The Beatles)
Mondegreen: "I wanna be a dork."
Correct lyric: "I wanna be adored." (The Stone Roses)

Mondegreen: "Life in the Vaseline"
Correct lyric: "Life in the fast lane." (The Eagles)
Mondegreen: "And donuts make my brown eyes blue."
Correct lyric: "And don't it make my brown eyes blue." (Crystal Gayle)
Mondegreen: "I'll never leave your pizza burning."
Correct lyric: "I'll never be your beast of burden." (The Rolling Stones)
Mondegreen: "The ants are my friends, they're blowing in the wind; the ants are blowing in the wind."
Correct lyric: "The answer my friend, is blowing in the wind; the answer is blowing in the wind." (Bob Dylan)

Pinker (1994) offers this mondegreen:

Mondegreen: "He is trampling out the vintage where the grapes are wrapped and stored."
Correct lyric: "He is trampling out the vintage where the grapes of wrath are stored." (The Battle Hymn of the Republic)

Lilly noted that he played the tape at a meeting of the American Association of Linguists, attended by almost 300 linguists who spoke 22 different languages. He tortured the linguists by playing the tape for 25 minutes (students grow restless after a few minutes). The linguists "heard" 2,730 different words in 22 languages.

Retaining

Memory is essential to the listening process. This may seem obvious once you ponder what it is that you do when you listen to a lecture in a college course. If you listen to the lecture and retain none of the information, of what value is it to you? All of those multiple-choice exams would truly become multiple-guess tests. You can't construct meaning from nothing. The information we retain when engaged in the listening process is the raw material from which meaning is constructed.

Naturally, our minds do not retain every morsel of information as we listen to someone. One study found that married couples remembered only 35% of what they discussed in the past hour (Sillars et al., 1990). Another study found that individuals recall only about 9% of what was discussed days earlier (Stafford & Daly, 1984). Hunt (1982) notes that, by the time college students receive their diplomas, they have forgotten, on average, almost 80% of what they learned. Part of the reason this occurs may be a result of cramming information into short-term memory, only to have it forgotten before it moves into long-term memory. Wurman (1989) calls this cramming process **information bulimia.** You're undoubtedly familiar with it. You binge on information to pass an exam and then purge it from your mind once the exam is over.

The forgetting curve (the rate at which we no longer retain information in our memory) drops rapidly at first but levels out and remains almost constant for many years thereafter (Bahrick, 1984). For example, students who took Spanish in high school or college, when tested 3 years later, had forgotten much of the vocabulary they had learned. After 3 years, however, forgetting leveled off, and retention of vocabulary showed only slight diminishment after 50 years (see Figure 7-1). Those students who took the most Spanish in school and learned it well remembered best. Even those students who hadn't used Spanish for years still retained a significant vocabulary if they learned it well initially.

Using information immediately enhances retention. "Use it or lose it," as they say in the memory business. If you immediately apply what you have learned in college to your life's profession or to your relationships, your retention will improve markedly and last longer. The forgetting curve will be far less pronounced.

Retention is important, but remembering everything you hear would be a curse. Imagine what it would be like forgetting nothing. Every telephone number, e-mail address, advertising jingle, slogan, song lyric, irritating noise, angry moment, embarrassing episode, and painful event would be available to clutter up your ability to think clearly and analytically. Imagine how this would affect your relationships with others. Wouldn't reliving every painful memory and embarrassing moment make it difficult for you to be optimistic and constructive in your relationships? Forgetting sometimes has a very constructive effect.

Russian psychologist Aleksandr Luria (1968) studied a Russian named Soloman Shereshevskii, a man who forgot nothing. He was incapable of conducting a normal conversation with another person. When he began a simple conversation, he became overloaded with a flood of memories only tangentially related to the topic of conversation. He would digress endlessly and swamp his listener with trivial asides and irrelevant details. He had difficulty concentrating and focusing his attention. He became easily scattered. So the next time you forget a fact for a test or feel embarrassed because you've forgotten a person's name, just remember how incoherent and scattered you might appear to others if you had an infallible memory.

We forget information for a variety of reasons. Sometimes we just don't pay attention. We are introduced to strangers, and we are concerned with the kind of

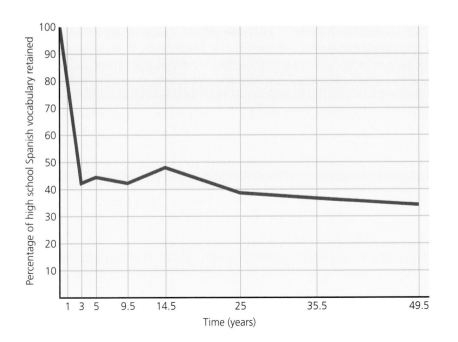

FIGURE 7-1 Long-Term Forgetting Curve (Source: Bahrick, 1984)

impression we are making on them. Their names glance off the edges of our memory and promptly skip irretrievably into space. We are forced to say, "I'm sorry, but I've forgotten your name." We also forget because we don't properly organize the information we hear. We don't attach the information to any meaningful concept, idea, event, or phenomenon. The numbers 1865, 1945, and 1953 don't mean much unless you realize that they are the ending dates of three significant American wars. You can remember the dates more easily knowing that. Forgetting also results from lack of motivation to listen carefully and remember. Imagine if your professor stated at the start of a lecture, "You don't need to know this for the test." Would you pack up your notebook, put away your pen, and hunker down in your seat with no concern about your attention drifting or your eyelids slamming shut?

We forget a great deal for many reasons. A perfect memory would be a curse, but what we do remember is vital to our ability to comprehend what another person communicates to us. As linguist Herbert Clark (cited in Hunt, 1982) observes, "We bring to bear an enormous amount of knowledge to even the simplest utterances, in order to comprehend them" (p. 119).

Whenever we listen, we depend on our memories to fill in the blanks. Speakers presume knowledge of their audiences. If you had no common experiences with others and no common language to communicate those experiences, you couldn't communicate even rudimentary messages effectively. Retention of information is an integral part of the listening process.

Responding

Responding is a third essential element of listening (Purdy & Borisoff, 1997; Barker & Watson, 2000). Listening is a transactional process between speaker and audience. Effective listening depends on both participants in the transaction. Speakers look for responses from listeners to determine whether a message is being processed or ignored. Without a response from the listener, we have no way of knowing whether listening actually occurs. We determine the quality and type of listening from the responses of listeners. These responses can be both verbal and nonverbal. As listeners, we indicate confusion by frowning or by asking a question for clarification. If listeners are staring out a window, doing a face plant onto the desktop, doodling, talking to the person in the next seat, or reading the sports page when you are talking, then listening to you probably isn't a top priority.

One study (Lewis & Reinsch, 1988) revealed that responsiveness is a key determinant of effective listening. Analyzing 195 incidents in medical and banking environments, researchers determined that listeners' attentiveness to the speaker was critical. Verbally, listeners exhibited attentiveness by answering questions and sharing ideas. Nonverbally, listeners exhibited attentiveness by maintaining eye contact and using facial expressions that showed interest (e.g., smiles, raised eyebrows).

Specific Listening Problems

Comprehending, retaining, and responding are the three elements of listening. Most people do not comprehend, retain, and respond competently. There are several specific problems that produce deficient listening: shift response, competitive interrupting, glazing over, pseudolistening, ambushing, and content-only responses.

Shift Response

Charles Derber (1979) conducted an extensive study of conversational narcissism. (Narcissus was a Greek mythological character who fell in love with his own image reflected in a spring.) **Conversational narcissism** is the tendency of listeners "to turn the topics of ordinary conversations to themselves without showing sustained interest in others' topics" (p. 5). "Well I've been talking long enough about me, so what do you think of me?" typifies the conversational narcissist (Aune et al., 2000). They are perceived by others to be socially unattractive and inept communicators (Vangelisti et al., 1990).

Derber tape recorded and transcribed 100 dinner conversations among 320 friends and acquaintances conducted in restaurants, dining halls, and homes. The predominant pattern found in these conversations was the strong inclination to employ the attention-*getting* initiative, called the *shift response,* as opposed to the attention-*giving* initiative, called the *support response* (see also Vangelisti et al., 1990). The **shift response** is a competitive vying for attention and focus on self by shifting topics. It is Me-oriented. The **support response** is a cooperative effort to focus attention on the other person. It is We-oriented. You can see the difference between the two responses in these two conversations:

BORIS: I'm feeling pretty depressed.

NATASHA: Oh, I felt really depressed last week when I flunked a math exam. (*Shift response*)

BORIS: I'm feeling really depressed.

NATASHA: Why are you feeling depressed? (*Support response*)

As you can see from these examples, the shift response sets the stage for a competitive battle for attention; the support response does not. Conversational narcissism can be exhibited by a single person or it can be a pattern of interaction by both parties in a conversation, neither of whom may be prone to shift responses. One person's shift response, however, likely will be countered with the other person's shift response, and a narcissistic transaction may ensue, as in this example:

BORIS: I love listening to jazz.

NATASHA: I hate jazz, but I love country. Don't you think country is more truly native to the U.S.? (*Shift response*)

BORIS: I think country is cornball. All those silly lyrics like "My baby left me high and dry and now I have altitude sickness and skin like a lizard" are for Gomers. Have you ever listened to jazz, I mean really listened to it? (*Shift response*)

NATASHA: No, and I don't plan to. It's just a bunch of noise. Sounds like kids first learning to play instruments. Let me play some country tunes for you. You'll like them if you put aside your prejudice. (*Shift response*)

In this conversation, the two individuals construct a narcissistic pattern of communicating. Each attempts to make his or her topic the focus of the conversation by quickly making a shift response. Neither party ever gets an opportunity to explore a topic he or she introduced.

Support responses encourage elaboration of the topic initially introduced. Three types of support responses encourage the speaker to explore the topic initiated.

They are the *background acknowledgment* (e.g., "Uh huh," "Really," "Yeah"), the *supportive assertion* (e.g., "That's great," "I didn't think of that," "You must have considered this carefully"), and the *supportive question* (e.g., "How is jazz different from blues?" "Why do you hate math?").

Conversational narcissism is a pattern of overusing the shift response and underusing the support response. Men more often than women adopt conversational narcissistic patterns (Derber, 1979). The shift response may be necessary in some conversations in which individuals drift from the main task. The shift response becomes a listening problem, however, when it becomes a patterned response. *The competent communicator primarily uses the support response, not the shift response.*

Competitive Interrupting

Interrupting is closely related to the shift response. Interrupting can be used to shift attention to oneself and away from the other person talking. One study found that interrupting was the second most frequent indicator of conversational narcissism, behind the shift response (Vangelisti et al., 1990). The difference between interrupting and the shift response, however, is that the shift response usually observes the "one-speaker-at-a-time" rule. **Interrupting** occurs when one person stops speaking when another person starts speaking (Tannen, 1994). Those who interrupt don't wait their turn. They step into the conversation when so moved. Also, while the shift response changes topics, an interrupter may break into the conversation and make a point directly relevant to the topic.

Interrupting can be competitive, just like the shift response. **Competitive interrupting** occurs when we dominate the conversation by seizing the floor from others who are speaking. Competitive interrupting can create reciprocal interrupting where both parties battle each other for conversational control.

Interrupting also can be used for a variety of reasons that are noncompetitive. Expressing support ("She's right"), showing enthusiasm for the speaker's point ("Great idea"), stopping the speaker to ask for clarification of a point ("Hold on! I'm lost. Could you give me an example to clarify that point?"), warning of danger ("Stop! You're going to tip over the computer"), and giving a group a break from a talkaholic's nonstop monologue all are noncompetitive forms of interrupting. Most interruptions are noncompetitive (see James & Clarke, 1993, for a review of 56 studies).

Listening problems occur with competitive interrupting but only rarely with noncompetitive interrupting. In competitive interrupting, the focus is Me-oriented. Interrupters are not concerned with listening to the speaker. The agenda of interrupters is to break into the conversation and make their own point. Competitive interrupting creates winners and losers in ordinary conversation. Fighting for the floor, trying to dominate the conversation, and hogging the stage by cutting off other speakers in midsentence creates rivalry, hostility, and, in some instances, reticence to continue with the conversation.

Do men interrupt more than women? Actually, they do not (Canary et al., 1997; James & Clarke, 1993). There is some evidence, however, that men and women interrupt for different reasons (Mulac et al., 1988; Stewart et al., 1996). *Men are more frequent competitive interrupters and women are more frequent supportive interrupters.* Nevertheless, a critical review of the research indicates that the differences in interrupting patterns between men and women are small (Canary et al., 1997). Typically, men and women mirror the interrupting patterns of their partners in conversation. If

Interpersonal arguments often produce competitive interrupting.

one person interrupts to seize the floor, the other person may interrupt to seize it back. If one person interrupts supportively, others may be encouraged to do likewise.

Glazing Over

The third most common behavior of the conversational narcissist and a prominent listening problem is what researchers call *glazing over* (Vangelisti et al., 1990). **Glazing over** occurs when listeners' attention wanders and daydreaming or sleeping occurs. Listening is an active process. You have to be committed to listening. As discussed previously, connecting bids are the glue that binds individuals in relationships (Gottman & DeClaire, 2001). When you glaze over, you give a turning away response to a connecting bid of a speaker, which produces a negative communication climate.

The average listener can think at a rate of about 500 words per minute, but the normal speaking rate is about 150 words per minute (Wolvin & Coakley, 1996). This leaves plenty of opportunity for daydreaming and glazing over. Listeners may benefit from a faster speaking rate. Studies have shown that there is no significant loss of message comprehension when the speaking rate increases to 275 words per minute (Orr, 1968). Characters in the TV programs "West Wing" and "The Gilmore Girls" regularly speak at a 250 to 300 words-per-minute rate. A lethargic speaking rate may put listeners to sleep. Picking up the pace may counteract glazing over by listeners. If the pace is slow, the listener should try to put the differential between the rate of speaking and thinking to good use. Think about the speaker's message. Apply the message to your life experience.

Pseudolistening

When Franklin Roosevelt was president, he once decided to test whether individuals whom he greeted in a receiving line actually listened to him. As each person was received, he remarked, "I murdered my grandmother this morning." Listeners typically responded, "Thank you," "How kind of you," and the like. Many people passed in the receiving line pretending to listen before someone actually listened to the president and retorted, "I'm sure she had it coming to her" (Fadiman, 1985). This is an example of pseudolistening. **Pseudolistening** occurs when someone pretends to listen. It is slightly different from glazing over. When listeners glaze over, they are not even pretending to listen. Falling asleep or staring blankly while another person is speaking shows no effort to disguise inattention to the message. Pseudolistening attempts to disguise inattention to the message. Responding with "Mmm-hmm," "Really," and "Uh-huh" as someone speaks fakes attention if one's mind is not focused on the speaker's message. Pseudolistening typically is easier to enact over the telephone when visual cues are unavailable.

Individuals pretend to listen for many reasons. Often we engage in pseudolistening to keep from making a partner upset with us. We don't really want to put any energy into listening to what he or she has to say, but we don't want to be accused of not listening because that could start a quarrel. So we nod our heads to indicate listening, when all the time our minds are out in the Andromeda galaxy floating far away from the topic of conversation.

Students can be skillful pseudolisteners. Pretending to listen to a boring lecture, nodding your head when the professor asks the class, "Does everyone understand what I just explained?" and focusing eye contact on the professor can fake listening. The listening process requires effort. *Effective listening necessitates focused attention.* We do not remember what has not received our focused attention (Box 7-2). If your attention wanders, you are not listening proficiently.

Pseudolisteners' attention is unfocused and drifts away. They remember none or next to none of the details of a conversation. Queried later, they look blankly at their inquiring partner, or they launch an offensive (e.g., "You never told me that"). Pseudolistening can be maddeningly frustrating for speakers because it is a form of turning away from a connecting bid.

Non Sequitur   **Wiley**

Box 7-2   Sharper Focus

Focused Attention

Listening requires focused attention. The airlines industry recognizes this. In an effort to get passengers to listen carefully to safety instructions at the beginning of flights, flight attendants have tried singing the safety message while accompanied by a ukulele, impersonating famous people while reciting the instructions, and even performing a rap version of the safety message (Riechmann, 2001). To make the point that we do not retain information unless our attention is focused, answer the following questions:

1. On which side of the Apple icon for Macintosh computers is the bite located, left or right?
2. How many sides on a stop sign?
3. In which hand does the Statue of Liberty hold her torch?
4. On which side of their uniforms do police officers wear their badges (to them, not to you)?
5. When you look at a dime, which way does Franklin Roosevelt face?
6. How many geometric shapes are in the CBS "eye" logo?
7. Is the top stripe on an American flag red or white?
8. What is in the center of the backside of a 1 dollar bill?
9. Every number key on the main portion of a standard computer keyboard has a symbol on it as well. What symbol is on the "5" key?
10. What is the lowest number on a standard FM radio?
11. Which of the following can be found on all current U.S. coins?
    a. "United States of America"
    b. "E Pluribus Unum"
    c. "In God We Trust"
    d. "Liberty"
12. When you rewind a videotape, does the tape fill up the left or right side of the cassette?

The correct answers (don't sneak a peak until you've finished) for these 12 questions are **1.** *right side*, **2.** *eight sides*, **3.** *right hand*, **4.** *left*, **5.** *faces left*, **6.** *two geometric shapes: a circle twice and a football shape*, **7.** *red*, **8.** *ONE*, **9.** *%*, **10.** *88*, **11.** *all of them*, **12.** *left side*.

How did you do? It is not unusual to answer many of these questions incorrectly. What you don't pay attention to because it isn't meaningful to you isn't remembered. A coin collector would answer the Franklin Roosevelt question correctly because coin collectors spend a great deal of time examining coins for minute details. It is part of their business. Most of us, however, pay little attention to the details on coins aside from recognizing what coin it is. Even this can be attended to rather casually, as many people discovered when they used Susan B. Anthony silver dollars as quarters, necessitating the withdrawal of the silver dollars from circulation.

For listening to be proficient, speakers should make their points meaningful to listeners. That which is meaningless, mere trivia, rarely is remembered. Answer this question for listeners: "Why should they care?" Listeners should focus their attention on what speakers are saying. This means coming prepared to listen by bringing a notepad or laptop computer to make notes or mentally reviewing key points made by the speaker.

Ambushing

We don't necessarily listen openly and without bias. Sometimes we ambush a speaker. **Ambushing** occurs when we listen for weaknesses and ignore strengths of a speaker's message. An ambusher's bias is to attack what the speaker says. We're looking for weaknesses and ignoring strengths. This is focused attention with prejudice. Ambushers may distort what a speaker says to gain an advantage. Ambushing is competitive and Me-oriented.

Some of the most obvious examples of ambushing occur in the political arena. Individuals running for political office are coached to ambush their opponents. It's called "going negative." The listener is looking to tear down his or her opponent. Journalists also can be ambushers. They're drawn to the mistakes made by public officials and celebrities (Tannen, 1998). They're listening to frame a story as a scandal, a blooper, or an egregious error.

Ambushing is not a problem of comprehension, although comprehension may be sacrificed when a person looks only for the negative. Ambushing is also not primarily a problem of retention. The listener is focused and attending. What is remembered, however, is very selective and not always representative. Ambushing is primarily a problem of responding. The listener responds with a rebuttal or refutation of the speaker. This twists the listening process into a wholly negative experience because it is a form of turning against a connecting bid made by a speaker.

Content-Only Response

A **content-only response** focuses on the content of a message, but it ignores the emotional side of communication. A content-only response comprehends the literal meaning of messages from others but doesn't recognize the feelings that ride piggyback. Consider this example:

BETTINA: I can't believe we're so far in debt.

JEREMY: I've been in worse trouble.

BETTINA: Look at these Visa bills, and the MasterCard is maxed out too.

JEREMY: Actually, we haven't hit the limit on the MasterCard yet. We have another $800 to go.

BETTINA: That's small comfort. What if we lose our house because we can't pay the mortgage?

JEREMY: We could use the MasterCard to buy food and pay some bills up to the $800 that's still short of the limit. Then we could use our paychecks to cover the mortgage next month.

Nowhere does Jeremy, the content-only responder, ever acknowledge Bettina's fears and concerns by providing turning toward responses to her connecting bids (e.g., "I understand your fear. I'm feeling very anxious too about our pile of debt."). Every response only increases her fears that they are in debt up to their eyebrows and that they may lose their home. Content-only responding ignores feelings. It is a form of turning away response to a connecting bid.

Competent Informational Listening

In the next three sections of this chapter, three types of listening will be discussed: informational, critical, and empathic listening. In this section, **informational listening** is defined as listening for comprehension of a speaker's message. Your goal is to understand what the speaker has said. When listening to others, it is usually better to be sure that you comprehend the speaker's message before you critically evaluate it. Too often we are prone to judge another person's ideas without fully understanding what the person actually said and believes. Accurate comprehension is more difficult than it may appear to be. Two problems—confirmation bias and the vividness effect—interfere with proficient informational listening.

Confirmation Bias

I was watching *Nightline* on TV. The issue being debated was compulsive suing. The first person questioned by Ted Koppel was a representative of the insurance industry. He told a story of a man who was seriously injured when an automobile went out of control and crashed into the phone booth he was occupying. The injured man sued the phone company for millions of dollars and won. The insurance man asserted that this was a classic case of a frivolous lawsuit. Obviously, the injured man sued the "deep pocket," the party with the cash, not the person responsible for the injury, namely, the driver of the automobile. As I listened, I began nodding my head in agreement and feeling annoyed at the verdict. Koppel, however, turned to the lawyer who represented the injured man and asked for his response. The lawyer presented a different set of facts. The phone company, according to the lawyer, had been notified on numerous occasions that the phone booth involved in the accident had a door that would jam and trap occupants inside the booth. When the automobile spun out of control, the man inside the booth saw the car coming toward him, tried desperately to exit the phone booth, but could not because the door jammed. The man inside was crushed by the automobile and permanently paralyzed. The phone company was held liable for negligence. Now I felt irritated with myself for not withholding my judgment until I had heard both sides of the issue.

This case is an example of confirmation bias. **Confirmation bias** is the psychological tendency to look for and listen to information that supports our beliefs and values and to ignore or distort information that contradicts our beliefs and values. As I listened to the first interview, I became incensed that someone would sue the phone company when clearly the person responsible for the injury was the driver of the car. This version of events supported my belief that Americans are suit-happy. When I heard the facts presented by the lawyer for the victim, however, I felt dumb for not having waited to hear the entire story.

Confirmation bias is a common problem (Gilovich, 1997). It is especially common in small groups (Schittekatte & Van Hiel, 1996). Group members have a strong tendency to "show interest in facts and opinions that support their initially preferred policy and take up time in their meetings to discuss them, but they tend to ignore facts and opinions that do not support their initially preferred policy" (Janis, 1982, p. 10). This confirmation bias often produces poor, sometimes disastrous decisions (Box 7-3).

As listeners, we constantly have to be vigilant, ready to counter confirmation bias. Try adopting the habit of waiting to draw a conclusion until you've heard dissenting viewpoints and then weigh the evidence before making a decision.

The Vividness Effect

In April 1999, 18-year-old Eric Harris and 17-year-old Dylan Klebold walked into Columbine High School in Littleton, Colorado, and began a 4-hr massacre of their fellow students. Armed with shotguns, semiautomatic handguns, a semiautomatic rifle, and 30 homemade pipe bombs, they eventually killed 12 students and a teacher. The siege ended when they killed themselves. The story was international news. Every newspaper and television station covered the story extensively for days. This horrific incident resurrected a national debate on gun control. New legislation restricting gun ownership was passed by the U.S. Senate 1 month after the Columbine shootings. The vividness of this single incident led many to believe that schoolchildren are in imminent peril across the country. A *Newsweek* poll of 757 randomly selected adults, taken just 2 days after the school massacre, found that 63% of the respondents thought a shooting incident at their children's school was very or somewhat likely (Anatomy of a Massacre, 1999). Is a shooting at school a likely event? So it would seem from the vividness of the reporting and the sensational nature of the crime.

Box 7-3   Focus on Controversy

Reliability of Children's Testimony in Child Abuse Cases: Confirmation Bias in Action

Margaret Kelly Michaels, a 26-year-old preschool teacher at the Wee Care Nursery School in New Jersey, was found guilty of 115 counts of sexual abuse on August 2, 1988. She had been accused of appalling behavior with her preschoolers over a 7-month period. Prosecutors shocked jurors with stories based on testimony of preschoolers. Michaels was accused of dancing nude in her classroom and of ordering her children to strip naked, whereupon she licked peanut butter off their genitals. She also was accused of forcing the children to drink her urine and of raping them with knives, forks, spoons, and Legos. Michaels was convicted on the testimony of 19 children. No physical evidence was produced to corroborate any of the children's startling stories of abuse, even though these acts were supposedly carried out in her open classroom in broad daylight with other adults wandering by. The plausibility of such out-rageous and numerous acts of abuse occurring openly without any adult noticing is highly dubious, but chil-dren's testimony can be quite convincing.

Every year approximately 125,000 substantiated cases of sexual abuse against children in the United States occur (Bruck et al., 1998). Unquestionably, this reprehen-sible treatment of children is a serious problem. In an effort to find and punish the transgressors, however, clear instances of confirmation bias have led to false accusations and convictions (Bruck et al., 1998; Ofshe & Watters, 1994; Loftus & Ketchum, 1994; Pendergrast, 1995). The Michaels case was one such instance. Sentenced to 47 years in prison, she was released after 5 years by a state appeals court on the ground that the children's tes-timony was unreliable.

In their understandable zeal to discover actual child abuse and punish the perpetrators, untrained or poorly trained therapists, attorneys, parents, teachers, and police can and have induced false memories of abuse (Bruck et al., 1998; Loftus & Ketchum, 1994; Ofshe & Watters, 1994). They often listen only to answers from children and adults that confirm their worst fears that abuse occurred. When interviewers begin with a belief that children have been molested, they can easily slip into confirmation bias, refusing to accept denials of abuse and insisting abuse must have occurred (Ceci & Bruck, 1995). Consider this excerpt of a child's testimony from a grand jury hearing in the Michaels case:

PROSECUTOR: Did she touch you with a spoon?

CHILD: No.

PROSECUTOR: No? O.K. Did you like it when she touched you with the spoon?

CHILD: No.

PROSECUTOR: No? Why not?

CHILD: I don't know.

PROSECUTOR: You don't know?

CHILD: No.

PROSECUTOR: What did you say to Kelly when she touched you?

CHILD: I don't like that (cited in Ceci & Bruck, 1995, p. 121).

The prosecutor ignores the child's denial of abuse, assumes abuse has occurred, confuses the child, cues the child as to the "right" response, and elicits an indirect confirmation of abuse from the child. Disconfirmation is disregarded (the child says, "No") and only confirmation is accepted.

Bruck and her associates (1998) found that those who interrogate children in child abuse cases selectively encourage statements that confirm suspicions of abuse by exhibiting vigorous head nodding and smiling or making statements such as "Good! Tell me more." They discourage denials of abuse in similar ways by shaking their heads, scowling, or making stern comments such as "Come on, you know something happened. Tell me." The prosecutor's question, "Did you like it when Kelly touched you?" assumes a fact clearly denied already by the child. It is erroneously suggestive. As Bruck and her associates note,

> One of the hallmarks of interviewer bias is the single-minded attempt to gather only confirmatory evidence and to avoid all avenues that may produce negative or inconsistent evidence. Thus, while gathering evidence to support their hypotheses, interviewers may fail to gather any evidence that could potentially disconfirm their hypotheses (p. 140).

This is biased informational listening, not an objective, dispassionate attempt to comprehend the truth.

Well-trained interviewers can avoid confirmation bias while questioning children in child abuse cases by asking questions that might disconfirm the allegations. Such questions as "Did anyone tell you that this happened to you?" "Did you remember this happening to you before you were told by someone that it happened?" and "Did you see it happen?" are disconfirming questions.

Box 7-3 Focus on Controversy (continued)

Employing competent informational listening skills is not always a matter of counteracting relatively benign instances of confusion or misunderstandings between people. Sometimes, terribly serious issues are involved. Some experts estimate that as many as 35% of accusations of sexual abuse of children turn out to be false (see Bruck et al., 1998). We all want to protect children from the scourge of child abuse, and we don't want to discourage children from revealing real abuse. Refusing to accept a child's accusation of abuse because the idea is too horrible to contemplate would use confirmation bias to protect abusers. Given the seriousness of the crime, however, we also do not want to make false accusations that needlessly destroy families. Effective informational listening can help guard against "making monsters" out of innocent people. Effective informational listening by those who initially suspect abuse (e.g., parents, teachers) and by those who

later investigate allegations is vital. We need to hear all relevant evidence to weigh it properly. Informational listening free of confirmation bias can help us all feel confident that those who are prosecuted, found guilty of child abuse, and punished truly received what they deserved.

Questions for Thought

1. Does the highly emotional nature of child abuse allegations contribute to confirmation bias? How?
2. Is it possible to maintain objectivity and be "dispassionate" when listening to a possible victim of child abuse? If not, how can we combat confirmation bias in such cases?
3. Is it ethical to avoid seeking disconfirming information when questioning children in child abuse cases?

The news each night fills the airwaves with graphic stories of murder and mayhem. It's enough to make you want to hide in your home. Yet the Columbine High School incident, as tragic and inexplicable as it was, occurred at a time when violent crime was plunging in the United States by about a third since 1993 (Glassman, 1998). There are about 15 million high school students in the United States attending 20,000 secondary schools. In the 5 years prior to the Columbine High School shootings, there were six similar incidences in schools (Glassman, 1998). Six! That's six too many, but it is not cause for national breast-beating about our violent youth. Including the Columbine incident, there were 32 students and three teachers shot and killed at elementary and secondary schools in the United States between 1997 and 2001 (Lott, 2001). That's less than one student death per 4 million students. These deaths were from gang conflicts, robberies, and accidents as well as Columbine-type events. During the same period, 53 students died while playing football for their school teams (Lott, 2001). Only 10% of schools register even one serious violent crime, on average, in a year (Glassman, 1998).

This is an example of the **vividness effect**—the tendency of graphic, outrageous, shocking, controversial, and dramatic events to distort our perceptions of the facts, resulting in our concluding that we have problems that are wholly out of proportion to the facts (Glasner, 1999). The vividness effect seriously distorts informational listening because the shocking example can negate a mountain of contradictory evidence. How many times have you avoided a class based solely on the claim of another student that the professor was "incredibly boring" or "sexist" or "terribly unfair"? Perhaps the student told a startling tale of poor behavior from the teacher. You might reply, "Wow! I hadn't heard that. Thanks. I'll make sure not to take his class."

A sample of one is hardly conclusive evidence upon which to base such choices, yet we do make such choices. Listening to information from a single source with a vivid tale to tell—possibly a biased one at that—is generally poor listening practice. If you seek out other students' opinions of the same professor, you might be surprised to discover that many may actually have very positive things to say, completely countering the single student with the negative opinion. There are exceptions, however, where you may need to take seriously a vivid tale, even if told by only one person. If you hear that someone is dangerous and potentially violent, even if it proves to be erroneous, you must give the information serious consideration until it is disproven. In general, be on guard for the vividness effect. Don't jump to conclusions based on a single dramatic example. Seek more information, ask questions, and research the issue before making a conclusion.

Competent Critical Listening

Listening involves more than accurately understanding the messages of others. Comprehension is an important first step in the listening process. Once we understand the message, however, we need to evaluate it. All opinions are not created equal. People used to think that the earth was flat, that pus healed wounds, that bloodletting cured diseases, and that drilling a large hole in an afflicted person's skull cured mental illness by letting evil spirits escape. A book published in 1902 entitled *The Cottage Physician*, written by a group of "the best physicians and surgeons of modern practice," offers some unusual advice. It claims that cataracts can be cured by generous doses of laxatives, tetanus can be treated effectively by "pouring cold water on the head from a considerable height," and difficulty urinating can be relieved with marshmallow enemas (cited in Weingarten, 1994).

We hear a dizzying variety of claims every day. We hear that most of us are raised in dysfunctional families, that 96% of Americans experience codependency, that psychics can make accurate predictions about our love lives, and that extraterrestrial beings have abducted some of our citizens and performed sexual experiments on them. (Goodfellow Rebecca Ingrams Pearson, a London firm, at one time offered an insurance policy for two extraterrestrial occurrences: abduction and alien impregnation. Cost: $155 a year [Insurance Policies, 1996].) How do we separate the likely facts from the almost certain fantasies and nonsense? We do it by listening critically. **Critical listening** is the process of evaluating the merits of claims as they are heard. A **claim** is a generalization that remains to be proven.

In this section, skepticism, probability, and the criteria for analyzing and evaluating claims will be discussed. As listeners, we need to know the difference between prime rib and baloney.

Skepticism

 See skepticism article on CD.

Critical listening begins with skepticism. Skepticism, unlike the media's version of it, is not simply finding fault with the claims of others. **Skepticism** is a process of listening to claims, evaluating evidence and reasoning supporting those claims, and drawing conclusions based on probabilities. Skepticism falls between the two extremes of true belief and cynicism.

True believers willingly accept claims by authorities or valued sources without question. They exhibit confirmation bias. They actively seek evidence (even if weak) that supports already accepted beliefs, and they ignore or distort contradictory evidence. True believers are belief driven, not evidence driven. They embrace a belief and refuse to change it no matter how much evidence refutes it.

Thirty-nine members of the Heaven's Gate cybergroup committed mass suicide in March 1997, blindly following the dictates of their leader, Marshall Applewhite.

Trephining was a primitive procedure that involved cutting a hole in a person's skull to release evil spirits or "mad thoughts." Clearly, some ideas are better than others, and it is the critical listener's responsibility to make such determinations. Our knowledge can build only if we critically evaluate claims and reject those that aren't supported by quality evidence.

Members were not interested in having their beliefs challenged by evidence that contradicted them. Their minds were locked shut (Gardner, 1997). They believed the Hale-Bopp comet was a sign that extraterrestrial spaceships were coming to pick them up after death to transport them to a higher plane of reality. No amount of evidence contradicting their beliefs could penetrate their minds. These were not unintelligent people. Some of them were highly educated computer whizzes. That's what makes true belief scary. Intelligent, highly educated individuals can close their minds to facts and evidence just like anyone else. You have to choose to unlock your mind and listen to the facts and evidence.

Cynics have a negative attitude. H. L. Mencken once described a cynic as a person who "smells flowers and looks around for a coffin" (Brussell, 1988, p. 126). Cynics are faultfinders. Both cynics and true believers have their minds on automatic pilot, never changing their direction. Cynics, however, act as though there is software in their heads that programs them to tear down and ridicule others. You don't qualify as a critical listener by cynically mocking others. Evaluate claims, not people. *Be hard on the claim, soft on the people making the claim* (Sagan, 1995). During a lifetime, each of us is likely to feel embarrassed at least once, probably several times, by the realization that we believed in something or someone that immediately should have struck us as silly.

Skeptics operate in the middle of the two extremes of true belief and cynicism. Skeptics approach each claim they listen to with a willingness to be shown the truth of the claim, neither blindly accepting nor sneering at the beliefs of others. Skeptics are evidence driven, not belief driven. If a used car salesperson told you, "This honey of a car has never had a problem," wouldn't you want to see evidence to support such a claim? A skeptic doesn't ridicule the salesperson for making the claim. Skeptics simply expect something more than a salesperson's say-so (e.g., maintenance records, engine tests, a mechanic's report). Skeptics are guided by evidence and reasoning.

Having drawn distinctions between true belief, cynicism, and skepticism, we must understand that true belief, as used here, does not simply mean "strong belief." Skepticism also does not mean "no belief." As Ruggeiro (1988) notes, "It is not the embracing of an idea that causes problems—it is the refusal to relax that embrace when good sense dictates doing so." *The key distinction between a true believer and a skeptic is not the strength of the belief but the process used to arrive at and maintain a belief.* True believers use confirmation bias and assertions of authority figures as primary avenues to belief formation and perpetuation. A true believer is an individual whose mind has slammed shut. Skeptics show a willingness to change beliefs, even strongly held ones. If a belief cannot withstand mounting evidence, skeptics don't ignore or distort the evidence (confirmation bias). They change the belief and all related claims. Skeptics do not change beliefs lightly or without a struggle, but they do not cling obstinately to erroneous beliefs.

So, how should a skeptic confront a true believer without belittling or showing contempt? Consider this dialogue:

TRUE BELIEVER: You should join my group.

SKEPTIC: Please correct me if I'm misinformed, but aren't you pressured to sell all of your possessions and give the proceeds to the group?

TRUE BELIEVER: Yes, that shows true commitment.

SKEPTIC: Doesn't it bother you that the leader of your group uses those proceeds to buy expensive cars and live a lavish lifestyle, while group members are required to wear inexpensive robes and live frugally?

TRUE BELIEVER: We believe our leader is the exalted one and should have, as you put it, "a lavish lifestyle." We are merely his servants.

SKEPTIC: It seems contradictory to me to teach commitment and to attack materialism but expect that only you will make sacrifices while your leader lives very comfortably without visible sacrifice.

TRUE BELIEVER: That simply shows how little you understand us and our leader.

SKEPTIC: Perhaps, but I'm trying to understand. Are you ever allowed to doubt the teachings of your leader?

TRUE BELIEVER: No! Doubt leads to confusion and weak commitment.

SKEPTIC: Well, this is where we really disagree, because I have serious reservations about a group that requires me to accept without question what a group leader teaches.

Throughout this dialogue, respect is shown to the true believer even though differences in belief are obvious and strong. You can disagree, even strongly, with a true believer without being disagreeable. Skepticism is a process for belief construction and validation. There can be reasonable disagreement even among skeptics. Show others respect when discussing beliefs, because few people take their beliefs lightly.

www.mhhe
● com/
/ **rothwell2**

See "Urban Legends"
activity on Online Learning
Center, chapter 7.

Probability Model

Skepticism rests on probabilities of truth. Whenever we make a truth claim (e.g., "Single women in their 40s have a worse chance of getting married than being kidnapped by a terrorist," "Men self-disclose less often than women," "Students who like their teachers give instructors higher evaluations"), we should first determine the degree of likelihood that the claim is true. Note the differences among these examples:

POSSIBILITY: You could receive an "A" grade in a class even though you flunked all the tests and assignments and rarely came to class.

PLAUSIBILITY: There is at least one other galaxy in the universe with life forms similar to us.

PROBABILITY: Leaping out of an airplane without a parachute from 3,000 feet will result in death.

CERTAINTY: All of us will die.

Each claim rests on the *likelihood* that it is true. The first is highly unlikely but still possible. A student could get an "A" grade in a class despite flunking everything assigned. A clerical error by the instructor or a computer glitch could produce such a result, but don't bet your educational future on such an unlikely event occurring. Likewise, you don't need to worry about a cow falling through the roof of a coffee shop and onto your lap while you're relaxing with friends. Why? Because the likelihood of such an occurrence is extremely remote at best. Nevertheless, it did happen. Ethem Sahin ended up in a hospital with a broken leg and a gash on his forehead from a cow that crashed through a roof of a coffee house in Nevsehir, Turkey, where Sahin was playing dominoes with friends (Falling Cow, 2001). Peter John Robinson slipped on ice, hit his head, and drowned in his cat's water bowl, which contained a mere inch and a half of liquid (Man's Fall, 2001). Do you need to fear that such a fate awaits you? Of course you don't because living your life based on possibilities is a surefire way to go crazy.

The second claim about life in other parts of the universe is more likely than the claim about receiving an "A." This is so because, instead of just blind luck or random chance, it can be supported by a rational argument. It is plausible that another galaxy has life forms similar to us. Astronomers tell us that there are approximately 100 billion galaxies, each with about 100 billion stars. With numbers that enormous, it doesn't defy logic to expect that life exists elsewhere. Nevertheless, this claim is not very probable without evidence, and we have no credible evidence of life in other parts of the universe (despite accounts of UFO sightings). We merely have intriguing speculation.

The third claim is a step up from a plausible argument. Not only is the claim plausible (i.e., people can injure themselves by falling from only an 8-ft ladder), it also is very likely to be true. Plentiful evidence shows that when people jump out of planes and their parachutes fail to open the results are almost always tragic. The human body isn't made to withstand such a fall. Nevertheless, although highly probable, the claim is not certain. On September 25, 1999, Joan Murray, a 47-year-old bank executive plunged 14,500 feet when her parachute wouldn't open during a sky dive. A reserve chute opened at 700 feet from the ground but became tangled and deflated. Murray hit the ground at an estimated speed of 80 miles per hour. She survived with multiple injuries. Two years later she resumed skydiving (Beating the Odds, 2002).

For a claim to be certain there can be no exceptions—ever. Our mortality seems certain, but there are few other claims that are arguably absolute. Consequently, a skeptic initially views claims of certainty as dubious.

Truth claims vary in likelihood from possible to certain. As we make claims of increasing likelihood, our burden of proof also increases. **Burden of proof** is the obligation of the claimant to support any claim with evidence and reasoning. *Who-*

ever makes a claim has the burden to prove it. Thus, if you claim plausibility, you must meet that standard of proof. If you claim probability, you must meet that higher standard of proof for us to have confidence in your claim. If you claim certainty, you have accepted an enormous burden of proof. Only a single exception disproves your claim of certainty. Even a few exceptions, however, will not disprove a probability because you claim high likelihood, not certainty (Box 7-4).

Sometimes speakers try to shift the burden to listeners by challenging them to "Prove that it is not true." When you listen to speakers make a claim, remember that the claim is theirs to prove. It is not yours to disprove until they have met their burden of proof.

Burden of proof increases as our claims move toward certainty. Thus, claims of probability that meet the burden of proof should be taken more seriously than those that merely meet the less burdensome plausibility or possibility standards. For instance, let's say that a stranger asks you to walk blindfolded across a busy freeway. Would you do it? Not unless you're eager to die. What if you saw another person do it successfully before you were asked? Would you do it then? One successful case shows that it is possible to walk blindfolded across a busy freeway and not collide with a speeding car that could distribute your bodily parts across several counties. Nevertheless, you would be a fool to try it, because possible doesn't mean likely, and one successful case is a weak standard of proof. The stranger meets his or her burden of proof by showing that it can be done, but he or she doesn't show with one case that it is likely others can also be successful. You should also weigh likelihood against

Box 7-4　Focus on Controversy

Skepticism and Open-Mindedness

In April 1993 the Roper Organization polled 992 adults and 506 high school students (Poll, 1993). Thirty-four percent of the adults and 37% of the high school students thought it was "possible that the Holocaust did not happen." Thirty-seven percent of the adults and almost half of the high school students did not know that the Holocaust was Hitler's systematic effort to exterminate the Jews, the disabled, gays, gypsies, and other humans who did not qualify as members of the "Master Race" during the Third Reich. A Zogby International poll of 1,200 Americans in May 2001, found that 7% of respondents believed the Apollo astronauts never landed and walked on the moon. An additional 4% weren't sure. If results were generalized to the entire U.S. population, about 20 million citizens doubt the moon landing. The Fox TV network even aired an hour-long program on February 15th, 2001, entitled "Conspiracy Theory: Did We Land on the Moon?" Striving for the sensational and achieving the nonsensical, the program implied that the moon landing was faked by the U.S. government.

Why do so many people believe that two of the most thoroughly documented events of the 20th century might not have happened? The answer might lie in a misunderstanding of what it means to be open-minded. During one period in my life, I explored myriad alternative medicines and therapies, partly out of curiosity and partly from a need to help a sick friend. I explored herbal remedies, homeopathy, polarity therapy, radiasthesia, dowsing, psychic healing, crystal healing, megavitamin therapy, pyramid power, and faith healing, among others. One consistent pattern emerged from my personal exploration. Whenever I expressed doubt about the validity of these alternative approaches to disease and afflictions, believers in the therapies and remedies denounced me as "closed-minded." At first I was bothered that others perceived me as closed-minded. It seemed that to my detractors being open-minded meant I had to accept without question what they wanted me to believe. My academic training in speech and debate, however, kept emerging. "Show me convincing evidence supporting your position," I said, "not just testimonials and opinions from biased sources eager to sell a product."

The poll on the Holocaust asked respondents if it was "possible" that the event never occurred. Perhaps respondents wanted to appear open-minded by allowing for the possibility that this event did not happen. Similarly, on talk shows, individuals who claim the Holocaust never happened "debate" Jews who survived the death camps. Talk show hosts justify this spectacle as an open-minded exchange of two opposing sides. This may have been the thinking of Fox network executives who aired the moon landing conspiracy program. They were just presenting the "other side." Student editors run ads from Holocaust deniers in college newspapers (Lipstadt, 1993). The editor of the *Georgetown Record* justified the appearance of such an ad by claiming that "there are two sides to every issue and both have a place on the pages of any open-minded paper's editorial page" (cited in Lipstadt, 1993).

Remaining open to obviously false claims, however, is not the sign of an open-minded person. As Lipstadt (1993) explains, "One can believe that Elvis Presley is alive and well and living in Moscow. However sincere one's conviction, that does not make it a legitimate opinion or 'other side' of a debate" (p. xvi).

The more a claim bumps against well-established knowledge and facts, the less plausible becomes the claim (Adler, 1998). It is possible, for example, that recurrent stories of alien abductions are true. Such accounts, however, must withstand the "vast evidence of the established physical laws that would have to be violated or strained" (Adler, 1998). Testimonials of alien abductions, even from sincere individuals, are unconvincing when weighed against certain facts. Visits by aliens require speed-of-light space travel—a monumentally implausible occurrence (Paulos, 1988). Credible alternative psychological explanations for accounts of alien abductions explain the testimonials and do not require rewriting the laws of physics (Adler, 1998).

We do not have the time, energy, and resources to listen equally to every opinion and claim. Those claims that have been studied and found deficient must be discarded unless truly impressive proof is produced to warrant a rehearing. Current knowledge of historical facts and scientific evidence contradicts claims that the earth is flat, that bloodletting cures disease, that drilling holes in a person's head cures mental illness, and that the Holocaust and the moon landing did not occur. A true believer of such things would hang on to such viewpoints despite the evidence. A skeptic would not.

Adler (1998) notes, "What truly marks an open-minded person is the willingness to follow where evidence leads. If the evidence against alien abductions and many other supernatural and paranormal speculations is overwhelming, then an open-minded person must reject them" (p. 44). Conversely, *a closed-minded person is someone who refuses to examine his or her beliefs when there is compelling evidence that contradicts the validity of those beliefs.* Clinging steadfastly to unwarranted beliefs can make you feel secure, and discarding beliefs that cannot withstand a preponderance of proof can be unsettling, even anxiety producing. Human knowledge and progress do not

Box 7-4 | **Focus on Controversy** (continued)

advance, however, by holding onto beliefs based more on wishful thinking than critical thinking.

There are, of course, customs and common practices that cannot be proven or disproven by any evidence. Many differences exist between cultures in what is valued and in how individuals communicate (see Chapter 4). Ethnocentrism is prejudice that elevates one's own culture while diminishing another culture because values and behaviors differ. Cultural preferences regarding the "right" and "wrong" way to address a person of status, greet a stranger, show respect for others' feelings, express emotions, or conduct oneself during courtship cannot be proved or disproved by evidence. These are untestable differences based on deep-seated cultural values that make human diversity interesting and challenging. Open-mindedness in this context requires a willingness to understand differences and to recognize that difference doesn't necessarily mean deficiency. Closed-mindedness in this context would be ethnocentrism. A closed-minded person devalues the customs and practices of another culture simply because they are different and fall outside his or her comfort zone. When traveling abroad, a closed-minded person judges how "advanced" or "primitive" a culture is by seeing how closely customs and common practices parallel those of his or her own culture.

Questions for Thought

1. Can you think of other claims besides Holocaust and moon landing denials and alien abduction stories that have been justified by appeals to open-mindedness? Creationism? Channeling? Astrology? Explain your answer.
2. Can you have too much skepticism and become closed-minded? Explain.
3. Should we give an open-minded hearing to claims that women are the inferior sex and men make poor parents?
4. How should an open-minded person deal with cultural practices that dehumanize, such as female circumcision?
5. Is it ethical to steadfastly maintain a belief that you know is wrong but that makes you feel comfortable nevertheless? Explain.

the consequences of failure. In this instance, the consequences could be serious injury or death.

Criteria for Evaluating Reasoning and Evidence

Critical listeners are skeptical listeners. Skepticism rests on probabilities of truth. The more probable the claim, the more valuable it is to listeners as a basis for decision-making, provided that the claimant meets his or her burden of proof. Proof is composed of reasoning and evidence. Thus, we determine if the burden of proof has been met by evaluating the reasoning and the evidence. There are three primary criteria, or standards, to use in such evaluations: credibility, relevance, and sufficiency. In this section, these criteria are discussed in terms of the **fallacies**—errors in evidence and reasoning—that demonstrate how not to meet these standards.

CREDIBILITY A key criterion for evaluating evidence as you listen to others make claims is credibility. The **credibility** of evidence used to support claims is determined by its trustworthiness and reliability. Quoting the Centers for Disease Control on the likelihood of a serious outbreak of the West Nile Virus is credible because the CDC is an objective, scientific body that studies diseases worldwide. They have a track record of providing dependable information. The CDC is called upon to investigate outbreaks of disease all over the world.

Evidence cited is often not credible, however. Several fallacies significantly diminish the credibility of evidence presented.

Questionable Statistic Some statistics cannot be accurate, but that doesn't prevent individuals and groups from manufacturing a statistic or making an attempt to

This anti-gay protester at the funeral of murdered gay college student Matthew Shepard expresses his point of view that "AIDS Cures Fags." Open-mindedness doesn't mean we have to listen to hateful bigotry.

count something. Dr. Edgar Suter (1994), national chair of the Doctors for Integrity in Policy Research, Inc., wrote in an article published in the *Journal of the American Medical Association* that "between 25 to 75 lives may be saved by a gun for every life lost to a gun." Sugarmann (2001), however, notes that there were 648,046 gun deaths in America in the final two decades of the twentieth century. If Suter's statistic on guns as lifesavers is correct, this means that as many as 48,603,450 Americans would have died in the same 20-year period if guns had not been available to Americans to protect themselves (648,046 × 75). This is almost *50 times more deaths* than the total American lives lost in battle in *all the wars in U.S. history*. One can only wonder why Great Britain, with its almost universal ban on guns, had only a few *thousand* homicides during the same period (Sugarmann, 2001). The skeptic must ask, "Does the statistic make sense?"

The skeptic must also ask, "How could you generate such a statistic accurately?" Consider the example of the number of homeless people in the United States. Every report on homelessness in this country tries to quantify the extent of the problem. As Crossen (1994) notes, however, estimates of the homeless have varied from 230,000 to 3 million, not exactly a precise count. There is simply no way to count the number of homeless with any precision because the homeless "are transient, wary of authority, and sometimes mentally ill or addicted to drugs" (p. 137). If our homeless shelters are overwhelmed by greater demand than supply of beds and food, we know there is a problem to be addressed. Even if we only fill those shelters to half or three quarter capacity, we still have a problem. There are better ways to make a case for aid to the homeless than manufacturing inflated and unreliable statistical estimates of the problem.

Biased Source   Special interest groups or individuals who stand to gain money, prestige, power, or influence if they advocate a certain position on an issue are biased sources of information. You should consider their claims as dubious. Look for a source that has no personal stake in the outcome of a dispute or disagreement, a source that seeks the truth, not personal glory or benefit. Consider these examples

(Crossen, 1994). Chocolate may actually prevent tooth decay, reported a newsletter from the Princeton Dental Resource Center. M&M/Mars—makers of chocolate snack foods—finances the center. Quaker Oats sponsored studies that reported reductions in cholesterol from oat bran. Manufacturers added oat bran to more than 300 of their products even though the reduction in cholesterol claimed was a paltry 3%. Nacho chips sprinkled with oat bran were proclaimed to be health food. Advertisers announced that oat bran had been added to toothpaste, licorice, and beer.

Bald men are three times more likely to suffer a heart attack than are men not follicly challenged, claimed a study sponsored by Upjohn Company, maker of Minoxidil, a hair restoration product. Drug companies do their own studies and almost always seem to find that their new drug outperforms older competitors (Rampton & Stauber, 2001). Bias seriously diminishes the credibility of a source.

Expert Quoted Out of Field of Expertise   Iben Browning, the chief scientist for Summa Medical Corporation, has a doctorate in physiology and a bachelor's degree in physics and math. He predicted a major earthquake for December 3 and 4, 1990, along the New Madrid Fault in the Midwest. Schools in several states dismissed students for these two days as a result of Browning's prediction. Browning had some scientific expertise but not in the area of earthquake prediction. In fact, earthquake experts around the country denounced Browning's predictions. No earthquake, large or small, occurred on the dates Browning predicted. Browning was not a credible source on earthquakes. Quoting experts outside their field of expertise is inappropriate.

RELEVANCE   Evidence used to support claims must have **relevance**—it must relate directly to those claims. Several fallacies fail the relevance test.

Irrelevant Statistic   Frank Lautenberg, a U.S. senator from New Jersey, claimed, "In 1996, 41 percent of some 42,000 deaths due to traffic crashes were alcohol-related" (cited in Mulshine, 1998). Does this mean that drunk drivers caused almost half of these 42,000 deaths? Lautenberg used this statistic to support legislation to lower the national standard for drunk driving from a blood alcohol level of .10 to .08. The statistic, however, is deceptive. Most of the deaths that were "alcohol-related" did not involve drunk driving. According to the National Traffic Safety Administration, 19%, not 41%, of fatalities involved a drunk driver (Mulshine, 1998). The 41% figure includes sober drivers and drunk pedestrians. It also includes any driver who had an alcohol level above .01. A driver who had a few swallows of wine and was involved in a car crash in which someone died would be included in the "alcohol-related" death statistic. The 41% figure is mostly irrelevant to and doesn't support the claim of drunk driving fatalities.

Ad Hominem Fallacy   The **ad hominem fallacy** is a personal attack on the messenger to avoid the message. It is a diversionary tactic. "There's an article in the student newspaper charging student government with misuse of student funds. Why should we listen to anything that rag prints?" This is an ad hominem fallacy because it doesn't directly respond to the claims made in the newspaper article; it merely disparages the newspaper. What if the paper is correct? Shouldn't the charges be considered?

Not all personal attacks are ad hominem fallacies. If a claim raises the issue of a person's credibility, character, or trustworthiness, the attack is then relevant to the claim made. Criticisms that led to Richard Nixon's resignation and Bill Clinton's impeachment involved legitimate questions about their character and credibility.

Ad Populum Fallacy   A 1997 national survey of first-year college students conducted by UCLA found that 56.4% opposed "affirmative action in college admissions" (cited in Lubman, 1998c). Arguing that affirmative action related to college admissions should be abolished because a majority of first-year students believe it should be abolished is an example of the **ad populum fallacy**—basing a claim on popular opinion. You should not judge a claim simply on the basis of how many people feel a certain way. A finding such as the one in the UCLA survey should cause concern among supporters of affirmative action and motivate campuswide discussions on the issue. It should not determine whether affirmative action is unfair or ineffective and should be abolished. Majorities can be and often are wrong in their judgments, a point Republicans kept making while they pushed impeachment of Bill Clinton in 1999 in the face of his 73% public approval rating.

SUFFICIENCY   The person who makes a claim has the burden to prove that claim. This means that sufficient evidence and reasoning must be used to support a claim. Sufficiency is a judgment. There is no precise formula for determining sufficiency. Generally, strong, plentiful evidence and solid reasoning meet the sufficiency criterion. More than 40,000 studies show that cigarettes are a serious health hazard (Advertising is Hazardous, 1986). Now that's sufficient proof.

Claims are often insufficiently supported. Several fallacies clearly exhibit insufficiency.

Inadequate Sample   Almost every day we read in the newspaper or hear on radio or television about some new study that "proves" coffee is dangerous, certain pesticides sprayed on vegetables are harmful, power lines cause cancer, or massive doses of vitamin C prevent colds. What's a person to believe? *A single study is insufficient to draw any general conclusion.* In science, studies are replicated before results are given credence because mistakes can be made that may distort the results. The

DILBERT   Scott Adams

DILBERT reprinted by permission of United Feature Syndicate, Inc.

greater the number of studies that show similar or identical results, the more sufficient the proof.

Some polls report results from a very small sample of people. In general, the margin of error in polls goes up as the number of people chosen randomly goes down. A poll of 1,000 people typically has a margin of error of about plus or minus 3%. This means that, if the poll says that 65% of respondents approve of the job the president is doing, the actual result, if every adult American were surveyed, would be between 62% and 68%. No poll is perfect, but increasing the sample size improves the chances of the poll being accurate. The national survey of 250,000 first-year students conducted at UCLA in 1997 had a margin of error of .6% (Lubman, 1998c).

Self-Selected Sample   Any poll or survey that depends on respondents selecting themselves to participate will provide results that are insufficient for generalizing beyond the sample. A **random sample** is a portion of the population chosen in such a manner that every member of the entire population has an equal chance of being selected. A **self-selected sample** attracts the most committed, aroused, or motivated individuals to fill out surveys on their own and answer polling questions. Printing a survey in a magazine and collecting those that have been returned is an example of a self-selected sample. Calling an 800 number to answer questions about politics or social issues is another example of a self-selected sample.

Shere Hite (1987) mailed 100,000 surveys to gather data for *Women and Love*. Her survey included 127 essay questions. Only 4,500 were completed and returned. Her most startling result was that a whopping 98% of the women who responded were dissatisfied with their relationships with men. Several national polls at the time completely contradicted this finding (Gallup & Gallup, 1989). Those women who filled out the survey had to be very motivated, probably by anger toward the men in their lives, to spend time answering 127 essay questions. Hite's results tell us about a group of women who are dissatisfied with the men in their lives, but her findings cannot be generalized to all women because her sample was self-selected, not random.

Testimonials   When a person praises a product that he or she has used, this is called a **testimonial.** Testimonials are not sufficient proof for a claim. One person can make a mistake and believe psychic, bare-handed surgery cured an ailment. A hundred such testimonials on psychic surgery don't make the claim any stronger because a hundred people can also be wrong. Testimonials are persuasive, which is why advertisers use them, but they are lousy proof for a claim. For every 10 people who claim a product was effective, there might be 1,000 who found the product worthless. Testimonials are confirmation bias in action. Advertisers use only the supportive testimonials. Resting your claim on testimonials is fallacious and insufficient proof.

Correlation Mistaken for Causation   A **variable** is anything that can change. A consistent relationship between two variables is called a **correlation.** Suppose a strong relationship was found between two variables, amount of exercise and degree of health, for example. Increased exercise and improved health seem related. Increase your exercise and your health improves. Can you conclude from this that increased exercise causes your improved health? No! *Correlation does not prove causation.* Increased exercise may correlate with improved health in adults, but there may be more to it. Adults who increase their exercise may also stop smoking, reduce fat intake, or reduce their stress at work at the same time. So was it the exercise, cessation of smoking, diet changes, stress reduction, or all of them combined that caused the improved health? Correlations suggest possible causation and may be worthy of further study, but correlations alone are insufficient reason to claim probable causation. Stephan Jay Gould (1981) notes that "the vast majority of correlations in our world are, without doubt, noncausal" (p. 242). Kids with big feet are better readers. Why? Because big feet cause reading proficiency? Not likely. Children with big feet are usually older, and older children have had more experience reading.

Of a sample of 100 college students, what if you found that 45 had eaten breakfast and then dumped their girlfriend or boyfriend the same day, but none of the 55 individuals who had skipped breakfast had dumped their girlfriend or boyfriend? Here's a perfect correlation (no exceptions). Incidence of breakfast eating is perfectly related to frequency of girlfriend/boyfriend dumping in a given population. Eat breakfast—dump girlfriend/boyfriend. Don't eat breakfast—keep girlfriend/boyfriend. Would you conclude that this perfect correlation was sufficient proof that eating breakfast causes a person to dump his or her girlfriend or boyfriend? Not unless you're a cereal manufacturer trying to boost sales.

All of us have a strong inclination to leap from correlation to causation. We don't see the insufficiency of such proof. "The invalid assumption that correlation implies cause is probably among the two or three most serious and common errors of human reasoning" (Gould, 1981, p. 242).

False Analogy   A claim based on an **analogy** alleges that two things that resemble each other in certain ways also resemble each other in additional ways as well. Thus, both things should be treated in similar ways. Consider this analogy: "In Turkey, farmers grow poppies as a cash crop. In the United States, farmers grow corn and soybeans for cash crops. Why outlaw poppies in the United States when we don't outlaw corn and soybeans?" Sound reasonable to you? Analogies become insufficient proof and fallacious logic when significant points of difference exist despite some superficial similarities between the two things being compared. These kinds of analogies are false. Poppies, corn, and soybeans are all cash crops, but that doesn't warrant similar treatment. This is a superficial similarity. Poppies are outlawed in the United States because they are a source of heroin, a dangerous drug. Corn and soybeans are grown in the United States to feed the world, not to produce narcotics. Poppies are not an indispensable crop. Corn and soybeans are indispensable crops. The world can do just fine without poppies, but millions would likely starve without corn and soybeans.

Sufficiency of proof is directly tied to the degree of your truth claim. As already noted, claims alleging possibility require less proof than claims alleging plausibility or probability. Claims of certainty allow no exceptions. Even one exception is sufficient to disprove a claim of certainty. *An extraordinary claim requires extraordinary proof* (Abell, 1981). A few UFO sightings are grossly insufficient to amend our laws of physics to account for alien visitation. Claims of cancer cures must have better proof than testimonials.

Competent Empathic Listening

Informational listening and critical listening achieve important goals for the competent communicator. Informational listening expands our knowledge and understanding of our world. Critical listening helps us sort through bad ideas to discover good ideas that will solve problems and help us make quality decisions that improve our lives. There are times, however, where the point of conversation is to establish a relationship with another person or to help them through an emotional event. These situations require empathic listening, or what some people refer to as *therapeutic*, or helpful, listening. **Empathic listening** requires us to take the perspective of the other person, to listen for what that person needs.

Response Styles

Rogers and Roethlisberger (1952) conducted a series of studies on response styles. Five styles emerged from their research. They are, in the order of their frequency of use: evaluation, interpretation, support, probing, and understanding. These five styles are the types of initial responses we make when another person comes to us with a problem, reveals a frustrating event, or experiences an emotional crisis. In this next section, these five styles, plus the advising response, will be examined in the context of empathic listening (Figure 7-2).

EVALUATIVE RESPONSE   A friend comes to you, obviously upset, and says, "I hate my job. I've got to find something different to do." You respond, "You haven't given the job much of a try. Perhaps you'd like it better if you put more effort into it." This is an **evaluative response**; it makes a judgment about the person's conduct. It assumes a standard of evaluation has or has not been met. As you read the evaluative response, perhaps you said to yourself, "I wouldn't respond that way." Perhaps not, but the most frequent response people make in situations like the one just presented is evaluation (Rogers & Roethlisberger, 1952).

A hypercompetitive, individualistic culture such as ours promotes the evaluative response. Competition focuses us on discerning weaknesses in our adversaries. Even when we are conversing with a friend, there is a tendency to focus on weaknesses. Competitors don't try to bolster their opponents. Adversaries try to diminish each other to win. Evaluating a friend who comes to you with a problem is nonempathic. It is a turning against response that promotes defensiveness. Your friend will feel worse, not better.

Evaluation is the least effective response when we need to be empathic. Harold Kushner, author of *When Bad Things Happen to Good People* (1981), makes this point:

> It is hard to know what to say to a person who has been struck by tragedy, but it is easier to know what not to say. Anything critical of the mourner ("don't take it so hard," "try to hold back your tears, you're upsetting people") is wrong. Anything

FIGURE 7-2   Listening Responses

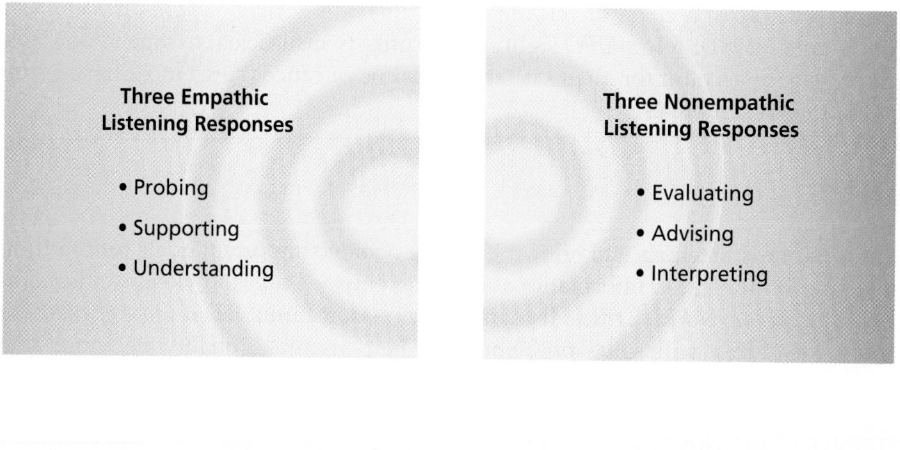

Three Empathic Listening Responses

• Probing

• Supporting

• Understanding

Three Nonempathic Listening Responses

• Evaluating

• Advising

• Interpreting

which tries to minimize the mourner's pain ("it's probably for the best," "it could be a lot worse," "she's better off now") is likely to be misguided and unappreciated (p. 89).

When you're suffering, the last thing you need is criticism and judgment.

ADVISING RESPONSE   "My roommate drives me crazy. She has so many odd quirks." How would you respond to this? If you would respond in this fashion, "Why don't you change roommates?" you would be offering advice. The **advising response** tells people how they should act. It is a common initial reaction to those who make a complaint or reveal a problem.

Men more than women tend to offer advice when others come to them with a problem or complaint (Tannen, 1990; Wood, 1994). Giving advice under these circumstances does two things (Wood, 1994). First, it fails to acknowledge the other person's feelings. Second, it communicates the superiority of the person giving the advice. Giving advice presumes that the person with the problem hasn't figured out the solution, so the listener offers advice. Take the perspective of the other person before giving advice. Does the person seem interested in receiving advice from you? Is that what he or she is seeking? Have you considered your advice carefully, or is it merely a glib response made without thoughtful examination?

INTERPRETING RESPONSE   When we give an **interpreting response** we express what we think is the underlying meaning of a situation presented to us. A friend says to you, "I don't understand why he says such embarrassing things to me in front of my family." You respond, "Perhaps he is just uncomfortable around your parents and doesn't really know quite what to say, so he says silly things that embarrass you because he's socially clumsy." This is an interpreting response. You are clarifying the meaning of the situation for the other person. Interpreting responses are what we pay counselors, psychiatrists, and therapists to do for us when we can't make sense of our relationships, feelings, conflicts, and traumas. The interpreting response is useful in some situations, but, like advising, it tends to ignore the feelings of the person. It also places the listener in a superior position. One can "play guru" too often if the interpreting response becomes frequent.

PROBING RESPONSE   The **probing response** seeks more information from others by asking questions. Several types of questions qualify as a probing response (Purdy & Borisoff, 1997). There is the clarifying question (e.g., "Can you give me an example of what you mean when you say that she is insensitive?"). There is the exploratory question that urges the speaker to examine possibilities posed by a problem or situation (e.g., "Can you think of some ways to defuse her anger?" "Can you think of any alternative besides resigning from your position?"). There is also the encouraging question that inquires about choices made and implies agreement at the same time (e.g., "You didn't have any other choice did you? Who could blame you for sticking to your principles?"). Probing responses show interest in the speaker by seeking more information from and showing attentiveness to the plight of the other person.

SUPPORTING RESPONSE   A **supporting response** acknowledges the feelings of the speaker and tries to boost the person's confidence. When a friend is nervous about starting a new job, you might offer reassurance (e.g., "First day on the job can be a little nerve-racking, but you have the skills to do the job really well.").

When a person is suffering the loss of a loved one, he or she needs empathy. In our struggle to help someone shoulder his or her burden, we may choose the wrong response. One survey (Davidowitz & Myricm, 1984) found that bereaved individuals considered 80% of the responses made to them during mourning to be unhelpful. Almost half of the responses were advice (e.g., "You need to get out more," "You have to accept his death and move on with your life"), but they were hardly ever perceived as helpful to the bereaved. Acknowledging and validating the feelings of the bereaved was the most helpful response (e.g., "I can see how much you miss her. She was a warm and sensitive person.").

UNDERSTANDING RESPONSE   The **understanding response** requires a listener to check his or her comprehension of the speaker's message (We discussed perception checking in Chapter 3.) by paraphrasing and perception checking. **Paraphrasing** "is a concise response to the speaker which states the essence of the other's content in the listener's words" (Bolton, 1979, p. 51). Paraphrasing is not a long-winded parroting of a person's message. Paraphrasing is concise and to the point. Here's an example:

FRANCINE: My roommate hums to himself while he studies. He hums stupid, irritating little tunes that stick in my head like annoying ads on TV. I'm trying to study, and I can't concentrate with his humming. I have a major exam in chemistry class tomorrow, and I'm worried that old hum-till-you're-dumb will screw up my chances of scoring big on the exam.

TERESA: You're worried about your chemistry exam, and your roommate's humming is a distraction.

FRANCINE: Yeah! Got any suggestions what I should do about him?

Paraphrasing helps a listener understand the essence of a speaker's message. Paraphrasing, however, should be used only occasionally during a conversation. Look for the significant points in a conversation and then paraphrase. Details and elaborations of important points usually don't require paraphrasing.

Now that you have read about these response styles, test yourself by identifying the listening response in Box 7-5.

Response Styles and Empathic Listening

Different responses produce different results. Some of these response styles are empathic and some are not.

EMPATHIC RESPONSE STYLES   Empathic listening is composed of probing, supporting, and understanding responses. All three put the focus on the speaker and are therefore confirming responses—they enhance the person's self-esteem and confidence. Hamachek (1982) explains:

> An understanding response is a way of letting a person know that you're listening to both the content of what's being said and the feeling accompanying it; a probing response lets a person know that you want to know more and, on a deeper level, that he or she is worth knowing more about; a supportive response is a way of saying that you care and that you hope things will get better (p. 214).

When building a relationship and connecting with a person are the principal goals of your communication, probing, supporting, and understanding responses establish trust, deepen the connections between you and the other person, and keep communication open.

Box 7-5 **Sharper Focus**

Distinguishing Listening Responses

Read the following situation and then identify the type of response for each statement. Mark **A** for advising, **E** for evaluation, **I** for interpreting, **P** for probing, **S** for supporting, and **U** for understanding.

> My boss is a total jerk. She's always giving me these huge projects to do and then yelling at me for not getting my other work done. She never has anything nice to say to anyone, and she actually times us when we take breaks to make sure we don't take longer than we're allowed. I feel like quitting.

_____ Aren't you being a little unfair? She can't be that bad.

_____ What have you tried so far to deal with your boss?
_____ Your situation is a classic power struggle.
_____ I think you should quit and find a job more to your liking.
_____ You feel overworked and underappreciated.
_____ I know you'll make the right decision because you usually know what is right to do.

Which response do you think would be the best? Second best?

Answers: E, P, I, A, U, S

NONEMPATHIC RESPONSES   Evaluating, advising, and interpreting responses tend to be disconfirming (they diminish the person and reduce confidence). They are nonempathic responses from the speaker's perspective (Hamachek, 1982). Should you, therefore, avoid such responses? Empathy is not always the type of listening that is appropriate in a given situation, so the answer is "no." Therapists interpret meaning for clients. Interpreting is an important listening response when a speaker is confused and wants clarity. Advising others can be constructive and helpful, especially if they seek our advice. Evaluating a person's self-destructive behavior may save that person's life.

COMMUNICATION COMPETENCE VARIABLES   Three variables influence the appropriateness and effectiveness of evaluating, advising, and interpreting responses. The first variable is frequency. _Frequency_ refers to how often you use disconfirming responses. Occasional evaluation, interpretation, or advice, especially in a strong relationship, will rarely cause more than a ripple of disturbance. Frequent use of such disconfirming responses, however, can swamp even resilient relationships.

A second variable is timing. _Timing_ refers to when you evaluate, interpret, or advise. "This is politics, pure and simple. You've handled them wrong. Stand up to these thugs." This statement begins with interpreting, follows with evaluating, and closes with advising—the triple crown of disconfirmation. Such a statement early in a relationship when the two parties hardly know each other would likely be received negatively. The same statement made much later in a relationship when the two parties are familiar with each other's style and trust each other might be received in a more neutral, even positive, way. Additionally, evaluating, interpreting, or advising responses used when a person is feeling fragile and in need of support will likely disconnect speaker and listener. Such responses can make a person feel inferior and diminished.

Finally, evaluating, advising, and interpreting responses are more appropriate and likely to be more effective when the speaker solicits them. _Solicitation_ refers to a request for evaluation, interpretation, or advice. A person may simply want to be heard, not told what to do. He or she may reject unsolicited advice, even resent it. "I already thought of that. It won't work" is a typical rejoinder to unsolicited advice. If individuals request such advice, however, they will more likely perceive it to be

CATHY/Cathy Guisewite

© 2001 CATHY GUISEWITE. Distributed by Universal Press Syndicate. www.ucomics.com.

helpful. Individuals who seek help from a therapist implicitly request an interpreting response. People rarely request evaluation, but if they do, it is more likely to be accepted than an unsolicited critique.

Summary

Listening is the most frequent type of communication any of us does on a daily basis. Listening is first and foremost an active process. You cannot comprehend information, retain it, or respond appropriately to what you hear from others without focused attention. Listening requires effort. Competent communicators avoid shift responses, competitive interruptions, glazing over, pseudolistening, ambushing, defensiveness, and content-only responses. The competent communicator recognizes when informational, critical, and empathic types of listening are appropriate and effective. Be an informational listener when the principal focus of the communication is learning or retaining information. Be a critical listener when you need to find solutions to problems or make decisions that have consequences for yourself and others. Be an empathic listener when you are trying to build or maintain a relationship with another person who comes to you with a problem or crisis.

Quizzes Without Consequences

Go to *Quizzes Without Consequences* at the book's Online Learning Center at **www.mhhe.com/rothwell2** or access the CD-ROM for *In the Company of Others*.

www.mhhe
● com/
/ rothwell2

Key Terms

ad hominem fallacy
ad populum fallacy
advising response
ambushing
analogy
burden of proof

claim
competitive
  interrupting
comprehension
confirmation bias

content-only
  response
conversational
  narcissism
correlation
credibility

critical listening
cynics
empathic listening
evaluative response
fallacies
glazing over
hearing
information bulimia
informational listening

interpreting response
interrupting
listening
probing response
pseudolistening
random sample
relevance
self-selected sample
shift response

skepticism
support response
supporting response
testimonial
true believers
understanding
 response
variable
vividness effect

See Audio Flashcards
Study Aid.

www.mhhe
● com/
/rothwell2
See Crossword Puzzle
Study Aid.

Suggested Readings

Hoffer, E. (1951). *The true believer*. New York: Harper & Row. This work still remains the classic book on fanatical thinking.

Kohn, A. (1990). *The brighter side of human nature: Altruism and empathy in everyday life*. New York: Basic Books. If you plan to research the topic of empathy, start with this book. Kohn presents the research on empathy clearly and effectively.

Lipstadt, D. (1993). *Denying the Holocaust: The growing assault on truth and memory*. New York: Penguin. The author expertly responds to the Holocaust deniers and shows the dangers of true belief. She also provides a nice history lesson in the process.

Rampton, S., & Stauber, J. (2001). *Trust us, we're experts*. New York: Jeremy P. Tarcher/Putnam. This is fascinating reading on the manipulation and distortion of expert scientific testimony and evidence.

Sagan, C. (1996). *The demon-haunted world: Science as a candle in the dark*. New York: Random House. Carl Sagan wrote this book just before his death. Like his other works, it is an articulate defense of science and human reasoning and a compassionate, yet direct, critique of magical thinking.

Tannen, D. (1998). *The argument culture: Moving from debate to dialogue*. New York: Ballantine. Tannen offers an interesting and insightful treatment of how U.S. culture predisposes people to attack rather than listen effectively to others.

Film School

Jerry Maguire (1996). Comedy/Drama; R ★★★★✔
Both Cuba Gooding Jr. and Tom Cruise turn in Oscar-caliber performances (Gooding won an Oscar) in this amusing, poignant story about a glib sports agent who falls on hard times. Examine this film for narcissistic listening, especially by the title character.

Inherit the Wind (1960). Drama; Not rated ★★★★★
This is an outstanding adaptation of the stage play depicting the Scopes monkey trial and its challenge to the Tennessee law forbidding the teaching of evolution in schools. Who are the true believers, cynics, and skeptics in the movie? Explain.

Ordinary People (1980). Drama; R ★★★★✔
Robert Redford's Oscar-winning directorial debut presents a family in crisis. Look for examples of listening problems, especially shift response, competitive interrupting, pseudolistening, ambushing, and content-only responses. Also notice response styles, especially evaluative, interpretive, and advising responses.

CHAPTER 8

Power: The Inescapable Communication Dynamic

P ower is inescapable in human transactions. "There is power in a word or a gesture. There is power when women and men live together, work together, talk together, or are simply in each other's company. There is power in a smile, a caress, and there is power in sex." There is also "power in how we choose to resolve our conflicts and how we negotiate the most intimate aspects of our lives" (Kalbfleisch & Cody, 1995, p. xiii). Relationships between parents and children, doctors and nurses, teachers and students, judges and lawyers, supervisors and employees, and coaches and athletes are hierarchical and fundamentally power oriented. Parents, doctors, teachers, judges, supervisors, and coaches have the power to tell others what to do. A person who speaks as an expert to a large group has power. Organizations and institutions are typically structured as hierarchies with the powerful at the top and the less powerful below. "Power plays a major part in the interactions occurring in organizational life" (Hollander & Offermann, 1990, p. 183).

Even in less hierarchical situations, power is ever-present. As noted in Chapter 1, every message has two basic dimensions: content and relationship. The content of a message communicates information regarding events and objects. The relationship dimension identifies, among other things, how power is being distributed between individuals. Power is constantly being negotiated during conversations with others. Consider this dialogue and the comments interjected in parentheses that indicate the power dynamics in the conversation:

Jennifer is washing the dishes.

"I'm tired of dealing with my mother's demands on me," begins Jennifer (*control is an issue*).

Geoff responds, "Don't let her make you feel guilty for not spending every holiday with her and your father" (*advising as a parent to a child*).

Jennifer says, "I'm not letting her make me feel guilty (*asserting control*). I just get emotionally exhausted having to explain over and over again why we aren't coming to her house on Christmas."

Geoff picks up a towel and begins to dry some dishes. "Tell her just once why we won't be coming for the holidays, then refuse to talk about it any further. Stand up to her" (*encouraging assertion of power*).

Jennifer scrubs a plate a bit more vigorously than necessary (*exhibiting tension when implicitly accused of being weak*). "It isn't a question of standing up to my mother (*rejecting Geoff's characterization of weakness*). You make it sound like I'm putty in her hands."

"Well, maybe not putty; more like sculpting clay," Geoff says with a chuckle (*reasserting weakness by Jennifer*).

"You're one to talk," says Jennifer. "You haven't stood up to your father in years. Why don't you practice what you preach?" (*takes the offensive in the battle to win the argument; asserts weakness by Geoff*).

Geoff moves next to Jennifer, looking down at her with an unpleasant expression on his face (*dominance posture*). He responds in a stern voice (*power in tone of voice*), "That's hitting below the belt."

"Now you know how it feels to receive such flip advice," Jennifer retorts (*continues with powerful offensive*).

Power, who has it, and how it is being exercised are central to this conversation. Power is the main topic of conversation as well as the subtext, the meaning beyond the words. Each person is struggling to define the main issue of contentiousness in an interpersonal tug-of-war for dominance. Both Jennifer and Geoff are quick to reject characterizations by the other of weakness. Offering advice becomes a source of dispute because to accept advice is perceived as an acknowledgment of subordination to the person advising. There is friction regarding who should be able to tell whom to do what.

There is no virtue in powerlessness. *You can't achieve your individual goals, resolve conflicts, or communicate competently in relationships without exercising power.* Feeling powerless creates apathy, shrivels our desire to perform at work, and strains personal relationships. It creates interpersonal disconnection, erodes self-esteem, and makes us ineffectual in most or all of our dealings with others (Lee, 1997). Feeling powerless can strangle our spirit and stifle our motivation to improve our lives and the lives of those we love. It can lead to self-destructive behavior or aggression toward others.

Understand, however, that Machiavellian manipulation to achieve self-centered, hypercompetitive goals is not being advocated. Nevertheless, our choice is not between using and not using power. "We only have options about whether to use power destructively or productively for ourselves and our relationships" (Wilmot and Hocker, 2001, p. 104).

The primary purpose of this chapter is for you to understand the significant role power plays in your relations with others so you can respond competently.

There are four chapter objectives:

1. to define what power is and is not and to explore the differences between types of power,
2. to describe the primary indicators and sources of power,
3. to examine problems that emerge from power imbalances and the challenges that these imbalances present to the competent communicator, and
4. to present competent communication strategies to balance power in our transactions with others.

> The primary purpose of this chapter is for you to understand the significant role power plays in your relations with others so you can respond competently.

Definition of Power

Power is the ability to influence the attainment of goals sought by yourself or others. This is a general definition. More specifically, this section explores the nature and forms of power.

The Nature of Power

Power does not reside in the individual. *Power is relational.* The power you exercise is dependent on the relationships you have with others. Teachers normally are granted more power than students in the classroom, but this power is quickly taken away when students refuse to pay attention to the teacher's requests or dictates. In some instances, bad student evaluations can invite dismissal of an instructor; good evaluations may produce promotion. Power is not a characteristic of any individual. Power is determined by our transactions with others.

Power is not dichotomous. We often identify individuals as powerful or powerless. This is not an accurate assessment of power distribution in a relationship. No one is all powerful or completely powerless, not even an infant, as many weary parents can attest to when they have tried to attend to their crying baby's needs in the middle of the night. If each person has some degree of power in a relationship, the appropriate question is not the dichotomous, "Is Person A powerful or powerless?" The apt question is, "How much power does Person A have compared to Person B?"

Forms of Power

There are three forms of power: dominance, prevention, and empowerment (Hollander & Offerman, 1990). **Dominance** is the exercise of power over others. Dominance is a competitive, win-lose transaction. This form of power results from dichotomous, either-or thinking. You're perceived to be either a winner or a loser in a power struggle.

Prevention is power used to thwart the influence of others. Prevention is the flip side of dominance. When someone tries to dominate you, you may try to prevent the dominance. Psychological reactance emerges. The willingness to say "no" can be formidable, even in the face of dominating attempts. Prevention power is competitive. Dominators and preventers engage in power struggles to become winners and to avoid becoming losers.

It is a false dichotomy to assume that power can be exercised only as dominance or prevention (to win or to avoid losing). There is a third alternative—empowerment. **Empowerment** is power derived from enhancing the capabilities and influence of individuals and groups. It is power used positively and constructively. It is a cooperative form of power. You do not have to defeat anyone to achieve personal or group goals. Empowered individuals feel capable, effective, and useful because they performed well, not because they beat someone. You become empowered by successfully accomplishing an important task. That accomplishment has an impact on you and on others (Thomas & Velthouse, 1990; Frymier and Shulman, 1996).

Differences in Forms of Power

The three forms of power—dominance, prevention, and empowerment— are considerably different from each other. Those who try to dominate see power as an active effort to advance personal goals at the expense of others. Power is a zero-sum contest. This means that, for every increment of power I gain, you lose an equivalent amount of power. From this perspective the power pie can't be enlarged, so the battle is for the biggest possible slice.

Those who seek to prevent domination by others see power as reactive. Prevention power is competitive. Individuals who attempt to prevent domination react to the power initiatives of others by fighting back. Preventive power is self-protective. You're trying to keep the slice of the power pie that you have and even enlarge your portion if possible by decreasing the portion of those trying to dominate (see Figure 8-1).

The dominance-prevention power struggle can be seen in commonplace transactions. Access to bathrooms on the job rarely poses a problem for white-collar workers, but for workers in factories, telephone-calling centers, food-processing plants, and construction sites, using the restroom when nature calls can be a serious power struggle, especially for women (Linder & Nygaard, 1998). Lawyers, business executives, and college professors don't need to ask for permission to relieve themselves, nor do they have their bathroom activities monitored. Employees on the lower rungs of the employment ladder, however, may not be so lucky. Workers who perform the heavy lifting and "grunt" work can be refused permission when they request a bathroom break; they can be timed with stopwatches while they are in the restroom; they can be disciplined for frequent restroom visits; they can even be hunted like quarry by supervisors if they remain in the stalls too long. The courts have ruled that these common practices by supervisors are not necessarily illegal (Linder & Nygaard, 1998). Workers in some instances have taken to wearing adult diapers while working on assembly lines because bathroom breaks are not permitted often enough. Increasingly, workers have fought back by complaining to supervisors, filing formal grievances, taking court action, and protesting their treatment. Train operators on the Norfolk Southern railway protested the lack of flush toilets by taking the waste-filled plastic bags they were forced to use and flinging them off their moving trains. Norfolk Southern responded by printing employee numbers on the bags and monitoring which employees brought back the full bags (Walsh, 2000). A dominance-prevention power struggle can quickly deteriorate into outlandish power tactics.

Those who seek to empower themselves and others see the power pie as expandable. When the power pie is expanded, there is more for everyone (see Figure 8-2). Thus, no zero-sum competitive game need take place. "Empowerment takes an abundance mentality—an attitude that there is plenty for everybody and to spare, and the more you share the more you receive. People who are threatened by the successes of others see everyone as competitors. They have a scarcity mentality. Emotionally they find it very hard to share power, profit, and recognition" (Covey, 1991, p. 257).

Empowerment is proactive. Individuals take positive actions to assist themselves and others in attaining goals cooperatively (Table 8-1). For example, a football team may have a great quarterback, but it takes a team to be successful and win games. If the offensive line performs poorly, the quarterback will be running for his life, not throwing touchdown passes. Future Hall of Fame quarterback Steve Young

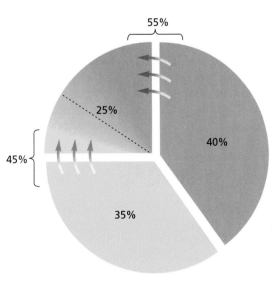

FIGURE 8-1 Power Struggle Dynamic

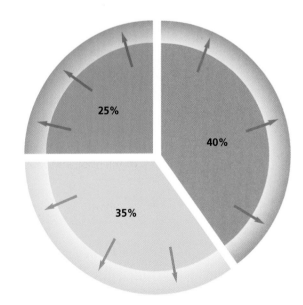

FIGURE 8-2 Empowerment—Expanding Resources and Enhancing Capabilities

DILBERT   Scott Adams

DILBERT reprinted by permission of United Feature Syndicate, Inc.

of the San Francisco 49ers became uncomfortably aware of this fact during the 1999 NFL season. His offensive line performed poorly in the first three games, and he was clobbered by opposing players. In a game against the New Orleans Saints, Young was smacked to the ground 21 times. In the third game, Young was hit by a defensive end who roared through the 49ers' line untouched. Young was knocked unconscious, suffered a serious concussion, and subsequently retired from the game. The team floundered the rest of the season without their star quarterback.

The empowerment perspective encourages improvement by working together, not against each other. By helping each other to improve blocking techniques, players on the offensive line improve the entire team's performance. Protecting the vulnerable quarterback so he can have time to spot open receivers, score points, and stay healthy benefits everyone. I also should note here that empowerment can occur even in the larger competitive arena, in this instance professional football. You can have intragroup (within the group) empowerment for the purpose of intergroup (between groups) competitive success. Intergroup rivalry is not necessary for intragroup empowerment, but different forms of power sometimes operate at the same time.

If you have a negative view of power, you are more than likely responding to the dominance form of power and its companion, prevention. It would be naïve, however, to argue that we could replace dominance with empowerment in all, or even in most, cases. If individuals in a relationship are satisfied with an unequal power distribution, empowerment may not be necessary. *Dominance is the primary form of power in a hypercompetitive society, and it will likely remain so.* Establishing a better balance between competition and cooperation, however, requires greater emphasis on empowerment.

Table 8-1 The Three Forms of Power		
Type	**Definition**	**Description**
Dominance	Competitive, hierarchical	Active: zero-sum
Prevention	Competitive, hierarchical	Reactive: zero-sum
Empowerment	Cooperative, egalitarian	Proactive: multisum

Indicators of Power

To understand the role of power in all of our transactions with others, we have to recognize its inherent presence. We can become adept at recognizing power dynamics by understanding three types of power indicators: general, verbal, and nonverbal.

General Indicators of Power

There are several general indicators of power. The first is *who can define others*. Typically, those people who define others are recognized as having power in relationships and groups. Teachers define students (e.g., smart, slow learner), physicians define patients (e.g., healthy, hypochondriac, addict), psychiatrists define clients (e.g., paranoid schizophrenic, psychotic), parents define children (e.g., incorrigible, obedient), and bosses define employees (e.g., hard worker, sluggard).

Definitional prerogative as an indicator of power can be seen from our attitudes about rape of men. The rape of women in the United States is an outrage recognized by government, social service agencies, and most Americans. The rape of men, however, is largely ignored, even made the subject of television sitcom humor. Official rape statistics compiled by the FBI and the Bureau of Justice Statistics exclude prisoner rapes. There is reason to believe, however, that the number of rapes of males by other males (mostly in prison) may be equal to or greater than the number of rapes of women by men (see Farrell, 1993; Mallory, 1999). Rape of both women and men is a brutal crime of dominance. The central point, however, is that the rape of men is virtually ignored because the victims are defined as "criminals."

Most of the men raped in prison have not been incarcerated for committing violent crimes. One such victim, Stephen Donaldson, was raped 60 times in 2 days while he was incarcerated on a charge for which he was later acquitted (participating in a Quaker "pray-in" at the White House). He subsequently became president of a national organization called Stop Prisoner Rape. He was infected with the AIDS virus when he was raped in jail, and he later died from the disease (Mallory, 1999). Prisoners, however, have no power to define rape inside prison as a crime or even as a serious problem to be solved. Prisoners are dependent on judges, prosecutors, and lawmakers to define prisoner rape as a criminal act worthy of sanction. We recognize those who can define the actions of others as more powerful than those who try to define the actions of others but are not accorded legitimacy.

A second general indicator of power is *who cares less about maintaining a relationship*. The **principle of least interest** indicates that the person who cares less about continuing a relationship is typically recognized as having more power (Waller & Hill, 1951). The person with the greater interest and investment in maintaining the relationship can be held hostage by his or her partner's lack of interest, forced to try resurrecting an intimacy that only one partner cares much to rejuvenate. The partner with the lesser interest is in the dominant position because of the implied or stated threat to terminate the relationship. The only person controlled by a threat to end a relationship is a partner who cares about maintaining the relationship.

A third general indicator of power is *whose decisions are followed*. Employees follow the directives of supervisors, not vice versa. Children obey parents. Wouldn't it be odd to see parents obeying children (e.g., "Dad! Be home by 10 o'clock and gas up the BMW before you return.")? We recognize those whose decisions are followed as having power.

Verbal Indicators of Power

Power is indicated by the way we speak and by how listeners evaluate these speech patterns. The speech of a less powerful person is often flooded with self-doubt, approval seeking, overqualification, hesitancy, and personal diminishment. Here are examples of speech patterns commonly viewed as relatively powerless in U.S. culture (Mulac & Bradac, 1995):

Hedges: "*Perhaps* the best way to decide is . . ." "I'm a *little* worried that this *might* not work."

Hesitations: "Well, *uhm*, the central point is . . ." "Gosh, *uh*, shouldn't we, *uhm*, act now?"

Tag question: "Dinner will be served at 6 o'clock, *okay*?" "This section of the report seems irrelevant, *doesn't it*?"

Disclaimers: "You may *disagree* with me, but . . ." "This idea is probably very *silly*, but . . ."

Excessive politeness: "I'm *extremely sorry* to interrupt your conversation, but . . ."

Powerless speech suggests lack of confidence, uncertainty, indecisiveness, vacillation, and deference to authority. It advertises a person's subordinate status. Powerful speech, by contrast, is generally direct, fluent, declarative, commanding, and prone to interrupt or overlap the speech of others. It advertises superior status, dynamism, and credibility (Haleta, 1996).

Powerful forms of speech are not always appropriate (see Box 8-1). Abusive and obscene language sounds powerful because it is shocking, but it will likely offend others. Sometimes deferential language is a sign of respect and not merely powerlessness. Even tag questions sometimes can be used powerfully. If your boss says, "You'll see that this is done, won't you?" it may be more a directive than a request. If so, the tag question is authoritative, not weak. Competent communicators understand that in some contexts it is important to use language that acknowledges another person's power.

Nonverbal Indicators of Power

Manchester, England became the first major British city to replace the traditional conical-shaped helmets worn by the police with more practical, American-style caps. Brian Mackenzie, president of the Police Superintendents Association, opposed the change. The helmet, he asserted, "provides stature, height, authority, and protection" (Hats Off, 1996).

Clothing is recognized as a strong indicator of power. We typically associate uniforms with power and authority. The "power suit" indicates to most people a stature and status associated with financial success and position in an organization. Tattered clothing scrounged from the trash communicates powerlessness associated with poverty.

Touch is another important nonverbal power indicator. The more powerful person can usually touch the less powerful person more frequently and with fewer restrictions (Henley, 1995). Sexual harassment laws recognize this difference and try to protect subordinates from tactile abuse.

Box 8-1 Sharper Focus

Gender, Culture, and Powerful/Powerless Language

Verbal indicators of power in U.S. culture show several clear gender differences. Men are typically more verbose, more inclined to give long-winded verbal presentations, and more talkative in mixed-sex groups than are women (James & Drakich, 1993). Talkativeness is associated with leadership. Men are more verbally aggressive than women (Nicotera & Rancer, 1994). They are more inclined to attack the self-concepts of others (dominance). Men are also more argumentative than women (Stewart et al., 1996), meaning that they are more likely to advocate controversial positions or to challenge the positions on issues taken by others. Women are inclined to view verbal aggressiveness and argumentativeness as strategies of dominance and control and as a hostile, competitive act (Nicotera & Rancer, 1994). Since men are more likely to seek status and women are more likely to seek connection in conversations (Tannen, 1990), these gender differences in verbal indicators of power are not surprising.

The issue of powerless versus powerful speech takes on more complexity when culture is added to the mix. What is viewed as powerful speech is culture specific. Japanese, for example, and members of most Asian cultures would view our version of powerful speech as immature because it indicates insensitivity to others and is likely to make agreement more difficult (Wetzel, 1988).

Collectivist Asian cultures desire harmony; the group is more important than the individual. In Western societies, verbal obscenity and swearing are perceived as powerful language. Individualistic Western cultures place high value on personal uniqueness. Verbal obscenity marks you as an individual willing to flout cultural values that discourage verbal obscenity. Japanese people do not use such language except in rare instances (De Klerk, 1991), but it is increasingly common among Americans.

When cultures clash over significant issues, these different views of powerful and powerless speech can pose serious problems. When negotiating teams from Japan and the United States meet, misunderstandings easily arise (Hellweg et al., 1994). The language of Japanese negotiators is rife with indirect phrases typical of a high-context communication style. Japanese negotiators use expressions such as "I think," "perhaps," "probably," and "maybe" with great frequency because they strive to preserve harmony and cause no offense that would result in loss of face for anyone (Samovar & Porter, 2001). American negotiators view this indirect language as powerless because they are more accustomed to the direct, explicit, "powerful" language of a low-context communication style.

Eye contact indicates a power difference. More powerful people stare more freely. Less powerful individuals must monitor their eye contact more energetically. A boss can show lack of attentiveness or interest by looking away from a subordinate, but a subordinate doing the same to his or her boss may invite a reprimand. Submissiveness is typically manifested both in the animal and people worlds by lowering one's eyes.

Space is a clear nonverbal indicator of power. The more powerful usually have more of it. Those who dream of winning the lottery imagine buying a large house, not a cramped studio apartment. The master bedroom in a house is reserved for the more powerful parents, and the children are given smaller bedrooms. The higher up in the corporate hierarchy you travel the bigger is your office space. Reserved parking spaces, part of the "parking wars" on college campuses across the United States, clearly designate power differences. Reserved faculty parking spaces often are closer to classroom and office buildings. Student parking spaces often are located somewhere in the next time zone.

In the spring term of 1999 a skirmish erupted over parking at Cabrillo College. Some faculty members were upset that students were "stealing" faculty parking spaces and that violators were not being ticketed sufficiently. The campus e-mail system was inundated for weeks by a debate on this controversy. Gated parking lots, entered only by inserting a special plastic card into a device that raises and lowers a gate, was one proposal circulated. One tongue-in-cheek proposal was that the

DILBERT Scott Adams

DILBERT reprinted by permission of United Feature Syndicate, Inc.

college dig a moat around faculty lots and toss in some crocodiles to keep out student violators. Space and power are clearly connected.

Much more could be added here, but the point seems clear. You can ascertain the relative distribution of power among individuals by observing general communication patterns and specific verbal and nonverbal communication.

Power Resources

Certain resources are utilized during transactions to exercise power. A **power resource** is anything that enables individuals to achieve their goals, assists others to achieve their goals, or interferes with the goal attainment of others (Folger et al., 1993). The range of power resources is broad. In this section the primary resources from which power is most extensively derived will be discussed.

Information

We live in the Age of Information, when information is power. Not all information, however, becomes a power resource. *Information has power potential when it is not easily or readily available.* Lawyers can charge eye-popping fees because they have information about the law that clients must have. Information that is restricted and scarce can be a powerful resource.

J. Z. Knight, a controversial woman who portrays herself as a celestial "channeler" in contact with a 35,000-year-old Cro-Magnon prophet named Ramtha, runs a School of Enlightenment in rural Washington (Conway & Siegelman, 1995). The main attraction for Ramtha devotees is to hear the "wisdom" of this prophet as he speaks to small gatherings of fascinated followers. Ramtha "speaks" in a guttural voice through Knight, who appears to be in a trance. Ramtha doesn't speak to just anybody. He speaks only to those who join Knight's enlightenment school (and presumably pay the hefty entrance fee).

It's not every day that you get an opportunity to hear from a 35,000-year-old guru from another spirit dimension. The scarcity of such elder prophets makes what Ramtha has to say more inviting. What Ramtha says, among other things, is that every orgasm brings you nearer to death (the same could be said, of course, for every breath you take). When you die, you should not seek the light because "light beings" are waiting and they will suck experience from your spirit and leave you to reincarnate with no memory of your last life. Instead, Ramtha urges, seek the darkness, the void.

If a 35-year-old guy named Fred provided the same information as Ramtha, do you think anyone would pay much attention? Many did pay attention to Ramtha, however, because his "wisdom" was viewed as scarce—it was restricted and accessible only through Knight (Conway & Siegelman, 1995). Knight makes it seem that the information is scarce and restricted because she allows only a select few to access it. Anybody, presumably, could hear Fred.

Information can be a positive power resource. Teachers are accorded stature because they have information that is valuable to students. Sharing this information can empower students. Ministers, priests, and religious leaders have information that brings them respect and prestige, and the information they share is spiritually empowering for laypersons. The information teachers and ministers share is a power resource because its access is restricted by the limited background and experience of those desiring the information. Teachers and ministers can translate the information and make it understandable.

Expertise

There is an old story told about an expert who was called in to fix a brand new diesel locomotive that wouldn't start. The railroad that owned the diesel engine requested an itemized billing once the expert had successfully finished his labor. His bill was for $1,500. He broke the bill into two items: $15 for swinging a hammer and $1,485 for knowing the right spot to hit and how to hit it. We pay big money to experts for knowing what to do and how to do it.

Information and expertise are closely related, but a person can have critical information without being an expert. You might possess a valuable technical report without being able to decipher any of the information. You may also know the law but not be capable of practicing it skillfully in the courtroom. Expertise is more than just having information. *An expert knows how to use the information wisely and skillfully.*

No individual or group could ever hope to function effectively without at some time requiring the services of experts. Families require the skills of financial advisers, roofers, carpenters, exterminators, counselors, physicians, hair stylists, mechanics, and those who repair our appliances, phones, computers, broken pipes, and broken hearts. Expertise can be a very positive power resource.

Expertise functions as a power resource under two conditions. First, the expert is perceived to *have the requisite skills, abilities, knowledge, and background* to function as a real expert. Normally, real expertise includes appropriate education and training, intelligence, experience, and demonstrated mastery of relevant information.

A second condition for experts is to *be considered trustworthy.* People everywhere are more influenced by experts who stand to gain nothing personally than they are by those who would gain personally by lying or distorting information (McGuinnies & Ward, 1980).

In the summer of 1992 the *National Law Journal* and LEXIS, a database service, conducted the most comprehensive national poll of jurors ever undertaken. Of the nearly 800 individuals who had recently sat on a jury, 95% said that they were impressed by expert testimony during a trial, and 70% felt that expert testimony

Augustana College students react to the O.J. Simpson "not guilty" verdict. Note the different reactions from black and white students. These partly reflect the level of trustworthiness accorded police testimony, a prime issue during the trial.

influences the outcome of a trial. Nevertheless, 51% of the jurors said that they didn't necessarily trust the testimony of police officers, and 70% of African American jurors felt police testimony was untrustworthy (Jurors' Views, 1993).

Legitimate Authority

See Video clip #7, chapter 8 on the CD.

Participants were told to deliver increasingly painful electric shocks to an innocent victim whose "crime" was merely making a mistake on a word association test. The purpose of this series of studies (Milgram, 1974) was to determine whether subjects would blindly obey a legitimate authority even when that authority ordered them to harm an innocent victim. No one, not the experimenters, groups of psychiatrists, college students, or middle-class adults, thought any of the participants would deliver the maximum shock of 450 volts. Nevertheless, two thirds of the participants in some of the studies obeyed the experimenter and delivered the maximum shock to the victim, who in some cases screamed in agony. No shocks were actually delivered, but the experiments were made to seem real, and none of the participants suspected trickery.

In all, 18 variations of these obedience-to-authority studies were conducted. More than 1,000 participants from all ages and walks of life took part. Other researchers replicated these studies in the United States and abroad, gaining as much as 85% compliance (Miller, 1986). It didn't matter if the innocent victim complained of a heart condition or demanded to be freed from the experiment; most participants obeyed the orders of the legitimate authority.

Would you shock this cute puppy? College students shocked a puppy like this one in a replication of the Milgram obedience studies. How do you explain the fact that all of the female subjects in this study shocked the adorable puppy?

In one of the more dramatic replications, participants were told to shock a cute fluffy puppy (Sheridan & King, 1972). Although the human victims in the other studies weren't actually shocked, the puppy did receive shocks (at reduced levels). Despite the disbelief commonly exhibited by my students that anyone would continue to shock an adorable puppy held captive in a box whose floor was an electrified grid, the results of the experiment duplicated those of previous studies. Three quarters of the subjects, all college students, were obedient to the end (54% of the men and 100% of the women).

Participants in the study delivered electric shocks, not because they were evil or sadistic, but because they couldn't resist legitimate authority (Milgram, 1974). The experimenter was the legitimate authority. He insisted that participants continue to deliver increasing levels of electric shock to the victims. A **legitimate authority** is someone who is perceived to have a right to direct others' behavior because of his or her position, title, role, experience, or knowledge.

The strength of legitimate authority can be seen outside the experimental laboratory. David Cline, a driver education instructor at Northern High School in Durham, North Carolina, resigned from his teaching post in October 1997 because of his irresponsible behavior. While acting as a driving instructor, he ordered a teenage student driver to chase a car that had cut them off. When they caught up to the offender, Cline jumped out of the car and punched Jon David Macklin in the nose. Macklin took off. Cline ordered the student driver to chase after him again, which the student did. A police officer pulled them over for speeding. The student broke traffic laws and endangered several people on the orders of a legitimate authority—her driver education instructor.

No individual possesses legitimate authority. This is conferred by others. Participants in the Milgram studies could have perceived the orders of the experimenter as illegitimate and refused to obey. Parents exercise legitimate authority over their children by virtue of their caregiver role. This is usually a positive use of power because most parents want what is best for their children. They typically use their legitimate authority to guide, protect, and teach their children.

Even if authority is granted by virtue of a formal title, position, or role, it must be perceived as legitimate to function as a power resource. Baby-sitters sometimes face this predicament. Parents put them in charge of their children, but the children's perception that the sitter is not a "real parent" can undermine this power resource.

The competent communicator must adopt the skeptical view and distinguish between appropriate and inappropriate use of authority. Blindly refusing to obey police officers, teachers, parents, judges, and bosses is as dangerous as blindly obeying authority. Ethical criteria—respect, honesty, fairness, choice, and responsibility—provide the means for determining when we should comply with and when we should defy authority. In the Milgram studies, the victims were pleading with participants to stop shocking them. The victims were given no choice, and the delivery of seemingly painful electric shocks showed little respect for and sensitivity toward the innocent victims of the experiment.

Rewards and Punishments

The role of distributing rewards and punishments can be an important source of power. Salaries, bonuses, work schedules, perks, hirings, and firings are typical job-related rewards and punishments. Money, freedom, privacy, and car keys are a few of the rewards and punishments found in family situations.

The power potential of punishment depends on the degree of certainty that the punishment will be administered. Idle threats have little influence on behavior. Parents who threaten spankings or denial of privileges—but never follow through—soon realize that their children have learned to ignore such impotent bluster. Punishment is a source of power if it can be, and likely will be, exercised.

Punishing, however, is delicate business. Punishing can be used positively to change behavior from antisocial to prosocial. Punishing, however, is coercive and reinforces dominance. Consequently, it easily triggers psychological backlash. Individuals on the receiving end of punishment typically rebel. Those who punish create interpersonal distance between themselves and those punished. We don't normally like our tormentors.

Reward as a power resource tends to induce rewarding behavior. If you disseminate rewards, you become more attractive in the eyes of those rewarded. This, of course, depends on whether the rewards are issued through a cooperative or competitive system. Rewards, especially when used to bribe a person to behave in a certain way, can be used as a strategy of dominance. "Do what I say and I'll buy you a computer" seeks compliance from the person rewarded.

Personal Qualities

We all know individuals who exert some influence over us without using any of the power resources already discussed. They exhibit personal qualities that we find attractive. Mother Theresa, the Pope, several U.S. presidents, and some sports figures, political leaders, teachers, and parents exhibit these personal qualities that draw people to them and make them positive role models. The constellation of personal attributes that people find attractive is often referred to as **charisma.**

Good looks, an attractive personality, dynamism, persuasive skills, warmth, and charm are some of the personal qualities that make an individual charismatic. There is no precise formula for determining charisma. What is attractive to you may be unattractive to others. Your friends may be flabbergasted by your choice for a date. Cult leaders Charles Manson, Marshall Applewhite, and David Koresh seem like lunatics to many, but others followed them unhesitatingly. Who can adequately explain the grief exhibited by Elvis worshippers on the 25th anniversary of his death in 2002? Many of the grief stricken weren't born until after Elvis died. The cult of celebrity and personality can be a very powerful resource.

Before leaving this section on power resources, consider one final point. None of the five resources—information, expertise, legitimate authority, punishments and rewards, and personal qualities—have inherent power. Power resources are not properties of individuals. *A person does not possess power but is granted power by others.* Your relationship partner, a group, or an organization must endorse the resource for it to be influential. Charisma means little in a job interview if a hiring committee prefers diligence, expertise, and efficiency. Charisma might look like flash without follow-through. A reward that nobody wants will influence no one. Information that is irrelevant to the needs of individuals or groups has no power potential. When Richard Nixon faced impeachment because of the Watergate scandal, he had to resign because the American people no longer endorsed the legitimacy of his presidency. Bill Clinton, however, weathered the impeachment storm because a significant majority of the American public opposed his removal from office. Power is transactional.

Problems of Power Imbalance

Chapter 2 cited research that showed the results of power imbalances on relationships: When men refused to share power with their wives, there was an 81% chance that the marriage would self-destruct (Gottman & Silver, 1999). When power is unequally distributed and dominance becomes the focus, power struggles often ensue (Wilmot & Hocker, 2001). In this section, four effects of dominance will be discussed: physical violence, verbal and nonverbal abuse, sexual harassment, and commonplace difficulties in ordinary transactions. With the exception of the last effect, all are part of what some researchers have called the "dark side" of communicating with others (Cupach & Spitzberg, 1994).

It is common practice in most human communication textbooks to ignore the dark side of communicating, or at most to make only passing mention of it. The desire to present communication transactions in a sunny, "positive" framework is understandable. Ignoring the dark side because it is unpleasant, however, makes communication textbooks seem sadly unrelated to the all too frequent experience of readers. As two communication experts observe, "To fully understand how people effectively function requires us to consider how individuals cope with social interaction that is difficult, problematic, challenging, distressing, and disruptive" (Cupach & Spitzberg, 1994, p. vii). As another puts it, the "dark side is integral to the experience of relationships, not separate from it" (Duck, 1994b, p. 6). Few problems in life, especially significant difficulties, are solved by ignoring them. If verbal and physical violence, abuse, and harassment were infrequent, insignificant occurrences, ignoring them here would be appropriate and welcomed. These problems, however, occur frequently in our communication transactions, and they are significant. We ignore them at our own peril.

Ultimately, this examination of the more unpleasant side of communicating with others has a very positive goal: to help you recognize the sometimes subtle encroachment of the dark side into your communication transactions. Such recognition is the first step toward preventing the dark side from intruding into your life.

Physical Violence

Violence in relationships, unfortunately, is not an uncommon occurrence. Studies show that **common couple violence,** or "the occasional violence that arises out of strong reactions to the escalation of a particular disagreement," is a mutual event with both partners engaging in equal amounts of violence (Klein & Johnson, 1997). It is appropriate to call couple violence "common" because about half of American couples have experienced some violence in their romantic relationships (Johnson, 1995; Klein & Johnson, 1997). This includes gay and lesbian relationships. Violence is as frequent and as intense in gay and lesbian relationships as it is in heterosexual relationships (Letellier, 1994; Renzetti, 1991; Waldner-Haugrud et al., 1997).

This is the image most people have when spousal or partner abuse is an issue. Hundreds of studies, however, reveal substantial violence is also initiated by women against their partners (see Box 8-2).

Box 8-2 | Focus on Controversy

Gender and Relationship Violence

Comedian Elaine Boosler once remarked, "When women are depressed, they either eat or go shopping. Men invade another country" (Ivy & Backlund, 2000, p. 44). Despite the widespread belief that men are usually the perpetrators of violence and women the victims, recent studies have challenged this perception. Farrell (1999) cites 53 studies on relationship violence that show, *without exception*, that men and women are equally violent. Archer (2000) conducted a meta-analysis of 124 studies involving almost 65,000 subjects and concluded that women resort to physical violence as often as men (see also George, 1994). Research also shows that men and women threaten violence about equally. One study of college students (Marshall, 1994) found that 77% of males and 76% of females had made threats of violence to their partners, and 72% of males and 79% of females had received threats of violence from their partners.

These findings startle many, and they have provoked white-hot debate among partisan groups. You probably should be surprised by these findings. Data that reveal high levels of female violence against men usually go unreported in the media (Farrell, 1999). Also, crime surveys conducted by the FBI and other governmental agencies understate the problem of female violence. Males are reluctant to label a physical attack by a female partner as a criminal assault (Archer, 2000).

Two principal responses have been offered to counter these surprising and consistent results (Berns, 2001). First, although the rates of violence are about equal for men and women, the severity of the violence may not be (Dobash et al., 1992). Certainly a woman slapping a man across the face is less severe than a man beating a woman with his fists. Numerous studies, however, reveal that women unleash "severe violence" on men more often than men similarly victimize women (Morse, 1995; Rollins & Oheneba-Sakyi, 1990; Russell & Hulson, 1992; Stets & Henderson, 1991; Straus & Kantor, 1994; Thompson, 1991). According to the U.S. Department of Justice Bureau of Justice Statistics (1998), women compensate for less physical strength by employing weapons (knives, iron skillets, guns) more frequently than do men.

The results of studies showing women inflicting "severe violence" on men more frequently than in reverse, however, is misleading. The most frequent acts of "severe violence" by women ("kicked," "bit," "tried to hit with something") rarely produce severe injuries (Straus & Kantor, 1992). Even seemingly identical acts of aggression ("hit with fist") can produce markedly different physical injuries because of men's greater physical strength (Christopher & Lloyd, 2000). Lardner (1997) claims that almost 10 times as many women as men are treated in

emergency rooms at hospitals for serious injuries inflicted by spouses or partners (see also Gelles, 1997). Although male victims may be hesitant to seek medical treatment for injuries inflicted by their female partners ("It's unmanly"), and they may lie about what caused the injuries (Farrell, 1999), it seems unlikely that all or even most of the difference in hospital treatments of serious injuries can be accounted for by these explanations.

The severity of the violence inflicted on women may also appear greater, on average, than that inflicted by women on men for three additional reasons. First, women must contend with spousal and partner rape (Christopher & Lloyd, 2000). Between 10% and 14% of women are raped by their intimate partners (Finkelhor & Yllo, 1985; Russel, 1982). Men simply do not have to concern themselves with rape by their female partners. Second, women are more frequently murdered by their male partners than in reverse. According to the U.S. Department of Justice Bureau of Justice Statistics (1994), of the approximately 1,500 spousal murders each year, women are the victims in 59% of the cases. This, however, should not obscure the fact that a substantial 41% of the homicide victims are male. Third, "patriarchical terrorism" (Johnson, 2001), the most extreme form of violence that aims to completely control and subdue one's partner, is almost exclusively male (97%).

Self-defense is a second reason offered to counter the consistent findings that relationship violence is mutual. Perhaps women use violence to ward off their male attackers. Undoubtedly this is true, but it also seems true that men ward off female-initiated attacks. The preponderance of evidence does not support the claim that female violence is predominantly used in self-defense. Numerous studies show that women initiate violence against their male partners more often than in reverse (Billingham & Sack 1986; Bookwala et al., 1992; Henton et al., 1983; Sorenson & Telles, 1991). As one study concluded, "Males who used force reported that they were more likely to be retaliating for being hit first, and female victims also reported this to be the case" (Follingstad et al., 1991, p. 56).

If self-defense does not adequately explain female violence, why are women more frequently and seriously injured? We might easily assume that the person with the severe injuries is the victim, and the partner that is relatively unscathed must be the initiator of the abuse. As two communication experts explain, however, "It cannot be presumed that women's behavior is self-defensive; women may initiate a flurry of violent but noninjurious acts, and men may respond with a single violent and injurious act" (Cupach and Canary, 1997, p. 185). Some

Box 8-2 **Focus on Controversy** (continued)

have even argued that female homicides of male spouses are "delayed acts of self-defense" precipitated by previous male battering. Research, however, does not support this as a reason for most partner homicides (Sommer et al., 1992; Straus, 1989, 1993).

Thus, in totality, the evidence supports several conclusions. First, there is frequent violence initiated by *both* women and men in relationships. Second, *both* men and women are victims of severe violence and injury. Women, however, suffer more injuries than men (Archer, 2000), they suffer more grievous injuries, they have the added fear of partner rape, and they are killed more often than men in domestic disputes. Third, women undoubtedly feel more menaced by the prospect of extreme violence by their male partners because they typically are physically weaker and are almost exclusively the victims of patriarchal terrorism (battering).

Some have argued that taking female aggression seriously may become a strategy to obscure men's violence (Berns, 2001). This is certainly not my intention. The fact that women violently attack men should make us no less concerned about men battering women. We should, however, be more concerned about female-initiated

violence than perhaps we are currently. Relationship violence should not be framed as a competition to determine who is the bigger victim, women or men. Our aim should be to stop the common couple violence. We cannot do that effectively if we look at only male abusers and female victims.

Questions for Thought

1. Are you surprised by the research results showing about equal frequency of violence from men and women? Why is the stereotype of male abusers and female victims so prevalent?
2. Farrell (1999) documents that the popular media censor research findings that show female frequency of violence equal to or exceeding male violence. Why would the popular media do this? Is this ethical for them to censor such research findings?
3. Do you agree that women probably feel more menaced by violence in relationships than men? Do you think men fear violence from their female partners as much as women fear violence from male partners?

www.mhhe
 com/
 rothwell2

See online Relationship Violence Questionnaire on Online Learning Center, chapter 8.

The issue of physical violence in relationships is muddied somewhat by the stereotype of the male abuser and female victim. (For a discussion of this highly charged issue of gender and violence in relationships, see Box 8-2.) Focusing attention primarily or exclusively on male perpetrators and female victims ignores the problem of mutual violence so common in this country. A serious discussion of relationship violence cannot be confined simply to male violence against women, as serious and disturbing as this problem is. Relationship violence is a broader problem of dominance-prevention power struggles.

An imbalance of power, whether actual, perceived, or desired, is a central element in relationship violence (Leonard & Senchak, 1996; Rogers et al., 1996; Sabourin, 1995). Violence is far more prevalent in relationships in which power is unequally distributed than in relationships in which the power distribution is relatively equal (Cahn & Lloyd, 1996; Coleman & Straus, 1986; Lloyd & Emery, 1993). One study concluded that "egalitarian marriages [equal distribution of power] have the lowest risk of intimate violence" (Gelles & Straus, 1988, p. 112).

Feelings of relative powerlessness can result from deficiencies in communication knowledge and skills (Infante et al., 1992). Difficulties in making claims and arguing those claims effectively in the midst of conflict are significant contributors to relationship violence (Infante et al., 1989; Infante et al., 1990). Such communication deficiencies produce a sense of relative powerlessness. Violence, in a perverse way, compensates for the communication deficiencies, especially if the deficient individual has a verbally adept partner.

Jealousy, rule violations, and perceived instances of disrespect are common sources of violence in relationships (Cupach and Canary, 1997). All of these involve an imbalance of power. In each case, the issue of control emerges. When rule violations occur, who has the "right" to punish transgressors? More powerful parents punish less powerful children for rule violations. When jealousy emerges, the jealous partner feels a loss of control. His or her partner is "threatening" the relationship. Violence may be the "desperate" act of a jealous partner trying to exert control where control has slipped away. When disrespect is exhibited, violence may be chosen to punish those who show disrespect. Those who perceive that they should be accorded status are most likely to become angered by disrespect. Violence then becomes an act of demanding respect where none has been shown.

Verbal and Nonverbal Abuse

Power struggles in relationships that take on a dominance-prevention quality do not always end in violence. In fact, more likely than not, no fists will fly, nor will any pots and pans. Partners will simply abuse each other verbally and nonverbally by tearing apart each other's self-esteem and self-worth. Communicating contempt for one's partner has a corrosive effect on a relationship (Gottman, 1994a, 1994b).

Contempt is intended to insult and emotionally abuse a person. A 36-year-old female trucking company executive describes men in power positions as "a bunch of shallow, bald, middle-aged men with character disorders. They don't have the emotional capacity it takes to qualify as human beings. One good thing about these white, male, almost extinct mammals is that they are growing old. We get to watch them die" (Gates, 1993, p. 49). Now that's contempt! When couples argue as adversaries trying to win a verbal exchange, contempt can easily become a verbal weapon, both for the dominant partner trying to exert control and for the weaker partner trying to equalize the power distribution.

There are four ways to communicate contempt (Gottman, 1994a, 1994b). First, contempt can be communicated by verbal insults and name calling. *Bastard, bitch, moron, jerk, imbecile, fathead,* and even cruder, more vicious insults are targeted at tearing apart the self-esteem of one's partner.

Second, hostile humor communicates contempt. Camouflaged as "only a joke," hostile humor, if you're the target, aims to make others laugh at your expense. "Marsha's so sweet I fear getting diabetes just being around her" and "Harry's a very passionate lover—of himself" ridicule the person shown contempt. Respect, a key ingredient of competent communication, is nowhere to be seen.

Third, mockery communicates contempt. You mock others by imitating them derisively. A woman says to her partner, "I really do love you," and her partner responds with a contorted facial expression and fake, exaggerated voice, "You really do love me." Mockery is meant to make fun of a person. It assaults that person's sincerity.

Fourth, certain body movements communicate contempt. Sneering, rolling your eyes, curling your upper lip, and using obscene gestures are all signs of contempt for your partner. Leaving the room while your partner or coworker is speaking to you nonverbally communicates contempt.

Sexual Harassment

Mike Hughes, a journalist, was eating breakfast at Bette's Ocean View Diner in Berkeley, California, one fall morning in 1991 while reading an article on freedom of the press in *Playboy* magazine. His waitress, Barbara (only name given), was highly offended and, with the assistance of the restaurant's manager, insisted that Hughes put away the magazine or leave. Hughes left. This incident was reported in the press. Demonstrators conducted a "read-in" in front of the diner to dramatize their opposition to censorship. Counter-demonstrators also showed in equal numbers to protest "pornography in the workplace." As Barbara explained, "I think pornography is offensive, and I feel pornography in my workplace is sexual harassment" (cited in Hentoff, 1992, p. 14).

Sexual harassment is an explosive issue. Part of its explosiveness comes from serious disagreements, illustrated by the Bette's Diner conflict, regarding what constitutes sexual harassment. One study asked female faculty and graduate students whether they had experienced 31 acts legally defined as sexual harassment. Almost 90% of the study participants had experienced at least some of these. Yet only 5.6% of the faculty and 2.8% of the graduate students surveyed answered "yes" to the question that directly asked them if they had been sexually harassed (Brooks & Perot, 1991; see also Mecca & Rubin, 1999; Shepela & Levesque, 1998). A similar result was found for male college students with only 1 of 40 labeling inappropriate behavior by their professor as sexual harassment (Kalof et al., 2001). The distinction between harassing communication and communication that is natural among friends, between romantic partners at work, or between teachers and students is not always clear (Witteman, 1993). Complimentary comments and gestures, nonsexual touching, and staring can be viewed either way. What is flirtation to one person may be harassment to another.

The law defines two principal types of sexual harassment: quid pro quo (you give something to get something) and hostile environment (Witteman, 1993). **Quid pro quo harassment** occurs when the more powerful person requires sexual favors from the less powerful individual in exchange for keeping a job, getting a high grade in a class, landing an employment promotion, and the like. **Hostile environment harassment** is not quite so obviously an abuse of power. The Supreme Court in 1986 endorsed the hostile work environment interpretation of sexual harassment. According to the Court's decision, employees have a right to work in an environment free from discriminatory insult, ridicule, or intimidation (Paetzold & O'Leary-Kelly, 1993). Recently, colleges and universities have expanded this ruling to include hostile learning environment to protect students.

The *Playboy* incident at Bette's Diner demonstrates the problem of interpreting what constitutes a hostile environment. Sexist language, sexual jokes, pictures of spouses in skimpy bathing suits at the beach, and pinups of either sex are banned in most workplaces. Complicating the issue further, consensual romantic relationships have been deemed sexual harassment at some colleges and places of employment. Some people perceive that such romantic relationships bestow on fellow workers or classmates benefits not justly earned, and they consider this a hostile environment issue. San Francisco State University in 1998 created a firestorm of controversy when it proposed to ban all romantic relationships between students and faculty, even if a student wasn't in the professor's class or under his or her supervision. Most students interviewed on campus felt that this violated their rights as adults to choose a romantic partner.

The hostile environment form of sexual harassment has some validity. A District of Columbia court awarded Elizabeth Reese $250,000 for damages incurred while she worked for the architectural design firm Swanke, Hayden, and Connell. Reese's male supervisor repeatedly made lewd comments to her, incessantly asked about her sex life, encouraged her to prostitute herself for the firm, and then told fellow workers that she had.

Sexual harassment is often more nonverbal than verbal, and it usually involves a power imbalance.

Power imbalances are at the heart of most sexual harassment (Dziech & Hawkins, 1998). Quid pro quo harassment is a clear instance of dominance, usually by more powerful males against less powerful females. Dealing with this kind of sexual harassment is extremely difficult because the harasser has legitimate authority and can punish the victim for openly complaining. Laws forbidding such behavior, policies that explicitly punish such harassment, and enforcement of laws and policies are all helpful in combating quid pro quo harassment. Firm, unequivocal rejection of such harassment by the target of an unwanted sexual advance is also an important communication approach. "Do not ever make sexual remarks to me" is an unequivocal rejection of the harassment.

Hostile environment sexual harassment typically flows from power imbalances as well. It is particularly prevalent where women try to compete in traditionally male occupations. Smith Barney, a Wall Street brokerage firm with 400 offices nationwide, established a pattern of hostile environment sexual harassment that led to a class action lawsuit by 25 female stockbrokers. Male employees gawked at the women's breasts and made lewd and suggestive remarks. Senior male managers in the Garden City, New York, office maintained a basement room dubbed the "Boom-Boom Room," where female employees were confronted with unwanted sexual advances, groping, and kissing on the lips. Women at work were sent condoms and food shaped in the form of penises. Plaintiffs claimed that their complaints to superiors were ignored. In some cases, women were punished with menial tasks and public humiliations for complaining. Pamela Martens, one of the plaintiffs, noted, "It's like they have a manual in their heads as to how to crush women" (Jackson, 1997). Even though the harassment often came from fellow brokers of equal position and power, most of the Smith Barney brokers were men. This put female brokers at a decided disadvantage when trying to combat the hostile "men's club" environment created by male brokers.

Combating hostile environment sexual harassment is difficult. Most often a dominance-prevention dynamic occurs. Sometimes the hostile environment is the product of incompetent communication, not ugly intentions (Bingham, 1991). A firm, clearly defined policy staunchly supported by those in power positions goes a long way toward diminishing this type of sexual harassment. With such a policy, those who are harassed can more safely and confidently reject poor treatment. Communication strategies of assertiveness, a threat of formal complaint, or deflection of sexual remarks by diverting discussion to neutral topics can be successful when hostile environment harassment is clearly not tolerated in the workplace or educational environment (Bingham, 1991).

Commonplace Difficulties

Power imbalances don't always lead to verbal or physical abuse and harassment. Many, perhaps most, instances of power imbalance never graduate to the dark side of interpersonal relationships. They remain part of the lighter side of personal difficulties experienced with others.

Consider the remote control wars. Invented for Zenith Corporation by Dr. Robert Adler, the remote control made its debut on June 8, 1956. The Consumer Electronics Manufacturers Association estimates that there are about 400 million remote controls in use, and guess who typically controls that use? According to a study conducted by sociologist Alexis Walker, president of the National Council on Family Relations, men are the predominant channel surfers, much to the displeasure of most women (cited in McCall, 1996). Numerous studies have found similar results (Bellamy & Walker, 1996). One woman in Walker's study expressed her frustration this way: "He just flips through the channels. It drives me crazy because he just goes through, and goes through, and goes through" (cited in McCall, 1996 p. D1). Walker herself recalls, "My parents bought a second TV set because my mother said to me, 'I will not watch TV with your father any more because of the way he uses that remote control'" (p. D1). Women told Walker that they videotaped their preferred shows to view at a later time so they could still be with their male partners while they watched sports.

When the issue of who is in charge of the remote control is confronted directly, a man may give control to his partner but then insist that she turn quickly to another channel to check on a sports score. The woman is still doing his bidding even though he is not actually pressing the buttons on the remote control.

Walker concludes that the balance of power at home, as reflected in the battle over the remote control, is still tilted in men's favor no matter how equal a couple sees their relationship. Men, however, are mostly unaware that they are in charge of the remote control. "I guess I don't think about it, I just switch the channel," said one man in the study (McCall, 1996, p. D6). "Power dynamics among couples are rarely conscious," explains professor Stephen Marks of the University of Texas at Austin. "He gets to watch it the way he wants to watch it, whether she's there or not. She has to watch by herself or the way he watches it. To put it in the most simple way, it's not fair" (p. D6).

Power imbalances are apparent in a wide variety of daily occurrences. Power imbalances at work are made apparent in a variety of ways. Bosses often refer to assistants by their first names but may be addressed by subordinates as "Mr. Burns" or "Ms. Simpson." The shift from work to personal talk is usually initiated by the most powerful person (Tannen, 1994). If the office manager takes a break and begins telling stories and chatting, everyone else in the office sees fit to follow suit. Taking breaks and chatting, however, can be perceived as goofing off unless sanctioned by a more powerful person. Such power imbalance can make employees wary, even resentful, of the "double standard."

Doctor-patient relationships are rarely equal. Patients wait for doctors, sometimes for unreasonably long periods of time, but doctors don't wait for patients. My doctor developed a reputation for mistreating his patients by making them wait for up to an hour and a half. On one occasion, after a tedious delay, I felt compelled to leave before seeing him, whereupon he raced out into the parking lot, chased me down, and cajoled me into returning for immediate treatment. The less powerful do have options.

Doctors usually wear white coats as symbols of their authority. Patients wear casual clothes, humiliating hospital gowns with a breezy backside, and sometimes no clothes at all, which can be embarrassing. Patients refer to the physician by title, such as "Dr. Schmidt" or "Dr. Martinez," not "Harry" or "Maria." The physician, however, often addresses the patient by his or her first name. This pattern is not always displayed, however, when the doctor is female. Some male patients may inappropriately try to upset the power imbalance by referring to female physicians informally (e.g., "Hi, Kate") or even by making lewd or suggestive remarks (Tannen, 1994). Such references are insulting, and they make the doctor's task of caring for the patient exceedingly difficult.

Apologies for mishaps or misdeeds are expected from the less powerful, reminding them of their subservient position. Children are expected to apologize to parents for cracking up the car, but parents do not normally apologize to their kids for a similar mishap, even though the children may be seriously inconvenienced by the car being out of commission. Nevertheless, apologizing can cement relationships between unequal individuals.

In brief review, an imbalance in power alters the way we communicate with others. Sometimes it produces violence and psychological abuse that can easily spiral out of control. An imbalance in power also creates an environment that is ripe for sexual harassment. Dominance, even when no violence or harassment occurs, still often produces friction, anger, wariness, awkwardness, strife, frustration, and an assortment of other difficulties in a wide variety of relationships. A central concern to any competent communicator must be how to balance the power more appropriately in relationships where power imbalances are counterproductive. This central concern is explored next.

Competent Communication and Balancing Power

The quick answer to relationship problems caused by power imbalances is to balance the power. This is easier said than done, especially when some individuals would rather maintain their dominance in relationships and groups. There are many ways to balance unequally distributed power; some that involve competent communication and others that are clearly incompetent communication.

Dominance-Prevention Power Balancing

Dominance-prevention power struggles produce several methods of balancing power. These methods are coalition formation, defiance, and resistance.

COALITION FORMATION Individuals form temporary alliances, called **coalitions,** to increase their power relative to others. Coalitions occur in group situations when there are disputes. Coalitions have been formed when group members jointly use their combined power to control a decision and to take action. One study (Grusky et al., 1995) found that arguments and disagreements in families lead to coalitions about 30% of the time. Coalitions can balance the power in a group when the relatively powerless use them to increase their strength. Coalitions can create power imbalances when the more powerful group members move to consolidate their strength by banding together against the weaker members.

In most families the father is considered the most powerful person, followed by the mother, then the oldest child, and then the younger siblings (Grusky et al., 1995). Parental coalitions are the predominate coalitions in a four-person family, and they are virtually unopposable. Such coalitions maintain the family structure and support the status differences between parents and children. The next most frequent coalition is composed of a parent and an older child. Children-only coalitions are the least frequent and are almost always unsuccessful (Grusky et al., 1995).

Coalitions may be useful in the political arena, but they can be destructive in family situations (Rosenthal, 1997). Coalitions create a "them versus us" competitive mentality. Parental coalitions are sometimes necessary to present a united front when a dispute with children arises. Parent-child coalitions, however, can disrupt the family structure. Parental stability is the most vital part of family stability. Asking children to choose sides in a dispute between parents can rip a family apart, especially if the issue is significant and the dispute is recurrent. It is usually more constructive and effective for parents to work out their differences without seeking allies among their children.

DEFIANCE   Low power persons sometimes overtly defy higher power persons. **Defiance** is unambiguous, purposeful noncompliance. It is a refusal to give in to those with greater power. Defiance is a prevention form of power in which one stands against those who attempt to dominate.

Defiance can be contagious. A defiant child can embolden siblings to defy parents unless the parents take effective action. A single worker who defiantly walks off

Defiance is an overt act of noncompliance. This lone unarmed man stands against tanks in the 1989 Tiananmen Square uprising in China. Most defiance is the product of a power imbalance, vividly evident here.

Box 8-3   Sharper Focus

Henry Boisvert Versus FMC Corporation

Henry Boisvert was an engineer who worked on the Bradley Fighting Vehicle, a controversial 25-ton military weapon that is part tank and part troop carrier. In the early 1980s, Boisvert began warning his superiors at FMC Corporation, a military contracting company in San Jose, California, that there were serious flaws in the Bradley (Mintz, 1998). Boisvert was concerned about safety problems, including the BFV's tendency to sink in water despite being advertised to the U.S. Army as an amphibious vehicle. Boisvert's efforts to include safety problems in testing reports were snubbed by FMC.

When Boisvert finally went public with his accusations that FMC had defrauded the federal government of billions of dollars for a military weapon that was unsafe and ineffective, his life became a nightmare. In 1986 he was fired from FMC. FMC labeled Boisvert a flake and a troublemaker, denying all of his accusations. Almost all of his friends, most of whom had worked at FMC, deserted him. He was unable to find work. He sent out 8,000 résumés, had 5 interviews, and received no job offers, even for low-level positions. Concerned that his phone was tapped and that FMC was responsible for burglarizing his lawyer's office, Boisvert constantly worried about his safety. Unable to find work, he went broke and exhausted his retirement fund.

For 12 years he fought FMC in court. Finally, in April 1998, a U.S. district court jury decided unanimously that Boisvert was right and awarded him millions of dollars in damages and fined FMC over $350 million, most of it to go to the federal government as repayment for the fraud. An Army veteran, Boisvert explained after the verdict, "I wanted a jury to make them pay the government back. I promise I'll give most of the money away. I'll set up trusts to help society. The bottom line was to save troops' lives. I was just hoping nobody got killed" (Mintz, 1998, p. A9).

Whistleblowers like Boisvert, who alert the public and government of fraud and criminal activity by businesses and corporations, face nasty consequences for their defiance of company orders to keep quiet. On December 10, 1993, CNN reported that 88% of whistleblowers suffer personal reprisals for their defiance. On March 6, 1989, CBS News reported that, partly because of pressures to keep quiet about abuses, 17% of whistleblowers studied lost their homes, 15% divorced, and 10% attempted suicide. It takes courage and resilience to defy those in positions of power.

---

the job may encourage a wildcat strike. Those in authority are anxious to halt defiance before it spreads.

Defiant individuals hoping to counter dominance from others occasionally convert an entire group to their point of view. If a person cannot be expelled from the relationship or group (e.g., family member), remaining unalterably and confidently defiant provides the best chance of successfully countering pressure to comply (Gebhardt & Meyers, 1995). When a group has the power to expel a person, however, remaining unalterably defiant will likely prove to be an impotent choice. Remaining uncompromisingly defiant until the group is about fed up and then switching to a more compromising position is an option likely to produce better results (Wolf, 1979).

Remaining uncompromisingly defiant risks straining friendships and jeopardizing relationships with partners, relatives, and coworkers (Box 8-3). Any time individuals are defiant, they run the risk of alienating those who disagree with them and sometimes even those who agree. Defiance is a highly competitive communication behavior. It will make a person a loser far more often than a winner simply because the very nature of defiance is disagreeable to those who want compliance, and they usually are the majority. In most cases, consider defiance an option of last resort.

RESISTANCE   Defiance is overt, unambiguous noncompliance. **Resistance** is covert, ambiguous noncompliance. It is often duplicitous and manipulative. Resisters are subtle saboteurs. The sabotage is ambiguous because truly successful resistance leaves people wondering if resistance even occurred.

Resistance, like defiance, is usually the choice of the less powerful. Resistance has an advantage over defiance. It is often safer to use indirect means of noncompliance than direct confrontation when faced with a more powerful person or group. Those who are defiant dig in their heels and openly cause trouble, but those who resist merely drag their feet.

There are several resistance strategies (Rothwell, 2001). Resistance strategies are sometimes referred to as *passive aggression.*

Strategic Stupidity   This is the playing stupid strategy. When children don't want to do what their parents tell them to, they sometimes act stupid when they know better. "But mom, I don't know how to fold the laundry" may simply be an effort to frustrate the parent who may give up in disgust and fold the laundry rather than show the child for the "bizillionth" time what should be plainly obvious.

Strategic stupidity works exceedingly well when the low-power person claims stupidity, is forced to attempt the task anyway, and then performs it ineptly. In one study of 555 married adults (Home Chores, 1993), 14% of the men admitted purposely botching house chores to get out of doing them again. The poor performance becomes "proof" that the stupidity is real. The passive aggressor can assert, "I told you I didn't know how to do laundry."

Loss of Motor Function   This resistance strategy is an effective companion to strategic stupidity. The resister doesn't act stupid, just incredibly clumsy, often resulting in costly damage. There is a mixed message here of resistance on one hand but apparent effort on the other. "I tried really hard not to let dishes slip out of my hands; I'm sorry I broke two plates" may be an honest apology from your housemate for accidental behavior. If it becomes repetitive, however, it may be an effort to avoid doing dishes.

The Misunderstanding Mirage   This is the "I thought you meant" or the "I could have sworn you said" strategy. The resistance is expressed "behind a cloak of great sincerity" (Bach & Goldberg, 1972, p. 110). Students sometimes excuse late assignments by using this strategy. "You said it was due Wednesday, not today, didn't you?" they'll say hopefully. The implied message is that, since this is a simple misunderstanding, penalizing the student for a late paper would be unfair.

Selective Amnesia   Have you ever noticed that some people are particularly forgetful about those things that they clearly do not want to do? This temporary amnesia is highly selective when used as a resistance strategy. Selective amnesiacs rarely forget what is most important to them. No outward signs of resistance are manifested. Resisters agree to perform the task—but conveniently let it slip their minds.

In a sophisticated version of this strategy the individual remembers all but one or two important items. A person shops for groceries and purchases all but two key items. Hey, no one's perfect. He or she remembered almost everything. The dinner menu, however, will have to be altered because the main course wasn't purchased.

Tactical Tardiness   When you really don't want to attend a meeting, a class, a lecture, or a party, you can show contempt by arriving late. Tactical tardiness irritates and frustrates those who value the event. It can hold an entire group hostage while everyone waits for the arrival of the person who is late. Consistently arriving late for class is disruptive, especially if the resister requests an update on material missed.

Tactical tardiness may be used on occasion by high power persons to reinforce their dominance and self-importance. Celebrities often arrive late to functions. They may hope to underscore their prestige by making fans wait for them.

Purposeful Procrastination   Most people put off doing what they dislike. There is nothing purposeful about this. Purposeful procrastinators, however, pretend that they will pursue a task "soon." While promising imminent results, they deliberately refuse to commit to a specific time or date for task completion. They delay completion of tasks on purpose. Trying to pin down a purposeful procrastinator is like trying to pin Jell-O to a wall—it won't stick. If those waiting for the task to be completed express exasperation, they appear to be nagging or fussing. Parents who try to get their kids to clean their rooms are often faced with this maddening strategy. When parents grow weary of monitoring their children's room-cleaning progress, they may give up in disgust and perform the task themselves or leave the room chaotic. This makes the resistance successful.

All six of these resistance strategies result from power imbalances. It is difficult to know for sure when such strategies are being used. A single occurrence of forgetfulness or tardiness doesn't indicate resistance necessarily, although resistance may be occurring. If the behavior becomes repetitive, it is safe to conclude that resistance strategies are being used.

Resistance strategies are underhanded, deceitful, and dishonest. This doesn't make for terribly competent communication. In extreme cases, resistance strategies may be the only feasible option available to prevent evil. In most instances, however, there are better ways to prevent dominance, as you will see later in this text. There are two principal ways for competent communicators to discourage resistance strategies, especially when the resistance is unjustified:

1. *Confront the strategy directly.* Use first-person singular language to describe the resistance strategy (see Chapter 2). Discuss why the strategy has been used and work cooperatively with the resister to find an equitable solution so resistance strategies are not employed.
2. *Thwart the enabling process.* We become enablers when we allow ourselves to become ensnared in the resister's net of duplicity. When we continue to wait for the tactically tardy, we encourage the behavior. If we perform the tasks for those who use loss of motor function or strategic stupidity, we reward their resistance and guarantee that such strategies will persist.

You thwart the enabling process by refusing to encourage the resistance. If staff members "forget" important items when shopping for office supplies, send them back for the items. Encourage them to make a list and check off items as they shop. If a person is persistently late for meetings, continue without them and do not interrupt the meeting to fill them in on missed information. Encourage them to be punctual. Continued tardiness may necessitate punishment or expulsion from the group. Refrain from rescuing those who use strategic stupidity or loss of motor function. Compensation for damage caused by such resistance strategies should be the responsibility of the resister.

Despite the negative aspects of resistance strategies, the primary focus should not be on how to combat resistance. Instead, focus on how to reduce power imbalances and dominance-submissiveness transactions that foster a desire to resist.

Empowerment and Balancing Power

Empowerment is a constructive form of power. Individuals become empowered by learning to communicate competently. Acquiring communication knowledge and developing a broad range of communication skills can give us confidence that we can adapt our communication appropriately whatever the context. We are empowered by this knowledge and these skills because they make more options available to us. In this section several ways to empower people will be explained.

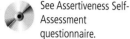

See Assertiveness Self-Assessment questionnaire.

DEVELOPING ASSERTIVENESS   The terms *assertive* and *aggressive* are often confused. **Assertiveness** is "the ability to communicate the full range of your thoughts and emotions with confidence and skill" (Adler, 1977, p. 6). Those who confuse assertiveness with aggressiveness tend to ignore the last part of this definition. Assertiveness isn't merely imposing your thoughts and emotions on others. Assertiveness requires confident and especially skillful expression of thoughts and emotions. Assertiveness falls between the extremes of aggressiveness and passivity and is distinctly different from both of them. Aggressiveness puts one's own needs first; you wipe your shoes on other people. Passivity underemphasizes one's needs; you're a doormat in a world of muddy shoes. Assertiveness considers both your needs and the needs of others.

Although assertiveness can be employed to defy others, it is primarily an empowering skill. We are most often assertive to assure that our needs, rights, and responsibilities are not ignored or to make a relationship or group more effective. Assertive individuals seek to enhance their significance in the eyes of others without alienating anyone. When passive, reticent individuals learn assertiveness, they become more productive contributors in groups. When aggressive individuals learn to be assertive, they are more likely to receive a fair hearing than if they try to bulldoze through what stands in their way.

Assertiveness may even save lives. The National Transportation and Safety Board recommended assertiveness training for cockpit crews. Several airline crashes were partially linked to lack of assertiveness by flight crew members who recognized pilot errors but were reluctant to correct the more powerful captain (Foushee, 1984).

Assertiveness involves four key steps (Bower & Bower, 1976):

1. *Describe* your needs, rights, and desires or the basis of your conflict with others. Use first-person singular language.
2. *Express* how you think and feel. "It upsets me when my ideas are ignored" is an example.
3. *Specify* the behavior or objective you are seeking. "I want to be included in future decision making" specifies the objective.
4. *Identify* consequences. The emphasis should be on the positive, not the negative, consequences. "I like working here, and I will continue for as long as I'm treated fairly" is better than "If you continue to treat me unfairly, I'll be forced to quit."

It is important to note that being assertive doesn't mean being impolite to others. Competent communicators show respect to others. You can remain firm and direct and still be unwaveringly polite and respectful.

Assertiveness isn't always appropriate. Asian cultures typically do not value the low-context directness that characterizes assertive communication. Standing up for yourself and speaking your mind are seen as disruptive and provocative acts likely to create disharmony. Women in highly masculine cultures (e.g., Japan, Venezuela, Italy) may also find that assertiveness poses problems for them because only men are expected to be assertive. Even in an individualistic culture like the United States where a low-context communication style is encouraged, overly persistent assertiveness can result in less favorable evaluations from supervisors, lower salaries, greater job tension, and greater personal stress than can less vigorous assertion of one's needs and desires (Schmidt & Kipnis, 1987). Assertiveness by battered wives can be potentially hazardous, even fatal (O'Leary et al., 1985). The competent communicator analyzes the context to determine the appropriate use of assertiveness.

INCREASING PERSONAL POWER RESOURCES   Individuals can empower themselves in numerous ways by developing their power resources. A woman who has been a homemaker may significantly empower herself by returning to college, earning a degree, and finding employment. The additional income benefits the entire family. Her self-esteem may be bolstered by the sense of independence resulting from a college education and employment in her field of study.

Husbands who assume a greater portion of the domestic chores and child-rearing responsibilities may increase their value in the family. They do not have to depend on the expertise of their partners to perform domestic activities competently. The stereotype of the bungling husband and father burning the dinner and falling prey to the antics of his children when his wife is away doesn't have to be the reality. Men can empower themselves to handle domestic responsibilities and tasks with dexterity. They don't have to become the passive victims of their own self-imposed ineptitude.

Developing expertise can be empowering. Learning computer skills can make you a valuable asset in a group or organization. Developing public speaking and interpersonal skills is empowering. Such skills open up new horizons, new capabilities, and options. Becoming informed on topics, especially if the information is specialized, can make you a valuable group member. The more we develop our personal power resources, the more empowered and significant we can become.

EMPLOYING COOPERATIVE ARGUMENTATION   When someone tells us that he or she just had an argument with another person, we usually perceive it to be a negative event. Arguments usually involve strong disagreements between "opponents" engaged in disagreeable verbal combat with a goal of "winning the argument" even if this means using unethical personal attacks, deception, and manipulation. It is little wonder that most people shrink from such unpleasant engagements. The willingness and ability to engage in argument, however, is a sign of one's degree of power. Those who feel highly capable in the arena of advocacy feel powerful. Those who feel ill equipped to so engage feel relatively powerless in such situations.

Makau and Marty (2001), however, offer an empowering alternative to the typical hypercompetitive argument; namely, cooperative argumentation. **Cooperative argumentation** is engaging in a process of deliberation with understanding and problem solving as ultimate goals. Cooperative argumentation focuses on the problem or issue, not the people deciding. Participants disagree without being disagreeable. Civility is the overarching principle that guides discussions. Critical listening is emphasized, not fighting for the floor to dominate the conversation. In typical arguments, there is a dominance-prevention power struggle with winners and losers. Cooperative argumentation balances the power by providing a supportive atmosphere in which all participants can feel free to join the discussion. Those who are hesitant to disagree are encouraged to participate. Having an opportunity to be heard can be profoundly empowering, especially to those unaccustomed to being taken seriously.

Cooperative argumentation is conducted in a supportive climate, whereas competitive argument produces defensiveness and a desire to counterattack or withdraw entirely from the clash of ideas. Thus, participants in cooperative argumentation describe objections they have to particular ideas instead of criticizing "rivals" to achieve a personal advantage. Participants problem solve instead of attempting to force other participants to agree. They assert their points of view instead of aggressively attacking those who disagree. They treat everyone as equals by eschewing arrogance. They are careful to avoid absolute statements that shut off discussion, and they let the force of their arguments change minds instead of employing manipulative strategies of influence, such as ridiculing a rival's idea or being deceptive about the weakness of a proposal. Participants engaging in cooperative argumentation also avoid the indifference of turning away responses and the hostility of turning against responses, concentrating instead on turning toward responses during deliberations and discussions.

SEEKING MENTORS AND NETWORKING   Mentors are knowledgeable individuals who have achieved some success in their profession or jobs and who assist individuals trying to get started in a line of work. Mentors can provide information to the novice that can prevent the mistakes of trial and error. Mentoring seems to be especially empowering for women in their rise to upper echelons of organizations (Noe, 1988). One study showed that women who have mentors move up the organizational ladder much faster than do women without mentors. Women also receive more promotions faster when they are assisted by mentors (cited in Kleiman, 1991). Mentors are important for women trying to advance to the highest levels of corporate leadership.

Networking is another form of empowerment. Individuals with similar backgrounds, skills, and goals come together on a fairly regular basis and share information that will assist them in pursuing goals. Networks, especially women's networks, also provide emotional support for members.

ENCOURAGING LEADERSHIP THAT EMPOWERS   Leaders can take actions that empower individuals and groups. Encouraging meaningful participation in decision-making, providing opportunities to perform complex and challenging tasks, giving greater responsibility, and providing opportunities to expand knowledge and expertise all empower individuals in groups and organizations (Burpitt & Bigoness, 1997). Teams evaluated as most innovative actively seek out, learn, and apply new knowledge and skills. Becoming a competent communicator is empowering.

Summary

Power is the ability to influence the attainment of goals sought by yourself or others. Power is inherent in all human relationships. There are three forms of power: dominance, prevention, and empowerment. Power imbalances produce several consequences: physical violence, verbal and nonverbal abuse, sexual harassment, and commonplace difficulties. Power imbalances also produce anger, frustration, wariness, and resentment in common everyday situations. Information, expertise, legitimate authority, rewards and punishments, and personal qualities are the primary power resources. Coalition formation, defiance, and resistance strategies are the chief power balancing approaches employed in dominance-prevention power struggles. Whereas dominance and prevention forms of power can produce "the dark side" of interpersonal relationships, empowerment is a very positive form of power. Becoming empowered is an important step in becoming a competent communicator. Empowerment is a win-win cooperative approach to power balancing.

Go to *Quizzes Without Consequences* at the book's Online Learning Center at **www.mhhe.com/rothwell2** or access the CD-ROM for *In the Company of Others.*

Quizzes Without Consequences

www.mhhe
● com/ **rothwell2**

---

assertiveness	defiance	power resource
charisma	dominance	prevention
coalitions	empowerment	principle of least
common couple	hostile environment	interest
violence	harassment	quid pro quo
cooperative	legitimate authority	harassment
argumentation	power	resistance

Key Terms

See Audio Flashcards Study Aid.

www.mhhe
● com/ **rothwell2**
See Crossword Puzzle Study Aid.

Suggested Readings

Farrell, W. (1993). *The myth of male power: Why men are the disposable sex.* New York: Simon & Schuster. This is a highly provocative polemic on the myth of the patriarchal society and the abuse of men written by a former board member of the National Organization for Women. I guarantee that this book will spark debate.

Farrell, W. (1999). *Women can't hear what men don't say.* New York: Tarcher/Putnam. This is another provocative book on gender and power. It will make you think.

Hoff-Sommers, C. (1993). *Who stole feminism? How women have betrayed women.* New York: Simon & Schuster. This extremely controversial attack on "gender feminists" challenges the notion that men are the enemy of women and that power must be seized from men to benefit women.

Wolf, N. (1994). *Fire with fire: The new female power and how to use it.* New York: Fawcett Columbine. Wolf, a self-proclaimed feminist, has written a nicely balanced treatment of power and how it relates to women.

Film School

Cool Hand Luke (1967). Drama; Not rated ★★★★★
Paul Newman wowed audiences with his portrayal of Luke, an irrepressible, spirited individual imprisoned and forced to endure a repressive southern chain gang. Analyze the instances of passive aggression and defiance that exemplify the point that no one is completely powerless.

Disclosure (1994). Drama; R ★★★★
Intriguing plot twist propels this film. Michael Douglas plays a business executive who files sexual harassment charges against his female superior. Analyze the issue of power imbalance and sexual harassment. Does it seem like a stretch to portray a man as the victim of sexual harassment?

One Flew over the Cuckoo's Nest (1975). Drama; R ★★★★★
The role of Randall P. McMurphy made Jack Nicholson an international star and earned him his first Oscar. This film depicts a power struggle in a mental institution. Analyze the dominance-prevention dynamic that propels the story. Does empowerment emerge?

CHAPTER 9

Technology and Communication Competence

Technology has become so much a part of our daily lives that communication cannot easily be separated from it. Canadian English professor Marshall McLuhan (1964, 1967) was the focal point for intense debate over electronic media and their effects when television was still a relatively new invention. Derisively labeled the "Oracle of the Electronic Age," the "High Priest of Pop Culture," and the "Metaphysician of Media," McLuhan gained notoriety partly because of his gift for creating memorable phrases. "The medium is the message," "the medium is the massage," and "the global village" are all McLuhan creations. Despite criticisms of McLuhan's point of view (see especially Davis, 1993)—a view that was essentially optimistic about electronic media and their potential contributions to humankind—McLuhan did shift the debate from a focus on media content to the media themselves.

Meyrowitz (1997) notes, "The spread of printing, radio, television, telephone, computer networks, and other technologies have altered the nature of social interaction in ways that cannot be reduced to the content of the messages communicated through them" (p. 196). Consider a few simple examples. Your partner sits at the breakfast table reading a newspaper while you try to engage him or her in a conversation. Does it matter what your partner is reading, or does the mere act of reading the newspaper interfere with interpersonal connection? Families that eat dinner in front of the television rarely engage in conversation. In fact, conversation during a television program is considered rude and will often provoke a collective "shush" from family members. Does it matter what the family is watching? The mere act of watching television can close off dialogue and opportunities for conversation. When children and parents spend hours alone in front of computer screens, does it matter whether they are playing video games, surfing the Internet, or catching up on office work? The mere use of communication technologies has the power to shape our lives in ways we may not notice.

The purpose of this chapter is to discuss the many ways communication technologies can influence our communication with others.

The purpose of this chapter is to discuss the many ways communication technologies can influence our communication with others.

There are three Chapter objectives:

1. **to examine trends in communication technologies,**
2. **to discuss the consequences of these trends on our communication with others, and**
3. **to offer ways competent communicators can cope with the impact of communication technologies.**

The content of messages transmitted via communication technologies does matter. Violent television programming and pornographic images on the Internet are subjects of heated debate and intense concern. You are probably familiar with the controversies surrounding these content issues. What you may not have pondered, however, is how the pervasive use of electronic communication technologies is changing our lives. Although the messages that we communicate electronically cannot be ignored, the emphasis of this chapter will be the opportunities and challenges presented to us by the increasing availability of electronic communication technologies.

Trends in Communication Technology

Recognizing trends in communication technologies can help you understand how these technologies affect your relationships with others and whether these effects are likely to continue or even grow more significant. There are two primary trends: (1) the use of electronic communication technology is becoming pervasive, and (2) the bias for speed in electronic communication technology has permeated our society.

Pervasiveness of Communication Technology

Put in its simplest form, a **technology** is a tool to accomplish some purpose, and a *communication* technology is a tool to communicate with others. Not all technologies are readily accepted when they first appear. A century ago, the United States Justice Department seriously advocated a ban on public ownership of automobiles because cars would allow criminals to flee from the scenes of their crimes (Neumann, 1999). The accelerated pace of public acceptance of new communication technologies is therefore remarkable.

See "How-Wired Are You?" survey on CD.

The Center for Policy Analysis notes that new communication technologies are reaching and being used by a significant portion of the U.S. population faster than ever. The telephone took 35 years to reach a quarter of the U.S. population; radio took 22 years, television 26 years, the PC only 16 years, the mobile phone 13 years, and the Internet just 7 years (Reeling in the Years, 1998). Virtually every home in the United

States has at least one television set, a radio, and a phone; most have more than one of each. More than 100 million Americans use cellular phones (Carpenter, 2000).

By the mid-1990s the Internet, hardly recognized by most Americans at the start of the decade, had emerged as a dominant communication system used by people from a variety of backgrounds. Seventy-one percent of all Americans used the Internet in 2002 (Chmielewski, 2003). Half of nonusers plan to go online. Despite concerns about a "digital divide" among races, half of Hispanic adults and 43% of African American adults were using the Internet by 2001 (Ostrom, 2001). Although females once lagged far behind males in computer and Internet use, by the year 2000, gender differences disappeared (Wood & Smith, 2001). Only the elderly seem more inclined to be "computer meek." Fewer than 15% of individuals 65 years or older are online, and Jupiter Communications, a New York technology firm, estimated in 2001 that only 17 million seniors would be cruising the Net by 2005, leaving 36 million who would not be Internet surfing (Atkins, 2001). Anxiety about dealing with complex technologies is the main reason for the reticence of seniors.

The pervasiveness of communication technologies truly has influenced our lives, and most individuals think it's a positive development. For example, a Gallup poll conducted in February 2000 reported that 72% of respondents believe that the Internet has improved their lives, only 2% believe it has made their lives worse, and 26% report no difference (Americans Say, 2000). This same sample reported that they use the Internet to obtain information (95%), to send and receive e-mail (89%), to shop (45%), and to visit chat rooms (21%).

Bias for Speed

Carrie Fisher, in her *Postcards from the Edge*, remarked, "Instant gratification takes too long." The pace of technological change is accelerating, and with it comes a bias for speed. In the first half of the 20th century a new major communication technology might have come along once in a decade or two. Now, with the digital world of computers, communication technology arrives more quickly and changes more rapidly. Bill Seawick of computer software giant Oracle Corporation says, "Technology is coming at such a fantastic pace that people have to learn new technologies every three or four months" (cited in Shenk, 1997, p. 86).

"Digital technology, the basis of today's new media technologies, represents the translation of all forms of content (text, images, audio, video, and other animation) into a form that is easily manipulated by computers. That sentence sums up developments in communication technologies for the last 20 years" (Klopfenstein, 1997, p. 22). The digital world of computers has merged with virtually all communication technologies, creating a communication revolution (DeFleur & Dennis, 1998). There are computer chips in televisions, radios, CD players, telephones, VCRs, DVDs, and fax and copy machines. Digitalization has made possible an integration of communication technologies unparalleled in human history. We now talk of interactive television, an unprecedented combination of communication technology that would merge cable, television, telephone, and computer technology. The Internet, which merges computer and phone (modems) technology, can be a medium of print, graphics, photography, video, or sound. It can be linear, one-way communication, or it can be interactive with chat rooms and e-mail permitting interchange between users. This technological merging has created an exhilarating but far different world of communication than existed just 2 decades ago.

What this accelerating technological change means to us is that communication competence has never been a bigger challenge. E-mail, Internet Web sites, cell phones, pagers, faxes, and Palm Pilots allow us to access information and connect with individuals all over the globe in ways that would have been difficult to imagine a half-century ago. *All of these technological advances in communication have an inherent bias: Faster is better* (Gleick, 1999).

A message sent in the form of a letter would take an average of 3 days to deliver if sent by standard mail. Regular mail became "snail mail" when Federal Express introduced overnight delivery service, and with the ready availability of e-mail, anything less than speed of light transmission became by comparison excruciatingly slo-o-o-o-o-w. James Gleick (1999), in his book *Faster: The Acceleration of Just About Everything*, notes that the television remote control "in the hands of a quick-reflexed, multitasking, channel-flipping, fast-forwarding citizenry, has caused an acceleration in the pace of films and television commercials" (p. 10). During the 1964 New York World's Fair, thousands of people stood in line at the AT&T pavilion to try Touch Tone dialing for the first time (Gleick, 1999). Dialing a 7-digit number on a rotary phone typically took about 10 seconds. Touch Tone could save about 7 to 8 seconds. Inevitably, the faster-is-better bias gave us the speed-dial button, saving additional precious nanoseconds (although programming it can wipe out any perceived aggregate time savings). Telephone answering machines come equipped with quick-playback buttons that compress speech so messages sound like callers are auctioneers on amphetamines.

Cell phones and pagers make us reachable at almost any instant, and they implicitly demand an instant reply. This is particularly true when the message is task oriented (Walther & Tidwell, 1995). The longer the interval between the initial message sent and the reply, the more excuses we feel compelled to offer for our "tardy" response. An immediate reply signals respect and interest. A delayed response or no response at all signals disrespect and disinterest. The cell phone and the standard phone are different in this aspect. When we call and leave a message on a home answering machine, we don't have the same expectation of an immediate reply. The party that we call is presumed to be away from home (unless we suspect that they are screening their calls). A cell phone, however, is portable. If the party called doesn't

Calvin and Hobbes   by Bill Watterson

answer, it appears deliberate. When we leave a message on a cell phone that identifies us, we are doubly insulted when the call is "ignored." There, of course, are good reasons individuals turn off their cell phones or do not respond promptly, but the ready availability of cell phones makes excuses for delaying the return call suspicious.

With the bias for speed comes an expectation of speed, which easily morphs into a need for speed (Shenk, 1999). With this need for speed often comes impatience, stress, frustration, and even anger at the relatively slow pace of anything that is less than instantaneous. Who can tolerate the relatively slow speed of the old dot matrix printers, for example, at one time thought to be a miracle of technological advancement, when laser printers can pump out professional looking copies as much as 20 to 30 times faster? As C. Leslie Charles, author of *Why Is Everyone So Cranky?* notes, "This constant accessibility and compulsive use of technology fragments what little time we do have, adding to our sense of urgency, emergency, and overload" (cited in Peterson, 2000, p. 2A). *Multitasking,* a term coined by computer scientists in the 1960s, becomes a necessity because it is the only way of "keeping up" with the increased pace of life. Have you ever sat at a computer terminal, read e-mail, and responded to e-mail while conducting a phone conversation? That's multitasking made possible by electronic communication technologies.

Each of us, of course, can choose the degree of technological immersion we wish to embrace. Many individuals have yet to embrace the cell phone. A study of 2,000 American households by the UCLA Center for Communication Policy's World Internet Project, reported that 16.8% of respondents claimed that they would not purchase a computer at any price. They "don't want to go online because everybody else is online" (Cole et al., 2000). The bias for speed inherent in communication technologies does not render us powerless to resist this bias, but it does make it increasingly difficult, especially as the technologies become ever more pervasive. If you have the option to send a message by writing a letter that requires addressing an envelope and affixing a stamp to the envelope before mailing it or to send the message by e-mail, which would you choose? One does not have to own a computer or learn PowerPoint, but as job announcements increasingly include requirements for computer skills and panels expect PowerPoint demonstrations during the interviewing process, rigidly refusing to become a "slave to technology" can seriously limit one's options. Speed is exhilarating, and humans have trouble resisting its allure (Gleick, 1999). Research can still be conducted the "old fashioned way," in a library searching through the stacks (and sometimes this is the only option). If your research could be conducted in a tenth of the time by hopping on the Internet and accessing the most recent, high-quality information, however, would you eschew the allure of speed for the "purity" of the dusty excursion through often outdated books?

Consequences of Communication Technologies

The history of communication technologies appears to be a simple process of adding new technologies on top of old ones. However, it is far more complicated than this. As Postman (1993) explains,

> A new technology does not add or subtract something. It changes everything. In the year 1500, fifty years after the printing press was invented, we did not have old Europe plus the printing press. We had a different Europe. After television, the United States

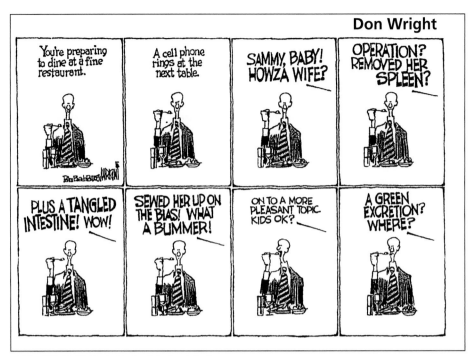

© Don Wright. Distributed by the Palm Beach Post.

was not America plus television; television gave a new coloration to every political campaign, to every home, to every school, to every church, to every industry (p. 18).

Consider what impact the cell phone has had on our lives. The cell phone is an amazing invention capable of connecting us to almost anyone in the world whenever we desire. Parents can keep track of their children more easily with cell phones. If there is a misunderstanding or confusion about children's planned activities, placing a call to their cell phone can remedy the problem quickly. In emergency situations the cell phone can be a lifesaver. Even knowing that you have a cell phone at the ready in case of an emergency can be comforting. Relatives and friends can be notified easily when you are running late for an engagement so they don't become worried or irritated by your tardiness. Parents can "tuck in" their children during a break in a late-night meeting. Business can be conducted more easily with cell phones.

There is a downside to the cell phone, however. In an elegant San Antonio, Texas, nightclub a jazz singer was entertaining the crowd when a cell phone rang. The patron answered the phone and then shushed singer Ken Slavin so the patron could hear the call. In Palo Alto, California, a food fight nearly broke out when one customer complained loudly about eight cell phone calls disrupting his meal. Actor Laurence Fishburne, in the middle of a Broadway play, felt compelled to break character and bellow at an audience member to turn off a cell phone. Solitary cell phone users can conduct conversations with phones pressed to their ears while bouncing off passers-by like balls in a pinball machine, seemingly oblivious to their surroundings. National Public Radio's "Car Talk" show has given away 60,000 "Drive Now, Talk Later" bumper stickers. Restaurants, theaters, and museums from coast to coast have begun creating "cell phone free zones" or banning cell phone conversations entirely by posting "No Cell Phones" signs at entrances. Teachers at all

www.mhhe
com/
rothwell2

See cell phone poll on the Online Learning Center, Chapter 9.

Box 9-1   Sharper Focus

Cell Phone Etiquette for the Competent Communicator

Cell phone manufacturer Nokia and several Web sites (http://computersathome.com/gsm/etiquette.html; *GetConnected.com*; www.letstalk.com/promo/unclecell/unclecell2.html) offer etiquette advice. Guidelines for using cell phones appropriately include the following:

1. Do not use a cell phone on a date, during a business meeting, or while conducting a face-to-face conversation unless you know that an emergency has arisen. Most people perceive interrupting face-to-face communication to take a cell phone call as rude and insensitive. It appears that your cell phone conversation takes precedence over your face-to-face conversation. That's insulting. Use the phone's caller ID function to screen calls, and let voice mail handle all calls that aren't clearly urgent.

2. Never use a cell phone in a restaurant, in a theater, or during any public performance when such use could disrupt others' enjoyment. If you absolutely must receive a call in such venues, switch to the vibrating ringer and take the call in a more private location.

3. When using a cell phone in public, do not raise your voice. Speak in a normal manner, not a "cell yell." Most individuals do not care to listen to your personal conversations.

4. Avoid using annoying rings such as popular tunes or sound effects. If you forget to turn off your cell phone during a public performance or a college class, the phone jingle merely amplifies the inappropriate ringing.

5. Do not use a cell phone while driving. It's likely to divert your attention from the safe operation of your vehicle. Pull off the road to take a call that seems urgent.

---

education levels regularly instruct students to turn off cell phones before classes begin. Cell phone etiquette has become a national, even an international issue. In 2001, Hong Kong's 7 million residents had more than 5 million cell phones. In response to complaints about cell phone disruption, the Office of Telecommunications in Hong Kong seriously considered silencing cell phones in select public places by jamming cell phone signals (Luk, 2001).

Cell phones have blurred the line between public and private space. Personal, private conversations formerly relegated to one's home, office, or possibly an enclosed phone booth now regularly take place in crowded restaurants, buses, airport waiting areas, and even public bathrooms. In March 2000, Wirthlin Worldwide conducted a survey and discovered that 39% of those polled would converse on a cell phone while conducting nature's business in a bathroom stall (cited in Carpenter, 2000). Etiquette, our rules of appropriate public communication, has not kept up with technological change (see Box 9-1).

In this section, significant consequences of both the prevalence of electronic communication technologies and their bias for speed will be explored. These consequences include information overload, proliferation of misinformation, and effects on our interpersonal relationships.

Information Overload

The recent cornucopia of information made available by advances in communication technologies, especially the Internet, certainly can be beneficial. Every academic discipline has its own plethora of Web sites, making information on vital and interesting subjects readily available. You can access abstracts and full text articles in scientific and educational journals and magazines on the Internet. Authoritative medical information on several reputable sites can assist you in deciding what action to take when you experience health problems. When you need to research a topic for a speech or term paper, the old excuse "I couldn't find anything on the

CATHY/Cathy Guisewite

© 2002 CATHY GUISEWITE. Distributed by Universal Press Syndicate. www.ucomics.com

subject" just won't work anymore. You can send e-mails to individuals of stature and acclaim from around the world, seeking answers to questions. The Internet empowers us by eroding barriers of time and space through speed of light information transmission from almost anywhere on the globe. It is at once exciting and daunting.

New challenges face us now that we all have ready access to this treasure trove of information. The amount of information we are exposed to each day is staggering. A study of more than 1,000 employees of Fortune 1000 companies found that workers send and receive 178 messages on average each day using e-mail, phones, faxes, pagers, and face-to-face communication (Ginsberg, 1997). Americans send 2.2 billion e-mail messages every day; there are 50,000 new books published each year in the United States; there are 12,000 newspapers, 22,000 magazines, and 600 million radios; and 98% of U.S. homes have at least one television set. More than half of the U.S. population has access to the Internet (Baran, 1999; DeFleur & Dennis, 1998; Levy, 2002; Turow, 1999). Add to this millions of fax machines, pagers, copy machines, and cell phones. All this technology pumps out information at a staggering rate. We can produce gigaheaps of data too voluminous for processing. "More information is generated in a 24-hour period than you could take in for the rest of your life. And as more people go online and add information to the Internet, we will rapidly approach a situation in which more information is generated on earth in one hour than you could take in for the rest of your life" (Davidson, 1996, p. 496).

EFFECTS OF INFORMATION OVERLOAD   Several specific consequences result from information overload (Shenk, 1997). These consequences are discussed next.

Affects Health and Relationships   The volume of information created and available to us daily impinges on our physical and interpersonal well-being. A survey of 1,300 business managers from the United States, Great Britain, Australia, Japan, and Singapore by Reuters Business Information found that 43% of senior managers felt that information overload made them ill (Businesspeople Suffering, 1996). Almost two-thirds of these respondents believed that their personal relationships had been diminished because of information overload at work. Another Reuters' study of 1,000 managers in the United States, Great Britain, Ireland, Germany, Hong Kong, and Singapore reported that 46% of individuals surveyed believed they work longer hours merely to keep pace with the cascade of information pouring down on them, and 61% believe that they receive too much information to be useful (Veitch, 1997). Information overload at work increases our stress, and this added stress can increase the likelihood of friction in our interpersonal relationships both at home and at work.

Impedes Critical Thinking   Too much information "thwarts skepticism, rendering us less sophisticated as consumers and citizens" (Shenk, 1997, p. 31). In Chapter 7, the importance of developing a healthy skepticism was explored. Our ability to exercise skepticism can be impeded by too much information coming at us too quickly. We simply don't have time to process the pile of information. Buried in an avalanche of data from the myriad communication technologies, we have a difficult time separating the garbage from the good stuff. Students recognize this immediately when they prepare speeches or research papers for class. Finding information on almost any subject these days is not the difficult part. Knowing when to stop searching and begin thinking about the organization of your speech or paper and the points you want to make is the difficult part. You can become so engrossed in finding information that you don't leave yourself enough time to think about the information you have gathered.

Promotes Indecisiveness   "The psychological reaction to such an overabundance of information . . . is to simply avoid coming to conclusions" (Shenk, 1997, p. 93). Bill Clinton was frequently accused of indecisiveness. "To listen to him speak extemporaneously about an issue is to witness a man able to grasp so much data, he frequently becomes engulfed in it" (p. 94). Clinton's seemingly endless hunger for facts and statistics could get him focusing on the trees but not the forest. Journalist Elizabeth Drew (1994, p. 79) noted that White House staffers complained to her that Clinton was fond of delivering "an intense seminar on government minutiae" every chance he got.

The paradox of the new Technological Age is that our world is speeded up enormously, yet our ability to make decisions individually and in groups is slowed down by the easily accessible megamountains of information. It's tough to be decisive when you're never sure if some new fact or statistic available to everyone in an instant will suddenly emerge to invalidate your point of view.

Creates Normalization of Hyperbole   Communication scholar Kathleen Hall Jamieson says that our society is experiencing a "normalization of hyperbole" (cited in Janofsky, 1995). **Hyperbole** is exaggeration for effect that is not meant to be taken literally. As we become evermore swamped in information, gaining the attention of an audience becomes a bigger challenge. Hyperbole is the solution for many. "Extreme measures to grab attention are not only condoned; they're admired. Outrageous behavior by individuals is rewarded with wealth and influence" (Shenk, 1997, p. 104). Dennis Rodman, Madonna, Roseanne, Eminem, Rush Limbaugh, Jerry Springer, and radio shock jocks Howard Stern and Don Imus all "pump up the volume" to get noticed and are amply rewarded. "Historically, discourteousness and vulgarity have always signified a lack of sophistication; garishness was considered tasteless and degrading. In today's attention-deficit society, however, people have learned that churlish behavior is the key to headlines, profit, and power" (Shenk, 1997, p. 104).

If practically everyone is shouting at us, grossly overstating the importance of their messages, and competing for our attention by being outrageous and sensational,

Futurists predicted that electronic communication technologies would create a "paperless society." So much for that fantasy. What has happened is an increasing problem of information overload.

how are we to take seriously any message that truly is urgent? If everything is made to be a crisis, how are we to cope? Regularly I receive junk mail with "URGENT" written repeatedly across the envelope. On the few occasions that I have actually opened the envelope, I was invariably annoyed to find a rather routine message asking me to renew a magazine subscription.

During the Clinton impeachment hearings, "legitimate" journalists anguished about the "tabloidization of journalism" in which sensational stories about political figures' private lives become front-page headlines. "The fast-food part of the modern media diet—conflict, celebrities, and catastrophe—exists in part because of burgeoning technology. To be heard above the din of growing competition, much of journalism today finds itself in tabloid mode, shouting and trivializing to attract attention" (Fulton, 1999, p. 63). Amidst this din, how can voices of rationality and balance be heard? The answer: not easily.

COPING WITH INFORMATION OVERLOAD   Coping with information overload can't be done by turning back the clock. Brian Lamb, founder and chairman of C-SPAN, identifies the problem succinctly: "You can't stop the process. It's the American way. Which part of the library or the Internet do you want to shut down? Let me tell you something: If we can't survive all the information that we're going to develop, then we're in real trouble. Because no one is going to stop writing books. No one is going to stop creating information" (cited in Shenk, 1997, p. 22). Coping with information overload is critically important, and there are several steps a competent communicator can take.

Screen Information   Be in charge of your own information environment. You can choose to ignore much of the flood of information that can drown you in pointless detail. You can screen e-mail automatically or manually. Simply delete messages that are irrelevant or trivial. I regularly delete messages without opening them. On average, I weed out about 75% of all the e-mail messages I receive simply by looking at the title of the message. You can also screen telephone messages. Let the caller leave a message on the message machine; that way you can decide if you want to take the call or ignore it. This puts you in charge, and it screens out telemarketers, solicitors, and people whose messages intrude on your private time at home. Purchase a readily available device that automatically deletes telemarketers' phone calls.

Break the E-Mail Feedback Loop You don't want to pile up messages in someone's e-mail box by sending confirmations that messages were received or by responding with brief courtesy replies such as "Thank you," "You're welcome," or "No problem." In face-to-face or phone conversations such polite terminations of conversations are the norm. E-mail, however, is trickier to end (Cohen, 2002). If you do not respond with confirmation or courtesy replies, how will the sender know for sure that you received the e-mail? Also, you don't want a nonresponse to seem rude or indifferent. Nevertheless, these brief confirmation or courtesy e-mails can double or triple the number of messages received, making e-mail management more difficult. The receiver of the e-mail may respond with a "Got it!" confirmation. The sender of the original message may then respond, "Great!" This may be followed by a "Thanks again" message, then a "You're always welcome," and so on in a seemingly endless feedback loop from which there seems to be no escape. Try preempting such e-mail exchanges by finishing a message with NRN (no reply necessary), or when making a request, finish the e-mail with "Thanks in advance." Use FYI (for your information) to indicate that no reply is expected.

Narrow the Search This is particularly useful advice when researching a speech or paper for class. If you search the Internet without a specific target, you will be overwhelmed. Narrow your search for information by having a clear, specific purpose in mind. You can best narrow the search for information by finding relevant patterns. As Klapp (1978) notes, "Once a pattern is perceived, 90 percent of information becomes irrelevant" (p. 13). **Pattern recognition,** the process of piecing together seemingly unrelated information into a plan, design, or whole picture, narrows your search for information. Once you discern a pattern, you know what information is irrelevant and useless and what information is on target. An effective outline for a speech or research paper establishes a pattern, allowing you to weed out the useless from the useful information.

De-Nichify Strive to be more of a generalist looking at the "big picture" than a specialist lost in an increasingly narrow world of detail. The more specialized we become to cope with information overload, the more limited our world becomes. As we become ever more specialized, we learn more and more about less and less. If everyone moves toward specialization, soon we will have very little to discuss with each other except maybe the weather.

Niches are specialized segments of an audience. Niche marketing targets a narrow segment of the total audience by focusing on a select portion of radio and television channels, magazines, newspapers, and the Internet. Shenk (1997) suggests "de-nichifying." Instead of subscribing to many magazines on specialized topics, for example, subscribe to one or two that are broad based. *Time* and *Newsweek*, for example, are general newsmagazines that provide a general overview of world news and controversial issues of the week. Some specialization is necessary to remain current in your field of endeavor, but balance the specialization with a general knowledge of the world. This is the philosophy behind most colleges' mandatory general education requirements, which are meant to supplement students' major coursework.

Proliferation of Misinformation

On June 5, 1998, the Associated Press news service and several sources on the Internet announced that comedian Bob Hope had died. The announcement was then brought to the attention of House Majority Leader Dick Armey, who notified Rep. Bob Stump, a member of the House Veterans Affairs Committee. An obituary was read on the House floor. The speech by Stump was telecast live by C-SPAN. Reuters news service issued a bulletin. A national ABC radio report lamented Hope's demise. Presented with this startling piece of "news," the very alive Bob Hope quipped, "They were wrong, weren't they?" (cited in Antonucci, 1998). Mark Twain once remarked that falsehood spreads halfway around the world before truth puts on its boots. In this age of electronic speed-of-light transmission, misinformation spreads more rapidly than Twain could ever have imagined.

COMMUNICATION OF NEWS A CNN and *Time* story alleging that the U.S. military used lethal nerve gas in a 1970 attack on defectors in a small Laotian village during the Vietnam War was retracted, embarrassing both news organizations (Getlin, 1998). This inaccurate story followed close behind other prominent cases of inaccurate or fabricated stories in reputable news media. Patricia Smith, a *Boston Globe* columnist, was fired for inventing quotes in four of her articles. Stephen Glass, a writer for the *New Republic*, was also fired for fabricating 27 stories. On May 11, 2003, the *New York Times* printed a 14,000-word article on "the widespread fabrication and plagiarism" of Jayson Blair, a *Times* reporter who was subsequently fired for his journalistic misdeeds (Mnookin, 2003).

Newsweek columnist Jonathan Alter (1998) succinctly summarized the causes of this proliferation of misinformation reported to the public: "Hype, cyberspeed, and 24-hour competition are bringing out journalism's worst" (p. 66). Competition comes not just from credible news organizations but also from the more peripheral and questionable outlets, such as Internet sites, tabloid papers, and talk radio. Robert Lichter, president of the Center for Media and Public Affairs in Washington, D.C., claims that the standard news media use too many unidentified sources and too much hearsay. Reporters aren't checking their facts because of competition to be the first person breaking the story. As Lichter explains, "People are afraid to hold on to every detail for fear that it will show up in the (Internet gossip) Drudge Report or on talk radio" (Antonucci & Quinn, 1998, p. A12).

Reporters should check facts before writing stories or broadcasting to avoid reporting misinformation. This is an ethical issue. Failure to take necessary precautions to stem the flow of misinformation is irresponsible. Obviously, journalists who fabricate stories and quotations are guilty of dishonesty. The combination of hypercompetitiveness in the news marketplace and the instant accessibility of information from an array of communication technologies, however, has lowered journalistic standards overall. As Ben Bagdikian, former assistant managing editor for the *Washington Post* and professor of mass media at the University of California, Berkeley, explains, "In the past, the degraded standards of non-serious media . . . would get into serious print and serious network news only after going through a careful editorial process. That filtering system has disappeared" (Antonucci & Quinn, 1998, p. A12).

The desire to break a story ahead of competitors has always been a driving force in the world of journalism, but it has taken on a new dimension. The 2000 presidential election circus is an apt example. Networks first announced that Al Gore had won Florida (and thereby the presidency), then retracted the announcement and declared George W. Bush the Florida winner only to be forced to retract again and declare the race "too close to call." An independent report by three journalists drew this scathing conclusion about this "debacle":

> Television news organizations staged a collective drag race on the crowded highway of democracy, recklessly endangering the electoral process, the political life of the country, and their own credibility, all for reasons that may be conceptually flawed and commercially questionable. . . . Their hyper-competition stemmed from a foolish attempt to beat their rivals to the finish line in calling state-by-state winners in the presidential election. . . . Those calls and their retractions constitute a news disaster that damaged democracy and journalism (Excerpts from the Report, 2001, p. A5).

Combine the problems associated with information overload (diminished critical thinking, indecisiveness, and hyperbole) with the hypercompetitiveness in the world of news and you have a formula for the proliferation of misinformation as never before.

INTERNET MISINFORMATION   The proliferation of misinformation is not just a problem in the communication of news. According to the U.S. Health and Human Services Department, about 43% of all Internet users seek medical advice from Internet Web sites (cited in McDermott, 1998). Bulletin Board Systems (BBS), a form of text-based communication in which contributors send messages to a single computer address and the messages are posted so visitors can access the messages at their discretion, are particularly vulnerable to misinformation when used by members of online support groups (Wood & Smith, 2001). Inaccurate, even harmful information can be posted by support group members acting as faux experts. Virtual therapy from nonprofessionals could have disastrous results.

Slick-looking Web sites touting a mixture of bat guano and huckleberry bark or some combination of "natural" herbs as a cure for serious ailments might influence a desperately ill, vulnerable individual to try unproven, even dangerous remedies. Web sites run by hucksters and charlatans can look as professional or more so than sites run by reputable experts and professional organizations. True Believers can proselytize on the Web, spreading misinformation worldwide. At the start of the new millennium, experts estimated that there were 500 hate group Web sites targeting their poisonous misinformation and calls for violence at individuals or groups identified by their ethnicity, religion, national origin, sexual orientation, gender, or disability (Etchingham, 2000). By 2001, that number had been revised upward to 600 such groups (Wood & Smith, 2001).

Deceit is also a common form of misinformation discovered in Internet chatroom conversations (Wood & Smith, 1999). Individuals concoct fake personalities and identities and even gender swap online without the knowledge of interactants. Although such deceit can be harmless fun, there are potential dangers. One study of online relationships found that a majority of individuals who established a personal relationship on the Internet eventually pursued the relationship by contacting their partner by telephone, through snail mail, or in face-to-face meetings (Park & Floyd, 1996). Disappointment is probably the mildest outcome of such deceit. (Barnes, 2001). Sexual predators have used Internet chat rooms to lure victims into face-to-face

© G. B. Trudeau. Distributed by Universal Press Syndicate.

meetings. Documented cases of child abusers using online chat rooms to entice kids to meet in person numbered 4,000 in the year 2001 (Camp-Flores, 2002). About 12% of children who meet strangers online follow up with offline in-person encounters. Thirteen-year-old Christina Long met a 25-year-old man at a mall in Danbury, Connecticut, in May 2002. She was strangled to death by her chat-room partner.

COMBATTING MISINFORMATION So what can you do about this spread of misinformation? What you can't do reasonably is slow down the transmission of information, censor the Internet, or reduce competition in the journalistic marketplace. Those are structural changes that bump against constitutional guarantees and consumer choice. The answer lies in becoming a more competent, skeptical consumer of information.

Seek Credible Sources of Information Ignore Web sites from questionable sources and obvious hate groups. Follow advice provided in Chapter 15 on "Cruising the Net Skeptically." Pay no attention to tabloid stories (except perhaps for amusement) unless they have been verified by more reputable news sources.

Question the Reliability of Any Unidentified Sources Reputable media increasingly use such dubious sources as "administrative sources" or "a person high in the State Department" to compete with peripheral news outlets. Misinformation, however, is easily spread when consumers can't determine the reliability of the information. Unidentified sources should be discounted.

Check Several Reputable Sources   The erroneous story of Bob Hope's death was not reported by all news organizations. CNN didn't report the initial announcement; neither did MSNBC. Reliance on a single source is always shaky. Hate groups regularly twist historical facts and manufacture big lies to further their agenda. Check neutral sources before accepting startling "facts" from any obviously biased source.

Be Extremely Careful About Pursuing Internet Relationships   Do not provide phone numbers, home addresses, or office locations to a chat-room partner. Take a friend along on any in-person meetings (not recommended) and meet in a public location. As a parent, monitor your children's Internet use or block access to chat rooms.

The proliferation of misinformation will continue and perhaps grow worse in the future. Our primary protection from the spread of falsehoods is to exercise skepticism and to be a critical listener as discussed in Chapter 7.

Interpersonal Effects

Communication technologies markedly influence our relationships with others and our lives in general. There are those who argue that e-mail, Internet chat rooms, cell phones, pagers, and fax machines bring us closer together because they increase communication. Others argue that all this technology doesn't create community but disconnection. Let's examine the interpersonal effects of communication technologies.

SOCIAL CONTACT   Time spent on the Internet can be quite productive. You can strengthen relationships, share information, and form groups with shared interests. Faculty members sometimes find that students more readily contribute points of view and ideas through e-mail than in class. Students aren't intimidated by what their peers will think when they are communicating directly with their teachers. When distance prevents physical contact with friends and family, phones and e-mail are useful substitutes. After the terrorist attack on the World Trade Center in 2001, people used the Internet to find out if friends and family members living in the New York City area were safe, especially when phone lines became jammed from heavy loads. Almost 18 million Americans telecommute to their jobs, working from their homes with computers, cell phones, and fax machines (Telecommuting, 1999). Potentially, this could save time commuting by car to work, and it offers an opportunity to interact with children and one's partner during lunch and work breaks. Parents sometimes purchase computers and connect to the Internet just to remain in touch with a son or daughter at college. A 3-year study in Sweden, Portugal, Great Britain, and Ireland shows that seniors get a psychological boost from online communication (cited in Marcus, 1999). Family therapist Howard Adelman encourages his older patients to use e-mail to counteract loneliness and depression. "Seniors are often depressed, and with depression comes withdrawal. E-mail brings them back to the world" (Marcus, 1999, p. 62).

Young people also find e-mail particularly useful and engrossing. Most teens have Internet access, and e-mail is their principal online activity (Silver & Perry, 1999). They mostly gossip with friends. Instant messaging is a popular service.

Users compile a list of friends, all of whom can chat online at the same time as their comments appear on screen. Fourteen-year-old Grace Doherty reveals, "I would totally say so many things online I would never say to someone's face" (cited in Silver & Perry, 1999, p. 57). That can be good or bad depending on what is said.

Instant messaging is popular with adults as well as teens. A survey of 50 Fortune 1000 companies found that 36% of employees used instant messaging to connect with other employees (Biggs, 2001). The downside of instant messaging, however, is that senders know that you are logged onto your computer, so if you do not respond quickly, even more so than is true with cell phones, it easily appears that you are purposely ignoring the sender.

Long-distance friendships can also develop over the Internet. One study surveyed Internet newsgroups to find out about personal relationships online (Parks & Floyd, 1996). Although newsgroups compose only about 20% of online participation by Internet users (Wallace, 1999), nearly two-thirds of newsgroup respondents reported that they had formed personal relationships with other newsgroup members. Only 7.9% of these respondents, however, reported romantic relationships from newsgroup participation.

Online support groups can also connect people who face troublesome physical or emotional problems (Barnes, 2001). "These groups are focused on a mutually recognized need for emotional support and feedback. Members offer each other encouragement in dealing with a medical or mental affliction that they share in common with other members of the group" (King, 1995). Individuals with physical limitations that make face-to-face support group participation difficult and individuals who could never get together in person because of geographic distances can meet in virtual support groups. A sense of community between otherwise highly diverse group members can develop online (Tal, 1994).

Using various communication technologies has many benefits, but there are also some serious drawbacks to consider. Most research shows that television watching reduces social contact and involvement (Brody, 1990; Neuman, 1991). The time spent viewing television displaces time spent engaging in social activities with friends and family. Isolation and fragmentation can easily occur when households have more than one TV set. Family members disperse to separate rooms to watch different television programs. Even though television is sometimes viewed in the presence of others, the quality of the social interaction is generally weak (Kraut et al., 1998). Talking during television watching interrupts the viewing. Conversation during commercial breaks invariably gets unplugged once the TV program continues. The social interaction is usually secondary to the television viewing. A similar critique has been launched against the Internet (see Box 9-2).

As previously discussed, cell phones can be highly disruptive when used inappropriately. In addition, phones can be a source of disconnection in ways similar to television and computers. When teens spend hours on the phone with friends, they disassociate themselves from the family. When parents spend a great deal of time on the phone talking business, the time is not spent with children and partners. The time spent using our technological toys is often time spent away from social contact with significant people in our lives. This can strain relationships and produce disconnection with those we count on for support, affection, and love.

Interpersonal relationships are formed online but the depth of these relationships certainly can be questioned, and since there is no physical proximity, you hardly know what is truth and what is fiction. "Love online can be fraught with

Box 9-2 Focus on Controversy

Cyberaddiction

On June 27, 1999, Kelli Michetti became enraged with her husband Robert for his excessive use of the Internet, especially his chats with women until 4 a.m. several days in a row. Kelli seized a meat cleaver and began whacking power cords on the computer, and then she started hacking at the computer terminal as her husband struggled with her. Kelli was arrested and charged with domestic violence (Women Angry, 1999).

The case of Sandra Hacker stirred national outrage when she was discovered neglecting her children so she could spend up to 12 hours a day online. She apparently would lock her children in a filthy room while she obsessively used the Internet (Bricking, 1997).

Cyberaddiction has become an issue of popular interest recently. Some evidence suggests that as many as 10% of Internet users in the United States are cyberaddicts. They average 38 hours a week online and about 4 hours of sleep a night (Baran, 1999). A large study claimed that the figure of cyberaddicts is closer to 6%, a smaller figure but still significant (Donn, 1999).

The University of Maryland in College Park began a counseling service for cyberaddicted students called "Caught in the Net." One study at the University of Glasgow in Scotland revealed that 16% of participants admitted they were irritable, restless, depressed, or tense if prevented from going online; 27% felt guilty about the time they spent online; 10% confessed that they neglected a partner, child, or a project at work because of their addiction (cited in Locke, 1998). Kraut and his associates (1998) found that, like television viewing, the Internet displaces time that could have been spent with family members and friends in conversation and social activities. This time displacement is particularly serious when Internet use becomes excessive. The Stanford Institute for the Quantitative Study of Society reported that, of the respondents who spent 5 or more hours per week on the Internet, 13% spent less time with family and friends, 26% talked less often with them on the telephone, and 8% attended fewer social events because of excessive Internet use (Stanford, 2000).

Some surveys, however, challenge whether Internet addiction even exists, and if it does whether it is a significant problem. The UCLA Internet study (Chmielewski, 2003) found that Internet use sacrifices time in front of the television, not social contact with friends and family members. Internet users reported that they watch 30% less television than nonusers. A 2000 Pew Internet survey of 3,500 adults found that 72% of Internet users had visited a friend or relative the previous day compared to 61% of non-Internet subscribers.

Whether Internet addiction is a real psychological disorder is open to question, even though the American Psychological Association has recognized it (Wood & Smith, 2001). The APA issued a press release in 1996 entitled "Internet Can Be as Addicting as Alcohol, Drugs, and Gambling, Says New Research." Dr. Kimberly Young (1996) conducted this new research. She studied 496 heavy users of the Internet. When she compared these subjects' Internet use to clinical criteria used to classify pathological gambling, she assessed 396 of the 496 subjects as Internet dependent.

Are there individuals who spend excessive time on the Internet at the expense of their interpersonal relationships? Undoubtedly there are (Barnes, 2001). Even those who spend less time watching television when they use the Internet may still ignore interpersonal relationships because of excessive Internet usage. The Stanford Institute study (Stanford, 2000) found that 59% of Internet users spend less time watching television, but 13% also spend less time with family and friends. Heavy Internet usage may bite into both time spent watching television *and* contact with friends and family. The Pew Internet survey also measured visits to friends and relatives as an operational indicator of social contact, but it merely compared Internet users and nonusers. It did not separate respondents according to degree of Internet usage. Heavy users may be much more prone to diminished social contact with family members and friends than are light users. The pervasiveness of Internet addiction is debatable, but "it is clear that there are negative effects associated with people who use the Internet disproportionately" (Wood & Smith, 2001, p. 104).

Questions for Thought

1. Do you think that Internet addiction is a serious problem? Have you ever spent excessive amounts of time on the Internet at the expense of your interpersonal relationships?
2. Is it likely that some Internet addicts spend large amounts of time developing interpersonal relationships online, not ignoring important relationships?

hazards. . . . People who are socially reticent are particularly vulnerable to false electronic proposals. Receiving numerous virtual accolades can make one ignore the risks of dealing with strangers" (Barnes, 2001, p. 145). Unlike the appealing romance portrayed in the movie *You've Got Mail*, there is little to recommend online romance. "Falling in love with a digital fantasy, rather than the real person that lives and breathes behind the monitor, is a common pitfall of net-inspired affairs" (Tamosaitis, 1995, p. 46). Love is a flesh and blood attraction between people, not a disembodied electronic fantasy.

Pagers, cell phones, fax machines, e-mail, and other electronic gadgets can be wonderful communication technologies if kept under control. The cell phone and pagers working in tandem, for example, can be an electronic lasso that binds a family together. Communication technologies, however, can also be what Shenk calls "electronic leashes" if we can never escape their intrusiveness. They can definitely reduce the amount of uninterrupted quiet time available to us where we pause from the daily routine of processing information and making decisions. A vacation can be transformed from relaxing time spent with one's partner or family into a "working vacation" with its stress and hustle if we are always connected to our jobs by pagers, cell phones, and e-mail.

CONFLICT   "E-mail, and now the Internet and the World Wide Web, are creating networks of human connection unthinkable even a few years ago. But at the same time that technologically enhanced communication enables previously impossible loving contact, it also enhances hostile and distressing communication" (Tannen, 1998, p. 239). A British study of more than 1,000 office workers found that 46% had reduced their face-to-face communication at work by using e-mail. Thirty-six percent sent messages by e-mail purposely to avoid face-to-face communication (cited in Locke, 1998). Using e-mail to avoid direct interpersonal contact may produce conflict.

Messages communicated by e-mail easily can be misinterpreted. Sarcasm, for instance, or teasing without the requisite tone of voice, facial expressions, and physical cues that signal how the message should be interpreted can be mistaken for serious personal attacks. **Emoticons,** graphic notations that indicate emotional information, can help in this regard. Emoticons for a smile ☺ or a frown ☹ can indicate a proper tone for a message (see Figure 9-1). Men, however, especially when conducting business by e-mail, may resist using emoticons because they are more closely associated with female communication patterns, and they may seem unprofessional. Emoticons also don't produce understanding if receivers are unfamiliar with them.

E-mail also reduces the natural constraints on incivility and hostility that come from facing a person directly. **Flaming** is a cyberterm for an abusive, attacking e-mail message. The same British study just cited found that 51% of the respondents

Emoticons

;-)	Wink		:-/	Skeptical
:-P	Sticking out one's tongue		:)	Happy
:-O	Screaming in fright; hair standing on end		:(	Sad
:-(	Frown		:((	Very Sad
:'-(	Crying		l-o	Yawning
%-)	Tired		:-x	One's lips are sealed

FIGURE 9-1   Emoticons
Emoticons act as social cues about online messages, substituting for vocal intonations and facial expressions. Here are some examples. For a more extensive list see www.computeruser.com/ resources/dictionary/ emoticons.html

had received flames, 31% had responded with a flame of their own, and 18% revealed that their relationships with fellow workers had disintegrated permanently after the exchange of flaming e-mail messages. The absence of normal constraints on incivility and hostility that come with in-person transactions (such as implicit rules against ugly public displays of anger), coupled with the ease and swiftness of e-mail, often lead to the detriment of relationships (Wallace, 1999). As Brin (1998) explains,

> Electronic conversations seem especially prone to misinterpretation, suddenly and rapidly escalating hostility between participants, or else triggering episodes of sulking silence. When flame wars erupt, normally docile people can behave like mental patients. . . . Typing furiously, they send impulsive text messages blurting out the first vituperation that comes to mind, abandoning the editing process of common courtesy that civilization took millennia to acquire (p. 166) .

Flaming is competitive, defensive communication. Those given to flaming often experience sender's regret—they wish they hadn't sent the angry, emotionally damaging message in the heat of the moment. Once it is sent, however, the damage is done. In September 2000, Qualcomm released its 5.0 version of the software Eudora with an enhancement called MoodWatch to address this concern. This new feature automatically signals e-mail composers when a potential flame occurs. When the e-mail composer is writing a message, a tiny ice cube icon remains in the window indicating that no flame has been detected. The moment the e-mail composer slips into potential flame territory, however, a chili pepper icon pops onto the user's screen. The most incendiary messages receive three chilies, and an author who attempts to send such a flame is warned, "Your message is the sort of thing that might get your keyboard washed out with soap" (Weber, 2000). Many business organizations have software that automatically censors potentially offensive words. Such approaches to flames, however, are only partial solutions, and they can be highly controversial (Yaukey, 2000).

So what can you do if using communication technologies severely reduces important social contact with others and increases hostile conflict? Here are two suggestions.

1. *Use communication technologies selectively.* If you find that communication technologies have become more of a leash than a lasso, plan for times during each day when you will have no access to any of these technologies. Turn off the pager or put it away. Shut off the computer, switch off the cell phone, and turn off the television set. Try simple conversation with another person with no technological distractions. Play a game, have a cup of coffee with a friend, take a walk, exercise, hike, shoot hoops, or just relax in a hot tub of water. Sometimes there simply is no substitute for personal, face-to-face contact, as anyone who has tried to conduct a long-distance relationship can attest. You can't hug, caress, or kiss a partner by e-mail, fax, or cell phone.

2. *Delay sending any e-mail message that has strong emotional content.* If you want to avoid sender's regret, delay sending any e-mail message you've written in the heat of the moment. I make it a standard practice never to send an angry message to anyone until I have reconsidered it at least overnight. I reread the message the next day before deciding to send, edit, or delete it entirely. Usually, upon reflection, I choose to delete the message. Flaming e-mail messages should always be put aside overnight. Never send an angry response to

Box 9-3   Sharper Focus

Netiquette

The competent communicator wishes to function within the social norms of a specific community. Certain communication norms specify appropriate behavior on the Internet. Barnes (2001) offers several guidelines for **netiquette,** etiquette on the Internet:

1. *Be brief.* Lengthy messages make e-mail management difficult and can be irksome. Get to the point.
2. *Flame off.* Common courtesy is expected of all netizens.
3. *Observe good form.* Observe grammar, spelling, and capitalization rules, and accepted spacing between words and paragraphs. Take the same care in composing e-mails that you would writing a standard letter. Such care demonstrates respect for the reader.

4. *Avoid spamming.* **Spamming** is sending unsolicited e-mail, especially advertisements for products or activities. Spamming clutters one's e-mail box.
5. *Assume publicity.* When composing e-mails, assume that anything written could be published on the front page of the local newspaper. If you'd be embarrassed if what you've written were published for all to see, consider carefully whether you should write it at all. Deletion of messages does not wipe out any trace of e-mails.

Although you can find exceptions to each of these guidelines, in most communication you should follow the guidelines carefully.

---

someone else's flame until you have had time to cool down. If an immediate response is required, simply ask for time to reflect on what was said and the way it was said.

3. *Do not use e-mail to fire or to reprimand an employee, to offer negative work appraisals, or to tender resignations.* These are highly personal matters and should be conducted face to face.
4. *Exercise etiquette on the Net.* See Box 9-3 for details.

Cultural Effects

In 1991, I visited Holland. After a long plane ride and a trip through Customs, I was anxious to find my hotel and relax. Once I found my hotel room and put away some of my things, I switched on the television set. I was surprised to see an episode of *Cheers* playing with Dutch subtitles. I switched channels. CNN was reporting the news in English.

Probably the biggest impact communication technologies have had on diverse cultures is a steady erosion of cultural integrity. It is difficult to maintain cultural values and viewpoints when an unending barrage of information and images is being transmitted from other cultures. This is sometimes referred to as **cultural imperialism**—"the invasion of an indigenous people's culture by powerful foreign countries through mass media" (Baran, 1999, p. 469). Cultures are expressing concern that their cultural identity is eroding.

CNN transmits to 800 million people in 60 countries. The 1991 Gulf War, NATO's conflict in Yugoslavia in 1999, and the dismantling of the Taliban in Afghanistan by the United States and its allies in 2001 were viewed all over the world on CNN. The BBC broadcasts all over the world in 40 languages. Radio Beijing from China does likewise. American movies and television programs are available worldwide. The proliferation of American films and programs concerns many cultures bothered by the heavy diet of violence and sex in most U.S. movies and TV series.

Box 9-4   Sharper Focus

China and the Internet

China traditionally has been closed off from the outside world. Anxious to protect its cultural values and way of life, China has severely restricted access to information from both outside and within China. With the development of the Internet, however, China faces a new challenge. Recognizing the growing connection between the Information Age and economic vitality, China has gone online with enthusiasm. About 50 million Chinese have access to the Internet, and the Chinese government is investing $54 billion in the expansion of its telecommunications system (Rubin, 1999).

Chinese officials hope to join the information revolution while controlling access to information that challenges cultural values and political points of view. Security officials block Web sites of foreign media or dissident Chinese groups outside the country. A Chinese citizen who wishes to access a foreign Web site must register and pledge not to read or disseminate information that imperils state security (Rubin, 1999). Cyberpolice read e-mail and block Web sites in most large cities in China.

These attempts to interrupt the free flow of information on the Internet are only partly successful (Platt, 2000). Banned material can be acquired from within China by accessing "proxy servers," computers located outside of China. Dissident materials can be e-mailed out of the country to proxies who can then send them back to Internet users inside China. At the moment, there is no imminent peril of government collapse from the Internet. In a decade, however, about 100 million Chinese will have access to the Internet. According to Minxin Pei, a scholar at the Carnegie Institute, "Party control of information will totally collapse. There will be a critical mass of informed people penetrating all segments of society, not just the elite. There will be a popularization of the Internet, more communication between groups. Popular resentment will grow" (cited in Rubin, 1999, p. P7).

What this will mean for China is difficult to predict. What it illustrates, however, is that the expansion and intrusion of communication technologies clearly disrupt cultural stability and the status quo. In a clear case of collectivist values, many other Asian countries have also attempted to control the Internet at the expense of individual freedom to use this technology as one sees fit (McDonald, 2001). The clash of cultures is apparent when the Internet makes all countries part of the global village. You may not be aware that almost half of all Internet users globally reside in the United States, with but a small percentage residing in South Asia (Wood & Smith, 2001). Our individualist values embrace easy access to communication technologies. Other cultures are more hesitant.

Consider just one commonplace example that illustrates the concern other cultures have regarding the ubiquity of the media invasion from the United States. American TV crime programs such as "Law & Order" and "NYPD Blue" apparently are affecting French citizens' perception of proper courtroom procedure. According to a poll in France, most French people think a judge should be addressed as "Your Honor" instead of the customary French form of address, "Mr. President." Many are also demanding warrants when police try to search their homes, even though no warrant is required under French law. These findings prompted a French official to exclaim, "It's a cultural catastrophe! French citizens don't even understand their own legal system anymore" (cited in France, 1997, p. 156).

Most countries impose quotas on media content from foreign countries. In 1989, for instance, the European Union mandated that 50% of all programming on European television had to be produced in Europe (Baran, 1999). Restrictions in China, Singapore, and a host of non-Western countries are even more rigid (Box 9-4).

Whether the global village will ultimately prove to be a boon or a bust for the people of the world remains to be seen. Unquestionably, our world will be a very different place as communication technologies become even more widely dispersed and utilized.

Cultural imperialism, the invasion of an indigenous people's culture by powerful foreign countries through mass media, is a real concern of nations worldwide. The Goddess of Liberty statue, remarkably similar to the Statue of Liberty, was made during a student protest in China in 1989. It shows the effect one culture can have on another when information is so readily available.

Summary

There are two primary trends in communication technologies: the pervasiveness of these technologies and the bias for speed. The consequences of these trends are far-reaching. Information overload has become a serious problem. The proliferation of misinformation has become widespread. Our relationships with others have been affected in both positive and negative ways, and cultural integrity has become an issue. The competent communicator still has control over technology. Control requires monitoring your use of communication technologies and understanding how these technologies influence your daily life. Communication technologies can solve problems or create new ones. It is up to us to choose.

Quizzes Without Consequences

Go to Quizzes Without Consequences at the book's Online Learning Center at **www.mhhe.com/rothwell2** or access the CD-ROM for *In the Company of Others.*

www.mhhe
● com/
/ **rothwell2**

Key Terms

See Audio Flashcards
Study Aid.

www.mhhe
com/
rothwell2
See Crossword Puzzle
Study Aid.

cultural imperialism	hyperbole	pattern recognition
emoticons	netiquette	spamming
flaming	niches	technology

Suggested Readings

Brin, D. (1998). *The transparent society: Will technology force us to choose between privacy and freedom?* Reading, MA: Addison-Wesley. This is an interesting book on how communication technologies have diminished our privacy.

Locke, J. (1998). *The de-voicing of society: Why we don't talk to each other anymore.* New York: Simon & Schuster. The author shows the marked impact communication technologies have had on society and individuals.

Postman, N. (1985). *Amusing ourselves to death: Public discourse in the age of show business.* New York: Viking Penguin. This is a provocative book on the nature of television and its impact on U.S. society. Postman has a definite point of view.

Shenk, D. (1997). *Data smog: Surviving the data glut.* New York: HarperCollins. This is the best work on information overload and its consequences.

Film School

EdTV (1999). Comedy/Drama; PG-13 ★★★➴
The effects of technology on interpersonal relations is depicted well in this Ron Howard film. Analyze the intrusive nature of technology and how it specifically intrudes on a developing romantic relationship.

You've Got Mail (1998). Romantic Comedy; PG ★★★★
Meg Ryan and Tom Hanks play two people who develop a romance via e-mail without having met each other in person. Explore the pitfalls and potential of an Internet romantic relationship.

PART TWO

Interpersonal
Communication

CHAPTER 10

Making Relationships Work

Our relationships with others can seem so fragile. According to the Rutgers University National Marriage Project, our nation's marriage rate has dropped 43% in the last 4 decades, to its lowest point ever recorded. The RUNMP also reports that only 37.8% of married couples are "very happy," down from 53.5% in 1973 (Fletcher, 1999). Divorce rates dropped slightly during the 1990s but currently are high. The unprecedented surge of women entering the workforce, acquiring college degrees, assuming an increasing percentage of management positions, and entering prestigious professions has afforded women a greater opportunity to leave unhappy relationships than at any other time in history (Coontz, 1997). Gay and lesbian relationships are even less durable than heterosexual marriages (Huston & Schwartz, 1995; Kurdek, 1998). Making relationships work in the long term, always a daunting prospect, seems more challenging than ever.

It may seem pleasant to envision a return to the "good old days" of the 1950s, depicted in television shows such as *Father Knows Best, Leave It to Beaver,* and *Ozzie and Harriet.* These shows presented an idealized picture of happy, intact families with manageable problems. Divorce was hardly ever mentioned, and single-parent families were a rarity. A Knight-Ridder poll (Thomma, 1996) found that 38% of respondents picked the decade of the 1950s as the best time for children to grow up (highest of any decade). According to a Gallup poll, 68% of respondents reported that it is tougher to have a good marriage today than it was for their parents' generation (Popenoe & Whitehead, 2001). More than half also question marriage as an institution because they believe that there are few good or happy marriages.

Yearning for the good old days, however, diverts attention from a deeper truth. The 1950s were good only for a small portion of our society. This "best decade" saw widespread racism, sexism, and homophobia. More than 27% of America's children lived in poverty, and almost half of African American families were impoverished (Coontz, 1997). Alcoholism, child abuse, and partner abuse were significant social problems that were mostly hidden from public view and largely ignored by social agencies. Leaving a bad relationship was not as acceptable in the 1950s as it is today.

One study (Wallerstein & Blakeslee, 1995) of present-day happily married couples found that only 5 of 100 spouses "wanted a marriage like their parents." The husbands "rejected the role models provided by their fathers," and the wives said that "they could never be happy living as their mothers did" (p. 15). It is unlikely that women's and men's expectations of marriage and employment will ever revert to the rigid gender roles of the past—the woman as the spouse who tends the house and the man as the sire of the shire. This means that *making relationships work now requires different answers from those offered in the past*.

Sustaining relationships has never been more challenging, and making friendships work is no exception. Friends engage in conflict more often than individuals who are not friends. These conflicts are satisfactorily managed in only about 30% of the cases (Davis & Todd, 1985). Faced with unsatisfactory outcomes, friends tend to part (Duck & Allison, 1978). Sustaining friendship during your college experience can be especially challenging given the typical high stress associated with a college education, the close proximity of dorm life, and the competitive atmosphere that often pervades college life.

Relationships at work can be equally challenging. One study found that almost 85% of respondents reported conflicts at work (Volkema & Bergmann, 1989). Working well with coworkers is frequently a condition for promotion; so managing our relationships with coworkers can be critically important (Fine, 1986).

Clearly, finding ways to make our relationships work is a big challenge. There is no magic formula, but *communication competence is central to the degree of relationship success we are likely to enjoy.* Although competent communication is no panacea for troubled relationships, as noted in Chapter 1, deficient communication aggravates problems that inevitably emerge in all relationships.

We know more about how competent communication can improve our relationships than at any previous time in our history. So let's explore what we've learned. *The primary purpose of this chapter is to discuss how to communicate more competently to sustain our relationships at home, at work, at school, and at play.*

There are four chapter objectives:

1. to describe the stages of relationship development and the communication patterns that emerge;
2. to explain communication dialectics inherent in relationships;
3. to address communication difficulties associated with intercultural relationships; and
4. to explore ways to improve our communication in relationships given the different stages, dialectics, and cultural differences that challenge us.

> The primary purpose of this chapter is to discuss how to communicate more competently to sustain our relationships at home, at work, at school, and at play.

Before we begin this exploration, let's clarify some terms. **Interpersonal communication** is dyadic communication; it is a transaction that takes place between two people. An **interpersonal relationship** is a connection two people have to each other because of an association (brother-sister), an attraction (friends), or a power distribution (boss-employee). A **personal relationship** is a close connection between two people that is characterized by strong emotional bonding and commitment. Our personal relationships, be they friendships, romantic couplings, or family associations, all seem to trigger a desire for closeness, a recognition that these relationships are special, and a wish that they continue for the long term.

Interpersonal communication occurs in both interpersonal and personal relationships, but not all interpersonal relationships qualify as personal. You and your boss may not even like each other, and maybe you stay as far away from each other as possible outside of the work setting. Nevertheless, you have a relationship with each other, if only a professional one, because of your interconnected roles.

Stages of Intimate Relationships

Understanding what makes relationships succeed or fail begins with a focus on stages of relationship development. Particular patterns of communication occur in each stage, allowing us to identify whether a relationship is progressing or deteriorating. Movement through the stages may be rapid, especially in the early stages, or it may be slow when one partner wants to move forward or backward but the other partner resists. It may not even be sequential because sometimes stages are skipped. Let's look at each of these stages, recognizing that this developmental model is descriptive of intimate relationships such as in romances and close friendships. Other relationships such as with family members and coworkers follow different patterns.

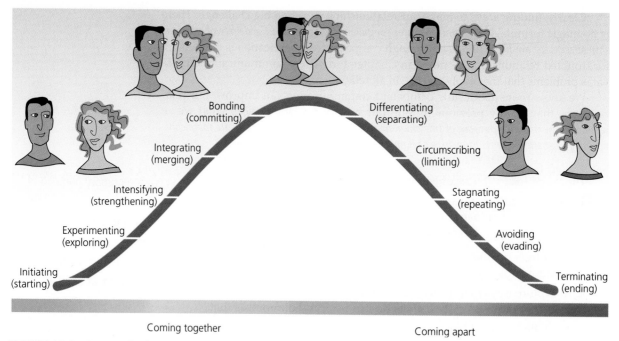

Bonding (committing)

Differentiating (separating)

Integrating (merging)

Circumscribing (limiting)

Intensifying (strengthening)

Stagnating (repeating)

Experimenting (exploring)

Avoiding (evading)

Initiating (starting)

Terminating (ending)

Coming together

Coming apart

FIGURE 10-1 Stages of Relationship Development

Coming Together Stages

Knapp and Vangelisti (1992) provide five "coming together" stages of intimate relationships. Figure 10-1 illustrates these stages.

INITIATING (STARTING)   Communication with others begins with a first step. Someone has to initiate contact. Physical attractiveness is often the impetus for initiating communication when a personal relationship is sought. It's important to note right from the start, however, that physical attractiveness is a weak basis for satisfaction in personal relationships. As one study found, "Although physical attractiveness may be the primary predictor of initial interaction, it does not appear to be as important as communication skills once the relationship is underway" (Zahahi & Duran, 1984, p. 56).

During the initiating stage, we are surveying the interpersonal terrain. We try to put our best foot forward by appearing friendly, open, and approachable. One study revealed the communication strategies that seem to work well during this stage when the intent is to explore the possibility of a blossoming personal relationship (Douglas, 1987). *Networking* (learning about a person from someone who knows him or her), *offering* (making yourself available for conversation by sitting in an adjacent seat or being in a place the person usually frequents), *approaching* (signaling an interest verbally or nonverbally with a smile or a self-introduction), and *sustaining* (keeping the conversation going by asking questions) all work well. Communication strategies that don't work well during this stage of personal relationship development include expressing deep feelings ("I'm afraid to love again"), keeping silent to create an air of mystery (there's no mystery in looking doltish), asking for big favors ("May I borrow $500?"), or diminishing oneself ("I'm very awkward when I first meet people").

EXPERIMENTING (EXPLORING)   In the experimenting stage we "audition" for the part of acquaintance, which may be a stepping stone to friendship. We experiment by engaging in small talk to discover areas of commonality: "What's your major?" "Can you believe how awful the weather has been?" "Have you worked at this job long?" We're casually probing, searching for ways to connect with others. All of us have superficial contacts with hundreds of people that never develop to any extent. Most of our transactions do not progress beyond the experimenting stage of development. They are fleeting contacts with no future.

INTENSIFYING (STRENGTHENING)   Relationships deepen at the intensifying stage. Individuals use a variety of communication strategies to intensify a relationship with another person (Taraban et al., 1998). The top 10 intensifying strategies in their order of frequency are (Tolhuizen, 1989)

See Intensifying Relationships Assessment on CD.

1. *Increased contact* (39.2%)—seeing or phoning partner more often
2. *Relationship negotiation* (29.1%)—openly discussing feelings about the relationship
3. *Social support and assistance* (26.1%)—requesting advice from a parent or friend
4. *Increased rewards* (17.6%)—doing favors such as doing partner's laundry or fixing partner's car
5. *Direct definitional bid* (16.6%)—asking for a commitment from partner
6. *Tokens of affection* (16.1%)—giving gifts, sending flowers, giving cards
7. *Personalized communication* (15.1%)—listening to partner or friend
8. *Verbal expressions of affection* (14.1%)—saying the big one: "I love you" or "You're really sweet"
9. *Suggestive actions* (13.1%)—flirting
10. *Nonverbal expressions of affection* (12.1%)—gazing, touching

Which of these strategies do you use most frequently? Women use relationship negotiation far more often than do men; men use direct definitional bid and verbal expressions of affection more often than do women (see also Owen, 1987).

The success of any of these strategies depends on the unique dynamics of a particular relationship. What works in one relationship may fail disastrously in another. Be careful not to move too quickly and exuberantly to intensify a relationship. You might panic your partner. Also, sensitivity to the signals given off (mostly nonverbally) by your partner is critical. We all give clues to the desirability and acceptance of intensifying strategies. Watch for the signals.

Trying to intensify a relationship is one thing; determining if the effort is working is quite another. Individuals conduct "secret tests" during the intensifying stage to check out the success of their intensification efforts (Baxter & Wilmot, 1984). *Endurance* requires a partner to tolerate unpleasant behavior such as criticism and inconvenient requests. If the tested party endures the test, commitment is assumed. *Public presentation* tests the intensity of the relationship through the introducing of one's partner as "my boyfriend" or "my girlfriend" to see if the partner is comfortable with the label. *Separation* tests the relationship by keeping the partners away from each other for a period of time to see if the relationship will remain viable. This, of course, is a risky test because although "absence makes the heart grow fonder," absence can also "make the heart wander" (Ivy & Backlund, 2000). *Third-party questioning* occurs when one partner asks a friend to check out the other person's depth of feeling about the relationship and then report the results to the tester. *Triangle tests* involve asking a friend to make the partner jealous by seeming to express interest in the partner concocting the test.

Women are more likely to employ these "secret tests" of a relationship. Separation and triangle tests are the most frequent choices. "The use of tests by females more than by males may reflect their greater relationship monitoring. . . . It is through secret tests that females monitor a relationship's pulse" (Baxter & Wilmot, 1984, p. 197). Nevertheless, *endurance, separation, and the triangle test are the least constructive.* The triangle test in particular is the most dangerous because trying to induce jealousy may sabotage a promising relationship. Public presentation and third-party questioning are relatively harmless ways to test the depth of a relationship.

INTEGRATING (MERGING)   The integrating stage fuses a relationship. Individuals seem to merge into a clearly distinct couple. Social circles of friends mix. A member of a couple displays nonverbal markers of intimacy, such as rings, pictures, pins, or clothing belonging to his or her partner. Self-disclosure is more revealing and potentially risky at this point. Couples share life goals and aspirations. A sexual relationship often occurs at this stage. Partners may begin living together, indicating that they have clearly moved beyond the "just friends" stage.

BONDING (COMMITTING)   The public ritual stage that institutionalizes the relationship is called *bonding.* In bonding, we are communicating to the world that we have a committed relationship. There is a public contract, of which marriage is the most obvious example. Although gay couples do not have this option in most states, any public announcement, ceremony, or proclamation that the relationship is considered exclusive and binding moves a couple into the bonding stage.

This stage usually signals a turning point. During the bonding stage, you are signaling the unique and exclusive nature of your relationship. You've made a decision to commit to your partner for the long term.

Turning points are key moments that move the relationship forward, such as sharing an interest, disclosing a personal secret, or lending your classic car that is in mint condition. Having sex, moving in together, or saying, "I love you" are typical turning points during the intensifying stage. Interestingly, almost half the time partners in heterosexual relationships do not identify the same turning points in their relationship (Baxter & Bullis, 1986). For example, having sex may be a momentous turning point for a woman that suggests a long-term intimate relationship, even marriage. For the majority of women (85%), emotional involvement is an absolute prerequisite for sex (Carroll et al., 1985). Conversely, many men may view sex as no turning point at all but just as a pleasant but not very significant event. Only a minority of men (40%) feel emotional involvement is a precondition for sex (see also Hatfield et al., 1989). Realizing for the first time that his female partner actually enjoys watching sports or backpacking in the wilderness, however, may be a turning point for a man.

As we all know, reaching the bonding stage does not guarantee that partners will remain bonded. Also, bonding is not an idyllic state. You may not wish to remain bonded with your partner. Nevertheless, Chapters 2 and 8 revealed five key communication skills that can improve your chances of remaining bonded with your romantic partner, if that is your desire:

1. *Make frequent connecting bids with your partner.* The more we bid, the more opportunities we have to connect and remain bonded.
2. *Emphasize turning toward responses to the connecting bids of your partner.* You do not have to turn toward every bid, but the majority of your responses should be turning toward, not turning away or turning against.

www.mhhe
● com/
/**rothwell2**

See "Close Relationship" quiz on the Online Learning Center, chapter 10.

3. *Strive for the "magic ratio" of 5:1 positive to negative communication in your relationship.* Remember, the negativity bias makes accentuating the positive a critical element of relationship maintenance.

4. *Avoid defensive and employ supportive communication patterns.* Defensive responses create distance between partners. They are not responses to real threats. You're not protecting the relationship; you're corroding it. Also, supportive communication doesn't mean always agreeing with your partner. You're supportive of the relationship, thus engendering closeness.

5. *Share power equally with your partner.* This is not only significant for heterosexual couples; several studies of gay and lesbian couples reveal that sharing relatively equal power leads to higher satisfaction and greater commitment (Eldridge & Gilbert, 1990; Kurdek, 1989; 1998). One survey of 3,000 married couples in the United States found that 64% reported that power is shared relatively equally in the marriage (Blumstein & Schwartz, 1983). Gays and lesbians report slightly less power sharing than heterosexual couples (Peplau & Cochran, 1980; Reilly & Lynch, 1990). In a study of college students, 48% of women and 42% of men reported equal power sharing in current dating relationships (Felmlee, 1994). Research also shows about the same level of power sharing in African American and Mexican American marriages as that found in Anglo American marriages (Peplau & Campbell, 1989).

Power is shared when partners accept each others' influence (Gottman & Silver, 1999). When partners disagree, they search for common ground. They problem solve; they discuss issues without insisting that one viewpoint be accepted outright. They do not try to dominate each other in a grab for power. Attempting to drown out a partner's expressed viewpoint, exhibiting contempt for his or her feelings, heaping criticism on, or trying to bully him or her into capitulating during an argument is the opposite of power sharing.

Coming Apart Stages

"Happily ever after" is a great finish to a fairy tale, but romantic relationships often don't move in just one direction—from friendly to intimate to happy to blissful. Relationships can move forward (coming together) or backward (coming apart), and the outcome is not inevitable. Couples who were once happy but become dissatisfied don't necessarily end their relationships. The direction of a relationship can turn around in an instant. A sexual affair can provoke a partner to leapfrog from bonding to termination, skipping four stages in between that are typical of a relationship that is coming apart. A friendship that is just beginning to intensify may fall apart suddenly because of an act of violence or a perceived betrayal of trust. Nevertheless, some relationships do dissolve slowly over time. The bonds that keep us together gradually fray and unravel. If you want to prevent the demise of a relationship, *recognizing the early stages of relationship deterioration can help.* Let's look briefly at the five coming apart stages.

DIFFERENTIATING (SEPARATING)   The first stage of disengagement is differentiating. Differences, not similarities, between partners, friends, relatives, or coworkers emerge.

HOMER: I thought you liked donuts.

MARGE: I just pretended to like them because I wanted to please you.

What were thought to be similarities are discovered to be differences. The pretense of being alike in most things begins to erode.

The orientation becomes more "Me" than "We." Assertions of individuality become more frequent. Conflict occurs, although differentiating can occur without conflict. Differentiating is an expected stage in romantic relationships. In the beginning of an intimate relationship partners may be inseparable. Later in the relationship such closeness may begin to feel smothering. A natural desire for some autonomy, some separateness, is probably inevitable. Giving each other "some space" may be a welcomed way to respond.

CIRCUMSCRIBING (LIMITING)   When we establish limits and restrictions on communication with our partner, we are circumscribing. Both the breadth and the depth of our communication become constrained. We perceive fewer topics as safe to discuss for fear of igniting a conflict, and the topics we address we discuss superficially. Communication interactions become less frequent.

STAGNATING (REPEATING)   Stagnating relationships experience the treadmill effect. Many miles are covered, but no destination is reached. Stagnating relationships aren't growing or progressing. The feeling is that "nothing changes." Communication becomes even more restricted, narrow, hesitant, and awkward than in the circumscribing stage. "We should talk about our relationship" is likely to provoke dread of yet another conflict with an unhappy outcome.

AVOIDING (EVADING)   In the avoiding stage, partners simply keep a distance from each other, hoping not to interact. They desire separation, not connection. Partners stay away from home by working late, or they spend more time with friends. If physical separation is not possible because children need to be parented, partners' communication may be impersonal and infrequent.

TERMINATING (ENDING)   Some relationships never terminate because they never get started. You greet a person, perceive no spark between you, and shuffle off in search of more promising prospects. Other relationships may take years, even decades, to terminate. This is the final pulling apart stage. The relationship is over—done, finished, ceased, dead, kaput.

In romantic partnerships, one or both parties choose to end the relationship. Who initiates its termination is about equal between men and women (Akert, 1998). Women, however, typically anticipate the demise of a relationship sooner than men, but men take the termination harder. Men are more depressed, lonely, and unhappy following the end of a personal, romantic relationship than women (Unger & Crawford, 1996). Regardless of whether men initiate the breakup or are dumped, they usually prefer not to "remain friends" with their ex-partners. Women more often wish to remain friends regardless of who initiated the dumping. When the initiation of the breakup is mutual, men and women are about equally desirous of remaining friends (Akert, 1998).

Sometimes termination can be narrowly avoided, but it isn't easy. As relationships fall apart, the desire to turn the direction around and rebuild the connection is typically stymied by the negative atmosphere that pervades the deteriorating relationship. It is difficult to short circuit a failing relationship and recapture the "magic" that once existed between people. We must apply all the suggestions for sustaining the bonds of relationships with extra vigor if we want to salvage a failing relationship. The primary suggestions are as follows (Gottman & DeClaire, 2001):

1. *Resist the temptation to reciprocate negative communication.* Fighting fire with fire will make toast of your relationship. Remain unconditionally constructive.
2. *Seek opportunities to praise, compliment, and bolster your partner.* Supportive communication is critical when a relationship begins to hit the skids. "You sure have been working hard," "You look nice," and "That place couldn't run without you" are examples of the type of communication that can begin to turn around a negative communication climate.
3. *Avoid at all costs turning away and turning against responses to connecting bids.* You don't repair relationships by choosing communication responses that tear apart bids that connect two people. Find every opportunity to make turning toward responses to bids of your partner.

Although there is a tendency to view the coming together stages of relationships as good and the coming apart stages as bad, this is not necessarily true. Some romantic relationships that appear promising initially prove to be less satisfying as the partners get to know each other better. Some relationships may even be destructive to one or both parties and should not progress. Terminating abusive relationships is positive, not negative. Sometimes relationship participants have to step back before they can step forward. Stages of relationships merely describe what is, not necessarily what should be.

Relationship Dialectics and Communication Competence

Relationships are often messy. As we move through the stages and become increasingly intimate, relationships will rarely follow the profile for textbook-perfect communication. Many romantic partners talk to each other on average for a mere hour a day, rarely self-disclose, often fight, even become violent verbally and sometimes physically, are less polite to each other than they are to strangers, and are more concerned with task accomplishment than with sharing intimacies (Baxter & Montgomery, 1996). We typically don't measure up to the ideal because romantic partnerships, close friendships, family relationships, and even work relationships face difficult contradictions every day. Communication theorists historically have tended to gloss over the contradictions inherent in relationships (Baxter & Montgomery, 1996).

In this section, the contradictory impulses, or dialectics, that push and pull us in conflicting directions in our relationships with others are addressed (Figure 10-2). Communication strategies for dealing with these relational dialectics competently also are discussed.

Dialectics Within Relationships

Dialectics are impulses that push and pull us in opposite directions simultaneously within our relationships with others. These contradictions create tension in relationships. With this tension comes an impetus for change. *Dialectics never disappear from relationships.* They are managed, not eradicated. There are three primary dialectics common to most personal relationships: connection-autonomy, predictability-novelty, and openness-closedness.

CONNECTION-AUTONOMY   The desire to come together with another person (connection) yet remain apart, independent, and in control of one's own life (autonomy) is called the **connection-autonomy dialectic.** We want to be an "us" without losing our individuality.

Adult children, for example, want to be connected to their parents in a loving relationship, but they usually rebel when parents interfere in their lives too much or make them feel as though they are still children to be supervised. As a relationship moves increasingly toward intimacy, the connection-autonomy dialectic becomes a central tension. Intimacy means connecting with another person emotionally. Intimacy requires greater We-ness than Me-ness, but intimacy doesn't require complete loss of self. Increasing levels of intimacy move us progressively toward greater connection with another person and away from autonomy. This can produce some anxious moments for individuals who become commitment phobic from fear of losing control of their lives.

Excessive emphasis on connection usually leads a person to feel smothered by his or her partner, parent, or personal friend, to feel entrapped and controlled by others, to have no life of his or her own. Excessive emphasis on autonomy, however, leads to complaints of insufficient time spent together, lack of commitment, and loss of affection (Baxter, 1994). Too much emphasis on either connection or autonomy can push a relationship into one of the stages of coming apart.

Workplace friendships pose an interesting challenge because the connection-autonomy dialectic emerges as a result of proximity. Working in the same office can provide many opportunities for people to connect and solidify a friendship. At the same time, however, daily contact with a friend at work may provide insufficient autonomy or separation and excessive connection (Bridge & Baxter, 1992). Romantic partners who also work together may find the connection-autonomy dialectic particularly troublesome. Opportunities for autonomy become fewer when you see your partner both at home and at work.

PREDICTABILITY-NOVELTY   Relationships require a fair degree of stability and constancy to survive; that is, they need some predictability. Families are a primary stabilizing force in most people's lives. Families provide an anchor in a sea of change. When marriages dissolve, it is not unusual for one or both partners in the breakup to seek comfort, even guidance, from parents. Some may even seek temporary refuge with parents until they can face life's tempests.

Predictability can be comforting. When you know what to expect, there are no unpleasant surprises. Predictability is stabilizing. When teenagers prepare a lavish meal for their parents and expect them to arrive home at 5:30 p.m., the last thing they want is for them to show up at a novel time, say 7:30 p.m. Predictability, however, does not produce pleasant surprises either, and it can induce boredom, possibly leading to the stagnating stage of a relationship. Teenagers, in particular, often come to see their families as suffocatingly predictable and unexciting. Spending a summer vacation with parents and siblings loses its allure during adolescence and may become unendurable when early adulthood hits. The **predictability-novelty dialectic** that flows from desiring both stability and change is a central concern in relationships.

Life in front of the television set can make a relationship overly predictable and boring, inviting a need for greater novelty. Novelty if not taken to an extreme can prevent a relationship from becoming stale and too predictable.

The early stages of relationships—initiating, experimenting, intensifying—are inherently novel. Everything seems new and different, and that can be exciting. Interacting with a new college roommate can be an interesting and challenging enterprise. Dating someone for the first time can be exciting because both individuals are exploring and discovering. A new romance brings change, and change can be thrilling and energizing. At some point, however, dating partners will often wish to settle into a long-lasting partnership to provide some predictability because of the comfort and stability it produces.

As relationships become long-term, the desire for novelty increases. Predictability, like an old shoe, can be comfortable but dull. To keep the spark in a relationship and avoid monotony, couples need to find ways to stimulate interest in each other. Similarly, friendships can grow stale without novelty: "We always sit around and gossip. Let's do something different for a change." We can become bored with our friends if activities and conversations with them become repetitive and predictable. Coworkers can seem tedious because you see them in the same situations doing mostly the same things, day in and day out. This can increase your desire to find new employment, with new coworkers, to counteract the tedium of predictability.

OPENNESS-CLOSEDNESS   U.S. culture encourages openness and discourages closedness (Klapp, 1978). We view an open mind and an open society with admiration. We usually view a closed mind and a closed society with disdain. Open expression of feelings and self-disclosure are necessary for bonding and intimacy to occur in a relationship. Some privacy, however, is also necessary if a relationship is to survive. This tension between accessibility and privacy is called the **openness-closedness dialectic.** The openness-closedness dialectic is an important dilemma that every relationship faces. How much self-disclosure and openness, candor or honesty, with your friends, family members, or romantic partner is enough, and how much is too much (see Box 10-1)? Indiscriminate self-disclosure strains most relationships and is incompetent communication. No effort is made to determine the appropriateness of the self-disclosure or to show appreciation for the audience. Telling your partner or friend personal information that he or she is not prepared to hear can doom the relationship. Excessive closedness, however, makes you a silent partner. Friendship and intimacy don't flourish when you share little with another person about who you are.

The openness-closedness dialectic takes an interesting twist when friendships are established at work (Bridge & Baxter, 1992). Close friends are expected to be open with each other. Organizational rules, however, may require confidentiality in certain circumstances, such as worker hirings, employee evaluations, and top-secret projects. In such instances, friends are pulled in opposing directions. "Go ahead and tell me who they plan to hire. I won't tell anyone" encourages openness based on friendship but collides with the ethical requirement to remain closed about confidential hiring details. If confidential information is spilled to a network of friends and if a supervisor gets wind of the infraction, your job security may become an issue. This could severely strain friendships. Similarly, if a friend at work told you that he or she had mismanaged a project or misused funds, imagine the dilemma you would face if your boss asked you to tell what you knew about such events.

The three relational dialectics discussed—connection-autonomy, predictability-novelty, and openness-closedness—typically emerge as more or less intense and challenging at different stages of a personal relationship (Baxter, 1990). During initial stages of a developing relationship, openness-closedness is of paramount concern. How much should you self-disclose to your friend or romantic partner? Is your self-disclosure reciprocated? These are real concerns. As a relationship becomes more established, however, connection-autonomy often predominates. Are you losing your identity and independence? Are you becoming distant from each other, burdened by the daily concerns of work and earning a living? Finally, as a relationship settles in for the long term, predictability-novelty often becomes a primary concern. Has the relationship become boringly predictable? Has either or both partners or friends changed so much since the beginning of the relationship that they seem like different people?

Dialectics With Outsiders

The dialectical tugs-of-war that push and pull us in opposite directions occur not only within relationships but also with outsiders. Anyone who is not directly involved in a specific relationship is considered an outsider. In a parent-child relationship, everyone who is neither the parent nor the child is an outsider. In a marriage, anyone outside of the marriage is an outsider, even a parent of either one of the spouses. We experience three primary dialectics with outsiders: inclusion-seclusion, conventionality-uniqueness, and revelation-concealment.

INCLUSION-SECLUSION   In a relationship with another person, we are pulled in two directions when outsiders enter the picture. We may want our partner to spend time with outsiders (inclusion), yet we may also want time alone together to nurture our relationship (seclusion). This is called the **inclusion-seclusion dialectic.** Including a larger network of friends and family can provide emotional support and encouragement that is highly supportive of the relationship. Too much involvement of outsiders, however, can provide few moments for relationship partners to connect. Thus, we may be torn between larger "family responsibilities" imposed by parents, in-laws, relatives, and friends, such as spending holidays together, and a desire to be alone with our partner without stress from outsiders.

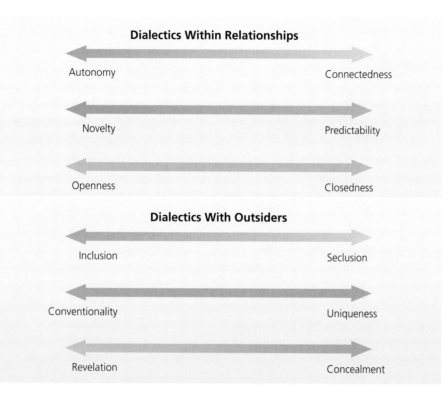

FIGURE 10-2 Relationship Dialectics

The desire for seclusion marks the relationship as special. Going camping with a friend with no one else invited says, "I want to spend time with just you." At the same time, friends and romantic partners may also desire inclusion and want relatives and friends to accept their relationship. Not including a partner in an invitation for a family get-together when your relationship is known would be insulting and hurtful. Failure of others to accept a romantic partner or friend is a common source of intense, even bitter conflict in the larger family network.

CONVENTIONALITY-UNIQUENESS   When we have relationships with others, we usually want to "fit in" and conform to certain family and societal expectations. Such conventionality just makes life less difficult generally. We're not bumping against how others believe we should act. Yet, by conforming to familial and societal expectations, our relationships may lose their sense of uniqueness, their special quality. They may begin to look like everyone else's relationships. When we are torn between wanting our relationships to be the same yet different, we are experiencing the **conventionality-uniqueness dialectic.**

Consider marriage, for example. The conventional institution of marriage has not lost its appeal for most people despite high divorce rates. Very few adults will live out their entire lives never having been married. Although the number of single parents in the United States numbers more than 12 million, with 2 million being single dads (Goldberg, 2001), single parenthood tends to be a temporary state. About three quarters of divorced parents remarry (Gottman, 1994a). Even cohabiting couples (unmarried partners living intimately together) are still relatively unconventional today. For every 100 married couples there are only 8 cohabiting couples

Box 10-1 | Focus on Controversy

Is Honesty Always the Best Policy?

You are gay. You are celebrating Christmas with your parents and siblings, and you want to bring your partner to the festivities. Your father is intensely homophobic. He is also recovering from a heart attack. Do you pretend that your partner is just a friend, or do you reveal the true nature of your relationship (revelation-concealment)?

Your spouse asks you whether you've ever had an affair. You have, but it ended 2 years ago. There is little chance that the affair ever would be discovered unless you told your spouse. Your spouse would be devastated to know you had cheated, even though you have no intention of ever being unfaithful again. Would you answer honestly (openness-closedness)?

Your close friend at work feels insecure about his body image. Your friend asks whether you think he is fat and unattractive. Your friend is very overweight and poorly groomed. Would you be honest (openness-closedness)?

You feel smothered by your partner. You have little time alone. When you plan outings with friends, your partner invites herself along. Do you tell your partner you need time alone or with friends, knowing that your partner will feel excluded (connection-autonomy)?

Dialectical forces pose a challenge to the oft-stated claim that honesty is always the best policy in relationships. The desire to be open, to reveal, and to connect with others pushes us toward honesty with our partners, friends, family, and coworkers. Nevertheless, circumstances also can pull us toward closedness, concealment, and autonomy. Pulled in this direction, we are inclined to lie to protect ourselves and others. The issue of lying brings into focus a principal dilemma we all face in relationships. Honesty is an important ethical guideline for the competent communicator and the cornerstone of trust, but relationship dialectics complicate the tidy but chirpy advice to "Just be honest."

Lying is widespread in the United States. One survey cited by NBC News on August 24, 1998, reported that 93% of employees "lie habitually" at work. A study by DePaulo and colleagues (1996) found that 147 participants told more than 1,500 lies in a 1-week period. Half the subjects were undergraduate students and half were members of the general public. Undergraduates lied in 1 of every 3 interactions they had with others. Nonstudent participants lied in 1 of every 5 interactions. Students lied to 38% of the people they interacted with; nonstudents lied to 30%.

Lying is pervasive but not because honesty is no longer valued. In fact, when asked to choose among telling a hurtful truth, telling a face-saving lie, or equivocating, only 6% chose lying, about 4% chose the truth, and over 90% opted for equivocation.

Equivocation occurs when our language permits more than one plausible meaning. For instance, when asked, "Do you like the dinner?" you might respond that "It is most unusual." The questioner can interpret the answer as either approval or disapproval. Equivocation spares the feelings of the questioner and avoids the brutal truth that you're tossing dinner into the dog dish at the first opportunity.

Even outright lies rarely are told to cause psychological damage to another ("So he'd look like a fool"). Fewer than 1% of lies told by college students and slightly more than 2% of lies told by nonstudent adults are of this damaging variety (DePaulo & Kasby, 1998).

Honesty is an important ethical standard for the competent communicator, but honesty can clash with respect for others. We don't always lie for self-centered reasons (to gain an advantage or manipulate others), and most of our fabrications are minor fibs, or "white lies," not whoppers. About a third of our lies (DePaulo et al., 1996) are told for altruistic reasons, such as to spare the feelings of a friend. When a friend or partner asks, "Am I fat?" you may lie by responding, "You're not fat. You look fine." The lie is meant to bolster your friend or partner's self-esteem.

Complete honesty can sound very good in the abstract, but total honesty can be hurtful and destructive, as amusingly illustrated by the Jim Carrey movie *Liar, Liar*. Psychology professor Bella DePaulo explains, "I can go as far as saying it would be a disaster if everyone tried to tell the truth all the time. If you tell the whole truth, you start alienating people. You'd have to go back and apologize because you've made a mess of your interpersonal relationships" (Lying Is Part, 1996).

So when is it appropriate to tell the truth, and when is lying acceptable? No absolute answer can be given. Several guidelines can assist you, however, in deciding whether to tell the truth or lie.

First, *honesty should be the norm, and lying should be the exception*. Communication with others would be chaotic if we could never trust what others say to us. Relationships must have a foundation of honesty even if an occasional lie for altruistic reasons seems warranted.

Second, *those who ask for honest answers must be prepared to accept the truth*. If not, then they probably shouldn't ask the question. If you can't accept a "Yes, you're fat" answer, don't solicit an honest response. Don't set yourself up to be hurt.

Third, *try to determine what the questioner is seeking*. This requires sensitivity—picking up signals from the person. If it is clear that the person is seeking support and encouragement, not absolute honesty, then a small lie may be appropriate.

Box 10-1 | Focus on Controversy (continued)

Fourth, *weigh the likely consequences of an honest response versus those of a lie.* Lying to a friend or spouse about his or her weight may encourage the person to continue an unhealthy lifestyle. An honest response may sting initially, but it may also motivate change.

Bok (1978) summarizes the issue well when she explains, "To say that white lies should be kept at a minimum is not to endorse the telling of truths to all comers. Silence and discretion, respect for the privacy and for the feelings of others must naturally govern what is spoken" (p. 76). *Honesty isn't always the best policy, but it usually is the best policy.*

Questions for Thought

1. How did you answer the questions posed in the four situations described at the beginning of this box? Explain your answers.
2. Do you agree that honesty is usually the best policy? Why or why not?
3. What would occur in your own relationships if dishonesty were the norm?

(Vobejda, 1998). A significant portion of cohabiting couples will eventually get married. The increased interest in marriage among gay and lesbian couples also illustrates the desire for some conventionality in relationships. Among gays, 85% view legal gay marriage as "very" or "somewhat important" (Leland & Miller, 1998). At the same time, couples typically want outsiders to view their relationships as unique. Talk of a "soul mate" and the "love of my life" expresses a desire to have a special relationship with a special "irreplaceable" person.

REVELATION-CONCEALMENT   Both intimate relationships and friendships face this dilemma: How much do we reveal to outsiders about the relationship, and how much do we keep private? This is the **revelation-concealment dialectic.** Revealing too much breaks the confidentiality that intimacy requires, but revealing too little denies the couple an important source of support and legitimation.

The revelation-concealment dialectic is a particular dilemma for gays and lesbians, as illustrated by one participant in a study by Dindia and Tieu (1996). This individual revealed, "I'm really struggling with this [who to tell] for about the past year. . . . I want to tell—hard to lie—hate to lie. Something pulls the other way [not telling], I don't know what" (p. 17). The military's "don't ask, don't tell" policy creates pressure to conceal same-sex relationships from outsiders. The military discharged 1,212 men and women in 2000 for violating this policy (Richter, 2001).

The "don't ask, don't tell" rule also operates outside of the military. Several participants in the Dindia and Tieu (1996) study reported that this rule guides disclosure of homosexuality with straight individuals. For example, one individual reported that she lived with her lesbian lover in an apartment directly above her parents. "They had to know but they didn't ask. So I didn't tell" (p. 35). This same person revealed that her brother and sister-in-law also knew but didn't ask.

The revelation-concealment dialectic is particularly significant when social stigma accompanies a revelation (See Box 10-2). Gay and lesbian teachers, for example, reveal their same-sex relationships at their own peril in most states. Few states have antidiscrimination laws to protect gay and lesbian teachers from being fired or

Box 10-2   **Sharper Focus**

Office Romances

The revelation-concealment dialectic is a key dilemma in office romances. A survey of 1,007 randomly selected adults, commissioned by the romance novel publisher Harlequin (cited in Jackson, 1999), found that almost 40% of employees admitted dating a coworker, and 39% of these romances, according to the American Management Association, result in marriage or long-term committed relationships (We Met, 1999). Most of the participants in office romances admitted to having sex with their office partner in the workplace—in a conference room, on their desks, or in the boss's office (one-fifth dated a supervisor)—making concealment of the relationship a tad more challenging. An additional 34% of workers in another study revealed that they might participate in an office romance if the opportunity arose (Steffans, 2001).

Despite their frequency and contrary to most couples' desire to announce their romance to friends and coworkers, office romances are often concealed from fellow workers and bosses (Eng, 1999). Only 13% of companies in the United States have a specific policy on workplace romances (Steffans, 2001). Although the great majority of

these policies ban romantic relationships between subordinates and supervisors, most companies have no such stricture. Nevertheless, most companies permit but discourage romantic relationships between employees.

A survey of 756 employees found that 8% of respondents were angered by workplace romances, and 47% felt that such relationships created an uncomfortable and awkward workplace environment (Staff, 1988). Supervisor-subordinate romances produce the strongest negative reactions from fellow workers (Powell & Mainiero, 1990). In another survey, 78% of female executives resented supervisor-subordinate romances, but only 21% resented romances between peers on the job (Mainiero, 1989). Concern about special treatment of subordinates by supervisors who are romantically involved creates the resentment. Fear of violating official workplace policies or informal taboos, gossip, and general disapproval and concern that fellow workers will levy accusations of sexual leverage to attain promotion encourage romantic couples in the workplace to hide their relationships as best they can (Witteman, 1993).

pressured out of their teaching jobs once their sexual preference becomes public knowledge (Irvine, 1998).

Dialectical Strategies

If a husband has more power than his wife, he does not have to understand her point of view or even listen to her position in a conflict. He can achieve greater autonomy, for instance, by simply telling his wife that he plans to spend more time with his male friends. Announcing choices, however, is a monologue, not a dialogue. Dialogue between partners in a relationship is at the center of dialectical management. Communication that discourages dialogue is "interactionally incompetent" (Baxter and Montgomery, 1996, p. 201). Dialogue is a conversation, not an announcement. It is a cooperative effort to find mutual solutions to problems. For dialogue to take place, both parties need to listen empathically to each other. As we review the strategies for managing relationship dialectics, keep in mind that none are likely to be effective without open and honest dialogue.

SELECTING (CHOOSING)   There is never an ideal balance point or "happy medium" between these polarities that pull us in two directions at once (Baxter & Montgomery, 1996). Attention to one of the two contradictory forces inevitably creates a stronger impulse from the other direction. Giving attention to one contradictory impulse while ignoring the other is called **selecting.** Constant attention to novelty leaves no time for establishing predictability in a relationship. Without some predictability, most people feel insecure in a relationship. One form of novelty, after all, could be that your partner decides you're too dull and he or she needs a different partner. Novelty can be exciting, but it doesn't provide predictability and security in relationships.

Likewise, focusing attention on autonomy leaves no room for connection. Intimacy suffers. Partners who spend most of their time pursuing career goals, hobbies, and personal interests separate from one another leave little or no time for developing intimacy. They become strangers living together. Friends who rarely see each other can become disconnected and distant. Coworkers who insist on being around you all the time at work can seem cloying and suffocating. When a coworker tries too hard to connect with you, he or she can induce a screaming desire to be alone.

Selecting can manage dialectics in certain circumstances. For instance, if both partners in a relationship see the value of novelty but agree that predictability, although unexciting, is safer and more secure, then their choice to emphasize one impulse and deemphasize its opposite may work. Also, couples may alternate between opposing impulses, selecting connection for a time, and then emphasizing autonomy, for example. They may spend a substantial, concentrated period of time engaging in activities together and then spend other times mostly separated, doing things that are not mutually satisfying. Partners sometimes hardly see each other they are so busy with their respective jobs and careers. They may purposely take a month-long vacation together to rekindle the connection that their mostly autonomous lifestyle has diminished.

Selecting, however, is the least effective method for managing relational dialectics because one need is sacrificed for its opposite (Baxter, 1990). Spending "quality time" together on a pleasurable vacation may not satisfy the partners' need to connect on a more regular basis. The residual "glow" from a wonderful vacation may not sustain a relationship for 11 months until the next dose of connection is administered. There may even be a relationship between the selection strategy and abuse. One study found that abusive couples primarily use selection to manage dialectical tensions (Sabourin & Stamp, 1995). Addressing both impulses is usually preferable to addressing one need at the expense of the other.

NEUTRALIZING (COMPROMISING)   Striking a compromise between opposing dialectical impulses by partially satisfying both impulses is called **neutralizing**. Partners negotiate some personal autonomy, for instance, but not as much as they desire. Consider the case of Gabriel and Alexis. Gabriel wants to spend time with his male friends at least twice a week. Alexis wants him home to help take care of the kids. She agrees to "guys night out" once a week in exchange for greater participation in putting the kids to bed. Neutralizing doesn't fully satisfy any of the conflicting needs in a relationship, but it may be satisfactory given the circumstances. After all, children require parenting. It is unlikely that any parent will have as much independent time as he or she might like.

SEGMENTING (CATEGORIZING)   When partners divide certain parts of their relationship into domains, or categories, they are **segmenting.** In dealing with the openness-closedness dialectic, for instance, partners may designate certain subjects as "off limits" for sharing with each other to reduce the possibility of hurting each other's feelings or provoking jealousy. For instance, previous boyfriends or girlfriends may be segmented as a taboo topic. How each partner spends money from his or her own bank account may also be categorized as off limits. With coworkers, confidential work information may be one area that is off limits. Office gossip about personnel files and hiring interviews can create dicey, even illegal, situations. Openness, however, would be encouraged in all areas other than those designated as removed from discussion.

Couples might also segment novelty and predictability in similar fashion. The weekends might be set aside for novel activities (trying a new sport, traveling to a new destination), whereas the weekdays might follow a predictable routine. Similarly, couples might set aside certain holidays to visit parents and relatives (inclusion) but keep certain special occasions, such as birthdays or New Year's, just for themselves (seclusion).

Segmenting is potentially one of the most effective means of managing relational dialectics because both partners' needs are being addressed on a fairly regular basis for the sake of the relationship (Baxter & Montgomery, 1996). Unlike neutralizing, where compromises have to be made and needs are only partially met, segmenting attempts to satisfy fully the needs of both individuals in the relationship through a joint effort.

REFRAMING (REDEFINING)   Sometimes we can take a seeming contradiction between two impulses and look at it from a different frame of reference. This change in perspective is called **reframing.** Lack of honest, open disclosure might be reframed as being tactful or using discretion. Time for yourself (autonomy) might be explained as connection because personal time may rejuvenate the bond between partners and lessen interpersonal friction. Predictability in a relationship might be presented as necessary for novelty to be appreciated when it occurs. A couple might view their relationship as unique because it has survived for an entire year, a new record for both partners, even though outsiders might view this as unspectacular and ordinary.

Reframing is a very sophisticated strategy for dealing with relational dialectics. It takes practice to create a new perspective on dialectical needs, but reframing has the potential to be very effective in addressing relational dialectics.

Effectively managing relational dialectics can be a complex process. Two points should be emphasized. First, *dialectics are not dichotomies*. In a relationship, you should not have to choose between openness or closedness, connection or autonomy, predictability or novelty. These should not be either-or choices but rather *both-and* choices (Baxter & Montgomery, 1996). Relationships need *both* openness *and* closedness, connection *and* autonomy, predictability *and* novelty, and so forth. Recognizing when one need requires more attention than its opposite shows sensitivity. Addressing the need effectively requires dialogue between partners.

Second, *approaching relational dialectics as a competition is self-defeating*. If one partner "wins" greater autonomy at the expense of the other partner's need for connection, then both lose because the relationship is diminished. Approaching relational dialectics as a competition is usually ineffective. None of the strategies for dealing with relational dialectics is likely to be successful without cooperative dialogue between partners.

Intimacy and Love

In the previous chapter the "dark side" of personal relationships was discussed. Our personal relationships also have a "bright side." Intimacy and love are two of the most fulfilling, satisfying experiences humans can enjoy. In this section, these two profound and significant aspects of personal relationships and the role communication plays in fostering both experiences will be explored.

Intimacy

We engage in many kinds of interpersonal relationships. What makes some of these relationships special is the intimacy shared between two people. **Intimacy** "is the feeling of closeness in a relationship—the degree to which a person can share feelings freely with another" (Schultz & Oskamp, 2000). Although intimacy is sometimes associated in the popular mind with sex ("We were intimate last night"), intimacy occurs in different types of relationships, some nonsexual and unromantic. One study (Berscheid et al., 1989) of several hundred college students found that respondents' "most intimate relationship" was with a romantic partner (47%), a friend (36%), or a family member (14%). In another study, three-quarters of college students reported that intimacy could occur without sex and romance (Floyd, 1996).

The dialectics of connection-autonomy and openness-closedness influence the communication of intimacy between partners. Intimacy is partially achieved through self-disclosure. If partners express too little self-disclosure and too much autonomy, intimacy cannot be experienced. Intimacy, however, is nurtured mostly by daily conversation, often of the chitchat variety (Andersen & Guerrero, 1998). Baxter (1992) refers to this as "intimate play." The use of affectionate nicknames, being silly together, conversing about daily activities at work, trying to organize child-rearing schedules, doing a crossword puzzle together, and teasing each other all serve to solidify a relationship and nourish intimacy. These are all turning toward responses that encourage closeness.

Men and women, however, do not always express intimacy in the same ways. Women typically draw close to one another through talking about personal matters and discussing experiences. When you equate intimacy with just self-disclosure, it would appear that women are better at establishing intimacy than men. Verbal self-disclosure, however, is not the only way of establishing intimacy. We can establish closeness in relationships by sharing activities or doing something helpful for our partners or friends. Men typically talk less about personal matters and share feelings less with other men, but they achieve closeness by sharing meaningful activities. Going on a hike, watching sports, or building a fence together are all ways that intimacy can be achieved. More than 75% of men in one survey reported that shared activities were their most important experiences with friends (Swain, 1989).

If styles of communicating intimacy differ between men and women, then it is important that the partners recognize this early in the relationship. Otherwise, misunderstandings will emerge. For example, a man fixes an annoying squeak in a door hinge that has bothered his female partner for some time. He assumes that she will recognize this as an act of affection because he perceives it as such. His partner, however, may see this as simple maintenance and not recognize it as an expression of intimacy. Thus, she experiences no act of closeness, and he likely feels perturbed that an act of affection went unrecognized. Men also may think that physical proximity (being in the same room; watching television while sitting on the same couch together) is intimate. Women may see this as the "lump on the couch." These style differences in communicating intimacy should be discussed. Unfortunately, men's greater aversion for such discussions often results in these conversations never occurring (Rubin, 1984).

Love

Richard Barnfield described it as "a fire, a heaven, a hell, where pleasure, pain, and sad repentance dwell." Germaine Greer called it "a drug." Helen Rowland said it is "woman's eternal spring and man's eternal fall." George Bernard Shaw, ever the cynic, saw it as "a gross exaggeration of the difference between one person and everybody else." Love almost defies definition, principally because there is not just one kind of love. Although we tend to think of love in terms of passion, not all types of love are passionate.

Robert Sternberg (1986, 1988, 1997) has offered his **triangular theory of love** to explain the different types (see Figure 10-3). The three elements of love according to this theory are intimacy, passion, and commitment. *Intimacy* has already been defined as feelings of closeness with another person. *Passion* refers to the drives that produce intense emotions. These drives include physical attraction, sexuality, need for nurturance, self-esteem, or even dominance. *Commitment* refers to a decision to continue a relationship long term. Different types of love are composed of varying combinations of these three elements. Sternberg offers seven types:

1. *Liking*—intimacy without passion or commitment, such as in a friendship
2. *Infatuated love*—passion without intimacy or commitment, such as "puppy love"
3. *Empty love*—commitment without passion and intimacy, such as stagnating, unsatisfying marriages
4. *Romantic love*—passion and intimacy without commitment, such as a romantic affair
5. *Companionate love*—intimacy and commitment without passion, such as a long-term marriage in which partners are more friends than lovers
6. *Fatuous love*—passion and commitment without intimacy, such as a "love at first sight" relationship
7. *Consummate love*—combining intimacy, passion, and commitment, such as the most satisfying adult relationships

It is not unusual for people to mistake passion for consummate love. Passion without intimacy or commitment, however, is more a "one-night stand" than a consummate love. In the absence of intimacy and commitment, passion can flame out quickly, leaving emptiness and disappointment. *Personal relationships that have the greatest longevity and satisfaction are those in which partners are constantly working on maintaining intimacy and reinforcing commitment to each other.* This is the companionate love of friendships that plays an integral part in making our lives rewarding.

Passion does not inevitably disappear as a romantic relationship grows over the long term, but the giddy levels of passion characteristic of early stages of romance realistically cannot be maintained for years (Tucker & Aron, 1993). As romantic relationships mature, passion becomes more episodic, appearing sometimes but seeming to disappear at others. When the fires of passion seem to flicker out occasionally or diminish overall, as they inevitably will, a long-term relationship is sustained by the warmth of intimacy and the security of commitment. Turning toward responses to connecting bids, supportive communication patterns, mutual self-disclosure, and empathic listening are important communication skills vital to intimacy and commitment. These skills say, "You are important to me, and I value our relationship."

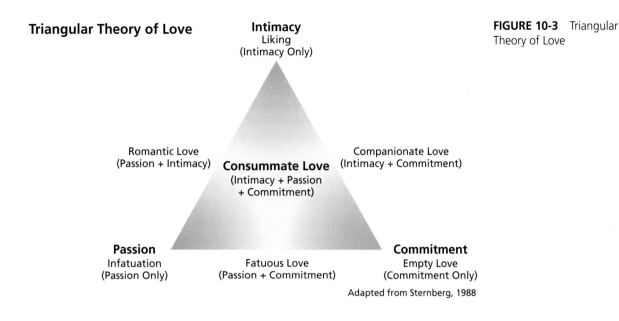

FIGURE 10-3 Triangular Theory of Love

Would you be willing to marry a person if you were not in love with him or her? In other words, is marriage an option for you if passion is missing in action (Regan et al., 1998)? There appear to be wide variations across cultures in answering this question. In one study (Levine, 1993), the willingness to marry without passion as a prospect varied from 4% in the United States, 5% in Australia, and 8% in England, to 49% in India and 51% in Pakistan. Romantic love is a significant, even vital basis for marriage in individualist cultures, but it is less important in collectivist cultures (Dion & Dion, 1996). Individualist cultures such as the United States value the right of each person to decide whom to marry. In collectivist cultures, however, the decision regarding whom to marry must involve the wishes and preferences of family members and other groups. That is why arranged marriages are common in such cultures. As Francis Hsu (1981) explains, when in love "an American asks, 'How does my heart feel?' A Chinese asks, 'What will other people say?'" (p. 50). In collectivist cultures, a marriage that would disrupt complex networks of existing relationships within families typically would not be attractive.

Intercultural Relationships and Communication Competence

Different cultures have different perspectives on love and intimacy. When individuals from cultures with different perspectives develop friendships or romantic relationships, difficulties inevitably arise.

Relationship dialectics, for example, don't disappear when members of different cultures mix. Dialectics can pose even more significant challenges for intercultural relationships than for individuals from the same culture. Individualist, low power-distance cultures such as the United States, for example, emphasize autonomy, openness, uniqueness, and novelty. Individual freedom is valued, and status differences are deemphasized. Collectivist, high power-distance cultures such as Singapore value harmony as a way of nurturing relationships. Conformity and group well-being are highly valued. Connection (within relationships), closedness (with outsiders), conventionality (following the rules), and predictability (stability) further harmony. In a collectivist culture autonomy, openness, uniqueness, and novelty are likely to upset cultural harmony.

Given the sometimes enormous perceptual differences, how do individuals from distinctly different cultures develop friendships and romantic relationships? Not easily!

Intercultural Friendships

The initial stages of a developing friendship between individuals from different cultures must address three problems (Martin & Nakayama, 1997). First, the differences in values, perceptions, and communication style can be troublesome. These are deep-seated, not superficial differences (Chapter 3). Second, anxiety is a common experience in the initial stages of any friendship, but intercultural friendships are likely to induce greater anxiety. We experience greater fear of making mistakes and causing offense when we are unfamiliar with the norms and rules of another culture. Third, overcoming stereotypes about a different culture and resisting the impulse to be ethnocentric can be difficult.

A study of American and Japanese students who were friends revealed some interesting ways to nurture intercultural friendships (Sudweeks et al., 1990). First, some similarities that transcend the cultural differences must be discovered, whether these are sports, hobbies, lifestyles, or political attitudes. Bridges must be constructed from common experience. Second, making time for the relationship is critical. It takes more time to develop a friendship with a member of another culture because we are typically drawn to others who are like us, not to those who are unlike us. Third, sharing the same group of friends can be very important. A shared group of friends can lend support to an intercultural relationship. Finally, capitalizing on key turning points (requesting a favor; revealing a personal secret) is especially vital in developing cross-cultural friendships. Reluctance to respond positively to a turning point may be perceived as an insult and might end the relationship.

Ultimately, cross-cultural friendships require more "care and feeding" (Pogrebin, 1987) than do friendships between similar individuals. More explaining and understanding must take place. "Mutual respect, acceptance, tolerance for the faux pas and the occasional closed door, open discussion and patient mutual education, all this gives crossing friendships—when they work at all—a special kind of depth" (Pogrebin cited in Gudykunst & Kim, 1992, p. 318).

Intercultural Romantic Relationships

Romantic relationships can be even stickier than friendships. Once the difficulties of developing a friendship have been overcome, additional problems can develop when romance flowers. Families may raise a stink about cross-cultural friendships, and romance may intensify this opposition (Kouri & Lasswell, 1993). Opposition from one's family isn't necessarily based on prejudice, although surely bigotry sometimes plays a part. Concerns about child-rearing styles, religious differences,

Cross-cultural relationships present unusual challenges for couples. Consensus, learning about and adopting aspects of each other's culture, is an effective strategy for meeting intercultural relationship challenges.

politics, gender roles, power issues, place of residence, and rituals and ceremonies may also increase opposition.

Romano (1988) identifies four strategies that are used in intercultural marriages. Submission is the most common strategy. One partner abandons his or her culture and submits to the partner's culture, adopting the religion, value system, politics, and so forth. This is rarely effective because individuals find it enormously difficult to erase their core cultural values and background. A second strategy, compromise, means giving up only part of one's cultural beliefs, values, and habits. This is also very difficult in most situations. Asking one partner to forgo Christmas decorations and celebration and the other partner not to observe the Muslim holy month Ramadan isn't likely to be a smooth compromise. A third strategy, obliteration, is sometimes used. Obliteration occurs when both partners attempt to erase their respective cultures from the relationship. This is difficult to accomplish, and it means avoiding basic support groups such as family and friends. Finally, there is consensus, which seems to work best. Consensus is based on negotiation and cooperation. Learning the partner's language, studying the religion, and learning about the cuisine erect bridges between partners. Consensus is built by emphasizing similarities and commonalities in relationships and by deemphasizing differences. Consensus is difficult even among culturally similar individuals. It is doubly difficult between culturally dissimilar individuals who plan to marry.

Summary

As we begin the new millennium, relationships are more challenging than ever. Every relationship travels through specific stages. Keeping a relationship from moving into the coming apart stages is a principal concern. Each relationship is challenged by dialectics, or contradictory impulses, pushing and pulling each partner in two directions simultaneously. Intercultural relationships are even more challenging. Individuals from collectivist cultures have a We-emphasis, but persons from individualist cultures have a Me-emphasis. This fundamental distinction in cultural values can put a strain on an intercultural relationship.

Quizzes Without Consequences

Go to Quizzes Without Consequences at the book's Online Learning Center at **www.mhhe.com/rothwell2** or access the CD-ROM for *In the Company of Others*.

www.mhhe
com/**rothwell2**

Key Terms

See Audio Flashcards
Study Aid.

www.mhhe
com/**rothwell2**

See Crossword Puzzle
Study Aid.

connection-autonomy
  dialectic
conventionality-
  uniqueness dialectic
dialectics
equivocation
inclusion-seclusion
  dialectic
interpersonal
  communication

interpersonal
  relationship
intimacy
neutralizing
openness-closedness
  dialectic
personal relationship
predictability-novelty
  dialectic
reframing

revelation-concealment
  dialectic
segmenting
selecting
triangular theory of
  love
turning points

Suggested Readings

Farrell, W. (2001). *Father and child reunion: How to bring the dads we need to the children we love*. New York: Jeremy P. Tarcher. Farrell has written another provocative book. This time he focuses on the crucial role fathers play in children's lives and how our society has made dads seem expendable.

Gottman, J. M., & Silver, N. (1999). *The seven principles for making marriage work*. New York: Crown. This is a very readable presentation of Gottman's groundbreaking research on marriage and divorce.

Gottman, J. M., & DeClaire, J. (2001). *The relationship cure*. New York: Crown. If you want more instruction on making relationships work, this is the book to peruse.

Annie Hall (1977). Romantic comedy; PG ★★★★★
This is Woody Allen's amusing, Oscar-winning take on relationships. Apply the
stages of relationships and dialectics material to the film.

My First Mister (2002). Comedy/drama; Not rated
An unusual relationship develops between the Albert Brooks and Leelee Sobieski
characters. Analyze their relationship using the triangular theory of love model.

Notting Hill (1999). Romantic comedy; PG-13 ★★★★⤙
This is the charming and extraordinarily entertaining story of a London bookstore
owner whose chance encounter with an internationally acclaimed American actress begins an on-again off-again romance. Analyze the complex, fitful development of their relationship in terms of the stages of relationships. Do the several
reversals of direction in the relationship between the Hugh Grant and Julia
Roberts characters coincide with the stages of relationships material presented in
this chapter? Explain.

Say Anything (1989). Comedy/drama; PG-13 ★★★⤙
A very appealing relationship movie with John Cusack providing most of the appeal. Analyze the stages of this relationship between Cusack's character and the
character played by Ione Skye.

The Story of Us (1999). Drama; R ★★⤙
Underrated, intense drama about a couple in crisis trying to raise two children.
Look for examples of dialectics and how these dialectics impact relationships

CHAPTER 11

Interpersonal Conflict Management

Experience tells us that conflict is often an unpleasant, even nasty business. Look up the word *conflict* in a thesaurus, and you find synonyms such as "discord," "disagreement," "struggle," "strife," "clash," "fight," "hostility," "disharmony," "adversity," "dissonance," and "opposition." You will have to look long and hard to find any positive meaning ascribed to conflict, perhaps because the original derivation of the word comes from the Latin *conflictus*, meaning to "strike together with force."

Research on marital conflict certainly doesn't paint a very cheerful picture. The more couples engage in conflict, the more they become verbally aggressive, and verbal aggression can provoke physical violence (Cahn & Lloyd, 1996). Conflict episodes often become more intense and ugly as conflict becomes more frequent. Marital conflict is also associated with a wide range of problems for children, including depression, weak academic performance, poor social skills, and discipline difficulties (Hetherington et al., 1998). These results are likely to be more serious as the frequency of conflict increases. Children of intact (nondivorced) families with frequent conflict, for example, have greater problems with psychological adjustment and self-esteem than do children living in low-conflict divorced families or nondivorced families (Amato & Loomis, 1995).

Conflict is an unavoidable fact of life. One study found that college students engage in conflicts, on average, seven times per week (Benoit & Benoit, 1987). Another study reported two substantial arguments per week between adolescents and parents, and three additional conflicts among siblings (Montemayor, 1986). In the same study, a quarter of the parents complained about conflicts with their teenagers, and a fifth of the adolescents claimed that they had "many serious" conflicts with their parents.

In the workplace, conflict is prevalent. A survey of 150 executives from Fortune 1,000 companies reported that 18% of management time is devoted to resolving conflicts (Employee Tiffs, 1996). "Conflict is a stubborn fact of organizational life" (Kolb & Putnam, 1992, p. 311). Organizations are "arenas for staging conflicts, and managers [act] as both fight promoters who organize bouts and as referees who regulate them" (Pondy, 1992, p. 259). One survey of 1,305 workers found that almost a third admitted to yelling at a coworker (Girion, 2000). "Workplace bullying" is rapidly increasing. Workplace bullying occurs when supervisors shout at subordinates and coworkers, criticize employees, and demoralize competent workers by taking away their responsibilities when work isn't performed exactly as ordered (Survey, 1998). According to a 1998 Justice Department report, almost 2 million people each year are also victims of violence in the workplace (Lardner, 1998). The United States has the highest incidence of homicide at work of any industrialized nation, averaging more than 1,000 murders per year (Survey, 1998).

Despite its frequency and negative potential, however, conflict can be a constructive force in relationships at home, at work, at school, and at play if managed competently. Conflict can appear ugly and destructive to us when it is frequent and we lack the skills necessary to manage it constructively. Conflict, however, can be a signal that change needs to occur for a relationship to remain vital. Women, but not usually men, may use conflict to provoke attention to a relationship problem and trigger discussion on a possible solution (Haefner et al., 1991). Conflict can also encourage creative problem solving in the workplace by raising tension, which may encourage an energetic search for innovative answers. Reducing the severity of conflict episodes by learning conflict management techniques is a key to constructive conflict (Canary et al., 1995).

Consequently, *the main purpose of this chapter is to discuss communication that provokes destructive conflict and communication that encourages constructive conflict.*

There are four chapter objectives:

1. to define conflict in both its constructive and destructive forms,
2. to describe the primary communication styles available for managing conflict,
3. to discuss which communication styles are most likely to encourage constructive conflict management, and
4. to discuss ways to manage conflict competently through anger management, forgiveness, and intercultural understanding.

> The main purpose of this chapter is to discuss communication that provokes destructive conflict and communication that encourages constructive conflict.

Definition of Conflict

Managing conflict competently begins with clear definitions of terms. In this section conflict in its general form is defined. Then its destructive and constructive aspects are explained.

General Definition

Janice Lightner is a student in Professor Leticia Winthrop's Human Communication intensive 4-week summer course. Professor Winthrop has a strict policy on attendance. Five absences result in an automatic "F" for the course. Janice has to fly from Eugene, Oregon, to Toronto, Canada, to attend the funeral of her grandfather. She must be absent from class for an entire week. The class meets every day of the week, so Janice will miss five classes. She approaches Professor Winthrop and asks her for an exemption from the attendance policy, explaining the unforeseen circumstances of her grandfather's sudden death. She promises to make up the work and miss no other classes. Professor Winthrop expresses regret but tells Janice that she will not pass the course if she misses a week of class. Janice becomes upset and tells Professor Winthrop that her attendance policy is unreasonable and unfair. Professor Winthrop defends the policy as essential for her students to learn difficult class material. They part feeling angry.

Conflict is the expressed struggle of interconnected parties who perceive incompatible goals and interference from one or more parties in attaining those goals (Folger et al., 1993; Wilmot & Hocker, 2001). The Professor Winthrop–Janice Lightner situation illustrates each element of this definition.

First, conflict is an *expressed struggle* between two or more parties. If Janice had accepted Professor Winthrop's attendance policy without confronting her about it, no conflict would have existed. Even if Janice had been angry about the policy, for a conflict to exist Janice had to indicate her unhappiness to Professor Winthrop in some fashion. The expression of the struggle could be obvious, such as Janice talking directly to Professor Winthrop. The expression could also be very subtle, even exclusively nonverbal, such as cold stares or slouching posture.

Second, conflict involves *interconnected parties*. The behavior of one party must have consequences for the other party. Professor Winthrop and Janice are interconnected. Janice faces a dilemma because of Professor Winthrop's attendance policy.

Professor Winthrop affects the choice Janice must make. Does she miss her grandfather's funeral so she can pass her class, or does she attend her grandfather's funeral and flunk the class? Janice affects Professor Winthrop because Janice is a disgruntled student challenging her attendance policy. Subsequently Professor Winthrop may wonder whether her policy is too harsh or unfair.

Third, *perceived incompatible goals* must be present for conflict to occur. The goals of Professor Winthrop and Janice seem to be incompatible. Professor Winthrop's goal is to have students attend class regularly so they can learn difficult material. Janice's goal is to attend the funeral without failing the class. Professor Winthrop's attendance policy and Janice's desire to attend her grandfather's funeral clash directly.

Finally, *perceived interference from parties* who pursue incompatible goals is necessary for conflict to occur. For two people to have a conflict, either one or both must interfere with the other's goal attainment. Professor Winthrop clearly interfered with Janice's goal to attend her grandfather's funeral without affecting her class grade. If Janice attends the funeral, she thwarts Professor Winthrop's goal. Janice will fall seriously behind in the class.

Perception plays an important role in conflict. Goals may not be incompatible, and goal attainment may not be interfered with by anyone. Nevertheless, if you act as though your goals are incompatible with your partner's goals and as though your partner is trying to interfere with your goal achievement, conflict will occur until perceptions are clarified and accepted.

Destructive Conflict

To most people, conflict always seems to be destructive. Conflict can make us angry, fearful, frustrated, and upset. These are feelings we don't usually like to experience, especially if the feelings are intense and frequent. Our communication, however, determines to what degree conflict is destructive or constructive.

Destructive conflict is characterized by escalation, retaliation, domination, competition, cross-complaining, defensiveness, and inflexibility (Wilmot & Hocker, 2001; Lulofs, 1994). When conflict is destructive, it spirals out of control. A conflict between two coworkers at the Fresh Vegetable Package Company in Denver, Colorado, is an example of destructive conflict. One worker accused another of throwing fruit at her because she had "laughed at her." The conflict escalated to vegetables, at which point the fruit thrower "for no reason" hurled a 4-inch diameter carrot. The victim, who was 5 months pregnant, complained about stomach pains and was rushed to Denver General Hospital. A detective investigating the altercation reported, "All she [the victim] wants is that the suspect leave her alone. I'm going to call up and talk to the supervisor and have the assailant moved from the dangerous weapon section—back from vegetables to fruit." No charges were filed against the assailant, presumably because it would have been difficult to prosecute the attacker for "assault with a deadly vegetable" (Isenhart & Spangle, 2000).

During destructive conflicts, participants lose sight of the initial goals. Hurting the other party becomes a primary focus. Complaints by one party are countered by complaints from the other party in a competitive one-upsmanship contest. This cross-complaining is "the most dysfunctional thing that people in conflict do" (Lulofs, 1994, p. 132) because it escalates conflict.

The ability to prevent the escalation of a conflict distinguishes the competent from the incompetent communicator. Not only is destructive conflict inappropriate and ineffective communication, it is unethical. Typical tactics employed during

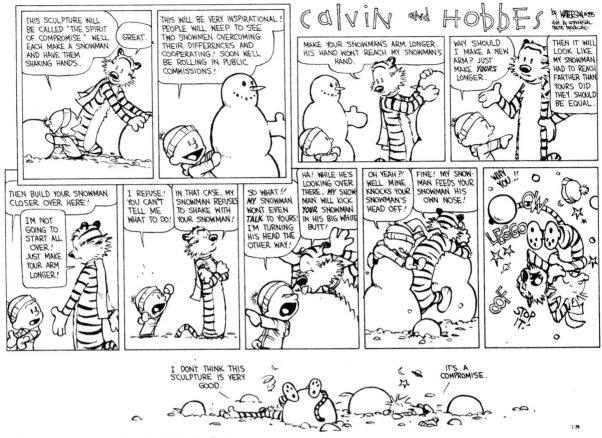

© 1995 Watterson. Distributed by Universal Press Syndicate.

destructive conflict include threats, intimidation, condescension, dishonesty, and personal assaults (verbal or physical). All of these tactics violate, at minimum, the standards of respect, honesty, and choice necessary for communication to be ethical (see Box 11-1).

Donohue and Kolt (1992) argue that the key to recognition of destructive conflict is the ability to say to oneself in the middle of a conflict, "Gee, I'm getting stupid" (p. 24). When you begin to lose sight of why you're battling with someone and you become petty, even infantile in your tactics to win an argument, you're getting stupid. When you can no longer think clearly because conflict triggers emotional reactions that clog the brain's ability to reason, then you are moving into destructive conflict territory. Gottman & Silver (1994) call this **flooding.** They define flooding this way:

> When people start to be flooded, they feel unfairly attacked, misunderstood, wronged, or righteously indignant. If you are being flooded, you may feel that things have gotten too emotional, that you just want to stop, you need to calm down, or you want to run away. Or you may want to strike back and get even. . . . The body of someone who feels flooded is a confused jumble of signals. It may be hard to breathe. People who are flooded inadvertently hold their breath. Muscles tense up and stay tensed. The heart beats faster and it may seem to beat harder. The flooded person longs for some escape and relief. (p. 112)

Men are far more likely to experience flooding than women.

FIGURE 11-1 Destructive Versus Constructive Conflict

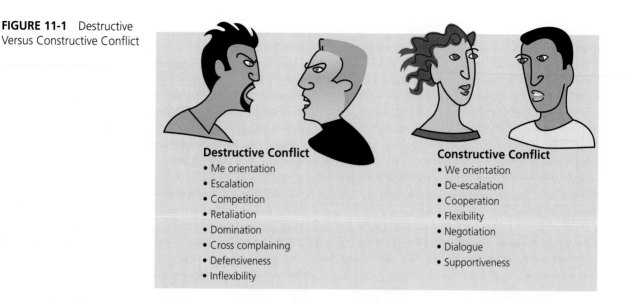

Destructive Conflict
- Me orientation
- Escalation
- Competition
- Retaliation
- Domination
- Cross complaining
- Defensiveness
- Inflexibility

Constructive Conflict
- We orientation
- De-escalation
- Cooperation
- Flexibility
- Negotiation
- Dialogue
- Supportiveness

The movie *War of the Roses* depicts escalation of conflict and "getting stupid" in uncomfortable detail. A couple, played by Michael Douglas and Kathleen Turner, in the midst of their divorce, savage each other and completely lose sight of any useful goals. They simply want to hurt each other. Each tries to dominate the other. Each character meets abuse with retaliation that ratchets the conflict to a higher level of stupidity. Their communication is completely inflexible and uncompromising. They destroy their house and each other in the process. One study (Ting-Toomey, 1983) found a *War of the Roses* pattern among couples dissatisfied with their marriages. Dissatisfied couples in this study often engaged in 10 turns of attack-and-defend communication. The dissatisfied couples didn't seem able to halt the escalation of the conflict, thus putting further strain on an already tattered relationship. This is a conflict pattern that sometimes spirals out of control.

Constructive Conflict

Conflict is sometimes constructive, not destructive. **Constructive conflict** is characterized by a We-orientation, cooperation, and flexibility (Wilmot & Hocker, 2001; Lulofs, 1994). The focus is on achieving a solution that is mutually satisfactory to all parties in the conflict. Participants work together flexibly to deal effectively with their conflicts by controlling and de-escalating them.

Dialectics in relationships, especially close relationships, often produce conflict. Dialogue is the chief means used to address dialectical conflict effectively. Destructive conflict shuts off dialogue, whereas constructive conflict embraces it. Tannen (1998) explains, "In dialogue, there is opposition, yes, but no head-on collision. Smashing heads does not open minds. . . . Even cooperation, after all, is not the absence of conflict but a means of managing conflict" (p. 26).

Constructive conflict doesn't mean we have to feel all warm and fuzzy as we work out our differences with others. Constructive conflict can be contentious, frustrating, and difficult. It is constructive, however, because the communication is competent. Participants employ supportive communication patterns. They are

Box 11-1 | Focus on Controversy

The Culture of Conflict

Our culture values debate and the exchange of opposing arguments on issues of controversy and conflict. There is a difference, however, between making an argument and having an argument. Making an argument—building a logical case supported by high-quality evidence—can be quite constructive (see the discussion on cooperative argumentation in Chapter 8). Having an argument typically involves engaging in a fight—expressing aggression toward others. Tannen (1998) maintains that our culture has become an "argument culture," not a culture that values argumentation. In an argument culture, the atmosphere is warlike. We see it often on daily talk shows or what Hughes (1993) calls "caterwauling freakshows." Such shows provoke conflicts and even stage them, and ugliness is the norm. Shouting, interrupting, and verbally or physically assaulting those who disagree replace serious discussion of issues.

Tannen claims that our argument culture promotes adversarial approaches to conflict. Despite the voluminous evidence that competitive, adversarial approaches to managing conflict are ineffective, disputes too often are litigated, not mediated. The courts are clogged with neighbor suing neighbor and strangers suing each other. According to the National Center for State Courts, approximately 15 million civil suits are filed each year in the United States. There is approximately one lawyer for every 50 people in this country. Compare that to Japan, a collectivist culture that values harmony and conflict avoidance, where there is approximately one lawyer for every 10,000 people (Berko et al., 1997). We are a litigious society.

Even children are getting into the act. Fourth-grader Ryan Rose hired attorney Monte Walton to fight for better food at his elementary school in Alcoa, Tennessee. "Me and my friends got mad because there was not anything to eat" (Fourth Grader, 1999). Fed up with week-old leftovers, cold food, and lack of "good stuff," 10-year-old Ryan hired Walton, paying him a $1 fee. Ryan's mom worked for Walton as a paralegal, so Walton took the case. Walton proposed adding hamburgers to the menu. The case was settled out of court.

Politics has become a battleground of incivility and nastiness. Republican Senator John McCain of Arizona noted, "When it gets nasty these days, it really gets nasty" (Dewar, 1997). When Bill Clinton was president, he called it the "politics of personal destruction." Democratic Senator Patrick Leahy of Vermont claimed, "Advice and consent has become harass and maim" (Dewar, 1997). The debacle resulting from the disputed 2000 presidential election was certainly not a departure from what has become the norm in politics. In such an atmosphere of hostility, criticizing and expressing contempt are mistaken for critical thinking. Cynicism, not skepticism, reigns supreme.

This cynicism became so serious that Congressmen Ray LaHood and Tom Sawyer put together a Bipartisan Congressional Retreat. This was a gathering of members of Congress whose purpose was to diminish "the toxic level of discourse in politics" and to halt efforts by both major political parties to "demonize the opposition" (Give Congress, 1999).

We are a culture immersed in conflict. This fact in and of itself is not a stunning revelation. How we approach conflict in this culture, however, is significant. Tannen (1998) presents a wealth of evidence supporting her claim that we live in an argument culture—we engage in destructive conflict. Tannen notes that our culture tends to devalue cooperative conflict management approaches even though they work better than more competitive, aggressive strategies. "It's as if we value a fight for its own sake, not for its effectiveness in resolving disputes" (p. 23).

Honest, open, energetic, lively debate on issues is constructive, but such debate cannot occur in an atmosphere of personal attack, viciousness, and win-at-all-cost tactics. The answer lies not in eliminating debate but in conducting debates as true exchanges of differing points of view. Venting aggression toward "enemies" is not constructive. Parties in conflict would be more successful if they tried harder to mediate disputes, not litigate them.

Questions for Thought

1. Do you agree that we live in an argument culture? Explain.
2. In your view, is an argument culture truly destructive? Does it have any merits? Is it the logical outcome of placing a high value on freedom of speech and individuality?
3. What steps, if any, should we take to address the argument culture?
4. Why do you think so many people are drawn to argument? What is the appeal of talk shows that encourage and incite ugly arguments?
5. Is engaging in argument ethical? Explain.

assertive, not aggressive or passive. They have an overriding commitment to cooperating, not competing. Thus, participants emphasize certain communication styles of conflict management, a subject discussed in the next section. Cooperative argumentation, not competitive tactics useful in a power struggle, is preferred. This means that certain rules of appropriate engagement during conflict might be helpful. Some examples are no personal attacks, never dismissing the other person's issue as trivial, never shouting, sticking to the point and not shifting the issue, and avoiding assigning blame (Jones & Gallois, 1989).

The distinctions between destructive and constructive conflict are perhaps most apparent during and after divorce, especially when children make contact between estranged parents unavoidable. Cooperative, mutually supportive co-parenting is the most advantageous communication pattern in such situations for both parents and children (Hetherington et al., 1998). Such co-parenting techniques reduce the frequency and severity of conflicts. Children adapt more effectively to their parents' divorce and accept remarriages more readily. Unfortunately, only about one quarter of divorced parents manage such conflicts constructively. An equal number maintain bitter, destructive conflicts with partners and children. The remaining estranged parents adopt a more indifferent, parallel co-parenting approach marked by infrequent contact (Maccoby & Mnookin, 1992).

When divorced parents express contempt for each other in front of children, insist that children choose sides in a conflict, use children as leverage in a power struggle with a former spouse, or ridicule their ex-spouse's new partner, they engage in destructive conflict. When divorced couples encourage children to have contact with both parents, focus on supportive communication patterns, and maintain respect for former spouses and their new partners even while they themselves disagree on important issues, they engage in constructive conflict.

We cement our relationships when we reconcile our conflicts cooperatively and supportively. When we try to impose our will on others in a competitive test of power and control, we propel ourselves toward the relationship graveyard where the pathetic remains of a once happy relationship are buried for eternity. In the next two sections, ways to manage conflict cooperatively are addressed.

Communication Styles of Conflict Management

Communication styles of conflict management have been the focus of much research. A **communication style of conflict management** is a typical way to address conflict. There are five communication styles: collaborating, accommodating, compromising, avoiding, and competing (Blake & Mouton, 1964; Kilmann & Thomas, 1977).

Collaborating (Cooperating)

The word *collaborating* is derived from two Latin roots—*cam* and *laborare*—that together mean "to work together." Thus, **collaborating** means working together to maximize the attainment of goals for all parties in a conflict. This is a cooperative style of conflict management. It is We- not Me-oriented. The collaborating style has three key components: confrontation, integration, and smoothing.

CONFRONTATION   The overt recognition of conflict and the direct effort to find creative ways to satisfy all parties in the conflict is called **confrontation.** It is an assertive strategy that is the opposite of avoidance. Confrontation brings the conflict out into the open for careful examination and discussion. Although mass media often use the term in a negative sense (e.g., "There was a violent confrontation between police and demonstrators"), this is not the meaning that applies here. Confrontation as a collaborating strategy should utilize all the elements of supportive communication already discussed (i.e., describe, problem solve, empathize, be honest, treat others as equals, and qualify your statements).

There is a huge gender difference in who is most likely to confront difficult relationship issues. Someone once quipped that, for men, the most terrifying statement in the English language is "Let's talk about our relationship." *In more than 80% of the instances of confrontation, women raise the issue, not men* (Gottman & Silver, 1999). Disparity in who raises the issue is not necessarily a sign of a troubled relationship; how men respond to the confrontation, not who initiates it, is a more important concern.

Confrontation, however, can be used excessively. Some conflicts are too trivial to warrant confrontation. Sometimes the timing is wrong. Individuals wake up irritable and need time to gather their thoughts. Confronting them before they've had their morning coffee or when they are late for a meeting at work will probably escalate a conflict. Confrontation is best attempted at a time when people are able to work on problems. Additionally, confrontation should be used judiciously, for important issues. Incessant confrontation can become annoying and counterproductive. "Can't you just let some things slide?" will be the likely response to excessive use of confrontation.

INTEGRATION   A collaborative strategy that meets the goals of all parties in the conflict is called **integration.** Two integrative tactics are expanding the pie and bridging.

Expanding the pie refers to finding creative ways to increase resources, typically money. Scarce resources often cause conflict (power struggles). These conflicts can easily degenerate into competitive clashes in which adversaries struggle to divide a woefully inadequate budget. *Bridging* considers the goals of all parties in the conflict and offers a new option that satisfies the interests of everyone involved.

A family I knew employed both strategies to resolve a conflict. The parents wanted to travel to Europe on vacation. The children wanted to camp in Yellowstone National Park as they usually did each summer. Initially, the parents tried to convince their children that they would enjoy a trip to Europe. The children countered that the trip would be too expensive so they shouldn't even consider it. The parents agreed that the trip would be expensive, but they claimed that going to Yellowstone and camping had become boringly repetitive since they had done that for the last five summers.

After a lengthy discussion, it became apparent that the children's primary interest was not as much in going to Yellowstone as it was in camping together as a family. The parents admitted that their primary interest was to expose their children to different cultural experiences and thus expand their horizons. Discussions revealed that the parents didn't mind camping through Europe. That sounded exciting and certainly less expensive than staying in hotels. The children became excited when it was suggested that the family could travel by ship to Europe and come home by plane. The ocean voyage sounded particularly appealing. This meant, however, that the cost of the vacation would be a problem. Further discussions led to the oldest child's suggestion that everyone in the family find extra jobs and earn additional money that they could pool for the trip. Everyone agreed, and for 6 months the family worked toward their goal to raise enough money to make the trip feasible. They were ultimately successful, traveled to Europe by ship, camped for a month in four countries, and returned by plane with memories of many adventures.

This family used both expanding the pie and bridging as integrative methods for resolving their conflict. Initially, it appeared that there was a conflict of two mutually exclusive interests (i.e., camping in Yellowstone and traveling to Europe). After confronting the problem directly, it became apparent that no real conflict of interest existed. The interests of all family members (i.e., camping and new cultural experiences) could be met with a little creative problem solving. They expanded the pie by pooling extra resources, and they bridged by creating a trip that satisfied all family members' real interests.

SMOOTHING   The act of calming the agitated feelings of others during a conflict episode is called **smoothing.** When tempers flair and anger turns to screaming or tears, no collaborating is possible. It is important to address inflamed emotions. Here is an example:

MARIETTA: (trying to hold back tears) It totally fries me that you never called to tell me where you were. I was a wreck all night wondering if you'd been in a terrible accident. How can you be so insensitive?

ALONZO: I'm really sorry. I didn't mean to worry you. I can understand why you're upset with me.

Smoothing addresses the emotional side of conflict. Smoothing can make integrative solutions possible by defusing emotionally volatile situations.

Gottman and Silver (1999) call smoothing *repair attempts*. They suggest a number of statements that are useful in short-circuiting escalating conflict. Among these are "Can I take that back?" "How can I make things better?" "I see your point," "Let's try that over again," and "I understand." They even suggest that you might want to be blatant about the repair attempt by straightforwardly announcing, "This is a repair attempt!" Such an announcement prevents repair attempts from being missed by a partner.

Research on collaborating as a conflict management style is consistently positive (Wilmot & Hocker, 2001). Collaborating produces better decisions than other styles, and participants typically are more satisfied with the decisions, the process, and the interpersonal relations developed during conflict management.

Accommodating (Yielding)

When we surrender to the needs and desires of others during a conflict, we are using the **accommodating** style. This is a nonassertive style of conflict management. It may appear that accommodating is We-oriented because the accommodator yields to others "for the sake of the relationship or group." This may be true in some cases, but yielding to others to maintain harmony can easily build resentment that one's own needs have been sacrificed. This can lead to a martyr complex and ultimately to bitterness and complaint.

Accommodating is most often the style of the less powerful. Less powerful individuals are expected to accommodate more often and to a greater degree than more powerful individuals (Lulofs, 1994). Employees are expected to yield to the requests or demands of their supervisors. Your boss is less likely to feel a need to accommodate your wishes. One mistake made by more powerful individuals, however, is failing to appreciate the value of accommodating even when yielding isn't required. When a person is clearly wrong about an issue or point of contention, it makes sense for the person to yield on it. This yielding demonstrates reasonableness and enhances the relationship with the other person. Yielding also makes sense if the issue is more important to the other person. This flexibility is an aspect of constructive conflict management. The roles may be reversed in the future, and it may be appropriate for the other party to yield. Accommodating by others is more likely when there is a history of mutual flexibility.

Accommodating can be a constructive and necessary style of conflict management. Yielding can sometimes maintain harmony in a relationship. A less powerful person may need to yield to a more powerful person to keep a job, maintain a relationship, or avoid nasty consequences. Nevertheless, being too accommodating can make you someone else's lackey.

Compromising

When we give up something to get something we are **compromising.** The compromising style of conflict management occurs most often between parties of relatively equal power. More powerful individuals do not usually consider compromising as necessary. They can dominate, and they often choose to do so.

Compromising emphasizes workable but not optimal decisions and solutions. Some have referred to compromising as a lose-lose style of conflict management because trade-offs and exchanges are required to reach agreement. Only some of the goals and needs are met in a compromise. Gain is counterbalanced by loss. As one anonymous wag put it, compromise is "a deal in which two people get what neither of them wanted." Pruitt and Rubin (1986) express this negative point of view when they argue that compromising arises "from two sources—either lazy problem-solving involving a half-hearted attempt to satisfy the two parties' interests, or simply yielding by both parties" (p. 29).

Despite these negative views, compromising may be the only feasible goal in a conflict of interest in which parties have relatively equal power. Half a loaf is better than starvation, so goes the thinking. Compromising can be a useful strategy when an integrative decision is not feasible, when issues are not critical, when essential values are not undermined, and when such a settlement is only temporary until a better solution can be found and negotiated.

Avoiding (Withdrawing)

When we sidestep or turn our back on conflict, we are **avoiding.** The avoiding style is exhibited in many ways (Lulofs, 1994). We avoid conflict when we ignore it or deny it exists, even though it does. When we shift topics so we don't have to address a conflict, we avoid. We may crack jokes to deflect a focus on disagreeable issues. We may quibble about the meaning of a word used by another who is probing uncomfortably into a subject of some dispute, or we may simply not respond to a question (turning away response).

A particularly powerful form of avoiding is stonewalling. **Stonewalling** is refusing to discuss problems or physically leaving when one partner is complaining, disagreeing, or attacking. Consider this example:

Men stonewall far more than women. Notice the differences in nonverbal communication between the man and the woman.

JUANITA: We need to talk about your reluctance to pick up after yourself. I'm frustrated every time I see your dirty clothes strewn across our bedroom.

ROBERTO: There's nothing to talk about. Get used to it.

JUANITA: There's plenty to talk about!

ROBERTO: No there isn't. (He leaves the room.)

Stonewallers often justify their withdrawal from conflict by claiming that they are merely trying to remain under control and not make the contentiousness worse by responding. Stonewalling can be extremely frustrating to those faced with the withdrawal. Stonewalling can also communicate disapproval, conceit, self-righteousness, and cold indifference, a defensive communication pattern.

Earlier it was noted that women far more than men confront issues in relationships that trigger conflict. Men, conversely, are far more prone than women to avoid such issues and withdraw (Canary et al., 1995). About 85% of the stonewalling in relationship conflicts comes from men (Gottman & Silver, 1994). Men more than women tend to withdraw from conflict partly because men are more likely to experience flooding (Gottman & Carrere, 1994). As a result, men stonewall in the hope that they can prevent flooding.

Avoiding is a frequently used conflict style. One study (Sillars et al., 1982) reports that students use avoiding in more than half of their conflicts. Another study (Larson, 1989) found that managers often avoid giving negative feedback to employees because they find it to be the most unpleasant and difficult task they have to perform. They are reluctant to stir up a conflict.

These flights from fights are usually not constructive. How can we heal a relationship when one party refuses to confront problems? Avoiding increases the frequency of marital disagreements because spouses repetitively revisit issues that don't get resolved (McGonagle et al., 1993). Managers who avoid critiquing employees' poor work performance typically become increasingly annoyed by the continued bad performance. When the annoyance rises to extremely high levels, they give feedback that is usually biting, sarcastic, harsh, threatening, and personal (Baron, 1988). This merely intensifies anger by both parties.

Couples that brag to others that they "never fight" may be avoiding underlying discord for the sake of appearances. Frequency of conflict alone does not indicate how healthy a relationship is or is not (Gottman & Silver, 1994). In fact, avoiding is a strategy often used by abused partners to keep from provoking violence from their abusers (Gelles & Straus, 1988). This avoidance creates a **chilling effect** wherein a partner low in power avoids discussing issues with his or her abusive partner that might trigger aggression (Roloff & Cloven, 1990).

Avoiding is not always an inappropriate and ineffective style of conflict management. We can avoid trivial issues without damage to our relationships. Avoiding "hot button" issues that trigger intense disagreements and hurt may also be appropriate. Reminding a partner of an affair confronted long ago dredges up anger and hurt feelings with no constructive outcome likely. The fact of the affair cannot be changed. Repeatedly reliving damaging events keeps partners prisoners of their history. If your choice is to stay in the relationship, then don't pick the scab. Let the wound heal. If unresolved anger persists, consider resolving it by talking to a third party.

Competing (Power Forcing)

When we approach conflict as a win-lose contest, we are competing. The competing or power-forcing style of conflict management flows from the dominance perspective on power. The competing style is exhibited in a variety of ways: by threats, criticism, contempt, hostile remarks and jokes, sarcasm, ridicule, intimidation, fault finding and blaming, and denials of responsibility (Wilmot & Hocker, 2001). All of these behaviors upset the ratio of positive to negative communication. As discussed in Chapter 2, at least a 5 to 1 ratio of positive to negative communication between partners is necessary to sustain a relationship (Gottman & Silver, 1994). The competing style of conflict management emphasizes the negative. The competing style is aggressive, not assertive. It is a Me-oriented style that is focused on winning a dispute at the other's expense. It is not confrontation as previously defined; it is an attack.

The essence of the competing style is pressuring others to change their behavior to your advantage. The more we try to force others to do our bidding, however, the more we ignite psychological reactance. Simply put, *the competing style has the greatest potential for destructive conflict because it can easily escalate a conflict even beyond stupidity and pointlessness.*

The chief flaw of the competing style is that the focus is on victory for oneself, not on a mutually satisfactory decision for all parties involved. The competing style attempts to create or to expand power imbalances in relationships. Chapter 2 outlined the deficiencies of competition. The competing style suffers from many of these same deficiencies.

Power forcing is sometimes an unavoidable conflict management style, but it should be a last resort in most situations, used only when other styles have proved to be ineffective or can't be used because of an emergency.

Managing Conflict Competently

In this section, we'll address how to transact conflict competently. Topics include appropriate and effective use of communication styles of conflict management, anger management, communicating forgiveness, and the communication challenges presented when cultures clash.

Communication Styles in Action

In my small group communication classes, the members of at least one group every semester approach me about problems they are having with one member. Typically, the group member is unreliable, fails to show for group meetings, and hasn't shared the group workload on class projects. Consistently, their first question to me is "Can we kick Josh, Jamie, Janine, or whomever out of the group?" When I ask if they have confronted this person and expressed the group's concerns and feelings, they admit that they have yet to confront their slacker. They avoid the problem because it makes them uncomfortable to confront, but when the problem keeps getting worse, they choose power forcing, the least effective style. This is not surprising in a hypercompetitive society.

Research shows clearly that the collaborating style is the most constructive and effective means of managing conflict (Phillips & Cheston, 1979; Tutzauer & Roloff, 1988). The number of disputes at Toyota's U.S. subsidiary, for instance, fell from 178 in 1985 to 3 in 1992 when the company instituted a problem-solving (collaborative) method for dispute resolution (Carver & Vondra, 1994). Satisfaction in romantic relationships is positively associated with the use of integration to manage conflict episodes (Canary & Cupach, 1988; Canary & Spitzberg, 1989). "Integrative solutions are almost always the most desirable. They tend to last longer and to contribute more to the relationship between parties and the welfare of the broader community than do compromises and agreements about how to choose the winner" (Fry & Fry, 1997, p. 12).

The competing style is the least effective. "Competitive strategies fail to address the long-term, underlying needs of relationships, organizations, or communities" (Isenhart & Spangle, 2001, p. 23). The avoiding style is only slightly better than the competing style (Canary & Spitzberg, 1987). One study by Markman (cited in Edwards, 1995) of 135 married couples, 21 of whom later divorced, showed that escalating conflicts into ugly verbal battles (competing) and refusing to face conflicts directly (avoiding) predicted divorce in almost every instance.

Collaborating depends on dialogue. Dialogue is central to the management of conflict provoked by dialectics in relationships (Baxter & Montgomery, 1996). Competing and avoiding both stifle dialogue. Competing sets up a power relationship that discourages dialogue. If you can force your point of view on others, you don't have to engage in dialogue. You can demand compliance. Those with less power also have little motivation to engage in dialogue. Expressing dissenting viewpoints might invite retaliation from the more powerful individual. Avoiding dialogue and controversial viewpoints becomes an act of self-protection in a competitive, power-imbalanced situation.

Despite the clear advantages of the collaborating over the competing style, research shows that *typically we use the least effective and most inappropriate style when trying to manage conflict*. One study compared the collaborative and competing styles

"Just another of our many disagreements. He wants a no-fault divorce, whereas I would prefer to have the bastard crucified."

in 52 conflict cases (Phillips & Cheston, 1979). Participants used the competing style twice as often as the collaborating style. In half of the cases, competing produced bad outcomes. In all cases in which participants used collaborating, the outcomes were good. Another study (Gayle, 1991) showed that only 5% of supervisors, middle managers, top managers, and administrators actually used the collaborating style in specific conflict situations. Instead, 41% of this same group selected competing, and 26% chose avoiding. This was true of both male and female supervisors and managers.

A key to appropriate and effective use of conflict management styles is more than how often you use a style. Timing is important. If you begin using a competing style, the likely result will be anger, hostility, and retaliation. Realizing that the competing style isn't working well, you may decide to try the collaborating style. Good luck! Once you have competed, it is much more difficult to cooperate. Suspicion and mistrust will permeate your transactions. It is far better to begin with the collaborating style. If collaborating does not work, you may have to use other styles to manage the conflict. If the issue is not very important, accommodating or avoiding might work. You could use compromising as an interim style until you find a more integrative solution. Ultimately, you may have to use the competing style.

The students in my small group communication course must first confront group members who are not producing and try to resolve the conflict cooperatively. If these efforts are unsuccessful, I do allow the students to inform their slacker that he or she will be booted out of the group unless these behaviors change. *Competing is the style of last resort, but you may have to use it when all other styles fail or are inappropriate.* Employees who are frequently tardy or absent, do not complete required work on time, and manifest a negative attitude may have to be fired if no other style changes their behavior. Divorce is often a power-forcing style, especially when one partner wants out of the relationship and the other does not. Nevertheless, divorce may be the last-resort solution to years of bitter conflict. It isn't pretty, but it may be necessary in some circumstances.

Communication Styles and Partner Abuse

The problem of partner abuse has been addressed (Chapter 8), but the relationship between partner abuse and communication styles of conflict management has not been discussed. *A person's style of handling conflict can be an important indicator of potential abuse early in a relationship.* The competing (power forcing) style is the most common style used in abusive relationships (Sabourin, 1995). Spotting potential abuse early can prevent abuse from emerging.

If a partner's chief style of resolving conflict is competing (power forcing), you should take this as a warning sign of possible future abuse. In particular, controlling behaviors, such as wanting to know whom you were with when you weren't with your partner, and trying to specify which friends you should associate with are troublesome power-forcing behaviors. Even if your partner presents these controlling behaviors as requests rather than demands at first, be concerned. Yielding to such requests or demands won't end disagreement, and it may feed the abuser's desire to control you.

Psychologically abusive communication such as contemptuous remarks, ridicule, and humiliating comments are dominance strategies aimed at keeping a partner "in line." Verbal threats of physical violence when resistance is offered, of course, are even more serious power-forcing behaviors. Verbal aggression often leads to physical aggression (Infante et al., 1992). Verbal aggression in relationships either precedes or accompanies physical violence in 99% of abuse cases (Straus & Sweet, 1992). Psychological abuse as an intimidating conflict strategy is dangerous and cause for alarm.

Accommodating is normally an ineffective conflict style to use when signals of possible abuse first appear. Yielding to power-forcing demands may be necessary in the immediate situation if one's partner is showing signs of losing self-control. Nevertheless, accommodating the demands of a partner out of fear for one's safety places the potential abuser in charge.

Compromising usually doesn't satisfy a potential abuser. Abusers, especially outright batterers, want total control and obedience (Jacobson & Gottman, 1998). There should be no compromise on the goal of eradicating verbal and physical aggression. Do not try to defend or rationalize "a little bit of abuse."

Avoiding is the most common style used by women to deal with physical abuse from their partners, especially patriarchal terrorism previously discussed (Gelles & Straus, 1988). Avoiding "hot buttons" that trigger violence in a partner reduces the frequency of physical violence in relationships. This style, however, is difficult to recommend except in the most dire situations in which avoiding might be a temporary expedient necessary for self-protection. As a long-term style, it is woefully deficient. It reinforces power imbalances and perpetuates domestic terrorism.

Confrontation is most effective for dealing with potential or actual abuse in relationships. As Gelles and Straus (1988) explain, "Delaying until the violence escalates is too late. A firm, emphatic, and rational approach appears to be the most effective personal strategy a woman can use to prevent future violence" (p. 159). They suggest confronting the very first incident of even minor violence and stating without equivocation that such behavior will not be tolerated and must never occur again.

In a study of college students, almost a third of college women admitted slapping their partners, and almost a fifth admitted slapping a partner in the face (Vitanza and Marshall, 1993). During my first year in college, I dated a woman who, when angry at me, would slap me in the face. The first time it happened, I avoided discussing it, mostly because I was embarrassed. When it happened a second time, months later, I still did not confront her. Finally, when it happened a third time, I confronted her. I described how it made me feel when she slapped me. I explained to her that when she slapped me my first reaction was to slap her back, but that might injure her physically. I further explained that I hated the feeling of wanting to strike her in retaliation. Finally, I said to her, "I cannot and will not hit you when you slap me, but you put me in an embarrassing and unfair position. You can hit me, but I can't hit back. What am I supposed to do?" She responded by saying that she had never considered her actions from my perspective. She promised never to slap me again, and during a long relationship, she never did. It is vital that even relatively minor acts of aggression be confronted before they escalate into tragic abuse. I should have confronted my partner sooner than I did.

If physical or psychological abuse continues after you confront it, you should seriously consider ending the relationship. Abuse that is excused, rationalized, or ignored almost always recurs and grows worse (Jacobson & Gottman, 1998). *The best way to handle abuse is assertively, directly, and unequivocally at the outset.* Partners can stop their abuse, but it is infinitely more difficult and more dangerous to stop it once it has become standard practice.

Once again, the evidence is clear. Cooperation has distinct advantages over competition. Collaborating has greater potential than power forcing for constructive management of conflict. Start with collaborating and work hard to make it work. Only when all else has failed should you consider competing or power forcing.

Anger Management

"She slurps when she eats soup—it makes me crazy." "He drives like a maniac. I hate it." "She squirrels money away like we're poor. We make plenty of money, but you'd never know it from the way she hoards it." "He never cooks a meal. He acts like I'm his personal chef and waitress all in one." The issues that create conflict are virtually infinite in number. Gottman (1979) found 85 different types of issues that trigger conflict for young married couples. Marriage counselor David Mace notes, "Marriage and family living generate in normal people more anger than those people experience in any other social situation in which they habitually find themselves" (cited in Tavris, 1989, p. 221). Conflict over serious issues or silly ones is a natural part of marriages and all close personal relationships. Anger is a frequent companion of such conflicts.

Learning to manage anger is an important step in managing conflicts competently. Ahrons (1994) notes that the chief difference between divorced parents who were effective co-parents to their children and those who were ineffective "was that the more cooperative group managed their anger better" (p. 145).

CONSTRUCTIVE AND DESTRUCTIVE ANGER   Twenty-nine-year-old Rene Andrews pulled onto I-71 near Cincinnati, Ohio, one fateful day in July 1997. Apparently upset by the way Andrews pulled into her lane, 24-year-old Tracie Alfieri attempted to pass Andrews on the right shoulder of the freeway, then passed on the left, cut in front of Andrews, and slammed on the brakes. Andrews swerved and crashed into a stopped tractor-trailer rig. Andrews died in this accident. Alfieri suffered multiple injuries, and her 6-month-old fetus died. Alfieri was convicted of aggravated vehicular homicide and was sentenced to 18 months in prison.

Road rage is an increasing problem in the United States. Ricardo Martinez, head of the National Highway Traffic Safety Administration, attributes 28,000 highway deaths each year to road rage (Wald, 1997). He claims that an increase in a "me first philosophy" is a primary cause of road rage. Clearly, road rage is an example of destructive anger.

www.mhhe
com/**rothwell2**

See "Self-assessment of Destructive Anger" quiz on the Online Learning Center, chapter 11.

Two conditions determine how destructive or constructive anger is (Adler & Towne, 1999). The first condition is the *intensity*, or relative strength, of the anger. Anger can vary in intensity from mild irritation to rage. Mild, even moderate anger can be constructive. It can signal the existence of a problem, and it can motivate necessary change. Rage, however, is destructive. Temper tantrums and screaming fits are never endearing. In relationships, rage frightens partners and children. In the workplace, rage is never appropriate because it "shows you've lost control—not to mention that it's tough to be articulate if you're having a conniption" (Black, 1990a, 1990b). Ranting and raving make you look like a lunatic. When used to get your way on an issue, rage is a power-forcing style of conflict management that will likely produce an equivalent counter response. *Rage times rage equals rage squared.*

Duration, or how long something lasts, is the second condition that determines to what degree anger is constructive or destructive. The length of an anger episode

Road rage produced four wrecked cars and three dead people in this horrific Washington, D.C., crash.

can vary from short-lived to prolonged. Quick flashes of temper may hardly cause notice by others. Even fairly intense expressions of anger, if short-lived, can make the point powerfully that you are upset. If your anger goes on for too long, however, you and anyone listening will lose sight of the issue that caused the anger. Protracted anger episodes can make conflict management extremely difficult. When expressions of anger are highly intense and long lasting, the combination can be extremely combustible.

There is a popular notion that venting one's anger is constructive and that suppressing anger is unhealthy. This notion led to the rapid growth of a Web site dubbed *Angry.Org*. Individuals were encouraged to vent their anger about almost anything. A more controversial Web site called *The Dick List* (Lohr, 1997) encourages women to express their outrage at men who inflicted pain and suffering on them by identifying a man's name and offering a brief description of his egregious behavior. The site developer explains, "I get a broad range of women, from teenagers to divorced housewives, who are finally getting a grip on their anger" (Lohr, 1997, p. 169).

See Destructive Anger exercise on CD.

The popular notion that venting one's anger is constructive is wrong. *Venting anger, or "blowing off steam," usually increases one's anger* (Baron, 1990; Tavris, 1989). Replaying our anger about past events, especially if the anger is unresolved, simply rehearses it. When we tell friends of past "injustices," blood pressure rises, heart beat increases, and the face flushes. You are experiencing the anger all over again. This doesn't put the anger to rest. It awakens it, pops it out of bed, and starts it doing jumping jacks.

ANGER AND ATTRIBUTION   In a study (Zillmann, 1993), a confederate of the experimenter acted as a rude assistant who insulted participants riding an exercise bike.

When provided a chance to retaliate by giving the rude assistant a bad evaluation that they thought would adversely affect his effort to get a job, all of the angry participants did so with enthusiasm. In another version of the experiment, however, another confederate told the rude assistant, just before the participants had a chance to retaliate, that he had a phone call down the hall. The rude assistant made a snide comment to the new confederate and left. The new confederate took the snide comment well, explaining to the participants that the rude assistant was under a great deal of pressure, worried as he was about his upcoming graduate oral exam. The participants' anger was defused in this instance, and they chose not to retaliate. Instead, they expressed compassion for the rude assistant.

Anger and the desire to lash out at others are choices. Imagine, for instance, that you are stopped at an intersection in your car and another car "steals" your right-of-way by moving into the intersection before you do. Do you get angry? Do you make an obscene gesture? Do you shout at the driver? Now imagine what your reaction would be if you saw that it was your best friend or your mother driving the car. Would your reaction be the same? Probably not. We can be righteously indignant, or we can choose to be calm, even amused, faced with the same stimulus.

Anger can be a thoughtful choice unless our anger reaches the level of rage (Zillmann, 1993). Rage floods our thought process: We can't think straight, and we "get stupid." Attributing meanings, causes, or outcomes to conflict events shapes the way we think about and respond to disagreements and perceived poor treatment. Attribution can influence enormously whether we get stupid or get smart on potentially volatile issues (Baron, 1990).

Intent and blame are two common forms of attribution that ignite anger (McKay et al., 1989). Trying to ascertain the intention of another person is mind reading, or "intention invention" (Stone et al., 1999). Unless a person tells us, we must guess what motivated them, and, unfortunately, we often assume the worst. Negative behaviors from others that we perceive to be intentional, not accidental, easily trigger our anger. Deliberately shoving someone is perceived to be more worthy of anger and hostility than accidentally tripping and knocking a person down while trying to regain your own balance.

Blaming someone for negative behavior is the companion of intent. If the behavior of others is intentional and negative, it "deserves" reproach. We can justifiably blame the person for unfortunate outcomes. If the behavior is not intentional, we can still blame the person for the outcome, but it doesn't seem as justified to be angry about it. How we frame potential conflict-producing events influences our emotional response.

Consider an example (Stone et al., 1999). A patient named Margaret had her hip replaced by a prominent surgeon, a man she perceived to be gruff and difficult to confront. When Margaret appeared for her first office visit following the surgery, she was informed that the doctor had unexpectedly extended his vacation. Margaret was furious. She imagined her doctor soaking up sun on some Caribbean island, probably with his wife or girlfriend. When Margaret returned for her postponed appointment, she asked her doctor curtly how his vacation had turned out. He replied that the vacation had been wonderful. "I'll bet," Margaret responded in a sarcastic tone. Her doctor, however, continued before Margaret had a chance to express her anger about being so cavalierly inconvenienced. "It was a working vacation. I was helping set up a hospital in Bosnia. The conditions there are just horrendous" (p. 47). Understandably, Margaret's anger subsided with this news.

FIGURE 11-2 Managing Anger

Managing Your Own Anger
• Reframe self-talk
• Speak and listen nondefensively
• Deliberately calm yourself
• Find distractions

Managing Others' Anger
• Be asymmetrical
• Validate the other person
• Probe
• Distract
• Assume a problem orientation
• Refuse to be abused
• Disengage

MANAGING YOUR OWN ANGER   There are several ways to defuse and de-escalate anger, both your own and others' (Figure 11-2). Try these suggestions for managing your own anger:

1. *Reframe self-talk.* Thoughts trigger anger. Reframing the way we think about events can deflate our anger before it has a chance to escalate (Baron, 1990). Very often we have no way to know whether the act of another person was intentional or not. Instead of assuming it was intentional, assume it was unintentional. "He probably didn't see me." "She looked stressed out." "Her day isn't going too well." This kind of self-talk reframes events as unintentional, even haphazard—not intentional.

2. *Speak and listen nondefensively.* Criticism, contempt, and cross-complaining ignite angry passions (Baron, 1990). Refuse to become defensive. Reframe criticism as a problem or challenge. Use supportive communication.

3. *Deliberately calm yourself.* Exercise some discipline, and refuse to vent your anger. You will feel your heartbeat increasing when your anger starts to rise. This is a signal that your anger is escalating. Check your pulse if you are uncertain whether you are feeling overwhelmed. A pulse rate that climbs 10% higher than your normal resting pulse rate is cause for concern. If your normal resting pulse is 80 beats per minute, be concerned if it increases to 88. If your pulse reaches 100, you are in the throes of flooding (Gottman & Silver, 1994).

    When you feel the adrenaline surge, deliberately take slow, deep breaths and concentrate on reducing your heartbeat. Count to 10 before responding. A cooling-off period may be necessary in serious cases. A cooling-off period works well to calm a person's anger (Goleman, 1995). Typically, it takes 20 minutes to recover from an adrenaline surge. Use the 20 minutes away from the person or situation that triggers your anger. Go for a walk, shoot a basketball, kiss a frog, or do whatever diverts your attention and moves you out of the situation. Return to discuss your anger with others only when you are certain that flooding has subsided. Then express your anger to others in a calm, descriptive manner (first-person singular language).

4. *Change your focus.* Don't rehearse your anger. Revisiting past injustices won't change your history. You can't get beyond old issues if you keep replaying them in your mind. Change your focus when old hurts resurface. Read the newspaper, watch television, or make plans for a family outing. Just get your mind off your anger for a little while (Rusting & Nolen-Hoeksema, 1998).

Don't attempt to learn all four of these suggestions at once. Pick one and work on learning it until it becomes virtually automatic. Then you can attempt a second suggestion, and so forth.

MANAGING THE ANGER OF OTHERS   You can defuse and de-escalate the anger of others so you can confront issues constructively. It is usually best to address the person's anger first and then deal with the substance of the dispute that triggers the anger (Donohue & Kolt, 1992). Dialogue cannot take place when tempers are white hot. Try these suggestions to defuse another person's anger and restore a climate conducive to dialogue:

1. *Be asymmetrical.* When a person is exhibiting anger, particularly if it turns to rage, it is critical that you not strike back in kind. Resist reacting signally to words of criticism. Be asymmetrical; that is, do the opposite. Counteract rage with absolute calm. Stay composed (Black, 1990a, 1990b). Hostage negotiators are trained to defuse highly volatile individuals by remaining absolutely calm throughout the negotiations and employing the smoothing technique to quiet the enraged person. Matching a person's rage with rage can produce ugly, violent outcomes.

2. *Validate the other person.* Validation is a form of the smoothing technique of collaborating. Let the person know that his or her point of view and anger have some validity, even though you may not agree with him or her. Validation is particularly vital for men to use because men tend to respond to a woman's emotional upset by becoming hyper-rational (Gottman, 1994b). Offering advice or trying to solve a problem while a person is extremely upset invalidates that person's feelings by ignoring them.

    You can validate another person in several ways. You can take responsibility for the other person's anger. "I upset you didn't I?" acknowledges your role in provoking anger. You can apologize. "I'm sorry. You're right to be angry" can be a very powerful validation of the other person. Don't apologize, of course, unless you really bear some responsibility. Sometimes a compliment can defuse another person's anger: "I actually think you handled my abrasiveness and moodiness rather well." Finally, actively listening to the other person and acknowledging what the person has said can be very validating. "I know it upsets you when I play my music too loudly while you're trying to study" makes the other person feel that he or she has been heard, even if conflict still exists.

3. *Probe.* Seek more information from the other person so you can understand his or her anger (McKay et al., 1989). When you ask a question of the angry person, it forces the person to shift from emotional outburst to rational response. Simply asking, "Can we sit down and discuss this calmly so I can understand your point of view?" can momentarily defuse another person's anger. If your partner

angrily criticizes you—"You're a jerk of epic proportions; a reigning king of the principality of jerkdom; you are the essence of jerkness the embodiment of all that is jerky"—listen and then probe. "Wow! Any chance you might give me some examples so I can understand why you think I'm such a jerk?" probes for specific information necessary to resolve the conflict.

4. *Distract.* When a person is really out of control, distracting that person by introducing a topic that shifts the focus can sometimes divert attention away from the source of the rage. A humorous quip, an odd question, pointing to some event unrelated to the anger, or requesting help on a thorny problem not associated with triggering the rage are ways to distract and short circuit the tirade.

5. *Assume a problem orientation.* This is a supportive communication pattern. This step should occur once you have calmed the angry person by the previous steps. Approach the emotional display as a problem to be solved, not a reason to retaliate. The question "What would you like to see occur?" invites problem solving.

6. *Refuse to be abused.* Even if you are wrong, feel guilty, or deserve another person's anger, do not permit yourself to be verbally battered (McKay et al., 1989). Abusive assaults are unproductive no matter who is at fault in a conflict. "I cannot discuss this with you if you insist on being abusive. I can see that you're upset, but name calling won't lead to a solution" sets a ground rule on how anger can be expressed.

7. *Disengage.* This is the final step when all else fails to calm a person's anger. This step is particularly important if the person continues to be abusive and enraged. Simply and firmly state, "This meeting is over. I'm leaving. We'll discuss this another time."

Keeping track of all seven of these steps, especially when faced with an enraged person, is too much to expect. Concentrate on one or two steps until you have learned them so well that they become a habit. Being asymmetrical is the crucial step, with validation a close second. You can learn the remaining steps gradually. Being asymmetrical provides the greatest chance of defusing the other person's anger and keeping yourself safe in the process (Box 11-2).

Anger is a central element in conflict. The constructive management of conflict can occur only when you keep anger under control. This does not mean squelching anger. A person can feel angry for excellent reasons. Anger acts as a signal that changes need to occur. Anger should not, however, be used as a weapon to abuse others. We need to learn ways to cope with and express anger constructively, not be devoured by it.

Typically it is best to express your anger directly to the person with whom you are upset, not to innocent bystanders (Tavris, 1989). Coming home and chewing out your roommate because your boss at work angered you is inappropriate. Express your anger when you have calmed yourself and can confront the person in a descriptive manner. Expressing anger is most satisfying when the behavior that caused the anger changes. Gaining behavioral change from others happens more often when both parties engage in constructive dialogue, taking the problem-solving approach to communication. Expressing anger is also most satisfying when there is no retaliation from the target of your anger. Power forcing, competing styles of expressing anger are likely to provoke retaliation. Collaborating, assertive styles of expressing anger are more likely to avoid retaliation and produce just solutions.

Box 11-2 **Sharper Focus**

Bill Gates Goes Ballistic

Bill Gates is enraged. "His eyes are bulging and his oversized glasses are askew. His face is flushed and spit is flying from his mouth. . . . He's in a small, crowded conference room at the Microsoft campus with 20 young Microsofties gathered around an oblong table. Most look at their chairman with outright fear, if they look at him at all. The sour smell of sweaty terror fills the room" (Moody, 1996, p. 12). Gates continues his tirade, flooded with anger, seemingly incapable of rational resolution of the problem. The anxious programmers seated around the table try to reason with him but to no avail. No one seems able to calm down their boss—except a diminutive, soft-spoken Chinese American woman. She maintains eye contact with Gates as everyone else in the room looks away. Twice she short circuits his outburst by addressing him in a calm, even voice. Gates is momentarily calmed by the woman's first attempt before

revving up again. Her second attempt makes him pause. He listens to her, thoughtfully considers what she has said, and then says, "Okay, this looks good. Go ahead." Crisis past, the meeting adjourns.

What this woman said to Gates was only slightly different from what several people in the room had been trying to say throughout his diatribe. What she said, however, was not nearly as important as how she communicated it. She responded asymmetrically to Gates's angry eruption. Gates was flooded and "acting stupid"; she was calm and able to think straight. Her tranquil demeanor broke through and quelled the outburst. It signaled that the intense anger was unnecessary. Blazing anger was extinguished by asymmetrical calm. Exercising self-control when faced with someone out of control can be very empowering.

Transforming Competing into Collaborating

Conflicts are transactional. What one party does affects the other party in a conflict. Defensive communication from one person can ignite defensive communication from another. Supportive communication from one person encourages supportive communication from others. It takes two to compete, and it takes two to cooperate. The big question is "What do I do when I want to cooperate, but the other person wants to compete?" In a hypercompetitive society, chances are good that you will have to address this problem more often than not. Knowing that collaborating works far better than competing in most conflict situations doesn't automatically mean that others will share your informed viewpoint.

Here are some suggestions for how you might transform a competitor into a collaborator:

1. *Always be "unconditionally constructive"* (Fisher & Brown, 1988). Refuse to be abused, but also refuse to be abusive. Don't return contempt with contempt, intimidation with intimidation. If others become abusive, remain civil. If they confuse issues to hide their weak position, clarify. If they try to intimidate you, don't bully back. Attempt to persuade them of the merits of your viewpoint. If they lie, neither trust nor deceive them. Remain vigilantly trustworthy at all times. If they don't actively listen to you, encourage them to listen carefully. Always listen actively and empathically to them. Meet defensive communication with supportive communication. This is not a guide to sainthood, although you probably deserve some small award for remaining composed when dealing with certain individuals. Remaining unconditionally constructive serves your own interests. As Fisher and Brown (1988) explain, "If you are acting in ways that injure your own competence, there is no reason for me to do the same. Two heads are better than one, but one is better than none" (p. 202).

Remaining unconditionally constructive during a conflict can be a huge challenge, but returning abuse with abuse merely angers both parties and produces destructive conflict. Reciprocal abuse also rarely produces very intelligent interchanges because flooding fogs the brain during shouting matches.

2. *Ask problem-solving questions* (Ury, 1993). Your goal is to move the other party from a power-forcing, controlling communication pattern to a problem-solving, collaborative pattern. One way to do this is to engage the other person in joint problem solving. Encourage joint effort to find an integrative solution. Ask "Why?" "Why not?" and "What if?" questions. "Why is it a problem for you that I don't talk much when I come home from work?" "Why not do it as I suggested? Can you see some problems?" "What if you let me do extra credit? What would happen?" You should not ask these questions, of course, as if you are cross-examining a terrorist on the witness stand.

3. *Confront the process* (Ury, 1993). Confronting the process can encourage collaborating. Don't attack; be assertive. Simply make an observation about the process. "Have you noticed that many times when I try to explain my point of view you interrupt me before I can finish my thought? Perhaps we can both agree to listen to each other without comment for 1 minute. What do you think?" If the other party gets nasty and belligerent, don't return fire. Address the process. "Do we really want to get nasty with each other? I don't see any good coming of it, do you?" This forces the other party to justify the nastiness, which is not an easy thing to do. Notice that the phrasing uses "we" to express inclusiveness. This removes the appearance of accusation. Sitting next to the person to discuss a family budget or credit card debt instead of across from him or her also nonverbally shows inclusiveness, not exclusiveness.

4. *Ask for advice* (Ury, 1993). "What would you do if you were in my position?" This requires some empathy—taking the perspective of the other person. "What do you suggest we do to satisfy both of our needs?" Again, the focus is on solving problems together and moving away from power-forcing strategies. To paraphrase Ury (1993), you're trying to bring others to their senses, not bring them to their knees.

Remaining unconditionally constructive is the most crucial of these four suggestions. It is the close companion of an asymmetrical response to anger. Don't try to learn all four steps at once. Concentrate on remaining unconditionally constructive first until it becomes second nature to you. Then gradually use and refine the other three suggestions, one at a time.

Forgiveness

One of the most starkly horrifying images of the Vietnam War is Associated Press photographer Nick Ut's picture of 9-year-old Phan Thi Kim Phuc running naked from her village, screaming in pain from a napalm attack that scorched 75% of her body with third-degree burns. Ut snapped the photo and then rushed the anguished little girl to a hospital, saving her life. Her two younger brothers died in the same napalm attack.

Kim Phuc spent 14 months in a Vietnamese hospital recovering from her terrible burns. When her wounds were washed and dressed, she lost consciousness from the excruciating pain. Even today, almost 3 decades later, the pain of those disfiguring wounds remains. "They are like a knife. They feel like they are cutting me" (as cited in Schultz, 1998).

In 1996 Kim Phuc brought a message of forgiveness to a Veteran's Day gathering at the Vietnam War Memorial in Washington, D.C. Addressing the crowd, she said, "Even if I could talk face to face to the pilot who dropped the bombs, I could tell him we could not change history. We should try to do good things for the present and the future to promote peace" (cited in Schultz, 1998). One veteran of the war, John Huelsenbeck, present at the ceremony said, "It's important to us that she's here, part of the healing process. We were just kids doing our job. For her to forgive us personally means something" (cited in Sciolino, 1996, p. A14). Kim Phuc exhibited Mark Twain's conception of forgiveness—"The fragrance the violet sheds on the heel that has crushed it."

Forgiveness plays an important role in resolving conflict and dealing with anger (Exline & Baumeister, 2000). Studies show that forgiveness seems to promote marital adjustment and satisfaction (Fenell, 1993; Woodman, 1991) and to reduce hostile anger (Williams & Williams, 1993). "Forgiveness is the final stage of conflict and is the one thing that is most likely to prevent repetitive, destructive cycles of conflict" (Lulofs, 1994, p. 288).

FORGIVENESS DEFINED   In Neil Simon's play *California Suite*, a woman catches her husband committing adultery and says to him, "I forgive you. And now I'm going to go out and spend all your money." Great line, but this isn't forgiveness. **Forgiveness** is "letting go of feelings of revenge and desires to retaliate" (Lulofs, 1994, p. 276). The focus of forgiveness is on healing wounds, not inflicting them on others.

Forgiveness is not simply forgetting what happened. How could Kim Phuc ever forget what happened to her? The painful scars covering her body remind her every day. Yet she forgave her attackers. Forgiveness is not excusing the behavior. When we forgive, we remove the desire to mimic the behavior we hate. Forgiveness is also not tolerating reprehensible behavior ("Oh, that's okay."). Kim Phuc clearly showed that she did not tolerate bombing innocent children in villages. The best indicator that you have forgiven someone for bad behavior is honestly wishing that person well when you think of them (Smedes, 1984).

Forgiveness, of course, is the opposite of the popular bumper sticker, "Don't get mad—get even." Forgiveness doesn't come easily. It is particularly difficult when the offense is severe, intentional, and repeated and the transgressor is unrepentant

Kim Phuc (center) as a child runs screaming down a Vietnamese road after suffering severe burns from napalm. As an adult, she meets John Plummer, an American officer who coordinated the bombing attack. Despite her lifelong suffering from her burns, she accepts his sincere apology.

(Exline & Baumeister, 2000). When a friend ridicules your style of dress or taste in music in front of others, it can hurt and make you angry, but you usually can forgive the insult easily. In fact, as Smedes (1984) explains, "It is wise not to turn all hurts into crises of forgiving. . . . We put everyone we love on guard when we turn personal misdemeanors into major felonies" (p. 15). Stealing your boyfriend or girlfriend from you on purpose with no apparent guilt, however, makes forgiving a bit more difficult.

Revenge may be our first impulse in response to transgressions, but seeking revenge doesn't resolve conflict. A movie such as *The First Wives Club* depicts revenge as a normal, even constructive response to the hurtful actions of others. This makes good entertainment, depending, of course, on your taste in movies. In the real world, however, revenge stimulates anger and perpetuates and escalates conflict. Revenge fantasies and blaming can lead to psychopathology, criminality, poor recovery from bereavement, and health problems (Exline & Baumeister, 2000).

THE PROCESS OF FORGIVENESS So how does forgiveness occur? Forgiveness is a process that occurs in stages. Smedes (1984) offers a four-stage model: We hurt, we hate, we heal, and we come together. Hurting and hating are natural results of the painful actions of others. Dwelling on the hating stage, however, paralyzes us. Hate is like a parasite drawing our life's energy from us, making us too weak to move forward. Our lives can become consumed by hatred for those who have inflicted pain on us. The only way to break free from the grip of hatred is to forgive. Forgiveness starts the healing process.

Perhaps you're thinking, "Easy for you to say, but there are just some things that can't be forgiven." Remember that forgiveness doesn't mean acceptance or tolerance of bad behavior by others. It doesn't mean you shouldn't get angry when you are mistreated. It also doesn't mean that you necessarily return to a relationship. Wishing a person well and no longer desiring revenge and retaliation won't necessarily mean that a relationship is salvageable. Think, though, what the alternative is to forgiving. Holding onto hatred and seeking revenge does nothing constructive to enhance your life. Hatred and desire for revenge are physically and psychologically damaging (Lulofs, 1994).

Mary Nell Verrett is the sister of James Byrd Jr., a 49-year-old African American who was beaten and dragged to death behind a pickup in Jasper, Texas, on June 7, 1998. Despite her terrible loss, Verrett eloquently testifies to the futility and danger of hating: "Our family has no use for destructive hate . . . it tears away at you. You become sick. You become a victim all over again. It can keep you from sleeping, eating, and thinking straight. It can keep you from going forward" (cited in Message of Hope, 1998, pp. 9–10). If Mary Nell Verrett can forgive what racist White men did to her beloved brother, and Kim Phuc can forgive the transgressors who inflicted unspeakable pain and suffering on her, surely we can forgive those who hurt us.

Forgiveness is a transactional process. Although some individuals can readily forgive others, it is extremely difficult for others to forgive. In such cases, what the transgressor does to encourage forgiveness can help. If you have inflicted pain, you can take two steps to initiate the forgiveness process. First, you can openly and sincerely accept guilt for what you have done. "What I did to you was wrong and totally unprovoked" expresses guilt. Second, you can apologize. "I'm very sorry for hurting you" is a short apology. An apology is a particularly important step that encourages forgiveness (McCullough et al., 1997). *Elaborate, sincere apologies work best when the transgression is serious* (Weiner et al., 1991).

The forgiveness process was manifested in a Santa Cruz County, California, courtroom at the sentencing of Bryce Kurek, an 18-year-old found guilty of drunken driving that caused an accident that killed three of his friends and paralyzed a fourth. Stricken by the horror of what he had foolishly and irresponsibly done, while weeping he issued this apology to the court and to the parents of his dead and injured friends: "I just want to say I'm so sorry for what I did. I just apologize with all of my heart and soul. It's all I can give you when I took so much from you. I can't imagine how it must feel to lose your child. I want to be punished, your honor, for what I've done. I know whatever I do it'll never bring them back, but it might ease the pain of the parents" (cited in Gammon & Clark, 1997, p. A4).

The apology was elaborate and sincere, and he accepted guilt by asking the judge to punish him. It did not excuse his behavior, and no one will forget what happened. All of the victims' parents lost their only children in the fiery crash. Nevertheless, Laurie Maze, mother of one of the victims, said after the judge passed sentence, "We never had revenge for him. We just wanted justice served. I hope he learns and matures and accepts the full responsibility of his actions" (Gammon & Clark, 1997, p. A1). Veta Jackson-Smith, also a victim's mother, actually pleaded with the court for mercy: "I want something good to come out of this instead of all this bitterness. It's enough of a sentence that he knows until the day he dies that he killed his friends" (p. A4). Judge Robert Yonts sentenced Bryce Kurek to 8 years in prison.

Others can start the forgiveness process, but ultimately we have to forgive in our hearts. *As the victims, we can forgive by reframing the event*. We recast the behavior that hurt us into an uncharacteristic departure from the norm. The hurtful act doesn't have to become a defining moment in our relationship with the other person. A friend can hurt us and still remain a friend. We can also reframe the event by attributing situational causes to the act. "He stole my money because he lives in desperate circumstances, not because he is evil" reframes the event for forgiveness. The parents in the Bryce Kurek tragedy might have reframed the event as "He was a kid who did a dumb, irresponsible act brought on by alcohol abuse, but before this event he was a good person and he probably still is."

The final stage of the forgiveness process is the coming together part. This step can continue the healing and nudge us toward closure so we can move on with our lives. Coming together occurs when the victim openly communicates forgiveness to the transgressor. "I forgive you. I have no desire for revenge" expresses forgiveness. A hug or some expression of affection, if possible, is also helpful in bringing parties together. In cases of serious transgressions, the transgressor may have to demonstrate his or her commitment to make amends (Tavris, 1989). Forgiveness doesn't mean that trust springs back immediately. If the transgressor, for instance, agrees to clean the house every week for 3 months without being asked, this might serve as an outward sign that regaining trust is important. This indicates that commitment to the relationship is firm.

Personal injury inflicted on us by others becomes a part of who we are, but it does not have to be the whole of who we are (Lulofs, 1994). Expressing forgiveness and acting in ways that show forgiveness can heal.

Culture and Conflict

The value differences between cultures discussed extensively in Chapter 4 highlight the potential for intercultural conflict. Misinterpretation of a person's intentions and behavior is common when value differences are pronounced. The ways individuals from different cultures manage conflict can pose significant problems as we become a more multicultural society (Box 11-3).

Individualist and collectivist values markedly influence the choice of communication styles of conflict management when conflict erupts. Consider differences between Chinese and Americans. Chinese culture, far more collectivist than American culture, emphasizes harmony as a goal. "The Chinese consider harmony as the universal path which we all should pursue. Only when harmony is reached and prevails throughout heaven and earth can all things be nourished and flourish" (Chen & Starosta, 1998a, p. 6). A conflict-free interpersonal relationship, therefore, is the ultimate goal (Chen & Starosta, 1998a).

The Chinese philosophy of harmonious relationships translates into a strong desire to avoid conflict with friends or members of in-groups (e.g., family). When conflicts are unavoidable, there is a preference for accommodating, not confronting, the dispute, so harmony is maintained (Chen & Starosta, 1998a). Handling a dispute ineptly can bring shame, a loss of face, not just on the individual but also on the

Box 11-3   Sharper Focus

Managing Cultural Conflicts

Two Japanese students, Norrie Kobayashi and Kentaro Ebiko, were raised in Japan but had lived in the United States for 3 years and had been dating each other for 7 months when they were interviewed. As you read this brief excerpt from their interview, notice how they attest to the influence on conflict management of the cultural value of collectivism, with its high-context (indirect, ambiguous) communication style.

QUESTION: According to researchers, there are considerable differences between the way conflicts are dealt with in the United States and Japan. Do you agree?

KENTARO: Definitely. In the U.S.A. being direct and expressive is very important. In Japan, just the opposite is true. You almost never talk about conflicts there, at least not openly.

QUESTION: If people don't talk about conflicts, how do they resolve them?

KENTARO: Sometimes they don't. In Japan the tradition is not to show your emotions. Outside appearances are very important. If you're upset, you still act as if everything is okay. So there are lots of times when you might be disappointed or angry with somebody and they would never know it.

QUESTION: Do conflicts ever get expressed?

KENTARO: They aren't discussed openly, assertively very often. But in Japan a lot more is communicated nonverbally. If you guess that the other person is unhappy from the way they act, you might try to change to please them. But even then you wouldn't necessarily talk about the conflict directly.

QUESTION: Norie, does Kentaro hide his feelings very well?

NORIE: No! He's more American than I am in this way. . . .

QUESTION: It sounds like you're less comfortable facing conflicts than Kentaro?

NORIE: That's right. I think it's partly my Japanese upbringing and partly just my personality but I don't like to confront people. For example, I was having a hard time studying and sleeping because one of my housemates would wash clothes late at night. I wanted her to stop, but I would never have talked to her directly. I asked my housemother to take care of the problem. Asking a third party is very common in Japan.

Source: Adler & Towne (1993). Used by permission.

---

individual's entire family. Thus, one must avoid stirring up trouble for fear of bringing shame to the family (Yu, 1997).

Conflicts with individuals from an out-group, however, are often handled quite differently among Chinese than are conflicts within the group. Although not the initial choice, competing is not an uncommon way to approach conflict with outsiders, especially if the interests of the opposing parties are highly incompatible. Vicious quarrels, even physical fights, are not uncommon in such circumstances (Chen & Starosta, 1998a; Yu, 1997).

Imagine the difficulty that would occur when an American and a Chinese try to resolve a conflict. Americans favor direct, competing or compromising styles of conflict management. These styles clash with the avoiding and accommodating styles initially favored by Chinese. Consider a slightly different intercultural conflict with similar difficulties. Tannen (1998) cites an example of a Japanese woman married to a Frenchman. The French love to argue; in fact, they may change topics at the dinner table until they find one that ignites a disagreement. For the first 2 years of marriage, this Japanese woman spent a great deal of time in tears. She tried accommodating her husband and avoided arguing with him. This seemed to frustrate him. He would try to find something to start an argument. Finally, she couldn't take it any more, and she began yelling at him. Her husband was thrilled. To him, starting an argument with his wife showed that he valued her intelligence and that he was interested in her. He considered enthusiastic debate between partners a sign of a solid relationship.

Many Middle Eastern and Mediterranean cultures favor a forceful, aggressive, argumentative style of communication typical of power forcing (Samovar & Porter, 2001). Native Americans in the United States find assertiveness too direct and aggressive displays of anger distasteful (Moghaddam et al., 1993).

The key to effective intercultural conflict management is flexibility. If you find yourself in a situation or relationship that calls for intercultural conflict management, try broadening your approach to conflict. Learn to use all communication styles well, not just those you are most comfortable with or used to using. Change to a different style when one style seems to clash with another person's cultural values. If you know that someone comes from a collectivist culture, don't abandon collaborating, but be prepared to seek accommodation wherever possible. In any case, recognize that competing is as ineffective and troublesome to use interculturally as it is to use intraculturally. When you make mistakes, and you will, be prepared to apologize. Seek forgiveness for embarrassing or shaming the other person. Elaborate apologies work best when the insult or embarrassment seems to be great. Above all, try to empathize with people whose cultural values and standards are different from your own. Consider their perspective and respect their right to disagree. Find ways to build bridges between culturally diverse individuals, not tear them down.

Summary

Most people view conflict with some dread. Conflict, however, can be constructive as well as destructive. Our communication determines the difference. Destructive conflict is typified by escalating spirals of conflict that can easily turn ugly. Constructive conflict is characterized by controlling or de-escalating conflict by using a We-orientation, cooperation, and flexibility in applying communication styles of conflict management. There are five communication styles of conflict management: collaborating, accommodating, compromising, avoiding, and competing. Collaborating has the greatest potential for appropriately and effectively managing conflict; competing has the least potential. Learning to control our anger and to manage the anger of others is an important part of dealing with conflict effectively. The final stage of conflict is forgiveness. Forgiveness is letting go of the desire for revenge and retaliation. Intercultural conflicts can be extremely difficult to manage because members of individualist and collectivist cultures differ dramatically in how they view conflict and how best to manage it.

Quizzes Without Consequences

Go to Quizzes Without Consequences at the book's Online Learning Center at **www.mhhe.com/rothwell2** or access the CD-ROM for *In the Company of Others.*

www.mhhe
com/ **rothwell2**

Key Terms

See Audio Flashcards
Study Aid.

www.mhhe
● com/
    /rothwell2
See Crossword Puzzle
Study Aid.

accommodating	compromising	forgiveness
avoiding	conflict	integration
chilling effect	confrontation	smoothing
collaborating	constructive conflict	stonewalling
communication style of	destructive conflict	
conflict management	flooding	

Suggested Readings

Fisher, R., & Brown, S. (1988). *Getting together: Building a relationship that gets to yes.* Boston: Houghton Mifflin. This is an extension of *Getting to Yes* in which collaborative principles of negotiation are applied to interpersonal relationships.

Fisher, R., & Ury, W. (1981). *Getting to yes: Negotiating agreement without giving in.* New York: Penguin. This is the bible of collaborative negotiation. Fisher and Ury have made a strong case for cooperative approaches to negotiation.

Stone, D., Patton, B., & Heen, S. (1999). *Difficult conversations: How to discuss what matters most.* New York: Viking. This is a very good treatment of how to keep conflict constructive.

Tavris, C. (1989). *Anger: The misunderstood emotion.* New York: Simon & Schuster. Tavris debunks many myths about anger and explores how to express it constructively.

Ury, W. (1993). *Getting past no: Negotiating your way from confrontation to cooperation.* New York: Bantam. Ury provides many creative ways to transform a competitive negotiation into a more cooperative one.

Film School

Chasing Amy (1997). Drama; R ★★★
If you don't like graphic language and descriptions, avoid this movie. Otherwise, there is much to analyze here. Are there dialectics that trigger conflict? Explain. What styles of conflict management are used predominately by the characters?

The War of the Roses (1989). Black Comedy; R ★★★★★
This is destructive conflict in graphic detail. Kathleen Turner and Michael Douglas play a wife and husband who go toe to toe in an increasingly mindless escalation of verbal and physical aggression. Identify instances that fit the definition of *destructive conflict.*

What's Cooking? (2000). Comedy/Drama; PG-13 ★★★↲
Diversity is not lacking in this portrayal of four interrelated couples trying to celebrate Thanksgiving. Look for the many dialectical sources of conflict. Is honesty always the best policy? Identify the communication styles of conflict management depicted in the film.

PART THREE

Group
Communication

CHAPTER 12

The Anatomy of Small Groups

www.mhhe
● com/
/rothwell2

See "Grouphate" activity on the Online Learning Center, chapter 12.

"A camel is a horse designed by a committee." Countless individuals have passed along this cynical witticism as a sage observation about groups. Similarly, J. B. Hughes comments, "If Moses had been a committee, the Israelites would still be in Egypt." Richard Harkness offers this: "What is a committee? A group of the unwilling, picked from the unfit, to do the unnecessary." Then there is this anonymous contribution: "Trying to solve a problem through group discussion is like trying to clear up a traffic jam by honking your horn" (Brussell, 1988).

Groups clearly suffer from bad public relations. It seems that almost everyone has a negative opinion about working in groups. Sorensen (1981) coined the term "grouphate" to describe this negative view. The most interesting finding from her research is that individuals who received the most instruction in communicating competently in groups had the most positive view of groups. Instruction in communicating competently in groups directly influences our perception of the group experience. As is true of so many things in life, if you do not have the knowledge and skills necessary to perform effectively and appropriately, the value you ascribe to the experience is low, and your enjoyment is diminished.

There are good reasons to feel negatively about groups. Often, they seem to be an impediment to decision-making and problem solving, not an aid. Probably everyone, however, can point to one, two, or a few very positive experiences with groups. The experience may have been with a sports team, a study group at school, your family, a project team at work, or with friends. The most successful teams are composed of individuals who love working in groups (Goleman, 1998). A basic question to ask is "Why are some group experiences unpleasant and others a joy?" Finding answers to this question is important because there is no escaping the group experience—regardless of how you feel about groups now.

Primary groups such as family and friends provide us with warmth, affection, support, and a sense of belonging. Social groups such as fraternities and sororities, athletic teams, and hobby or special interest groups share a common purpose or pursue common goals. Service groups such as PTAs, Kiwanis and Lions clubs, Habitat for Humanity, and many campus clubs help others. Self-help/support groups empower individuals to deal with addictive behavior or physical or mental illness or to make life transitions. There is a self-help group for almost every medical disorder identified by the World Health Organization (Balgopal et al., 1992). In California alone there are approximately 4,000 self-help/support groups, and in the United States about 7.6 million people participate in such groups (Lieberman & Snowden, 1993). "The self-help and support group phenomenon reminds us of the importance of groups in meeting human needs" (Kurtz, 1997, p. xiii).

"Most of the important decisions that affect your work life are made by groups" (Tropman, 1988, p. 7). Work teams have become increasingly popular in organizations across the United States. Work teams are self-managed groups that work on specific tasks or projects within an organization. Nearly half of all U.S. employees will participate in work teams (Freeman, 1996).

Study groups are an outgrowth of cooperative learning strategies. Study groups are an increasingly popular way to learn academic course material by sharing knowledge and understanding with other students. A Harvard University study found that college students learn more "when they do at least some of their studying in small groups rather than logging long, solitary hours of study" (Fiske, 1990, p. A1).

This is not an exhaustive list of groups, but the point is clear. There is no escaping groups, so we had best learn how to make them a positive experience.

A positive group experience begins with knowledge of how groups function. *The primary purpose of this chapter is to learn how to improve your communication in groups by understanding the nature of small groups.*

> **There are three primary chapter objectives:**
> 1. to explore the advantages and disadvantages of communicating in groups,
> 2. to analyze the structure of small groups, and
> 3. to learn communication strategies that can improve the small group experience.

The primary purpose of this chapter is to learn how to improve your communication in groups by understanding the nature of small groups.

Let's begin by defining what a group is. A **group** is composed of three or more individuals interacting for the achievement of some common purpose(s) who influence and are influenced by one another. Two people qualify as a couple or dyad, not a group. Communication between two people is typically viewed as an interpersonal transaction, not a group transaction. Also, a group is not merely any aggregation of people, such as 10 strangers standing in line waiting to buy tickets to a rock concert. These strangers are not standing in line to achieve a common purpose, such as helping each other buy tickets. The same is true for a crowd in a shopping mall or a collection of people waiting to board a plane. In both cases the presence of other individuals is irrelevant to the achievement of a common purpose, which is buying clothes or traveling from point A to point B. *To qualify as a group, three or more people must succeed or fail as a unit in a quest to achieve a common purpose.* The essence of a group, therefore, is a We-orientation, not a Me-orientation. Any of these examples, of course, could qualify as a group if circumstances required united action to achieve a mutual goal.

The focus here is on small groups, but trying to draw a meaningful line between small and large groups is problematic. Communication theorists typically set the upper limit on small groups at about 12 (the size of most juries). There is no absolute number, however, that clearly demarcates small from large groups. It seems more appropriate to define groups in terms of process, not number of individuals. *Groups are small as long as each individual in the group can recognize and interact with every other group member.* Recognition means knowing who is in the group and remembering something about their specific behaviors when the group met.

Pros and Cons of Groups

It is easy to be cynical about groups, but groups offer significant benefits as well as disadvantages. Both advantages and disadvantages of groups will be addressed in this section.

Group Size

With groups, size matters. All small groups are not created equal. A group composed of 3 members doesn't function the way a group of 10 does. As the size of the group increases, complexity of group transactions and decision-making increase enormously. The possible number of interpersonal relationships between group members grows exponentially as group size increases. Bostrom (1970) provides these calculations:

Group Size	Number of Possible Relationships
3	9
4	28
5	75
6	186
7	441
8	1,056

A triad, or three-member group, has 9 possible interpersonal relationships, a four-person group has 28 possible relationships, and so forth as shown in Figure 12-1.

The relationship member A has with member B may not be the same as the relationship member B has with A. Member A may see the relationship with member B as close; B may see it as just a work relationship, no more. Different perceptions of relationships increase the complexity of transactions among group members. Individual members also can have very different relationships with two or more other members (see 7, 8, and 9 in Figure 12-1). Adding even one member to a group is not an inconsequential event. As newscaster Jane Pauley once observed on the "Today" show, "Somehow three children are many more than two."

Several disadvantages emerge as groups increase in size and complexity. First, the number of nonparticipants in group discussions increases when groups grow much beyond six members. Reticent members may be intimidated by the prospect of speaking to a group, especially a large one. Second, larger groups easily become factionalized. Members of like mind may splinter into smaller factions, or subgroups, to withstand the pressure from other members to conform to the majority opinion on an issue. Third, larger groups may take much more time to make decisions than smaller groups. With more members, there are potentially more voices to be heard on issues being discussed. Finally, even scheduling a meeting at a time when all members are available can be a daunting task when groups grow large. Schedule conflicts are almost inevitable with groups of more than 8.

FIGURE 12-1   Number of Possible Relationships in a Group of Three

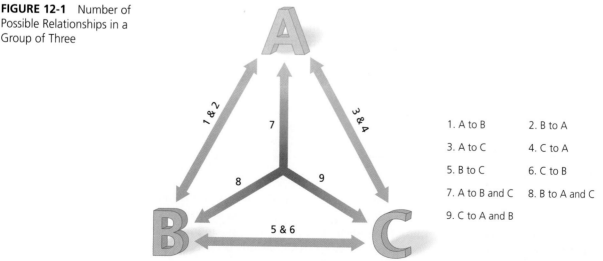

1. A to B
2. B to A
3. A to C
4. C to A
5. B to C
6. C to B
7. A to B and C
8. B to A and C
9. C to A and B

Smaller groups avoid the disadvantages of larger groups. They are less complex and factionalized and more efficient than larger groups. Small groups, however, can be too small to be effective. Too few members may provide too few resources to make decisions and solve problems effectively. A larger group of, perhaps, 7 can provide more input and has a potentially greater knowledge pool to assist in decision making. Complex, politically charged issues may require much larger groups (10 or more) just to give a voice to all interested factions.

So what is the ideal group size? Offering a precise number would be arbitrary and debatable. Instead, *the smallest size capable of fulfilling the purposes of the group should be considered optimum*. Each group experience is unique. The key point is to keep groups relatively small to reap the greatest advantages. As groups grow in size, complexity and potential difficulties increase.

Support from Groups

Support and self-help groups have become a national phenomenon. The diversity of such groups is astonishing. Alcoholics Anonymous, the original self-help group, has been imitated by groups such as Depressives Anonymous, Gamblers Anonymous, Cocaine Anonymous, Batterers Anonymous, Impotents Anonymous, Prostitutes Anonymous, Families Anonymous, Parents Anonymous, and Overeaters Anonymous. There are groups for most addictive behaviors, physical or mental illnesses, life transitions (e.g., Recently Divorced Catholics), and friends and relatives of those with a problem (e.g., Adult Children of Alcoholics). Support groups range from the conventional to the bizarre.

Some of the more unusual support groups include Hot Flashes (for menopausal women), Good Tidings (for women who continually fall in love with priests), Crossroads (for male transvestites), and Compulsive Shoppers. An unnamed support group was organized in 1993 by a hypnotherapist to assist the poor unfortunates who have been abducted by extraterrestrials (the ultimate illegal aliens) and lived to tell about it. Even distraught rock fans, grief-ridden at the news of a recently departed rock star, can find a support group, such as the group that formed after the Grateful Dead's Jerry Garcia died in 1995.

Most support and self-help groups are small, and even the larger organizations such as Alcoholics Anonymous operate from local chapters whose group meetings typically include 8 to 12 members (Kurtz, 1997). Research on support groups reveals that they give emotional support to members, impart information, share experiences, convey a sense of belonging, and teach methods for coping with problems common to the group (Kurtz, 1997). In a word, *support groups empower members*. This is a significant advantage of groups.

The attraction to support groups is more than sharing a common bond brought about by similar problems. It is also the desire to learn how to solve difficult problems and to cope with life's tribulations with the help of support, comfort, and advice from fellow sufferers.

Synergy

Synergy is the product of cooperation within a group. The end product of efforts by group members working cooperatively isn't necessarily just the sum of those individual efforts. Sometimes the whole is greater than the sum of its parts. **Synergy** (*syn* = together + *ergon* = work) occurs when the work of group members yields a greater total effect than the sum of the individual members' efforts could have produced. When this joint action of group members produces performance that exceeds expectations based on perceived abilities and skills of individual members, synergy has occurred (Salazar, 1995). Synergy is like combining cancer-fighting drugs to produce far greater effects than taking the drugs separately could produce. This is the basis of chemotherapy.

A June 23, 1998, *NBC News at Sunrise* report provides an apt example of synergy. A Little League team in Tucson, Arizona, called the Diamondbacks, was composed of players no other teams wanted because they were considered misfits that were not good enough to play. These misfits compiled a perfect record of 18–0 to win the league championship. The group effort far exceeded expectations of success based on the individual abilities of the players.

How does synergy happen? It occurs primarily through teamwork based on cooperation and the We-orientation. Individuals work together, unselfishly, in a coordinated effort to achieve a common goal. Rafael Aguayo (1990) draws from his own experience as a Little League soccer coach to explain how synergy occurs. Aguayo emphasized having fun, improving skill levels, and teamwork. He deemphasized winning. Before each game he told his players that scoring goals and winning weren't important. Playing hard, improving skills, and acting like a team were important. After a game, he would ask his players, "Who scored that first goal?" At first, the player who scored the first goal would raise a hand. "No!" Aguayo would cry. "We all scored that goal. Every person on a team is responsible for scoring a goal." Then he repeated his question, "Now, who scored that goal?" All the players on the team raised their hands. Aguayo never singled out any player as better than any other. Instead, he gave every team member a "best player" trophy at the end of the season. Each player got to be captain at least once. What were the results of this experiment in cooperation, teamwork, and a We- not Me-orientation? Synergy was the result. In the 4 years Aguayo coached Little League soccer, his team lost only a single game.

Even in a larger competitive environment, cooperation can thrive. Aguayo's coaching philosophy echoed that of legendary college basketball coach, John Wooden. "Many people are surprised to learn that in 27 years at UCLA, I never once talked about winning. . . . I always taught players that the main ingredient of stardom is the rest of the team" (cited in Aguayo, 1990, p. 99). Wooden's teams never had a losing season. In his final 12 years of coaching at UCLA, his teams won 10 national championships, 7 in a row (both current records). His teams hold the world record for the longest winning streak in any major college sport—88 games without a loss. Groups don't have to be a hateful experience. Sometimes groups can surpass our wildest expectations. The synergy produced through teamwork can make the group experience joyful.

Groups don't always produce synergy, however. Sometimes groups produce results that are beyond bad. This is called *negative synergy*. **Negative synergy** is the joint action of group members that produces a result worse than that expected based on perceived individual abilities and skills of members (Salazar, 1995). Negative synergy is like mixing alcohol and tranquilizers, which can cause accidental death. The mixture is far worse than the sum of the effects produced when taking each separately.

I give cooperative exams in my classes. Group members work on the exam together and turn in a single answer sheet. An individual accountability test, which

THE FAR SIDE® BY GARY LARSON

**"And so you just threw everything together?
Mathews, a posse is something
you have to *organize*."**

sets a minimum standard of performance to earn the group grade, follows the group exam. Most groups score much higher than the average of individual test scores (synergy) and often higher than any member of the group scores on the individual test. Occasionally, however, negative synergy occurs. On one exam all the groups but one scored in the 80s or 90s. One group of six, however, scored 50. Their group score was actually lower than the average of their individual scores. The group performed worse than any group member. I had listened to their discussion during the test, and I heard members talk the group into choosing incorrect answers. The group was capable of scoring much higher on the test, but lack of motivation, poor communication in the group, lackluster preparation, and conflict diminished their result.

Synergy won't magically occur simply because individuals form a group. A single expert on a technical topic can provide better advice than a group of uninformed members. If you have a legal question, go see a good lawyer. Seeking legal advice from a group of friends who know next to nothing about the law is inviting disaster. Nevertheless, groups can often produce exceptional results because members can share the labor required to research even technical or complex subjects, they can pool knowledge and share information, and they can correct errors more readily because there are more heads devoted to spotting mistakes and misjudgments (Rothwell, 2001). As the Japanese proverb says, "None of us is as smart as all of us."

Social Loafing

Social loafing is one of the most common complaints about working in groups. Members do not share the same level of commitment to the group and the task. Those who are fully committed, even inspired to work in the group, become demoralized and frustrated by the apathy and disinterest shown by one or more group members. **Social loafing** is the tendency of individuals to reduce their work effort when they join groups. Social loafers "goof off" when tasks need to be accomplished. They miss some meetings and show up late to others. They fail to complete tasks important to overall group performance. Social loafers exhibit scant effort because of weak motivation, disinterest in the group, or poor attitude. Social loafing is not the same as shyness. Shy individuals may have a strong motivation to work in the group but are reticent to participate in discussions because of communication anxiety or fear of disapproval. Shy members may attend all meetings and never be tardy.

Social loafing is a serious disadvantage of working in groups. *Social loafing increases with group size.* One study (Latane et al., 1979) asked participants to clap and cheer "as loud as you can." These efforts were measured as individuals, as dyads (two partners), and as four- or six-person groups. Dyads performed at 71% of each person's individual capacity, four-person groups at 51%, and six-person groups at only 40%. Social loafing occurs because individual group members often do not see the connection between their personal effort and the outcomes desired by the group (Karau & Williams, 1993).

Social loafing occurs in a broad range of groups working on a variety of tasks. Males and females of all ages and from many different cultures may be social loafers. Social loafing is more common in an individualist culture such as that of the United States than it is in collectivist cultures such as those of Singapore, China, Thailand, Pakistan, and Indonesia (Early, 1989; Gabreyna, 1985). People in individualist cultures are not as heavily influenced as those in collectivist cultures by what the group might think of a person's effort. Individual group members may establish their "uniqueness" by showing how uninvolved they can be, even in the face of group pressure to perform. In collectivist cultures, however, pleasing the group, maintaining group harmony, and submerging individual accomplishment for the sake of the group encourage strong group commitment and discourage loafing. The collectivist attitude is "Don't let the group down." Lackluster performance by loafers could bring loss of face.

How can you diminish or eliminate the disadvantage of social loafing associated with group work? Motivation is the root of this problem. There are no magic formulas, no simple list of do's and don'ts that will motivate loafers.

Before discussing what might motivate loafers, let's be very clear regarding what doesn't motivate others. Exhortations from motivated group members usually have no lasting effect on loafers. This is analogous to hiring a "motivational speaker" to lecture employees in the workplace. Kohn (1993) sums up the failure of this approach: "At best, the result is a temporary sense of being re-energized, much like the effect of eating a doughnut. When the sugar high wears off, very little of value is left in the system" (p. 187). Cheerleading doesn't address a loafer's lack of interest in the group and its tasks. It assumes that every member can be inspired, even if the group task is tedious.

Performance evaluation also is unlikely to jump-start a loafer, especially if it is tied to some kind of reward system (Aguayo, 1990; Kohn, 1993). Grading a group member's effort, aside from creating the obvious difficulties of determining objective criteria for such an evaluation, creates a defensive atmosphere. This is especially true when the appraisal results in a punishment. In the workplace, performance evaluations are often tied to wages and other forms of compensation. Exceptional work earns a bonus. Poor appraisal of a worker typically results in no pay increase or even a pay reduction. Consultant Peter Scholtes (1990) says, "Using performance appraisal of any kind as a basis for reward is a flat out catastrophic mistake" (p. 46). The likely result of such schemes is demotivation of workers given mediocre or poor appraisals for lackluster performance.

Any step that creates a competitive, defensive environment is unlikely to motivate social loafers (Kohn, 1993). Kohn (1993) offers "the three C's of motivation" that encourage cooperation, not competition. The three C's are collaboration, content, and choice. These are aspects of teamwork, a subject to be discussed in detail in Chapter 13.

Collaboration is the cooperative style of conflict management. It is also synonymous with teamwork (LaFasto & Larson, 2001). Developing teamwork and cooperation can motivate loafers because they no longer see themselves as individuals separate from the group. They identify with the group. Groups that achieve success and receive rewards for such success typically have little problem with loafers. This is especially so when each group member perceives that his or her individual effort is necessary for the group to succeed (Karau & Williams, 1993). If a group member's individual performance can be identified separately from the group's, social loafing also decreases (Karau & Williams, 1993). When a group member has been given a specific task to perform and he or she does not complete the task because of weak effort, the entire group notices. Not wanting to let the team down can be a powerful motivator.

Content refers to the group task. What work are group members asked to perform? "Idleness, indifference, and irresponsibility are healthy responses to absurd work," claims Frederick Herzberg (cited in Kohn, 1993, p. 189). Few group members will be motivated to work on tasks that hold no interest for them. Granted, not all tasks can be motivating. Some tasks have to be performed even though they are dreary, tedious jobs. Nevertheless, busywork and paper chasing should be kept to a minimum so the totality of a group's work is viewed as involving and interesting. Group members need to see the value of performing a task before they are likely to take responsibility for meeting their individual obligations to the group effort. Social loafing decreases when group members see work as meaningful (Karau & Williams, 1993).

Choice is a nice complement to content. One way of making group projects and tasks challenging and interesting to group members is to allow as much choice as possible. Try letting group members choose which part of a project they would most like to tackle. Arbitrarily imposing task assignments on group members will quickly produce loafing, even grumbling. Let group members participate in decision making. That's what encourages teamwork and cooperation. Group tasks become meaningful when members have a say in what is done and how it is accomplished.

Kohn's three C's provide general principles for motivating group members and discouraging social loafing. Teamwork is the overall solution.

Meetings

The major difference between meetings and funerals is that "most funerals have a definite purpose. Also, nothing is ever really buried in a meeting." So claims

Mitchell's Law says: "Any problem can be made insoluble if enough meetings are held to discuss it." Meetings can be exhausting, especially if they are aimless and unproductive. The meeting monster can be tamed with some careful planning and appropriate strategies.

humorist Dave Barry (1991, p. 311). Many people perceive having to attend meetings as a serious disadvantage of group work. Grouphate is nourished by the prevalent belief that group meetings are mostly a waste of time. Studies have found that about a third of the time spent in meetings is wasted, costing billions of dollars to organizations and businesses (Green & Lazarus, 1990; Lazar, 1991). Business consultant Mitchell Nash (Dressler, 1995) identifies six common complaints made about group meetings: (1) the meeting has an unclear purpose, (2) participants are unprepared, (3) key individuals are absent or tardy, (4) discussion drifts into irrelevant conversation, (5) some group members dominate discussion, and (6) the decisions made are not implemented.

Meetings don't have to be time wasters. Whoever chairs a meeting can take steps to make the meeting productive and efficient. Here are some suggestions:

1. *Don't call a meeting unless no other good alternative exists.* If immediate action is required, group participation is essential, group members are prepared to discuss relevant issues, and main players can be present, then hold a meeting. If objectives can be met without a meeting, don't meet. One of life's little pleasures is the surprise notification "Meeting has been cancelled."
2. *Identify the specific purpose of the meeting.* Notify each group member of where the meeting will be held and when and how long it will likely last. Let participants know if they should bring certain materials or resources to the meeting. Encourage each member to be prepared to discuss important issues. Typically, only about a quarter of group members are prepared most of the time for meetings (Green & Lazarus, 1990).
3. *Prepare a clear agenda* that lists the topics of discussion in the order that they will be addressed. Include a time allotment for discussion of each issue (Box 12-1). Provide accurate, concise information on issues discussed.

Box 12-1 Sharper Focus

A Sample Agenda for Group Meetings

Meeting of the Student Senate
November 15
Boardroom
2:00–4:00 p.m.

Purpose: Biweekly meeting

I. Meeting called to order

II. Approval of the minutes of last meeting (5 minutes)

III. Additions to the agenda (2 minutes)

IV. Committee reports
   A. Student clubs committee (5 minutes)
   B. Student transportation committee (5 minutes)
   C. Student activities committee (5 minutes)

V. Officers' reports

A. Treasurer's report (3 minutes)
B. President's report (10 minutes)

VI. Old business (previously discussed but unresolved)
   A. Campus security problems (15 minutes)
   B. Cost of textbooks (10 minutes)
   C. Parking garage proposal (10 minutes)
   D. Student credit card proposal (5 minutes)

VII. New business
   A. Hate speech on campus (15 minutes)
   B. Expanding the bookstore (10 minutes)
   C. Open access computer use (10 minutes)
   D. Student elections (5 minutes)

VIII. Agenda building for next meeting (5 minutes)

IX. Adjournment

4. *Above all, keep the discussion on track.* Don't allow drift. Aimless discussion sucks the life out of meetings. Also, do not allow any member to hog the stage. Encourage participation from all members.

5. *Start the meeting on time and be guided by the "what's done is done" rule* (Tropman, 1996). Do not interrupt the flow of the meeting by bringing latecomers up to speed except to indicate which item on the agenda is under discussion. Latecomers can be filled in briefly after the meeting or during a break if necessary. Instructors don't restart classes each time a student comes in late. Nothing would get accomplished. Concerts aren't stopped in midstream to accommodate those who amble in late. Movies aren't rewound and begun again when latecomers appear 20 minutes into the movie. Punctuality discourages late arrival, especially when the meeting moves forward and isn't derailed by tardiness.

6. *Do not discuss an issue longer than the time allotted unless the group decides to extend the time.* This prevents talkaholics from pointlessly extending the meeting well beyond expectations. Three of four meetings don't end on time (Green & Lazarus, 1990). Meetings that end ahead of time are cause for celebration; those that end late are cause for exasperation.

7. *Take a few minutes at the end of the meeting to determine if all objectives were accomplished.* Two thirds of meetings fail to accomplish stated objectives (Green & Lazarus, 1990). Schedule time in the next meeting to consider any unresolved issues.

8. *Distribute minutes of the meeting to all participants as soon as possible.* The minutes should indicate what was discussed, who said what, what action was taken, and what remains to be discussed and decided.

You can slay the meeting monster and quell grouphate if you follow these simple steps to keep meetings efficient and productive. Meetings do not have to be a torture.

The advantages of working in groups are many. Groups can pool knowledge and information, correct errors often missed by an individual working alone, accomplish broad-range tasks by sharing the load among members, and, above all, empower group members and produce synergy. The main disadvantages of groups—factionalism, scheduling conflicts, negative synergy, social loafing, and wasting time in meetings—are correctable. The group experience can be unpleasant if we allow it to be, but it does not have to be that way.

The Structure of Small Groups

Every group has a discernible structure. In this section group structure, which is composed of the relationship between task and social dimensions, norms, and roles will be examined.

Task and Social Dimensions

Every group has two primary interconnected dimensions. The **task dimension** is the work performed by the group and its impact on the group. The **social dimension** consists of relationships among group members and the impact these relationships have on the group.

Walter V. Clarke Associates, a consulting firm, conducted a study of more than 700 professional athletes, NFL draft choices, and college players. The study found that skill at performing tasks is not enough to be successful in groups (cited in Goleman, 1998). Gifted athletes who haven't mastered how to work cooperatively with group members can create havoc. Athletes who listened poorly, wouldn't take directions, and came late to meetings were rated by their coaches as being less motivated, harder to coach, less talented, and less likely to be leaders. Although technical, task-oriented skills are important, a study by the U.S. Department of Labor Employment and Training Administration (Carnevale, 1996) showed that the critical skills are all socially oriented—oral communication, interpersonal communication, and teamwork abilities (see also Goleman, 1998).

Productivity is the goal of the task dimension. The extent of a group's productivity is determined by the degree to which it accomplishes its work efficiently and effectively. **Cohesiveness** is the goal of the social dimension. The extent of a group's cohesiveness depends on the degree to which members identify with the group and wish to remain in the group (Langfred, 1998).

One national survey (Silva, 1982) found that the cohesiveness of sports teams was the number one concern of coaches. This was so because cohesiveness and productivity (performance) are interconnected; one affects the other (Cohen & Bailey, 1997). High cohesiveness alone doesn't guarantee group success, but it seems to be a necessary condition for successful task accomplishment. When groups lack cohesiveness, their productivity typically suffers. Small groups of exceedingly talented individuals will not accomplish tasks well if interpersonal relations among members are immersed in disharmony, anger, resentments, hostilities, and rivalries (Goleman, 1995). Low cohesiveness almost always dooms a group to poor performance and low productivity. Members who do not like each other and wish they weren't a part of the group will typically exhibit feeble effort and poor performance. Competitiveness among group members, especially when combined with time pressure to accomplish tasks, diminishes cohesiveness (Klein, 1996).

Group members can be so cohesive, however, that they become too concerned with maintaining harmony. When members avoid disagreement because they fear disrupting group cohesiveness, they may sacrifice error correction. This is one aspect of groupthink, a problem discussed in Chapter 13.

Finding the proper balance between productivity and cohesiveness is a persistent dialectical struggle in all groups. Too much focus on productivity can strain interpersonal relationships within a group. Too much focus on cohesiveness can lead to anemic effort on the task. Strong cohesiveness combined with a strong group work ethic is an effective combination (Langfred, 1998). Both task and social dimensions should be addressed, not one at the expense of the other.

Norms

Every group, large or small, has norms that guide behavior. **Norms** are rules that indicate what group members have to do (obligation), should do (preference), or cannot do (prohibition) if they want to accomplish specific goals. Norms regulate group behavior. In this section small group norms are discussed. Types of norms, their purpose and source, and conformity to norms are explored.

TYPES OF NORMS   There are two types of norms: explicit and implicit. **Explicit norms** specifically and overtly identify acceptable and unacceptable behavior. Explicit norms are typical of a low-context communication style. You want group members to know unambiguously what behavior is expected, preferred, and prohibited, so you tell members explicitly. No smoking signs posted around campus and in public buildings indicate an explicit norm. Laws of society and by-laws of a group are explicit norms. When your instructor tells the class not to interrupt a student during discussions or to attend regularly and be on time, he or she is providing explicit norms.

In small groups, however, most norms are implicit. **Implicit norms** are observable patterns of behavior exhibited by group members that identify acceptable and unacceptable conduct. Examples might include all group members sitting in the same seats for every meeting, not eating or drinking during meetings, dressing neatly, being polite, avoiding sarcastic or offensive humor, or not saying anything derogatory about any other member. These patterns indicate implicit norms. There is no book of rules on how to behave in such meetings, yet members all act as though there were.

Implicit norms may become explicit on occasion, especially when there is a norm violation. Instructors rarely feel compelled to tell students at the beginning of a school term that loud talking during lectures is unacceptable. This is an implicit norm that is taken for granted. It is unlikely that you would find such a rule in the college catalogue, on the schedule of classes, or on a syllabus. If students have ignored this implicit rule, however, instructors may make the implicit norm explicit by pointedly telling the class that talking while a lecture is in progress should cease.

PURPOSE OF NORMS   The primary purpose of norms is to achieve group goals. Shimanoff (1992) provides the example of Overeaters Anonymous to illustrate the

Imagine if the people on the left were at a rock concert and those on the right were dressed (or undressed) for an opera. It doesn't work, does it? Every social situation has norms for appropriate attire and conduct.

goal-oriented nature of norms. Losing weight is the principal goal of Overeaters Anonymous groups. Norms help achieve this goal. Members are permitted to talk about food only in general terms (carbohydrates, proteins, and so forth) but not in terms of specific foods (such as candy bars, burgers, or ice cream). The norm is based on the assumption that references to specific foods will induce a craving for those foods and make losing weight more difficult. References to foods in general terms, presumably, will produce no such cravings. Apparently you won't hear the refrigerator calling your name when merely talking about carbohydrates, but mention Ben and Jerry's ice cream and there better be an unobstructed path to the Frigidaire or somebody's going to get trampled.

See Video Clip #8 on CD.

CONFORMING TO NORMS   Group members tend to conform to group norms. **Conformity** is the inclination of group members to think and behave in ways that are consistent with group norms. In a study of bulimia (Crandall, 1988), conformity was found to be a primary element of this eating disorder. Bulimia is a problem in certain social groups such as cheerleader squads, dance troupes, sports teams (e.g., gymnastics), and sororities. These social groups establish norms that promote this binge-and-purge behavior. Instead of seeing bulimia as a bizarre and abnormal practice, the groups studied by Crandall promoted bulimia as a reasonable method of weight control. Group norms even prescribed a preferred rate of binging and purging. Popularity within the groups depended on conforming to this standard.

Box 12-2 | Focus on Controversy

Crying in the Workplace

Members of the Committee on Workplace Conditions are meeting to construct a proposal to present to management for improvement of job-related conditions. The discussion becomes heated and members' anger begins to show. One member begins speaking slowly to the group, chokes back tears, apologizes for this display of emotion, and then succumbs to the intensity of the moment and cries openly.

As this scene was described, did you see an image of a woman or a man crying? What if the crying group member had been a man? Would you make the same assessment of this person as you would if the member were a woman?

Crying in the workplace may seem to be only an unusual, extreme reaction to stress, but it is actually quite common. In a survey of 1,305 workers, *23% reported crying at work* (Girion, 2000). Women far more than men are inclined to tear up or openly cry in the workplace (Domagalski, 1998; Hoover-Dempsey et al., 1986). Crying at work is usually an expression of anger and frustration caused by perceived mistreatment. Domineering, uncivil behavior is the most common reason for tears in the office (Domagalski, 1998). In one study, women indicated that they could imagine themselves shedding tears in the workplace but not yelling, arguing, or "telling someone off" (Hoover-Dempsey et al., 1986). Some of these women said they were ashamed when they cried, others were confused by it, but all of them felt bad about crying at work during and after the episode. Common perceptions of women who cry in the workplace, especially in male-dominated work environments, are that "women are not tough enough" and that "their crying is unprofessional" (Murphy & Zorn, 1996).

Men far more than women express their anger in the workplace with outbursts of yelling, venting, and rage (Domagalski, 1998). Although this is often not condoned, such outbursts may foster the image of a tough, unyielding individual capable of withstanding any pressure to change. Crying in the workplace, however, does a man no good. "Crying in the office may undermine a woman's credibility as a tough professional, but it can destroy a man's reputation on both personal and professional levels" (Murphy & Zorn, 1996, p. 217).

Crying at work is a violation of an implicit norm. As Kathryn Black unequivocally states (1990) in *Working Woman* magazine, "It's [crying] a response that doesn't belong in the office" (p. 88). A person is expected to act differently at work than at home. Crying can interrupt, even halt a meeting at work. People might perceive shedding tears as manipulative—trying to achieve a goal by making others feel uncomfortable (Hoover-Dempsey et al., 1986). Crying in front of coworkers or strangers, especially during group meetings, can leave everyone feeling helpless and uneasy. Group members are usually not prepared to deal with tears and often can't offer much comfort or assistance in a public forum. Crying at home, however, will not be branded as unprofessional behavior. An individual will also likely get greater support and comfort at home than at work when crying. Men can cry at home usually without fear of being labeled "weak" or "too emotional." Norms at home and at work differ.

With an ever-increasing number of women entering the job market, the issue of how to deal with tears in the office and on the job becomes more relevant. Male supervisors report that the mere anticipation of a woman crying causes them great discomfort and induces them to soften criticism or withhold feedback (Murphy & Zorn, 1996). They are unaccustomed to dealing with this nonconformity. Crying is mostly a reflection of anger, as is yelling, slamming doors, and "chewing out" someone. All of these behaviors can be disruptive in the workplace. The advice provided in Chapter 11 on dealing with anger also applies to crying. Domineering, uncivil communication is the usual cause of crying at work. Eliminate or substantially reduce the cause of crying at work, and crying will become a rare issue of concern. Competent communication treats people with respect and thus reduces the need to cry, yell, or pound inanimate objects.

When crying does occur, all parties to the event can choose to ignore it and continue with the group discussion, take a brief break to allow the person shedding tears to regain composure and perhaps receive comfort and support from others in a more private venue, or acknowledge the tears (Black, 1990a, 1990b). The person who cries might say, "I am crying because I'm angry, but I want to continue discussing this issue until it is resolved." Acknowledging the tears while remaining firmly resolved to produce constructive outcomes may eventually lead to a relaxation of the restrictive norm against crying at work.

Questions for Thought

1. Do you agree with Black that crying is always inappropriate in the workplace? Explain your answer.
2. Can you think of any circumstances under which crying at work might be constructive?
3. How should we deal with the stereotype that "real men don't cry" on the job?

Even members who did not initially feel a desire to binge and purge buckled under group pressure and followed the crowd.

Members conform to group norms for two principal reasons: to be right and to be liked (Cialdini & Trost, 1998). We typically do not want to suffer the embarrassment of being wrong in front of our group so we look to the group for information on correct behavior. Conformity can keep lines of communication open. Sources of information are likely to be shared when we conform to group norms. Failure to conform, however, can lead to the severing of informational sources that may be critical to meeting personal goals within the group. We also are inclined to strive for acceptance from our group. We "go along to get along." Social acceptance, support, and friendship are often the rewards for conformity. Nonconformity typically triggers a negative response from the group such as social ostracism, personal attack, or expulsion (Box 12-2).

Group conformity is strongest when cohesiveness is high, when members expect to be in the group for a long time, and when members perceive that they have somewhat lower status in the group. Groups have little leverage against members who are not committed to the group, don't plan on remaining in the group for long, or have high status that gives them "the right" to occasional nonconformity.

Roles

Roles and norms are interconnected. Small group **roles** are patterns of behavior that members are expected to exhibit. The expectation tied to a role is based on a group norm. We expect leaders to guide the group. If they don't, we usually view them as ineffective.

There are two general types of roles: formal and informal. **Formal roles** assign a position. Formal roles are a standard part of the structure of organizations. Titles such as "president," "chair," or "secretary" usually accompany formal roles. Formal roles do not emerge naturally from group transactions; they are assigned. Normally, an explicit description of expected behaviors corresponds to each formal role.

In small groups, roles are mostly informal. **Informal roles** identify functions, not positions. They usually emerge naturally from group transactions. The informal roles a group member plays are identified by observing patterns of communication. If a member often initiates group discussion, the member is playing the role of initiator-contributor. The group does not explicitly tell a member how to play an informal role. Groups do, however, indicate degrees of approval or disapproval when a member assumes an informal role.

Informal roles are generally divided into three types: task, maintenance, and disruptive roles (Benne & Sheats, 1948; Mudrack & Farrell, 1995). Task roles advance the attainment of group goals. The central communicative function of task roles is to extract the optimum productivity from the group. Maintenance roles address the social dimension of small groups. The central communicative function of maintenance roles is to gain and maintain group cohesiveness. Disruptive roles are Me-oriented. They serve individual needs at the expense of group needs and goals. Group members who play these roles often deserve the label "difficult group member"(See Box 12-3). The central communicative function of disruptive roles is to focus attention on the individual.

Because competent communicators recognize the interconnectedness of task and social dimensions of groups, they look for the optimum balance between task and maintenance roles to achieve group success. They also avoid disruptive roles.

Box 12-3   Sharper Focus

Dealing with Difficult Group Members

In one of my small group classes, six women formed a group to work on a class project. Their communication was warm, friendly, and harmonious. They appeared enthusiastic about working together. They brainstormed a long list of ideas for their project and settled on one option within a short period of time. The following class period, a male student needed to join a group because he had missed the previous class. He joined the all-women group because other groups in the class were already somewhat larger. This new group member single-handedly transformed a harmonious, task-effective group into an experience in frustration. This particular individual enjoyed telling sexist jokes, making derogatory remarks to the other members, and fighting any suggestions that were not his own. He proudly (and loudly) proclaimed to the entire class that he was the "leader of a chicks group." He also told his astonished group members that he "hoped PMS wouldn't be a problem" when they worked on their project.

The women were stunned. After class, they all approached me and requested that this disruptive individual be assigned to another group. I turned down their request, not wanting to pass the problem to another group. When I asked what steps they had taken to deal with their difficult group member, they confessed they had taken none. This is not unusual. When faced with a difficult group member, ridding the group of the troublemaker is a common first response. As previously discussed, however, the power-forcing conflict style should be used as a last resort, not a first option.

Difficult group members exhibit a wide variety of troublesome behaviors. Table 12-1 provides a common list of such behaviors. The male student who disrupted the previously all-female group adopted the fighter-controller and clown roles.

The pervasiveness of troublesome group members is significant. A 1991 survey of U.S. employers conducted by the Harris Education Research Council found that 40% of employees do not work cooperatively with fellow employees (cited in Goleman, 1998). Their communication patterns are defensive, not supportive. They are not team players but Me-oriented individualists. They diminish the group performance by disrupting social relationships. Difficult group members can destroy group cohesiveness.

So what should you do about difficult members? You can take several steps (Rothwell, 2001).

1. *Make certain a cooperative climate has been created by the group.* Are communication patterns supportive or defensive? Is meaningful participation encouraged? Are all group members treated with respect? Is there an interdependence of goals and division of labor and resources? Troublesome group members can be a cancer that threatens the health of a group. Problems associated with troublemakers will spread if the group climate is competitive and defensive.

2. *Don't encourage disruptive behavior.* Laughing nervously at a disrupter's offensive "jokes" encourages the antisocial behavior. All six women laughed nervously at the disrupter's sexist jokes and remarks. He became convinced that the women actually appreciated his humor. He had no antenna to pick up fairly obvious signals from his group members that they were offended and embarrassed by his behavior. When all group members filled out a feedback form weeks later, his self-assessment showed that he believed the female group members thought he was funny and liked his humor. He was flabbergasted when all six women wrote on their feedback form that his humor was offensive and disruptive.

   Don't allow the disrupter to dominate conversations, interrupt other members, or in any way intimidate the group. Giving the troublemaker a soapbox only encourages the bad behavior. Simply ask the disrupter to wait his or her turn, respect other members, and listen.

3. *Confront the difficult person directly* (see Chapter 11). If the entire group is upset with the disrupter, the group should confront the troublemaker. Follow the guidelines for supportive communication when confronting a difficult member.

4. *If all else fails, remove the disrupter from the group.* In one study (Larson & LaFasto, 1989) of 75 diverse teams, a very clear message emerged: "There is no longer any room on teams for people who cannot work collaboratively" (p. 71). Ruth Rothstein, who at the time of the study was CEO of Mt. Sinai Hospital in Chicago, summarized this point of view:

   One person who doesn't work well with others can set the team off into oblivion. One person like this can ruin a team. When that happens, you give feedback to [confront] that individual and help them make the necessary changes. But if they can't adapt, then you have an obligation to remove them from the team. Otherwise, the rest of the team can become pretty resentful (p. 71).

If the troublesome group member cannot be removed for some reason, keep interactions with this person to a minimum. No matter what, be

Box 12-3 **Sharper Focus** (continued)

unconditionally constructive. Do not reciprocate the bad behavior of the disrupter. Model constructive communication. If you must remain in a group with a difficult member, imitating the disrupter's troublesome behavior will not improve the situation.

So how did the six women in my class manage their disruptive member? None of them would confront him directly, despite my prompting. All of them, however, remained unconditionally constructive. They eventually stopped laughing nervously at his "jokes," and they refused to be bullied by him. Since there were six of them and only one of him, they managed to silence him on several occasions by ignoring his disruption and focusing on the task, thereby giving him no soapbox and no appreciative audience. They all performed wonderfully during their group presentation to the class. He, on the other hand, embarrassed himself by performing ineptly. Sometimes the most you can hope for is containment, not transformation, of the disrupter.

Table 12-1 identifies some common task, maintenance, and disruptive roles found in small groups (Benne & Sheats, 1948; Mudrack & Farrell, 1995; Rothwell, 2001). This list is not exhaustive.

Assuming appropriate task and maintenance roles during group discussion is a matter of timing. A devil's advocate is not needed during initial discussion. You do not want to kill potentially creative ideas by immediately challenging them. A harmonizer-tension reliever is needed when conflict emerges and threatens to derail the group discussion. It is irrelevant if there is no tension and disharmony. Disruptive roles embody incompetent communication. Deal with those who act out disruptive roles the way you would approach difficult group members.

Role playing is a fluid process. A group member may play several informal roles during a single meeting. Groups usually function better when members exhibit flexibility by playing several roles, depending on what is required to make the group effective. **Role fixation,** in which a member plays a role rigidly with little or no inclination to try other roles, will decrease group effectiveness. The chosen role will be appropriate only some of the time but irrelevant or inappropriate most of the time. Every group needs an energizer, but no group needs an energizer all of the time. Constant cheerleading grows tiresome. If that is the only role a member chooses to play, the member will be mostly an annoyance for the group.

Leadership

Gibb (1969) notes, "Almost every influential thinker from Confucius to Bertrand Russell has attempted some form of analysis of leadership" (p. 205). Scholars, philosophers, social scientists, communication theorists, and even novelists have shown an interest in leadership. The first recorded use of the word *leadership* appeared in writings about political influence in the British Parliament more than 200 years ago. Egyptian hieroglyphics had a symbol for *leader* about 5,000 years ago. As many as 600 books are published each year on leadership. "In fact, over the last twenty years authors have offered up over nine thousand different systems, languages, principles, and paradigms to help explain the mysteries of management and leadership" (Buckingham & Coffman, 1999, p. 53). One communication scholar estimates that nearly 8,000 studies have been published on group leadership (Pavitt, 1999).

Table 12-1 Sample of Informal Roles in Small Groups

Task Roles

1. *Information giver*—provides facts and opinions; offers relevant and significant information based on research, expertise, or personal experience
2. *Information seeker*—asks for facts, opinions, suggestions, and ideas from group members
3. *Initiator-contributor*—provides ideas; suggests actions and solutions to problems; offers direction for the group
4. *Clarifier*—explains ideas; defines the group position on issues; summarizes proceedings of group meetings; raises questions about the direction of group discussion
5. *Elaborator*—expands the ideas of other group members; helps the group visualize how an idea or solution would work if the group implemented it
6. *Coordinator-director*—pulls together the ideas of others; promotes teamwork and cooperation; guides group discussion; breaks group into subgroups to work effectively on tasks; regulates group activity
7. *Energizer*—tries to motivate group to be productive; a task cheerleader
8. *Procedural technician*—performs routine tasks such as taking notes, photocopying, passing out relevant materials for discussion, finding a room to meet in, and signaling when allotted time for discussion of an agenda item has expired
9. *Devil's advocate*—gently challenges prevailing viewpoints in group to test and evaluate the strength of ideas, solutions, and decisions

Maintenance Roles

1. *Supporter-encourager*—offers praise; bolsters the spirits and goodwill of the group; provides warmth and acceptance of others
2. *Harmonizer-tension reliever*—maintains the peace; reduces tension with gentle humor; reconciles differences between group members
3. *Gatekeeper*—controls the channels of communication, keeping the flow of information open or closed depending on the social climate of the group; encourages participation from all group members and open discussion

Disruptive Roles

1. *Stagehog*—recognition seeker; monopolizes discussion and prevents others from expressing their points of view; wants the spotlight
2. *Isolate*—withdraws from group; acts indifferent, aloof, and uninvolved; resists inclusion in group discussion
3. *Fighter-controller*—tries to dominate group; competes mindlessly with group members; abuses those who disagree; picks quarrels, interrupts, and generally attempts to control group proceedings
4. *Blocker*—expresses negative attitude; looks to tear down other members' ideas without substituting constructive alternatives; incessantly reintroduces dead issues
5. *Zealot*—attempts to convert group members to a pet cause or viewpoint; delivers sermons on the state of the world; exhibits fanaticism; won't drop an idea that has been rejected or ignored by group
6. *Clown*—interjects inappropriate humor during discussions and meetings; engages in horseplay; diverts attention from the group task with comic routines

The leader is often thought to be the most important group role. Geier (1967) interviewed 80 U.S. students, males and females, who participated in 16 discussion groups. Seventy-eight of the students said that they would like to be the leader of their group. This is not an unexpected result in an individualist culture in which status associated with the leader role provides an opportunity to enhance one's ranking in the social hierarchy. In this section the role of leader and the exercise of leadership will be discussed.

Definition of Leadership

There are almost as many definitions of *leadership* as there are individuals discussing this role. Most definitions share several components, however (Northouse, 1997; Rothwell, 2001). Leadership is primarily a social influence process. Leaders influence followers, but what kind of influence do leaders exercise? Is it the "ability to inflict pain" on followers, as one corporate executive claimed in a 1980 *Fortune* magazine article? Is this influence "power over other people," which "enables a man to do things, to get things, to accomplish feats that, by himself, are unattainable"? (Fiedler, 1970). Sidestepping the obvious sexism of Fiedler's view, his definition presents leadership as dominance of followers. This is the competitive viewpoint of leadership.

A different viewpoint, consistent with an earlier definition of *communication*, is that leadership is a transactional influence process. This means that the influence is a two-way process negotiated between leader and potential followers. The influence occurs with the "consent of the governed." Leaders influence followers, but followers also influence leaders, making demands on them to meet expectations and evaluating their performance in light of these expectations.

Leadership is also goal oriented. The influence exercised by leaders has to have a purpose. That principal purpose is group goal achievement. This frames leadership as a We-oriented, not a Me-oriented role.

Finally, leadership is fundamentally a communication process. Leadership is exercised and influence is achieved through communication with group members. The communication competence of leaders, therefore, is an important part of leadership.

In summary, the main elements of leadership are that it is an influence process that is transactional, goal-oriented, and dependent on competent communication. A simple definition of leadership can be derived from these elements. **Leadership** is a transactional influence process whose principal purpose is group goal achievement produced by competent communication.

Leader Emergence

In formal groups and organizations, the role of leader is often assigned. In certain cases, it is a formally elected position. In some small groups the leader role is designated (chair of a committee), but in most small groups a leader emerges from group transactions. Emergence of a leader is an important event in the life of a small group. Geier (1967) studied 16 small groups for 4 months. In 5 of these groups a leader did not emerge, and none of these groups was successful in completing tasks and tending to social relationships. All of the groups in which leaders did emerge were successful.

Leader emergence is a process of elimination (Bormann, 1990). Small groups typically know what they don't want in a leader but are less certain about what they do want. The first to be eliminated from consideration for the leader role are quiet, uninformed, seemingly unintelligent and unskilled members. Group members who express strong, unqualified assertions and those perceived to be poor listeners are also quickly eliminated as candidates for the role of leader (Bechler & Johnson, 1995). A second phase of this process of elimination rejects bossy, dictatorial members and individuals with irritating or disturbing communication styles.

If a leader hasn't emerged after these two phases, the group typically looks for a member who provides a solution to a serious problem or helps the group manage a crisis. Members who are perceived to be effective listeners also frequently emerge as leaders during this stage (Johnson & Bechler, 1998). A member may acquire a lieutenant, an advocate who promotes him or her for the leader role. This member will become the leader unless another member acquires a lieutenant. If there are competing lieutenants, a stalemate may ensue and no clear leader will emerge.

Groups expect more from leaders who emerge naturally from group transactions than they do from assigned leaders (Hackman & Johnson, 1996). Emergent leaders are held to a higher standard, and failure is tolerated less because the group has more invested in their chosen leader. How the leader performs reflects well or badly on the group. When an outsider (i.e., supervisor, executive) assigns a leader to a group, gaining credibility with group members may be the biggest hurdle for the leader. Gaining credibility to become leaders and to function effectively as leaders in groups is especially difficult for women and ethnic minorities (see Box 12-4).

Effective Leadership

Emerging as leader of a group and exercising effective leadership may be distinctly different processes. Emergent leaders aren't always effective leaders. In this section, several perspectives on leadership effectiveness will be discussed.

TRAITS PERSPECTIVE   Do you have the "right stuff" to be an effective leader in small groups? That is the core question of the traits approach to leadership. This is the "leaders are born, not made" perspective. The first systematic scientific investigations of leadership looked for a list of traits that distinguish leaders from followers. **Traits** are relatively enduring and distinctive characteristics of a person that are displayed in most situations. There are physical traits such as height, weight, physical shape, physique, and beauty or attractiveness. There are personality traits such as being outgoing or sociable. There are traits associated with inherent capabilities such as intelligence and quick-wittedness. There are traits associated with consistent behaviors such as integrity, trustworthiness, and confidence.

Hundreds of studies have generated separate lists of traits that characterize leaders (see Northouse, 1997). Tall, attractive individuals seem to have an advantage in becoming leaders. Charisma, a constellation of traits that a group finds attractive in a leader, is often thought to be an essential quality for an effective leader.

Several problems with the trait perspective, however, make it only marginally insightful. First, certain negative traits can predict who will not become leader, but positive traits don't permit accurate predictions regarding who is likely to emerge as leader and exhibit effective leadership. Tall, attractive individuals may have an advantage over short, unattractive individuals in a competition for leader emergence. Nevertheless, this doesn't explain why Bill Gates is the richest person in the world and runs the powerful Microsoft Corporation. Diminutive Barbara Boxer and Barbara Mikulski became U.S. senators. Ross Perot, twice a serious candidate for

Box 12-4 | Focus on Controversy

Gender and Ethnicity: The Glass Ceiling and the Brick Wall

Group bias against women and ethnic minorities is still an issue in leader emergence. Groups tend to favor white men when selecting and evaluating leaders (Forsyth et al., 1997; Shackelford et al., 1996). This bias in choosing group leaders occurs despite impressive evidence that women and men exhibit equivalent leadership effectiveness (Eagly et al., 1995), and one study showed that African Americans (male and female) were perceived to have more leadership ability than Whites (Craig & Rand, 1998).

Significant gains have been made in women's rise to positions of leadership in the workplace. Women held 15.7% of the 13,673 corporate officer positions in Fortune 500 companies in 2002, an increase from 8.7% in 1995 (Files, 2002). Almost half (49%) of all managerial and professional positions in the United States are held by women (White, 2002). Almost 11 million women are paid more than their male spouses. That's one in three wives who outearn their husbands (Avila, 2001). Nevertheless, the **glass ceiling,** an invisible barrier of subtle discrimination that excludes women from top leadership positions in corporate and professional America, remains. Women occupy only 24% of senior management positions in U.S. government service (Kampeas, 2001). As of the end of 2002, only 6 women were CEOs for the 500 largest companies in the United States (Files, 2002). Once women do climb to the highest levels of corporate America, the pay disparity between male and female executives is stark. Female senior executives earn, on average, only 67 cents for every $1 paid to male senior executives (Armas, 2000).

Although the "common wisdom" is that men are the main impediment to female advancement into leadership positions, this may not be entirely true. Since 1975, periodic Gallup polls have consistently shown that men accept female bosses more readily than do women (Moore, 2002). In fact, a 2002 Gallup poll showed the smallest male-female gap since 1975. When asked to state either a preference for a male or female boss or to indicate no preference (either is equally acceptable), 70% of male respondents and 66% of female respondents either preferred female bosses or had no preference (Moore 2002). Stating a preference in a survey, however, and actually working well with a female boss may be quite different. Although women have made gratifying advances in the workplace, in the competitive work environment women will continue to have difficulty shattering the glass ceiling for some time to come.

The situation for ethnic minorities gaining important leadership positions is not very encouraging. In 2001, African Americans occupied only 7.1% of senior management positions in the federal government, and Hispanic Americans occupied a mere 3.1% of such positions. This is actually a better record than that in the private sector, which hires far fewer minorities for senior management positions (Kampeas, 2001). Only three African American males were CEOs of Fortune 500 companies in 2001 (Rethinking Black Leadership, 2001). Although there is virtually no pay disparity between African American males and White males in lower status jobs, as jobs become more prestigious (doctors, lawyers, managers), a large pay disparity emerges. Black men in the better occupations earn as little as 72 cents for every $1 earned by white men in the same occupation (Tran, 2001). Asian Americans, despite their phenomenal success in scientific and technical fields, are less likely than Whites or African Americans to rise to positions of leadership in those prestigious fields (Tang, 1997). Female ethnic minorities face the toughest time emerging as leaders because they face a double bias. Their predicament is closer to a "brick wall" than a glass ceiling (Smith, 1997). There were no African American female CEOs of Fortune 500 companies in 2002. Only 163 ethnic minority women, or 1.6% of the total, were corporate officers in Fortune 500 companies in 2002. Of the 163 women, 106 were African American, 25 were Hispanic, and 30 were Asian (Files, 2002).

Any approach to reducing gender and ethnic bias in leader emergence is best aimed at empowering all members in a group so each has a greater chance of being chosen group leader. A competitive power struggle for leadership is unlikely to prove successful for women and minorities who are often badly outnumbered at the outset.

Women and ethnic minorities can improve their chances of emerging as group leaders in several ways (Rothwell, 2001):

1. *Increase the proportion of women and ethnic minorities in groups* (Shimanoff & Jenkins, 1996). This is known as the Twenty Percent Rule (Pettigrew & Martin, 1987). Discrimination decreases when at least 20% of group membership is composed of women or minorities. Flying solo is the most difficult position for women and minorities (Taps & Martin, 1990). Being the only woman or minority in a group can brand a person as a "token," thus diminishing his or her chance of emerging as leader. In some circumstances, increasing the representation of women and ethnic minorities may require a power-forcing style as a last resort to produce change, but at the outset it may be merely a matter of sensitizing the group to the need for greater diversity in membership.

BOX 12-4 | Focus on Controversy (continued)

2. *Encourage mingling and interaction among members before choosing a leader.* Getting to know group members while working on a project puts the emphasis on individual performance instead of gender and ethnicity (Haslett, 1992).
3. *Emphasize task-relevant communication during group discussions.* Play task roles. This can be empowering. Task-oriented female group members are as likely to become small group leaders as are task-oriented male group members (Hawkins, 1995). This suggestion applies primarily to work groups. Support groups may prefer a more social-oriented leader.
4. *Women and minorities should be among the first to speak in the group, and they should speak often* (Shimanoff & Jenkins, 1996). In the United States leaders are expected to speak often and to initiate conversation in groups. One study of all-male groups (Kelsey, 1998) found that "token" White males (one White male, three Chinese males) were judged to be leaders in every instance, whereas "token" Chinese males (one Chinese male, three White males) were never seen as leaders. The key factor was not ethnicity, however,

but degree of participation. Token White males spoke much more often and longer than did the majority Chinese males in every instance. Speaking first and often marks a person as leadership material in U.S. culture.
5. *Hone communication skills and become a competent communicator* (Hackman & Johnson, 1996). Communication is the core of leadership, and communication skills are empowering. The best communicators have the best chance of emerging as group leaders.

Questions for Thought

1. Have you experienced discrimination in small groups that prevented you from emerging as leader? Discuss the ethics of this discrimination.
2. Will men easily accept greater representation of women and ethnic minorities in groups? Explain.
3. Can power struggles for leader emergence be avoided by the steps suggested, or do you think they are inevitable?

president of the United States and a billionaire businessman, is often described as "jug-eared" and "squeaky-voiced." Fellow Texan Molly Ivins (1992), a columnist, described Perot as "a seriously short guy who sounds like a Chihuahua" (p. 38). Who would have predicted on the basis of traits alone that Jesse "The Body" Ventura would become governor of Minnesota in the 1998 election? As one pundit described him, "He's a shaved-head, muscle-bound, ex-pro wrestler with the voice of a carnival barker" (Thomas, 1998, p. P3). Garrison Keillor, host of the public radio program "A Prairie Home Companion," gives an even less flattering description: Ventura is "this great big honking bullet-headed shovel-faced mutha who talks in a steroid growl and doesn't stop" (cited in Ventura, 1999, p. A2). Traits aren't very accurate predictors of leader emergence and effective leadership.

Second, traits may cancel each other. Physical attractiveness and sociability may be outweighed by lack of integrity. Intolerance may cancel charisma. How does one predict which traits will be most important with which group? Researchers can't even agree on which traits are universal attributes for all effective leaders (Northouse, 1997).

Third, certain traits may be necessary but not sufficient for emerging as an effective leader. Fiedler and House (1988) claim that "effective leaders tend to have a high need to influence others, achieve, and they tend to be bright, competent, and socially adept, rather than stupid, incompetent, and social disasters" (p. 87). Intelligence, social and verbal skills, integrity, sense of humor, confidence, or other traits may influence a group. Such traits, however, are not sufficient for effective leadership. Why?

The trait perspective on leadership explains very little. What do Jesse Ventura, former governor of Minnesota, and Condoleeza Rice, George W. Bush's national security advisor, have in common that would explain their leadership? Certainly not looks, personality, gender, ethnicity, education, physical size, vocal quality, or a host of other traits.

Because *leadership is not a person; it's a transactional process* (Hollander, 1985). A leader must have followers. Labeling the traits of an individual as characteristic of leadership when there is no followership "is no more leadership than the behavior of small boys marching in front of a parade, who continue to strut along Main Street after the procession has turned down a side street toward the fairgrounds" (Burns, 1978, p. 427).

If a person possesses requisite leadership traits, why doesn't he or she become an effective leader in all groups? Ross Perot and Steve Forbes tried to translate their leadership in business to the political arena. Both were unsuccessful presidential candidates. Traits that prove effective in one context may prove to be ineffective in other arenas. The trait perspective is too limited in scope to explain much about leadership effectiveness.

STYLES PERSPECTIVE   There are two principal leadership styles. The **directive style,** originally called *autocratic,* puts heavy emphasis on the task dimension with slight attention to the social dimension of groups. Member participation is not encouraged. Directive style exhibits an imbalance of power. Directive leaders assume that they have greater power than other group members. Such leaders tell members what to do, and they expect compliance. The **participative style,** originally called *democratic,* places emphasis on both the task and social dimensions of groups. Task accomplishment is important, but social relationships must also be maintained. Unlike the directive style, which uses the dominance form of power, the participative style is empowering. Group members are encouraged to participate meaningfully in discussions and decision-making. Participative leaders work to improve the skills and abilities of all group members.

Initially, researchers thought the participative style would prove to be superior. Research results, however, have been mixed (Gastil, 1994). Both directive and participative leadership styles can be productive. Although the participative style fosters more member satisfaction than does the directive style (Van Oostrum & Rabbie, 1995), the difference is neither large nor uniform (Gastil, 1994). Some groups don't want their leaders to be participative. The military wouldn't function effectively if every soldier got to vote on the wisdom of a military action: "All those in favor of attacking the heavily armed enemy on the ridge signal by saying aye; those opposed, nay. Okay, the nays have it."

High power-distance cultures tend to expect and prefer the directive leadership style (Brislin, 1993). In such cultures, the participative style may not work as well as the directive style. The directive style also tends to be more effective when groups face stressful circumstances or time constraints, whereas the participative style is usually more effective in nonstressful situations (Rosenbaum & Rosenbaum, 1985). These research results indicate that effectiveness of leadership style depends on the situation.

SITUATIONAL PERSPECTIVE   No single style of leadership will be suitable for all situations. Thus, effective leadership is contingent on adopting the style appropriate for each situation. The Hersey and Blanchard situational leadership model is one of the most widely recognized approaches to leadership effectiveness (Hersey & Blanchard, 1988). Hersey and Blanchard have subdivided the directive and participative leadership styles into four types: telling, selling, participating, and delegating. As Figure 12-2 indicates, the telling style emphasizes task, the selling style emphasizes

FIGURE 12-2 Situational Leadership Model: The Telling (S1), Selling (S2), Participating (S3), and Delegating (S4) leadership styles related. (Source: Situational Leadership is a registered trademark of the Center for Leadership Studies, Inc. Reprinted with permission. All rights reserved.)

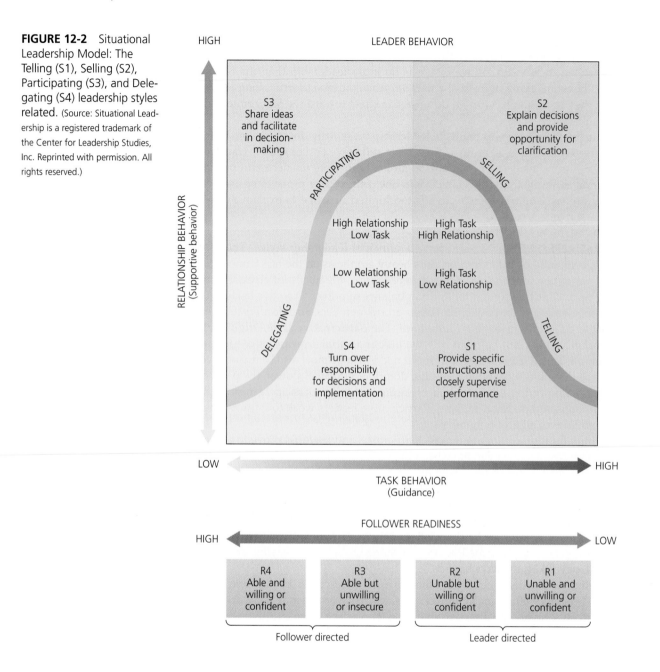

both task and relationships, the participating style emphasizes relationships, and the delegating style has little focus on either task or social dimensions of groups. The key situational variable that every leader must consider in determining which style is appropriate is the readiness level of followers. **Readiness** is composed of the ability of group members, their motivation, and their experience with relevant tasks. Lots of experience and strong motivation to accomplish a task aren't enough if a member's ability is poor. Likewise, substantial ability and experience don't compensate for weak motivation.

When the readiness level of followers is low, the telling and selling styles are most appropriate. As readiness levels increase, effective leaders choose the participative and delegating styles. When someone is hired for a job, for example, effective leaders begin diagnosing the readiness level of the employee. Readiness levels vary from R1 (unable, unwilling, and lacking confidence) to R4 (able, willing, and confident). Normally, a person at the R1 level would not be hired. Who would want someone of this caliber? Thus, the telling style would mostly be used with an employee whose readiness level falters because of stress, personal trauma, or technological advances beyond the employee's abilities. Using the telling style with an able worker would seem like micromanaging. The selling style requires interaction between leader and follower. This style would normally be used with a new employee as the supervisor and the employee begin to establish a relationship. With greater readiness comes a further shift in leadership style. The participating style is appropriate for the worker who now knows the ropes and has sufficient readiness to offer suggestions and engage in decision making. Finally, when the readiness level is high, an effective leader steps out of the way and delegates responsibility and decision making to the worker.

Although the research to support this perspective is somewhat skimpy (Northouse, 1997), the situational leadership perspective makes intuitive sense. One leadership style does not fit all situations. An effective leader matches the style with the readiness level of followers and the group as a whole. Newly formed groups require greater supervision and direction than experienced groups. Experienced, capable groups work best when leaders are "guides on the side." They offer relational support and encouragement but allow the group to perform its task without much interference. Leaders can become more directive (telling or selling) if groups or individual members slip in their readiness levels because of stressful events or personal difficulties. This means that leaders should be sensitive to signals from group members that readiness levels have diminished and that a different style of leadership is required.

COMMUNICATION COMPETENCE PERSPECTIVE   Other leadership perspectives offer useful insights about leadership effectiveness. Effective leadership, however, is ultimately a matter of communication competence. No set of traits, particular styles, or matching of styles with situational readiness will be effective without competent communication. The most effective leaders are the most proficient communicators. As Hackman and Johnson (1996) conclude, "Extraordinary leadership is the product of extraordinary communication" (p. 81).

The We-orientation of the communication competence model is crucial for leadership effectiveness. Larson and LaFasto (1989) studied 75 highly diverse teams (e.g., mountain climbing, cardiac surgery, and professional football teams). Their conclusion was unequivocal: "The most effective leaders . . . were those who subjugated their ego needs in favor of the team's goal" (p. 128). Bennis and Nanus (1985) interviewed 90 successful leaders from a broad range of environments and concluded that "there was no trace of self-worship or cockiness" among these leaders (p. 57). Effective leaders try to empower group members, not stand out as dominant and deserving of adoration or blind obedience. Garfield (1986) interviewed more than 500 top leaders and concluded that they use three primary skills: delegating, stretching the abilities of team members, and encouraging thoughtful risk taking. All three skills empower group members. As Larson and LaFasto (1989) concluded, "leaders create leaders" (p. 128).

Box 12-5 Sharper Focus

"Chainsaw Al" Dunlap and Aaron Feuerstein: The Challenge of Ethical Leadership

He wrote a self-promoting book entitled *Mean Business*. He developed a reputation for coldheartedness. As CNN financial correspondent Peter Viles observed in a December 8, 1998, report, "If one man symbolized the ruthless restructuring trend of the 1990s, it was Al Dunlap, known as the pit bull who would attack any cost, lay off any unit in order to protect shareholder value" (cited in Fields, 1998). Dunlap's slash-and-burn approach to management earned him several unflattering labels including "Rambo in Pinstripes" and "Chainsaw Al."

Albert Dunlap is a notorious CEO whose standard approach to "turning around" a faltering company includes slashing costs by "downsizing," increasing stock values, and selling off the remaining carcass (Fields, 1998). In the process, thousands of workers lose their jobs. Dunlap slashed 18,000 jobs at Scott Paper Company and cut more than half of the 12,000 employees at Sunbeam. His 3-year, $70 million contract with Sunbeam prompted him to brag, "You can't overpay a great executive. . . . Don't you think I'm a bargain?" In his book, Dunlap has this to say about workers who lose their jobs from his downsizing strategy: "Those whose jobs will be eliminated in a restructuring should still consider the outcome philosophically and have enough confidence in themselves to know they will have opportunities somewhere else. A company is not your high school or college alma mater. Don't get emotional about it" (Dunlap, 1997, p. 272). Those are the only consoling words from the multimillionaire CEO. "Don't get emotional," he tells displaced workers who must figure out how to support their families after their abrupt termination of employment.

Once the darling of stockholders who were anxious to avoid a financial disaster, Dunlap was fired in June 1998 as CEO of Sunbeam, maker of appliances. His trademark downsizing strategy didn't work at Sunbeam (Sloan, 1998). Stock value initially shot up and then faltered. The company continued to lose money, and directors lost faith in Dunlap's methods. The remaining employees at Sunbeam reportedly cheered when they heard the news that Dunlap was fired.

Aaron Feuerstein is a boss of a completely different sort. Given the Lincoln Award for Ethics in Business in 1997, Feuerstein, the 70-year-old owner of a textile company, Malden Mills, in Lawrence, Massachusetts, saw his business gutted by a fire in 1995. His family, board of directors, and other executives advised him to collect the insurance money and forget about his mill. Feuerstein ignored their advice. He maintained his entire workforce of 2,400 employees on his payroll while the mill was rebuilt. It cost him $1.5 million per week. Demonstrating an extraordinary sense of ethical responsibility, Feuerstein believed that if he closed his mill for good, the city of Lawrence would die with it. "I wasn't going to be the guy to finish it off. We have a responsibility to our community. Keeping the mill open helps to keep the town alive" (as cited in Amparano, 1997, p. E3). Feuerstein chose not to downsize. His reward was loyalty and commitment from the workers whose jobs were saved. Before the fire, workers produced, on average, 130,000 yards of fabric each week. When the mill reopened, workers produced 200,000 yards of fabric per week. Ethical, compassionate leadership is good business.

Competent communication is critical to effective leadership because groups are affected enormously by the leader. A leader sets the emotional tone of the group. Top executives who fail as leaders exhibit insensitivity to others, are brutally critical, and are too demanding (Goleman, 1998).

As the young leader of the team that developed the Apple Macintosh computer in the early 1980s, Steve Jobs was less than sensitive to team members. He was noted for what was dubbed by team members "management by walking around." Jobs would appear without warning, walk around and look at members' work, and then make caustic criticisms. His favorite critique was, "This sucks!" (Bennis & Biederman, 1997). Jobs' youth and immature leadership style prompted the joke "What's the difference between Apple and the Boy Scouts?" Answer: "The Boy Scouts have adult supervision" (cited in Bennis & Biederman, 1997, p. 81).

When a leader expresses rage, shows disrespect for members, berates those who make mistakes, humiliates members in front of the group, and exhibits arrogance and pettiness, the entire group is tarnished by this incompetent communication (Goleman, 1998). Such emotional outbursts and insensitivity ripple throughout the group. Birgitta Wistrand calls it "emotional incontinence" (see Goleman, 1998). When leaders fail to control themselves emotionally, members become hesitant, anxious, fearful, angry, and depressed. Box 12-5 provides a comparison of two leaders, one who showed coldheartedness, and another who exhibited extraordinary sensitivity and kindheartedness.

Effective leaders create a supportive climate, encourage open communication, stimulate cooperation and a collaborative spirit, show empathy, and express optimism and a positive attitude (Goleman, 1998). "Going thermonuclear" is not an option for an effective leader. Effective leaders adapt to changing circumstances and a variety of styles and personalities.

Summary

Grouphate is a prevailing problem. Communication competence is central to our attitude about groups. Those who have little communication training typically find the group experience daunting and frustrating. Those who learn to communicate competently typically find the group experience far more positive.

Many benefits can be derived from working effectively in groups. Members can pool information and knowledge to produce better decisions. Groups can tackle broad-range, complex problems that would overwhelm a person working alone. Groups can empower members and produce synergy. The main disadvantages of groups—factionalism, scheduling conflicts, negative synergy, social loafing, and wasted time in meetings—are all correctable once there is an appreciation and understanding of how effective groups function.

The structure of small groups is composed primarily of norms and roles. Norms are rules that govern the behavior of group members. Roles are patterns of behavior that group members are expected to exhibit. The leader role is central to group structure. Playing the role of leader, however, does not equate with effective leadership. Effective leadership is not a person; it is a transactional process. Effective leadership requires competent communication. Leaders should be sensitive to the changing needs and situations within the group, assume the appropriate style for a given situation, and resist displays of competitive, defensive communication when dealing with group members.

Quizzes Without Consequences

Go to Quizzes Without Consequences at the book's Online Learning Center at **www.mhhe.com/rothwell2** or access the CD-ROM for *In the Company of Others.*

**www.mhhe
.com/
rothwell2**

Key Terms

See Audio Flashcards
Study Aid.

www.mhhe
● com/
/ **rothwell2**
See Crossword Puzzle
Study Aid.

cohesiveness	implicit norms	readiness
conformity	informal roles	role fixation roles
directive style	leadership	social dimension
explicit norms	negative synergy	social loafing
formal roles	norms	synergy
glass ceiling	participative style	task dimension
group	productivity	traits

Suggested Readings

Abramson, J. (1994). *We, the jury: The jury system and the ideal of democracy*. New York: Basic Books. This is the best single work on one of the most important small groups in our society—the jury.

Adams, Richard. (1972). *Watership Down*. New York: Avon. Adams has written an allegorical story about rabbits, but it is so much more than this. All the elements that constitute small groups are contained in this highly entertaining novel.

Burns, J. (1978). *Leadership*. New York: Harper & Row. This is an excellent general work on leadership in the political arena.

Singer, M. (1995). *Cults in our midst: The hidden menace in our everyday lives*. San Francisco: Jossey-Bass. Singer discusses small groups gone wrong.

Film School

The Great Santini (1980). PG rated
This film is an exceptional example of role fixation and what it can do to a family. The main character, Bull Meechum (Robert Duvall), treats his family members like military recruits.

A League of Their Own (1992). Comedy/Drama; PG ★★★↗
Director Penny Marshall's amusing and engaging treatment of the first women's professional baseball league is highly entertaining. Analyze leadership styles, especially those used by the Tom Hanks character. Does he change leadership styles as the movie progresses?

Pleasantville (1998). Comedy/Drama; PG ★★★★★
The two main characters (played by Tobey Maguire and Reese Witherspoon) are zapped into the black-and-white world of the 1950s. This is a trippy little movie with a nice message. Analyze the impact of norms on behavior and the reactions to nonconformity.

Twelve Angry Men (1957 or 1997). Drama; PG-13 ★★★★★
Either version of this film is terrific. This is the classic jury movie, copied many times but never equaled. Examine the pros and cons of groups by analyzing the communication of jury members.

CHAPTER 13

Teambuilding and Teamwork in Small Groups and Organizations

On March 27, 1977, a Dutch KLM 747 aircraft (flight 4805) crashed into a Pan American 747 (flight 1736) shortly after takeoff at the Tenerife airport in the Canary Islands. Of the 614 passengers, 583 were killed in the crash, the worst commercial airline disaster in history. Numerous small mistakes accounted for the crash, but overall there was a serious lack of teamwork among crew members on the KLM flight. Weick (1990) observed that "the KLM crew acted less like a team than like three individuals acting in parallel" (p. 580).

Following a series of airline mishaps, the Federal Aviation Administration investigated Delta Airlines in 1987. The FAA's report stated, "There is no evidence that Delta's crews are (on the whole) either unprofessional or purposefully negligent. Rather, it was observed that crew members are frequently acting as individuals rather than as members of a smoothly functioning team" (cited in Whitkin, 1987). About 80% of airline crashes result from poor communication and lack of effective teamwork among crews (Goleman, 1995). Technical proficiency of crews is insufficient to prevent disasters. Crew training now emphasizes teamwork and cooperation as an equally important aspect of crew effectiveness.

Developing effective teams is an important concern for all of us, not just for those who hop on an airplane and brave the sometimes not-so-friendly skies. Most of us have our first exposure to teams from early participation in sports. Basketball, baseball, softball, football, ice hockey, field hockey, and soccer provide common experiences with teams for millions of girls and boys, women and men, every year. In addition, theater productions in high school and college require team effort, as do fund-raising activities to support college clubs and service groups. Also, group projects in college classes are most successful when approached from a team perspective.

Perhaps our most important and long-term exposure to teams, however, occurs in the workplace. "Today's business environment is so complex and in such a continual state of change that success often depends on the outputs of teams or work groups rather than the efforts of a single person" (McCann & Margerison, 1996, p. 50). A national survey of 750 top U.S. companies found that 71.4% of respondents listed "ability to work in teams" as an essential employment qualification (cited in DuBois, 1992). The Center for Creative Leadership conducted a study of top U.S. and European executives whose careers went sour. They found that the inability to build and lead teams was the common reason for executive failure (Spencer & Spencer, 1993).

Every team is a group, but not every group is a team (Hackman & Johnson, 2000). There are three primary distinctions between small groups and teams. First, teams commonly exhibit a higher level of cooperation and cohesiveness than standard groups. Teams are inherently We-oriented. Each member develops skills "for the good of the team." A forward may have to switch to playing center to help his or her basketball team, even though this may mean scoring fewer individual points. Teams may function within a competitive, intergroup environment, but to be successful they depend on intragroup cooperation. Second, teams normally consist of individuals with more diverse skills. Not everyone can be a goalie in soccer or a pitcher in baseball. A team requires complementary, not identical, skills. Third, teams usually have a stronger group identity. Teams see themselves as an identifiable unit with a common mission. Thus, a **team** is "a small number of people with complementary skills who are equally committed to a common purpose, goals, and working approach for which they hold themselves mutually accountable" (Katzenbach & Smith, 1993b, p. 45).

Boards of directors, standing committees, student and faculty senates, and similar groups are not usually teams. These groups often lack cohesiveness and cooperation, and group members may have similar rather than diverse skills. Members are asked to attend periodic meetings at which discussion occurs and an occasional vote is taken, but members do not have to work together. In fact, contact with fellow members may never take place except indirectly and formally during meetings.

Some groups may pit members against each other, thwarting the possibility of teamwork. The House Judiciary Committee in 1998 sent four articles of impeachment against President Bill Clinton to the full House for a vote. Members of the Judiciary Committee voted along party lines—every Republican voted for impeachment, every Democrat voted against. This committee clearly was not a team. Members did not work together to accomplish a common goal; in fact, the two parties seemed to pursue contradictory goals. There was little cooperation exhibited throughout the proceedings and less cohesiveness. Committee members acted as adversaries, not team members.

Although some groups are not and will never become teams, most groups can profit from acting more teamlike. The more teamlike small groups become, the more likely they will function effectively. Teams embody a central theme of this text—that cooperation in human communication arenas has distinct advantages. These benefits of cooperation should be exploited far more than occurs at present. Thus, *the principal purpose of this chapter is to examine ways to build teams and promote teamwork with competent communication.*

There are two chapter objectives:

1. to explore constructive ways to build the structure of teams, and
2. to explain how to develop teamwork in small groups by managing team conflict, engaging in creative problem solving, and avoiding groupthink.

> The principal purpose of this chapter is to examine ways to build teams and promote teamwork with competent communication.

Teambuilding

Teams share a common structure. Building a team means building that structure. In this section the specific structure necessary to build effective teams will be explored.

Establishing Goals

Teambuilding begins with goal setting (LaFasto & Larson, 2001). A team needs a purpose, and goals provide that focus. Goals should be clear, challenging, and cooperative.

CLEAR GOALS   An ancient Chinese proverb states, "If you don't know where you are going, then any road will take you there." Groups that have no particular focus drift aimlessly. They achieve little because little is planned. Without exception, every effectively functioning team studied by Larson and LaFasto (1989) had clear, identifiable goals, and members had a clear understanding of those goals. Vague goals such as "do our best" or "make improvements" provide no clear direction. "Complete the study of traffic congestion on campus by the end of the term" or "raise $100,000 in donations for a campus child care center within one year" are clear, specific goals. For a group to become a team, clearly focused goals are essential.

Romig (1996) found one department in an organization had developed 60 goals to achieve in a single year. This department accomplished none of its goals but threatened the future of the entire organization by throwing huge sums of money aimlessly in all directions. Too many goals can diffuse effort and scatter group members. A few clear goals are preferable. Each member should be able to recite from memory the primary goals of the team. All team members must have a shared mission and a common vision. *Goals for a team work best when they are clearly stated and limited in number.*

CHALLENGING GOALS   Accomplishing the trivial motivates no one. Groups need challenging goals to spur interest among members. Challenging goals can stretch the limits of group members' physical or mental abilities. Problems never faced nor solved present a challenge. Finding solutions to problems when time is short and the need is urgent can also challenge a group. Groups are elevated to teams when they see their mission as important, meaningful, and beyond the ordinary.

The team that developed the original Macintosh computer had this elevated sense of purpose. Randy Wigginton, a team member, puts it this way: "We believed we were on a mission from God" (cited in Bennis & Biederman, 1997, p. 83). Steve Jobs, the team leader, promised team members that they were going to build a computer that would "put a dent in the universe" (p. 80).

COOPERATIVE GOALS   In individualist cultures such as the United States, the cooperative aspects of teambuilding are a bit more challenging than in collectivist cultures such as those of Singapore, China, and Malaysia. Competitive goal structures abound in the United States. Developing cooperative goal structures can seem perplexing initially.

There are several elements that compose cooperative goals (see Box 13-1). First, cooperative goals require interdependent effort from group members. This is achieved by all members working together in a coordinated fashion.

Second, cooperative goals necessitate a We-orientation. A study at Cambridge University of 120 teams found that assembling highly intelligent team members didn't produce stellar results (Belbin, 1996). High-IQ members were intensely competitive. Instead of working together, they exercised their intellectual abilities by striving to impress each other with their brilliance. Each member's individual status became more important than any group goal. Teams composed of members with more ordinary intellectual abilities outperformed the high-IQ teams. They exhibited a We-orientation by putting personal agendas aside for the sake of team goals. The result was synergy. The most common complaint registered in the Larson and LaFasto (1989) study of teams was that some team members were self-oriented, not team oriented. Putting personal goals ahead of team goals weakens group resolve and diminishes cohesiveness. Teams need unified commitment from all members. "The essence of a team is common commitment. Without it, groups perform as individuals; with it they become a powerful unit of collective performance" (Katzenbach & Smith, 1993a). Those members who do not demonstrate sufficient

Box 13-1   Sharper Focus

The U.S. Women's Olympic Basketball Team

The crowd of 32,987 in Atlanta was on its feet cheering wildly as the final seconds ticked away. The U.S. women's basketball team had soundly defeated its longtime nemesis, Brazil, for the gold medal in the 1996 Olympic games. Brazil, a powerful team that had humbled previous U.S. teams in the 1991 Pan America games, the 1992 Olympics, and the 1994 world championships, was no match for the smooth teamwork of the U.S. women. The final score was 111–87. The U.S. total was the most points ever scored by a women's basketball team in the Olympics.

The U.S. women's success was achieved primarily by establishing cooperative goals from the outset. Sportswriter Ann Killion (1996) summed it up when she attributed the U.S. women's success to "setting [their] sights on a goal and working for it [and] sacrificing one's self for the team" (p. D1). Tara VanDerveer, the U.S. women's basketball coach, explained her team's success this way: "There's a stereotype that women can't work together. What makes this special is that people had a team agenda. They weren't individuals. This team put the gold medal as their mission" (Killion, 1996, p. D3).

The road to the gold medal was long and difficult. The team traveled 100,000 miles during the year prior to the Olympic games to play international powerhouse teams such as China and Russia. Players endured intensive physical training. They participated in a teambuilding experiment in Colorado Springs. Players and coaches walked on parallel cables 30 feet above ground as the cables gradually split wider apart and participants were forced to rely on each other to keep from falling. As a result of a carefully constructed teambuilding effort, the women's team won all 52 preparation games and then scored wins in all 8 Olympic contests for a perfect 60–0 record.

The 1996 U.S. women's basketball team set a clear, focused, challenging goal for itself. Players wanted to win the Olympic gold medal. To achieve this overriding goal, they set cooperative goals such as putting the team above individual stardom and glory and committing themselves to a full year of training and preparation to achieve their mission. In the process, these capable women demonstrated that, even in the intensely competitive arena of international sports, success requires substantial cooperation.

---

commitment and effort necessitate the use of suggestions for dealing with social loafers and difficult group members (Chapter 12).

Third, goals established by team members, not imposed by outsiders or a team leader, usually gain greater commitment (Romig, 1996). Cooperative goals are the product of member participation. It is very difficult for members to get excited about goals foisted on them. If members have little say in determining team goals, they may have little interest in or commitment to those goals.

Developing a Team Identity

James Carville, chief strategist for Bill Clinton's 1992 presidential campaign, knew how to create a team identity. Self-described as the "Ragin' Cajun" from Louisiana, Carville ran the "War Room" team. The team name was Hillary Rodham Clinton's idea, and it gave the team an instant identification.

The War Room was the political nerve center of the Clinton campaign. Located in Little Rock, Arkansas, the team responded to every perceived threat, every attack from the Bush campaign, every stumble or miscue by Clinton with lightning speed. As Carville put it, "You create a campaign culture, and ours was based on speed" (cited in Bennis & Biederman, 1997, p. 93).

The War Room team's identity combined speed with informality. The T-shirt was part of the War Roomers' uniform. Carville liked wearing one that read, "Speed kills . . . Bush." He also wore ragged jeans with holes. There was a constant air of immediacy and high drama. Team members ran to copy machines, they didn't walk. Carville promoted a 24-hour-a-day sense of urgency. Like him or hate him, and he does have vociferous detractors, Carville unquestionably built a remarkably effective team.

Group identity is an important part of building a team. There isn't a single way to do this. Often team identity is fostered by a uniform or style of dress common to team members. A team name is not essential, but it helps. An identifiable style of behaving, such as the War Room's focus on speed, also creates an identity, especially if the style is different from other groups. Offering awards and prizes for team accomplishments, creating rituals and ceremonies unique to the group, establishing a clearly identifiable space that belongs to the team, and sometimes creating an air of secrecy all contribute to team identity. Every team will create its own identity in its own way. Part of being an effective team, however, is building that identity early in the group's life.

Designating Clear Roles

Roles emerge informally in most small groups, but teams require greater structure than groups in general. Group members won't function as a team if they are uncertain of the roles they are supposed to play. A team of lawyers will divide the responsibilities among members. One lawyer may be the chief researcher (information giver). Another may write the legal briefs (clarifier-elaborator). A third may challenge the briefs to find flaws in the arguments (devil's advocate), and a fourth lawyer might direct the entire team (leader). In each case team members are given specific responsibilities befitting their talents, experience, and expertise. The team leader often makes this assignment of roles, but in some cases team members will volunteer to play specific roles.

Poor role clarity can produce confusion, duplication of effort, and overall weak group performance. Team members need to demonstrate coordinated activity to be successful. Clear designation of roles can produce high performance. Dr. Don Wukasch, a respected open-heart surgeon, describes what happened when a hurricane hit the Texas Heart Institute while his surgical team was performing a heart operation:

> A hurricane again—the power went out, and the patient was on the heart-lung machine. When the power goes off, the heart-lung machine goes off. You have about a minute or two before the patient starts to die. I didn't know we had them, but there are hand cranks under each heart-lung machine. The team started cranking, and within 15 seconds we were going at normal. Here again, no panic, just a smooth operation. That's real professionalism. That's a high-performance team (cited in Larson & LaFasto, 1989, p. 54).

Each member of the surgical team played his or her part in the performance of a successful operation. No one tried to play all the roles. Every team member had a specific set of tasks to perform well, and all roles were coordinated. Clearly defining each team member's role is critical to team effectiveness.

Using the Standard Agenda

Decision-making and problem solving without structure will usually waste enormous amounts of time and produce negligible results for teams (Romig, 1996). Without a structure for decision-making, teams often leap to consideration of solutions before adequately discussing and exploring the causes of problems. This leads to ineffective decision making (Hirokawa, 1985). Thus, successful teams have a systematic, structured method of decision-making and problem solving, as do groups in general; unsuccessful teams do not (LaFasto & Larson, 2001). The Standard Agenda (See Figure 13-1) provides one such highly effective method consisting of six steps:

1. *Identify the goal(s).* Establish a clear, specific goal or goals. Let's say that your team has a project assigned in your group discussion class. Your instructor has told the class that each group must choose a project from a list of five options. The group's overall specific goal might be to choose an option that will earn the team an "A" grade. A secondary goal might be to work on a project that interests all group members.

2. *Analyze the problem.* When we analyze a problem we break it down into its constituent parts. We examine the nature of the problem. The group project assigned in class might produce an analysis of the pros and cons of the five options available. Team members might consider how much research will be required and what information is readily available for each option, how much time the group has to do the necessary research, how much background knowledge is necessary to do the project well, and how interested members are in each option.

3. *Establish criteria.* Criteria are standards for judgment, guidelines for determining effective decision-making and problem solving. When I visited the National Gallery of Modern Art in Washington, D.C., I was immediately drawn to a huge painting. The entire canvas, which covered most of an interior wall, was painted off-white except for a solitary red dot about the size of a basketball in the lower right quadrant. Why was this painting chosen as special enough to hang in the National Gallery? Why would the National Gallery pay tens of thousands of dollars for such a painting? Could it be the reputation of the painter? Perhaps its attention-getting quality made it a worthy choice. I couldn't help thinking that I could duplicate this work. "If I can do it, it can't be great art" has always been my starting criterion for assessing the relative merit of artworks. Knowing what criteria art experts who chose this painting used to make their decision would have helped me understand why their choice made sense. I never found out what criteria were applied to this painting, and my appreciation of its merits remains minimal.

    Without establishing criteria in advance of final decisions, it is very difficult to gauge whether group choices will likely prove to be effective. In the case of a class project, the instructor will normally provide the specific criteria for the groups. In other circumstances, the group should discuss criteria and choose three to five before proceeding with the next step. Criteria should answer the question "What standards should be met for the decision/solution to be a good one?" Some criteria for a group project in a class might be (1) stay within the prescribed time limits for the class presentations, (2) exhibit clear organization, (3) use at least one clear attention strategy and cite at least three credible sources of information during each group member's presentation, and (4) employ one visual aid per member's speech. The extent to which the group meets these criteria will determine whether members all earn an "A" on their project.

4. *Generate solutions.* When weighing the merits and demerits of each project option, don't assume that the objections to each option can't be solved. Let's suppose that the group is torn between two options: exploring a campus problem such as parking or researching an international problem such as rain forest

FIGURE 13-1 The Standard Agenda

The Standard Agenda

✔ Identify the goal

✔ Analyze the problem

✔ Establish criteria

✔ Generate solutions

✔ Evaluate solutions, make final decision

✔ Implement decision

depletion. Initially, the parking problem might seem a less satisfactory choice. Finding credible sources and sufficient quality information in the limited time available for preparation might seem to be insurmountable impediments. If the group has a greater interest in the parking problem than in rain forest depletion, however, group members might brainstorm possible solutions to these impediments. Perhaps the group could conduct a campus survey to generate credible information if a lack of such information might be a problem. School officials and campus security could be interviewed.

5. *Evaluate solutions and make the final decision.* Before team members decide which option to choose for their project, the group should consider each option in terms of the criteria. Which option will best allow the group to achieve its goals? Will exploring a campus problem such as parking or an international problem such as rain forest depletion best permit the group to reach its goal of an "A" grade? Which option is most interesting to group members? The likelihood of satisfying the criteria will allow group members to make a reasonable decision.

It is particularly important during this step that group members consider both the positive and negative aspects of each choice. Groups often become enamored with a solution without considering **Murphy's Law,** which is that anything that can go wrong likely will go wrong.

When Boeing Corporation builds an airplane, designers account for Murphy's Law in the plans. An airplane with four engines is designed to fly temporarily with but a single engine. Boeing doesn't expect three engines to malfunction during the same flight, but, just in case, it is better to err on the side of safety. Expect the unexpected and build it into your team decision.

The enormously successful Mars rover Sojourner, which explored the surface of Mars in 1997, was repeatedly tested for Murphy's Law (Shirley, 1997). Sojourner's task was to take pictures, measure the chemistry of rocks, and discover how difficult it is to drive on the Martian soil. The rover, which looked

Team members prepare the Mars rover Sojourner for another test in the sandbox in anticipation of Murphy's Law.

like a microwave oven on six wheels, had to cost no more than $25 million to build—an unheard of pittance for an interplanetary spacecraft. Sojourner had to weigh less than 22 pounds and survive in 150-degrees-below-zero temperatures. These specifications for the rover were daunting, yet the rover was built within these restrictions. The rover operated at a peak power of 16 watts, but most of the time at a mere 8 watts, the equivalent of your ordinary bathroom nightlight. In an April Fool's issue, *Road and Track* magazine compared the rover to high-performance automobiles. It estimated the rover's top speed to be 0.0037 miles per hour. These severe limits caused many in the Pathfinder Mars project to doubt the ability of the rover to accomplish its mission.

   An engineer named David Gruel was assigned the task of sabotaging the rover in any way he could imagine to test the probability of success for the mission. A model of the rover was tested in a "sandbox" that simulated the Mars surface. Gruel created difficult terrain for the rover to overcome. The Sojourner team, headed by Donna Shirley, successfully maneuvered Sojourner around every obstacle. By the time Sojourner actually landed on Mars, the team was confident the rover would be up to the task. Expected to operate for about a week, Sojourner lasted for almost 3 months and traveled more than 100 meters on the surface of Mars—ten times as far as thought possible—before failing batteries ended the mission (Shirley, 1997).

6. *Implement the decision.* To implement the team's decision, the group divides labor among the members in a coordinated fashion. Each member must be

given a clear role to perform that contributes to the eventual implementation of the team decision. One or two members might do interviews, another might write and conduct a survey, other members might research the parking problem. All of these tasks are interdependent. Leave any out and successful implementation may be jeopardized. Merely talking about doing the project doesn't get it done. Deadlines for completion of each stage of the project should be set so all members know what is expected of them and when the product of their labor is due. Members should then discuss the results, condense the material into usable form, and organize the presentation of results to outsiders.

Some teams don't stick rigidly to the Standard Agenda. They may jump around some from step to step. Two points are critical, however. First, explore the problem thoroughly before considering any solutions or options. Second, establish criteria before making any decisions.

Employing Decision-Making Rules

Choices have to be made at every step of the Standard Agenda. How those decisions will be made depend on rules of decision-making. There are three chief decision-making rules for small groups and teams: unanimity or consensus, majority rule, and minority rule. Each has its benefits and drawbacks.

CONSENSUS   Some groups operate under the unanimity rule. This is usually referred to as *consensus decision-making*. **Consensus** is "a state of mutual agreement among members of a group where all legitimate concerns of individuals have been addressed to the satisfaction of the group" (Saint & Lawson, 1997, p. 21). Juries are one example of consensus groups. Criminal trials in most instances require all jurors to agree. All legitimate concerns of jurors must be addressed to achieve a consensus. If jurors ignore a legitimate concern, even a single dissenter can hang the jury and force a retrial or dismissal of charges.

Consensus requires unanimity, but it doesn't mean that every group member's preferred choice will be selected. Consensus is reached when all group members can support and live with the decision that is made. This means that group members interact cooperatively. Members exhibit give-and-take during discussions. Some team members may have to modify a preferred choice before every team member can climb aboard and sail with the decision. Conversely, giving in too easily will negate the value of the unanimity rule. Airing differences of opinion is constructive. It takes a team effort to achieve a consensus (Box 13-2).

There are several advantages to using the unanimity rule to structure decision-making. First, consensus requires full discussion of issues, which improves the chances that quality decisions will be made. Every group member must be convinced before a decision becomes final. Minority opinions will have to be heard. Those who disagree can't be ignored because they can stymie the group. All points of view must be considered. Second, team members are likely to be committed to the final decision and will defend the decision when challenged by outsiders. Dissenters may undermine a group decision that is less than unanimous. Third, consensus usually produces group satisfaction. Members typically are satisfied with the decision-making process and the outcome.

The unanimity rule has two chief drawbacks. First, consensus is very difficult to achieve; the process is time-consuming and sometimes contentious. Members can

Box 13-2   Sharper Focus:

How to Achieve a Consensus

Achieving a consensus is a major challenge for any team. Here are several suggestions that can guide a team toward achieving consensus (Hall & Watson, 1970; Saint & Lawson, 1997):

1. Follow the Standard Agenda and use suggestions for running productive meetings. Consensus requires structured deliberations, not aimless conversation.
2. Encourage supportive patterns of communication throughout discussions. Discourage defensive patterns that creep into discussions.
3. Identify the pros and cons of a decision under consideration. Write these on a chalkboard, large tablet, or transparency for all to see.
4. Discuss all concerns and try to resolve those concerns to everyone's satisfaction. Look for alternatives if concerns remain.
5. Avoid arguing stubbornly for a position. Be prepared to give where possible. Look for ways to break an impasse.
6. Ask for a "stand aside." *Standing aside* means a team member still has a reservation about the decision but does not feel that it warrants continued opposition to the final decision.
7. Avoid conflict-suppressing methods such as coin flipping and swapping ("I'll vote for your proposal this time if you vote for mine next"). A straw vote to ascertain the general level of acceptance for a decision or proposal is useful, but the goal should be unanimity.
8. If consensus cannot be reached, seek a supermajority (at least two-thirds agreement). This at least captures the thrust of consensus decision making by requiring substantial, if not total, agreement.

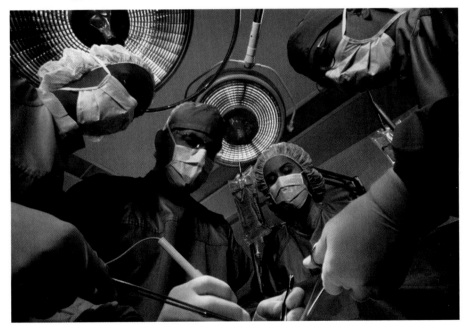

Consensus would be inappropriate for a surgical team performing an operation. Split-second decisions have to be made, so there is no time for lengthy discussion to achieve unanimity.

become frustrated by the length of deliberations and perturbed with holdouts who resist siding with the majority. Second, consensus becomes increasingly unlikely as groups grow larger. Teams of 15 or 20 will find it difficult to achieve consensus on anything.

Consensus is not the only way teams make decisions, but consensus decision-making is useful when team policy, priorities, and goals are being considered (Romig, 1996). Consensus is most relevant for important team decisions.

Many choices made by team members, however, do not require consensus. The team does not need to reach a consensus on where research should be conducted to gather information. Presumably, the team member who plays the information seeker role will be knowledgeable about where to look. Members can provide suggestions, but insisting on a consensus in such situations micromanages team members and will likely build resentment. If consensus cannot be reached, other decision-making rules can be used to break a deadlock.

MAJORITY RULE   The most popular method of decision-making in the United States is majority rule. The U.S. political system is dependent on it. Majority rule has important benefits. It is efficient and can provide rapid closure on relatively unimportant issues. In large groups, majority rule may be the only reasonable way to make a decision. Unlike consensus, majority rule won't produce a deadlock. Once a majority emerges, a decision can be made.

Majority rule also has significant disadvantages. First, majorities sometimes support preposterous positions. Majorities have supported racism, sexism, and homophobia at various times in the history of the United States. The majority in the South accepted slavery as a "peculiar institution" worth defending. Prior to 1920, the majority in the United States thought women should not be allowed to vote. A majority of the adult U.S. population supported the roundup of Japanese Americans

THE FAR SIDE®   By GARY LARSON

"Okay, Williams, we'll just vote. ... How many
here say the heart has four chambers?"

and their internment in camps during the Second World War. Sometimes the "tyranny of the majority" can produce awful decisions.

Second, groups using majority rule may encourage a dominance power dynamic within the team. Those with the most power (the majority) can impose their will on the less powerful minority. This could easily lead to a competitive power struggle within the team, thereby eroding team identity and team spirit.

Third, majorities may be tempted to decide too quickly, before proper discussion and debate have taken place, squelching the chance of creating synergy. Groups can make reckless, ill-conceived decisions. Minority opinion can be ignored.

Typically, teams use majority rule only when consensus is impossible or when quick decisions about commonplace issues must be made. A consensus decision regarding where, when, and for how long the team should meet is useful, but bogging down from lengthy discussions about such "housekeeping" tasks will quickly grow old. A simple majority vote may prove satisfactory to move the team along.

MINORITY RULE Majorities don't always make decisions in small groups and teams. Occasionally, a group will designate an expert to make the decision for the group. Sometimes a group merely advises a leader but doesn't actually make decisions (coaching staff on sports teams). The leader can choose to listen to the advice or ignore it. On rare occasions a forceful faction can intimidate a group and assert its will on the majority.

Minority rule has serious disadvantages. First, a designated expert can ignore group input or simply not seek it. Second, members may engage in power plays to seek favor with the leader who makes the decision. Third, team members will likely have weak commitment to the final decision because they had little participation in the process.

Minority decision-making may be warranted in some circumstances. Eisenhardt (1989) studied eight microcomputer companies. These companies used the unanimity rule with minority rule as a backup when they considered discontinuous change decisions in the high-velocity computer industry. **Discontinuous change decisions** involve major changes that depart significantly from the direction the team is taking currently. In business, wanting to start a new product line, offer a new service, or move location are examples of discontinuous change decisions. These are unlike **continuous changes,** which are merely extensions of previous decisions (ordering a greater quantity of a product or staying open an hour longer on weekends).

Consensus with qualification is a two-step decision-making process. First, the team tries to reach a consensus on the discontinuous change. If the team reaches consensus, the decision is made. If they cannot reach consensus, a supervisor, manager, or expert makes the final decision, using input from all team members. Thus, consensus with qualification begins with the unanimity rule and ends with minority rule.

Training and Assessment

Assessments of individual team members' productivity and performance should not be tied to wages, salaries, and promotions or demotions. This will quickly fracture a team and destroy motivation. Nevertheless, overall team performance and productivity should be assessed, especially in light of any training members might receive.

Formal training of teams is an important part of teambuilding. A college course can provide such training for student groups, but in the workplace training is often imported from outside sources. Goleman (1998) notes, however, that despite millions of dollars spent on training each year, business and corporate training programs are rarely assessed for their effectiveness.

"The world of training seems prone to whims and infatuated with fads" (Goleman, 1998, p. 249). The 1960s and early 1970s saw the rise of "encounter groups" and "sensitivity training," wherein thousands of employees were "trained" by sometimes obnoxious individuals with dubious backgrounds. These training sessions encouraged (some would say intimidated) participants to vent raw emotions. No evidence emerged that this form of training helped workers perform better on the job, and some studies showed damaging effects for some participants (Galanter, 1989; Singer, 1995).

Many current training programs are little better. Nevertheless, it is increasingly likely that you will be required to participate in team training as a condition of your employment. Requiring employees to participate in training that has not been shown to be effective and that could be damaging to participants raises serious ethical issues that should concern you (Box 13-3).

Before teams engage in training, members should seek evidence of program effectiveness that goes beyond "happy sheets" indicating how much participants liked the training and what about it they liked most. As Goleman (1998) points out, *liking* doesn't equal *learning*. Popularity rating sheets favor slick, cleverly packaged programs that are fun and entertaining. Whether they produce better teams and teamwork is questionable. The best evidence of effectiveness of training programs is an objective pre- and posttraining test that targets specific skill performance. Are the teams more productive after the training than before? Programs that cannot provide such data should be approached with caution. Training and assessment of team effectiveness are key components for structuring teambuilding. Done correctly, teams can flourish.

Teambuilding depends on proper structure. Establish clear, challenging, and cooperative goals; develop clear roles for each member; use the Standard Agenda to guide decision making; attempt to reach consensus whenever it is possible and practical; and train members to function as a team. Effective teambuilding, however, doesn't guarantee proficient teamwork.

Teamwork

Teamwork is the process of members exercising competent communication within the framework of teams. Teamwork operates within the structure erected by teambuilding. All the necessary structures for teambuilding may exist without teams working effectively. How members communicate within the team structure strongly influences the level of teamwork proficiency.

Competent communication is the essence of teamwork. Some of the key aspects of communication competence particularly relevant to teamwork that we already discussed are establishing a constructive climate, empowering team members, exercising a healthy skepticism without showing contempt for different viewpoints, using empathic listening, choosing the most effective conflict management style, employing situational and competent leadership, and managing anger effectively. Expanding on these discussions, this section explores three topics relevant to teamwork: conflict management in teams, creative problem solving, and defective teamwork (known as *groupthink*).

Box 13-3 | Focus on Controversy

Questionable Training, Dubious Ethics

Training on the job may involve far more than conveying nuts-and-bolts information on the technical aspects of tasks you will be expected to perform. Approximately $150 million is spent each year by U.S. businesses on sometimes controversial team training programs (Singer, 1995). These training programs include a surprising conglomeration of fads and fanciful notions to incite worker motivation and build teams. According to the Equal Employment Opportunity Commission (EEOC), a federal oversight agency, team training programs have included aura readings, biofeedback, faith healing, guided visualization, meditation, mysticism, therapeutic touch, yoga, and fire walking (lighting a fire under team members was never meant to be taken literally). The list of dubious training programs is long and controversial: Actualizations, Direct Centering, the Forum, Lifespring, MSIA/Insight Training Seminars, PSI World, Silva Mind Control, Sterling Management Systems, and Transformational Technologies are just a sample. Singer (1995) claims that "most of these programs do not provide the skills training they advertise" (p. 211). The skills training that some of them provide includes meditation, neurolinguistic programming, biofeedback, unusual relaxation techniques, visualization, trance inductions, and "attack therapy," which promotes suspension of critical listening and in some cases challenges employees' religious beliefs (Singer, 1995).

New fads and untested training programs spring up every year. Goleman's (1995) excellent best-selling book, *Emotional Intelligence*, stimulated the emergence of new training programs that purport to teach teambuilding by developing the emotional intelligence of workers. Goleman (1998) notes that such a program is "often only a repackaging or slight remodeling of a program they had offered before under another name" (p. 258).

Many training programs have come under fire. As Singer (1995) notes, "Besides making complaints to the EEOC, many employees have filed civil suits objecting to training program content or related pressures at the workplace. Some lost their jobs by objecting. Other employees have suffered psychological decompensation as a consequence of what occurred in the training programs" (p. 191).

Mandatory training programs whose effectiveness is unproven and techniques are questionable may violate several ethical standards discussed in Chapter 1. Many of the training programs are deceptively packaged as workshops on job-related skills and teambuilding when they are actually confrontational, psychologically intense therapy groups (Singer, 1995). Such deceptive packaging violates the ethical standard of honesty. Team members should know what to expect before entering such a program.

Some trainers are openly abusive to trainees (Singer, 1995). This abuse violates the ethical standard of respect. No team member should have to endure abusive remarks from trainers as a requirement for continued employment.

Finally, the mandatory nature of many programs forces team members to endure training that seems pointless or offensive. Coercing members to participate in questionable training programs violates the ethical standard of choice. Aside from the ethical concern, forced training programs usually produce lackluster participation from team members, resentment instead of an enthusiastic desire to learn new skills, and even exit from the team (Goleman, 1998).

The best programs are not one-size-fits-all types of training in which every team member, regardless of differences in individual skill level or motivation, is given identical instruction. Programs with proven records of effectiveness allow team members to choose for themselves from a menu of possible training experiences tailored to their individual needs (Goleman, 1998). This menu could include such work-related skills as empathic listening, anger management, creative decision-making techniques, or dealing with difficult team members.

Questions for Thought

1. Should a team member have an absolute right to refuse training if he or she views it as objectionable? Why or why not?
2. Should training programs ever be a requirement of employment? Explain.
3. What should be done with team members who refuse to receive training because they view it as objectionable or pointless, even though they are deficient in certain skills?

Conflict Management in Teams

Managing conflict in interpersonal relationships can be daunting. The challenge is considerably magnified when teams enter the picture. As the size of groups increases, complexity increases exponentially. The potential for conflict and the complexity involved in managing it effectively are markedly different for a team of 3 members than for a group of 10, 15, or more. Working out differences with a partner can be tough; working out differences with half a dozen or more team members can produce a four-aspirin headache.

One study (Rath & Strong, 1989) of 22,600 employees of Fortune 500 companies found that subjects rated conflict management as the part of their work that provoked the most dissatisfaction. Team members can follow a number of steps to improve conflict management (Romig, 1996).

PICK THE APPROPRIATE TIME   As a general rule, handling a conflict early prevents it from erupting into a more serious problem at a later time. Nevertheless, trying to manage a team conflict when members are hungry, tired, or severely stressed from deadline pressure can backfire (Romig, 1996). An ideal time may never emerge, but look for the best opportunity to deal with a conflict. This may mean postponing a confrontation for a day until members are more rested, less stressed, and have full stomachs.

MANAGE FEELINGS   Many of the best teams are composed of members with very diverse skills and personalities (Shirley, 1997). This diversity, however, can be a mixed blessing. Diversity provides a deep reservoir of resources for the group, but with diversity sometimes comes friction and intense conflict. Personality clashes within teams are not uncommon. When disagreements erupt into angry exchanges among members, managing this anger effectively is critical for the entire team. Emotionally charged debates characterized by angry outbursts and bad feelings can erode teamwork (Goleman, 1998). Team members all have to feel responsible for quelling angry outbursts during discussions and disagreements. This means following suggestions already presented for defusing anger and rage, such as remaining unconditionally constructive and asymmetrical, especially when strong disagreements emerge.

CREATE A CONSTRUCTIVE CLIMATE   Competition within a team destroys teamwork (LaFasto & Larson, 2001). Merit pay schemes, contests to determine who is the best team member, and comparison ranking of employees by grading their performance all encourage team members to work against others to gain an advantage and garner recognition. Create a constructive climate instead. Make turning toward not turning away and turning against responses to connecting bids from team members. Use supportive communication patterns (Chapter 2). Create a We- not a Me-oriented climate. Basketball coach John Wooden said it well: "It's amazing how much can be accomplished if no one cares who gets the credit" (cited in Aguayo, 1990, p. 100). Teamwork is cooperation in action.

USE APPROPRIATE STYLES OF CONFLICT MANAGEMENT   The most appropriate conflict management style for teams is collaboration (LaFasto & Larson, 2001). Unlike some other types of groups, teams are set up for members to work together collaboratively. Some initial research suggests that the collaborative style of conflict management is used by team members more frequently than other conflict styles (Farmer & Roth, 1998). The interdependence of goals, clearly defined role structure, and team identity all encourage a cooperative approach to conflict management.

On occasion, however, teams may find other conflict styles useful or even necessary. The point to remember is that conflict management is most successful when team members begin with styles that have a high probability of success, using lower probability styles as a last resort. This means beginning with collaboration, accommodating where possible, compromising only when no integrative decision emerges from creative problem-solving efforts, avoiding issues only when it would be counterproductive to confront them, and using the power-forcing, competitive style when no other style works and issues must be resolved.

Creative Problem Solving

Four deer hunters hire the same float plane every hunting season, fly into northern Maine, and "bag" a deer apiece. This season is no different. The pilot of the plane looks at the four deer carcasses and informs the hunters that he can't fly all the men and deer in one trip. The hunters complain, the pilot resists; the hunters complain more strenuously, the pilot wavers. They finally load the plane. The pilot taxies the plane across the lake, guns the engine, picks up speed, and lifts off. A few minutes into the flight the plane crashes. The men crawl from the wreckage and one hunter asks, "Where are we?" The pilot looks around and answers, "Looks like we're about 100 yards from where we crashed last year."

Groups can get into ruts. Creative problem solving requires breaking free from thinking that is repetitive, ritualistic, and rigid. The rigid thinking that characterizes the hunters' problem solving is an impediment. They continue to repeat the same mistake because their thinking is stuck.

In this section, we'll explore ways to unstick a team's thinking so that creative, original, and effective solutions to problems can be devised. Creative problem solving is a vital aspect of teamwork. As Carnevale and Probst (1998) note, "Successful conflict resolution often requires that disputants develop novel alternatives, new perspectives, and a fresh outlook on the issues. Creative problem solving is often required in negotiation" (p. 1308). Solving problems is a primary purpose of teams, and doing it effectively requires creativity.

PROMOTING TEAM CREATIVITY   Several conditions can promote creative problem solving. First, *a cooperative expectation is most conducive to creativity*. Competitive expectations can freeze thinking (Carnevale & Probst, 1998). When group members anticipate an adversarial exchange, thinking often becomes rigid, and counterproductive power struggles can distract the team. "An individual who anticipates competition may use precious cognitive resources in the effort to beat the other negotiator rather than develop creative optimal solutions. Cognitive resources may be used to plan, strategize, and coerce rather than to problem solve and collaborate" (p. 1308). A cooperative expectation can unfreeze thinking. Team members have little reason to be combative, and the focus is on solving a problem together to everyone's satisfaction.

Second, *creativity is promoted by challenges*. As the adage says, "Necessity is the mother of invention." Trying to discover a solution to a previously insoluble problem can stir the creative juices. Attempting to do what others have not been able to accomplish can be a powerful motivator.

Third, *creativity flourishes when there is a moratorium on judging ideas*. Create an atmosphere in which any idea, no matter how zany, can be offered without fear of ridicule. Ideas must be evaluated for their practicality and effectiveness, but instant assessments are creativity killers (Goleman, 1998). Team members should withhold critiques of ideas until there has been an opportunity to explore a solution and to tinker with it.

Fourth, *relaxing deadlines as much as possible can free team members' thinking*. Creativity can flourish under pressure, but relentless and unreasonable deadlines can panic a team. Panic doesn't usually spur creativity, but it can lead to a mental meltdown.

Fifth, *a fun, friendly atmosphere usually promotes creativity best* (Goleman, 1998). Fun relaxes team members and reduces concerns about power, status, and esteem. Having fun is the great equalizer among diverse individuals. Having fun means modifying some nonessential rules. Casual dress instead of more formal work attire may help signal a looser, friendlier, less power-conscious atmosphere.

www.mhhe
 com/ rothwell2

See "Brainstorming"
Activity Chapter 13, Online
Learning Center.

SPECIFIC METHODS Team creativity is enhanced by structured methods of problem solving (Romig, 1996). Edward DeBono (1992), author of several books on creativity, argues that unstructured creativity "is a dead end. It appears to be attractive at first, but you really can't go far. There are systematic structured approaches to creativity that I believe have more substance" (p. 37).

The first and most popular structured approach is brainstorming. **Brainstorming** is a creative problem-solving method characterized by encouragement of even zany ideas, freedom from initial evaluation of potential solutions, and energetic participation of all group members. The brainstorming method was originally introduced in 1939 by Alex Osborn, an advertising executive. Team members produce the best results when several rules are followed:

1. *All members should come prepared with initial ideas.* Most research that shows disappointing results from group brainstorming excludes this vital first step (Rothwell, 2001). Team members must be prepared adequately to brainstorm in the group. Provide necessary background information to all team members. Make certain the problem is clearly defined. Each member generates ideas prior to team interaction.

2. *Don't criticize any idea during the brainstorming process.* Idea slayers, such as "You can't be serious," "What a silly idea," "That'll never work," "We don't do it that way," and "That's crazy," will quickly defeat the purpose of brainstorming. This is especially true if the more powerful members make these criticisms of ideas offered by less powerful, hesitant members. An air of equality is important for productive brainstorming. If less powerful members concentrate on what more powerful members will think of them, they will be overly cautious about contributing ideas. Prohibiting instant evaluations of ideas can reduce initial reticence to participate fully in brainstorming sessions because all ideas are treated as equal during the brainstorming.

3. *Encourage freewheeling idea generation.* The more ideas the better. Even zany ideas may provoke a truly terrific solution to a problem by causing team members to think "outside the box." You want team members to expand their thinking and to think in new ways. This is where the fun atmosphere is important. A loose, relaxed, enjoyable brainstorming session encourages freewheeling idea

generation, and it can minimize power distinctions among members. When team leaders are as zany and relaxed as other members, power is momentarily equalized in the group. Team members see the leader as "one of them." This can be empowering for the more hesitant, cautious members.

4. *Don't clarify ideas during the idea generation phase.* That will slow down the process. Clarification can come later.
5. *Piggyback on the ideas of others.* Build on suggestions made by team members by modifying or slightly altering an idea.
6. *Record all ideas for future reference.* Don't edit any ideas during the initial phase of the brainstorming.
7. *Encourage participation from all team members.* Keep the brainstorming fun and fast paced so all members will want to offer suggestions (Box 13-4).

Nominal group technique is a second structured method of creative problem solving. **Nominal group technique** involves these steps:

1. Team members work alone to generate ideas.
2. The team is convened and ideas are shared in round-robin fashion. All ideas are written on a chalkboard, tablet, or easel. Clarification of ideas is permitted, but evaluation is prohibited.
3. Each team member selects five favorite ideas from the list generated and ranks them from most to least favorite.
4. Team members' rankings are averaged, and the ideas with the highest averages are selected.

Initial research comparing nominal group technique and brainstorming found a surprising result: Nominal group technique produced ideas in greater quantity and quality than brainstorming despite the popularity of brainstorming (Diehl & Stroebe, 1987). Other researchers, however, criticized this and subsequent studies that concurred with these initial findings (Sutton & Hargadon, 1996). The artificiality of untrained laboratory groups with no history of working together brainstorming ideas for an outcome members had no apparent interest in constituted the main criticism (Offner et al., 1996). More recent research shows brainstorming is as effective or slightly more effective than nominal group technique in generating a high number of ideas and high quality ideas when a trained facilitator guides the group and when a videotape of effective versus ineffective brainstorming is shown to group members prior to idea generation (Kramer et al., 2001).

Brainstorming offers, *in addition to the generation of creative ideas, more benefits than the nominal group technique.* Brainstorming tends to be more exciting and fun, it can create an organizational climate in which employees can feel free to take risks, it can impress clients with its vitality and creativity, and it can encourage talented and highly skilled employees to remain in an organization (Sutton & Hargadon, 1996). The nominal group technique is more impersonal than brainstorming, tends to be less fun and involving, and does not capitalize on the benefits of working in groups. It may be a relevant option, however, when teams experience substantial unresolved interpersonal friction and tension but need to make creative choices now. Brainstorming, because of its emphasis on high participation, may prove to be ineffective in such an atmosphere.

A third method of creative problem solving is reframing. **Reframing** is the creative process of breaking rigid thinking by placing a problem in a different frame of

Box 13-4 **Sharper Focus**

Brainstorming in Action

"Encourage Wild Ideas" reads the sign on the wall of each brainstorming room at IDEO Product Development in Silicon Valley, California. Brainstorming rooms are sanctuaries for creativity in which product design teams composed of engineers, industrial designers, and behavioral psychologists hurl ideas back and forth in a frenzy of mental activity (O'Brien, 1995). IDEO brainstormed designs for the Macintosh Duo docking system for laptops, Levolor blinds, virtual reality headgear, AT&T's telephones and answering machines, and a host of other diverse products (Myerson, 2001). One of its most notable and early accomplishments was the design for the Apple computer's original point-and-click mouse. Steve Jobs, Apple's driving force in its early days, went to Xerox first for the design. Xerox had a crude idea for a mouse, but it would have cost the consumer $1,200. This wasn't very practical for a computer that would cost only $1,000. Next, Jobs consulted Hewlett-Packard engineers, who claimed it would take 3 years to design a practical mouse, and it would cost the consumer $150. Jobs finally consulted David Kelley, owner and president of IDEO. Kelley assembled a team and in 3 weeks designed a workable mouse. "We made the outside from a Walgreen's butter dish. It cost $17 to make," explains Kelley (O'Brien, 1995, p. 14).

Brainstorming is a key element in designs concocted by IDEO. Faced with the problem of an electric car that is so quiet it would likely cause accidents because no one would hear it approaching, the brainstorming team at IDEO attacks the problem with relish. "How about tire treads that play music?" one team member offers. "Different tread patterns will play different tunes," offers another. "How about a little Eric Clapton?" another chimes in, and the ideas flow, one piggybacked on another.

Presented with the challenge to design a commuter coffee cup that allows a person to pedal a bicycle without spilling the drink, the brainstormers rapidly fire questions at the customer who requests the product. "Do you want to sip or suck the coffee as you ride?" "Sip," is the response. The brainstormers quickly draw designs of 15 contraptions, among them a "camelback" that puts a container with a plastic hose in a backpack, a coffee cup

with a temperature gauge attached to a helmet, and a "Sip-o-matic" with a suction valve. The Sip-o-matic is a hit with the customer. The brainstorming atmosphere is kept lighthearted and zany. No idea is too goofy during the idea generation phase of the brainstorming session, and all ideas are written on "writeable walls." Brainstormers repeatedly piggyback on the ideas of other team members, and all team members are totally engrossed, enjoying the challenge.

Brainstorming can be an integral part of a corporate culture as it is at IDEO, pictured here, not merely a creative problem-solving technique.

reference. A service station proprietor put an out-of-order sign on a soda machine. Customers paid no attention to the sign, lost their money, and then complained to the station owner. Frustrated and annoyed, the owner changed the sign to say that sodas are $5. No one since made the mistake of putting money in the soda pop dispenser. The proprietor reframed the problem. Instead of wondering how to get customers to recognize that the machine was out of order, the owner changed the frame of reference to what would make customers not want to put money in the dispenser. Reframing opens up possible solutions hidden from our awareness by rigid thinking.

Levi Strauss, a huge manufacturer of jeans, faced a troublesome dilemma when it learned that two of its sewing contractors in Bangladesh were employing child laborers. Human rights activists pressured the company to take a stand against this abuse of children. They wanted Levi Strauss to insist that the contractors cease using underage children in the factories. The company investigated the situation, however, and discovered that no longer employing the children wasn't necessarily a good decision. The children would be impoverished if they lost their jobs, and some might even be driven into prostitution. Levi Strauss could have viewed this dilemma rigidly as a dichotomy, a choice between two opposites. Instead, the company reframed the problem by seeking a solution that neither fired the children from their jobs nor kept them working while they were underage. The company kept the children on the payroll while they attended school. Then it hired them again when they reached legal working age (Sherman & Lee, 1997). Reframing can produce creative solutions to seemingly intractable problems.

Reframing a team dispute from a competitive, adversarial contest of wills to a cooperative problem to be solved by mutual effort and goodwill can prevent conflict from becoming destructive. Trying to win a contest and trying to solve a problem involve distinctly different frames of reference.

When teams become stumped by narrow or rigid frames of reference, asking certain open-ended questions can help reframe the problem so new solutions might emerge. "What if . . . ?" is a very useful question. "What if we don't accept the inevitability of worker layoffs and downsizing?" "What if we tried working together instead of against each other?" "What if management is telling the truth about the budget?" All these questions encourage a different frame of reference and a different line of thinking. Additional reframing questions include the following:

Why must we accept what we've been told?
Why are these the only choices?
Could there be a different solution than the one we've discussed?
Can the problem be described in any other way?
Is there any way to make this disadvantage an advantage?

Brainstorming, nominal group technique, and reframing are three useful methods of creative problem solving. In some instances, methods can be combined, such as brainstorming ways to reframe a problem before brainstorming ideas to solve the problem.

Groupthink

How could the United States have been caught sleeping when the Japanese executed a sneak attack on Pearl Harbor, resulting in the worst naval disaster in U.S. history? Why did John Kennedy and his cabinet advisers ever launch the Bay of Pigs invasion? After all, 1,400 Cuban exiles were facing a 200,000 strong Cuban army in a fruitless attempt to overthrow Fidel Castro. Kennedy lamented afterward, "How could I have been so stupid to let them go ahead?" (cited in Janis, 1982, p. 16). Add to these disasters the escalation of the Vietnam War under Lyndon Johnson, the

Nixon Watergate scandal, Jimmy Carter's failed mission to rescue hostages in Iran, the Iran-Contra scandal during the Ronald Reagan presidency, and the space shuttle Challenger disaster and you have a list of major fiascoes produced by teams. These are all examples of wretched teamwork.

Each of these events is an instance of "groupthink" (Janis, 1982; Mansfield, 1990). **Groupthink** is teamwork gone awry. It is a process of group members stressing cohesiveness and agreement instead of skepticism and optimum decision-making. Too much emphasis is placed on members being "team players," and too little emphasis is placed on the group making quality decisions. Consensus seeking, cooperation, and cohesiveness are all part of teamwork, but these normally vital and constructive aspects of teamwork can produce terrible consequences when taken to an extreme.

Groupthink has several specific characteristics (Janis, 1982; Mohamed & Wiebe, 1996; Street, 1997). First, disagreement is discouraged during group discussions because it is viewed as disruptive to team cohesiveness. Second, there is a strong pressure to conform so there is at least the appearance of team unity. The team usually has a self-appointed "mindguard" whose task is to discourage ideas and viewpoints that might threaten team unity. Dissenters are pressured to be "team players." Third, the group lacks a structured decision-making process that encourages consideration of divergent options and opinions. Confirmation bias is prevalent. Lack of structured decision-making combined with a high concern for maintaining team cohesiveness produces poor group decisions (Mullen et al., 1994). Fourth, there is an in-group–out-group competitive team mentality. Everyone who is not a team member is considered part of the out-group. This in-group–out-group mentality gives rise to feelings that the team is morally superior to out-groups; outsiders are often negatively stereotyped or branded as evil. An offshoot of this in-group–out-group view of the world is a strong team identity that gives members a feeling of pride and prestige from belonging to the team (Street, 1997).

Janis (1989) offers four suggestions to prevent groupthink and to produce effective teamwork. First, the team can consult an impartial outsider with expertise on the problem discussed. This reduces the danger from excessive cohesiveness, which leads to poor team decisions. This is sometimes why consultants are hired from outside an organization or group to give advice and counsel.

Second, to reduce pressure on team members to conform, the team leader can withhold his or her point of view during early discussions. In this way, the appearance of dominance in power relationships between a more powerful team leader and less powerful members is avoided, and members are more inclined to express honest opinions.

John Kennedy, anxious to avoid committing another blunder after the Bay of Pigs fiasco, instituted leaderless group discussions with his advisory team. On occasion, especially during the early stages of team discussion when alternatives were brainstormed, Kennedy would leave the group. This proved to be especially effective during the 1962 Cuban Missile Crisis when the United States and the U.S.S.R. took the world to the brink of nuclear war over the U.S.S.R.'s secret installation of nuclear missiles in Cuba. Ted Sorenson, an Executive Committee member who worked on the crisis, noted, "One of the remarkable aspects of those meetings was a sense of complete equality. . . . I participated much more freely than I ever had . . . and the absence of the president encouraged everyone to speak his mind" (cited in Janis, 1982, p. 144).

Third, the team can assign the devil's advocate role to a specific member. This can combat the excessive concurrence seeking typical of groups that slide into groupthink. The devil's advocate challenges any decision the group is likely to make to test the ideas.

Fourth, the team can set up a "second chance" meeting in which members can reconsider a preliminary decision. This allows team members to reflect on any proposal and avoid making impulsive decisions.

Teams in Organizations

Organizations in the United States have changed markedly in the last decade or so. The trend has moved from "hierarchical, function-based structures to horizontal, integrated workplaces organized around empowered individuals and self-directed work teams" (Graham & LeBaron, 1994, p. xi). This trend is discussed in this section. To understand the trend, you must know some basics about traditional organizational structure in the United States. Then the move toward "flattening the hierarchy" with self-managed teams is explained.

Traditional Structure of Organizations

What began as a very small business in 1937 with a half-dozen employees grew into 30,000 establishments worldwide employing about 1 million workers, exceeding any other American organization, public or private. One of every eight workers in America has at some time been employed by this organization (Schlosser, 2002). Can you guess what it is? If you guessed McDonald's you are correct.

Small groups sometimes grow into large organizations, and with the transition come changes in structure. Small groups typically operate with an informal structure. A meeting of a three-person group certainly doesn't require formal communication rules such as Robert's Rules of Order. Communication is usually conducted informally as conversation rather than formally as public presentations. Procedures for managing conflict also remain informal. There is little need for formal grievance procedures. The three group members can usually handle their differences through discussion and a meeting. They also can easily share power.

As groups increase in size, complexity increases. Thus, when small groups become large groups and eventually organizations, structure typically becomes more formal to cope with increased complexity. Individuals receive formal titles with written job descriptions. Power is distributed unevenly. Those with the most prestigious titles typically are accorded the most status and decision-making power. The larger the organization, the more likely it is that the structure will become **hierarchical,** meaning that members of the organization will be rank ordered. This pyramid of power has those at the top—the CEOs, presidents, and vice-presidents—wielding the most power, with middle managers coming next, followed by the "worker bees" or low-level employees (See Figure 13-2).

With greater formal structure come changes in communication (Adler & Elmhorst, 2002). Formal communication networks emerge. In most organizations, low-level employees' communication with those at the top of the power pyramid is restricted. If everyone in the McDonald's organization, all 1 million workers, felt free to e-mail those at the top, information overload would overwhelm decision

FIGURE 13-2
Communication in
Traditional Organizations

FIGURE 13-2
Communication in
Traditional Organizations

makers. Formal lines of communication, or networks, are established to control information flow. These chains of command can make **upward communication**—messages that flow from subordinates to superordinates in an organization—very difficult. Typically, there are risks for low-level employees who communicate with bosses, especially if the information is negative. Criticism and complaints can get you fired, ostracized, or perceived as a troublemaker or a doofus. Messages from down below also can become distorted or diluted as they are transmitted upward through layers of gatekeepers who screen messages before they arrive at their final destination. Managers, for example, may decide to censor messages or ignore them entirely so they never reach top decision-makers because such messages may cast managers in an unfavorable light. Problems "down in the trenches" may remain unknown among top-level decision makers until real disasters emerge. Upward communication is very important to the success of an organization, but the more formal an organization's communication networks, the more difficulties employees are likely to have communicating successfully up the organizational structure.

Downward communication—messages that flow from superordinates to subordinates in an organization—also can be problematic, especially in larger organizations. Communicating policy changes, giving rationales for assignments, explaining proper procedures and practices for the smooth running of the organization, motivating workers, and offering sufficient feedback to subordinates so they know when they have performed well and when improvement is needed are vital messages. What you don't want in an organization is what former United Airlines president Ed Carlson called NETMA—Nobody Ever Tells Me Anything.

Horizontal communication—messages between individuals with equal power in organizations, such as office workers in the same department—is another common communication pattern in organizations. Horizontal communication coordinates

DILBERT reprinted by permission of United Feature Syndicate, Inc.

tasks, aids problem solving, shares information, enhances conflict management, and builds rapport (Adler & Elmhorst, 2002).

An organizational culture guides decision-making and problem solving. An **organizational culture** is a particular way of doing things, certain shared values, and specific ways of talking about the organization (Hanna & Wilson, 1998). For example, Starbucks Coffee, an organization that began in 1971 with a single store and rapidly grew to more than 2,300 outlets, tries to "imprint values" on its employees. As former Starbucks CEO Howard Schultz explains, "Whether you are the CEO or a lower-level employee, the single most important thing you do at work each day is communicate your values to others, especially new hires" (Schultz & Yang, 1997, p. 81). Some of the values Schultz attempted to imprint on employees included a passion for quality coffee, superior customer service that creates a bond with coffee consumers, recognition that employees are the organization's greatest asset, creation of a comfortable climate for casual social interaction, concern for local communities and the environment, and constant innovation. Employees are referred to as "partners," suggesting that they are more than worker drones. Other organizations refer to employees as "associates," and employees at Disneyland are called "cast members" to reflect corporate values.

Prodded by the economic success of Japan and lagging economic growth in America, organizational cultures began to change in the early 1980s. Attempts to "flatten the hierarchy" gathered proponents. American organizations rushed to establish **quality circles**—teams composed of employees who volunteer to work on a similar task and attempt to solve a particular problem. Here employees became problem solvers, not mere worker bees who were told what to do and expected "to check their brains at the door." This initial attempt to squash the pyramid of power in most organizations by recognizing and encouraging employees to act as partners in problem solving and decision-making didn't prove to be the panacea expected. Typically, these teams had little or no authority to make decisions or implement proposed solutions to problems. Most quality circles were restricted to analyzing a problem and offering recommendations to management for improvements. Management, accustomed to making decisions without much employee input, often ignored the recommendations of the quality circles. Organizational cultures had not fully embraced the flattened hierarchy, and quality circles were a halfhearted attempt to reduce the power distance between those at the top and those at the lower levels of an organization. By the mid-1980s, quality circles had failed "in more than 60 percent of the American organizations in which they have been tried" (Marks, 1986, p. 38). Many organizations abandoned quality circles within a year of initiating them (Dubrin et al., 1989).

Self-Managed Work Teams

Self-managed work teams—self-regulating groups that complete an entire task—emerged as a true manifestation of flattened hierarchies in organizations. Self-managed work teams, after sufficient training and education, share responsibility among members to plan, organize, set goals, make decisions, and solve problems. How they manifest a flattened hierarchy is the subject of this section.

Self-managed work teams embrace empowerment (Graham & LeBaron, 1994). Employees are empowered when organizational structure is transformed from the traditional pyramid of power through which information and decisions flow downward to lower-level workers, to a more open system of shared information, communication in all directions (upward, downward, and horizontally) with few gatekeepers obstructing the information flow, and participation in decision-making and problem solving by low-level workers (Teubner, 2000). Power distance within the organization is substantially reduced but not eliminated. CEOs and presidents still oversee the organization, but establishment of self-managed teams makes power distances less obvious. In a traditional organization, when a problem arises low-level workers wait until a manager or foreperson solves the problem. In self-managed teams, the team members assume the responsibility for solving the problem. Communication is mostly horizontal among team members.

Self-managed teams are likely to be successful only to the extent that the organizational culture embraces a flattened hierarchical structure (LaFasto & Larson, 2001). "Autonomy becomes the dominant value of the organizational culture and the emphasis is on employees' 'moral responsibility' to act in the best interests of the organization" (Teubner, 2000, p. 8). Instead of functioning as mere "cogs in a wheel," employees take ownership of decisions and take pride in the performance of the organization. Leadership within the organization must loosen the reins of control to make this happen. This means not only permitting low-level decision-making, but also encouraging such meaningful participation. It's one thing to claim that an organization has a flattened hierarchy; it's another to actually implement such a structure. When managers, used to giving directives in a traditional organizational structure, are required to step back and let the group decide, the managers may find it difficult or even impossible to accept. Similarly, employees who are accustomed to taking orders may find the transition to being a participant in decision-making awkward and ambiguous. Without sufficient training in collaboration and teamwork, self-managed teams will flounder.

Self-managed teams provide several benefits to an organization. These benefits include improvement in work procedures and methods; improvements in service and quality of products; increased outputs; enhanced decision-making quality; greater attraction to the organization and greater retention of employees; reduced need for management and supervisory staff; and greater staffing flexibility (Boyett & Boyett, 1998; Teubner, 2000). These benefits, of course, will not materialize if team training is insufficient, if some team members strongly resist a participative decision-making process, if conflicts are managed poorly and competitively, if team meetings become inefficient time wasters, or if teams are indecisive from fear of failure or reprimand from superordinates. Initially, an organization must exhibit patience as teams learn from mistakes. The benefits of effective self-managed teams will eventually serve as the best refutation of initial concerns and criticisms.

Summary

Teams are cooperative groups. Teambuilding provides the structure for teams: clear, challenging, and cooperative goals; clear roles; use of the Standard Agenda; consensus decision-making whenever possible; and team training. Teamwork is competent communication in the context of teams. Teamwork often requires creative problem solving. There are three structured methods of creative problem solving: brainstorming, nominal group technique, and reframing. Groupthink is poor teamwork in action. Groupthink occurs when team members place too much emphasis on cohesiveness and concurrence. Finally, small groups sometimes become large organizations. Organizations have a formal structure that is traditionally hierarchical. Recent efforts to flatten organizational hierarchies have produced increasing numbers of self-managed teams. These teams are empowerment in action.

Quizzes Without Consequences

Go to Quizzes Without Consequences at the book's Online Learning Center at **www.mhhe.com/rothwell2** or access the CD-ROM for *In the Company of Others*.

www.mhhe
● com/
/ **rothwell2**

Key Terms

brainstorming
consensus
continuous changes
discontinuous change
  decisions
downward
  communication
groupthink

hierarchical
horizontal
  communication
Murphy's Law
nominal group
  technique
organizational culture
quality circles

reframing
self-managed work
  teams
team
teamwork
upward
  communication

Suggested Readings

Goleman, D. (1998). *Working with emotional intelligence.* New York: Bantam. This is
  an excellent treatment of how to build teamwork in the workplace.

Larson, C., & LaFasto, M. (1989). *Teamwork: What must go right, what can go wrong.*
  Newbury Park, CA: Sage. This is a highly readable work on teams.

LaFasto, M., & Larson, C. (2001). *When teams work best: 6,000 team members and leaders tell what it takes to succeed.* Thousand Oaks, CA: Sage. This is the single best
  work on teams and teambuilding, rich in data and insights.

Film School

The Dream Team (1989). Comedy; PG ★★★★✔
This laugh-a-minute comedy about four escaped mental patients on the loose in
New York City in search of their mugged psychiatrist is a gem. Analyze team-
building and teamwork as depicted in this engaging comedy.

Remember the Titans (2000). Drama; PG ★★★★✔
Denzel Washington plays a high school football coach who must integrate his team
in the face of racism and ignorance. Analyze how Washington accomplishes the
feat of molding a championship team from warring factions in this film based on a
true story.

The War Room (1993). Documentary; PG ★★★★
This documentary on the 1992 Clinton presidential campaign earned an Oscar
nomination. Whatever your political leanings, this is a fascinating inside look at
politics in action. Analyze how Clinton's campaign team capitalized on the elements of teambuilding and teamwork to forge a winning combination.

PART FOUR

Public
Speaking

CHAPTER 14

Beginning the Speech Process

Freedom of speech is the bedrock of a democratic society. Virtually every major and minor protest that occurs in our sometimes tumultuous society relies on public speaking to move the populace. The entire history of student protest in this country exhibits the power of public speaking. From the "Free Speech Movement" at Berkeley in 1964, through the Vietnam War era, and continuing with the battle on college campuses over racism, sexism, and "politically correct" speech, students have depended on public speaking to produce change. Ideas have to be framed, issues have to be crystallized, and arguments have to be made for change to occur. Public speaking is a powerful and essential method for accomplishing this.

It is difficult to identify a profession that does not rely on or benefit from competent public speaking. Teaching, law, religion, politics, public relations, marketing, and business are communication-oriented professions. They require substantial knowledge and skill in public speaking. Company recruiters and business consultants uniformly recommend that job seekers develop public speaking skills (Patterson, 1996).

Average citizens are frequently called upon to give speeches of support or dissent at public meetings on utility rate increases, school board issues, and city or county disputes. Toasts at weddings or banquets, tributes at awards ceremonies, eulogies at funerals for loved ones and friends, and presentations at Tupperware parties or before other sales groups are additional common public speaking situations. One survey found that 55% of adults had given a speech during the previous 2 years (Kendall, 1985). College courses in diverse disciplines increasingly require oral presentations as class assignments. Those students who have public speaking knowledge and skills enjoy an enormous advantage in college courses when presentations in front of the class are required.

Competent public speakers know how to present complex ideas clearly and persuasively, keep an audience's attention, make reasonable arguments, and support claims with valid proof. They also move people to listen, to contemplate, and to change their minds. This is an impressive array of knowledge and skills for anyone to possess, and its application is virtually boundless. When would a person not find such public speaking knowledge and skills useful? Nevertheless, most people are uncertain how to begin the constructing of a speech.

The principal purpose of this chapter is to explore the initial steps involved in beginning the public speaking process.

The principal purpose of this chapter is to explore the initial steps involved in beginning the public speaking process.

There are three chapter objectives:

1. to analyze the causes of speech anxiety and consider ways to control stage fright,

2. to discuss topic selection and development, and

3. to explain how to analyze your audience so your message resonates with listeners.

The communication competence model will guide us throughout the discussion of public speaking. Public speakers must make choices regarding the appropriateness and likely effectiveness of topics, attention strategies, style and delivery, evidence, and persuasive strategies. When you are giving a speech, you must be sensitive to the signals sent from an audience that indicate lack of interest, disagreement, confusion,

Changing the collective mind of an audience is a cooperative effort. You may win the debating points but receive a chorus of boos from the audience if you don't appreciate this fact.

enjoyment, support, and a host of additional reactions. This allows you to make adjustments during the speech, if necessary. A committed public speaker must expect to spend generous amounts of time and energy preparing to speak to an audience. Finally, ethics is always an important part of giving speeches. Effectiveness of a speech must be tempered by ethical concerns. What works may not always be honest, respectful, responsible, noncoercive, or fair.

Additionally, public speaking is primarily a cooperative, interdependent transaction between the speaker and his or her audience. A speaker needs to think in terms of what will induce an audience to work with, not against, him or her. When an audience turns against a speaker and exhibits a collective desire to engage in an adversarial contest of wills, the speaker is almost always the loser. Speakers who project an image of arrogance, superiority, and dogmatism—competitive communication patterns—usually turn an audience against them. An effective public speaker takes the perspective of the audience (empathy) and works with that perspective to frame issues and ideas that will resonate with listeners. As many experienced public speakers can attest, you can "win" all the debater points but lose the audience if listeners just don't like the attitude you project. As the process of public speaking unfolds in the next few chapters, keep uppermost in your mind that *cooperation— working with an audience and building goodwill—is a key to public speaking success.*

Speech Anxiety

Speech anxiety, or *stage fright* as it is sometimes called, "refers to those situations when an individual reports he or she is afraid to deliver a speech" (Ayres & Hopf, 1995). Speech anxiety is often discussed in a chapter on speech presentation. It is included in this initial public speaking chapter, however, for two reasons. First, when a speech assignment is given, most individuals are immediately concerned about speech anxiety. This concern can powerfully occupy one's mind and adversely affect one's ability to prepare a speech. Second, managing speech anxiety effectively requires specific preparation for the potentially stressful event of giving a speech. If you wait until you actually give your speech before considering what steps to take to manage your anxiety, it is usually too late. Simply put, you need a clear plan for managing your speech anxiety, and the most effective plan begins to take shape very early in the public speaking process.

Speech Anxiety as a Problem

As an undergraduate, I took a persuasion course that required several speeches. During one speech assignment, I observed a startling instance of speech anxiety. A young woman, bright and articulate outside of class, was terrified to give her speech. As if hoping for some cataclysmic natural disaster to strike and save her from the even worse fate of having to give her speech, she waited until all the other students had performed. Facing her audience from behind a podium, she opened her mouth and began to speak. All that came out was a breathy sound but no words. She grabbed her throat and then swallowed hard and began again with the same result. At first, I believed she was merely gaining the audience's attention. I was curious to see how she would make this display relevant to her topic. Soon, however, I realized that I was witnessing a very unusual case of intense speech anxiety, so extreme that this terrified student actually lost her voice momentarily.

The professor quickly diagnosed the problem and gently told his anxious student to take her seat and see him after class. Remarkably, her voice returned as soon as she sat down. She met with the professor and discussed several ways to control her anxiety. In the next class period she gave her speech in full voice and received the enthusiastic applause of her classmates. In three decades of teaching public speaking to thousands of students, I have never witnessed a repeat occurrence of such extreme speech anxiety, but this example should provide you comfort. *Even in the worst cases of speech anxiety there is an effective, relatively simple remedy.*

Speech anxiety is a significant problem for most people. Motley (1995) found that about 85% of the population fears public speaking. Another study found that approximately 70% of the general population experiences moderately high to very high speech anxiety (Richmond & McCroskey, 1989). My own surveys of college students in public speaking courses show that the vast majority, often everyone in class, experiences at least some nervousness before giving a speech. Even college

DILBERT   Scott Adams

DILBERT reprinted by permission of United Feature Syndicate, Inc.

Box 14-1 **Sharper Focus**

Stage Fright Among Great Speakers and Performers

Those who are unaccustomed to performing in front of the public usually experience anxiety. Those accustomed to public performance, however, also often experience stage fright. One survey (cited in Hahner et al., 1997) revealed that 76% of experienced speakers have stage fright before performing. Biographies of famous speakers such as Demosthenes, Cicero, Abraham Lincoln, Henry Clay, Daniel Webster, and Winston Churchill reveal that these giants of history had such a strong desire to overcome their fear of public speaking that they took every opportunity to mount the speaker's platform. Actor Harrison Ford was so terrified to speak in front of an audience that he studied acting to overcome his fear. Singer Carly Simon, however, succumbed to her stage fright, refusing to perform in live concerts for 5 years until she finally took steps to manage her performance anxiety. Legendary Oscar-winning actor Laurence Olivier suffered such intense stage fright that he forbade cast members to look him in the eye while he was acting. Willard Scott, sometime weatherman and most of the time vaudeville act on NBC's "Today" show, experienced such intense stage fright that he hyperventilated on camera. Nicole Kidman, Adam Sandler, Gwyneth Paltrow, Jennifer Aniston, Cameron Diaz, Natalie

Portman, Liv Tyler, Matt Damon, Barbra Streisand, Madonna, Randy Travis, and Luciano Pavarotti are just a few performers who have admitted that they have stage fright before performing.

If you experience speech anxiety, don't feel alone. You're in good company. Even the professionals must learn to manage their fear of performing in public. I. A. R. Wylie, novelist and lecturer, offers this observation about stage fright: "Now after many years of practice I am, I suppose, really a 'practiced speaker.' But I rarely rise to my feet without a throat constricted with terror and a furiously thumping heart. When, for some reason, I am cool and self-assured, the speech is always a failure" (cited in Bradley, 1991, p. 36). Speechwriter Peggy Noonan (1998) notes that Ronald Reagan "was always nervous before he spoke. Good performers always are, because they're serious about what they're doing and want badly to do well" (p. 11). As Edward R. Murrow, acclaimed radio and television commentator, explained, "The best speakers know enough to be scared. . . . The only difference between the pros and the novices is that the pros have trained the butterflies to fly in formation" (cited in Osborn & Osborn, 1997, p. 56).

instructors must manage speech anxiety. One study revealed that 87% of psychology instructors experience speech anxiety when teaching (Gardner & Leak, 1994). Sixty-five percent of these same instructors rated their most severe case of speech anxiety between "definitely unpleasant" and "extreme."

Take any four individuals and odds are that two of the four have some butterflies in their stomachs prior to a speech. The third individual has anxiety that is bothersome but not incapacitating. The fourth individual has anxiety so severe that he or she is almost paralyzed by fear of giving a speech. These individuals will avoid classes that require oral presentations, skip meetings, refuse job promotions, or even change jobs or occupations to escape public speaking. The fear of public speaking is one reason most colleges and universities make a public speaking course mandatory. If taking such a class were left as an option, the great majority of students would avoid it because of fear (Box 14-1).

Symptoms of Speech Anxiety

We often fear what we do not understand. Information can be empowering because it can provide choices for us. Learning how to manage speech anxiety gives you opportunities to excel in front of an audience. Remaining uninformed about managing your speech anxiety reduces your chances of exhibiting competent public speaking skills. Understanding speech anxiety so you can learn to manage it begins with identifying common symptoms associated with speech anxiety and exploring why these symptoms occur.

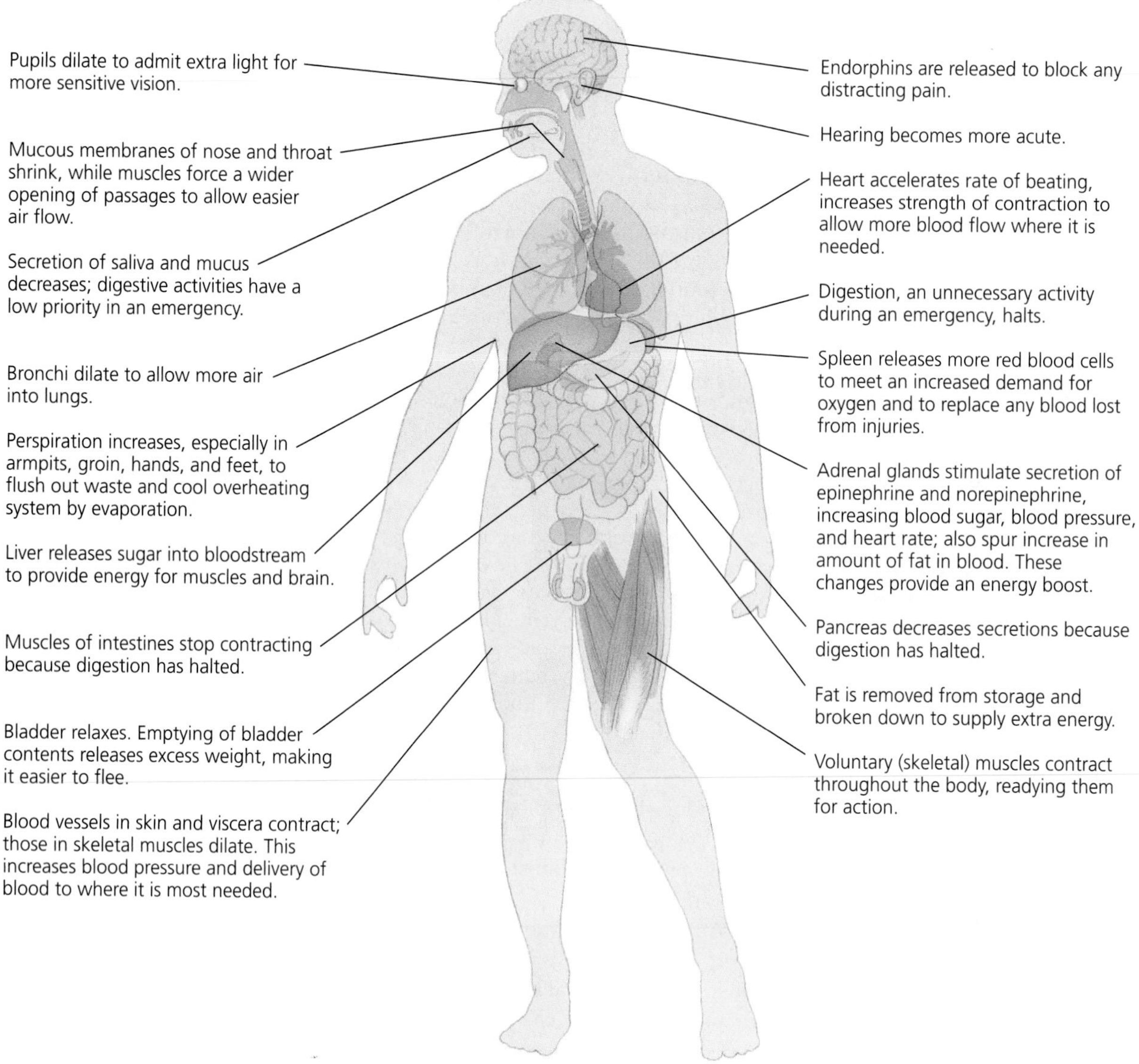

Pupils dilate to admit extra light for more sensitive vision.

Mucous membranes of nose and throat shrink, while muscles force a wider opening of passages to allow easier air flow.

Secretion of saliva and mucus decreases; digestive activities have a low priority in an emergency.

Bronchi dilate to allow more air into lungs.

Perspiration increases, especially in armpits, groin, hands, and feet, to flush out waste and cool overheating system by evaporation.

Liver releases sugar into bloodstream to provide energy for muscles and brain.

Muscles of intestines stop contracting because digestion has halted.

Bladder relaxes. Emptying of bladder contents releases excess weight, making it easier to flee.

Blood vessels in skin and viscera contract; those in skeletal muscles dilate. This increases blood pressure and delivery of blood to where it is most needed.

Endorphins are released to block any distracting pain.

Hearing becomes more acute.

Heart accelerates rate of beating, increases strength of contraction to allow more blood flow where it is needed.

Digestion, an unnecessary activity during an emergency, halts.

Spleen releases more red blood cells to meet an increased demand for oxygen and to replace any blood lost from injuries.

Adrenal glands stimulate secretion of epinephrine and norepinephrine, increasing blood sugar, blood pressure, and heart rate; also spur increase in amount of fat in blood. These changes provide an energy boost.

Pancreas decreases secretions because digestion has halted.

Fat is removed from storage and broken down to supply extra energy.

Voluntary (skeletal) muscles contract throughout the body, readying them for action.

FIGURE 14-1   The Fight-or-Flight Response

Physiologist Walter Cannon labeled the physiological defense-alarm process triggered by stress the "fight or flight response." Physiologically, animals and humans are equipped with the same defense system for dealing with stress. The myriad physiological changes that are activated by a threat prepare both animals and humans to either fight the threat or flee the danger.

The fight or flight response produces a complex constellation of physiological symptoms (Figure 14-1). Some of the more pronounced symptoms are as follows (Zimbardo, 1992):

Dilated pupils (to accommodate far vision)
Accelerated heart beat and increased blood pressure (to increase oxygen supply)

Blood vessel constriction in skin, skeletal muscles, brain, and viscera (to cut off blood supply to less necessary functions)

Increased perspiration (to generate cooling)

Bronchial tube dilation (to increase oxygen supply)

Inhibited digestion (to eliminate unnecessary energy drain)

Stimulated glucose release from the liver (to increase energy supply)

Increased blood flow away from extremities and to large muscles (to supply oxygen and glucose to major muscles used to fight)

Tightened neck and upper back muscles (to prepare for fighting)

Stimulated adrenal gland activity (to generate alertness, motion, and strength)

Spleen release of red blood corpuscles (to aid in clotting a wound)

Bone marrow stimulation to produce white corpuscles (to fight possible infection)

Some of the more prominent corresponding verbal and nonverbal symptoms of speech anxiety are as follows:

Quivering, tense voice, and weak projection (because of constricted throat muscles)

Frequent dysfluencies such as "uhms" and "ahs" (because of restricted blood flow to the brain causing confusion of thought)

Rigid, motionless posture (because of constricted muscles of legs and torso)

Flailing arms, tapping fingers, shaky hands, aimless pacing, side-to-side swaying (because of adrenaline surge)

Dry mouth, sometimes called "cotton mouth," which makes speaking difficult (because of digestive system shutdown)

The physiological symptoms make sense if you are about to grapple with a crazed grizzly or sprint from a rampaging bull, but they don't seem especially relevant to making a speech. Increased perspiration (cooling), respiration (oxygen), glucose (energy), and blood flow to major muscles (strength) would certainly help with the grappling and sprinting. Shutting down functions not immediately relevant to fighting or fleeing also makes sense in an emergency. You do not need to waste energy digesting your burger and fries when dealing with a sudden danger. Digesting can be postponed until the threat is past (Box 14-2).

What, though, does the fight or flight response have to do with performing a speech in front of an audience? Neither fighting nor fleeing is considered an appropriate response to the stress of public speaking. The sight of a student wrestling with an instructor or bolting from the classroom when he or she is called to begin a speech would be startling. Granted, some of the physiological responses to threat are relevant to public speaking. If the speech is lengthy, the room hot and stuffy, and the occasion momentous, increased glucose, respiration, perspiration, and adrenaline will help you sustain yourself throughout such a challenging task. Adrenaline can also assist you in performing at a peak level. Clothes saturated with perspiration, increased red and white corpuscles, a quivering voice, dry mouth, shaky hands, rigid posture, nausea, and a pounding heart are unnecessary and often distracting when making a speech—unless a real threat to life and limb truly exists (an unlikely classroom occurrence).

Our autonomic nervous system controls physiological responses to a perceived threat. When a person experiences stress from whatever source, the autonomic nervous system reacts reflexively, initiating the fight or flight response. The process is

Box 14-2   Sharper Focus

Odd but Common Symptoms of Speech Anxiety

Several physiological manifestations of speech anxiety occur often, and they may perplex you. Why do we suffer that fluttery feeling in the pit of our stomachs known as *butterflies*? Why do goose bumps appear when we're anxious about making a speech? The expression "getting cold feet" refers to extreme reticence to perform certain actions, but why do individuals giving speeches often literally get cold feet?

Chemicals, notably adrenaline, secreted into the bloodstream when fear is aroused in humans are responsible for butterflies. These chemical secretions shut down the digestive system, so our undigested food sits in our stomachs like globules of grease floating on top of dishwater. Digestion is relatively unimportant when compared to threats to a person's well-being, so digestion is temporarily postponed until the threat subsides.

The pimply effect on your skin that erects the hairs on your arm is known as *goose bumps*. It is an evolutionary relic from our ancient ancestors who had furry bodies. Erecting body hair increases insulation, thereby conserving body heat. In nonhuman mammals, erecting body hair is a means of defense against an opponent. A cornered cat, for instance, will erect its fur, making it appear much larger and therefore more menacing to an opponent.

Human body hair is too short to be of much use either to insulate or to appear formidable, so goose bumps serve no relevant purpose, especially to public speakers. Your goose bumps will not likely terrify anyone or keep you warm, but they do remind us of an evolutionary connection to our ancient past.

Cold feet (and cold hands for that matter) are caused by what physiologists call *peripheral vascular constriction*. In plain English, blood vessels in our extremities (hands and feet) narrow, reducing the blood flow. During stress, blood flow shifts away from the periphery of the body and the digestive tract toward the large muscle groups in the torso and legs where it is needed most for fighting or fleeing.

like a light switch. You have two choices—on or off. You may prefer a dimmer switch that gives a proportional response to stress, but your body prepares for the worst-case scenario. After all, what begins as a seemingly harmless event may balloon into a life-or-death struggle. Best to play it safe, so goes the internal logic of your body's fight or flight response. Thus, your anxiety may feed on itself, even spiral out of control. You sweat profusely even when the room isn't hot, your heart races and your respiration increases even though you're standing still, and the meal in your stomach, undigested, feels like you swallowed a chunk of radial tire.

Causes of Dysfunctional Speech Anxiety

Dysfunctional speech anxiety occurs when the intensity of the fight or flight response prevents an individual from performing effectively. **Functional speech anxiety** occurs when the fight or flight response is managed and stimulates an optimum presentation. *The degree of anxiety and our ability to manage it, not anxiety itself, determine the difference.* Speakers who experience low to moderate anxiety that is under control typically give better speeches than do speakers who experience little or no anxiety (Motley, 1995). Low to moderate anxiety means the speaker cares about the quality of the speech. Anxiety can energize a speaker and enhance performance. You will present a more dynamic, forceful presentation when energized than you will when you feel so comfortable and unchallenged that you become almost listless.

Causes of dysfunctional speech anxiety fall primarily into two categories: self-defeating thoughts and situational factors. Let's briefly examine each.

SELF-DEFEATING THOUGHTS   Some individuals see giving a speech as a challenging and exciting opportunity, whereas other individuals see it as an experience equivalent to swallowing a live snake. How you think about speaking to an audience will largely determine your level of stage fright.

There are three self-defeating ways of thinking about public speaking. First, *fear of catastrophic failure* can be a serious problem. This fear does not result in mild problems such as a brief stutter or a momentary lapse of memory. It can result in a complete collapse. Those with irrational fears of catastrophic failure can experience heart rates that exceed 200 beats per minute (Motley, 1995). Thinking irrationally about a speech presentation wildly exaggerates potential problems. Those with irrational fears predict not just momentary memory lapses but complete mental meltdowns (e.g., "I know I'll forget my entire speech, and I'll just stand there like a goober."). They fear that audiences will not just think that their ideas are questionable or even wrong but also will laugh, hoot them off the stage, and view them as fools. Minor problems of organization are magnified into graphic episodes of total incoherence and nonstop babbling. Predictions of catastrophes are irrational. I personally have listened to more than 10,000 student speeches. I have witnessed some unimpressive speeches, but not more than a handful of these speeches qualified as outright disasters, and the obvious cause of the disaster in each case was total lack of preparation.

A second form of self-defeating thought is *perfectionist thinking*. Perfectionists anguish over every perceived flaw and overgeneralize the significance of even minor defects:

"I totally failed—I forgot to preview my main points."

"My knees were shaking. The audience must have thought I was out of control."

"I feel like an idiot. I mispronounced the name of one of the experts I quoted."

Flawless public speaking is a desirable goal, but why beat up on yourself when it doesn't happen? Even the most talented and experienced public speakers make occasional errors in otherwise riveting and eloquent speeches. Martin Luther King Jr. stumbled twice during his famous "I Have a Dream" speech. Who noticed? Ironically, the imperfections so noticeable to perfectionists usually go unnoticed by most people in the audience.

A third form of self-defeating thought that increases speech anxiety is the *desire for complete approval* from an audience. Comedian Bill Cosby offers an interesting observation regarding complete approval: "I don't know the key to success, but the key to failure is trying to please everybody." All of us desire approval, especially from those whose opinions we value. It is irrational thinking, however, to accept nothing less than complete approval from an audience. You cannot please everyone, particularly if you take a stand on a controversial issue. Making complete approval from your audience a vital concern merely sets you up for inevitable failure. When you set standards for success at unreachable heights, you are bound to take a tumble.

ANXIETY-PROVOKING SITUATIONS   Several anxiety-provoking situations are relevant to public speaking (Figure 14-2). First, the *novelty of the speaking situation* can easily make us tense. When we do not know exactly what to expect because the situation is new to us, we feel anxious. As you gain experience speaking in front of groups, the novelty wears off and anxiety diminishes.

A second anxiety-provoking situation is *conspicuousness*. I have polled more than 1,000 students in public speaking classes. When asked what causes their speech anxiety, most identify being "on stage" or "in the spotlight." Being conspicuous, or the center of attention, increases most people's anxiety. We feel as though

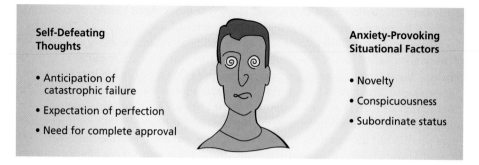

we are under a microscope being meticulously examined. As the size of an audience grows, we feel our conspicuousness increasing. The solution to anxiety provoked by conspicuousness is to develop confidence through experience that we can be successful in front of a large audience.

A third anxiety-provoking situation is *subordinate status.* When placed in a situation in which some or all of your audience has higher relative status than you, tension can mount. Students appearing before boards of trustees for the college or speaking to the faculty senate can easily feel intimidated and nervous. Again, preparation and practice are vital means of dealing with this anxiety-provoking situation.

These causes of speech anxiety, both self-defeating thoughts and anxiety-provoking situations, can produce a spiraling effect that feeds on itself. We begin by viewing a speech as a performance. This, in turn, stimulates physiological arousal. We then interpret the physical symptoms as fear, which triggers irrational thoughts, which stimulates more intense physical symptoms, greater fear, more irrational thoughts, and so forth (Motley, 1995). *The key to managing speech anxiety is to prevent the spiral of fear from ever occurring.*

Strategies for Managing Speech Anxiety

There is one surefire way to experience absolutely no anxiety prior to and during a speech. Simply don't care about the quality of your speech at all. You'll be very relaxed, but you'll also give a crummy speech. Your goal should not be to eliminate speech anxiety. Your goal should be to manage the anxiety that you do experience and use it to energize and stimulate peak accomplishment.

Many individuals have suggested strategies for managing speech anxiety; some are simple and others complex. Laurence Olivier sometimes swore at his audience backstage hoping to replace anxiety with anger. Willard Scott tried sticking a pin in his butt, hoping to startle away the stage fright. He also tried screaming off camera before giving weather reports on the "Today" show (not a very practical strategy for students in a classroom setting). Imagining members of your audience nude or clothed in their underwear or in diapers is a strategy offered so frequently by people that it almost amounts to folk wisdom. All of these suggestions have some merit, particularly if they work for you. They are unquestionably limited solutions, however, because they are diversionary tactics rather than strategies that directly address the primary causes of speech anxiety. In this section several ways to manage your speech anxiety are discussed.

PREPARE AND PRACTICE   Public speaking is a novel experience loaded with uncertainty for the inexperienced. Novices fear catastrophic failure because they don't know quite what to expect. Preparation and practice build self-confidence. As is true in almost anything you do, whether it is conversing with strangers at social gatherings or playing a musical instrument in front of a crowd, you tend to be less anxious when you are confident of your skills. You fear making a fool of yourself when you don't know what you're doing. You won't appear foolish if you have learned the requisite skills to present a speech effectively. You'll remove most of the novelty and uncertainty from the speaking experience when you are adequately prepared. So prepare your speech meticulously, and practice it before speaking in class to reduce your anxiety (Menzel & Carrell, 1994). Present it to friends. Present it to your dog. Practice it while taking a shower. Give it in your car on your way to class. *Practice, practice, practice!* When you've practiced your speech "enough," practice it again.

Speaking experience, of course, won't reduce anxiety if you stumble from one traumatic disaster to the next. Preparation is absolutely critical. If you make speech after speech, ill prepared and untrained, don't expect your anxiety to diminish. Your dread of public speaking will become dysfunctional. "Practice makes perfect" if it is practice based on knowledge of effective public speaking. Without requisite knowledge, practice will make perfectly horrible any speech that you give because you will be rehearsing incompetent public speaking.

Read the chapters in this text on effective public speaking. Listen to the advice of your instructor as you prepare and present speeches. *There is no substitute for preparation and practice.* If you do both, most of your anxiety will melt away and your confidence will soar (Ayres & Hopf, 1995).

GAIN PROPER PERSPECTIVE   Irrational, self-defeating thoughts are a primary cause of dysfunctional speech anxiety. How we think about our anxiety largely determines its level. One study (cited in Motley, 1995) compared three groups of anxious speakers that were randomly divided. A metering device that monitored the heart rate of speakers as they made their presentations was attached to the podium in plain view of the speakers. High, normal, and low anxiety zones were clearly designated on the metering device for speakers to see as they spoke. Each speaker delivered a prepared speech, and researchers monitored actual heart rates. What the speakers didn't know was that researchers had rigged the heart monitor to give false readings to the speakers. Members of one group saw high heart rate readings on the monitor, members of a second group saw low heart rates on the monitor, and the third "control group" gave speeches while the monitor was turned off. The results were dramatic. Speakers who saw high heart rate readings did experience elevated heart rates. Speakers who saw low heart rate readings on the monitor experienced diminished heart rates. Control group speakers experienced varied heart rates. You can exaggerate your anxiety by concentrating on your symptoms and thinking your anxiety is severe.

There are three phases to speech anxiety symptoms (Motley, 1995). There is the *anticipation phase* in which your symptoms elevate just prior to giving your speech. The *confrontation phase* occurs when you face the audience and begin to speak. There is a tremendous surge of adrenaline, your heart rate soars—sometimes to 180 beats per minute, perspiration increases, and so forth. The *adaptation phase* kicks in soon after the confrontation phase, within 60 seconds or fewer. Adaptation takes place even more swiftly for low-anxiety speakers, usually within 15 to 30 seconds. During

FIGURE 14-3 Heart Rate Patterns of Typical High- and Low-Anxiety Speakers (Motley, 1995)

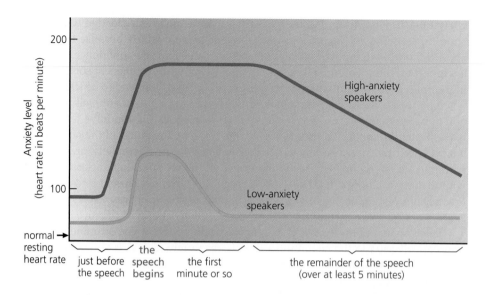

this phase symptoms steadily diminish, reaching a comfortable level within a couple of minutes (Figure 14-3).

Knowing the phases of anxiety allows you to gain a proper perspective on your experience of speech anxiety. First, recognizing that your anxiety will diminish dramatically and quickly as you speak should provide some comfort. Second, if you learn to monitor your adaptation, you can accelerate the process. As you begin to notice your heart rate diminishing, say to yourself, "It's getting better already . . . and better . . . and better." *Anxiety levels, even for the inexperienced, high-anxiety speaker, will diminish rapidly.*

Another aspect of gaining proper perspective is learning to recognize the difference between rational and irrational speech anxiety. A colleague of mine, Darrell Beck, concocted a simple formula for determining the difference: *the severity of the feared occurrence times the probability of the feared occurrence.* This formula gives a rough approximation of how much anxiety is rational and when you have stepped over the line into irrational territory. You approximate severity by imagining what would happen if catastrophic failure did occur. Would you fear for your life? Would you leave the country? Would you hide from friends and family, afraid to show your face? Would you drop out of college? Would you enter a convent or become a Trappist monk and take the vow of silence? None of these choices seems reasonable.

You gain perspective regarding the severity of your anxiety by deciding what's the worst that could befall you if disaster struck and you bombed the speech. You might drop the speech class, but even this is unlikely. Students are an understanding lot (this is not high school), and you'll have other opportunities in class to redeem yourself. Even a lousy speech doesn't warrant significant life changes. A few moments of disappointment, mild embarrassment, or discouragement because you received a mediocre grade is about as severe as it gets. Then, when you consider the probability of the "worst-case scenario" occurring, you should realize that there is not much to concern you. High severity times low probability equals pointless anxiety. *Concentrate on the probable (low severity), not the merely possible (high severity).*

Peggy Noonan (1998), a professional speechwriter, confesses that she had a phobia about public speaking that kept her from making her first speech until she was 40 years old. She learned to control her speech anxiety primarily by putting it in proper perspective. She explains it this way:

> (One) thing that has helped me is realizing that if I fail utterly, if I faint, babble, or spew, if people walk out flinging the heavy linen napkins onto the big round tables in disgust . . . my life continues as good as it was. Better. Because fewer people will ask me to speak. So flopping would be good for me. The minute I remember this I don't flop (p. 191).

Even individuals for whom English is a second language will benefit from gaining a proper perspective. Giving a speech in a second language can increase anxiety (McCroskey et al., 1985). There is an unrealistic expectation that English should be spoken perfectly. I have witnessed hundreds of speeches by nonnative speakers of English. Never once have I observed an audience of college students be rude to that speaker because his or her English was not perfect. Normally, students admire a speaker who tries hard to give a good speech in a relatively unfamiliar language. They usually listen more intently as well. Working yourself into a lather over an impending speech simply results from a lack of proper perspective.

ADOPT A NONCOMPETITIVE COMMUNICATION ORIENTATION   Desiring complete approval, fretting over your conspicuousness onstage, and feeling intimidated by status differences with listeners all occur when you view public speaking as a performance. Reframe this performance orientation of the high-anxiety speaker. Replace it with a communication orientation. Motley (1995) makes the case for reframing this way: "I have never encountered an anxious speaker who did not have a performance orientation, or one whose anxiety was not substantially reduced when the communication orientation replaced it. Very simply, changing your overall approach to public speaking is the key to reducing and controlling the anxiety" (p. 49).

A **performance orientation** emphasizes the "do's" and "don'ts" of speaking. Anxious speakers have inflated concerns about saying "ah" or "uhm" too many times. They worry about gestures, vocal inflection, eye contact, posture, and a myriad of style and delivery problems. They worry that word choice won't be precise, so they memorize the speech or read from a manuscript. Memorization increases anxiety (you worry about forgetting parts of your speech), and reading creates an artificial speaking style. This all places the focus on impressing critics and scoring style points, not on connecting with the audience and communicating your message.

Giving a speech isn't the Olympics, and you're usually not competing to score more points than someone else. Your audience won't hold up cards indicating your score immediately after you sit down. Granted, your speech instructor will likely give you a grade on your speech, but even here the performance orientation is counterproductive. No speech instructor expects silver-tongued oratory from novice speakers. Your instructor expects you to make mistakes, especially during your first few speeches. Speech classes are learning laboratories, not speech tournaments. Dump the performance orientation. It makes a speech into a contest. Most, perhaps all, of the speeches you will ever give will be evaluated on their own merits, not competitively in relation to someone else's speech. The competitive performance orientation feeds perfectionist thinking.

The irony is that you will perform better as a speaker if you move away from the competitive performance orientation (Motley, 1995). Your speaking style and delivery will seem more natural, less forced and stiff. When conversing with a friend or stranger, you rarely notice your delivery, gestures, posture, and so forth. You're

The communication orientation works well to reduce anxiety because you connect with your listeners. The focus becomes clearly communicating your message, not your fear of public speaking.

intent on being clear and interesting, even having some fun. Approach your speech in the same way.

The **communication orientation** focuses on making your message clear and interesting to your listeners. The communication orientation is audience centered, not self-centered. Focus on communicating with your listeners, not impressing them with your oratorical ability. What good is a speech that leaves audience members impressed with your style and delivery but confused about your ideas? Be concerned first with substance and only secondarily with stylistic eloquence. As Motley (1995) counsels, "Make the message clear and interesting and leave the performance ego out of it" (p. 63).

One way to reinforce the communication orientation approach to your speech is to practice your speech conversationally. Find a friend or loved one with whom you feel comfortable. Find a private location and sit in chairs or on a couch. Using a conversational style, just begin describing the speech that you have prepared. Don't actually give the speech. Merely converse about the speech—what the speech is about and how you plan to develop it. Use notes if you need to but refer to them infrequently. In subsequent practice sessions with your listener, gradually begin to introduce elements of the actual speech (an introduction only, for example). Eventually, deliver the entire speech while sitting down. Finally, present the entire speech standing, using only an outline of the speech for reference. This conversational approach to practicing your speech emphasizes the communication orientation.

Does the communication orientation work? *When compared to other methods of anxiety reduction and control, the communication orientation is the most successful* (Motley, 1995). Simply concentrating on communicating with an audience, not impressing them, reduces anxiety levels of speakers from high to moderately low.

The first three methods for reducing and controlling your speech anxiety work so well that little else needs to be said. Nevertheless, a few other methods are discussed because they are your insurance policy—included just in case you need them.

USE COPING STATEMENTS   Coping statements shift the thought process from negative to positive. Negative disaster thinking triggers high anxiety. You stumble at the outset of your speech and say to yourself, "I knew I couldn't do this well" or "I've already ruined the introduction." Try making coping statements when problems arise. "I'm past the tough part," "I'll do better once I get rolling," and "The best part is still ahead" are examples of positive coping statements. Make self-talk productive, not destructive.

USE POSITIVE IMAGING (VISUALIZATION)   Prepare for a speech presentation by countering negative thoughts of catastrophe with positive images of success. Some call this *visualization.* Create images in your head that picture you giving your speech fluently, clearly, and interestingly. Picture your audience responding in positive ways as you give your speech. Inexperienced speakers typically imagine what will go wrong during a speech. Exercise mental discipline and refuse to allow such thoughts to creep into your consciousness. Keep imagining speaking success, not failure.

TRY SYSTEMATIC DESENSITIZATION   This method of managing anxiety is very effective. Its chief drawback, however, is that it is time-consuming. **Systematic desensitization** is a technique used to control anxiety, even phobias, triggered by a wide variety of stimuli (Ayres & Hopf, 1995). You can manage fear of snakes or heights effectively using this method.

Systematic desensitization involves incremental exposure to increasingly threatening stimuli coupled with relaxation techniques. Applied to giving speeches, you would make a list of perhaps 10 steps in the speaking process, each likely to produce an increased anxiety response. Find yourself a comfortable, quiet place to sit. Read the first item on your list (e.g., your speech topic). When you experience anxiety, put the list aside and begin a relaxation exercise. Tense your muscles in your face and neck. Hold the tensed position for 10 seconds and then release. Now do the same with your hands, and so on until you've tensed and relaxed all the muscle groups in your body. Now breathe slowly and deeply as you say the word, "Relax" to yourself. Repeat this for 1 minute. Pick up the list and read the first item. If your anxiety remains pronounced, repeat the process. If your anxiety is minimal, move on to the second item (e.g., organizing your speech material) and repeat the tense-and-relax procedure. Work through your entire list of 10 items, stopping when you are able to read the final item (e.g., beginning the introduction of your speech) without appreciable anxiety. Use systematic desensitization several days in a row before your actual speech presentation. Your anxiety level should fall to lower levels.

www.mhhe
com/
rothwell2

See relaxation activity on the Online Learning Center, Chapter 14.

▆▆▆ Topic Choice and Analysis

A frequent concern of students that is a close second to speech anxiety is choosing a topic for a speech. In some instances you may be asked to give a speech on a particular subject because of your expertise (e.g., a nurse is asked to give a speech on flu shots; a student volunteer for "Food Not Bombs" is asked to speak on the local homeless problem). If you become an expert on some topic, organizations or groups may ask you to speak on that topic. In these instances the speech topic is chosen for you. In a speech class, however, the choice, within broad limits, will likely be up to you. In this section, how to choose a topic that is appropriate for you, your audience, and the occasion will be discussed. How to narrow your topic to a specific purpose statement, whether you've been assigned a topic or chosen one yourself, will also be explained.

See "Topic Helper" on CD.

Exploring Potential Topics

Choose a bad topic, and you are stuck with a bad speech. Choose a good topic, and the potential for a great speech looms large. How do you systematically explore potential topics for a speech? There are three primary ways: Do a personal inventory, brainstorm ideas, and scan popular periodicals and newspapers.

DO A PERSONAL INVENTORY Begin your exploration of appropriate topics by looking within yourself. What interests you? Make a list of every topic you can think of that you find interesting. What are your hobbies (e.g., woodworking, whittling, building model airplanes, doll collecting)? What sports do you play (e.g., tennis, racketball, softball, ice skating)? List any unusual events that have occurred in your life (e.g., caught in a tornado, observed a bank robbery). Have you done any volunteer work (e.g., for Habitat for Humanity, United Way, American Cancer Society)? What form of entertainment interests you (e.g., romantic movies, rap music, dancing, rodeo, car shows)? Do you have any special skills (e.g., surfing, cooking, carpentry, sewing)? Have you traveled to any interesting places (e.g., London, Paris, Cairo, Moscow)? Have you met any exciting people (e.g., rock stars, political leaders, professional athletes, actors)? What's the worst thing that's ever happened to you (e.g., divorce, serious illness, car accident, death of a relative)? What's the best (e.g., met your romantic partner, won a scholarship, saved someone's life)? How do you spend your free time (e.g., reading novels, hiking, watching TV, playing video games, exploring the Internet)? This list contains many possible choices for a speech topic.

BRAINSTORM Your personal inventory won't necessarily provide an immediate topic for your speech. You will probably need to brainstorm additional possibilities. Take your list of things that interest you, examine it, then choose five topics that seem most promising. Write down each topic on a separate list, and for each topic brainstorm new possibilities. For example, brainstorm "trip to London" by letting your mind free-associate with any related topics, such as double-decker buses, driving on the left, the Thames River, British accent, Parliament, Buckingham Palace, Princess Diana's death, royalty, Hyde Park, Soho, British money, and British rock groups. Each of these topics is rather general. Consider each one, and try to brainstorm a more specific topic. British money, for example, might lead to a comparison of

British money to American currency. Driving on the left could lead to an interesting presentation on why the British drive on the left yet we drive on the right. Parliament could trigger a comparison between the U.S. Congress and the British Parliament. If this approach does not generate excitement, try a third method—scanning.

SCAN MAGAZINES AND NEWSPAPERS   There is no shortage of magazines and newspapers readily available to you for scanning potential speech topics. Pick up a copy of *Newsweek, Time, Consumer Reports, Life, Sports Illustrated, Psychology Today, Entertainment, Muscle Media,* or any popular magazine. Look at the table of contents and leaf through the articles. Don't spend time reading the articles. You're scanning quickly just to get ideas. If you see a promising topic, write it down and note the magazine, the article, and the date. Do the same with newspapers. Your library will have local, national, and international newspapers filled with hundreds of potential topics for speeches.

Analyzing Appropriateness of Topic Choice

Appropriateness and effectiveness are key elements of the communication competence model. Choosing a topic that is inappropriate for a particular audience virtually guarantees that your speech will be ineffective. Appropriateness is contextual. A speech topic that works in one instance may be an abysmal failure in another instance. There are three central elements to consider when analyzing the appropriateness of your topic choice: speaker, audience, and occasion.

SPEAKER APPROPRIATENESS   If you choose a topic merely to fulfill an assignment but you find it uninteresting, even tedious, then it is not appropriate for you, the speaker. Choose a topic that interests or excites you. An appropriate topic for you can motivate your desire to research the topic and build a quality speech. An inappropriate topic for you will make researching and constructing your speech drudgery. If you're interested and excited about your topic, you can communicate that to your audience. It is a rare individual who can take a topic that he or she finds as dull as watching slug races and successfully fake interest in it to an audience. If you think the subject is dull, what must your audience think?

Some topic choices are not suitable because of who you are. You and the topic may be a poor or awkward fit. A White person speaking of the "Black experience in America" is an awkward fit. Similarly, young people talking about "what it's like being old" sounds goofy. Men speaking about female menopause is also awkward. A flabby, out-of-shape individual speaking about the wonders of weight lifting doesn't work (unless it is meant to be a humorous speech). No matter how gifted you are as a speaker, some topics will sink your chances of presenting an effective speech. Choose a topic that suits your interests and fits who you are.

AUDIENCE APPROPRIATENESS   Public speaking is transactional. A speaker and his or her audience are interconnected and influence each other. The appropriateness of a topic is largely audience centered. Over the years, my colleagues have shared many horror stories about student speeches that were startlingly inappropriate. Almost every speech instructor has heard at least one speech by a male student on "how to score with the babes." One student gave a speech on "how to assassinate someone you hate." Another student gave a distasteful speech on "proper methods of inducing vomiting after a big meal." My colleagues and I have heard speeches on "spitting for distance," "effective nail biting techniques," "harassing the homeless," "opening a beer bottle with your teeth," "constructing a bong," "maintaining your 'pot' plants," and "shoplifting techniques that work." These topics are inappropriate because they are offensive, trivial, or demeaning or they encourage illegal, unethical behavior. Most of them are pointless, adolescent silliness.

There are other reasons a topic might be inappropriate for an audience. An audience may find a topic choice difficult to relate to or appreciate. Giving a speech on how to surf to an audience living in Kansas is an awkward fit. A topic can also be too technical or complex. Students occasionally try to justify creationism and refute evolution by referring to the second law of thermodynamics. Their explanation is almost always incorrect and confusing to the audience because it requires an understanding of physics.

The increasingly multicultural makeup of audiences, especially student audiences, presents another source for inappropriate topic choice. Homogeneous audiences composed of highly similar individuals are rare these days. College campuses in particular are a heterogeneous conglomeration of diverse cultures. Even without intending to, a topic choice can be insulting to individuals from other cultures or cocultures. Giving a speech on religion or politics should be approached cautiously lest insult be given to those with different cultural perspectives.

OCCASION APPROPRIATENESS   When you're speaking at a particular event, your topic choice must be appropriate to the occasion. A topic choice should meet the expectations of your audience concerning what is appropriate. A graduation ceremony invites topics such as "employment possibilities for the future," "skills for success," and "thinking in the future tense." A sermon at a Sunday religious service warrants a topic related to ethical or moral behavior. Don't choose a topic unrelated to the occasion. It won't fulfill audience expectations. Soliciting support for a political cause at a graduation ceremony or an awards banquet will get you booed off the stage. The occasion dictates the appropriateness of a topic choice.

Eleven days before the 2002 national election, Paul Wellstone, Democratic U.S. senator from Minnesota, died in a plane crash along with his wife, Sheila, their daughter Marica, and three other victims. With the expectation that former U.S. Senator Walter Mondale would replace Wellstone on the ballot, the memorial service for Wellstone, attended by 20,000 people, became a pep rally for the Mondale campaign. In a "eulogy" for Wellstone, Rick Kahn made this plea, "Can you not hear your friend calling you, one last time, one step forward on his behalf, to keep his legacy alive and help us win this election for Paul Wellstone?" (Wilgoren, 2002). Most of the crowd sprang to its feet and began chanting, "Mondale! Mondale!" With many Republicans and independents in attendance, this burst of partisanship ignited a firestorm of controversy. Jesse Ventura, the Independent Party governor of Minnesota, left in a huff, remarking that he found the transformation of a solemn memorial service into a political pep rally "disturbing." For days afterward, Republicans bitterly complained that the Democrats had exploited a tragedy for political purposes. Jeff Blodgett, Wellstone's campaign manager, publicly apologized for the turn of events. Even to more neutral parties, the transformation of this occasion from a memorial into a political rally appeared inappropriate, even unseemly. The occasion dictated that the topic of focus should be memorializing Wellstone, not choosing to jump-start Mondale's campaign.

Narrowing the Topic

Sometimes you are given a very broad topic on which to speak. Other times you find an interesting topic, but it is too broad and general for the time available to speak. Narrowing your topic to fit the audience and the occasion is a significant task for any speaker.

STAY WITHIN THE TIME LIMIT   President Woodrow Wilson, a former college professor and the only U.S. president to earn a PhD, took his public speaking very seriously. A reporter interviewed him once regarding his speech preparation. "How long do you spend preparing a 10-minute speech?" Wilson was asked. Wilson replied, "About two weeks." "How long do you spend preparing an hour-long speech?" the reporter queried. "About a week," answered Wilson. Surprised, the reporter then asked Wilson how long he prepared for a 2-hour speech. Wilson replied, "I could do that now." Giving a long-winded speech takes less effort than narrowing the speech to fit neatly into a shorter time allotment.

Once you have settled on a general topic that is appropriate for you the speaker, the audience, and the occasion, begin narrowing the topic to fit your time limit. A 5-minute speech obviously requires much more narrowing than a 15-minute speech. You can't accomplish a great deal in only 5 minutes. Take the general topic and brainstorm more specific subtopics. For example, a general topic such as "the cost of a college education" is very broad and could easily require half an hour to explore in any depth. Break down this general topic into these more specific subtopics for a much shorter speech: problems with financial aid, how to get a scholarship, part-time student employment, the high cost of textbooks, room and board fees for campus living, college tuition, and college fees.

Don't choose a topic that is so broad and complex that you couldn't possibly do it justice in the time allotted. Heed Mark Twain's observation that "Few sinners are saved after the first 20 minutes of a sermon." *Staying within your time limit is critical.* Long-winded speeches, no matter how well constructed and delivered, won't be effective if the audience expects a short presentation (see Box 14-3). If you are asked to address a luncheon meeting of a civic organization and you are scheduled for a 15-minute presentation, narrow your focus to fit that time limit. You'll be addressing a roomful of empty chairs if you go much beyond the time limit. People attending luncheon meetings often have only an hour for the entire meeting, of which your speech is but a small part.

CONSTRUCT A PURPOSE STATEMENT   Once you have narrowed a general topic into more specific subtopics, identify a general purpose and compose a specific purpose statement. A **general purpose** is an infinitive phrase that identifies the overall goal of your speech; it tells the audience why you're giving the speech (to inform, describe, explain, demonstrate, persuade, memorialize, entertain, eulogize).

The general purpose will be given to you if your speech is a classroom assignment (e.g., give a demonstration speech). If you have no direction from others, you must decide what general purpose is appropriate for the audience and occasion. Once you have determined the general purpose, decide what will be your central idea (sometimes referred to as your *theme*). The **central idea** identifies the main concept, point, issue, or conclusion that you want the audience to understand, believe, feel, or reach. The central idea becomes the one concise thought, separate from all the details provided in the speech, that audience members are likely to remember.

Box 14-3 Sharper Focus

The Never-Ending Speech

His speech was scheduled to last no more than 15 minutes. Bill Clinton, at the time the 41-year-old governor of Arkansas, had the political plum of the 1988 Democratic National Convention in Atlanta. A gifted speaker, his nominating speech for presidential candidate Michael Dukakis could have provided Clinton with invaluable publicity and national stature. Instead, it turned into a disaster. His speech lasted more than twice as long as his scheduled time allowed. With convention delegates growing restless in anticipation of the acceptance address by Dukakis, Clinton droned on despite increasing annoyance throughout the convention hall. Some delegates began chanting, "Give him the hook" and "Wrap it up." Jim Wright, the convention chair, at one point edged close to Clinton and admonished him to finish his address. Even the television networks switched from showing the speech to shots of delegates drawing their forefingers across their throats in a "cut" signal. CNN focused its camera on the red podium light glaring at Clinton to stop speaking. In desperation, convention officials turned off the TelePrompTer hoping to shut down the single-minded Clinton. Clinton received his most enthusiastic cheer when he said, "In closing . . . ".

Massachusetts delegate William Bulger joked during the speech, "When this started I was a young man."

After the speech finally ended, a network executive taped a hand-lettered sign onto the front of an Atlanta phone book that read, "Transcript of Gov. Clinton's Speech." On the "Tonight Show" with Johnny Carson a few nights after his speaking disaster, Clinton joked, "It was not my finest hour or even hour-and-a-half." Clinton was given his topic (i.e., nominate Dukakis), but he failed to narrow it sufficiently for the occasion, and it doomed his presentation.

Bill Clinton never seemed to learn from his disastrous 1988 speech. His 2000 State of the Union speech took 1 hour and 29 minutes to deliver, proving that he did not heed the words of an anonymous wit who observed that "the brain can absorb only what the seat can endure."

Clinton is capable of great eloquence in flourishes, but he can't sustain eloquence for more than an hour, nor can media-saturated audiences easily maintain their attention for his excessively lengthy speeches. Abraham Lincoln's Gettysburg Address, considered one of the great American speeches, lasted about 2 *minutes*. Famed orator Edward Everett, who preceded Lincoln, gave a 2-hour-plus speech. He later wrote Lincoln, "I shall be glad if I could flatter myself that I came as near to the central idea of the occasion in two hours as you did in two minutes" (cited in Noonan, 1998, p. 65).

We compose a specific purpose statement when we have a clear central idea in mind. A **specific purpose statement** is a concise, precise declaration composed of simple, clear language that encompasses both the general purpose and the central idea and indicates what the speaker hopes to accomplish with the speech.

> *Topic:* Cost of a college education
> *Narrowed Topic:* The high cost of textbooks
> *General Purpose:* To inform
> *Central Idea:* Complaining about the high cost of textbooks is not as helpful as knowing why textbooks are so expensive.
> *Specific Purpose Statement:* To explain the three primary reasons textbooks are expensive

Once you have constructed your specific purpose statement, test its appropriateness and likely effectiveness. Ask the following questions:

1. *Is your purpose statement concise and precise?* A long, wordy statement will confuse listeners or put them to sleep. You should be able to phrase an effective purpose statement in 15 words or fewer. If your purpose statement is much beyond 15 words, rephrase it until it is more concise and precise.
2. *Is your purpose statement phrased as a declarative statement?* Phrasing a purpose statement as a question asks your listeners to provide the answers (e.g., "Why are textbooks so expensive?"). Make your purpose statement declarative

(i.e., declare the direction of your speech) and begin with an infinitive phrase (i.e., to inform, to persuade, to celebrate, to teach, to demonstrate, to eulogize).

3. *Is your purpose statement free of figurative language?* Keep your purpose statement plain and direct. Figurative language is fine for the body of your speech, but it can be confusing in a purpose statement. For example, "To tell you why textbooks are the golden fleece of education" will likely leave some of your listeners scratching their heads and saying, "Huh?" to themselves.

4. *Is your purpose statement more than simply a topic?* "To inform my audience about the cost of textbooks" is a topic statement, not a specific purpose statement. What about the cost of textbooks? Listeners are provided with no direction for your speech. Give them a direction. Tell them specifically what you seek to accomplish. "To discuss the feasibility of a private college bookstore as a way to lower textbook prices" is a purpose statement with a direction.

5. *Is your purpose statement practical?* Can your listeners accomplish what you ask them to do? "I want to teach you to be a top-notch computer programmer" will not happen in a single speech, not even a lengthy one. "My purpose is to inform you about the many changes in the new tax code" is too technical and complex for a single speech to an audience of mostly uninformed taxpayers. Make your specific purpose statement practical: "I want to convince you that taking a computer programming course is worthwhile."

Now you know how to choose a topic; determine its appropriateness for the speaker (you), the audience, and the occasion; and construct a specific purpose statement that appropriately narrows your topic for the time allotted. The next step is analyzing your audience.

Audience Analysis

A well-known and high-priced speaker was invited to address the Cabrillo College faculty. She was articulate, poised, and dynamic. For 45 minutes she told stories and anecdotes that brought frequent laughter from her audience. It appeared that she had succeeded admirably in presenting a speech. Faculty broke into groups following the speech to discuss the subjects the speaker had raised. Unlike the apparent positive response the speaker received during her speech, an avalanche of criticism followed. The chief complaint was that the speaker had entertained everyone but hadn't presented substantial material that warranted a generous speaker fee. The speech was so dissatisfying for most that the college was hesitant for several years afterward to invite any outside speaker to address the faculty. This speech failed, not because it wasn't prepared well or presented skillfully, but because it was poorly suited to the audience. A competent speech is far more than good style and delivery. Your thoughts have to resonate with an audience.

Edmund Muskie, former U.S. senator from Maine, once remarked, "In Maine we have a saying that there's no point in speaking unless you can improve on silence." Improving on silence requires careful audience analysis. Almost 2,500 years ago Aristotle wrote, "Of the three elements in speechmaking—speaker, subject, and person addressed—it is the last one, the hearer, that determines the speech's end and object" (cited in Cooper, 1960, p. 136). Meeting the expectations of your audience is a key element in competent public speaking. This is a cooperative effort between speaker and listeners. You are working with your listeners, not against them.

A speaker who berates his or her audience for some perceived wrongdoing invites angry responses from listeners. Teachers who lecture students on their inadequacies create a defensive, competitive communication climate. Making adversaries out of your audience rarely produces a positive result for a speaker. Think of audience analysis as the process of discovering ways to build bridges between yourself and listeners, to identify with their needs, hopes, dreams, interests, and concerns. In general, you construct your speech with the audience always in mind. Effective speakers mindfully craft their presentations based on the goals they seek to achieve, the relational status between them and listeners, and the constraints of the situation. Thus, knowing your audience well is a key concern for any speaker. In this section, types of audiences and audience composition will be discussed.

Types of Audiences

Begin analyzing your audience by considering what type of audience will hear your speech. *There are four general types of audiences: captive, committed, concerned, and casual.*

CAPTIVE AUDIENCE   A captive audience assembles to hear you speak because they are compelled to, not because they expect entertainment or intellectual stimulation. A required speech class is an example of a captive audience. Formal ceremonies, luncheon gatherings of clubs and organizations, and most meetings conducted in places of business are other examples of captive audiences (e.g., training sessions). Power, especially in its dominance form, can be an issue with captive audiences. Listeners may attend a speech only because those with greater power (supervisors, teachers) insist. This can easily trigger psychological reactance and establish a competitive, defensive environment in which listeners initially view the speaker as an annoyance and cause for complaint.

A captive audience presents a special challenge to a speaker. Gaining and maintaining the interest of a captive audience, engaging listeners actively, is a primary consideration for the speaker. When listeners would just as soon be elsewhere, snaring their attention and keeping them listening to you is no small accomplishment.

COMMITTED AUDIENCE   A committed audience voluntarily assembles to hear a speaker because they want to invest time and energy listening to the speaker's thoughts and being inspired by his or her words. A committed audience usually agrees with the speaker's position already and is presumably interested since they voluntarily appeared to hear the speech. Listeners who gather for Sunday sermons, political rallies, and social protest demonstrations are all examples of committed audiences. Gaining and maintaining the interest and attention of a committed audience is not nearly as difficult as doing the same with a captive audience. Inspiring action, persuading, and empowering listeners to act decisively are primary considerations for a speaker addressing a committed audience, not stirring interest or seeking agreement. Committed listeners want to be inspired to act, and, as the speaker, you want to "rally the troops," provide listeners with a "can do" attitude, and motivate change.

CONCERNED AUDIENCE   A concerned audience is one that gathers voluntarily to hear a speaker because they care about issues and ideas. A concerned audience is a motivated audience. Unlike a committed audience, however, listeners haven't

This is an example of a casual audience that assembled for a street performance.

attended the speech to show commitment to a particular cause or idea. Concerned listeners want to gather information and learn. Listeners who gather for book and poetry readings or lecture series are examples of concerned audiences. A primary consideration for a speaker addressing a concerned audience is to be informative by presenting new ideas and new information in a stimulating and attention-getting fashion. Concerned listeners may eventually become committed listeners.

CASUAL AUDIENCE A casual audience never anticipates being an audience in the first place. A casual audience is composed of individuals who are picked as listeners because they happen to be milling about or they're passing by and hear a speaker, stop out of curiosity or casual interest, and remain until bored or sated. Individuals wandering in front of the student union, sitting on the steps of a government building having lunch, or walking in a park on a sunny day might be a casual audience for a speaker. Street performers snare passersby to create an audience. A primary consideration for a speaker addressing a casual audience is to connect with listeners immediately and create curiosity and interest. Unlike a captive audience that feels compelled to act as listeners, members of a casual audience are free to leave at a moment's whim.

When I was in Bath, England, in 1995, I happened upon a street performer, or *busker*, as they are called in England. The busker was entertaining his casual audience composed primarily of tourists and shoppers. He gathered an audience mostly with clever banter, corny jokes, audience interaction, and whimsical tricks. Curious about the gathering crowd and happy to be entertained after a long day of sightseeing and shopping, I joined the audience. Within minutes I was picked out of the crowd to "assist" the busker in performing one of his "daring" tricks. My job was to tie the busker's hands tightly behind his back with a chain, put a bag over his head, and count to 30 while the performer "escaped" from his confinement while on his knees with his head submerged in a 1-gallon bucket of water. Immediately following his successful "underwater escape," a reporter from the BBC television network pulled me aside and asked if I would agree to be interviewed for a BBC documentary on buskers in England. The reporter wanted the "American viewpoint" on busking. I agreed to be interviewed. I was a casual member of an audience who ended up on British television.

Each type of audience—captive, committed, concerned, or casual—presents its own challenge to a speaker. Each audience has its own expectations that a speaker must address to be successful.

Audience Composition

Your speech should be prepared with your audience always in mind, so knowing something about your audience is critical. The appropriateness of your remarks and their effectiveness with a specific audience depend in large part on connecting with your listeners. Again, you are working cooperatively with your audience, not competitively against your listeners. Connection comes from framing your speech to resonate with listeners. This means shaping your material to address the expectations, interests, knowledge, needs, and experiences of audience members. You may have an opportunity to survey listeners and determine some of this important information about your audience. Students sometimes poll classmates about issues and problems before composing their speeches. Often, however, you must make educated guesses about an audience based on **demographics**—characteristics of an audience such as age, gender, culture and ethnicity, and group affiliations. Let's briefly consider each of these demographics.

AGE The average age of an audience can provide valuable information for a speaker. College instructors, for instance, must speak to the experience of college students, and most of you weren't even born before 1980. This means that most of you have no direct experience of the Vietnam War, Watergate, eight-track tapes, ditto machines, or manual typewriters and only fleeting recollection of a time when wristwatches did nothing more than tell time. E-mail was only a futurist's fantasy, and automobiles could be repaired without computer technology. But you've never known a time when space travel wasn't possible, color television didn't exist, computers wouldn't fit on a desktop or in your hand, phones couldn't be carried in a purse or pocket, overnight mail wasn't available, ATMs weren't readily accessible in foreign countries, and copy machines weren't everywhere.

It is difficult for most of you reading this text to imagine a time not very long ago when indoor shopping malls were rare and people carried transistor radios in their shirt pockets. The primary age of your audience tells you quite a bit about the experiences they haven't had as well as the experiences they have had. As a speaker, develop the content of your speech in such a way that it speaks to the experience of audience members. References to insider trading, mutual funds, problems of leadership in corporations, and planning retirement accounts don't speak directly to the experience of a young audience. Older audiences, however, may relate to detailed explorations of such topics.

GENDER Gender differences in perception and behavior do exist, as discussed in Chapter 3. You need to be careful, however, not to assume too much from these differences. For instance, during political elections women in the United States tend to place greater emphasis on issues such as education, health care, and social justice, whereas men tend to emphasize economics and military security. Nevertheless, effective audience analysis means that you present your material in a way that interests all audience members.

Develop your speech from different perspectives to include all audience members. A speech on sexual harassment, for instance, could be linked to both men and women by discussing effects on victims (typically women but sometimes men) and offering ways to avoid charges of sexual harassment (usually involving men). In addition, men can relate indirectly to the indignity and powerless feelings associated with sexual harassment by seeing what wives, girlfriends, or daughters experience when victimized. Men don't want to see the women they love or care about subjected to indignity and injustice.

In addition, sensitivity to an audience may require judicious attention to language when framing issues. Consistently referring to leaders as "he," "him," or "his," as in "A leader must inspire, and he must motivate his followers," excludes women. Similarly, referring to elementary school teachers as "she" or "her," as in "A third grade teacher works hard and she spends long hours with her students," excludes men. Try to speak in more inclusive terms, using "him or her" or plural forms such as "they" (see Chapter 5).

ETHNICITY AND CULTURE Throughout this textbook the role of ethnicity and culture in communication transactions has been made apparent. Ethnicity and culture are no less important for the public speaker analyzing his or her audience.

Students who fail to analyze the multicultural makeup of college audiences can create embarrassing speaking situations. Despite my efforts to encourage sensitivity to individuals from diverse cultures, I have witnessed several student speeches that ignited awkward, even hostile, moments in class. One Jewish student gave a speech on peace agreements in the Middle East. She referred to Palestinians as "terrorists and warmongers." This did not sit well with several Arab students in the class. You can question and debate policies and issues without resorting to insults and sweeping generalizations. Take care not to offend a chunk of your audience if you hope to have receptive listeners.

GROUP AFFILIATION The groups we belong to tell others a great deal about our values, beliefs, and points of view. Membership in the National Rifle Association usually indicates a strong belief in the right of gun ownership and a somewhat conservative political bent. Membership in the National Organization for Women usually indicates a strong belief in equal rights for women and a somewhat liberal political point of view. Listener membership in clubs, sororities, fraternities, national honorary societies, or educational groups provides you with information about your audience. This information can be vital in shaping your speech, as you will see in chapters 17 and 18.

Sensitivity to your audience's expectations, needs, values, interests, and beliefs is a necessary component of competent public speaking. Sensitivity means picking up clues about your listeners so you can successfully frame your speech. Picking up clues about your audience is the first part of the process of speech construction.

Summary

Managing speech anxiety is frequently the first and paramount concern of novice public speakers. Virtually all beginning speakers experience substantial anxiety. Your goal is not to eliminate anxiety but to control it and use it to energize your speaking. Self-defeating thoughts and anxiety-provoking situations trigger speech anxiety. There are many speech anxiety management methods available. The most effective methods include preparing and practicing diligently, gaining proper perspective, and replacing the competitive performance orientation with the noncompetitive communication orientation. Speech preparation also includes topic choice and analysis. The effectiveness of your speech will depend in large measure on the appropriateness of your topic choice. A topic should be appropriate to you the speaker, your audience, and the occasion. Narrow your topic to fit the time allotted by constructing a specific purpose statement. Finally, every speech should be tailored to your specific audience. A speech can be both a tremendous success or a dismal failure depending on the audience. In public speaking, the "one size fits all" approach doesn't usually work.

Quizzes Without Consequences

Go to Quizzes Without Consequences at the book's Online Learning Center at **www.mhhe.com/rothwell2** or access the CD-ROM for *In the Company of Others.*

www.mhhe
● com/**rothwell2**

Key Terms

See Audio Flashcards Study Aid.

www.mhhe
● com/**rothwell2**
See Crossword Puzzle Study Aid.

central idea
communication
  orientation
demographics
dysfunctional speech
  anxiety

functional speech
  anxiety
general purpose
performance
  orientation

specific purpose
  statement
speech anxiety
systematic
  desensitization

Hentoff, N. (1992). *Free speech for me, but not for thee.* New York: Harper Perennial. Hentoff forcefully argues the importance of public speech.

Jamieson, K. (1988). *Eloquence in an electronic age.* New York: Oxford University Press. This is a wonderful treatment of the importance of the spoken word and the new challenges offered by television.

The Candidate (1972). Drama; PG ★★★✦
In this slightly dated but still insightful look at a political campaign, Robert Redford plays the appealing, charismatic candidate. Analyze the speeches Redford makes to a variety of audiences. How do his speechwriters shape his speeches to appeal to diverse audiences?

Four Weddings and a Funeral (1994). Romantic comedy; R ★★★★
This is Hugh Grant at his most appealing as his character falls in love with an attractive American (Andie MacDowell). His inability to express his feelings to her thwarts any relationship until he has attended four weddings (including that of MacDowell's character) and a funeral. Note the severe case of speech anxiety exhibited by the novice priest (Rowan Atkinson). Analyze the "toasts" at the weddings for their appropriateness to the audience and occasion.

CHAPTER 15

Developing a Speech

It was the 60th annual convention of the California Federation of Teachers. Keynote speaker Charles Kernaghan, director of the National Labor Committee, was addressing an audience of California teachers. His central idea (theme) was that extreme poverty of much of the world's workforce accrues from economic globalization and the exploitation of workers. His speech was a rousing anti-sweatshop call to arms. Kernaghan held up garment after garment produced overseas, and he told stories of the workers who made these garments, noting that much of the clothing produced overseas is sold to young people in the United States. He claimed that 20 million American teenagers spend $155 billion a year on clothing, and college-age youth spend $268 billion a year. He provided a striking example of the exploitation of garment workers, most who are between the ages of 6 and 16. Referring to a Nike pricing document from the Dominican Republic, he noted, "There are 22 steps to the production of a T-shirt, which in total take 6.6 minutes, or 11% of an hour's labor. The worker gets 8 cents for that time—0.3% of the retail price. Advertising that same shirt costs them $2.32. They spend 32 times more on branding (brand identification) than they do on the worker" (cited in Anti-Sweatshop Activist, 2002, p. 4). He argued that young people "have a right to ask, how do the people live who produce the clothes they wear?" (p. 4). Kernaghan discussed the Students Against Sweatshops movement in the United States and its hundreds of chapters on college campuses. The audience cheered when he thundered, "These kids are on fire!" Kernaghan brought his audience to their feet when he concluded, "There can never be peace without social justice, or in a world with child labor" (p. 4).

Kernaghan's speech was masterful and an enormous success. "Of all the speakers at the 60th annual convention, none stirred delegates as deeply as Charles Kernaghan" (p. 4). His speech was successful for several reasons. First, the CFT convention had as one of its prime themes a concern for social justice. Kernaghan's keynote address was well suited to this theme. As members of a powerful teachers' union, listeners were receptive to his message that nonunion workers can be and are exploited as "cheap labor." He knew his audience and tailored his message to audience members' expectations, values, and beliefs. Second, he evidently researched his topic very carefully. He had the facts to support his claims. Third, he used very effective attention strategies. His speech was not a dry recitation of facts and figures; it was a passionate presentation that was at times intense, startling, and vital in its depiction of the plight of garment workers in countries around the world. He told stories about young women he interviewed who worked in deplorable sweatshop conditions. They struggle to stay alive on a day's wage of $4.80 when it costs them $1.14 for bus fare to and from work, 91 cents for breakfast, and $1.37 for lunch, leaving them $1.38 after expenses. Fourth, his conclusion didn't just fade out. He ended with an appeal that resonated with his audience and produced a rousing standing ovation. Clearly, Kernaghan developed his speech thoughtfully and carefully so it would be a smashing success with CFT members. *The primary purpose of this chapter is to explore the fundamental audience-centered process of developing a speech.*

The primary purpose of this chapter is to explore the fundamental audience-centered process of developing a speech.

There are four chapter objectives:

1. to discuss ways to research your speech,
2. to identify how to outline and organize your speech,
3. to identify ways to gain and maintain the attention of your audience, and
4. to discuss how to develop an effective introduction and conclusion to your speech.

Researching the Topic

Researching your topic should be a focused undertaking. Wandering aimlessly through a library or searching randomly on the Internet will waste time and accomplish little. In this section, how to research a speech topic is explained.

The Internet

The Internet has quickly become a primary source for research. Unfortunately, it is very difficult to separate information from misinformation on the Internet (see Box 15-1). To conduct competent Internet research you need to be familiar with search tools and tips for using these tools (Courtright & Perse, 1998; Hock, 1999; Maloy, 1999).

SEARCH TOOLS When researching a speech topic on the Internet, you have several search tools from which to pick. Often you'll begin with a search engine. A **search engine** is an Internet tool that computer generates indexes of Web pages that match, or link with, key words you type in a search window. There are far too many search engines to provide an exhaustive list here. A comprehensive list of search engines can be found at the Library of Congress Web site (www.lcweb.loc.gov/global/search.html). Some of the more popular search engines are as follows:

See "Internet Primer" on CD.

> AltaVista (www.altavista.com)
> Ask Jeeves (www.askjeeves.com)
> Excite (www.excite.com)
> FastSearch (www.alltheweb.com)
> Google (www.google.com)
> HotBot (www.hotbot.com)
> InfoSeek (www.infoseek.com)
> Lycos (www.lycos.cs.cmu.edu)
> Northern Light (www.nlsearch.com)
> Snap (www.snap.com)
> Webcrawler (www.webcrawler.com)

There is no search engine that accesses more than about a third of what is available on the Internet. If one engine fails to provide what you're looking for, try another one.

A **directory** is an Internet tool that generates edited indexes of Web pages that match, or link with, keywords you type in a search window. The important difference between a search engine and a directory is that a directory has a person trained in library or information sciences choosing prospective sites based on their quality. *Search engines are more likely than directories to provide overly broad, often irrelevant sites.* Two popular directories follow:

> TradeWaveGalaxy (www.einet.net)
> Yahoo (www.yahoo.com)

A **metasearch engine** will send your key word request to several search engines at once. These engines work best when your request is a relatively obscure one, not a general interest topic. When you want to narrow your search to about a dozen sites, try using a metasearch engine. Some popular metasearch engines are as follows:

> Dogpile (www.dogpile.com)
> InvisibleWeb (www.invisibleweb.com)

Box 15-1   Sharper Focus

Cruising the Net Skeptically

In April, 2002, I received the following e-mail:

> These are actual comments made on students' report cards by teachers in the New York City public school system. All teachers were reprimanded but boy, are these funny!!

1. Since my last report, your child has reached rock bottom and has started to dig.
2. I would not allow this student to breed.
3. Your child has delusions of adequacy.
4. Your son is depriving a village somewhere of an idiot.
5. Your son sets low personal standards and then consistently fails to achieve them.
6. The student has a "full six-pack" but lacks the plastic thing to hold it all together.
7. This child has been working with too much glue.
8. When your daughter's IQ reaches 50, she should sell.
9. The gates are down, the lights are flashing, but the train isn't coming.
10. If this student were any more stupid, he'd have to be watered twice a week.
11. It's impossible to believe that the sperm that created this child beat out 1,000,000 others.
12. The wheel is turning but the hamster is definitely dead.

Although the Internet is a phenomenal resource of high-quality information, it also offers a great potential for spreading misinformation. Confident that the "actual comments" in the e-mail would not have been made by public school teachers, especially on a report card, I used the Internet to check on the credibility of this report. I chose one of the comments, typed it verbatim in the search window of the Google search engine, and found something quite interesting. I located Web sites that printed the same list of comments but claimed that the list was garnered from British military officer fitness reports, employee performance evaluations, military performance appraisals, and appraisals of federal employees. There were 672 Web sites dating as far back as 1997 that printed this list of comments and attributed them to various sources (some sites had added comments to the list). The list is almost certainly a hoax.

The Internet is a rich source of rumor, gossip, and hoaxes. One hoax promised that the first 13,000 people to forward an e-mail message sent to them would win cash or trips to Disneyland. Author Kurt Vonnegut's commencement address to college graduates at MIT was printed on the Internet in its entirety. In it Vonnegut counseled graduates to "wear sunscreen. If I could offer you only one tip for the future, sunscreen would be it." He also advised graduates to "floss." Vonnegut exposed the address as a fake. He never addressed graduates at MIT (Harmon, 2001).

Following the terrorist attack on the Twin Towers in New York City, a message began circulating widely on the Internet that French astrologer Nostradamus predicted the World Trade Center's destruction in 1654. The message claimed that the infamous seer composed this prescient verse: "Two brothers torn apart by chaos, while the fortress endures, the great leader will succumb. The third big war will begin when the big city is burning." Aside from the highly ambiguous nature of this supposed prediction, Nostradamus composed no such verse (Liu, 2001). Nostradamus also died in 1566. A similar bogus Nostradamus prediction appeared on the Internet soon after the Space Shuttle Columbia disaster in February 2003.

In the hours immediately following the Trade Center catastrophe, a rumor circulated on the Net that a man on the 71st, 82nd, or 100th floor of the collapsing tower rode the falling debris to safety. Not surprisingly, it never happened (check the validity of Internet rumors at www.snopes2.com).

Singer Mariah Carey was victimized twice by bogus Internet hoaxes. In 1996, the following quote was attributed to her: "When I watch TV and see those poor, starving kids all over the world, I can't help but cry. I mean, I'd love to be skinny like that, but not with all those flies and death and stuff." In 1999, another fabricated quotation was attributed to Carey. The claim was made that Carey was one of the first celebrities to comment on the death of King Hussein of Jordan. "I'm inconsolable at the present time. I was a very good friend of Jordan. He was probably the greatest basketball player this country has ever seen. We will never see his like again" (Mariah "Quote" Spreads, 1999).

How do you separate the high-quality information on the Internet from the hokum? Follow these four easy steps that should remind you of the criteria for evaluating evidence—credibility, relevance, and sufficiency—discussed in Chapter 7.

First, *consider the source*. Are you looking at medical information from the Mayo Clinic or from Frank the taxi driver who lives in Hoboken? An author's name without accompanying credentials is suspicious. You may be able to find the credentials of an author by consulting *Biography Index* or by logging on to Virtual Reference Desk (http://thorplus.lib.purdue.edu/reference/index.html)

Box 15-1 **Sharper Focus** (continued)

or ProfNet's Expert Database (www.profnet.com). In some instances no source is identified for an article. In such cases be doubly cautious. Check to see if sources are cited in the article, and make a quick check of some of them to see if they exist and are credible.

Second, *try to determine if the source is biased*. No matter what the source, if the Web site uses a hard sell to peddle products, therapies, or ideas, be wary. Look for sites that have no vested interest, no products to peddle, and no axe to grind. Look at the Web site address. If it is a *.gov* or an *.edu* site, this means that the Web site is sponsored and maintained by a governmental or educational institution with a reputation to protect. If the address is a *.com* site, it is commercial and therefore more likely to be biased. Web sites with *.org* in their addresses are sponsored by organizations with varying credibility.

Third, *determine whether the document is current*. There is a tendency to believe that anything on the Internet is recent, but this is frequently not the case. Web sites will sometimes indicate when the site was last updated. Many documents will indicate the date at the top or at the end of the document. You can also make a rough estimate of the currency of the document from the recency of the information contained in the article.

Fourth, *assess the accuracy of information on the Web site*. Are the statistics credible? Are the statistics representative of the group or organization referenced? Do the facts and evidence presented contradict other reputable sources?

MetaCrawler (www.metacrawler.com)
SavvySearch (www.savvysearch.com)

Because there is much on the Web that is irrelevant, misinformed, or even plain nutty, people have created virtual libraries to provide more selective, higher-quality information. A **virtual library** is a search tool that combines Internet technology and standard library techniques for cataloguing and appraising information. Virtual libraries are usually associated with colleges, universities, or organizations with strong reputations in information dissemination. Compared to other search tools, virtual libraries provide fewer Web sites and a more narrow focus, but the information has been carefully screened so it is more credible. Some of the more popular virtual libraries are as follows:

Infomine (www.infomine.ucr.edu)
Internet Public Library (www.ipl.org)
Librarian's Index to the Internet (www.lii.org)
Social Science Information Gateway (www.sosig.ac.uk)
WWW Virtual Library (www.vlib.org)

A shortcut to a narrow search on a speech topic is to bypass search engines, directories, and virtual libraries and head to a specific Web site that is likely to provide the information that you need. Some credible research Web sites on the Internet that might be suitable for your research are as follows:

Government Sources
www.census.gov/ (U.S. Bureau of the Census stats)
www.ed.gov (education issues)
www.ecology.com/ (ecological issues)
www.naic.nasa.gov/fbi/ (FBI's information on law enforcement)
www.infoctr.edu/fwl (links to all major government Web sites)
www.census.gov/pub/statab/www (superior site for data on life in the
  United States from the Statistical Abstract)

www.mhhe
● com/ rothwell2

See "Fastpolitics.com" Activity, Chapter 15 of the Online Learning Center.

Health and Medicine Sources

www.healthcentral.com (Dr. Dean Edell and others)
www.cdc.gov/ (health and disease issues)
www.mayohealth.org (Mayo Clinic's Health Oasis)
www.ama-assn.org/consumer.htm (American Medical Association)
www.intelihealth.com (Johns Hopkins University)
www.nih.gov/ (National Institutes of Health)
www.quackwatch.com (health fraud issues)

General Information

www.ap.org (Associated Press news)
www.nytimes.com (The New York Times)
www.boston.com/globe (The Boston Globe)
www.phillynews.com (The Philadelphia Inquirer)
www.abcnews.com (ABC News)
www.cnn.com (CNN news, current events)
www.galaxy.einet.net/galaxy/Reference/Quotations.html (greatest quotations)
www.cc.columbia.edu/acis/bartleby/bartlett/ (great quotations)
www.refdesk.com (variety of information)
www.straightdope.com/index.html (unusual information)
www.fastpolitics.com (political information)

Education

www.apa.org (psychology)
www.public.asu.edu/corman/infosys (International Communication
    Association)

Ethnic Issues

www.mit.edu/activities/aar/aar.html (Asian American special interests)
www.aawc.com (African American special interests)
www.hanksville.org/NAresources (Native American history, language, art,
    and so forth)
www.rcf.usc.edu/~cmmr/Latino.html (Latino/Hispanic American interests)

INTERNET SEARCH TIPS   Information overload is a significant problem when you conduct only a general search on the Internet (see Chapter 9 for a more detailed discussion of information overload). A recent search on AltaVista for Web sites on "information overload" produced 190,569 sites. The same search on Google produced 394,000 sites, but FastSearch produced an astounding 481,154,472 sites. Obviously, such a high number of sites, usually presented in an order based on how many times any one or all of the key words appear in a document on the site, is unhelpful.

See "Guide to Electronic Research" on CD.

There are several tips that will aid you in narrowing your search. First, *click on the "Help," "Frequently Asked Questions," or "Search Tips" button* on the Internet search tool's homepage. Instructions will appear on screen for using the search engine, directory, or virtual library effectively. Second, *try placing key words in quotation marks.* This will narrow the search to documents that contain all keywords in the order in which you have typed them, omitting documents in which those words randomly appear. Third, *try adding plus (+) signs before key words.* For example, type +college"information overload" into the Google search window. The + sign before *college* limits the search to sites containing information overload at colleges. Fourth, *add words that further limit the search.* Notice what occurs as I add words to my search on the Google search engine:

The Library of Congress is the world's largest library, housing more than 120 million items, including 18 million books, 2.5 million recordings, 12 million photographs, 4.5 million maps, and 54 million manuscripts. In a wonderful blend of the old and the new, some of the Library's resources are accessible via the Internet at http://www.loc.gov/ or http://catalog.loc.gov/. "I couldn't find anything on my topic" used to be a problem for students. Not anymore.

> information overload (394,000 sites)
> "information overload" (122,000 sites)
> +college"information overload" (13,800 sites)
> +community+college"information overload" (7,670 sites)
> +California+community+college"information overload" (1,260)
> +Santa+Cruz+California+community+college"information overload"
>   (110 sites)

Fifth, *do a subject search.* Many Web homepages will have lists of subjects. Clicking on one of the subjects will produce subcategories. Clicking on one of these subcategories will produce even smaller subtopics and so on until you find the Web sites that work for you.

Research on the Internet can be highly productive, but the search needs to be focused and planned. Follow these five tips and you will save time and usually find much of what you need to build an effective speech.

Libraries

Your college library is still a primary research resource. The Internet is a wonderful resource, but there are books, documents, and reference works in libraries that can't be found on the Internet. College libraries also are computerized, and most allow students to access the Internet on library computers. Thus, college libraries provide "one stop shopping" for information on speech topics.

Every college library offers one or more tours of its facility. Take the tour. Even if you are already knowledgeable about using a library, the tour will familiarize you with where materials are located in a specific library.

LIBRARIAN Begin researching early. A frenzied attempt to research your speech topic in the library the night before your presentation will jump-start your anxiety and prove to be a less than satisfactory experience. If you do not know quite where to begin, ask the librarian; there is no better single source of information on researching a speech topic. I have consulted the reference librarians at Cabrillo College on dozens of occasions while researching this textbook. They are the experts on information location. Use them. Do not expect the librarian to do your research for you, but he or she will guide you on your journey through the maze of information.

LIBRARY CATALOGUES For decades the card catalogue was a standard starting point for most research. The card catalogue, listing all books contained in the library on 3 × 5 cards categorized by author, title, or subject, is rapidly becoming a dinosaur. The old card catalogues have been computerized in almost all libraries in the United States.

The computer catalogue, like its predecessor, lists books according to author, title, and subject. An important distinguishing characteristic of the computer catalogue is that it enables you to do a keyword search. Type in "mountain climbing" and a list of titles will appear related to this subject. You can also keyword search by author names. Computer catalogues will also indicate if the book is available or checked out, saving you time.

PERIODICALS The research bible for many students is *The Reader's Guide to Periodical Literature*. This reference provides current listings for articles in more than 250 popular magazines in the United States. Articles are listed by both author and subject. There is also a computer version of *The Reader's Guide*. It is entitled *Reader's Guide Abstracts and Full Text*. This computer version is faster to use, and it includes a brief abstract, or summary, of the listed magazine articles and full-text articles from more than 100 periodicals.

There are many other periodical indexes. Some examples are *InfoTrac Magazine Index* (magazines on current affairs, science, art, education), *Public Affairs Information Service* (journal articles and government documents), *Hispanic American Periodicals Index* (Hispanic American interests), *Index to Black Periodicals* (African American issues), *Women's Resources International* (women's issues), *ABI/Inform* (business and management journals), *ERIC* (education materials), *Social Sciences Index* (sociology, psychology, and so forth), *Psychological Abstracts* (psychology), and *ProQuest General Periodicals Ondisc* (general interest and scholarly periodicals). Check with your librarian to discover which of these are available at your college library.

NEWSPAPERS Newspapers are one of the richest sources of information on current topics available. Your college library will undoubtedly subscribe to the local newspaper. *The New York Times Index* is a valuable resource. Database indexes for newspapers include *Newsbank Index*, the *InfoTrac National Newspaper Index*, and *UMI's Newspaper Abstracts*.

REFERENCE WORKS Encyclopedias are standard references used for researching a wide variety of topics. The most widely known encyclopedias are the *Encyclopaedia Britannica*, *Colliers's Encyclopedia*, *World Book Encyclopedia*, and *Encyclopedia Americana*. Many encyclopedias can be accessed by computer. Microsoft's *Encarta* is a popular CD-ROM encyclopedia.

Other useful general reference works are *Statistical Abstracts of the United States*, *World Almanac*, *Monthly Labor Review*, *FBI Uniform Crime Report*, *Vital Statistics of*

Box 15-2 | Focus on Controversy:

Ethics and the Plagiarism Problem

Joseph Biden, a U.S. senator from Delaware, was running for president of the United States in 1987. Biden, a gifted orator, was given a decent chance of securing the Democratic nomination. His candidacy went into the dumpster, however, when news accounts revealed that Biden had plagiarized his conclusion to a speech he had given at the Iowa State Fair. His conclusion was lifted almost verbatim from a speech by British Labor Party leader Neil Kinnock. Biden had even cribbed Kinnock's personal history. For example, Kinnock asked rhetorically, "Why am I the first Kinnock in a thousand generations to be able to get to university? Why is Glenys [his wife] the first woman in her family in a thousand generations to be able to get to university?" (cited in Jamieson, 1988, p. 221). Biden's conclusion asked rhetorically, "Why is it that Joe Biden is the first in his family ever to go to a university? Why is it that my wife, who is sitting out there in the audience, is the first in her family to ever go to college?" (p. 222). Biden was not the first in his family to receive a college education (Jamieson, 1988).

Confronted with the charge of plagiarism, Biden claimed that the similarity between his speech and Kinnock's was merely coincidental. The news media, however, sensed a bigger story and discovered that Biden had also lifted passages from speeches by Hubert Humphrey and Robert Kennedy. Biden was further damaged by his admission that he had plagiarized while he was a law student at Syracuse University. Biden's presidential campaign came to a screeching halt.

Some might pass off Biden's plagiarism as a lot of huffing and puffing about very little. Plagiarism, however, is unethical behavior. Speaking someone else's words without giving attribution is dishonest and disrespectful and, therefore, incompetent communication. How do we know who the real Joe Biden is if he speaks the unattributed words of another and even assumes someone else's personal history to sound eloquent?

Biden was guilty of selective plagiarism, or stealing portions of someone else's speech or writings. That is bad enough, but plagiarism becomes even more serious when entire speeches are stolen and presented as one's own. Some students usually attempt such blatant theft of another's words because they've left the development of their speech until there is too little time to conduct adequate research. Research early and remove any temptation to plagiarize. Stealing someone's words is pilfering a part of that person's identity. That is never an inconsequential act.

Questions for Thought

1. Do you agree that Biden deserved to be denounced for his plagiarism and to fall out of the presidential race?
2. Chapter 10 argued that honesty was not always the best policy. Does this mean that plagiarism is sometimes permissible? Explain.

---

the United States, *Facts on File, The Guinness Book of World Records,* and *Who's Who in America.*

References for government related information include *Monthly Catalogue of United States Government Publications, Congressional Quarterly Weekly Report, The Congressional Record, The Congressional Digest,* and *The Congressional Index.*

Interviews

Charles Kernaghan interviewed many young workers who labor in sweatshops to produce garments for mostly young American consumers. He didn't rely just on the say-so of others, even of experts. He went to the victims directly to research the speech he would give before the California Federation of Teachers.

Research interviews are sometimes a very productive resource for your speeches. Interviewing local artists about painting techniques or about standards for determining the difference in quality between a Picasso painting and a 3-year-old's crayon drawing could be quite useful. Interviewing an expert on hybrid car technology might be a great place to begin your research on this topic. Experts can often guide your search by telling you where to search and what to avoid.

Student speakers often assume that no expert would want to be interviewed by just a student. That is usually untrue, especially when you consider how many experts are college professors on your campus.

If your topic is a campus issue, such as parking problems or theft of car stereos, interviews with the campus chief of security could provide valuable information for your speech.

INTERVIEW PLAN   No research interview should be conducted without a specific plan of action. Your plan should include what you hope to find out, who you will interview and why, a specific meeting time and place arranged with the interviewee, and prepared questions that will likely elicit helpful information. Avoid questions that ask the obvious or tell you what you already know. Avoid leading questions such as, "You couldn't possibly believe that this campus has no parking problem, could you?" Also avoid hostile or belligerent questions such as, "When you screwed up the arrest of that student accused of stealing car stereos on campus, did you make the arrest because you are biased against Middle Eastern people?" Ask difficult questions if you need to, but be respectful to the interviewee. Open-ended questions are usually a good way to begin a research interview. Consider a few examples:

Do you believe we have a parking problem on campus?
Has there been an increase in campus theft recently?
What actions should be taken to prevent campus theft?
How many parking citations have been made this year?
Have more citations been given this year than in previous years?
Do you have any wisdom on what should be done about campus parking?

INTERVIEW CONDUCT   The manner in which you conduct yourself during the interview will usually determine whether the interview will be a success and provide useful information. Dress appropriately for the interview. Sloppy or bizarre dress will likely insult the interviewee. It's disrespectful to the person who is doing you a favor by agreeing to be interviewed. Always be on time for your meeting. If you are late the interview may be cancelled. Never tape record your interview without the expressed permission of the interviewee. Stay focused and don't meander into unfruitful side discussions. Take careful notes. Stay within the allotted time for the interview. Thank the interviewee for answering your questions. Review your notes after the interview and write down any additional clarifying notations that will help you remember what transpired during the interview.

Researching, whether you use the Internet, comb through the library, or interview experts or individuals with a personal and relevant story to tell, can be a time-consuming process. Start early and do a focused search for information.

Competent Outlining and Organizing

Does a poorly organized speech make a speaker less effective with an audience? The answer is a resounding "yes." The quality of speech organization directly influences how well your listeners understand your key points (Thompson, 1960). A very disorganized speech arouses negative perceptions from your listeners. Speakers who

A speech outline is like a set of blueprints for constructing a house. It provides a coherent step-by-step plan. You wouldn't attempt to build a house without blueprints. You shouldn't attempt to build a speech without an outline.

are well organized impress listeners as more credible than speakers who are disorganized. A speaker who doesn't seem able to connect two thoughts together doesn't inspire confidence. Recall how frustrating it is to listen to a disorganized instructor present a rambling lecture. Note taking becomes chaotic. Learning is impaired. Impressive research on a topic is mostly wasted effort if your speech presents the fruits of your research in a disorganized fashion. Mastering effective outlining methods and organizational formats is a significant skill for the competent public speaker.

Effective Outlining

The organizational process begins with an understanding of the rudiments of outlining your thoughts. There is a standard form of outlining that has stood the test of time. Standard outlining follows a few basic criteria for appropriate formatting.

See "Outline Tutor" on CD.

SYMBOLS   Standard outlining form uses a specific set of symbols:

I. Roman numerals for main points
  A. Capital letters for primary subpoints
    1. Standard numbers for secondary subpoints
      a. Lowercase letters for tertiary subpoints

Each successive set of subpoints is indented to separate visually the main points from the primary, secondary, and tertiary subpoints. Thus, you would not format an outline as follows:

I. Main point
A. Primary subpoint
1. Secondary subpoint
a. Tertiary subpoint

FIGURE 15-1 The Outlining Process of Organizing a Speech

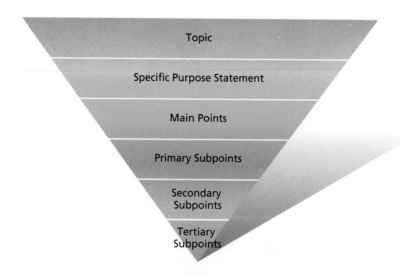

You can readily see that lack of indentation merges all of your points and easily can lead to confusion for the speaker.

COHERENCE Logical consistency and clarity are qualities of an effective outline. Your outline should flow from your specific purpose statement. When developing your outline, think of your speech as an inverted pyramid with the base on top and the apex on the bottom (Figure 15-1).

Begin with your topic, narrow the topic to your specific purpose statement, and develop main points from that purpose statement, which break down further into subpoints. Work from the most general to the most specific. Consider this example:

[TOPIC] The aging U.S. population
[CENTRAL IDEA] Longer lifespans pose new challenges.
[SPECIFIC PURPOSE STATEMENT] To explain in what ways longer lifespans stress fragile support systems for elderly Americans.

I. [MAIN POINT] Americans are living longer than ever before.
II. [MAIN POINT] Longer lifespans stress fragile support systems for the elderly in three significant ways.

Coherence requires that main points flow directly from the specific purpose statement. Subpoints, however, should also flow from main points. For example, look at the development of Main Point I:

I. [MAIN POINT] Americans are living longer than ever before.
    A. [PRIMARY SUBPOINT] The average lifespan of an American is at its highest level in history.
    B. [PRIMARY SUBPOINT] Americans are living increasingly to 100 years old and beyond.

Each primary subpoint flows from the main point on "living longer."

Each primary subpoint can be further divided into secondary subpoints that flow from primary subpoints. Consider this example:

A. [PRIMARY SUBPOINT] The average lifespan of an American is at its highest level in history.
   1. [SECONDARY SUBPOINT] The average lifespan of an American is a record 77 years old.
   2. [SECONDARY SUBPOINT] The average lifespan of an American has increased from 69 years old just 2 decades ago.
B. [PRIMARY SUBPOINT] Increasingly, Americans are living to 100 years old and beyond.
   1. [SECONDARY SUBPOINT] A record 30,000 Americans are 100 years old or older.
   2. [SECONDARY SUBPOINT] There will be an estimated 800,000 Americans at least 100 years old by the year 2050.

Following this pattern of working from the most general to the increasingly specific will assure coherence.

If primary subpoints relate directly to a main point, secondary subpoints relate to primary subpoints, and tertiary subpoints relate directly to secondary subpoints, every point will then flow logically from the specific purpose statement.

COMPLETENESS   Your first attempt to outline your speech will prove to be more successful if you use complete sentences. Complete sentences communicate complete thoughts. A word or phrase may suggest a thought without communicating it completely or clearly. Consider this example:

PURPOSE STATEMENT: To explain hazing (initiation rituals).

I. Hazing
    A. Campus hazing
    B. Military hazing
    C. Corporate hazing

II. Solutions
    A. Laws
    B. Policies
    C. Penalties
    D. Education

This word and phrase outline creates informational gaps and questions that can't be answered by merely referring to the outline. The purpose statement provides no direction. What will be explained? Will you explain how to do hazing? Why it is a problem? How it can be controlled? Why it shouldn't be controlled?

The main points and subpoints are no clearer. Main Point I is about hazing, and subpoints indicate three types: campus, military, and corporate. Still, no direction or complete thought is communicated. Are these three types of hazing serious problems? Should they be prevented? Should we find them amusing? Should we encourage hazing on campus, in the military, and in the corporate world? Main Point II suffers from the same problem. Solutions are suggested, but solutions imply a problem has been described when no problem is indicated in the previous main point or in the purpose statement. If a problem exists, what type of legal, policy, and educational solutions are offered? This remains unclear.

Consider how much more complete a full sentence outline is when compared to the incomplete and confusing word and phrase outline:

PURPOSE STATEMENT: To explain specific ways to prevent the problem of hazing.

I. Hazing is a growing problem in the United States.
   A. More than 50 deaths and numerous injuries have occurred from hazing on college campuses in just the last decade.
   B. The number of hazing incidents in the military and corporate arenas requiring intervention by authorities has doubled in the last decade.

II. There are several ways to prevent hazing.
   A. Hazing could be outlawed in all states.
   B. College, corporate, and military policies could ban hazing rituals specifically.
   C. Penalties for violations of laws and policies could be increased.
   D. Students, employees, and soldiers could receive instruction on the dangers of hazing and the consequences of violating laws and policies banning the practice.

BALANCE   Each main point deserves substantial development. This does not mean that you have to allot an equal amount of time during your speech to each main point. Nevertheless, you want a relatively balanced presentation. If you have three main points in the body of your speech, don't devote 4 minutes to the first main point and only 1 minute or less to your two remaining main points. Such a lopsided time allotment means either that your second and third main points aren't really main points at all or that you haven't developed your last two main points sufficiently. Increase the development of main points given insufficient treatment, combine points insufficiently developed into a single point and give the point some beef, or drop the two underdeveloped points and replace them with more substantial points.

DIVISION   Main points divide into subpoints. Note the plural on *subpoints*. Logically, you don't divide something into one. You divide a pie into two or more pieces. Likewise, you divide main points into two or more subpoints.

Incorrect Version

I. Main point
   A. Primary subpoint

II. Main point
   A. Primary subpoint
      1. Secondary subpoint

Correct Version

I. Main point
   A. Primary subpoint
   B. Primary subpoint

II. Main point
   A. Primary subpoint
   B. Primary subpoint
      1. Secondary subpoint
      2. Secondary subpoint

If you can't divide a point into at least two subpoints, this should signal to you that your point probably doesn't need division or that the point isn't substantial enough. It's time to rethink the development of your speech (Box 15-3).

Even when you have only a single example to illustrate a point, the principle of division still applies:

I. Professional baseball players' salaries are astronomical.
   A. Average player salaries are slightly more than $1 million per year.
   B. Example: Alex Rodriguez makes $25 million per year.

You can't generalize from a single example, so don't let your example dangle as a subpoint all its own.

Box 15-3 **Sharper Focus**

A Student Outline: Rough Draft and Revision

Constructing a competent outline can be a struggle, especially if you don't understand appropriate outlining form and criteria. Your initial attempts to outline a speech may prove challenging, and first attempts may produce seriously flawed results. Don't despair. Outlining is a process that trains our minds to think in an orderly fashion. It takes time to learn such a sophisticated skill.

Compare this rough draft of a student outline to the revised outline constructed by the same student (my comments appear in *italics*):

Rough Draft Outline

SPECIFIC PURPOSE STATEMENT: To eliminate the drug problem by making drug testing mandatory. (*Where's your central idea? You overstate the potential outcomes of mandatory drug testing. Try significantly reducing drug use, not "eliminating the drug problem." General purpose is only implied—will you try to convince us?*)

I. The drugs among society. (*No clear direction is provided. What do you want to say about "the drugs among society"? Also this is not a complete sentence.*)
   A. The effects of drugs. (*Are you concerned with only negative effects? Unclear! This is not a complete sentence.*)
      1. The immediate effects of drugs.
      2. The permanent effects of drugs. (*1 and 2 are not complete sentences.*)
   B. The effects of using drugs. (*This seems to repeat A above. Do you have a different idea in mind? Unclear! This is not a complete sentence.*)
      1. Memory loss.
      2. Addicted babies.
      3. Brain damage.
      4. Physical harm. (*1–4 are not complete sentences.*)
II. Ways to solve drug abuse. (*Your purpose statement indicates only one solution—mandatory drug testing. Stay focused on your purpose statement.*)
   A. The first step is to be aware of the problem. (*"Awareness" doesn't seem related to mandatory drug testing. Let your purpose statement guide your entire outline.*)
      1. Establish drug testing in all companies.
      2. Establish stricter laws against drug users.
      3. Start more drug clinics. (*Good use of complete sentences. Subpoints 1–3 do not relate directly to "A"—they are not kinds of awareness. Subpoints 2 and 3 also seem unrelated to mandatory drug testing. These are coherence problems.*)

(*You have an A point without a B point—problem of division. Also, main point II is less developed than main point I—problem of balance.*)

Revised Version

CENTRAL IDEA: Drug use in the workplace is a serious problem requiring a new approach to solving this problem.

SPECIFIC PURPOSE STATEMENT: To convince my audience that every place of employment should start a mandatory drug testing program. (*This is a much improved purpose statement. "Every place of employment," however, seems a bit drastic. Try narrowing the application of your proposal to workers who might jeopardize the health and safety of others if drugs were used—airline pilots, bus drivers, etc.*)

I. Drug use in the workplace is a serious problem. (*Good clear main point.*)
   A. Drug use in the workplace is widespread.
      1. Many employees in large companies use drugs.
      2. Many employees in factories use drugs.
   B. Drug use in the workplace is dangerous.
      1. Workers injure and even kill themselves.
      2. Customers have been injured and killed. (*Doesn't the risk go far beyond customers? If a plane crashes on a neighborhood because the pilot was loaded on drugs, dead and injured include far more than customers.*)

(*This entire main point with its subpoints is much improved. One question—are you focusing only on drugs used on the job or do you include drug use that occurs hours before starting work?*)

II. Mandatory drug testing in the workplace will reduce drug abuse. (*This is a solid second main point that flows nicely from your purpose statement.*)
   A. Drug testing will catch drug users.
      1. Testing is very accurate.
      2. Drug testing will provide absolute proof of drug use by workers. (*"Absolute proof" seems overstated. Try "solid proof."*)
   B. Drug testing will prevent drug use in the workplace.
      1. Workers will worry about getting caught using drugs.
      2. Drug testing can prevent drug users from being hired.

(*Second main point is coherent, balanced, and divided appropriately, and complete sentences were used throughout. One final question: What do you propose should happen to employees who use drugs? Rehabilitation? Immediate job termination?*)

Competent outlining requires proper use of symbols, coherence, completeness, balance, and appropriate division of points. An outline maps the flow of a speaker's ideas. A perfect outline, however, does not guarantee a perfect speech. A speaker's points may be clearly presented, but they may be incorrect, misleading, or distorted. Supporting materials (discussed in Chapters 7 and 16) must bolster a speaker's points. Nevertheless, clearly outlining your speech is an important step in the public speaking process.

Competent Organization

Taking a large, complex body of information and making it understandable to listeners is a big challenge. Finding an appropriate pattern for the information is a key to effective comprehension by your listeners. There are several patterns for organizing a speech. The most common ones used in U.S. culture are topical, chronological, spatial, causal, problem-solution, and problem-cause-solution.

TOPICAL PATTERN   A topical pattern shapes information according to types, classifications, or parts of a whole. Consider this example:

PURPOSE STATEMENT: To explain the three types of prisons in the United States.

   I. The first type is minimum security.
  II. The second type is medium security.
 III. The third type is maximum security.

A topical pattern doesn't suggest a particular order of presentation for each main point. You could begin with maximum security and work to minimum security prisons as easily as the reverse.

CHRONOLOGICAL PATTERN   Some speeches follow a time pattern. A chronological pattern suggests a specific sequence of events. When speeches provide a biographical sketch of an individual, explain a step-by-step process, or recount a historical event, chronological order is an appropriate pattern of organization. Consider this example:

PURPOSE STATEMENT: To explain the renovation plan for our local downtown city center.

   I. The old Cooper House and Del Rio Theatre will be demolished.
  II. Main Street will be widened.
 III. A Cinemax theatre complex will replace the Del Rio Theatre.
  IV. A new, twice-as-large Cooper House will replace the old Cooper House.

Each main point follows a logical sequence. You don't replace buildings on the same sites until the old buildings are demolished. There is a sequence that must be followed.

SPATIAL PATTERN   Some speeches provide information based on a spatial pattern. This spatial pattern may be front to back, left to right, north to south, top to bottom, or bottom to top. Explaining directions to a particular place requires a spatial order, a visualization of where things are spatially. Explaining how the Brooklyn Bridge was built would necessitate starting the explanation at the base of the bridge and working up spatially.

PURPOSE STATEMENT: To explain how to load a backpack for camping.

  I. Certain items must go on the bottom of the pack.

  II. Some items are best packed in the middle.

  III. There are several items that pack well on top.

  IV. A few items fit well lashed to the outside of the pack.

The outline focuses on segments of space. Actually loading a backpack while you explain your four points is an essential visual aid.

CAUSAL PATTERN   Humans look for causes of events. A standard organizational pattern is causes-effects or effects-causes. The causes-effects pattern looks for why things happen and then discusses the consequences. Consider this example:

PURPOSE STATEMENT: To explain the causes and effects of yearly flu viruses.

  I. There are several causes of yearly flu viruses.

  II. Flu viruses result in serious illness and death for millions of people worldwide.

Your speech can also begin with the effects of an event and then move to what caused the event:

PURPOSE STATEMENT: To show that grading systems create learning deficiencies at the elementary school level.

  I. There are serious deficiencies in student learning from grades 1 to 6.

  II. Grading systems promote these learning deficiencies.

PROBLEM-SOLUTION PATTERN   The problem-solution organizational pattern explores the nature of a problem and proposes a solution or possible solutions for the problem:

PURPOSE STATEMENT: To argue for a flat income tax to replace the current graduated income tax.

  I. The present income tax system has several serious problems.

  II. A flat income tax will solve these problems.

PROBLEM-CAUSE-SOLUTION PATTERN   The problem-cause-solution organizational pattern expands on the problem-solution pattern by exploring causes of the problem and addressing these causes in the solution:

PURPOSE STATEMENT: To argue for a government-sponsored program to prevent hearing loss among teenagers and young adults.

  I. Teenagers and young adults are suffering serious hearing loss.

  II. There are several causes of this hearing loss.

  III. A government-sponsored program to prevent hearing loss is critical.

All of the organizational patterns discussed here are commonly used in the predominant U.S. culture. Other cultures and co-cultures, however, may use additional patterns (Jaffe, 1998). Space does not permit an explanation of less standard, though valid, forms of speech organization. Learning the standard forms of organizing, however, is an excellent beginning for the novice public speaker.

Gaining and maintaining the attention of your audience requires planning and thought. If the audience sleeps through your speech, you may as well have spent your time talking to your dog (who may be more eager to listen).

Gaining and Maintaining Attention

A youth minister, Melvin Nurse, at the Livingway Christian Fellowship Church International in Jacksonville, Florida, wanted to make his point emphatically that sin is like Russian roulette. To draw attention to this point during his sermon to 250 parents and youngsters, he placed a .357-caliber pistol to his temple and pulled the trigger. Nurse apparently expected that the blank cartridge in the pistol's chamber would cause him no harm. Unfortunately, in front of his wife and four daughters, the blank cartridge flew apart on impact and shattered Nurse's skull. He died making his point. His attempt to gain attention was successful but with a disastrous result (Minister, 1998).

Gaining and maintaining the attention of your audience is a central task of any speaker, but it must be accomplished in a constructive manner. Your efforts to grab and hold the attention of your audience should enhance your presentation, not detract from it. *Gaining and maintaining the attention of your audience doesn't just happen magically. It has to be an integral part of your speech development.* As you put together your speech, make your specific choices of illustrative material, of examples, and of supporting points partially with an eye cast toward riveting your audience's attention. This takes planning and thought. In some instances, you may need to do further research to find more attention-grabbing material to jazz up the interest level of your speech.

Nature of Attention

Attention is a focused awareness on a stimulus at a given moment. Attention is not the same as listening, although it is related (Chapter 7). You can attend to a message without comprehending, retaining, or evaluating it, but without attention no listening takes place. Attention is a necessary but not sufficient condition for listening.

Attention is inherently selective. Approximately 99% of all stimuli received by our brains is filtered out as irrelevant (McAleer, 1985). Gaining and maintaining attention is a process of directing a listener's awareness toward the stimulus you provide and steering the listener away from competing stimuli. Herein lies the challenge. How do you induce an audience to attend to your message and ignore all others? When competing stimuli (kinds of noise) are everywhere, how can any speaker effectively gain and maintain an audience's attention?

A speaker can gain the attention of listeners by appealing to specific characteristics of stimuli that draw attention. These include appeals to that which is novel, startling, vital, humorous, or intense. Each of these characteristics will be explored in the next section, but it is important to note first that *gaining and maintaining the attention of listeners is not the exclusive responsibility of the speaker.* Communication is transactional. Listeners have a responsibility to make a concerted effort to pay attention to a speaker and not be diverted by competing stimuli. Nevertheless, a great deal of the responsibility for dealing with selective attention rests with the speaker. You are failing as a public speaker if your listeners must force themselves to stay focused on your message. Don't make listening to you a struggle; make it a pleasure.

Attention Strategies

Appealing to specific characteristics of stimuli can gain attention. When you plan these appeals in advance, they become strategies.

NOVEL APPEAL Audiences are naturally drawn to the new and different. Novelty attracts attention. The commonplace can produce a comalike stupor. Recognizing this means never beginning your speech with a snoozer, such as "My topic is . . ." or "Today I'd like to talk to you about . . .". Stimulate interest in your subject before giving your purpose statement.

There are several ways to make novel appeals to stimulate attention. First, *sprinkle your speech with unusual examples that illustrate important points.* For instance, consider using real examples such as these pulled from a newspaper story:

> "The check is in the mail" used to be the standard ploy to ward off bill collectors. Not so anymore. Delinquent customers have adopted more original stalling tactics. Collection agencies have received excuses from the bizarre to the ridiculous. One woman claimed that she had run over her husband with a car, breaking both of his arms thereby making it impossible for him to write checks. Another woman living in Fargo, North Dakota, claimed that she slipped on her way to the post office, lost her checks in the snow, and was forced to wait until the spring thaw before retrieving them. A flower-shop owner insisted that she couldn't pay her bills until someone died and had a funeral. "Business should pick up soon," she said hopefully. Then there was the businessman who placed his own obituary in the local newspaper and promptly sent the clipping to his creditors. These are silly excuses for failing to pay one's bills, but mounting personal debt is no laughing matter.

Compare this opening to the more commonplace opening "I want to talk to you about how to handle personal debt." The more novel opening invites attention. The commonplace opener encourages a nap.

A second way to make a novel appeal is to *tell an unusual story.* Newspapers are filled with novel stories that can snare listeners' attention. Consider this example:

Novelty is an exceptional attention strategy, and so is humor.

Supermarket customer Etharine Pettigrew was enraged that a woman named Vickie Lemons went through the express checkout line with more than 10 items. Despite the fact that Lemons had been motioned to enter the express line by the cashier, the violation apparently was more than Pettigrew could take. Pettigrew slashed off half of Lemons's nose with a pocketknife in a fit of "shopper's rage." Pettigrew was charged with second-degree reckless endangerment, and Lemons had to undergo reconstructive surgery to repair her nose. Civility in America has been replaced by uncivilized, violent behavior, and it is time to address this problem.

The example invites attention because it is unusual, yet it is presented as typical of a larger problem.

A third way to interject novelty into a speech is to *use colorful phrasing or unusual wording*. Notice how an ordinary expression of a point of view can be transformed by a cleverly phrased statement.

> **Ordinary:** Most books are carried for fewer than 60 days by bookstores unless they become best-sellers.
> **Novel:** The shelf life of the average book is somewhere between milk and yogurt. (Calvin Trilling)
> **Ordinary:** Choosing the right word is important.
> **Novel:** The difference between the right word and the almost right word is the difference between lightning and the lightning bug. (Mark Twain)

Be careful that your colorful wording doesn't push the bounds of good taste. Valerie Rose (2001), a student at Butte Community College, in an otherwise excellent speech presented at the 129th Annual Interstate Oratorical Association contest, pushed the limits to the point of "too graphic" with this conclusion to her speech:

> Today, we've mucked our way through the problems, causes, and solutions regarding sewer deterioration, and one thing should be very evident. IT happens. The bowels of this nation are in turmoil, and we need to pay attention to what's coming out of our manholes, unlike Brenda and Mike Martin. For our safety, this isn't a problem that we can turn our noses up at—it requires two-ply action (p. 7).

STARTLING APPEAL   Shake up your audience. Stun them out of their complacency. Surprise your listeners. A startling statement, fact, or statistic can do this effectively. Consider two examples. Aaron Unseth (2001) began his first-prize speech at the 2001 Interstate Oratorical Association contest this way:

> "My commander gave me a gun, cocked it, and said: 'Kill him.' The prisoner was standing about five feet away. He was crying, begging, 'Don't shoot me, please don't shoot.' I had no feelings. I just fired." These words are from an interview in the *World Press Review* of December 1999 with veteran soldier Tejan Bockarie; a veteran soldier who happens to be 11 years old. Unfortunately, this young boy from Sierra Leone is not a rare exception. You see, Tejan is one of at least 300,000 children—both boys and girls—under the age of 18 who are actively participating in 36 ongoing or recently ended armed conflicts around the world. The *Scientific American* from June of 2000 reports that many of these under-age warriors are between the ages of 10 and 14 and there have even been documented cases of children as young as 7 years old entering armed combat (p. 100).

This is a great opening to a speech. It makes you sit up and pay attention because it is so startling and disturbing.

Box 15-4   Sharper Focus

Inappropriate Use of the Startling Appeal

A Southern Illinois University speech student splashed gasoline on himself and ignited the explosive fuel as part of a demonstration speech. He was quickly sprayed with a fire extinguisher that was mounted on a wall in the hallway outside the classroom, and he was wrapped in a wet sheet the student had brought with him to class. Ricardo de la Pietra, a graduate student conducting the speech class, said that the student had asked permission to "do something special" but hadn't indicated exactly what (Berko, 1996). The student suffered first- and second-degree burns and was taken to a hospital.

Kate Logan, a graduating student at Long Trail School in Dorset, Vermont, stunned her audience of 200 faculty, friends, classmates, and parents when she shed all of her clothes during her speech at the graduation ceremony. Logan, 18, spoke of her "journey on a road less traveled" that inspired her individuality (Naked, 1998). As she spoke, she tossed away her cap and white gown, exposing her naked body to the startled assembly. A spokesperson for the school had this response: "This incident was overwhelmingly inappropriate and is not reflective of our student body."

Simply startling your audience to gain attention, even to make a point, isn't always appropriate. Startling an audience should enhance your speech and your personal credibility with the audience, not detract and distract from these goals.

Every speech instructor remembers notable examples of student miscalculations in using a startling appeal to gain an audience's attention. For instance, one student punched himself so hard in the face that he momentarily staggered himself and produced a large bruise under his eye (the speech was on violence in America). Another confused student fired blanks with a real handgun at his student audience. Classmates shrieked and scattered in all directions, fearing for their lives.

The competent public speaker exercises solid judgment when choosing to startle his or her listeners. *The speaker's goal should not be to gain attention by being outrageous or irresponsible or by exercising poor judgment.* The competent public speaker considers the implied or stated rules of a speech context when choosing attention strategies. Gaining attention by performing illegal acts violates explicit rules of society established to protect people, sometimes from their own foolishness. An audience can turn on a speaker and become an adversary, not an ally, when angered or offended. Startle an audience, but make certain your attention strategy is appropriate.

Kathy Levine (2001), a student at Oregon State University, offers this startling revelation in her speech on dental hygiene:

> As the previously cited *20/20* investigation uncovered, the water used in approximately 90% of dental offices is dirtier than the water found in public toilets. This means 9 out of 10 dental offices are using dirty water on their patients. Moreover, the independent research of Dr. George Merijohn, a periodontist who specialized in dental waterlines, found that out of 60 randomly selected offices from around the nation, two-thirds of all samples taken contained oral bacteria from the saliva of previous patients (p. 77).

Startling statements, facts, and statistics can be unsettling (wondering if I'm rinsing my mouth with someone else's saliva when I go to the dentist certainly disturbs me). They are meant to alarm, shock, astonish, and frighten an audience into listening intently to what you have to say (Box 15-4).

THE VITAL APPEAL   We attend to stimuli that are meaningful to us, and we ignore stimuli that are relatively meaningless to us (Chapter 7). Your principal challenge as a speaker is to make your message meaningful to your listeners so they will pay attention to your speech. Problems and issues that vitally affect our lives are meaningful to us. In this sense, audiences tend to be Me-oriented. Listeners heed warnings when a societal problem affects them personally. The AIDS epidemic was slow to seize the attention of the average American when it was erroneously thought to be a "gay disease." When the disease became rampant in the general population of heterosexual males and females, however, more people started to pay attention.

When attempting to grab the attention of your listeners, don't just make a general appeal, citing the seriousness of the problem for nameless, faceless citizens. Personalize the appeal to all of your listeners. Jake Gruber (2001), a Northern Illinois University student, did exactly this when he stated in his speech on heart disease in women, "Whereas one in 28 women will die of breast cancer, one in five will die of heart disease. And guys, before you take the next nine minutes to decide what you'll eat for lunch, ask yourself one question: what would my life be like if the women who make it meaningful are not there? Clearly, this is an issue that concerns us all" (p. 16). Make your topic a vital concern for all of your listeners. Vital concerns that affect us personally focus our attention.

HUMOROUS APPEAL "We've childproofed our house, but they keep finding a way in." Everyone enjoys a good laugh. Humor is a superior attention strategy when used adroitly. Humor is everywhere. It is on television, in books, newspapers, and magazines, and in your own personal experiences. Incorporating humorous anecdotes, quotations, and personal stories into your speech will help keep the audience attentive and on your side.

There are several guidelines, however, for using humor competently as an attention strategy:

1. *Don't force humor.* If you aren't a particularly funny person and have never told a joke without omitting crucial details or flubbing the punch line, avoid humiliating yourself. Listening to a speaker stubbornly try to be funny without success can be an excruciatingly uncomfortable experience for all involved.

   The inability to tell jokes, however, does not rule out humor as an attention strategy. You can include humorous quotations, funny stories you've heard from others, or amusing occurrences in your life to amplify or clarify points. Just don't set them up as canned jokes. Avoid using a lead-in such as "I heard a really funny story" or "Let me tell you a hilarious experience I had." It isn't necessary to signal to an audience that you plan to be funny. That simply sets you up for an embarrassing moment if the audience doesn't share your sense of humor.

   Here's an opening to a speech that uses humor by simply relating examples that many people might find amusing:

   > John McKay was a highly successful football coach at the University of Southern California. He was also the woefully unsuccessful coach of the NFL's Tampa Bay Buccaneers in their first years of existence. The Bucs under McKay's coaching lost their first 26 games before they broke into the win column at the end of their second season. McKay had a gift for making light of events that might send the rest of us over the edge. Asked by a sportswriter in the midst of his team's record losing streak what he thought about the "execution of the Bucs' offense," McKay quipped, "I'm all for it." On another occasion he noted, "I said on my TV show sportswriters didn't know a quarterback from a banana stand, and someone sent me a crate of bananas. This week, I'm going to say most sportswriters don't know a quarterback from a Mercedes." During one of the Bucs' training camps, McKay was told that a placekicker named Pete Rajecki said that he was struggling with his field goal kicking because McKay made him nervous. McKay responded, "I don't think he's got much of a future here because I plan on going to all the games."

   You don't have to tell jokes to use humor effectively in a speech. Use other people's humor, and audiences will appreciate you making them laugh.

2. *Use only relevant humor.* Humor should amuse listeners while illustrating a point in your speech. The humorous story, anecdote, quotation, or personal experience that makes a relevant point saves you from embarrassment if the audience doesn't laugh. You can act as if no humor was intended. You just wanted to illustrate your point. Here is an example of humor that doesn't make a relevant point:

> A middle-aged businessman, burned out from overwork, decides to take a year's leave of absence from his job to search for the meaning of life. He reads every philosophy book he can find, travels the world, takes college courses, and meditates. After 9 months he still hasn't discovered the meaning of life. Then he hears about a guru living on a mountaintop in Nepal who supposedly has the answer. With renewed vigor he uses his final 3 months of leave and his remaining savings to find the guru. With great anticipation, the businessman begs the guru to tell him the meaning of life. "My son," the guru begins, "the meaning of life is—(pausing for dramatic effect)—a waterfall!" Stunned, the businessman berates the guru. "You mean I came all this way and exhausted my savings only to be told this gibberish that life is a waterfall?" The guru looked pained, and replied, "You mean it isn't?"
>
> This is my favorite story and I can see that it has put you in a looser mood. That's good because what I want to discuss with you today can make you tense. I want to discuss the reasons people are afraid of heights.

Making an audience laugh or loosen up isn't sufficient justification for using a humorous story, especially a lengthy one. Humor needs to be relevant to the main purpose of your speech.

Making humor relevant is not difficult. All you need to do is tie the humor directly to a main point, principal theme, or purpose statement. Consider this example:

> Someone once said, "I want to die peacefully in my sleep like my grandfather. Not screaming in terror like his passengers." You've all experienced it—the nerve-wracking anxiety every time you see an old person behind the wheel of a car. Last month the National Transportation Agency reported that elderly drivers are the second most dangerous group of drivers, exceeded only by very young drivers. I want to convince you that greater restrictions on elderly drivers should be instituted to protect us all.

The humor is simple, and direct, and it leads to the purpose statement.

3. *Use good taste.* Glib one-liners and slapstick do not mesh well with funeral services. Sexist, racist, and homophobic "jokes" exhibit poor taste and lack of ethics. Offending an audience with ridicule or sarcasm may produce laughter, but it will win few allies. (A formal "roast," however, has as its purpose the sarcastic ridicule of a respected individual who agrees to be roasted.) Coarse vulgarities, obscenities, and sick jokes invite anger and hostility from many listeners. Humor that rests on stereotypes and put-downs may alienate vast sections of an audience, making the speaker the target.

A speaker I heard recently cracked this "joke" to his mixed-sex audience: "What's the difference between a terrorist and a woman with PMS? You can negotiate with the terrorist." Watching the audience's reaction was instructive. Some laughed. Some started to laugh and then thought better of it. Others not only didn't laugh, they booed the speaker. The speaker seemed surprised by the mixed response and searched for a graceful recovery. He never found one.

4. *Consider using self-deprecating humor.* This type of humor that makes gentle fun of one's own failings and limitations can be very disarming when you are speaking to a hostile audience. It is a huge challenge to get a hostile audience to pay attention and listen to you. Self-deprecating humor can help.

On May 21, 2001, in the very early days of his presidency, George W. Bush was the commencement speaker at the Yale University graduation. An alumnus who had partied hard and earned mediocre grades during his stint at Yale, Bush faced his most hostile audience. More than 170 faculty members boycotted the graduation ceremony and scores of graduates greeted Bush with protest signs. At the time, many on college campuses thought Bush to be an illegitimate president because he had "stolen" the election from Gore who won the popular vote. Yale was giving the president an honorary degree during the ceremony, which outraged many.

Not known for his great oratorical abilities, Bush exceeded expectations by using self-deprecating humor successfully. He encouraged mediocre students with the comment, "You, too, can be president of the United States." Referring to his party animal reputation while at Yale, Bush remarked, "If you're like me, you won't remember everything you did here. That can be a good thing." Making fun of his penchant for using tortured syntax and inventing words, Bush said that he had studied haiku, a Japanese style of poetry, while at Yale. "As I recall, one of my academic advisers was worried about my selection of such a specialized course. He said I should focus on English. I still hear that a lot" (Hutcheson, 2001, p. 7A). Bush likely did not change many people's minds about his fitness for office or qualifications for an honorary degree from Yale, but he defused the overt hostility, and his audience listened to his speech because it is difficult to exhibit anger when you're laughing, especially when the person you dislike is the one making you laugh.

INTENSITY We are drawn to the intense. **Intensity** is concentrated stimuli. It is an extreme degree of emotion, thought, or activity. Relating a tragic event, a moving human-interest story, or a specific instance of courage and determination plays on the intense feelings of your audience.

At the 1996 Democratic National Convention, Vice President Al Gore made the centerpiece of his speech a lengthy, detailed, emotional account of the final painful days of his sister's life as she died from lung cancer caused by years of smoking cigarettes. Although some listeners felt Gore's appeal to intensity was melodramatic and manipulative, others were moved to tears. Life can have its intense moments, and relating some of them can rivet an audience's attention as long as the appeal doesn't become excessive.

You can create intensity in ways other than telling powerful stories and examples. Several delivery techniques capitalize on intensity; these techniques will be discussed in Chapter 16.

Gaining and maintaining the attention of the audience is a critical challenge for any speaker. Attention doesn't just happen; you have to plan it carefully.

▨ Introductions and Conclusions

The beginning and ending of your speech can be as important as the body of your speech. Getting off to a good start alerts your audience to expect a quality

This picture epitomizes intensity. It is also startling and novel. An African American woman protects a White Ku Klux Klan member from an angry mob.

presentation. Ending with a bang leaves a lasting impression on your listeners. Great introductions and conclusions don't just happen; they need to be developed before you present the speech. In this section the requirements for effective introductions and conclusions are addressed.

Requirements for Competent Introductions

There are four principal requirements for a competent introduction to a speech: Gain attention, make a clear purpose statement, establish the significance of your topic, and preview your main points. Before explaining each requirement, you should consider that these requirements in some cases might overlap. Your attention strategy may establish the significance of your topic and purpose statement, making additional focus on significance redundant. Some gatherings for speeches make unnecessary a direct reference to significance during the introduction because the audience has assembled in recognition of the significance of the topic (e.g., ceremonies commemorating the victims of the September 11 terrorist attack on the World Trade Center). Nevertheless, make certain that you address directly all four requirements of an effective introduction if no such exceptions exist.

GAIN ATTENTION   In the previous section, general attention strategies were discussed that you could use throughout your entire speech. For the introduction to your speech, however, there are more specific suggestions:

1. *Begin with a clever quotation.* A speaker could open with a clever quotation and convert it to the specific purpose statement as follows:

   > President John F. Kennedy, in a speech at a White House dinner honoring several Nobel Prizewinners, said, "I think this is the most extraordinary collection of talent, of human knowledge, that has ever been gathered together at the White House with the possible exception of when Thomas Jefferson dined alone."
   >
   > President Kennedy deftly complimented his esteemed honorees without becoming effusive in his praise. He demonstrated skill in giving compliments. Complimenting others is an important but often overlooked way to cement interpersonal relationships, build teamwork, and promote goodwill among coworkers and friends. Giving compliments unskillfully, however, can provoke embarrassment and awkwardness among people. Today I will discuss three effective techniques for giving compliments.

2. *Ask a rhetorical question or questions.* A question asked by a speaker that the audience answers mentally but not out loud is called a **rhetorical question.** Imagine if one of your classmates began his or her speech this way:

   > When you walk downtown and are approached by a street person begging for change, do you make a donation? When you pull off a freeway or interstate and see a person holding a cardboard sign reading, "Money for food—just a little help, please," do you reach into your wallet or purse and help the less fortunate? When members of the Salvation Army stand in front of stores during Christmas shopping season ringing their bells and asking for donations, do you drop change into their pots? Have you ever wondered what happens to the money donated to the poor? Well, I plan to inform you where that money goes and on what it is spent.

   Rhetorical questions involve the audience and invite interest in the subject. Rhetorical questions can personalize a topic. Make sure, however, that your rhetorical questions are meaningful and not merely a commonplace device to open a speech. "Have you ever wondered why our college doesn't have a field hockey team?" is likely to produce a "not really" mental or even verbal response from the audience. The question doesn't spark interest if interest is already lacking.

3. *Tell a relevant story.* Storytelling captivates the attention of audiences of all ages. We love to hear good stories, especially when they make a point relevant to the purpose statement. Tara Kubicka (1995), a student at Moorpark College, began her speech with this relevant story:

   > Brian Clark was the kind of son that all parents dream of having, a star football player, junior class president, 3.8 GPA, and a devoted brother. Sounds too good to be true, right? Early one afternoon at football practice, Brian collapsed, and tests revealed that he had advanced leukemia and the only thing that would help him would be an immediate bone marrow transplant. Against all hope a match was found—Brian received his life-saving transplant. The story doesn't end there, however. You see the donor died 9 months later of complications stemming from AIDS-related pneumonia. Brian's donor had been infected with the HIV virus and now . . . so was Brian (p. 9).

Tara went on to develop her case that postsurgical infections following transplantations are a serious problem.

4. *Refer to remarks introducing you to your audience.* In some cases, your planned introduction may need to be altered slightly following remarks made about you by the person introducing you to the audience. A simple, clean reference to those remarks is sufficient before launching into your prepared speech. Walter Mondale, former U.S. senator from Minnesota, had a standard response when he was extravagantly introduced to an audience: "I don't deserve those kind words. But then I have arthritis and I don't deserve that either" (cited in Noonan, 1998, p. 148). Former President Lyndon Johnson also had a standard line prepared if the introduction of him to an audience was effusive in its praise: "That was the kind of very generous introduction that my father would have appreciated, and my mother would have believed" (cited in Noonan, 1998, p. 148). Following an underwhelming, bland introduction of him to his audience, Mondale would begin, "Of all the introductions I've received, that was the most recent."

5. *Begin with a simple visual aid.* Carrie Clarke (1995), a student at Southern Utah University, began her speech with a simple visual aid apparent from her introductory sentence:

> When I flip this coin, I have a 50–50 chance of getting heads. You have the same odds of getting a qualified physician in an emergency room (p. 103).

She used a simple visual aid to draw in her audience and make her point.

MAKE A CLEAR PURPOSE STATEMENT   Purpose statements were discussed in some detail in Chapter 14. The purpose statement provides the blueprint for your entire speech, guiding the audience as they listen to the points you make. Imagine a classmate giving this introduction to his or her speech, and notice the blending of the opening attention strategy and the purpose statement:

> Matthew Shepard, a gay 21-year-old University of Wyoming student, was lured away from a bar in October 1998 by two young males pretending to be gay. Shepard was then robbed, beaten senseless, and tied to a fence outside of Laramie, Wyoming, and left for dead. He was found in a coma, and 5 days after his horrific assault Shepard died. This tragic instance of gay bashing aroused the entire nation. At his funeral, more than a thousand mourners showed up to pay their respects to "this gentle soul," as he was described by those who knew him. During the funeral, however, a dozen protesters stood across the street from the church holding signs that read, "No Tears for Queers" and "Get Back in Your Damn Closet." It was a tasteless and insensitive protest, and incidences like this one might make us inclined to support legislation that bans such hate speech. I hope to convince you, however, that outlawing hate speech will produce three significant disadvantages.

The opening example invites attention because it is intense, and it leads directly to a clear purpose statement.

ESTABLISH TOPIC SIGNIFICANCE FOR THE AUDIENCE   Audiences tend to be Me-oriented, not We-oriented. When told about a local, national, or international problem, listeners typically want to know "How does this affect me?" As a speaker, you must answer that question. During your introduction, establish the basis for why listeners should be concerned about the problem, information, or demonstration central to your purpose. If you are an avid golfer, surfer, card player, quilter, or woodworker, your audience will see your enthusiasm for your topic. Why should the audience be enthusiastic, though, if they haven't ever tried such activities or if they proved to be inept when they did try? Relate your purpose statement to your audience. For example, suppose your listeners never considered playing golf because it seemed uninteresting. You could make the topic relevant and significant to your listeners this way:

> Mark Twain once said that golf was a good walk spoiled. For many of you that may seem true. Most members of my family tell me that watching golf on television is as exciting as watching mold form on rotting food. I beg to differ with these assessments. Golf can be a wonderful activity to watch and play. Golf is a good walk, but it is only spoiled if you lack knowledge of the strategy behind the game and your skill level is deficient. Understanding the strategy, and learning to play golf well can make for an extremely enjoyable few hours of recreation in the bright sun and fresh air. Also, millions of dollars worth of business are negotiated on the golf links every day. By not learning to play golf, men and women have restricted their ability to compete in the business world. Learning how not to make a fool of yourself while swinging a driver or blasting out of a sand trap when your big business opportunity comes could save you tons of embarrassment and just might seal a deal. Even if you don't foresee a business deal on the horizon, it's never too early to begin learning the game in case your big chance comes unexpectedly. To put it succinctly, golf can be entertaining and it can enhance your life physically, psychologically, economically, and occupationally.
>
> I can't teach you to play golf well in a 5-minute speech. You'll want to find a qualified golf instructor to help you do that. I can, however, briefly explain four qualities to consider when choosing a golf instructor.

PREVIEW THE MAIN POINTS   Previewing your main points is the final requirement of an introduction. A preview presents the coming attractions of your speech. A speech will normally have two to four main points that flow directly from the purpose statement. Consider this example:

> I want to explain how you can save money when purchasing a new car. There are three ways: First, you can save money by comparison shopping; second, by lowering your interest payments; and third, by purchasing at the end of the year.

Although the purpose statement and the significance can be reversed in order, attention is always the first requirement. The preview is the final requirement of an introduction. Note how all four aspects of a competent introduction are present in this example:

> [ATTENTION] Orville Delong, a 57-year-old Canadian maintenance worker, was playing golf on July 12, 1998, when a meteorite the size of a baseball whizzed by his ear at an estimated speed of 124 miles per hour. "At first we thought somebody was shooting at us," commented Delong. University of Toronto geology professor John Rucklidge speculated that the meteorite probably originated in an asteroid belt between Mars and Jupiter. Is Delong's near-death experience with a meteorite merely a freak event, or do we all have something to fear from rocks falling out of the sky and imperiling life on earth? We are indeed imperiled. [PURPOSE STATEMENT] That is why I want to convince you that a space-based shield from meteorites is critical to our human survival.
>
> Meteorites are fragments of meteoroids that reach earth before burning up in the earth's atmosphere. Meteoroids streaking through the earth's atmosphere are

commonly referred to as shooting stars. [SIGNIFICANCE] Earth has already had many significant direct encounters with meteorites. In 1908 the famous Tunguska meteorite scorched a 20-mile area of Siberian forest and flattened trees. In 1947 a meteorite exploded into fragments in eastern Siberia leaving more than 200 craters. In 1992 a 27-pound meteorite crumpled the back end of a Chevrolet in Peekskill, New York. In June 1998 a one-ton meteorite smashed into Turkmenistan, south of Russia, leaving a 20-foot-wide crater.

The need to create a shield against meteorites is real and urgent. [PREVIEW] I will explore three points to convince you that this is true. First, the probability of earth experiencing a catastrophic collision with a meteoroid is very high. Second, current efforts to address this problem are woefully inadequate. Third, a space-based shield is the only sensible alternative.

This introduction satisfies all four requirements for an effective introduction. It presents a novel attention strategy. The purpose statement is clear and concise. Significance is clearly developed by making the entire audience feel imperiled by the threat. Finally, the preview is direct and concise and sets up the body of the speech.

Some speech experts suggest that there is a fifth requirement for a good introduction: *establishing the credibility of the speaker.* Mentioning to your audience that you have surfed for 10 years, worked as an auto mechanic for 3 years, or have a degree or certificate in computer science would likely induce your listeners to grant you credibility on those subjects. If you have expertise relevant to your purpose statement, don't hesitate to tell your audience. Student speakers and laypersons, however, often cannot establish their credibility in this way during the introductions to their speeches. They may have no particular experience or expertise on a subject that would produce initial credibility with an audience. Speakers may simply have a strong viewpoint and an intense desire to affect decision making. Even informing an audience that you have conducted extensive research on the subject can sound self-serving. Why not let your evidence and command of the facts make that point obvious, and leave it at that?

You create credibility primarily by developing your purpose with logic and supporting materials throughout the body of your speech. If you sound as though you know what you are talking about, listeners will be inclined to perceive you as credible. Establishing credibility in this way, however, takes an entire speech, not merely a few statements during the introduction. Credibility is discussed in greater detail in Chapter 18. At this point, however, you should view establishing credibility as one possible element of an introduction but not as an absolute requirement.

Requirements for Competent Conclusions

Conclusions should do what introductions do, except in reverse. Your conclusion should create a sense of unity like completing a circle. You want your introduction to begin strongly, and you want your conclusion to end strongly. *Do not end abruptly or apologize for running short on time, or ramble until you fizzle out like a balloon deflating.* Be as organized about your conclusion as you are with your introduction.

SUMMARIZE THE MAIN POINTS   In your introduction you preview your main points as a final step. In your conclusion you summarize those main points, usually as a first step: "In brief review, we learned a little history of the martial arts, I explained how to choose a qualified martial arts school, and I demonstrated some common martial arts defense techniques." Summarizing your main points during your conclusion reminds the audience of the most important points in your speech.

REFER TO THE INTRODUCTION   If you used a dramatic story or example to begin your speech, referring to that story or example in your conclusion provides closure. This is how Moorpark College student Tara Kubicka (1995) concluded her speech on tainted organ transplants:

> Clearly, by examining the problems associated with the unregulated organ industry and the factors leading to this tragedy, we can see that such steps are necessary. Only then can we insure that when the Ruth Glor's and Brian Clark's of the world receive their long awaited saving transplant that it is indeed life saving and not a death sentence (p. 11).

She finished by making reference to opening examples that she used to grab the attention of her audience.

MAKE A MEMORABLE FINISH   You begin your speech with an attention strategy, and you should end your speech in similar fashion. *The same attention strategies that grab listeners' attention in your introduction will work as well in your conclusion.* Misty Williams, a student at Southwestern Oklahoma State University, ends her speech on caffeine addiction this way: "Awareness of the health related effects and the addictive nature of caffeine might prevent each and every one of us from one day having to stand and say, 'My name is Misty, and I am a caffeine addict'" (p. 71).

A clever quotation, a rhetorical question, a moving example, or a humorous statement make effective attention grabbers for introductions. They serve the same purpose for effective conclusions. Chris Lahna (2001), a student at Miami University, finished a speech on expert testimony in court trials this way:

> Judge Raul A. Gonzalez stated in the *Los Angeles Times* of November 6, 2000, that "a person with a degree should not be able to testify that the world is flat, that the moon is made of green cheese, or that the earth is the center of the solar system." Today, we explored the problem of expert testimony and its causes. We finally offered solutions to improve the validity, reliability, and trustworthiness of expert testimony in the future. Playwright and social critic George Bernard Shaw once said, "No man can be a pure specialist without being in the strictest sense, an idiot." Only by remembering this principle will we be able to recognize the true value of expertise and the danger of its perversion (p. 67).

Both quotations provide a novel, interesting finish to the speech.

One final note about conclusions: They should be memorable, but don't make them memorable by rambling on and on until your audience wants to conclude your existence. Be concise and to the point when finishing your speech. Your conclusion should be about 5% of your total speech. Don't diminish the effect of a great speech with a bloated, aimless conclusion.

Summary

Speech development is audience centered. Speech appropriateness and effectiveness are largely dependent on developing a speech that resonates with your specific audience. Effective speech development begins with effective research on your topic. The Internet and your college library are rich resources for researching speech topics. In some instances a personal interview with experts or interesting people who have experience relevant to your purpose statement will supplement Internet and library research.

The first challenge for any speaker is to gain the attention of listeners, then to maintain it throughout the speech. If no one pays attention to your speech, you might as well not give it. An effective introduction is vital to the success of your speech. The introduction establishes the basis for an audience to listen to the whole presentation. An effective conclusion is also important because you want to finish your speech in a memorable way. Outlining and organizing the body of your speech clearly and precisely are essential parts of the speech development process. An organized, clearly outlined speech will build your credibility as a speaker, and it will improve the audience's comprehension of your message.

Quizzes Without Consequences

Go to Quizzes Without Consequences at the book's Online Learning Center at www.mhhe.com/rothwell2 or access the CD-ROM for *In the Company of Others.*

www.mhhe
● com/
/**rothwell2**

Key Terms

See Audio Flashcards
Study Aid.

www.mhhe
● com/
/**rothwell2**

See Crossword Puzzle
Study Aid.

attention	metasearch engine	virtual library
directory	rhetorical question	
intensity	search engine	

Suggested Readings

Noonan, P. (1998). *Simply speaking: How to communicate your ideas with style, substance, and clarity.* New York: HarperCollins. A highly readable work on how to develop a speech. Noonan was Ronald Reagan's speechwriter.

Shachtman, T. (1995). *The inarticulate society: Eloquence and culture in America.* New York: The Free Press. The author presents a nice discussion of the progressive loss of eloquence in public speaking and why this has occurred.

Bulworth (1998). Comedy; R ★★★✔
Warren Beatty plays a disillusioned U.S. senator. In an impulsive act of seeming self-destruction, he begins to tell audiences the literal truth. He uses a variety of attention strategies in his speeches. Identify these strategies and determine whether you think they worked for or against him.

Malcolm X (1992). Drama; PG-13 ★★★★★
This is Spike Lee's impressive portrayal of African American activist Malcolm X. Analyze the speeches given in the film. Are the introductions/conclusions effective? Explain.

All the President's Men (1976). Drama; PG ★★★★★
In the days when the Internet was only a futurist's dream, Bob Woodward (Robert Redford) and Carl Bernstein (Dustin Hoffman) do research the hard way. Identify how these reporters who exposed the Watergate scandal during the Nixon presidency managed to extricate important information from key individuals during repeated interviews.

CHAPTER 16

Presenting a Speech

S uccessful acting is largely a matter of presentation. Shakespeare's great litera-ture, spoken by an inept actor, can sound like gibberish. A joke told badly pro-duces a collective groan from an audience. Some people can butcher a terrific line, and others can make an ordinary line thigh-slappingly funny. Poetry read poorly can leave listeners preferring fingernails on a chalkboard; poetry presented skillfully can be a sublime experience. The greatest script, the wittiest joke, and the cleverest poetry are diminished or enhanced by how they are presented. Likewise, the effec-tiveness of a speech can depend largely on its presentation. Even ordinary ideas can seem extraordinary when said well. As James Russell Lowell notes poetically,

Though old the thought and oft exprest,
'tis his at last who says it best.

The primary purpose of this chapter is to examine how to present a speech competently.

The primary purpose of this chapter is to examine how to present a speech competently.

There are three chapter objectives:

1. **to explore how to present supporting materials capably,**
2. **to discuss how to develop an effective style of speech presentation, and**
3. **to examine the basic elements of a proficient delivery.**

Presenting Supporting Materials

A bridge is only as strong as its supporting structure. Provide a weak supporting structure and the bridge will collapse. Likewise, a speech without supporting mate-rials is weak and risks failure. Supporting materials include examples, statistics, and testimony. In Chapter 7 you learned about the fallacious use of examples, sta-tistics, and testimony of authorities. Remember, *criteria for evaluating supporting materials are credibility, relevance, and sufficiency.* Before presenting a speech, briefly review this material.

Having access to valid supporting materials doesn't necessarily mean, however, that you will use them effectively. The competent communicator presents support-ing materials for a speech in the most effective manner possible. To examine how to present supporting materials effectively, let's take a closer look at the purposes and the presentation of supporting materials.

Purposes of Supporting Materials

We use supporting materials to accomplish four specific goals: to clarify points, to amplify ideas, to support claims, and to gain interest. This is an audience-centered process. Work with your listeners cooperatively, not against them competitively. You are trying to "win over" your listeners and gain allies with the help of your supporting materials.

CLARIFY POINTS   When you don't understand a point made by someone, it is cus-tomary to ask, "Can you give me an example?" An example can clarify your point. Consider this example:

Classifying "races" according to skin color is like categorizing books in a library by the color of their covers. What value would there be in such an artificial grouping? What would it tell us about the content and substance of the book itself? Skin color is a superficial human trait that reveals nothing significant about the content of the group. We might as well have a freckle-faced race, a short or tall race, maybe a bow-legged, bald-headed, or protruding belly button race. No one seriously suggests that these inherited physical traits should be the basis of racial designations, yet who can be heard laughing at the suggestion that a Black, White, or Yellow race exists?

The speaker's point is clarified by the profusion of examples. Merely asserting that skin color makes a poor basis for differentiating human groups leaves listeners guessing as to the basis of such a claim. Providing clear examples lessens opportunities for listener misunderstanding.

AMPLIFY IDEAS   Supporting materials can amplify ideas, making them seem important, and thereby producing greater impact on an audience. Amanda Taylor (2000), a student at the University of Florida, in a speech at the 2000 Interstate Oratorical Association contest, used evidence well to amplify her claim that drowsy drivers are a serious road hazard.

> The February 6, 2000, issue of the *Washington Post* explains that over 100,000 accidents occur every year by drivers who fall asleep at the wheel. And of those, 10,000 end in fatalities. That's equivalent to taking 25 Boeing 747's, filling them up with people, and then crashing them. During a personal interview on April 4, 2000, Roger Browers, the executive director of the North Central Florida Safety Council, explained that, while the problem of people driving while drowsy is not a new one, it's not a diminishing one either (p. 13).

Without the supporting materials, the claim that drowsy drivers are a serious road hazard can easily be ignored. Supporting testimony, facts, statistics, and examples amplify claims and encourage listeners to pay attention.

SUPPORT CLAIMS   A claim without evidence is like a haystack in a hurricane—it is blown apart from lack of support. **Claims** are generalizations that must be established with supporting evidence. Speakers who make claims without supporting evidence diminish their credibility. In the 1988 presidential campaign, televangelist Pat Robertson, a Republican candidate, seriously damaged his credibility when he made numerous unsupported claims that were wild in the extreme. Among those unsupported claims were that he knew an impotent man who gave AIDS to his wife, and "the only thing they did was kiss" (Rivals Blast Robertson, 1988). He asserted that a person could catch AIDS from an infected person who sneezes in a crowded room. He further asserted that there were nuclear missiles in Cuba and that nine American hostages in Lebanon "could have been rescued" because their location was known (Robertson Sets Off, 1988). All of these claims were false and unsupported by evidence.

During an interview on NBC's *Meet the Press* in October 1998, billionaire Ross Perot—Reform Party candidate for U.S. president in 1992 and 1996—accused President Clinton of "emotional instability" and "using cocaine." When pressed by interviewer Tim Russert for proof, Perot was unable to provide any evidence, but he repeated his assertions again. Such wild, unsubstantiated assertions are unethical because they are dishonest, unfair, and disrespectful. If you have the proof, provide it. If not, don't make the claim. George H. W. Bush said it well when he was accused by Pat Robertson of using dirty campaign tactics to win the Republican presidential nomination in 1988: "Stand up like a Southern gentleman with a little evidence. I'd like to see an apology or proof" (cited in Rivals Blast Robertson, 1988).

Quality evidence can establish a claim. Notice how Shelomi Gomes (2000), a student at William Rainey Harper College, in a speech at the 2000 Interstate Oratorical Association contest, bolsters the claim that levels of noise in America have reached toxic proportions:

> Noise has become toxic. According to *Consumer Reports* September 1999, toxic noise is the reason why an estimated 12 million Americans suffer full or partial hearing loss. . . . The Centers for Disease Control and Prevention in their 1999 report states that between 1971 and 1995, hearing problems have increased by 30% among Americans ages 35 to 45, and 25% among those aged 18 to 35. Last November the *Journal of the American Medical Association* published a report showing nearly 20% of young people aged 6 to 19 had hearing loss (p. 28).

Clearly, claims supported by quality evidence strengthen a speech.

GAIN INTEREST   Clarifying, amplifying, and supporting the points in your speech are important goals that can be satisfied by using supporting materials. Perhaps less central, but still helpful, is the use of supporting materials to gain the interest of listeners. Much has already been said about gaining and maintaining the attention of an audience. The same characteristics of attention can be applied to using supporting materials. A startling quotation, a novel example, or a vital statistic, for instance, can keep an audience listening to your speech. Gaining the interest of your listeners is not the most important use of supporting materials. If you have two pieces of evidence that prove a claim, however, and one is dry and dull and the other is phrased in a novel way that will likely get notice from listeners, why not use the more attention-getting supporting material?

Effective Presentation of Supporting Materials

Using supporting materials effectively is a challenge. There are specific ways to make each type of supporting material effective with audiences (See Figure 16-1).

EXAMPLES   The well-chosen example is often memorable for audiences and may have a great impact on listeners. There are two types of examples: hypothetical and real examples.

A **hypothetical example** describes an imaginary situation, one that is concocted to make a point, illustrate an idea, or identify a general principle. Hypothetical examples help listeners envision what a situation might be like or they call up similar experiences listeners have had in the absence of a historically factual illustration. *As long as the hypothetical example is consistent with known facts, it will be believable.* Note how this hypothetical example is consistent with known facts:

> Imagine that you are working at your desk at your place of employment. Suddenly the air is filled with noxious odors. You begin to cough and gasp for air. Your eyes become irritated and they start to water. You are exposed to ammonia fumes, chemical acetate, hydrogen sulfide, methane gas, hydrogen cyanide, nitric oxide, formaldehyde, and dozens of other substances that are irritants, poisons, or carcinogens. Would you shrug your shoulders and endure these potentially lethal toxins? Would you support "smokers' rights" to pollute your air with such hazardous substances? Although laws

have been passed across the United States banning smoking in the workplace, the one workplace where employees typically cannot escape the hazardous risks of second-hand smoke is the local bar. Bars and taverns across this country, with few exceptions, force their employees to endure second-hand smoke in total disregard of their health. Congress must ban smoking in all bars and taverns.

A hypothetical example can help an audience visualize what might occur. Imagine what it would be like to experience a hurricane, tornado, or tsunami. What would happen to you if you suddenly lost your job, were laid up in a hospital for 3 months, or became permanently disabled? These hypothetical examples help listeners picture what might happen and motivate them to take action that might prevent such occurrences.

A **real example** is an actual occurrence. Real examples are factual, so they are more difficult to discount than hypothetical examples. A real example can personalize a problem. Hypothetical examples can be discounted; real examples are not so easy to ignore. If a speaker talks about his or her personal experience, it can rivet an audience. There is an immediacy about real examples. Just picture the different responses you would have to a speaker saying, "I could become an alcoholic and so could all of you" and to one saying, "I am an alcoholic, and if it happened to me it could happen to you." Real examples have more credibility than hypothetical examples.

There is a skill to using examples effectively. First, examples must be *relevant* to the point you make. A young Abraham Lincoln, acting as a defense attorney in a courtroom trial, explained what "self-defense" meant by using a relevant story to clarify his point. He told the jury a story about a man who, while walking down a country road with pitchfork in hand, was attacked by a vicious dog. The man was forced to kill the dog with his pitchfork. A local farmer who owned the dog asked the man why he had to kill his dog. The man replied, "What made him try to bite me?" The farmer persisted, "But why didn't you go at him with the other end of the pitchfork?" The man responded, "Why didn't he come at me with the other end of the dog?" (cited in Larson, 1992, p. 181). Lincoln made his point that the degree of allowable force is dependent on the degree of force used by the attacker.

Second, examples should be *vivid*. A vivid example triggers feelings and provokes strong images (Pratkanis & Aronson, 2001). Kittie Grace (2000), a student at Hastings College, in a speech that took second place at the 2000 Interstate Oratorical Association contest, uses a vivid example to evoke a strong image on her main theme that hotels in America are unsanitary:

> According to the August 8, 1999, H*otel and Motel Management Journal* or *HMMJ*, in Atlantic City, New Jersey, two unsuspecting German tourists shared a motel room which had been cleaned that morning, but a foul smell permeated through the room. After the third complaint, housekeeping cleaned under the bed finding the body of a dead man decomposing, all because housekeeping failed to clean under the bed in the first place (p. 86).

Third, examples should be *representative*. Kittie Grace went on to present voluminous evidence that significant numbers of people are getting sick and dying from unsanitary conditions in hotels and motels in the United States because of negligent housekeeping. The staff rarely clean under the beds, and poorly cleaned rooms become "a biological banquet for bugs and bacteria that cause us physical harm" (p. 87). The example of the dead body graphically represented just how negligent the housekeeping can be. She does not claim that dead bodies will be found under hotel beds on a regular basis.

Speakers often like to generalize from one or two vivid examples. If these examples are not truly representative, however, then the speaker makes a hasty generalization. A **hasty generalization** is a broad claim based on too few or unrepresentative examples. John Hinkley, who shot Ronald Reagan, successfully pleaded insanity. Dan White, who killed San Francisco mayor George Moscone and city supervisor Harvey Milk, successfully argued the "Twinkie Defense" (junk food made him murder two people). Based on these two high-profile cases, we easily leap to the conclusion that the insanity defense is widely used and often successful. A survey (Jeffrey & Pasework, 1983) of college students and nonstudent residents revealed that, when asked to estimate how often the insanity plea is used by defendants in criminal trials, they estimated 33% and 38%, respectively. Yet fewer than 1% of defendants attempt such a defense. These same survey participants were asked to estimate how often the insanity defense is successful when tried. Both groups estimated 45%, yet the truth is that only 4% of such pleas are successful (Jeffrey & Pasework, 1983). The Hinkley and White cases are vivid examples. They stick in our minds because they are dramatic, but they are not representative of what normally occurs in criminal trials.

Vivid examples can influence an audience far beyond their legitimacy as proof. Vivid examples that are unrepresentative have the power to distort the truth. *When using vivid examples, make sure that they are truly representative.*

STATISTICS Statistics are measures of what is true or factual expressed in numbers. A well-chosen statistic can amplify an idea quickly, support claims, show trends, correct false assumptions, validate hypotheses, and contradict myths, perhaps not as dramatically and memorably as a vivid example but often more validly.

You've probably heard the now-famous remark of Prime Minister of England Benjamin Disraeli that "there are three kinds of lies—lies, damned lies, and statistics." Certainly statistics can be manipulated to distort truth. There are four ways to use statistics effectively, however, without being accused of lying with statistics.

First, *use accurate statistics accurately.* Bill Clinton claimed that 80,000 lobbyists were roaming the halls of Congress, a figure originated by a university professor who admitted he had made it up (Crossen, 1994). The statistic itself should be accurate, but the speaker should also use a statistic accurately. News media and even health care professionals commonly claim that a woman's chance of developing breast cancer is 1 in 9. That, however, is the cumulative probability of getting breast cancer if a woman lives to an age of 85 years or older. The chances of developing breast cancer by age 50, however, are about 1 in 52, or less than 2% (Paulos, 1994). The risk gradually increases beyond the age of 50. Scaring young women into getting mammograms every year when their chances of getting breast cancer are slim is an unnecessary expense and creates unreasonable fear.

Statistics that are inaccurate or inaccurately used can seriously jeopardize intelligent decision making. As Crossen (1994) notes,

> The consequences range from trivial to profound. Maybe they [consumers] bought the wrong car; unless it was a Corvair, what real difference did it make? . . . But maybe they elected the wrong mayor, governor, or even president. Maybe they got the wrong treatment for their disease; maybe they did not stop smoking; maybe they starved themselves on diet pills; maybe they exonerated a polluter or acquitted a murderer; maybe they lost their life savings; maybe they could not solve their society's gravest problems (p. 37).

Statistical accuracy can be a roadmap for decision-making. Statistical inaccuracy can be like a 10-car pileup.

Second, *make statistics concrete.* Dr. Dennis Mangano, head of the research team at San Francisco Veterans Affairs Medical Center, used concrete examples to describe what it is like to undergo noncardiac surgery. Such surgery typically raises a patient's heart rate from a normal resting rate of 60 to 70 beats per minute to 90 to 110 beats per minute, often lasting for days: "It's like running 10 marathons in a row. It's like being on a treadmill for 100 hours" (cited in Puzzanghera, 1996, p. A28).

Large statistics don't always communicate meaning to listeners. For example, the difficulty of sending a spaceship to even the star closest to Earth is hard to grasp. Alpha Centauri, the nearest star, is 4.4 light years from the Sun; that's equivalent to about 26 trillion miles (Angier, 2002). These statistics are so large that they have little meaning beyond "really big." Dr. Geoffrey Landis of the NASA John Glenn Research Center in Cleveland, however, provides a concrete referent for us. The Voyager interplanetary probes, the fastest objects humans have ever launched into space, travel at approximately 9.3 miles per second. "If a caveman had launched one of those during the last ice age, 11,000 years ago, Landis observes, "it would now be only a fifth of the way toward the nearest star" (Angier, 2002). Landis doesn't merely present the statistics. He presents them effectively by providing a clear, concrete explanation that gives perspective.

An effective way to make some statistics concrete is to use comparison to provide a point of reference. Consider two examples. The $110 million supercomputer at the Lawrence Livermore National Laboratory has the ability to perform 12.3 trillion calculations in a second (Supercomputer, 2001). This statistic may seem fairly concrete, but notice how much more effective the statistic becomes when you make these comparisons: "The supercomputer is roughly as powerful as 50,000 of the desktop computers regular people use. It can store the equivalent of 300 million books, or 6 Libraries of Congress" (p. 1B). Consider another example of making statistics concrete by using comparison. In the two decades from 1980 to 2000, the average pay of workers in the United States increased 66%. The average pay of CEOs of the 365 largest U.S. companies rose 1,996% during the same time period. This means that the average worker pay of $24,668 in 2000 would have been $120,491 if their wages had increased by the same percentage the CEOs' salaries did since 1980 (Overholser, 2001).

Third, *stack statistics for impact.* Jon Celoria (1997), a student at William Carey College, effectively stacks statistics for maximum impact in a speech on counterfeit airline parts:

> *Aviation Week & Space Technology* of July 29, 1996, reports that since 1978, U.S. air traffic has grown ten times faster than the inspector force employed by the FAA. As a result, the FAA's nearly 3,000 inspectors currently have the unthinkable task of overseeing 7,300 jets, 200,000 other planes, 4,700 repair stations, 650 pilot training schools, 190 maintenance schools, and nearly 700,000 active pilots (p. 80).

This is an impressive stack of statistics supporting the point that thwarting the flood of bogus airline parts is an impossible task for inspection teams.

Stacking statistics should be used only to create an impact on the central points in a speech. An audience will tune out from a wearying mountain of statistics.

Fourth, *use credible sources for every statistic to build believability among your listeners.* As noted in Chapter 7, biased sources diminish the quality and the credibility of

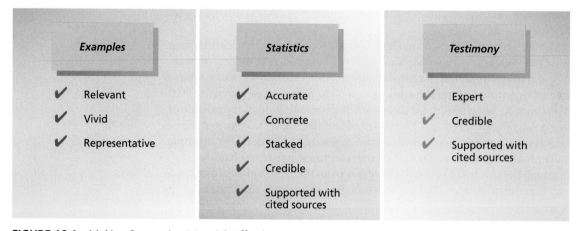

Examples	*Statistics*	*Testimony*
✔ Relevant	✔ Accurate	✔ Expert
✔ Vivid	✔ Concrete	✔ Credible
✔ Representative	✔ Stacked	✔ Supported with cited sources
	✔ Credible	
	✔ Supported with cited sources	

FIGURE 16-1 Making Supporting Materials Effective

a statistic. National polling agencies such as Gallup, Harris, and Roper are credible sources of polling statistics. They have no vested interest in the outcome of their polls and surveys, and they have established a strong reputation for accuracy. *Objectivity* and *accuracy* are essential for sources to be credible.

Speakers often cite credible sources for some but not all statistics used. Make it an automatic practice that every time you use a statistic you cite a credible source for that statistic. Listeners should never be given the opportunity to say to themselves, "I wonder where the speaker got that statistic."

TESTIMONY Testimony from experts provides important supporting material. Experts can help laypeople sort fact from fantasy. Expert testimony, however, must be credible. This requires a complete citation of the expert source. *A complete source citation includes, as a minimum,*

1. the name of the expert,
2. the expert's specific title or expertise, and
3. publication and date of the expert's statement.

See Bibliography Formats for Citation on CD.

All of these elements of a complete citation will establish the credibility of the expert testimony. You should be skeptical of any expert testimony that does not include such details.

Brian Eclov (1997), a student at Bartlesville Wesleyan College, in a speech on life insurance fraud, shows how to cite expert testimony: "In the August 1996, *Money* magazine, the president of the Consumer Federation of America, Bob Hunter, comments, 'What we often have is the illusion of regulation'" (p. 108). The citation is concise, yet complete. You could easily find this reference if you wished.

The Internet is a rich source of expert testimony, but the Internet itself is not an authority. It is a medium of communication. "According to the Internet . . ." is way too general a citation. That's like citing your fax machine. Citing a specific NBC news program on TV, however, or a specific issue of a particular newspaper or magazine is better. Quoting the actual experts on the program or in the articles is best.

◼️◼️ Competent Style

British author Oscar Wilde once said, "One's style is one's signature always." Your speaking style reveals an identity. It is part of who you are. A speech is a combination of substance and style. Your **style** is composed of the words you choose to express your thoughts and the ways you use language to bring your thoughts to life for an audience. A verbose style may tag you as boring. A clear and precise style may identify you in the minds of listeners as interesting or instructive. A vivid style may identify you as exciting, even inspiring. Take your style seriously because it is the picture that you project to your audience. Your style may leave a more lasting image with your audience than any specific points you make in your speech. In this section the differences between written and oral style and the primary elements of an effective and appropriate style will be discussed.

Oral Versus Written Style

The oral and the written word have distinct differences, which you should consider when speaking to an audience. First, *when we speak, we usually use simpler sentences than when we write.* An audience must catch the speaker's meaning immediately. When you read a sentence, however, you can reread it several times if necessary to discern the correct meaning and even consult a dictionary if you do not know the meaning of certain words. In a speech, very complex sentence structure can confuse even the speaker, who may get entangled in a thicket of words and lose track of grammar and meaning.

Second, *oral style is more personal and less formal than written style.* When speaking, you can look directly into the faces of your listeners. If you sense that they do not understand your point, you can adjust by rephrasing your point, adding an example, even asking your audience if they are confused. None of this can occur with the written word. Feedback is immediate from listeners, but feedback from readers is delayed and often nonexistent. The speaker and the audience influence each other directly. If you crack a joke and no one laughs, you may decide to dump other attempts at humor. Spelling errors only occur in written language. Grammar mistakes may go unnoticed when words are spoken but may jump off the page when words are written. More slang and casual forms of address creep into spoken language than appear in written form. We tend to be more conversational when we speak than when we write.

Audience expectations for speakers are different from those they have for writers. A speech is a cooperative, transactional effort of speaker and listeners. Speakers and listeners have to work together and make adjustments for a speech to be appropriate and effective. Speakers affect listeners, and listeners affect speakers. Cooperation is less of a factor with the written word. A writer must anticipate how readers will likely respond but can only hope his or her thoughts resonate with readers. A speech and an essay seem very similar, as hundreds of my students will attest when they write a manuscript speech. The two, however, can be quite different (Box 16-1).

Standards of Oral Style

Oral style is effective and appropriate when it fulfills certain criteria. In this section these criteria and some examples of effective oral style will be presented.

Box 16-1   Focus on Controversy

Women and Public Speaking: When Silence Isn't Golden

In the Middle Ages, women who dared speak in public risked "branking," a primitive form of humiliation in which a metal bit and a muzzle were strapped into the offending woman's mouth. Thus encumbered, the poor woman was either tied to a post in the village square or paraded through the town for public derision. In 17th-century America, a woman who offended colonial society by speaking publicly could be dunked in any available body of water. When raised, sputtering and breathless, she was given two choices—agree to curb her offending tongue or suffer further dunkings. In Boston during the same century, women who gave speeches or spoke in religious or political meetings could be gagged (Jamieson, 1988). The mere presentation of a speech by a female in public was considered "unwomanly" and invited scorn, ridicule, and humiliation (Levander, 1998).

Historically, female speech has been pejoratively labeled to keep women silent. "Nags," "shrews," "fish-wives," "gossips," and "magpies" are just some of the unflattering labels used to silence women. Prominent linguist Otto Jesperson (1924) characterized female speech as "languid and insipid" (p. 247). Societal institutions were mounted against women to curb their public speaking. As Jamieson (1988) explains,

> To hold speech of women in check, the clergy, the courts, and the keepers of the medical profession devised labels discrediting "womanly" speech. "Heretics!" said the clergy. "Hysterics!" yelled the doctors. "Witches!" decreed the judges. "Whores!" said a general chorus. "Harpies!" exclaimed those husbanding their power over women's names and property. These names invited the silence that in earlier times had been ensured by force (p. 69).

So intent were men on silencing women that in the 18th and 19th centuries a ridiculous fiction was propagated that women who insisted on speaking in public would become sterile. Even as recently as the early 1970s, Congresswoman Patricia Schroeder felt it necessary to tell a hostile constituent, "Yes, I have a uterus and a brain, and they both work" (cited in Tolchin & Tolchin, 1973, p. 87). Public speaking is significant for a lot of reasons, but contemporary men and women can only laugh scornfully at the nonsensical notion that public speaking could be a method of population control.

The relentless ridicule of female public speaking of the past, reaped from a dominance power perspective that accorded men rights and privileges not available to women, carries into more recent times. Madeleine Kunin,

first female governor of Vermont and later Assistant Secretary of Education and the U.S. ambassador to Switzerland, commented on the most difficult part of her transformation from private citizen to public official— speech presentations: "The fearful idea that by speaking out I would no longer be a good girl, that my words might antagonize those who heard me, was deeply rooted. If I said the wrong thing at the wrong time, I risked punishment: I might not be liked. Worse yet, I would not be loved" (Kunin, 1994, p. 63). Kunin gives testimony to the power of society's constricting labels applied to the female voice. Women have had to fight a history of put-downs and punishment for daring to open their mouths and give voice to their ideas and perspectives.

The battle to legitimize the female voice continues even today. The weapons of opposition no longer include gags, muzzles, and dunking, nor are the intimidating labels as frequent or brazenly offensive. The strategy to restrict female speech is far subtler. The "feminine style" of speaking, characterized as "personal, excessive, disorganized, and unduly ornamental" has been devalued in favor of the "masculine style," characterized as "factual, analytic, organized, and impersonal" (Jamieson, 1988, p. 76; see also Levander, 1998).

Exhibiting toughness by employing the rhetoric of fire and sword (masculine style) is the standard by which our society has judged political speech (Jamieson, 1988). When Congresswoman Geraldine Ferraro debated George Bush in the 1984 vice presidential debate, she felt it necessary to adopt the masculine style and appear tough and analytical. Female political candidates, until very recently, have adopted the masculine style of speaking traditionally favored in the male-dominated political arena. This can be problematic for women, however, who are often judged on a double standard. Former United Nations Ambassador Jeanne Kirkpatrick explains the predicament:

> If I make a speech [in the United Nations], particularly a substantial speech, it has been frequently described in the media as "lecturing my colleagues," as though it were somehow peculiarly inappropriate, like an ill-tempered schoolmarm might scold her children. When I have replied to criticisms of the United States (which is an important part of the job), I have frequently been described as "confrontational" (cited in Campbell & Jerry, 1987).

The marriage of television and politics offers a unique opportunity for women. Television favors a narrative, personal, self-disclosive, dramatic or feminine style of

Box 16-1 Focus on Controversy (continued)

speech (Jamieson, 1988). The adversarial, competitive, data-driven, impersonal, aggressive masculine style can come across on television as abrasive, unfriendly, and sometimes bland. It can disconnect an audience, especially female viewers. Ironically, Ronald Reagan helped legitimize the feminine style. His was a personal, narrative, dramatic style more typically associated historically with female speech. Bill Clinton blended the two styles, mingling narrative, self-disclosive, and dramatic elements with detailed explanations of policies and issues supported with copious amounts of data.

Women have had to learn the masculine style of speech to compete effectively in the political forum. Men have typically avoided, even derided, the feminine style. Women are in a unique position to combine the best of both styles. They can blend their acquired masculine style (analytical, organized, data-based) with their traditional feminine style (personal, narrative, dramatic) of speaking, thus exploiting positive aspects of both styles. Men are late to appreciate the feminine style and are thus likely to find television more challenging than women do.

Questions for Thought

1. If television is well suited to the feminine style of speaking, why should women blend both feminine and masculine styles?
2. How can men adopt the feminine style suitable for television without appearing awkward or weak?

CLARITY In Chapter 5, abstract language, connotation, jargon, and euphemism were addressed. Language that conceals rather than reveals is stylistically weak because it confuses listeners. Oral style works more effectively when language is clear and understandable. That is why you were previously counseled when using abstract terms (e.g., *freedom, rights, justice*) to operationalize them. Give them concrete, understandable referents. Try to avoid words that may trigger explosive connotations in the minds of listeners and ignite signal reactions. Use jargon carefully. Avoid it when possible if your audience is likely to be unclear about the meaning of the terminology. Use euphemisms rarely.

Clarity comes from a simple, concise style. John F. Kennedy asked his speechwriter, Ted Sorensen, to discover the secret of Lincoln's Gettysburg Address. Sorensen noted this: "Lincoln never used a two- or three-syllable word where a one-syllable word would do, and never used two or three words where one word would do" (National Archives, 1987, p. 1). He was simple and concise. Inexperienced speakers may think that big ideas require big words. When listeners start noticing the big words, however, the big ideas shrink into the dark shadows of obscurity. Don't try to impress an audience with a vocabulary that sounds as though you consulted a thesaurus on a regular basis. Remember, oral style requires greater simplicity than written style.

A clear style is a simple style, but simple doesn't mean simplistic. Abraham Lincoln spoke simply yet profoundly. Lincoln's second inaugural address included this memorable line: "With malice toward none, with charity for all, with firmness in the right as God gives us to see the right." The words are simple, yet the meaning is profound, even moving. If your style is too simple, however, your sentences will sound choppy. Use variety in your style so your words flow. Including an occasional complex sentence or more challenging vocabulary can work well. Although Lincoln used a simple, clear style, his sentence structure and phrasing were not always simple. In his Gettysburg Address, he included several lengthy, complex sentences. He also included this sentence: "We cannot dedicate, we cannot consecrate, we cannot hallow this ground." He could have said, "We cannot set aside for the special purpose of honoring, we cannot make holy this ground." Always choosing simple vocabulary

www.mhhe
com/ rothwell2

See "The Online Speech Bank" Activity, Chapter 16, of Online Learning Center.

may cause wordiness. Sometimes more challenging vocabulary provides an economical use of language. By occasionally using more sophisticated vocabulary, Lincoln spoke more concisely, clearly, and eloquently. If in doubt, however, default to simple sentence structure and vocabulary.

PRECISION   Baseball great Yogi Berra once observed this about the game that made him a household name: "Ninety percent of this game is half-mental." Berra also said, "Toots Shore's restaurant is so crowded nobody goes there anymore." Berra was not renowned for his precise use of the English language. Nor was Deborah Koons Garcia, wife of the Grateful Dead's Jerry Garcia, when she remarked, "Jerry died broke. We only have a few hundred thousand dollars in the bank" (cited in White, 1998).

You, however, should be precise in your use of language. Choose words that express precisely what you mean, not "sort of" what you mean (See Box 16-2).

A precise style is an accurate style. Adlai Stevenson, twice a candidate for president of the United States and a gifted public speaker, had just finished a speech before the United Nations when a woman approached him excitedly and said, "I really enjoyed your talk; it was without exception superfluous!" Before Stevenson could respond to the woman's unintended characterization of his speech as unnecessary, she continued, "Will it be published?" "Yes," replied Stevenson. "Posthumously." "Good," said the woman. "The sooner the better" (cited in Rand, 1998, p. 282). Stevenson probably did not feel flattered by the woman's unintended encouragement that he die soon so his speech could be published. Using and understanding the precise denotative meaning of words is important if you want your style to build your credibility, not diminish it.

Precision is one strong reason to avoid sexist language (see Chapter 5). Aside from its bigotry, sexist language is imprecise and often inaccurate language usage. Where once businessman, policeman, fireman, and postman fairly accurately reflected a society with few female executives, police officers, firefighters, and letter carriers, this is no longer true. Use language precisely. Eliminate sexist language.

VIVIDNESS   Simple, concise, precise use of language doesn't mean using words in a boring fashion. A vivid style paints a picture in the minds of listeners and makes a speaker's ideas memorable. William Gibbs McAdoo, twice an unsuccessful candidate

ZITS   Jerry Scott & Jim Borgman

© Zits Partnership. Reprinted with Special Permission of King Features Syndicate.

Box 16-2 | Focus on Controversy

The Ethics of Deleting Presidential Verbal Goofs

George W. Bush has been satirized and ridiculed repeatedly for his mangling of the English language. His imprecise use of words diverts attention from his main message and draws attention to his style difficulties. Here are just a few examples of his imprecise use of language:

The vast majority of our imports come from outside the country.
If we don't succeed, we run the risk of failure.
I believe we are on an irreversible trend toward more freedom and democracy—but that could change.
Republicans understand the importance of bondage between a mother and child.
A low voter turnout is an indication of fewer people going to the polls.

With the frequency of errors by the president, an ethical issue surfaced in 2002. White House transcripts began deleting or correcting his mistakes (Milbank, 2002). In a Bridgeport, Connecticut, speech on April 9, 2002, the president said that he wanted every American to volunteer for "4,000 years" when he meant 4,000 hours. In a speech the day before, President Bush was booed and heckled repeatedly during a speech in Knoxville, Tennessee. He faltered repeatedly, stopping and starting his speech numerous times. The official White House transcript corrected the first mistake and deleted the heckling and the many false starts by Bush, making the speech appear to be relatively fluent and without vocal opposition. These alterations in the official transcript put out by the Bush administration, all meant to make the president appear to be more fluent and less prone to imprecision in his speech, creates an ethical concern. The official transcripts are meant to be historical documents. It is clearly dishonest to doctor that historical record.

Although this issue surfaced during the Bush presidency, Congress has long practiced such doctoring of the historical transcript. Lawmakers regularly "revise and extend" speeches delivered on the floor of the U.S. House and Senate before they're printed in the *Congressional Record*. The printed speeches are often not the actual presentations verbatim, and on occasion a speech is printed that was never delivered. Should politicians be allowed to edit mistakes from the historical record to make themselves look good like many popular magazines airbrush blemishes from pictures of models and celebrities?

Questions for Thought

1. Should we be concerned that politicians doctor the official transcripts of their speeches?
2. Should politicians be absolutely truthful about what appears in official transcripts of speeches? Is this just a little harmless tinkering with historical truth?
3. Is this a greater distortion of truth than ghostwritten speeches—words put in the president's and politicians' mouths by speechwriters?

for the Democratic nomination for president, vividly described the speeches of President Warren G. Harding this way: "His speeches left the impression of an army of pompous phrases moving over the landscape in search of an idea. Sometimes these meandering words would actually capture a straggling thought and bear it triumphantly a prisoner in their midst, until it died of servitude and overwork." The words are simple and the point is clearly drawn. The style, however, is quite vivid.

Consider the difference vivid style makes by comparing the phrasing of several famous statements with plainer versions of the same statements:

VIVID: "Friends, Romans, countrymen, lend me your ears." (Shakespeare's version of a speech by Mark Antony)

PLAIN: "Friends, Romans, countrymen, may I please have your attention?"

VIVID: "Don't fire until you see the whites of their eyes." (Colonel William Prescott at the Battle of Bunker Hill)

PLAIN: "Don't shoot until they get really close."

VIVID: "I have a dream." (Martin Luther King)

PLAIN: "I have an idea."

Jesse Jackson and Ann Richards both have vivid styles, but in different ways. Neither could adopt the vivid style of the other and appear genuine.

VIVID: "I have nothing to offer but blood, toil, tears and sweat." (Winston Churchill, The Battle of Britain)

PLAIN: "I have nothing to offer but a struggle."

There are many ways to make your speech style vivid. Among these are the use of metaphors and similes, alliteration, parallelisms, and antithesis.

Metaphor and Simile   Figures of speech use words or phrases in a nonliteral sense or unusual manner to produce vividness. Metaphors and similes are two main figures of speech. A **metaphor** is an implied comparison of two seemingly dissimilar things. In a speech delivered on January 6, 1941, Franklin Roosevelt said that selfish men "would clip the wings of the American eagle in order to feather their own nests." Jesse Jackson, a candidate for the presidential nomination for the Democratic party in 1988, used vivid metaphors in his speech to the convention of delegates. In reference to the plight of poor children living in the Watts neighborhood of Los Angeles, he said, "Their grapes of hope have become raisins of despair." Referring to his own life, he said, "I was not born with a silver spoon in my mouth. I had a shovel programmed for my hand." Patrick Buchanan, a Republican candidate for president, in a speech at the Republican National Convention in 1992, characterized the Democratic National Convention held weeks before as a "giant masquerade ball [where] 20,000 radicals and liberals came dressed up as moderates and centrists in the greatest single exhibition of cross-dressing in American political history." You can differ with the point of view expressed by each of these speakers, but clearly all three speakers created vivid images that brought their ideas to life.

Be careful not to mix your metaphors lest your vivid imagery sound laughable. A **mixed metaphor** is the use of two or more vastly different metaphors in a single expression. Famous movie producer Samuel Goldwyn once remarked, "That's the way with these directors. They're always biting the hand that lays the golden egg." Mixed metaphors can sound goofy and be just a little difficult to imagine.

A **simile** is an explicit comparison of two seemingly dissimilar things using the words *like* or *as.* Curt Simmons described what it was like pitching to Hank Aaron: "Trying to get a fastball past Hank Aaron is like trying to get the sun past a rooster." Bill Clinton, in a speech at Galesburg, Illinois, on January 23, 1995, used simile in an amusing way: "Being president is like running a cemetery; you've got a lot of people under you and nobody's listening."

Similes can enhance a speech, but not if the similes are shopworn phrases that were clever when first spoken but have become tired from overuse. "Naked as a jaybird," "dumb as a post," "dull as dishwater," "strong as an ox," and "smooth as a baby's butt" are picturesque phrases, but they have become clichés.

Create your own unique similes and metaphors, but don't create picturesque figures of speech that offend and insult listeners. Similes and metaphors can be offensive. Hitler once compared Jews to "maggots on rotting flesh." His point was ugly and so was his figurative language. Using figures of speech is your opportunity to play with language, but play with it carefully.

Alliteration   When Spiro Agnew was vice president of the United States during the Nixon presidency, he became famous for phrases such as "nattering nabobs of negativism" and "pusillanimous pussyfooters." These were examples of **alliteration,** the repetition of the same sound, usually a consonant sound, starting each word. The problem with Agnew's use of alliteration, however, was that most listeners couldn't decipher what he had said because he loved to use silver dollar words when nickel and dime words would have been more effective.

Vice President Al Gore used alliteration to make his point that democracy is not well served by "going negative" during political campaigns: "We should not demean our democracy with the politics of distraction, denial, and despair." Before he became secretary of state, Colin Powell used alliteration in a speech on volunteerism delivered in Philadelphia on April 28, 1997, when he said, "As you've heard, up to 15 million young Americans today are at risk. They are at risk of growing up un-skilled, unlearned or, even worse, unloved. They are at risk of growing up physi-cally or psychologically abused. They are at risk of growing up addicted to the pathologies and poisons of the street." As first lady, Hillary Clinton likewise used al-literation to enliven her point that hatred should be fought by everyone: "In a nation founded on the promise of human dignity, our colleges, our communities, our coun-try should challenge hatred wherever we find it."

Alliteration can create a captivating cadence. Don't overuse alliteration, how-ever. A little alliteration is appropriate. Frequent alliteration could become laughable.

Parallelism   A parallel construction has a similar arrangement of words, phrases, or sentences. This parallelism creates a vivid rhythm. Here are some examples:

> The denial of human rights anywhere is a threat to human rights everywhere. In-justice anywhere is a threat to justice everywhere. (Jesse Jackson)

> Today, we have a vision of Texas where opportunity knows no race or color or gender. . . . Tomorrow, we must build that Texas.

> Today, we have a vision of a Texas with clean air and land and water. . . . Tomor-row, we must build that Texas.

> Today, we have a vision of a Texas where every child receives an education that allows them to claim the full promise of their lives. Tomorrow, we must build that Texas. (Ann Richards, former Governor of Texas)

> We shall fight on the beaches.

> We shall fight on the landing grounds.

> We shall fight in the fields and in the streets.

> We shall fight in the hills.

> We shall never surrender. (Winston Churchill)

As is true of any stylistic device, a little goes a long way. *Be careful not to overuse par-allel constructions.*

Antithesis   Charles Dickens began his famous novel *A Tale of Two Cities* with one of the most memorable lines in literature: "It was the best of times; it was the worst of times." This is an example of the stylistic device called **antithesis,** the use of oppo-sites to create impact. Barbara Bush offered this example of antithesis: "Your success as a family, our success as a society, depends not on what happens at the White House, but on what happens inside your house." Perhaps the most famous example of antithesis in public speaking is from John F. Kennedy's inaugural address in 1961: "Ask not what your country can do for you; ask what you can do for your country." The effectiveness of antithesis is in the rhythmic phrasing. Four months before his inaugural address, Kennedy made this statement: "The new frontier is not what I promise I am going to do for you. The new frontier is what I ask you to do for your country." This also used antithesis, but it wasn't memorable. The phrasing wasn't as easily remembered. It seemed more verbose. Be concise when using antithesis.

In review, the principal standards of stylistic effectiveness are clarity, precision, and vividness. You can learn much about style by examining competent speakers who follow these standards. Ultimately, however, your style must be your own.

Trying to mimic the style of Jesse Jackson by copying his rhythmic phrasing would sound silly. Jesse Jackson's style is uniquely his own. Work on clarity, precision, and vividness by listening to successful speakers, but explore what fits you well. Metaphors and similes may come easily to you, but antithesis may seem artificial and awkward. Develop your own style by experimenting. Try including metaphors in your conversations with others. Play with language informally before incorporating stylistic devices in your formal speeches. Remember, your style is your signature.

Delivery

Cornell University psychology professor Stephen Ceci had been receiving average student evaluations of his teaching. He decided to change his delivery of class lectures. He spoke more loudly than usual, varied the pitch of his voice more dramatically, and gestured more emphatically than normal. The student ratings for his class and his instruction went up dramatically, from an average of between 2 and 3 on a 5-point scale to a 4 plus (Murray, 1997). Ceci was perceived by students to be more effective, knowledgeable, and organized because of the change in delivery. Surprisingly, students found the textbook more interesting to read and Ceci's grading policy (unchanged) fairer than in previous terms when he had used a more commonplace delivery. Students also believed they had learned more material even though their test scores were identical to those of previous classes in which his delivery was commonplace. Does delivery make a difference? Unquestionably it does.

The next section begins with a brief discussion of common delivery problems. Then various methods of delivery that can be used by a speaker are explored.

Common Delivery Problems

Inexperienced public speakers often fail to notice problems of delivery that interfere with the effectiveness of their message. Most are commonplace problems that are easily corrected with practice.

WEAK EYE CONTACT   Eye contact can be riveting. It is an important part of gaining and maintaining the attention of your audience. Direct, penetrating eye contact with listeners can be quite intense. If you doubt this, try staring at someone for a prolonged period of time. The intensity can be quite powerful. When you do not look directly at your audience, listeners' minds can easily wander. Inexperienced speakers have a tendency to look at the ground, above the heads of their listeners, or at one side of their audience or the other but not both, or they bury their heads in their manuscript. When you zero in on listeners by making eye contact, it is difficult for listeners to ignore you. When you rarely look at your audience, you allow your listeners' attention to drift.

Simple ways to improve eye contact include the following:

1. Be very familiar with your speech so you won't get pinned to your notes or read from a manuscript.
2. Practice looking at your entire audience, beginning with the middle of your audience, then looking left, then right, and then to the middle again, and so forth. With practice (an imaginary audience will do fine) your eye contact will become automatic.

MONOTONE VOICE   Some individuals have very little range in their voices when giving a speech. Their voices sound flat and uninteresting. Strive for vocal variety, not a monotone voice. You can avoid attention-killing monotony by raising and lowering the pitch of your voice. The singing voice has a range of pitch from soprano to bass. Similarly, you can vary your speaking voice by moving up and down the vocal range from high sounds to lower sounds and back.

You can also avoid monotony by varying the loudness or softness of your voice. A raised voice signals intense, passionate feelings. It will punctuate portions of your presentation much as an exclamation point punctuates a written sentence. Using vocal volume to gain attention, however, can be overdone. As Mark Twain noted, "Noise proves nothing. Often a hen who has merely laid an egg cackles as if she laid an asteroid." Incessant, unrelenting, bombastic delivery of a message irritates and alienates the audience. Speak loudly only when you have an especially important point to make. All points in your speech do not deserve equal attention.

Speaking softly can also induce interest. When you lower the pitch and loudness of your voice, the audience must strain to hear. This can be a nice dramatic twist to use in a speech, if used infrequently. Vocal variety signals shifts in mood and does not permit an audience to drift into the hypnotic, trancelike state produced by the white noise of the monotone voice. Practice vocal variety on your friends during casual conversations. Experiment with different voice inflections, volume, and pitch.

VOCAL FILLERS   A common delivery problem is the tendency to include **vocal fillers**—the insertion of *uhm, ah, like, you know, know what I mean, whatever* and other variants that substitute for pauses and often draw attention to themselves. A Geneva, Nebraska, high school senior, Jessica Reinsch, won a $1,000 prize in the Nebraskaland Foundation's "you know" contest for recording a 15-minute radio interview during which that phrase was used 61 times (Best English Lesson, 1999). The fluency of your delivery suffers mightily when you use vocal fillers more than occasionally. Almost all speakers use vocal fillers once in a while, and an audience will not notice infrequent use. Frequent use, however, may be the only part of your speech that is memorable. Practice not using vocal fillers during casual conversation with friends and family. Focus on how often other people use vocal fillers during conversation. Practice your speech in front of a friend or videotape it. Have your friend tap a pencil on a table every time you use a vocal filler during your practice speech. When you review the videotaped practice speech, count the number of vocal fillers. With time, you will eliminate the habit.

RAPID PACE   Steve Woodmore of Orpington, England, spoke 637.4 words per minute on a British TV program called *Motor Mouth*. Sean Shannon, a Canadian residing in Oxford, England, recited the famous soliloquy "To be or not to be . . . " from Shakespeare's *Hamlet* at a 650-words-per-minute clip. Most speakers, however, are unintelligible when speaking faster than 350 words per minute, and most audiences become twitchy when a speaker motors along at much above 250 words per minute. As mentioned in Chapter 7, a very slow speaking pace (about 125 words per minute) can induce a stupor in an audience. Speaking pace should be lively enough to keep attention but not so fast that you appear to have consumed too many espressos. A speaking pace of 175 to 200 words per minute is usually appropriate. Without actually measuring your speaking pace, *you can get a rough idea of the appropriate pace by enunciating your words carefully and pausing to take breaths without gasping for air.*

Pausing occasionally not only slows your pace, but also can be used for dramatic emphasis. Prolonged silence is intense for most people. Silence punctuates important points in your speech. A pregnant pause—silence held a bit longer than would be usual if you were merely taking a breath—interjects drama into your speech and spotlights what you are saying. It calls attention to an especially important point you want to make.

AWKWARD BODY MOVEMENTS   A speaker stands before an audience, grabs the podium in a viselike grip (white knuckles clearly visible to everyone), assumes an expressionless face reminiscent of a marble statue in a museum, and appears to have feet welded to the floor. This is an example of too little body movement that calls attention to itself and diminishes a speaker's effectiveness. Excessive body movement or variation, however, also detracts from a speech. Aimlessly pacing like a caged panther, wildly gesticulating with arms flailing in all directions, or awkwardly wrapping legs and arms around the podium is distracting. Strive for a balance between excessive and insufficient body movement. The general guideline is "everything in moderation." *An animated, lively delivery can excite an audience, but you don't want to seem out of control.* Your posture should be erect but not so much that you look like a soldier standing at attention. Slumping your shoulders, crossing and uncrossing your legs, and lurching to one side with one leg higher than the other are awkward movements that call attention to themselves. Practice speaking in front of a mirror or videotape your practice speech to determine whether you make any of these awkward movements.

Proper gesturing can be a concern for the inexperienced public speaker. Don't let it overly concern you. Unless you have adopted some really odd or distracting gestures while speaking, your gestures will rarely, if ever, torpedo your speech. Let gestures emerge naturally. You don't need to plan gestures. As Motley (1995) explains, gestures "are supposed to be non-conscious. That is to say, in natural conversation we use gestures every day without thinking about them. And when we do consciously think about gestures, they become uncomfortable and inhibited" (p. 99). Focus on your message and your audience, and the gestures will follow.

DISTRACTING BEHAVIORS   This is a catchall category. There are dozens of possible quirky behaviors that speakers can exhibit, often without realizing that they are distracting an audience's attention from the message. Playing with change in your pocket while speaking is one example. Playing with a pen or pencil is another. Sometimes a speaker will click a ballpoint pen and not even realize it. Occasionally a speaker will tap the podium while speaking. Distracting behaviors can easily be eliminated. Don't hold a pen in your hand and you won't play with it while speaking. Take change out of your pocket before speaking if you have a tendency to jiggle coins when you put your hand in your pocket. Distracting behaviors won't destroy a quality speech unless the behavior is beyond weird (See Box 16-3). Nevertheless, eliminating them will help create the impression of a polished presentation.

Methods of Delivery

There are several methods of delivery, each with its own pros and cons. The four methods discussed here are manuscript, memorized, impromptu, and extemporaneous speaking.

Box 16-3   Sharper Focus

When Presentation Interferes with Substance

She crawled on her hands and knees across the courtroom floor while the jury watched transfixed. She kicked the jury box, cried, flailed her arms, and screamed. One journalist said she "behaved like she needed a rabies shot during the trial" (Hutchinson, 2002, p. 9A).

Defense attorney Nedra Ruiz's style and delivery before the jury in the emotion-charged trial of Marjorie Knoller and Robert Noel in the highly publicized 2002 dog mauling murder case in Los Angeles became a subject of considerable comment. Laurie Levenson, a law professor at Loyola University in Los Angeles, remarked, "Most people I talk to just shook their heads. To put it mildly, her style is unusual. It's borderline bizarre" (Curtis, 2002, p. A4). Some observers felt Ruiz's client, Margorie Knoller, who was convicted of second-degree murder in the case, might have a successful appeal based on poor legal representation. As Levenson explained during the trial, "There's a pretty decent defense here, but it's getting lost in her (Ruiz's) mannerisms and her theatrics. She's not smooth. She's not polished. She crosses the line from what I think is effective advocacy to cheap theatrics" (Curtis, 2002, p. A4).

At one point in the trial, Ruiz asked prosecution witness Janet Coumbs to stand and show how tall one of the dogs that savagely attacked and killed Diane Whipple was when he licked Coumbs's face (presumably to show how friendly the dog normally acted). Ruiz acted as the dog (again) and placed her "paws" on Coumbs's shoulders. A startled Judge Warren, apparently concerned about Ruiz's extreme style and delivery, instructed, "I think we'll leave it to the jury's imagination about the licking" (Mikulan, 2002).

This is a case of style and delivery subverting substance. Ruiz's style lacked clarity and precision. She was disorganized during her presentations before the jury. Her delivery was animated to the point of distraction for the jury. Her body movements appeared almost out of control. She exhibited vocal variety but to the point of being shrill. One of the jurors, Don Newton, remarked after the trial that Ruiz's flamboyant performance was "in some ways counterproductive. She was so scattered at times and it threw you off" (May, 2002, p. 8A).

Nedra Ruiz's presentation was vivid and memorable during her animated defense of Marjorie Knoller in a dog mauling trial. Nevertheless, it was so extreme, including crawling like a dog, that she was more distracting and comical than effective.

MANUSCRIPT SPEAKING Speakers often refer to "writing their speeches." In my lifetime I have delivered thousands of speeches. No more than a handful were written word for word. Remember that oral and written styles have distinct differences. It is very difficult to write a speech for oral presentation that won't sound like an essay read to an audience. I often tell my students that I do not have to look at a speaker to know immediately that the speaker is reading his or her speech. A read manuscript has a distinct sound and rhythm. Effective speeches are not merely spoken essays. An essay read to an audience can sound stilted and overly formal.

A manuscript speech may be an appropriate method of delivery in certain situations. If you must be scrupulously precise in your phrasing for fear of being legally encumbered or causing offense, then a manuscript may be necessary. Political candidates spend millions of dollars for television and radio ads. They cannot tolerate mistakes in phrasing or wordy speeches. Their speeches are precisely written and delivered from a TelePrompTer, an electronic device that scrolls a manuscript speech, line by line, for the speaker to read while looking right at the audience or the television camera. A television audience does not see the manuscript scrolling in front of the speaker. Most speakers, however, neither need a TelePrompTer nor have access to one.

It takes extensive practice to present a manuscript speech in such a way that an audience is not aware that the speaker is using the manuscript. A chief drawback of manuscript speaking is that the speaker can get buried in the manuscript and fail to establish eye contact with an audience. Reading to an audience can disconnect the speaker from the listeners. Another drawback is that digressions from the prepared manuscript are difficult to make smoothly, yet such changes may be critical if the audience does not respond well to a portion of the speech. Generally, manuscript speaking should be left to professional speakers who have substantial experience using this delivery method.

MEMORIZED SPEAKING Some speakers attempt to memorize their speeches. This is nothing more than delivery of a manuscript speech without the manuscript in front of the speaker. Aside from overcoming the problem of weak eye contact so prevalent with manuscript speaking, all of the limitations of manuscript speaking remain—and new problems arise. The obvious disadvantage of memorized speaking is that you may forget your speech. Awkward silences while you desperately attempt to remember the next sentence in your speech can cause great embarrassment for speaker and listeners alike. Generally, memorized speaking should be discouraged. Memorizing a few important lines in a speech may be useful, but memorizing an entire speech requires far too much energy. A memorized speech usually sounds memorized—artificial, not natural.

IMPROMPTU SPEAKING An **impromptu speech** is a speech delivered off the cuff, or so it seems. There is little or no obvious preparation. You are asked to respond to a previous speaker without warning or to say a few words on a subject or issue without advance notice. Although impromptu speeches can be challenging, a few simple guidelines can help.

First, *anticipate impromptu speaking.* If you have any inkling that you might be called on to give a short speech on a subject, begin preparing your remarks. Don't wait until you are put on the spot.

Second, *draw on your life experience and knowledge for the substance of your remarks.* F. E. Smith once remarked that "Winston Churchill has devoted the best years of his life to preparing his impromptu speeches." Churchill had clarified his ideas and points of view in his mind. When called on to speak in an impromptu fashion, he was already prepared to say what was on his mind. Life experience is preparation for impromptu speaking. Draw from that experience.

Third, *formulate a simple outline for an impromptu speech.* Begin with a short opening attention strategy—a relevant story, a humorous quip you've used successfully on other occasions, or a clever quotation you've memorized. State your point of view or the theme for your remarks. Then quickly identify two or three short points that you will address. Finally, summarize briefly what you said. You are not expected to provide substantial supporting material for your points during an impromptu speech, but if you have some facts and figures memorized, you will impress your audience with your ready knowledge. Impromptu speaking is usually more informal than a standard speech, so be conversational in tone and presentation.

EXTEMPORANEOUS SPEAKING Most public speaking classes stress extemporaneous speaking, usually called "extemp" speaking for short. An **extemp speech** is delivered from a prepared outline or notes. There are several advantages to extemp speaking. First, even though fully prepared in advance, *an extemp speech sounds spontaneous* because the speaker does not read from a manuscript but instead glances at an outline or notes and then puts his or her thoughts into words on the spot. In this sense, extemp speaking falls between impromptu and manuscript speaking. It sounds impromptu and has the detail and substance of a manuscript speech without being either.

Second, *extemp speaking permits greater eye contact with the audience.* The speaker isn't buried in a manuscript with his or her head down. Of course, an outline can take on the form of a manuscript if it is too detailed. It is possible to write an entire speech, word for word, on a 3 × 5 index card. In such cases, the manuscript is merely tiny.

Eye contact is easy when you are speaking from brief notes or a brief outline. Typically, a speaker prepares an extemp speech by constructing an outline composed of full sentences. The speaker delivers the speech, however, from an abbreviated outline composed of simple words or phrases that trigger complete thoughts and ideas. Extemp speaking appears more natural than manuscript speeches and is usually more organized and substantial than impromptu speeches.

Third, *extemp speaking allows the speaker to respond to audience feedback as it occurs.* You can adjust to the moment-by-moment changes in audience reactions much more so than with manuscript or memorized speeches.

The one drawback of extemp speaking is that learning to speak from notes or an outline takes practice. Inexperienced speakers tend to worry that they will forget important elements of their speech if it isn't all written down. There is no substitute for practicing extemp speaking. Once you learn how to do it, you may never want to use any other method of delivery.

In summary, the general guidelines for effective delivery are to use direct eye contact, vocal variety, few if any vocal fillers, moderate pace and body movement, and the extemporaneous method of speaking. Eliminate distracting mannerisms, and avoid manuscript and memorized speaking until you become an experienced public speaker.

Here is one final note about delivery: *Delivery should match the context for your speech.* Like every other aspect of public speaking, delivery is audience centered.

The appropriateness of your delivery is dependent on certain expectations inherent to the occasion and purpose of your speech. A eulogy calls for a dignified, formal delivery. The speaker usually limits body movements and keeps his or her voice toned down. A motivational speech, however, requires a lively, enthusiastic delivery. Your voice is loud, body movements are dramatic, eye contact is intense and direct, and facial movements are expressive. During a motivational speech, the podium is usually moved aside or ignored and the speaker moves back and forth across a stage or even moves into the audience. An after-dinner speech or "roast" calls for a lively, comic delivery. Facial expressions consist mostly of smiles, and gestures may be gross or exaggerated for effect. A speaker's voice may be loud, even abrasive, for effect. There is no one correct way to deliver a speech but many effective ways. Match your delivery to the speech context.

Summary

How a speaker presents a speech can be as important as the substance of the speech. Three aspects of speech presentation were discussed in this chapter: using supporting materials effectively, developing an appropriate and effective style, and developing a competent delivery. The three primary supporting materials are examples, statistics, and testimony. Each can be made effective by following the guidelines provided. Effective and appropriate style should meet three standards: clarity, precision, and vividness. Finally, there are common problems of delivery that become more frequent with some methods of delivery and less frequent with others. The four main methods of delivery are manuscript, memorized, impromptu, and extemporaneous speaking. Most common problems of delivery occur with manuscript, memorized, and impromptu speeches. Extemporaneous speaking has many important advantages compared to the other three methods of delivery.

Quizzes Without Consequences

Go to Quizzes Without Consequences at the book's Online Learning Center at **www.mhhe.com/rothwell2** or access CD-ROM for *In the Company of Others*.

www.mhhe
com/
rothwell2

Key Terms

alliteration	hypothetical example	simile
antithesis	impromptu speech	style
claims	metaphor	vocal fillers
extemp speech	mixed metaphor	
hasty generalization	real example	

See Audio Flashcards Study Aid.

www.mhhe
com/
rothwell2

See Crossword Puzzle Study Aid.

Suggested Readings

Crossen, C. (1994). *Tainted truth: The manipulation of fact in America*. New York: Simon & Schuster. This is an excellent treatment of the importance of credible use of evidence.

Gilovich, T. (1991). *How we know what isn't so: The fallibility of human reason in everyday life*. New York: The Free Press. The author does a wonderful job of presenting common fallacies of reasoning and evidence in a very entertaining way.

Film School

And Justice for All (1979). Dark Comedy/Drama; R ★★★✦
Al Pacino's character delivers a very famous speech ("You're out of order") in a courtroom. Analyze his style and delivery for appropriateness and effectiveness.

To Kill a Mockingbird (1962). Drama; Not rated ★★★★★
Gregory Peck's character is a lawyer in a small Southern town who defends a black man accused of raping a white girl. Peck earned an Oscar for his touching performance. Analyze the lengthy speech delivered to the jury for its style and delivery. Contrast the style and delivery with that of the Al Pacino character in *And Justice for All*.

CHAPTER 17

Informative Speaking

The advent of electronic technologies has ushered in the Information Age. Richard Wurman (1989) contends that "information has become the driving force in our lives" (p. 32). We have greater access to information than at any other time in human history. The ease with which we share information and misinformation is highlighted by a simple statistic: Americans send approximately 2.2 billion e-mail messages every day (Sklaroff, 1999). (Chapter 9 discussed this in detail.)

Crawford and Gorman (1996) use the metaphors of surfing, swimming, and drowning to underline the need to manage information effectively. Although discussing information in the context of electronic technology, their metaphors seem applicable to informative speaking. An informative speech with too little information is unsatisfying to an audience. This is analogous to surfing, merely skimming the top of a subject without delving deeply. Presenting too much information is analogous to drowning, swamping an audience in a tidal wave of information too voluminous for anyone to appreciate or comprehend. An informative speech works best when the speaker swims in the information, finding the right balance between too little and too much information for the audience.

In Chapter 14, the issue of swimming, not drowning or surfing in information, was discussed in a general way when the process of narrowing a topic was explained. Chapter 15 further refined this issue in discussion about outlining and organizing a speech. This chapter focuses on constructing and presenting a specific type of speech—the informative speech.

Informative speaking is a common event. One survey found that graduates from five colleges in the United States ranked informative speaking as the top skill most critical to job performance (Johnson & Szczupakiewicz, 1987). Another survey found that 62% of those surveyed claimed they used informative speaking "almost constantly" (Wolvin & Corley, 1984). Teachers spend the bulk of their time in the classroom speaking informatively. Managers speak informatively at meetings. Military officers give briefings. Religious leaders speak informatively when organizing fund drives, charitable activities, and special events. Students give informative presentations in a wide variety of courses and disciplines. Competent informative speaking is a valuable skill.

The principal purpose of this chapter is to discuss how to construct and present informative speeches competently.

The principal purpose of this chapter is to discuss how to construct and present informative speeches competently.

There are four chapter objectives:

1. **to distinguish between informative and persuasive speaking,**
2. **to explore the different types of informative speeches,**
3. **to examine guidelines for competent informative speaking, and**
4. **to discuss ways visual aids can be used to enhance informative speeches.**

Distinguishing Informative from Persuasive Speaking

No clear line can be drawn between informative and persuasive speaking. In general, however, *an informative speech focuses on teaching an audience* something new, interesting, and useful. You want your listeners to learn. *A persuasive speech focuses on convincing listeners to change their viewpoint and behavior.* You want your listeners to act.

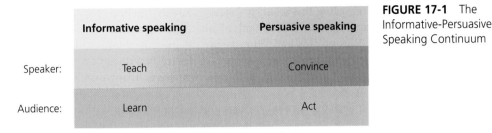

FIGURE 17-1 The Informative-Persuasive Speaking Continuum

However, don't think of informative and persuasive speeches as dichotomous. They differ more by degree than by kind. A teacher, for example, is primarily interested in informing students, but controversial issues arise and the teacher may need to advocate for a particular theory or perspective. Teaching isn't purely informative. Nevertheless, several specific distinctions between informative and persuasive speeches can help you understand where a speech falls on the informative-persuasive continuum (Figure 17-1).

Agenda-Setting Function

The news media perform an **agenda-setting function**—they don't tell us so much what to think as what to think about. We pay more attention to the stories carried on the news than to those that are ignored. In similar fashion, informative speeches direct an audience to think about a specific topic. If an informative speech is effective, it focuses a spotlight on subjects about which listeners may know little or nothing. Are you concerned about identity fraud? Ever heard of it? Imposters find your name and Social Security number by rummaging through your trash or in some other way, apply for credit cards using your name but a different address, and run up huge bills without your knowledge. It's fraudulent, but it can take years to clear your credit rating. If you didn't know about this fast-growing crime in the United States, you might be concerned after hearing an informative speech on the subject. The agenda has been set. You now think about the subject and maybe even take steps to protect yourself from such fraud.

The mere presentation of information to an audience may convince listeners to act differently. If you hear a speech informing you of the pros and cons of hybrid cars, you might be encouraged without any prompting from the speaker to investigate such cars further or even buy one. If a speaker relates a personal story about the rewards he or she experiences teaching young children, you might begin to consider teaching as a profession, even though the speaker never makes such an appeal. A blurry line is all that separates informative from persuasive speeches.

Noncontroversial Information

Informative speeches do not usually stir disagreement and dissension. A speech describing several ways listeners could save money on textbook purchases won't likely arouse animated disagreement. Mostly, your audience will be thankful for the information. Still, some subjects ignite disagreement without prompting. Mention alternative medicine to some individuals and they have a signal reaction, displaying contempt and disgust. A study by Dr. David Eisenberg (An Intense Look, 1998), an assistant professor of medicine at Harvard University, found that Americans visit alternative practitioners almost twice as often as medical doctors each year. Simply reporting this result to listeners already inclined to view alternative medical treatments with disdain might incite strong criticism. Nevertheless, presenting both sides on this and other issues, as most journalists report the news, tries to teach something new, interesting, or useful but doesn't advocate a point of view. This makes the speech essentially informative. If, however, the speech draws conclusions regarding which side is correct after weighing the evidence, then an informative speech moves a bit more in the direction of persuasion.

Precursor to Persuasion

An informative speech may arouse listeners' concern about a subject. This concern may trigger a desire to correct a problem. The informative speech may act as a precursor, or stepping stone, to a subsequent persuasive speech advocating strong action. This may not even be the intent of the initial speaker. In fact, the speaker may not even have perceived a problem that someone in the audience detects.

For example, do you know who Otis Blackwell was? He died May 6, 2002, at the age of 70. Otis Blackwell was credited with writing more than 1,000 songs that were recorded by such international stars as Elvis Presley, Ray Charles, Billy Joel, The Who, Otis Redding, James Taylor, Peggy Lee, and Jerry Lee Lewis (Edwards, 2002). His songs sold more than 185 million copies. He wrote "Return to Sender" and "All Shook Up" (Presley hits), "Great Balls of Fire" (a Lewis hit), "Handy Man" (a Taylor hit), and "Fever" (a Peggy Lee hit). Providing further details about the life of this remarkable African American talent would be an interesting informative speech. Someone listening to such a speech, however, might wonder why mainstream America is mostly oblivious that Blackwell ever lived. A persuasive speech that advocates teaching more African American history to American college students might be triggered by an informative speech on Otis Blackwell.

If you are given an assignment by your speech teacher to present an informative speech to the class, are told by your boss to make a report to a committee or group, or are asked to explain a new software package to novice computer users, remember that your focus will be on teaching, not convincing your listeners. The more neutral and evenhanded your presentation, the more essentially informative it is. When you take a firm stand, present only one side without critique, or advocate a change in the behavior of your listeners, you have moved into persuasive territory.

The competent public speaker recognizes when persuasion is appropriate and when the specific context calls for a more informative presentation. When teachers use the classroom as a platform for personal advocacy, they may step over the not always clear line between informative and persuasive speaking. Advocacy on issues directly relevant to the teaching role—such as advocating the scientific method as a means of critical thinking—is appropriate. Advocacy of "correct" political points of view, however, can run dangerously close to proselytizing, or converting the "unbelievers," not teaching. Again, it is a matter of degree.

Types of Informative Speeches

The issue of what constitutes an informative speech becomes clearer when you look at different types of informative speeches. Three types of informative speeches are reports, lectures, and demonstrations. There is some overlap among the types, but each type has its own unique qualities.

An officer gives a military briefing to soldiers, using a map as an essential visual aid.

Reports

A report is usually a brief, concise, informative presentation that fulfills a class assignment, updates a committee about work performed by a subcommittee, reveals the results of a study, provides recent findings, or identifies the latest developments in a current situation of interest. Students give reports in classes and during meetings of student government. Scientists give reports on research results. Press secretaries give reports, or briefings, to members of the mass media. Military officers give briefings to fellow officers and to the press. Visual aids are sometimes useful when making a report. Videotape of laser-guided missiles striking targets in Iraq in 1991 and 2003, Yugoslavia in 1999, and Afghanistan in 2001 were used extensively during press briefings to detail the progress of these wars fought by the United States. Maps and charts were used often to explain strategy and to assess the effectiveness of the air campaigns.

Lectures

Students are most familiar with this type of informative speech, having heard hundreds of lectures from numerous instructors. A lecture is an informative speech whose principal purpose is to explain concepts and processes or to describe objects or events. Unlike reports, lectures can vary widely in length, from as little as 5 or 10 minutes to several hours. Also unlike most reports, lectures work best when they are highly entertaining. Attention strategies discussed extensively in Chapter 15 are extremely important to the success of a lecture. Maintaining the attention of a sometimes captive audience for long periods of time is a huge challenge. Celebrities, famous authors, politicians, consultants, and experts of all types use the lecture platform to share ideas. They often earn a fat check in the process.

Demonstrations

A demonstration is an informative speech that shows the audience how to use an object or perform a specific activity. Dance teachers demonstrate dance steps while explaining how best to perform the steps. A salesperson demonstrates how a product works. Cooking and home improvement television programs are essentially demonstration speeches. Demonstration speeches require the speaker to show the object or to display the activity for the audience. A demonstration is not a mere description of objects or activities. If you are going to give a speech on martial arts, show the audience specific movements and techniques, don't just ask the audience to imagine them. A speech on how card tricks and magic are performed must actually demonstrate each trick slowly and clearly so the audience can understand.

These three types of informative speeches can overlap. A report may occasionally veer into a demonstration to help listeners who are having trouble understanding. A teacher typically lectures for a majority of a class period, but the teacher may do demonstrations to add variety and make a point more memorable and meaningful. I have given a fairly lengthy demonstration of a polygraph, or lie detector machine, using student volunteers, to drive home several points related to nonverbal communication and connotative meaning related to words. It never fails to engender interest, even fascination, from the class. Years later students tell me they still remember that particular demonstration and what it showed.

Guidelines for Competent Informative Speaking

In general, informative speeches work best when the information presented is clear, accurate, and interesting. In this section we'll discuss the general criteria for competent informative speaking.

Organize Carefully

Because the primary purpose of an informative speech is to teach, organization of the speech is vitally important. Any of the standard organizational patterns discussed in Chapter 15 can work well, depending on your topic and purpose statement. Several additional organizational tips are also useful.

BASIC STRUCTURE The basic structure of most speeches, especially informative ones, divides them into an introduction, body, and conclusion. The introduction grabs attention, explains the significance of the topic to the audience, provides a clear purpose statement, and previews the main points of the speech. The body of the speech, which takes the most time to present, develops the main points previewed in the introduction. The conclusion provides a quick summary of the main points, usually makes reference to the introduction, and offers a memorable finish.

This basic structure may seem unusual to individuals from cultures or co-cultures accustomed to high-context communication patterns. In high-context cultures speakers typically do not provide such explicit organization when communicating messages to audiences. A purpose statement and main points won't normally be precisely stated. Listeners are expected to understand the principal message of a speech from the context. Previous knowledge about the speaker and the message help listeners interpret meaning.

The United States, however, is a low-context culture. There is a general expectation that messages will be communicated explicitly and that ambiguity will be kept to a minimum. Because of this prevailing expectation, individuals from high-context cultures will be more effective public speakers in the United States if they organize their speeches explicitly, fulfilling standard requirements for a competent introduction, body, and conclusion. Explicit organization by a speaker can also help listeners from cultures whose native language is not English to understand the speaker's message.

DEFINITION OF KEY TERMS   Key terms, especially unfamiliar or technical ones, should be defined clearly and precisely. For example, do you know what *hemochromatosis* is? How about *endocrine disruptors?* Jennifer Bazil (1997), a student at West Chester University, gave a speech on hemochromatosis. She defined the term, unfamiliar to most listeners, in this way: "Hemochromatosis is a genetic blood disorder resulting in iron overload. It begins to take effect when an error in the metabolic system causes people to absorb too much iron from their diet" (p. 119).

Adam Childers (1997), a student at the University of Oklahoma, did an equally effective job when he defined endocrine disruptors as "human-made chemicals that have an uncanny ability to mimic some of the human body's most powerful hormones" (p. 103). Even though most people have a passing familiarity with the term *hormone,* many may have a difficult time giving a precise definition. Childers anticipated this and defined hormones as "little more than messengers of the endocrine system. They are released by the pituitary gland, and then they circulate throughout the body, telling different cells what to do. For example, the hormone adrenaline tells our heart when to beat faster" (p. 104). This is a nice definition of hormones. You can picture what hormones do in the body.

SIGNPOSTS AND TRANSITIONS   Signposts and transitions both have the same purpose. They guide the listener during a speech. Although not unique to informative speeches, signposts and transitions are extremely important when the principal aim is to help listeners understand. They may be especially helpful to listeners whose native language is not English. **Signposts** are organizational markers that indicate the structure of a speech and notify listeners that a particular point is about to be addressed. **Transitions** connect what was said with what will be said. They are bridges between points. Box 17-1 offers examples of typical signposts and transitions.

INTERNAL SUMMARIES   When you say, "Summary," most people think of a final wrap-up to a speech or essay. There is another type, however, called an *internal summary,* that is useful for both informative and persuasive speeches. An **internal**

Box 17-1 Shaper Focus

Examples of Signposts and Transitions

Signposts		Transitions	
My first point is	The key points are	So what does this mean?	In similar fashion
My second point is	In summary	For example	Why should we care?
My principal concern is	In review	Nevertheless	Naturally
There are three points to explore	Next	Along the same lines	Of course
Let me begin by	Finally	Consequently	Therefore
Please note	Consider this point carefully	Consider the following	On the one hand
My final point	There are two ways	Afterwards	Accordingly
		Unfortunately	Yet
		Instead	In addition
		Conversely	Hence
		Specifically	In other words
		Thus	A better way
		Once again	

summary restates a key point or points in a speech. It occurs in the body of the speech, not in the conclusion. Internal summaries help listeners follow the sequence of ideas, connecting the dots so the picture drawn by the speaker comes into focus. Lauren McGarity (1997), a student at Rice University, makes a nice internal summary of key points detailing a problem with medical privacy, or the right of patients to have their medical records protected from public scrutiny and use: "Thus, the powerful movement toward cost containment in health care, combined with the inadequacy of current legislation dealing with medical privacy, means that patients now face a privacy nightmare virtually every time they walk into a doctor's office" (p. 129). She then continues her speech by offering possible solutions to the problem.

Use Supporting Materials Competently

Much has been said in previous chapters about the use of supporting materials. In this section, how to use supporting materials in an informative speech is discussed.

AVOID FALLACIES This is a reminder to review the material in Chapter 7 on fallacies. No matter how interesting your informative speech might be, presenting misinformation to your audience is not competent public speaking. Avoid fallacies.

CITE SOURCES COMPLETELY Cite a credible source for each statistic you use, unless the statistic is common knowledge and widely accepted (e.g., number of senators in the U.S. Congress). One of the most frequent mistakes made during informative speeches is to provide statistics without a credible source or any source at all. Also, speakers may not cite sources completely. Provide the source, the source's qualification if not immediately obvious, and the date of the citation. Do the same for every authoritative source you use to supply important factual information or to present expert testimony. Cite your source even if you are merely paraphrasing the expert's precise statement.

Karmen Kirtley (1997), a student at Sheridan College in Wyoming, presents these supporting materials in her speech on funerals:

"The average funeral costs between $5,000 and $10,000; this means that most of us will spend 20 to 40 percent of our yearly income on an average funeral" (p. 155).

"Every year in our country, two million people die; eighty percent of them are buried, occupying over 3,000 square miles of land each year" (p. 156).

"A survey done by the San Francisco Chronicle showed that 85% of us want simple, inexpensive funerals . . ." (p. 155).

In the first two examples, Kirtley offers no source for several important statistics. Although the statistics appear credible, why raise any doubt by failing to cite a quality source? In the last example Kirtley provides no date. There is no way to judge how current or out of date the information is. Also, the survey from the *Chronicle* does not give a sample size—85% of how many people surveyed want inexpensive funerals? These are minor imperfections in an otherwise effective speech because they occur infrequently, but such minor flaws can become major if they are a frequent occurrence. Kirtley presented a strong speech, well organized and generally well supported, but the few instances of no source or incomplete source citations diluted the effectiveness of an otherwise strong, high-quality speech.

Your initial citation of a source should be complete, but you can abbreviate subsequent references to the same source to avoid tedious repetition, unless the abbreviation might cause confusion (e.g., two articles from the same magazine). Teresa Jascob (1997), a student at Ohio State University, does it this way: "According to the same *Chicago Tribune* article . . ." (p. 98). Sara Hefling (1997), a student at South Dakota State University, abbreviates the source as follows: "As *The Human Rights Watch* report tells us . . ." (p. 123). Jennifer Sunstrom (1997), a student at University of Wisconsin–Eau Claire, offers this form of abbreviating a source: "According to the previously cited *ABA Journal* . . ." (p. 153).

CITE SOURCES IN THEIR FIELDS OF EXPERTISE   When you cite sources on a subject requiring expertise, make sure you provide the experts' qualifications so listeners know you are quoting them in their fields. Failure to do this gives listeners no reason to grant expertise to the source. Jessica Lauren Pasel (2001), a student at Purdue University, cites many quality sources in her speech on controlled burns by the U.S. Forestry Service. The expertise of some of her sources, however, cannot be determined. "Clenton Owensby claims in the *Kansas City Star* of October 1, 2000" may appear to be an adequate citation, but we have no idea who Clenton Owensby is. "Wally Covington of Northern Arizona University" is another incomplete citation of a source. Is Wally Covington a professor of environmental studies or a student at NAU expressing an opinion? "Robert Nelson, author of 2000's *A Burning Issue*" is another citation that appears complete but isn't. Who is Robert Nelson? Is Nelson an expert or merely someone interested in making a buck by writing a book?

Use sources that are clearly credible in a field central to your subject. Adam Childers (1997), a student at the University of Oklahoma, does a nice job of citing scientific and medical sources on his topic of "hormone hell." He cites, among others, specific articles in *Environmental Health Perspectives, Nature,* the *New England Journal of Medicine, Lancet,* and the *British Medical Journal.* All of his sources are credible, respected, and authoritative on the subject of endocrine systems and hormones.

CHOOSE THE MOST INTERESTING CREDIBLE SUPPORTING MATERIALS   Learning doesn't usually occur when listeners are bored or uninterested in the subject matter.

This doesn't mean you should substitute colorful but weak supporting material for strong but bland material. Your first consideration when choosing supporting materials should be their credibility and strength. Nevertheless, strong, credible, but interesting supporting material is the best of all choices. Startling statistics, dramatic examples, and clever quotations by experts add interest to a speech that could become tiresome with dull and lifeless supporting materials. Use the strategies presented in Chapter 16 for effective use of supporting materials to enliven an informative speech. (For a model informative speech see Box 17-2.)

▓▓▓ Competent Use of Visual Aids

See Video clip #9 on CD.

We can surf, swim, or drown in information. There is little reason to use visual aids if our information on a subject merely skims on the surface. A speech on apple farming doesn't require a picture of an apple split in half unless the speaker plans to present information at a much deeper level than merely identifying readily apparent parts of this common fruit (skin, core, seeds, and so forth). Visual aids can be exceedingly helpful, however, in preventing an audience from drowning in data. A simple chart or graph can make complex information readily understandable to listeners. Visual aids can help speakers and listeners swim, not surf or drown, in information. In this section the benefits and types of visual aids available as well as presentational media and the guidelines for competent use of visual aids are presented.

Benefits of Visual Aids

Visual aids provide several benefits for a speaker. First, they can clarify difficult points or descriptions of complex objects. Actually showing an object to an audience can help listeners understand. Try explaining a motherboard for a computer or the internal combustion engine without a visual aid. Second, visual aids gain and maintain audience attention. A dramatic photograph of an anorexic teenager can rivet attention during the opening of a speech on eating disorders. Third, visual aids can enhance speaker credibility. Presenting impressive statistics in a graph, chart, or table can drive home an important point in your speech. Fourth, visual aids can improve your delivery. Novice speakers find it difficult to stray from notes or a manuscript. A good first step to take toward an extemporaneous delivery is to make reference to a visual aid. When you are showing an object, a chart, a graph, or some other visual aid, you move away from reading your speech. You assume a more natural delivery when you explain your visual aid to your listeners. Fifth, visual aids can reduce speech anxiety. When you make reference to a visual aid, you shift the focus of your listeners from you to the visual aid. You don't feel so spotlighted when the audience shifts back and forth between looking at you and viewing the visual aid. Finally, visual aids are memorable. Demonstration speeches rely heavily on visual aids. We can remember a magic trick, a martial arts move, or the proper way to arrange flowers when we have actually seen them demonstrated.

Types of Visual Aids

There are several types of visual aids, each with its advantages and disadvantages. Both strengths and limitations of each type are discussed in this section.

Box 17-2   Sharper Focus

Outline and Text of an Informative Speech

Here is an outline and the text of an informative speech. Each incorporates the suggestions offered for constructing a competent informative speech.

Introduction

I. *Attention strategy:* Use startling examples.
   A. Describe the Spanish flu pandemic of 1918–1919.
   B. Refer to the 1957 Asian flu pandemic and 70,000 deaths.
   C. Mention the 1968 Hong Kong flu pandemic.
   D. Note the 1976 and the 1997 flu scares.
II. *Significance:* We should all be concerned about yearly flu viruses for two reasons.
   A. A serious flu epidemic could strike again.
   B. Everyone is susceptible to flu viruses each year.
III. *Central idea:* Flu is a serious problem, but there are effective ways to prevent contracting this yearly disease.
IV. *Purpose statement:* To inform my audience about ways to prevent contracting the flu.
V. *Preview:* Three main points will be discussed.
   A. Flu viruses pose serious health hazards to all of us.
   B. Flu viruses are difficult to combat.
   C. There are three primary ways to prevent contracting the flu.

Body

I. Flu viruses pose serious health hazards to everyone.
   A. Ordinary, annual flu viruses are killers.
      1. On average, 20,000 Americans die each year from the flu.
      2. Flu kills more people each year than AIDS.
   B. Flu viruses can make you very sick.
      1. Flu produces symptoms such as high fever, sore throat, aches, cough, and severe fatigue.
      2. More than 100,000 victims are hospitalized each year during an average flu season from flu complications.
      3. "Stomach flu," however, is a misnomer.
   C. Flu viruses are highly contagious.
      1. Children easily catch the flu.
      2. Children infect adults.
      3. Adults spread flu to coworkers.
      4. Another pandemic is a virtual certainty.

II. Flu viruses are difficult to combat.
   A. "Influenza" was thought to be the "influence" of the stars, making it exceedingly difficult to combat.
   B. There are many strains of flu, even in a single flu season.
      1. There are two types of flu: types A and B

   2. There were three strains of flu during the 2002–2003 flu season: A/Moscow, A/New Caledonia, and B/Hong Kong
   C. Occasionally a flu virus will mutate, causing a pandemic.

III. There are three primary ways to prevent contracting the flu.
   A. Stay generally healthy.
      1. Get exercise.
      2. Eat nutritionally balanced meals.
      3. Avoid crowds during flu season.
   B. Get a flu shot.
      1. Flu shots are 70%–90% effective.
      2. Flu shots could prevent 80% of deaths and serious complications if everyone got immunized.
      3. Flu shots cannot cause the flu.
   C. Take an antiviral prescription drug.
      1. Antiviral drugs are almost as effective as vaccines.
      2. An antiviral drug is an effective option for those who fear shots or have allergic reactions to eggs.

Conclusion

I. Provide summary of main points.
   A. Flu viruses can be hazardous to humans.
   B. Combating flu viruses can be difficult.
   C. Flu viruses can be prevented.
II. Make reference to the introductory example of Spanish flu.
III. Give a memorable finish by using a quotation and making a reference to this annual plague.

Bibliography

Brody, J. (2001, October 23). An easy means of prevention: Flu shot. *The New York Times*. [Online]. Available at http://www.nytimes.com/2001/10/23/health/anatomy/23BROD.html?rd=.

Facts about flu. (1998, January 14). Press release, Centers for Disease Control.

Garrett, L. (1994). *The coming plague: Newly emerging diseases in a world out of balance*. New York: Penguin Books.

Haney, D. (1998, November 8). Researchers breaking new ground on flu front. *San Jose Mercury News*, p. 10A.

Kolata, G. (1999). *Flu: The story of the Great Influenza Pandemic of 1918 and the search for the virus that caused it*. New York: Farrar, Straus & Giroux.

Box 17-2 **Sharper Focus** (continued)

Prevention and control of influenza. (2002, May 5). Recommendations of the Advisory Committee on Immunization Practices (ACIP). [Online]. Available at http://www.cdc.gov/mmwr/preview/mmwrhtml/rr5103a1.html.

Recer, P. (1995, July 25). Experts warn of threat to humans posed by reinvigorated diseases. *Associated Press*, p. 1A.

Stracher, A., & Kendler, J. S. (2002, April 4). The influenza virus: Understanding your enemy. [Online]: Available at http://drkoop.healthology.com/focus_article.asp?f=xmipressfeed&c=influenza_virus.

The Annual Plague

It killed 21 million people worldwide and sickened 1 billion more, half the world's population at the time, according to Laurie Garrett, health and science writer for *Newsday* and the award-winning author of the 1994 book *The Coming Plague*. [CREDIBLE SOURCE] Garrett tells us that half-a-million Americans died of the disease in a single year, a greater loss of life than Americans suffered in all of the wars in the 20th century combined. [USE OF STARTLING STATISTICS GAINS ATTENTION; COMPARISON MAKES STATISTIC CONCRETE] The virus was so severe that some died from it within 1 day, a few within hours. Women who boarded the New York subway at Coney Island, feeling only mild fatigue, were found dead when the subway pulled into Columbus Circle 45 minutes later. [VIVID, REAL EXAMPLE MAKES STATISTICS MORE CONCRETE AND PROVOKES STRONG, MEMORABLE IMAGE] This lethal disease began in Europe and spread to every corner of the globe. Almost 20% of the population of Western Samoa died from the illness, and entire Inuit villages in isolated parts of Alaska were wiped out.

What was this killer disease? [TRANSITION] The Black Death of the 14th century revisiting the human species? Some biological warfare agent? Cholera, smallpox, or diptheria? [RHETORICAL QUESTIONS INVOLVE AUDIENCE, CREATE CURIOSITY] None of these were the cause of this massive loss of life. The global killer was the flu! [STARTLING STATEMENT FOR MOST LISTENERS] That's right, the so-called Spanish flu of 1918–1919 caused this pandemic, or worldwide epidemic. According to Gina Kolata, science reporter for *The New York Times* and author of the 1999 book *Flu*, victims of this disease suffered agonizing deaths from high fever and fluid that filled their lungs, causing them to drown. [VIVID DESCRIPTION KEEPS ATTENTION]

In 1957, a flu pandemic struck again. Laurie Garrett [ABBREVIATED SECOND REFERENCE TO SOURCE] notes that 70,000 Americans died from the Asian flu, and millions more were incapacitated for weeks by this illness. In 1968, yet another flu pandemic, the Hong Kong flu, felled the human population. The Hong Kong flu hit the United States with sledgehammer force, sickening a huge portion of the country. [USE OF COLORFUL LANGUAGE; EXAMPLES MAKE A NOVEL OPENING TO GRAB ATTENTION] In 1976, the Swine flu initially was feared to be a return of the Spanish flu, but it never developed into a serious illness. Finally, Gina Kolata [ABBREVIATED SECOND REFERENCE TO SOURCE] notes that in 1997 a potential pandemic was narrowly averted after a "bird flu" infected human victims in Hong Kong, which necessitated the immediate destruction of 1.2 million chickens to stop the deadly virus from spreading.

Why should we care about flu epidemics of the past? [RHETORICAL QUESTION INVOLVES AUDIENCE, MAKES TRANSITION] There are two good reasons to be interested in such notable events: (1) a flu pandemic could strike again, and (2) everyone in this room is a potential victim of a deadly flu virus. [SIGNIFICANCE OF TOPIC TO THE AUDIENCE IS ESTABLISHED] Since every person here probably has suffered from the flu at least once, you'll want to listen carefully as I inform you about ways to prevent contracting the flu. [CLEAR PURPOSE STATEMENT] I have three main points: I will show that flu viruses are a serious health hazard, that flu viruses are difficult to combat, and that there are three ways to prevent the flu. [CLEAR, CONCISE PREVIEW OF MAIN POINTS; PROBLEM–CAUSE–SOLUTION ORGANIZATIONAL PATTERN USED]

Let's begin by discussing the serious health hazards produced by a normal flu season. [SIGNPOSTING FIRST MAIN POINT] Even ordinary flu viruses that hit the United States every year between the months of October and April are killers. According to a May 5, 2002, report by the Advisory Committee on Immunization Practices, or ACIP, prepared for the National Center for Infectious Diseases, in an average flu season 20,000 people die from this affliction. [STARTLING STATISTIC MAINTAINS ATTENTION AND INTEREST; USE OF CREDIBLE SOURCE FOR ALL STATISTICS] Annual flu, directly or indirectly, kills more people than AIDS. [COMPARISON MAKES STATISTIC CONCRETE]

Most of you won't die from a common flu virus, but you may wish you were dead. [TRANSITION] Typical flu symptoms include high fever, sore throat, intense muscle aches, congestion, cough, and severe fatigue. My friend Terry once described how he feels when he gets the flu: "It's like being suddenly hit by a speeding car, catapulted into a concrete wall, roasted in an oven, then forced to participate in the Iron Man marathon. Death by comparison seems pleasant." [VIVID USE OF SIMILES; INTENSITY USED TO MAINTAIN ATTENTION] Symptoms of flu

Box 17-2 **Sharper Focus** (continued)

can last from a few days to several weeks. The flu can often lead to severe complications, such as bronchitis and pneumonia, which may require hospitalization. According to the 2002 ACIP report [ABBREVIATED SECOND REFERENCE TO SOURCE], more than 100,000 flu victims are hospitalized each year during an average flu season.

Although nausea sometimes occurs with the flu, the "stomach flu" is a misnomer. According to a January 14, 1998, press release from the Centers for Disease Control, severe vomiting is rarely a prominent symptom of flu. [CREDIBLE SOURCE] The so-called stomach flu is actually a gastrointestinal illness caused by microorganisms that cause food poisoning. So if you're "tossing your cookies" or "clutching the porcelain throne," it is unlikely that you have contracted the flu. [VIVID SLANG TO KEEP ATTENTION]

In addition to having severe symptoms [TRANSITION], flu is hazardous to humans because it is highly contagious. According to Daniel Haney, science reporter for the Associated Press, in a November 8, 1998, article in the *San Jose Mercury News*, young children are "flu incubators." [CREDIBLE SOURCE] Haney continues, "In epidemiological terms, children are in the same category as ticks, rats, and mosquitoes: they are vectors of disease." [COLORFUL QUOTE] Medical columnist for *The New York Times*, Jane Brody explains why this is so in her October 24, 2001, column: "Lacking immunity to flu viruses, children are most likely to acquire the virus, spread it among themselves, and transmit it to others." Day care centers and classrooms are flu breeding grounds where sick children spew the virus everywhere by coughing, sneezing, and wiping their runny noses. [VIVID DESCRIPTION CREATES ATTENTION] Children also bring the flu home and infect adult parents who pass it along to coworkers, and so it spreads throughout the population.

An average flu season can kill thousands and sicken millions in the United States. The threat of a not-so-average flu season, however, a full-blown flu pandemic, is real. No one can predict exactly when another severe flu outbreak will occur, but Dr. Adam Stracher, a medical doctor and flu expert interviewed on April 4, 2002, for the healthology.com Web site, notes that severe flu outbreaks occur on average about every 10 to 30 years. [CREDIBLE SOURCE; TESTIMONY OF EXPERT] Since the last severe outbreak occurred in 1968, you can see that we are past due for another pandemic. It is clear that flu viruses pose a serious health hazard for all of us because flu can cause death and widespread suffering. [INTERNAL SUMMARY OF MAIN POINT]

Naturally [TRANSITION], we're all interested in why flu is an annual event about as welcome as flies, frogs, and the other plagues God visited upon the ancient Egyptians in the biblical story of the Exodus. This brings me to my second main point [SIGNPOSTING MAIN POINT], which is that flu viruses are difficult to combat.

Previous centuries produced many theories as to the cause of flu. Influenza, *flu* being the shortened version of this term, reflects the 15th-century astrological belief that the disease was caused by the "influence" of the stars. According to Laurie Garrett [CREDIBLE SOURCE], prominent American physicians of the time thought the 1918 Spanish flu might have been caused by nakedness, fish contaminated by Germans, Chinese people, dirt, dust, unclean pajamas, open windows, closed windows, old books, or "some cosmic influence." [HISTORICAL EXAMPLES ARE NOVEL ATTENTION GETTER]

Unlike our predecessors [TRANSITION], we know that a virus causes flu, but a flu virus is difficult to combat. There are many strains, not just a single type. For instance, according to the 2002 ACIP report, there were three strains of flu in 2002 and 2003: A/Moscow, A/New Caledonia, and B/Hong Kong. Flu strains are divided into A and B types and designated by the principal city where the flu is first reported. There are many strains of flu because flu viruses continually change over time. Sometimes they change their genetic structure only slightly. This genetic "drift" means that your immune system's antibodies, produced to fight a previous flu, will not combat the disease as well when exposed to a slightly altered virus. Occasionally, a flu strain will mutate, altering the genetic structure of the virus so greatly that human antibodies from previous exposures to flu will be useless. Type A flu viruses are usually more serious than type B, partly because, according to the ACIP report [CREDIBLE SOURCE], type A viruses genetically drift more rapidly than type B flu viruses. According to Laurie Garrett [CREDIBLE SOURCE], the pandemics of 1918, 1957, and 1968 were mutated flu strains. [REFERENCE TO EARLIER EXAMPLES PROVIDES CONTINUITY TO THE SPEECH; CREDIBLE SOURCE] The changing structure of flu viruses and their many strains make finding a cure very challenging. [INTERNAL SUMMARY OF MAIN POINT]

So what can be done about the yearly flu until a lasting cure is discovered? [USE OF RHETORICAL QUESTION TO INVOLVE AUDIENCE; TRANSITION] This brings me to my final main point [SIGNPOSTING MAIN POINT] that there are three primary ways to prevent catching the flu. First [SIGNPOSTING SUBPOINT], stay generally healthy. Those in a weakened or vulnerable physical state, such as the very young, the elderly, those with chronic health conditions, and pregnant women, are most likely to catch the flu. Magdalene Vulkovic, chief pharmacist at the University

Box 17-2 **Sharper Focus** (continued)

of Houston Health Center, on its Health Center homepage, April 1999, states, "Exercise, proper diet, and plenty of rest will lessen your chances of catching the flu." [CREDIBLE SOURCE; TESTIMONY OF EXPERT] Also, avoid large crowds and confined spaces as much as possible where flu sufferers can spread the disease. Airplanes, classrooms, and offices are flu factories. [ALLITERATION FOR VIVIDNESS]

Second [SIGNPOSTING SUBPOINT], a yearly flu shot is the best preventive. The 2002 ACIP report notes that flu shots are 70% to 90% effective in preventing flu among healthy adults, and according to the 1998 CDC press release [ABBREVIATED CITATION], close to 80% of deaths from flu and its complications could be prevented with mass immunization each year. [CREDIBLE SOURCES; CREDIBLE STATISTICS] Because flu viruses change, last year's vaccination won't protect you against this year's flu strains.

Despite common belief, a flu shot cannot give you the flu because, as the CDC press release explains, flu shots contain no live virus. [CREDIBLE SOURCE; TESTIMONY OF EXPERT] The most frequent side effect is brief soreness at the site of the shot.

For those who get weak in the knees at the simple sight of a syringe, there is hope on the horizon. [COLORFUL LANGUAGE; USE OF ALLITERATION; TRANSITION] The 2002 ACIP report notes that an effective flu vaccine that you spray up your nose has been tested and is currently awaiting approval by the Food and Drug Administration. Its side effects are minimal, especially when compared to some things people shoot up their noses. Pain phobics take note—it doesn't hurt!

A third way to prevent catching the flu is to take an antiviral drug. There are four FDA approved antiviral drugs, all with unpronounceable names. The 2002 ACIP report [CREDIBLE SOURCE] documents that these prescription drugs are almost as effective as vaccines in preventing the flu, but "these agents are not a substitute for vaccination." The antiviral drugs have an added benefit, however. Again according to ACIP, they can shorten the duration of the flu by one or more days and reduce the severity of the symptoms if taken immediately after the onset of the flu. So for those individuals who faint at the thought of receiving a shot or who cannot be vaccinated because of allergic reactions to eggs (a component of the vaccine), antiviral drugs are a good option.

In review [SIGNPOST], I have shown that flu viruses can be hazardous to humans, that combating flu can be difficult, but that catching the flu can be prevented. [SUMMARY OF MAIN POINTS] I began with a reference to the 1918 Spanish flu. Nobody knows where the Spanish flu virus went or whether it will surface again. [REFERENCE TO THE SPANISH FLU EXAMPLE IN THE INTRODUCTION GIVES CLOSURE TO THE SPEECH] As Gina Kolata notes, "Perhaps, as we grow almost smug about influenza, that most quotidian of infections, a new plague is now gathering deadly force. Except this time we stand armed with a better understanding of the past to better survive the next pandemic." Until we find a lasting cure for the flu, we'll have to be vigilant in our effort to prevent this annual plague. [CLOSING QUOTATION ATTENTION STRATEGY; REFERENCE TO SPEECH TITLE, "ANNUAL PLAGUE," MAKES A MEMORABLE FINISH]

OBJECTS Sometimes there is no substitute for the actual object of your speech. A demonstration on tying different types of knots really requires a rope, not a mere drawing of knots in a rope. Tying knots is a process that is dependent on a specific object. "Imagine me tying a knot in a rope" just doesn't work for the audience. Giving a speech on how to pack the most camping supplies and necessities into a backpack can't be effectively demonstrated without the backpack and some supplies.

There are limitations, however, to the use of objects as visual aids. Some objects are too large to haul into a classroom or even an auditorium. Some objects are not available for show. A speech on building a bullet train in the United States similar to those in Europe and Asia may benefit from a visual aid, but you surely can't drive a real train into a classroom or auditorium. Students have given speeches in my class on surfing. A few have attempted to bring in surfboards as visual aids for their speeches. One student wanted to show how the size of surfboards has changed over the years, so he hauled in four different-sized surfboards. His immediate problem

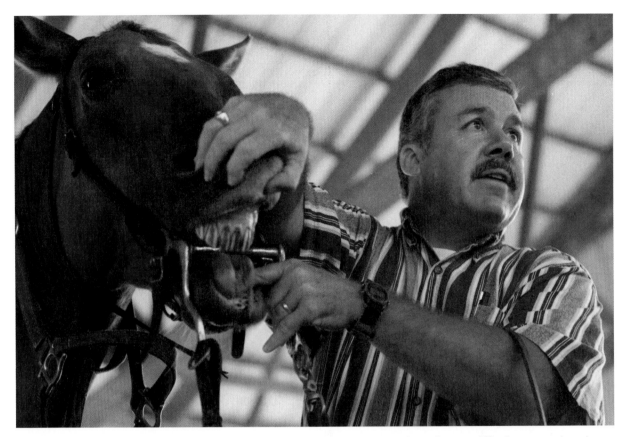

A live animal may be an effective visual aid in certain circumstances, but animals can be very difficult to control, and many are impractical for classroom demonstrations.

was that his longboard hit the ceiling when he placed it on its end, punching a hole in the ceiling tiles.

Some objects are illegal or dangerous or potentially objectionable to at least some audience members. One of my students long ago thought it was a good idea to bring in a live marijuana plant he had been cultivating as a "show-and-tell" object. Another student wanted to show students "how to roll a doobie." He began his speech by pulling out a plastic bag of marijuana and papers to roll a joint. In both cases, the speech had to be halted because the objects were illegal. Firearms, poisons, combustible liquids, or sharp objects are dangerous. One student wanted to give a speech on "the dangers of pornography." She asked me in advance, thank goodness, if she could bring in explicit pornographic photographs as a visual aid. I nixed her idea. Offending an audience with a visual aid, as abortion protesters often do with graphic pictures of aborted fetuses, can easily backfire and call into question a speaker's credibility and good taste. Simply exercise responsible judgment. Check for rules or laws that could invite trouble before using any visual aid that seems questionable.

Inanimate objects are usually preferable to living, squirming objects. Puppies are unfailingly cute and great attention grabbers, but they are also very difficult to control. One student brought a puppy to class for her speech. The puppy whined, barked, and howled throughout her presentation. At first it was cute. After 5 minutes

A normal bottle of Botox, a diluted poison used to reduce facial wrinkles, is about the size of an adult's thumb. The hugely enlarged model held by a representative of a company marketing Botox is a far more impressive visual aid than the real thing.

the audience was thoroughly annoyed. My student ended her speech as the puppy urinated on the classroom carpet.

Some living objects can frighten audience members. A live snake, especially one not in a cage, will make some audience members extremely uneasy, even agitated. One student brought a live tarantula to class for her speech. She let the spider walk across a table as she presented her informative speech. Audience members were transfixed—not by what she was saying but by the hairy creature moving slowly in front of them.

MODELS When objects relevant to your informative speech are too large, too small, expensive, fragile, rare, or unavailable, models can often act as effective substitutes. A speech on dental hygiene is an apt example. Speakers usually bring in a larger-than-normal model of a human mouth full of teeth. It isn't practical or effective to ask for a volunteer from the audience to open wide so the speaker can show the volunteer's teeth to everyone. The teeth will be too small to see well, especially for audience members in the back row. Such a demonstration will also be extremely awkward. The speaker may have to point out tooth decay, gum disease, and fillings in the volunteer's mouth—not something most people want others to notice, much less have spotlighted.

Demonstration speeches on cardiopulmonary resuscitation (CPR) require a model of a person. You can't ask for an audience member to serve as a victim for the

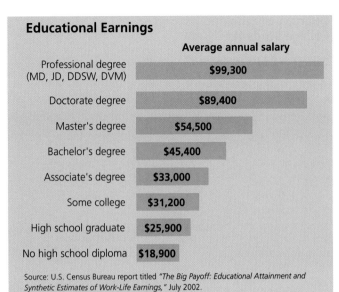

FIGURE 17-2 A Bar Graph Illustrating the Monetary Advantage of Education

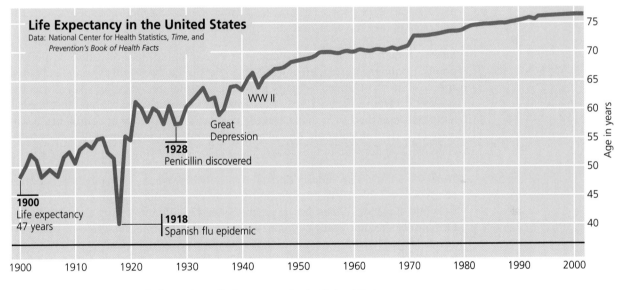

FIGURE 17-3 A Line Graph Illustrating Life Expectancy in the United States (Source: *San Jose Mercury News.*)

demonstration. Pushing forcefully on a person's chest could be dangerous and potentially embarrassing.

GRAPHS A graph is a visual representation of statistics in an easily understood format. There are several kinds. Figure 17-2 is a bar graph. A bar graph compares and contrasts two or more items or shows variation over a period of time. Bar graphs can make a dramatic visual impact. Figure 17-3 is a line graph. A line graph is useful for showing a trend or change over a lengthy period of time. A pie graph depicts a proportion or percentage for each part of a whole. Figure 17-4 is a pie graph.

Quantity of Smoking Among College Students

How many cigarettes per day?

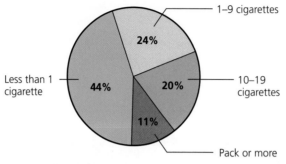

Source: Harvard School of Public Health

Graphs are effective if they are uncluttered. Too much information in a graph makes it difficult for an audience to understand. A graph must be immediately understandable to an audience. For a person reading a newspaper, a detailed graph is useful because the person has time to examine it carefully. During a speech, your audience can't take the time, and you don't want them to.

MAPS   A map helps audience members see geographic areas that make important points. Commercial maps are normally too detailed to be useful as visual aids for a speech. The most effective maps are large, simple, and directly relevant to the speaker's purpose. Figure 17-5 is an example of an effective map. Some speakers attempt to draw their own maps, but the proportions and scale of continents, countries, or bodies of water are often badly represented. A map should be exact to be effective. You don't want the United States to look three times bigger than Asia.

TABLES   A table is an orderly depiction of statistics, words, or symbols in columns or rows (see Table 17-1). A table can provide easy-to-understand comparisons of facts and statistics. Tables, however, are not as visually interesting as graphics. Tables can also become easily cluttered with too much information. Table 17-2 is an example of a table with too much information for a speech. Two or three tables could be made from the information in this single table.

Tables will be a visual distraction if the headings are too small to read, the columns or rows are crooked, and the overall impression is that the table was hastily drawn. With readily available computer technology there is little excuse for amateurish-looking tables.

PHOTOGRAPHS   The many photographs included in this textbook underline the effectiveness of this visual aid to make a point, clarify a concept, and draw attention. When objects are too big or unwieldly, unavailable, or too fragile to use as visual aids, photographs may serve as effective substitutes. Instead of bringing the wiggling, fussing, barking, urinating puppy to class, perhaps several photographs of the cute pet will suffice. Instead of violating the law by displaying a real marijuana plant in class, show a photograph of the plant.

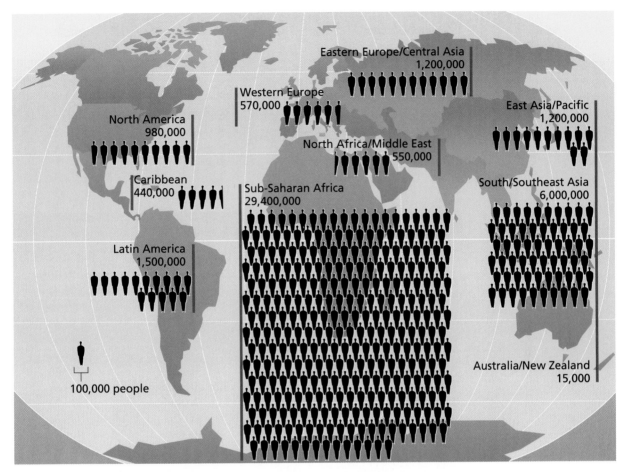

FIGURE 17-5 A Map That Illustrates Distribution of AIDS Victims Worldwide

Photographs have some drawbacks. They may need to be enlarged, and this can be expensive. Postage-stamp-size photographs are worthless as visual aids for an informative speech. When a speaker says to his or her audience, "So as you can see in this photograph," and no one can because the photograph is minuscule, the photo becomes not an aid but an embarrassment. The photograph should be large enough for everyone in the audience to see easily.

DRAWINGS When photographs are unavailable, a careful drawing might be an effective substitute. Drawings of figures performing ballet moves or pole-vaulting techniques could be instructive for an audience. If the drawings are sloppy, distorted, small, or appear to have been drawn by a 5-year-old with no artistic talent, find a different visual aid. Figure 17-6 is an example of an effective drawing.

Visual Aids Media

There are many media, or means of communicating, with visual aids. The most frequently used media are discussed next.

Table 17-1 Average Salaries of Male/Female University Faculty, 2002

	Men	Women
Professor	$85,437	$75,425
Associate Professor	$61,055	$56,883
Assistant Professor	$51,268	$47,446
Instructor	$37,456	$36,001
Lecturer	$44,143	$39,729

Source: American Association of University Professors

Table 17-2 Top Major League Baseball Salaries and Team Record, 2002

	Player	Salary	Team	W-L Record
1	Alex Rodriguez	$22,000,000	Texas Rangers	72-90
2	Carlos Delgado	$19,400,000	Toronto Blue Jays	78-84
3	Kevin Brown	$15,714,286	L.A. Dodgers	92-70
4	Manny Ramirez	$15,462,727	Boston Red Sox	93-69
5	Barry Bonds	$15,000,000	S.F. Giants	95-66
6	Sammy Sosa	$15,000,000	Chicago Cubs	67-95
7	Derek Jeter	$14,600,000	N.Y. Yankees	103-58
8	Pedro Martinez	$14,000,000	Boston Red Sox	93-69
9	Shawn Green	$13,416,667	L.A. Dodgers	92-70
10	Randy Johnson	$13,350,000	Arizona Diamondbacks	98-64
11	Greg Maddux	$13,100,000	Atlanta Braves	101-59
12	Larry Walker	$12,666,667	Colorado Rockies	73-89
13	Albert Bell	$12,368,790	Baltimore Orioles	67-95
14	Bernie Williams	$12,357,143	New York Yankees	103-58
15	Mo Vaughn	$12,166,667	New York Mets	75-86

Sources: asp.usatoday.com/sports/baseball/top25.aspx?year=2002
sports.yahoo.com/mlb/standings

CHALKBOARD OR WHITEBOARD Every student is familiar with the chalkboard or whiteboard. The chalkboard or whiteboard is a useful visual aid medium when time and resources don't permit the use of more sophisticated media. Chalkboards and whiteboards are widely available and allow great flexibility. You can illustrate tables, drawings, and graphs on them. If you make a mistake, you can immediately and easily erase them.

Chalkboards and whiteboards, however, do have several serious drawbacks. The quality of the table, drawing, or graph on a chalkboard is usually inferior. Students are sometimes tempted to draw on a chalkboard or whiteboard during their speeches, consuming huge portions of their allotted speaking time creating visual aids. If a student uses the chalkboard or whiteboard prior to his or her speech, the class waits impatiently while the speaker creates the visual aid. It is too time-consuming. Most instructors discourage the use of either as a visual aid medium.

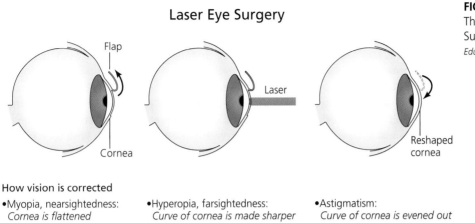

Laser Eye Surgery

Flap
Cornea

Laser

Reshaped cornea

How vision is corrected

- Myopia, nearsightedness: *Cornea is flattened*
- Hyperopia, farsightedness: *Curve of cornea is made sharper*
- Astigmatism: *Curve of cornea is evened out*

FIGURE 17-6 Drawings That Illustrate Laser Eye Surgery (Source: *Eye Surgery Education Council*)

POSTER BOARD   A poster board is a very simple medium for visual aids. Available in most college bookstores or stationery outlets, you can draw, stencil, and make graphs or tables on poster board. Making the poster appear professional, however, is a primary challenge. Posters are usually attached to an easel for display. Simply standing them on a chalk tray will usually result in the poster curling at the top and flopping onto the ground. Tape it to a wall if no better option exists.

HANDOUTS   Handouts are a popular form of visual aid. A table, map, drawing, or even a photograph can be distributed on a handout. One significant advantage of a handout is that the listeners can keep it long after the speech has been presented. It can serve as a useful reminder of the information presented.

Handouts have several potential disadvantages, however. Passing out a handout in the middle of your speech wastes time, breaks the flow of the speech, and can be a huge distraction, making it difficult to regain audience attention. If your listeners are busy reading your handout while you're speaking, they will not be attending to your message. You may have moved on to speaking about a new point while audience members are still reading your handout on a previous point.

Distribute a handout just prior to giving your speech if the handout will be an integral part of your presentation. If the handout is necessary for explanation of important points throughout your speech, it will not distract but will assist audience members to maintain focus and increase their understanding of your message. Sometimes you can distribute a handout after the speech has ended. A handout with names, e-mail addresses, and phone numbers of organizations or agencies that can provide additional information on your subject is most effective after your speech. You can distribute a handout during a speech if you are lecturing for a long time (1 to 2 hours). During short speeches (5 to 10 minutes), however, don't distribute handouts.

PROJECTION EQUIPMENT   There are several options available for projecting images onto a large screen. An opaque projector is a relic from another age that still has its uses. An opaque projector enlarges pictures from magazines, newspapers, and books, or it enlarges photographs onto a screen. Its greatest advantage is that no special preparation is necessary to use the equipment. You don't have to spend significant amounts of money to enlarge pictures that are too small to be effective visual aids. The opaque projector does the temporary enlargement.

The opaque projector does have several disadvantages. First, it is a clunky piece of equipment. It is awkward to use, especially if you have no experience with it. The bulb is very hot, so pictures placed in the projector can easily burn or curl if left in it too long. A more recent alternative to the opaque projector is the visualizer. It is much more compact but more complicated to use.

Another piece of projection equipment is the slide projector. This takes preparation to use effectively. Slides must be developed and placed in a circular tray right side up. Slide projectors provide beautiful enlarged pictures on a screen. If you need a picture and none is available, a slide projector allows you to take your own picture and blow it up on a screen for the audience. Slide projectors, however, are notorious for causing problems. Slides sometimes jam in the tray, bulbs burn out in the middle of presentations, and the tray sometimes fails to advance to the next slide.

Overhead projectors are yet another type of projector that can be used to display enlarged images. They are widely used because they are easy to use, relatively problem free, and flexible. You place a transparency on the overhead projector, which enlarges your image by projecting it on a wall or screen. Transparencies are very easy to prepare. Whatever you can photocopy you can make into a transparency. The relative ease of use of this equipment tempts speakers to overdo the number of transparencies they use during a speech. Be careful not to substitute transparencies for an actual speech.

VIDEOTAPE   A videotape excerpt from a movie or a segment from a videotape you shot yourself can be a valuable visual aid. Videotapes can be dramatic, informative, and moving. They often are great attention grabbers. Videotapes used during an informative speech, however, have several limitations. First, the sound on a videotape will compete with you, the speaker, for attention. Shut off the sound when you are trying to explain a point while the tape is playing. Second, a videotape with its dramatic action can make your speech seem tame, even dull, by comparison. It is tough to compete with a Hollywood production. Third, *a videotape isn't a speech.* I have to remind my students of this often. There is a real temptation to play a videotape as a major portion of a speech without making any narration or direct reference to the tape while it is rolling. A videotape should not be a substitute for your speech. If you use a videotape excerpt during your speech, be certain that it is properly cued so you won't have to interrupt the flow of your presentation by looking for the right place to start the tape. Use only very short video excerpts.

See the PowerPoint Tutorial on CD.

COMPUTER-ASSISTED PRESENTATIONS   By now you should be familiar with the many options available for computer-assisted presentations. PowerPoint is probably the most widely available and utilized example of this visual aid medium. Space does not allow a "how-to" explanation for using this technology (see CD-ROM tutorial). For relatively short presentations (5- to 10-minute speeches) this technology is probably overkill. For longer speeches (1-hour lectures) computer-assisted presentations can be wonderful. The biggest drawbacks are the time it takes to prepare the presentation using this technology, the potential for glitches to occur during the actual speech, and the tendency to become so enamored with the software capability that you fail to devote as much effort to the actual speech. Organizations such as the Pentagon have instructed employees to curtail the use of PowerPoint presentations because they turn meetings into marathon sessions (McGinn, 2000). As chief executive of Sun Microsystems, Scott McNealy ordered a ban on all PowerPoint demonstrations. The ban was never enforced, but more and more business conferences are prohibiting PowerPoint presentations because they place too much focus on the bells and whistles—the surface "gee whiz" computer capabilities—and too little on the content (Zuckerman, 1999). As Cliff Nass, associate professor of communication at Stanford University, observes, "Try to imagine the 'I have a dream' speech with PowerPoint" (Zuckerman, 1999, p. 9). Consider carefully whether multimedia presentations are appropriate and whether they really enhance the content of your presentation.

See "Checklist for Preparing and Delivering an Informative Speech" on CD.

Guidelines for Competent Use

Poorly designed and clumsily presented visual aids will detract from, not aid, your speech. Here are some guidelines for the competent use of visual aids.

KEEP AIDS SIMPLE   Complex tables, maps, and graphics can work well in print media such as magazines and newspapers. Readers can closely examine such visual aids. Listeners do not have the same option. Complex visual aids do not work well for speeches, especially short ones, in which the information needs to be communicated clearly and quickly. Your audience will be intent on figuring out a complex visual aid, not on listening to you speak. Keep visual aids simple.

MAKE AIDS VISIBLE   The general rule for visual aids is that people in the back of the room or auditorium should be able to see your visual aid easily. If they can't, it is not large enough to be effective. Audience members should not have to strain to see words or numbers on your visual aid. Your audience will quickly grow uninterested in your visual aid if it is not large enough to be seen easily.

MAKE AIDS NEAT AND ATTRACTIVE   I had a student who realized 5 minutes before his speech that a visual aid was required for the speaking assignment. I actually saw him take his lunch bag, pour out the contents, and with a black marker pen quickly sketch a drawing on it for his visual aid. When he gave his speech and showed his lunch bag drawing, audience members had to stifle their laughter. Don't embarrass yourself by showing a visual aid of poor quality. When you use a visual aid, you want it to look neat and attractive. This means you have to take time to prepare it. Sloppy, last-minute drawings, posters, tables, and the like won't suffice.

DON'T BLOCK THE AUDIENCE'S VIEW   A very common mistake even professional speakers make is to block the audience's view of a visual aid. Standing in front of your poster, graph, drawing, or table while you talk to the visual aid, not to your audience, is awkward and self-defeating. You want your audience members to see the visual aid. Your audience should not have to stand and move across the room to see it, crane their necks, or give up in frustration because you're blocking their view. Simply stand beside your poster, drawing, graph, or videotape while you explain it to the audience. Point the toes of your shoes toward the audience and imagine that your feet are nailed to the ground. If you don't move your feet, you will continue to stand beside, not in front of, your visual aid. Talk to your audience, not to your visual aid.

www.mhhe com/ rothwell2

See "Avoiding Visual Aids Distractions" Activity, Chapter 17 of the Online Learning Center.

PUT THE AID OUT OF SIGHT WHEN NOT IN USE   Cover your poster or drawing, graph, or photo when not actually referring to it. Simply leaving it open to view when you no longer make reference to it or showing it way before you actually use it distracts an audience. You want the focus on you. Shut off the overhead or slide projector, VCR, or opaque projector when you are finished using the visual aid. Turn them on only when actually referring to the slides, photos, drawings, and so forth.

PRACTICE WITH AIDS   Using visual aids competently requires practice. At first, using a visual aid may seem awkward, even unnatural. Once you have practiced your speech using a visual aid, however, it will seem more natural and less awkward. Practice will also help you work out any problems that might occur during your speech.

DON'T CIRCULATE YOUR AIDS   Don't pass around photos, cartoons, drawings, objects, or anything that can distract your audience from paying attention to you while you're speaking. If audience members want to see your visual aid again, let them approach you after the speech for a second viewing.

Summary

Informative speaking is central to teaching, business, religious practice, and a host of other common events in our lives. Informative speaking teaches, whereas persuasive speaking primarily moves an audience to act. Reports, lectures, and demonstrations are the main types of informative speeches. Organization and use of supporting materials are vital to the success of an informative speech. Using visual aids competently will also enhance your informative speeches.

Quizzes Without Consequences

Go to Quizzes Without Consequences at the book's Online Learning Center at **www.mhhe.com/rothwell2** or access the CD-ROM for *In the Company of Others.*

www.mhhe
● com/
 / **rothwell2**

Key Terms

agenda-setting function
internal summary
signposts

See Audio Flashcards
Study Aid.

www.mhhe
● com/
 / **rothwell2**
See Crossword Puzzle
Study Aid.

Mathews, J. (1998). *Escalante: The best teacher in America.* New York: Henry Holt. This is a nice biographical treatment of famous high school math instructor Jaime Escalante, subject of the movie *Stand and Deliver.* It shows informative speaking in action.

Dead Poets Society (1989). Drama; PG ★★★⌏
Robin Williams delivers an effective performance as an English teacher in a private New England prep school. Evaluate his use of the lecture format for informative speaking.

Dangerous Minds (1995). Drama; PG ★★⌏
Michelle Pfeiffer, probably miscast, plays a teacher in an inner city school. Contrast her character's informative speaking with that of the Robin Williams character in "Dead Poets Society."

CHAPTER 18

Persuasive Speaking

During most of 1998 and part of 1999, Americans and others from around the globe witnessed the peculiar spectacle of presidential impeachment. Special prosecutor Kenneth Starr had charged President Clinton with "high crimes and misdemeanors" resulting from the president's sexual affair with intern Monica Lewinsky. House Judiciary Committee members voted along straight party lines for impeachment. The Republican members fought to impeach the president, and the Democratic members defended the president. Both sides battled to frame the issues to their advantage. Ultimately, the goal was to win the hearts and minds of the American people.

Representative Henry Hyde, chairman of the House Judiciary Committee, in his opening speech before the committee, framed the issues in this case succinctly: "Do we still have a government of laws and not of men? . . . Do we have one set of laws for the officers and another for the enlisted?" (Trounstine, 1998). Representative John Conyers, the highest ranking Democrat on the Judiciary Committee and a staunch defender of the president, framed Clinton's defense this way in his opening speech: "The idea of a federally paid sex policeman spending millions of dollars to trap an unfaithful spouse . . . would have been unthinkable prior to the Starr investigation" (Abramson, 1998).

Persuasive speaking occupied center stage throughout the contentious proceedings in the House and again in the climactic stage before the full U.S. Senate. The impeachment trial was a war of words, an oratorical duel between rival political parties. One of the most effective speakers was Cheryl Mills, a little-known White House deputy counsel. She became a brief sensation for her eloquent defense of the president on the obstruction of justice charge. Even Republicans who favored impeachment offered congratulations for her spirited and well-reasoned persuasive speech. Ultimately, the majority of senators and the American public found the case for impeachment unconvincing.

The battle to impeach Bill Clinton reaffirmed the importance of persuasive speaking in our democracy. When issues large and small are considered, those with persuasive speaking skills are an invaluable asset. One study (Bennett, 1995) found that, when economists totaled the number of people whose jobs depend predominantly on persuading people—lawyers, counselors, managers, administrators, salespersons, and public relations specialists—persuasion accounts for 26% of the gross domestic product of the United States. Turn on the television and you will see persuasive speaking everywhere. CNN interviews individuals every day who engage in persuasive speaking before the cameras. Most talk shows display persuasive speaking from panelists and audience members, although many persuasive attempts are dismal efforts by unskilled and untrained speakers. *Court TV* and several "people's court" programs show average citizens defending themselves in court cases.

The primary purpose of this chapter is to explore how to construct and present a competent persuasive speech.

The primary purpose of this chapter is to explore how to construct and present a competent persuasive speech.

There are two chapter objectives:

1. to explain the foundations of persuasion and
2. to discuss persuasive strategies that speakers can use effectively.

▨▨ Foundations of Persuasion

Almost 2,500 years ago, Aristotle systematically discussed persuasion in his influential *The Rhetoric*. The scientific study of persuasion, however, began little more than a half-century ago in the United States. Much has been learned from the 50-plus years of research on persuasion. In this section the foundations of persuasion, which have been derived from scientific research, are explored. This will provide a basis for discussing specific persuasion strategies.

Defining Persuasion

Persuasion is a communication process of converting, modifying, or maintaining the attitudes, beliefs, or behaviors of others. As a communication process, persuasion is transactional. This means that speakers influence listeners, but listeners also influence speakers. Thus, persuasive speaking is not merely a speaker motivating listeners in a linear, one-way direction. If it were, pointing a gun at your audience and threatening to shoot anyone who refused to sign a petition or contribute money to a social or political cause would be persuasive. In such an instance the audience would have little or no influence on the speaker. Most people and scholars, however, would perceive threatening violence as coercion, not persuasion.

So what is the difference? *The essential difference between coercion and persuasion is the perception of free choice* (Strong & Cook, 1990). Those who coerce seek to eliminate choice by force or threats of force. Those who persuade seek to limit choice to the most acceptable options by using logical and emotional appeals. Logical and emotional appeals can influence listeners, but listeners are still free to choose what to believe and how to behave. As noted in Chapter 1, coercion raises serious ethical concerns because it takes away free choice.

Persuasive speaking is a communication process of convincing through open and honest means, not of compelling by use of force. Coercion is the dominance form of power in action. When listeners can choose for themselves which attitude to accept or which behavior to perform, they are in charge of their decision-making. This means that listeners have to cooperate with speakers for persuasion to occur. If listeners refuse to pay attention to the speaker, ignore the persuasion effort, or fail to heed the speaker's advice or plea, persuasive speaking fails.

Goals of Persuasion

Persuasive speaking can have several goals. Choosing the appropriate goal for the situation will largely determine your degree of success or failure.

CONVERSION Psychologist Muzafer Sherif and his associates (1965) developed the **social judgment theory** of persuasion to explain attitude change. Their theory states that when listeners hear a persuasive message they compare it with attitudes they already hold. The preexisting attitude on an issue serves as an **anchor,** or reference point. Surrounding this anchor is a range of possible opinions an individual may hold. Positions a person finds tolerable form his or her **latitude of acceptance.** Positions that provoke only a neutral or ambivalent response form the **latitude of noncommitment.** Those positions the person would find objectionable because they are too far from the anchor attitude form the **latitude of rejection.** Figure 18-1 depicts this range of possible opinions on an issue.

Strongly agree	Agree	Indifferent	Disagree	Strongly disagree

Anchor:

Guns are dangerous and cause widespread violence in the United States.

Latitude of acceptance:

All handguns should be banned.
All guns should be licensed.
There should be a mandatory waiting period before purchasing any gun.
Guns for sporting events, carefully monitored, are permissible.
Standard hunting rifles should be licensed only to individuals with no felony convictions.

Latitude of noncommitment:

The Second Amendment to the U.S. Constitution gives every citizen the right to "keep and bear arms."

Latitude of rejection:

Handguns should not be licensed.
There should be no mandatory waiting period to buy a gun.
Citizens should be able to purchase automatic and semi-automatic firearms.

FIGURE 18-1 Range of Possible Opinions on an Issue *A preferred position on an issue is the anchor. Positions that fall within the latitude of acceptance are less desirable but acceptable given the anchor position. A position will fall within the latitude of noncommitment when an individual has no opinion about the position because he or she lacks knowledge or information, or the individual has ambivalence (feelings pro and con simultaneously). Positions that fall within the latitude of rejection clearly contradict a person's anchor position.*

Research by Sherif and his colleagues (1965) found that persuasive messages that fall within a person's latitude of rejection almost never produce a change in attitude. The further away a position is from the anchor attitude, the less likely persuasion will be successful. This is especially true when the listener has high ego involvement with the issue. **Ego involvement** refers to the degree to which an issue is relevant or important to a person (Littlejohn, 1999).

Social judgment theory strongly suggests that setting conversion as your goal for persuasion is unrealistic. Conversion asks listeners to move from their anchor position to a completely contradictory position. This is especially unlikely when you seek conversion with a brief persuasive speech. Students often make the attempt to convert the "unbelievers" in speeches on abortion, religion, and other emotionally charged topics. Such efforts are doomed from the start. Unless a significant emotional event occurs, such as a death of a loved one, divorce, or winning the state lottery, conversion almost never happens from a single persuasive attempt. A staunch member of the National Rifle Association may become a convert to gun control when a son or daughter is killed by a handgun. Absent such an emotional event, however, an NRA member is unlikely to become a gun control advocate from hearing a 10-minute persuasive speech, no matter how eloquent. Conversion, then, is an unrealistic goal for most persuasive speeches. Attempting to convert an audience with a brief persuasive speech is inviting failure.

MODIFICATION A more realistic goal for persuasion is modification of an attitude or behavior. Positions that lie at the outer fringes of a listener's latitude of acceptance may become the new anchor position as a result of a persuasive speech. For example, very restrictive gun control legislation may be a person's anchor. A strong persuasive speech, however, may realistically modify this person's position to an outright ban on all handguns. Once the person embraces this position, it may become the new anchor. Subsequent persuasive efforts may move the anchor incrementally until the person eventually accepts a complete ban on ownership of all guns. Notice that the

Controversial Nation of Islam leader Louis Farrakhan speaks to his followers. One goal of persuasive speaking is maintenance of existing points of view, sometimes called "preaching to the choir."

change in attitude occurs bit by bit. It is rarely a one-shot effort. *Modification of attitudes and behavior is an appropriate, realistic goal for a persuasive speech.*

MAINTENANCE When most people think of persuasion, changing attitudes and behavior immediately come to mind. Much persuasion, however, does not aim to produce change. Most advertising of well-established products, such as Coke, McDonald's, or the Toyota Camry aims to maintain buying habits of the public. The goal is to keep consumers purchasing products over and over. In political campaigns, initial persuasion is usually aimed at "securing the base." This means motivating Democrats to keep voting for Democratic candidates and to keep Republicans voting for Republican candidates. The message is "Do what you've been doing." Sunday sermons usually change few minds because most people who attend a church service require no change of heart. They already believe the religious dogmas articulated by the minister, priest, or rabbi. "Preaching to the choir," however, can inspire the faithful, energize believers, and reinforce preexisting attitudes. Maintaining current attitudes and behavior is a valid and realistic goal of persuasive speaking.

Part of maintaining current attitudes and behavior of an audience is inducing resistance to **counterpersuasion,** or attacks from an opposing side. Inducing resistance to counterpersuasion helps maintain current attitudes.

There are two principal ways to induce resistance to counterpersuasion. First, *forewarn* an audience that an attempt to change their attitudes, beliefs, or behavior will occur (Gass & Seiter, 1999). One study (Fukada, 1986) forewarned one group of participants that they would hear a message aimed at provoking fear about syphilis; another group received no such forewarning. The forewarned group was less likely to get tested for syphilis than the group that received no forewarning. Bob Dole forewarned voters in the 1996 presidential election that Bill Clinton would try to scare the elderly about the possible demise of Social Security. Prosecution and defense attorneys often use forewarning in their opening statements to juries. When we are very aware of persuasive attempts, psychological reactance emerges and produces resistance (Fukada, 1986).

A second way to induce resistance to persuasion is to *inoculate* your audience (McGuire, 1964). When we inoculate individuals against disease, we expose them to a weakened version of the virus to trigger an immune response. Likewise, inoculating an audience to counterpersuasion exposes listeners to a weakened version of counterarguments. Studies aimed at preventing teenagers from starting to smoke cigarettes found that merely mentioning arguments for smoking (e.g., smoking is cool; peers will like you) and then refuting these weakly presented arguments did induce resistance to peer persuasion to start smoking (Pfau & Van Bockern, 1994). The inoculation, however, must occur between elementary and high school, or it is too late to prevent teen smoking.

Attitude-Behavior Consistency

An **attitude** is "a learned predisposition to respond favorably or unfavorably toward some attitude object" (Gass & Seiter, 1999, p. 41). An attitude sets our minds to draw certain judgments. Our attitudes and our behaviors aren't always consistent. For example, energy conservation is socially desirable. Few people would argue that consumers should waste energy. One study found that 85% of those surveyed considered the energy crisis serious (Costanzo et al., 1986). This same study, however, found little relationship between stated attitudes on the energy crisis and actual conservation of energy. As the authors of this study conclude, "People who cite conservation as the single most important strategy for improving our energy future are no more likely than others to engage in energy-conserving behaviors. This finding is consistent with other research on the tenuous link between attitudes and behavior" (p. 522). Most Americans believe the Ten Commandments should guide our lives, yet everyone violates at least some of the commandments as though they were merely the Ten Suggestions.

Very often changing attitudes is not sufficient. It is behavior that needs to change. If 100% of adults at risk for catching AIDS believe that using a condom every time they have sex is very desirable (attitude) but fewer than half actually practice safe sex (behavior), the AIDS epidemic will continue to spread wildly.

Why aren't our attitudes and behaviors always consistent? Several variables affect how consistent our attitudes and behaviors are likely to be.

PERSONAL EXPERIENCE   *Attitudes that are formed from personal experience usually conform closely to actual behavior* (Fazio, 1986). Those that are shaped more indirectly by media images or by what friends and others have told us tend to be inconsistently related to actual behavior. These "secondhand attitudes" (Gass & Seiter, 1999) usually serve as weak predictors of behavior because, when people are faced with actual situations, their secondhand attitudes are more borrowed than personal. You may steadfastly avoid drinking alcohol because you have experienced firsthand what alcoholism can do to a family. If your attitude about alcohol is mostly formed from watching public service announcements on the dangers of alcohol, however, when prodded to drink by friends and peers you may cave in to the pressure more easily.

PERSONAL IMPACT "How does this affect me personally?" is a common question that pops into listeners' minds while hearing a persuasive speech. Previous chapters stressed establishing the significance of a topic to an audience. From the standpoint of persuasion, if you want your listeners to act, not just nod their heads in mindless agreement, make them feel personally affected by the problem you describe (Smith, 1982). Poverty may be a significant national issue, but if your audience has never experienced poverty directly, how do you get them to take action to address this issue? Connect it to their lives. Who pays for poverty? We all do—in blighted neighborhoods, through increased crime, through heavier taxes to pay for welfare, and through embarrassment that the wealthiest nation on earth can't take care of its own people, especially our children.

EFFORT REQUIRED NBC News reported on April 8, 1999, that 60,000 children died in car accidents in the 1990s. The backseats of cars are not "child friendly," according to this report, because car seats for children often are not used or are improperly installed. Parents may understand that car seats protect children from injury in accidents. They may uniformly agree that children should be strapped into car seats for their own protection. Nevertheless, parents often do not act in accordance with this belief. Why? The primary reason is that the car seats are difficult and time-consuming to install. This same NBC report noted that car manufacturers have developed a prototype car seat that folds down from the standard backseat. No installation is required, and strapping a child into this seat is quick and easy.

Despite the best intentions, attitudes and behavior will often be inconsistent because consistency may require too great an effort to perform the behavior (Smith, 1982). Recycling our cans, bottles, and newspapers is too labor intensive if we have to separate each item into separate bins, load them into the trunks of our cars, and then drive to the nearest recycling center to unload the waste. Increasingly, however, communities around the country are recognizing the benefits of curbside recycling. Participation in recycling programs grows explosively when recycling is no more difficult than hauling a trash bin to the curb in front of our homes. In Santa Cruz, California, the recycling bin looks the same as the garbage can, except it is a different color. Up and down the block recycling bins dot the landscape on trash day. The effort to recycle is minimal, so compliance is almost universal.

California began a program in July 1998 to assist low-income families in acquiring basic health insurance covering medical, dental, and eye care for as little as $3 a month. By the end of the year a mere 10% of the 400,000 eligible families had signed up (Kaplan, 1998). Clearly, the 90% who failed to enroll had no opposition to the program. It provided a huge benefit to all eligible families. The principal problem was that completion of a 28-page application form was required for enrollment. The state trimmed the application form to 4 pages in the spring of 1999 and increased the payments to nonprofit agencies that assisted eligible families in filling out the forms, all to ease the burden of applying. Participation in the program mushroomed.

When trying to persuade an audience to act on a problem, find the easiest ways for listeners to express their support. Signing a petition or donating a dollar on the spot is an easy way to show support. Asking listeners to write a letter to members of Congress, however, will usually fail to produce much compliance. Most people do not have the time and energy to find the address of their congressperson, assuming they remember who that person is, write a letter, address an envelope, and mail the letter at a post office. (This is one reason members of Congress have established Web sites and e-mail addresses. E-mailing a member of Congress is easier than mailing a letter.) Asking listeners to canvass neighborhoods, call strangers on the phone to solicit support for a cause or a candidate, or raise money for a program is met with resistance because of the effort required to perform the behavior. Far less participation in such activities should be expected as a result.

Consider how Sean McLaughlin (1996), a student at Ohio University, offers simple, yet effective, solutions for the problem of food poisoning:

> First, wash hands well and wash them often. . . . If you prefer to use sponges and dishcloths, be sure to throw them in the dishwasher two or three times a week. Also, try color coding your sponges—the red one for washing dishes and a blue one for wiping up countertops. . . . Experts also suggest using both sides of a cutting board—one side for meats and the other side for vegetables. And those who wash dishes by hand, be careful. Scrub dishes vigorously with an antibacterial soap and rinse with hot water. Air drying is preferred to drying with a towel. . . . Finally, and perhaps the best advice—don't become lax when it comes to food safety in your home. Don't write your congressperson, write your mom. As we have seen today, re-educating yourself and spreading the word on kitchen safety can significantly reduce chances of food poisoning (p. 75).

The speaker provides several easy steps that will protect us from food poisoning. One step, air drying dishes, actually reduces labor. Towel drying requires effort; air drying requires merely waiting.

Solutions to serious problems cannot always be simple and easy to implement. Nevertheless, try to offer ways that even complex solutions can be implemented in relatively simple, straightforward steps.

Elaboration Likelihood Model

This textbook emphasizes mindful consideration of our communication with others. The communication competence model gives prominence to appropriateness, which requires mindful, conscious attention to explicit and implicit, often subtle communication rules within cultures. This book stresses sensitivity to cues from others during communication transactions. Ethical considerations also require mindfulness. When faced with numerous persuasive messages bombarding us every day, however, we have difficulty being mindful about each message. The truth is that we can be persuaded whether we are in a mindful or a mindless state.

 See Video clip #11 on CD.

Petty and Cacioppo (1986a, 1986b) developed the **elaboration likelihood model** (ELM) of persuasion to explain how attempts to persuade can be processed mindfully or relatively mindlessly. According to ELM, listeners cope with the bombardment of persuasive messages by sorting them into those that are important, or central, and those that are less relevant, or peripheral. The *central route* requires mindfulness. We scrutinize the content of the message for careful reasoning and substantial, credible evidence. We consider and weigh counterarguments. Questions come to mind, and we desire more information (elaboration). The *peripheral route* is relatively mindless. We give little attention to processing a persuasive message. We look for mental shortcuts to make quick decisions about seemingly peripheral issues. Credibility, likeability, and attractiveness of a persuader, how other people react to the message, and the consequences of agreeing or disagreeing with the persuader are some of the shortcuts we use in the peripheral route.

To illustrate the two routes to persuasion, let's say that you are on a date. You and your partner are about to order dinner at a nice restaurant. The waiter suggests several specials, all of them meat or fish. He even volunteers which one is his favorite. Your partner orders first. She is very careful to choose only vegetarian dishes from the menu. She asks the waiter whether an entrée is cooked in animal fat, whether there is any butter in the pasta, and whether the sauce contains any dairy products. Your date turns to you and says with an animated delivery that you should eat vegetarian because it is healthier and reduces animal deaths. You have no strong opinion on the subject, but you are very attracted to your date. You tell the waiter, "I'll have what she ordered." Your date used the central route to decide her order. She was very mindful of her decision. She considered her decision very carefully because it was important to her. You, on the other hand, used the peripheral route. The decision was relatively unimportant to you so you based your order on a cue unrelated to the menu, the waiter's preference, or the arguments offered by your date. You ordered vegetarian because your date was attractive and you hoped to gain favor with her.

Listeners use both central and peripheral routes when processing persuasive messages. This is called *parallel processing* (Petty et al., 1987). Listeners will tend to choose one route over the other, however. Which route will most likely be favored depends on two things: (1) the individual's motivation to think about the persuasive message, and (2) the individual's ability to process the information presented. Personal experience with an issue and its impact in relation to attitude-behavior consistency has already been discussed. These two factors, however, also influence whether central or peripheral routes will be chosen for processing persuasive messages.

The more personal the issue is to us and the greater the perceived impact is on us, the more central will be the processing. Persuasive messages perceived by listeners to be tangential to their interests and largely inconsequential to their lives will usually receive peripheral processing. Also, some persuasive messages are too complex and require technical knowledge to evaluate. Do you really understand the Second Law of Thermodynamics when creationism and evolution are debated? In such cases, our ability to use central processing is limited. Typically, we'll use peripheral cues, such as how other audience members respond to the messages.

Clearly, *central processing of persuasive messages should be encouraged.* Central processing is what skeptics do when presented with a persuasive message. It fits the communication competence model snugly. Central processing also produces more long-lasting persuasion than peripheral processing does (Gass & Seiter, 1999). If you purchased an ionizing air filtering system primarily because you found the salesperson very attractive, the product might sit in a box unopened or you might return it later for a refund. If you purchased the ionizing air filtering system because you read the literature, pondered the scientific research, and received credible answers to your questions, however, you would want to try the product as soon as possible. You might purchase additional units, especially if the ionizer performed as expected.

You can increase central processing by making issues relevant to listeners' lives. Simplify complex, technical issues for lay audiences. If listeners understand the basic concepts, they can analyze the arguments and evidence you present. Even highly involved listeners, however, will use both central and peripheral processing.

Because of time constraints and information overload, we sometimes have no choice but to use peripheral processing. Persuasive strategies that typically trigger both central and peripheral routes to persuasion are discussed in this chapter.

Culture and Persuasion

The scientific investigation of persuasive speaking is a peculiarly Western interest. In China and other Asian countries, for instance, spirited debates to influence decision making have been viewed as relatively pointless. Debates create friction and disharmony and usually end inconclusively (Jaffe, 1998). Persuasion works best when it is adapted to the cultural context. Persuasive strategies that may successfully change attitudes and behavior in an individualistic country such as the United States may not be so successful in collectivist countries.

One study (Han & Shavitt, 1994) examined slogans used in magazines for their cultural persuasiveness. The study considered slogans such as these (see also Gass & Seiter, 1999):

1. The art of being unique
2. We have a way of bringing people closer together.
3. She's got a style all her own.
4. The dream of prosperity for all of us
5. A leader among leaders
6. Sharing is beautiful.

Which of these slogans do you think would work best in individualist cultures, and which would work best in collectivist cultures? When comparing the United States and Korea, the study found that slogans like the first, third, and fifth were used more in the United States and were more persuasive than the others. These three appeal to individual success, personal benefits, and independence. Slogans like the second, fourth, and sixth were used more in Korea and were more persuasive than the others. They appeal to group harmony, cooperation, and collective benefit.

Another study (Wiseman et al., 1995) found that in attempts to convince roommates to quiet down, individuals from the United States preferred direct statements such as "Please be quiet," "You are making too much noise," or "If you don't quiet down, I'll be as noisy as possible when you are trying to study." These statements pay little attention to face saving or harmony. They address individual needs. Persons from China, however, used more indirect strategies of persuasion, such as hinting that less noise would be preferred or making statements invoking group awareness ("Your noisiness shows a lack of consideration for others").

Clearly, your choice of persuasive strategies should be influenced by the diversity of your audience. It is only one element of the complex persuasion equation, but it is an important element.

Persuasion Strategies

See Video clip #10 on CD.

Consideration of all possible persuasive speaking strategies would require a lengthy book. In this section a few of the most prominent and effective persuasive strategies are discussed.

Enhance the Speaker

Our first impression of a speaker may be our last. If listeners draw an unfavorable impression of a speaker, all the crafty, carefully planned persuasive strategies won't matter. Persuasive speaking begins with enhancing the speaker. You can accomplish this in several ways.

ESTABLISH IDENTIFICATION WITH THE AUDIENCE Kenneth Burke (1950) wrote, "You persuade a man [or woman] only insofar as you can talk his language by speech, gesture, tonality, order, image, attitude, idea, identifying your ways with his" (p. 55). Burke considered **identification,** the affiliation and connection between speaker and listeners, the essence of persuasion (Griffin, 2003). Larson (1992), revealing Burke's influence, defines persuasion as "the co-creation of a state of identification or alignment between a source and receiver" (p. 11).

Likeability A key element of identification is likeability of the speaker. If we perceive the speaker as likeable, our compliance and assent are more probable than if we do not like the speaker (Cialdini, 1993). A *USA Today*/CNN/Gallup tracking poll conducted October 6–8, 2000, several days following the first presidential debate between Al Gore and George W. Bush, found that Bush padded a small lead over Gore. The respondents generally rated Gore smarter than Bush, but they liked Bush more (Benedetto, 2000). Catholic University of America political scientist Mark Rozell explained that Gore's "smart alecky" debate performance was a key factor in producing the slide in his polling numbers. "Voters found his demeanor snide, rude, and offensive, characteristics they don't like in a president." He continued, "Gore just came across as not very likeable, while Bush, verbal stumbles and all, just seemed more human (Benedetto, 2000, p. 1A).

Stylistic Similarity We tend to identify more closely with those individuals who appear to be similar to us. One way to appear similar is to look and act the part. This is called **stylistic similarity.** We can dress, look, and speak similarly to our audience. A bureaucrat from the Department of Agriculture visits farmers in Kansas wearing an expensive suit and carrying a briefcase. Do you think farmers will likely give this person a nanosecond of their time? He doesn't look, dress, or probably even speak like them. Repeatedly, Bill Clinton and Al Gore in the 1992 and 1996 presidential campaigns "dressed the part" when they visited farmers, factory laborers, and construction workers. When visiting Midwest farmers, both Clinton and Gore wore jeans and casual shirts, sat on hay bales to chat informally with the folks that gathered, and played down the formality of the presidential office and campaign. Lamar Alexander, a Republican candidate for president in 1996, wore flannel shirts almost everywhere he campaigned in New Hampshire to create a folksy image in a mostly rural state. His supporters began wearing identical flannel shirts to show their solidarity with him. All these candidates attempted to identify with their audiences by dressing and acting similarly to their listeners.

Sometimes dressing the part, however, can make you look lame. The 1988 Democratic presidential candidate, Michael Dukakis, was persuaded by his advisers to climb aboard an army tank dressed in army fatigues and a tank commander's hat. This "photo opportunity" was supposed to create an image that Dukakis, despite his liberal credentials, was a strong supporter of the military. Actually, he looked

During political campaigns, stylistic similarity, in this case wearing plaid, creates identification.

like Snoopy from the "Peanuts" comic strip. This poor attempt to identify with more conservative elements of the electorate backfired. The more contrived dressing the part appears to be, the less likely it will connect with the audience. Dressing informally, for example, must be complemented by a relaxed, informal style of speaking and presenting oneself, or it will seem phony.

When the situation is formal, dress and speak formally. Avoid slang and verbal obscenity. When the situation is informal, however, shift styles and speak, dress, and act informally. Speaking, dressing, and acting very formally in an informal setting, such as in a tavern or in a wheat field, disconnect a speaker from his or her audience. Speaking, dressing, and acting informally in a formal setting, such as at a banquet dinner or at a prestigious awards ceremony, may insult your audience.

Substantive Similarity   A second way to develop the perception of similarity with your audience is to shape the substance of your speech to highlight similarities in positions, values, and attitudes with them. This **substantive similarity** creates identification by establishing common ground between speaker and audience. If listeners can say, "I like what I'm hearing," they can identify with the speaker. Often you are trying to change listeners' attitudes and behavior, but your point of view and proposed action may not be similar to your audience's. In such cases, it is helpful to build bridges with your audience by pointing out common experiences, perceptions, values, and attitudes before launching into more delicate areas of disagreement. Listeners will be more inclined to hear your more controversial viewpoints if they initially identify with you.

Notice how Geraldine Ferraro, the first female vice presidential candidate, tries to connect not merely with convention delegates but also with the much larger television audience in her acceptance speech to the 1984 Democratic National Convention:

Box 18-1 Sharper Focus

The "Spread Fred" Campaign

The 1998 campaign for the U.S. Senate in Vermont produced a striking example of how far identification can carry you. Fred Tuttle, a 79-year-old retired farmer, ran against a well-financed Republican named Jack McMullen. McMullen spent almost $500,000 trying to win the nomination and eventually run against incumbent Democrat Patrick Leahy. Tuttle spent $200. He held 5-cent-a-plate fundraisers (4 cents for seniors). Tuttle defeated McMullen by 10 percentage points. How did he do this? Vermont voters identified with Tuttle but were turned off by McMullen, whom they saw as an outsider. McMullen had moved from Massachusetts to Vermont a year prior to the campaign so he could run for the Senate seat.

Tuttle's low-key style and straightforward message resonated with voters. His style of dress and campaign approach were uniformly casual. His message was simple and direct: "Vermont for Vermonters." He made developers and people who moved into Vermont from another state key issues in the campaign. As Paul Dreher, an architect and Vermont voter explained, "McMullen was an out-of-stater. A lot of people are coming in here and buying our land, and posting 'no hunting' signs, and a sense of community is being lost. They're trying to re-create the gated community, and we don't like it" (cited in Higham, 1998).

Everywhere Tuttle campaigned crowds would ask for his autograph. "Spread Fred" bumper stickers were everywhere. Even Leahy, Tuttle's eventual opponent, found him attractive. Tuttle was simply a likeable guy. Leahy had dinner with Tuttle and they campaigned together. Tuttle, in his open and honest style, divulged at one point, "I'll probably vote for Senator Leahy. He's a wonderful man. He's done a wonderful job" (cited in Higham, 1998). Leahy won by a comfortable margin, but Tuttle demonstrated that identification can be a powerful persuasive strategy.

Last week, I visited Elmore, Minnesota, the small town where Fritz Mondale [Ferraro's running mate] was raised. And soon Fritz and Joan will visit our family in Queens. Nine hundred people live in Elmore. In Queens, there are 2,000 people in one block. You would think we would be different, but we're not. Children walk to school in Elmore past grain elevators; in Queens, they pass by subway stops. But, no matter where they live, their future depends on education—and their parents are willing to do their part to make those schools as good as they can be. In Elmore, there are family farms; in Queens, small businesses. But the men and women who run them all take pride in supporting their families through hard work and initiative. On the Fourth of July in Elmore, they hang flags out on Main Street; in Queens, they fly them over Grand Avenue. But all of us love our country and stand ready to defend the freedom that it represents (Ferraro, 1992, pp. 365–366).

Ferraro takes what seem to be, on the surface, vast differences that separate her from her audience and finds commonalities in each instance to establish identification between herself and her listeners.

Identification takes the peripheral path to persuasion (Box 18-1). The appeal is based on liking the speaker and finding familiar themes, values, and perceptions. Yet identification can act as a precursor to central processing of persuasive messages. Audiences are more likely to concentrate on the message, analyze it carefully, and be moved by the arguments when they can identify with the speaker.

BUILD CREDIBILITY Tonya Harding endorsed Nike athletic equipment but was quickly dumped by the company when her involvement in the assault on fellow skating competitor Nancy Kerrigan was revealed. O. J. Simpson was a spokesman for Hertz rental cars until he was accused of killing his wife. The instant these celebrities lost credibility, they lost their endorsement contracts. The credibility of the speaker can make a huge difference when persuasion is attempted. Speakers who lack credibility persuade few. Credibility of a speaker is part of the peripheral route to persuasion. Listeners who are relatively uninvolved in an issue are more influenced by speaker credibility than are listeners who are highly involved (Reardon, 1991).

O'Keefe (1990) defines **credibility** as "judgments made by a perceiver (e.g., a message recipient) concerning the believability of a communicator" (pp. 130–131). In *The Rhetoric,* Aristotle identified the ingredients of credibility, or **ethos** in his terminology, as "good sense, good moral character, and good will." Recent research affirms Aristotle's observation and expands the list of dimensions somewhat. The primary dimensions of credibility are competence, trustworthiness, dynamism, and composure (Gass & Seiter, 1999; Strong & Cook, 1990). Let's take a closer look at each of these dimensions.

Competence refers to the audience's perception of the speaker's knowledge and experience on a topic. Competence addresses the question "Does this speaker know what he or she is talking about?" When speakers identify their background, experience, and training relevant to a subject, they can enhance their credibility (O'Keefe, 1990). Citing sources of evidence used, speaking fluently, and avoiding vocal fillers ("uhm," "ah," "like," "you know") also enhance credibility (O'Keefe, 1990).

Trustworthiness refers to how truthful or honest an audience perceives the speaker to be. Trustworthiness addresses the question "Can I believe what the speaker says?" We don't feel comfortable hiring a dishonest plumber, electrician, or carpenter. We hesitate to buy anything from a salesperson we perceive to be dishonest. Detective Mark Fuhrman repeatedly testified during the O. J. Simpson trial that he never uttered the "N-word." Later in the trial it was revealed that he had used the racist epithet dozens of times during tape-recorded interviews with Laura McKinney, a screenwriter. His credibility was destroyed by this revelation, and the prosecution's case suffered seriously from his apparent dishonesty.

Trustworthiness, however, may not be as important as competence in some situations. A Field poll of 1,005 Californians conducted 1 month after Bill Clinton was acquitted on impeachment charges showed an interesting interplay between competence and trustworthiness. Fifty-two percent of the respondents viewed Clinton as not very honest or not honest at all, and only 38% said they liked him (cited in Ostrom, 1999). Sixty-eight percent of the same sample of Californians, however, approved of the job Clinton was doing. Poll director Mark DiCamillo interpreted the results by comparing Clinton to former president Jimmy Carter: "Jimmy Carter was well-liked as a person but wasn't seen as effective. And that's what you're hiring (a president) to do" (p. A10). Credibility is a constellation of dimensions. Trustworthiness is important in a president but apparently not as important as doing the job competently and producing beneficial results for the American people.

One way to increase your trustworthiness is to argue against your self-interest. If you take a position on an issue that will cost you money, a job, a promotion, or some reward or benefit, most listeners will see you as presenting an honest opinion. They're more likely to trust what you have to say than to trust someone who stands to gain from arguing a particular position. Few people trust the explanations for rapid increases in gas prices provided by spokespeople for the oil companies. Quite simply, the oil companies make profits when gas prices are inflated. Their self-interest diminishes their credibility.

Dynamism is a third dimension of credibility. It refers to the enthusiasm and energy exhibited by the speaker. Sleepy, lackluster presentations by speakers lower credibility. If a speaker tries to convince an audience that a serious problem exists but seems almost uninterested in the subject, credibility will be a real issue. Hucksters on infomercials are invariably enthusiastic about the products they sell. Sometimes they are overly enthusiastic, bordering on frenzied. Too little dynamism can hinder persuasion, but too much can also turn off an audience.

Speakers who are dynamic inspire audiences. They seem self-confident, charismatic, and comfortable in front of an audience. They are articulate, powerful speakers. Mario Cuomo, Jesse Jackson, and Ann Richards are examples of dynamic speakers.

A final dimension of speaker credibility is **composure.** Audiences tend to be influenced by speakers who are composed, meaning they are emotionally stable, appear confident and in control of themselves, and remain calm even when problems arise during a speech. Clint Eastwood has made composure a trademark part of his image in films. During emergencies, we are more likely to listen and to be influenced by a person who is composed than by someone shrieking or raging at us.

Former member of Congress Patricia Schroeder held a press conference to announce her candidacy for the 1992 presidential race. During that announcement she lost her composure and cried. Hers was the shortest-lived presidential candidacy in U.S. history. It was over as she announced it. Breaking down at a press conference when merely declaring your intent to run for public office doesn't inspire confidence from most listeners. Ross Perot lost his composure on a few occasions during the 1992 presidential race, becoming angry and attacking the press. His poll ratings dropped each time.

Displaying emotion overtly, however, does not always destroy a speaker's credibility. Too much composure may be perceived as hard-heartedness or insensitivity. Shedding tears at a funeral or expressing outrage at an atrocity may enhance your credibility with some listeners. The appropriateness of displaying composure depends on the context.

All four dimensions of credibility operate together. George W. Bush surprised his many critics when, as president, he handled the considerable challenge presented by the terrorist attack on the World Trade Center. His critics did not expect a competent, composed, or dynamic response from Bush. They expected a "bumbling" president. What most people perceived, however, was a president performing his job capably, with confidence and skill. Although sometimes given to excessive cowboy references ("wanted dead or alive"), he struck a strong tone in his public statements without losing his composure in angry outbursts against those who attacked the United States. He took decisive action against the terrorists, which established his dynamism. He said he would send American forces into Afghanistan to combat the terrorist network harbored by the Taliban, and he did just that. He thus appeared trustworthy. His approval ratings soared from around 55% before the terrorist attack to an astounding 90%. Republicans, Democrats, and Independents all gave Bush high ratings for his handling of this traumatic incident. Bush's approval ratings a year later remained high at around 70% (Gallup, 2002).

Strength in some dimensions may be overridden by weakness in even one dimension. A Gallup poll taken in May 1999 found that four of five respondents thought Al Gore was a good husband and father, and most thought he was honest, trustworthy, caring, and experienced. Thus, Gore scored well in trustworthiness and competence. The majority of respondents, however, also felt that Gore was uninspiring, even dull (cited in Jacobs, 1999b). Gore's perceived lack of dynamism became a key weakness in his unsuccessful pursuit of the presidency.

Build Arguments

A great deal has been said about the importance of logic and evidence to speakers and listeners. In this section, however, building arguments based on logic and evidence, what Aristotle called **logos,** are addressed with a specific focus on persuading audiences.

TOULMIN STRUCTURE OF ARGUMENT Arguments are the essence of a strong persuasive speech. Audiences aren't persuaded just by logic and evidence, but weak reasoning and shaky evidence leave your claims open to challenge. The central path to persuasion travels through arguments. Mindful listeners will examine your arguments closely, looking for strengths and weaknesses. Strong, compelling arguments can be highly persuasive, especially to skeptics.

An argument or "train of reasoning" is composed of several parts (Toulmin et al., 1979):

1. *Claim*—a generalization that requires support
2. *Data*—the grounds, or support, for the claim. Statistics, testimony of experts, and verifiable facts are data
3. *Warrant*—the reasoning that links the data to the claim. It is usually implied, not stated explicitly
4. *Backing*—the data that support the warrant
5. *Reservations*—exceptions or rebuttals that diminish the force of the claim
6. *Qualifier*—the degree of truth to the claim (possible, plausible, probable, highly probable)

Everyday reasoning follows this pattern known as the *Toulmin structure of argument* (Figure 18-2; Freeley, 1996). For example, suppose you are a guy who wants to date a supermodel. Your train of reasoning might proceed as follows:

CLAIM: I can date supermodel Jasmine.

DATA: I am a brainy, average looking, very nice guy with an average income.

WARRANT: She dates brainy, average looking, very nice, sensitive guys with average incomes.

BACKING: The last three guys she dated were brainy. Two of them had college degrees, and one had a Ph.D. All three were average looking according to five girls I asked at random. All three had very average incomes and drove 3- or 4-year-old sedans. I read interviews with Jasmine in which she said that all of these guys were very nice and sensitive, caring human beings.

RESERVATIONS: She's a supermodel who could date almost any guy she wanted. I'm a stranger to her. I don't know anyone who is friends with her who could introduce me. She has a bodyguard who could inflict grievous bodily harm on my person if I tried to approach her. I can't just call her. She might think I'm a stalker.

QUALIFIER: *Possibly* she would accept a date—when pigs can fly.

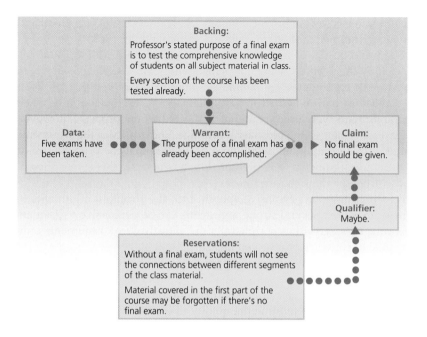

FIGURE 18-2 *The Toulmin Structure of Argument*

Persuasive speeches incorporate a series of claims. The primary, overriding claim for a persuasive speech is called a **proposition.** The proposition becomes the essence of your persuasive purpose statement. Propositions define and focus the argument, limit the issues that are relevant, and set standards for what should be addressed (Inch & Warnick, 1998).

There are three types of propositions: fact, policy, and value. A **proposition of fact** alleges a truth ("Lax sex education is a primary cause of high teen pregnancy rates"). A **proposition of policy** calls for a significant change from how problems are currently handled ("Smoking should be banned from all public places"). A **proposition of value** calls for a judgment that assesses the worth or merit of an idea, object, or practice ("Capital punishment is immoral"). Main arguments, or the chief reasons offered to support a proposition, are secondary claims. When asked why smoking in public places should be banned, you might list several main reasons:

1. Secondhand smoke is dangerous to nonsmokers.
2. Secondhand smoke is annoying to nonsmokers.
3. Smokers violate nonsmokers' rights to breathe unpolluted air.
4. Employees in bars and restaurants cannot escape the smoke even if they so desire.

QUANTITY AND QUALITY OF ARGUMENTS The number and quality of arguments advanced for a proposition can be factors in persuasive speaking. One study (Petty & Cacioppo, 1984) tested to what degree students could be persuaded that requiring completion of comprehensive examinations as a condition of graduating from college is a good proposal. Student groups were told either that the exams would begin in 1 year (meaning they would have to take the exams) or in 10 years (meaning they would not have to take the exams). Presumably, those directly affected by the proposal (must take the exams) would scrutinize the persuasive message, whereas those unaffected by the proposal would see the message as peripheral and use the number of arguments, even if weak, as decision-making cues.

The quantity and quality of arguments made a big difference. Mindful students directly affected by the proposal were not persuaded by nine weak arguments. In fact, the more weak arguments they heard, the more they disliked the proposal. They were persuaded only when strong arguments were used, especially when many strong arguments were used. Students unaffected by the proposal, however, used peripheral processing of the persuasive message. The quality of the arguments did not matter to this group. They were more persuaded that the proposal was a good idea when nine arguments were presented than when only three were offered, no matter how strong or weak the arguments.

When constructing your persuasive speech, pick the strongest arguments to support your proposition. Several strong arguments can be persuasive to listeners who process your message either peripherally or centrally. Weak arguments only have the potential to convince uninvolved listeners.

The strength of an argument depends primarily on the strength of your warrant, as indicated by the quality of your evidence and reasoning. In Chapter 7 fallacies in the use of evidence and reasoning were explained. Three criteria—credibility, relevance, and sufficiency—determine the quality of evidence and reasoning. We say that a claim is "unwarranted" when these standards are poorly met. When you present statistical evidence to support a claim, the underlying warrant is that the statistics are from credible sources, relevant to your claim, and sufficient to convince people to accept your claim. If this proves to be untrue, your argument is weak. When a speaker claims a causal relation from only a correlation, for example, he or she provides an insufficient logical connection between the data and the claim.

In the supermodel example, the data at first may appear to be completely irrelevant to the claim. Why would a supermodel want to date a brainy, sensitive, average-looking guy with a moderate income? The warrant tries to make the connection between the data and the claim. It is only partly successful. The claim is probably unwarranted. Review the specific fallacies that arise from failing to meet the criteria for use of evidence and reasoning.

You build a persuasive case by identifying your proposition (primary claim) and by establishing main arguments (secondary claims). Support all claims with evidence. Otherwise, mindful, skeptical listeners will find your persuasion deficient and unconvincing. Several strong arguments will persuade listeners who are processing your message using either the peripheral or central routes.

Induce Cognitive Dissonance

When we want to persuade others to change their attitudes or behavior, one of the most common strategies is to point out inconsistencies between two attitudes or between attitudes and behavior. A student asks her professor for more time on an assignment. The professor says no. The student retorts, "But you gave extra time to Jim. Why won't you give me the same extension?" The professor sees herself as a very fair-minded person. Faced with this apparent inconsistency in the treatment of two students, the professor feels tense and uncomfortable. Festinger (1957) called this unpleasant feeling produced by seemingly inconsistent thoughts **cognitive dissonance.**

Whenever a person holds two inconsistent ideas, beliefs, or opinions (cognitions) at the same time, or when an attitude and a behavior are inconsistent, dissonance occurs (Pratkanis & Aronson, 2001). Parents often confront this persuasive strategy from their children. "Why can't I stay up past midnight on weekends? You let Tommy when he was my age." "Why do I have a curfew? You never gave a curfew to Billy or Caroline."

We want to be perceived as consistent, not hypocritical or nonsensical, so dissonance emerges when inconsistencies are pointed out to us. If we view ourselves as unbiased but laugh at a sexist joke, some dissonance will likely surface. If we consider ourselves honest but use a copy machine at work for personal projects, we will likely experience some dissonance, especially if the inconsistency is pointed out to us.

"Cognitive dissonance is a motivating state of affairs. Just as hunger impels a person to eat, so does dissonance impel a person to change his opinions or his behavior" (Festinger, 1977, p. 111). *According to this theory, you have to awaken dissonance in listeners for persuasion to occur.* Without dissonance, there is little motivation to change attitudes or behavior. Therefore, the strategy for the persuader is to induce dissonance in the audience and then remove the dissonance by persuading listeners to change their attitudes or behavior in the direction desired.

> The [persuader] intentionally arouses feelings of dissonance by threatening self-esteem—for example, by making the person feel guilty about something, by arousing feelings of shame or inadequacy, or by making the person look like a hypocrite or someone who does not honor his or her word. Next, the [persuader] offers one solution, one way of reducing this dissonance—by complying with whatever request the [persuader] has in mind. The way to reduce that guilt, eliminate that shame, honor that commitment, and restore your feelings of adequacy is to give to that charity, buy that car, hate that enemy, or vote for that leader (Pratkanis & Aronson, 2001, p. 44).

Does inducing dissonance change behavior? It certainly can if used effectively. Several studies have shown that condom use to prevent AIDS and other sexually transmitted diseases can be increased significantly by inducing dissonance (Aronson et al., 1991; Stone et al., 1997).

Important decisions arouse more dissonance than less important ones (Gass & Seiter, 1999). Pointing out to a teacher that he or she was not consistent when grading a test could elicit varying degrees of dissonance. If the inconsistency involves a single point on a 100-point exam, the teacher can easily downplay the inconsistency as minor and inherent to any subjective grading system. If the inconsistency involves an entire grade difference and seems based on sex bias, however, the dissonance could be quite large.

Notice how Gary Allen (1996), a student at Northeastern State University, uses cognitive dissonance on the topic of drug testing in the military:

> The final problem is caused by a double standard, because a program is only as good as the goal it achieves. While alcohol is universally recognized as the most commonly abused drug, the military does not test for alcohol as regularly as for other drugs. . . . Soldiers caught drunk on the job are given 45 days extra duty, that is work that must be performed after the regular duty day, they have a letter put into their permanent file, and they are returned to light duty. Yet the soldier who receives a positive [drug] test result is, currently, kicked out of the military with a dishonorable discharge. Let me say that again. Everyday soldiers are required to undergo a test of their innocence without

Tall professional basketball players look small in contrast to extremely tall Margaret Dydek. The contrast effect as a persuasive strategy works similarly. What appears to be a huge commitment or investment may seem relatively small when contrasted to a much larger commitment or investment.

suspicion of guilt. The soldier who is found guilty is kicked out and marked for life with a dishonorable discharge, while soldiers drunk on the job, endangering everyone's life, are returned to duty with a slap on the hand (p. 82).

Here the speaker points out a glaring inconsistency to induce dissonance in the audience. Supporting such a "double standard" is hypocritical and unjust, so the speaker implies. One could argue that there is a big difference between alcohol and other drugs—namely, legality. Nevertheless, as regards possible dangerous effects of utilization, an inconsistency does seem apparent. Cognitive dissonance can be a very effective persuasive strategy.

Use the Contrast Effect

You're a salesperson and a woman comes into the dress store where you work. Most of your pay is based on commission, so you want to sell as much merchandise as you can at the highest prices possible. Do you show the woman the inexpensive dresses first, then gradually show her more expensive dresses, or do you begin with very expensive dresses probably outside of her price range and then show her less

Box 18-2 Sharper Focus

An Exercise in Contrast

Although this example is a letter, you can easily see how this strategy could apply in a persuasive speech (Cialdini, 1993, p. 14).

Dear Mother and Dad:

Since I left for college I have been remiss in writing and I am sorry for my thoughtlessness in not having written before. I will bring you up to date now, but before you read on, please sit down. You are not to read any further unless you are sitting down, okay?

Well, then, I am getting along pretty well now. The skull fracture and the concussion I got when I jumped out of the window of my dormitory when it caught on fire shortly after my arrival here is pretty well healed. I only spent two weeks in the hospital and now I can see almost normally and only get those sick headaches once a day. Fortunately, the fire in the dormitory, and my jump, was witnessed by an attendant at the gas station near the dorm, and he was the one who called the Fire Department and the ambulance. He also visited me in the hospital and since I had nowhere to live because of the burnt-out dormitory, he was kind enough to invite me to share his apartment with him. It's really a basement room, but it's kind of cute. He is a very fine boy, and we have fallen deeply in love and are planning to get married. We haven't set the date yet, but it will be before my pregnancy begins to show.

Yes, Mother and Dad, I am pregnant. I know how much you are looking forward to being grandparents and I know you will welcome the baby and give it the same love and devotion and tender care you gave me when I was a child. The reason for the delay in our marriage is that my boyfriend has a minor infection which prevents us from passing our premarital blood tests and I carelessly caught it from him. I know that you will welcome him into our family with open arms. He is kind and, although not well educated, he is ambitious.

Now that I have brought you up to date, I want to tell you that there was no dormitory fire, I did not have a concussion or skull fracture, I was not in the hospital. I am not pregnant, I am not engaged, I am not infected, and there is no boyfriend. However, I am getting a "D" in American History and an "F" in Chemistry, and I want you to see those marks in their proper perspective.

Your loving daughter,
SHARON

expensive dresses? Which will net you the biggest commission? According to research on the contrast effect, you'd make a better choice if you began with expensive and moved to less expensive (Cialdini, 1993). The **contrast effect** says listeners are more likely to accept a bigger second request or offer when contrasted with a much bigger request or offer. If shown a really nice dress that costs $250, most shoppers will balk at purchasing it because it is "so expensive." If shown a $475 dress first, however, and then shown the $250 dress, the second dress seems less expensive by contrast with the first. Once the $250 dress is purchased, "accessorizing" it with $30 worth of jewelry, scarves, or whatever will seem like very little by contrast.

The contrast effect, sometimes referred to as the **door-in-the-face** strategy, is used in all types of sales. I once purchased a recliner for $250. It was not "on sale." About 2 months later I was browsing through a furniture store and spotted the same recliner advertised as part of a "giant blowout sale." The price tag showed $800 marked out, then $600 marked out, then $475 marked out, and finally the "sale price" of $400. A casual customer who hadn't shopped around might see this recliner as a super bargain. The price had been cut in half. Yet this store was asking $150 more than what I paid for the same recliner at the regular price from another store. Cialdini (1993) provides an apt example of the contrast effect in action in parent-child persuasion (Box 18-2).

As a strategy to use in a persuasive speech, *the contrast effect works well when you are presenting your solution to a problem.* For example, say you have argued that injuries and deaths from guns pose a serious problem in the United States. You could begin the solution portion of your speech this way:

> Clearly, gun violence in the United States requires a major change. I propose that Congress ban all guns. All individuals who own guns must turn them in to local law enforcement agencies within 3 months from the implementation date of this proposal. Failure to do so will be a felony punishable by a year in prison and a $5,000 fine. Production of ammunition for guns of any sort will stop immediately. Banning guns and ammunition is the way to significantly reduce injuries and death from firearms. Britain has done it, so has Japan, with terrific results. Shouldn't we as a nation do likewise?
>
> Although a total ban on private ownership of guns would be very beneficial, it probably isn't entirely practical in this country. Perhaps instead we should close the loopholes in the Brady bill, merely making guns more difficult to own. . . .

Peruse the sample speech at the end of this chapter for another example of the contrast effect (Box 18-3).

Try Emotional Appeals

We are not like Spock or Data on *Star Trek*. Although logic and evidence can be enormously persuasive, especially for highly involved listeners, emotional appeals—what Aristotle termed **pathos**—are also powerful motivators. There isn't a pure distinction between reasoning and emotion; they overlap. Even logic and evidence can produce emotional reactions from listeners.

ETHICS AND EMOTIONAL APPEALS   Are emotional appeals ethical? It depends. Shouldn't we be angry about racism, sexism, homophobia, and all manner of injustice? Shouldn't we fear terrorism, drunk drivers, food poisoning, and gun violence? Shouldn't we feel guilt about the treatment of Japanese Americans during World War II? Emotional appeals are not inherently unethical just because they aren't a logical appeal. An emotional appeal is considered to be a peripheral route to persuasion, and the central route should be encouraged. Nevertheless, emotion in the service of logic and truth can equal constructive action to do good. Emotional appeals motivate action. They also create attention so we might listen more intently to a clearly reasoned and supported argument. *Emotional appeals are ethical as long as they complement the central route to persuasion. Emotional appeals in the service of fabrications, distortions, and rumors are unethical.* Emotional appeals should not be a substitute for logic and evidence. If an emotional appeal contradicts sound logic and solid evidence, then it becomes the tool of the True Believer.

GENERAL EMOTIONAL APPEALS   Appeals to freedom, pride, honor, patriotism, sex, guilt, and shame all have their place as persuasion strategies that ignite emotional reactions and change behavior (Gass & Seiter, 1999). Appeals to anger also may prove to be quite persuasive, although little research exists to prove this. Consider how Kristin Michael (1997), a student at the University of Northern Iowa, uses an anger appeal on the subject of corporate welfare:

> What is truly outrageous, though, is that according to the Cato Institute, a conservative think-tank, an estimated $85 billion in the form of direct federal subsidies and tax breaks is funneled into thriving, multi-billion dollar corporate giants each year. And

This is a fear appeal on the dangers of cigarette smoking combined with an anger appeal against the tobacco industry. The combination of appeals can be highly persuasive.

where does this $85 billion a year go? The Walt Disney Corporation, whose profits in 1995 exceeded $1 billion, received $300,000 in federal assistance last year for fireworks. McDonald's continues to receive $2 million annually to market Chicken McNuggets in the Third World, and defense manufacturer Lockheed Martin billed the government for $20,000 worth of golf balls, as an "entertainment" expense, according to the Boston Globe, July 7, 1996.

Citizens will attend public meetings in droves when angered by an increase in energy rates or a perceived injustice. Anger is a strong motivation to act. Unquestionably, however, fear is the number one emotional appeal used to persuade audiences to change attitudes and behavior.

FEAR APPEALS "Don't put that in your mouth. It's full of germs." "You'll poke your eye out if you run with those scissors." "Don't ever talk to strangers. They may hurt you." "Never cross the street before looking both ways. You could be killed." From childhood we are all familiar with fear appeals. Our parents give us a heavy dose to keep us safe and out of trouble. Do fear appeals work? Yes, they do. In fact, despite earlier research that indicated that excessively intense fear appeals could backfire, more recent research (Dillard, 1994; Witte & Allen, 1996) indicates that the more fear is aroused in listeners, the more vulnerable they feel, and the more likely they will be convinced (Gass & Seiter, 1999). But will they act on the fear appeal or become paralyzed into inaction because of the seeming insoluble problem that causes the fear?

Five conditions determine whether high fear appeals will likely produce constructive action (Gass & Seiter, 1999). First, *listeners must feel vulnerable*. We don't all fear the same things. Teenagers may not be frightened by the risk of contracting lung cancer from smoking cigarettes, but they may fear social disapproval from their peers. Public service announcements presenting smokers as disgusting, uncool, and sickeningly smelly may trigger greater fear than any health threat. Some people are frightened by the ready availability of guns in the United States. Other people take comfort from having the security and protection of a Smith and Wesson.

THE FAR SIDE® BY GARY LARSON

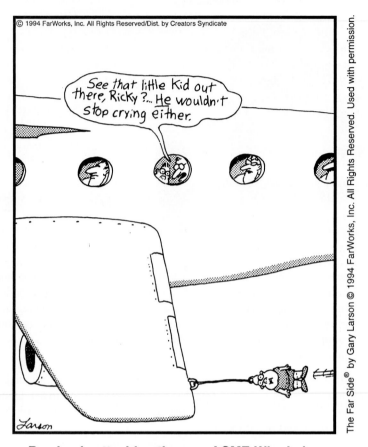

By simply attaching the new ACME Wingbaby, airlines can significantly improve their passengers' overall comfort.

Second, *a clear specific recommendation for avoiding or lessening the danger is important* (Aronson, 1999). A vague recommendation (fight corruption) is not as effective as a specific recommendation (vote for Proposition 45).

Third, *the recommendation must be perceived as effective.* The "Just Say No" campaign against drugs was a slogan, not a solution (Pratkanis & Aronson, 2001). Imagine kids being pressured by peers to take drugs. What would they likely fear most—the risk of the drugs or the threat of social disapproval from not going along with their peer group?

Fourth, *listeners must perceive that they can perform the actions recommended.* Again, the effort required to perform the behavior is a key variable. Giving up meat entirely for the rest of your life to avoid the danger of high cholesterol may not be possible for most people. The effort is too great. Cutting meat consumption in half, however, may be realistic.

Notice how Holly Sisk (1997), a student at George Mason University, uses a high fear appeal combined with an almost effortless solution:

In 1994 over five hundred Washington state residents were stricken by the e-coli bacteria. The story you probably didn't read, however, was that 49 of those patients never ate the tainted meat. They merely touched someone who had. The February 5, 1996, Wall Street Journal estimates that every year food poisoning cases from poor hand washing results in over 32 million illnesses and nearly four thousand deaths. . . . Over the last few years, Americans have made changes in their health. We've stopped smoking, started having safer sex, and changed our eating habits. But hand washing is a thirty second procedure that is the #1 daily thing you can do to protect your health. So if ten minutes of reasons haven't convinced you to spare those thirty seconds, my hands are clean (pp. 143, 145).

Finally, studies have shown that *fear appeals are more persuasive when combined with high-quality arguments* (Gleicher & Petty, 1992; Rodriguez, 1995). The fear appeal becomes more believable when it is bolstered by credible arguments.

In conclusion (Witte, 1998), fear appeals can be highly effective motivators of behavior but only under certain conditions. When listeners perceive a threat to be low, no action is likely. The speaker's fear appeal must be strong and demonstrate the threat to have a personal impact on individuals to arouse concern. When listeners perceive the personal threat to be high but view the solution as ineffective or too difficult to implement, denial ("We can't do anything anyway, so why worry?") or rationalization ("You've got to die of something") typically neutralizes the fear-arousing message. Finally, when listeners perceive the personal threat to be high and the solution to be effective and relatively easy to implement, fear-arousing messages will likely be successful in producing constructive action.

Use a Persuasive Organizational Pattern

How you organize your persuasive speech can have a major effect on its potential to convince listeners. There are two primary persuasive organizational patterns: two-sided speeches and Monroe's motivated sequence.

TWO-SIDED SPEECHES   Is it better to present arguments in favor of your proposition and ignore opposing arguments, or should you make your case and then refute opposing arguments? Until recently, this question produced contradictory research results, but newer studies by Allen (1991, 1993) provide a clear answer. Two-sided persuasive speeches are more effective than one-sided speeches in convincing listeners to change attitudes.

A two-sided organizational pattern begins with a presentation of main arguments supporting your proposition. After you have laid out your case, answer common objections, or opposing arguments, to your case. This, of course, means that you need to anticipate what an audience might question about your position. Answering opposing arguments is called **refutation.**

There are four steps to refutation. First, *state the opposing argument.* "A common objection to colleges shifting from a semester to a quarter system is that not as much subject matter will be covered each term" is a statement of an opposing argument. Second, *state your reaction to the opposing argument.* "This isn't true. Courses that meet 3 hours per week could meet 5 hours per week under the quarter system" is a statement of response to an opposing argument. Third, *support your response with reasoning and evidence.* Refutation requires the same standards of reasoning and evidence that are relevant to any claim asserted. Fourth, *indicate what effect, if any, opposing*

www.mhhe ● com/ **rothwell2**

See "Online Influence Test," Chapter 18 of the Online Learning Center.

Two-sided persuasion is more effective at changing attitudes and behavior than one-sided persuasion. Ignoring the opposition can make one-sided persuasion seem largely irrelevant.

arguments have had on the strength of your case. If some disadvantage will occur from your proposal, admit it, but weigh the damage against the claimed advantages of your proposal. "No quarter system is perfect. Yes, students will be pressured in some instances to work more intensely in a condensed period of time. Overall, however, the advantages of a quarter system—greater number and variety of courses, more diversity of instructors, better vacation schedules, and greater retention and success rates—far outweigh the minor objections to my proposal." The sample speech at the end of this chapter provides a detailed example of two-sided organization (Box 18-3).

MONROE'S MOTIVATED SEQUENCE The Monroe motivated sequence was first designed for sales presentations. It is a persuasive organizational pattern with five steps (Gronbeck et al., 1998):

1. *Attention*: Create interest; use attention strategies.
2. *Need*: Present a problem to be solved and relate it to your audience.
3. *Satisfaction*: Provide a solution to the problem that will satisfy your audience.
4. *Visualization:* Provide an image for your audience of what the world will look like if your solution is implemented.
5. *Action:* Make a call to action; get the audience involved and committed.

 See "Checklist for Preparing and Delivering a Persuasive Speech" on CD.

The sample speech in Box 18-3 provides an extended example of the Monroe motivated sequence.

Box 18-3 Sharper Focus

A Sample Outline and Persuasive Speech

A sample outline and text of a persuasive speech are presented here. This is approximately a 15-minute persuasive speech. That is a longer speech than most in-class presentations but shorter than many public presentations. This somewhat lengthier speech is presented to provide a more comprehensive illustration of several persuasive strategies.

The speech presented here uses the Monroe motivated sequence organizational format. Steps in this sequence are identified in square brackets. Annotations identify specific persuasion strategies.

Introduction

I. [*ATTENTION STEP*] Begin with notable examples of big money in college sports.
   A. CBS paid NCAA $6.2 billion for TV rights for basketball championship.
   B. Notre Dame has $45 million television contract.
   C. BCS bowl games produce $100 million to NCAA.
   D. Some universities have $30 million athletic budgets.
   E. Coors pays $5 million to University of Colorado, and Nike pays $5.6 million.
   F. All bowls have a corporate logo except the Rose Bowl.

II. Proposition: to convince you that colleges and universities should significantly reduce the scale of their athletic programs.

III. Establish significance to the audience.
   A. All college students partially pay for athletic programs with fees and taxes.
   B. Student scholars must compete with student athletes for scholarships.
      1. Duke University gave $4 million to athletes but $400,000 to students for academic merit.
      2. The University of North Carolina gave $3.2 million to athletes but $636,000 to students for academic merit.

IV. Preview the main points.
   A. Athletic programs contradict the educational mission of colleges.
   B. A specific plan will be offered to solve this problem.
   C. Common objections to such a plan will be addressed.

Body

I. [*NEED STEP*] Big-time intercollegiate athletic programs contradict the educational mission of colleges and universities.

   A. Athletic prowess, not academic ability, is often given priority.
      1. Athletes are given scholarships to play ball.
      2. Chris Washburn was a notable example.
      3. SAT scores for athletes are, on average, 200 points lower than for nonathletes.

   B. Student nonathletes and athletes alike are academically harmed by the contradiction.
      1. Student scholars may be bumped from academic admittance to make space for the student athlete with lower academic qualifications.
      2. Admitting marginal students because of their athletic ability is also harmful to the athlete and the college.
         a. Athletes struggle to survive academically.
         b. Colleges spend resources on tutors.
         c. Athletes often take "hideaway curricula."

   C. Colleges' primary mission is often diminished by athletic department deficits.
      1. Most colleges suffer big athletic department deficits.
         a. Only a handful make any money.
         b. The deficit for NCAA colleges is $1 billion annually.
         c. Deficit figures do not include huge coaches' salaries.
         d. Deficits will likely continue even with the CBS and BCS contracts.
      2. Huge deficits threaten academic programs.
         a. Deficits siphon precious resources from academic programs.
         b. Tulane University is a notable example.

II. [*SATISFACTION STEP*] Take the money out of college sports.
   A. Drop all college sports entirely (contrast effect).
   B. The real plan is as follows:
      1. Provide no scholarships based on athletic ability.
      2. Student athletes must maintain minimum 2.5 GPA.
      3. Team practice sessions will be limited to 10 hours per week.
      4. No corporate sponsorships, logos, names on arenas, and so forth allowed.
      5. No money from TV rights will go to college athletic programs.
      6. College coaches will be paid instructor salaries.

Box 18-3 Sharper Focus (continued)

7. Football and basketball must be self-supporting; no general college funds may be used.
8. NCAA will enforce these provisions using probation, suspension of sports program, or banishment from a league.

C. Three common objections to this proposal will be addressed.
1. Objection 1 is that disadvantaged student athletes will lose scholarships and be denied an education.
   a. This is true.
   b. Total number of student scholarships will not decrease.
   c. Student athletes will realize importance of academics.
2. Objection 2 is that career training for pros will be lost.
   a. This is also true, but colleges shouldn't be farm teams for sports corporations.
   b. A minuscule percentage go on to be professionals.
3. Objection 3 is that sports fans lose an entertainment source.
   a. There will still be college sports programs.
   b. There will still be gifted athletes entertaining us.
   c. There just won't be big money distorting academics.

III. [*VISUALIZATION STEP*] Imagine what it will be like when money is removed from college sports.
A. Colleges won't need to reduce or eliminate academic programs because of athletic department deficits.
B. More scholarship money will be available for academic merit.
C. Colleges will no longer contradict their mission.
D. Student tuition and fees will not be raised to pay for athletics.
E. Failure to implement this plan means increased deficits, hypocrisy, and reductions in academic programs.

Conclusion

I. [*ACTION STEP*] Take action now.
A. Make summary of main arguments.
1. Big money has corrupted college sports, thwarting colleges' academic mission.
2. The proposed plan takes the money out of college sports.
3. Common objections were found to be meritless.
B. Take action.
1. Contact your student representatives.
2. Sign the petition to be sent to the NCAA.
C. Memorable finish: Begin the dialogue; stop the hypocrisy!

Bibliography

Byers, W. (1995). *Unsportsmanlike conduct: Exploiting college athletes.* Ann Arbor, MI: The University of Michigan Press.

Eitzen, D. (1997, December 1). Big-time college sports. *Vital Speeches,* pp. 122–126.

Eitzen, D. S. (2000, September). Slaves of big-time college sports. *USA Today Magazine,* pp. 26–30.

Frank, R., & Cook, P. (1995). *The winner-take-all society.* New York: Free Press.

Hennessy, J. L., & Keohane, N. O. (2003, January 14). Universities must require athletes to make the grade. *San Jose Mercury News,* p. 6B.

Simons, J. (1997, March 24). Improbable dreams. *U.S. News & World Report,* pp. 46–52.

Sperber, M. (1999). *Beer and circus: How big-time college sports is crippling undergraduate education.* New York: Henry Holt.

Sperber, M. (1998). *Onward to victory: The crisis that shaped college sports.* New York: Henry Holt.

Will, G. (2001, August 12). Athletes don't graduate? Neither do other students. *San Jose Mercury News,* p. 7C.

Zimbalist, A. (2001, September). Only the few would benefit. *On Campus,* p. 4.

Zimbalist, A. (2001). *Unpaid professionals: Commercialism and conflict in big-time college sports.* Princeton, NJ: Princeton University Press.

Box 18-3 **Sharper Focus** (continued)

Get Big Money Out of College Sports

[*ATTENTION STEP*] Columnist George Will, in the August 12, 2001, issue of the *San Jose Mercury News*, reports that CBS will pay $6.2 billion to the National Collegiate Athletic Association from 2003 to 2013 to broadcast the men's college "March Madness" basketball tournament. Will also reports that Notre Dame University has a 5-year contract with NBC for $45 million to air their football games. Murray Sperber, chair of the National Alliance for College Athletic Reform and author of the 2000 book *Beer and Circus*, a critique of big-time intercollegiate athletics, notes that the BCS bowl playoff games for college football bring in $100 million a year in revenue to the NCAA. Sociology Professor Emeritus Stanley Eitzen of Colorado State University, in the December 1, 1997, issue of *Vital Speeches* observes, "Some university athletic budgets have surpassed $30 million a year, more than the entire budgets of many colleges."

Corporate sponsorship of college athletics has never been greater. Coors Brewing Company paid $5 million to the University of Colorado for naming its new fieldhouse "Coors Events Center." The university also receives $5.6 million in shoes, apparel, and cash from Nike. All football bowl games except the Rose Bowl now have corporate names attached, such as the John Hancock Sun Bowl and the Nokia Sugar Bowl. Clearly, college sports are big business.

Is this increasing commercialization of college sports compatible with the educational mission of institutions of higher learning? Professor Eitzen in his 1997 speech observes, "Big-time college sport confronts us with a fundamental dilemma. Positively, college football and basketball offer entertainment, spectacle, excitement, festival, and excellence. Negatively, the commercial entertainment function of big-time college sport has severely compromised academia. Educational goals have been superseded by the quest for big money. And, since winning programs receive huge revenues from television, gate receipts, bowl and tournament appearances, boosters, and even legislatures, many sports programs are guided by a win-at-any-cost philosophy."

Let's be honest: College athletics, especially Division I, big-time football and basketball programs, are a commercial entertainment venture far removed from the educational mission of colleges and universities. College sport has become so gigantic that it distorts the priorities of colleges and universities and compromises their educational mission. The June 26, 2001, report of the Knight Foundation Commission on Intercollegiate Athletics and the 2001 report of the National Alliance for College Athletic Reform both concur with this assessment. Because this is a serious problem, I will try to convince you that colleges and universities should significantly reduce the scale of their athletic programs. [*PROPOSITION OF POLICY*]

Every college student listening to me speak today is affected by this commercialization of college sports. [*PERSONAL IMPACT*] It is you who partially pay for big-time athletic programs with student fees and taxes. Student scholars are forced to compete against student athletes for scholarships and resources. Murray Sperber, in his 1998 book *Onward to Victory*, states that "many big-time sports schools spend much more money on grants for jocks than on academic merit scholarships." He cites two notable examples. Duke University awarded $4 million for 550 athletes, but only $400,000 in academic merit scholarships for its 5,900 other undergraduates. Likewise, the University of North Carolina gave $3.2 million to 690 athletes, but only $636,000 in merit scholarships for its 15,000 other students. Not only is there increased competition for scholarships, but also academic programs central to your educational goals and dreams may be jeopardized by huge deficits incurred by athletic programs, especially those with losing records.

I can guess what some of you are thinking. "He wants to reduce college athletic programs because he hates jocks and was a geek who always lost at sports." Not true! Baseball and basketball were my two favorite sports, and I earned my share of trophies and accolades playing both. I am an avid 49ers fan, and I grew up worshipping the L.A. Dodgers. You may not appreciate the teams I chose to support, but clearly I do not propose reducing the scale of college athletics because I hate sports. [*IDENTIFICATION*] A college education, however, can open the doors of success for each and every one of you. It is your ticket to a better future. College sports should never serve as a substitute for academic success or impede any student's chance to acquire the best education possible, but the commercialization of college athletics threatens to do just that. [*PERSONAL IMPACT*]

Let me make several arguments to support my proposal to significantly reduce the scale of college athletic programs. Please listen to these arguments before making

Box 18-3 Sharper Focus (continued)

a judgment. I will show how athletic programs contradict the educational mission of colleges. I will offer a specific plan to rectify this serious problem. Finally, I will respond to primary objections you may have to my proposal.

[*NEED STEP*] Returning to my first argument, that athletic programs contradict the educational mission of colleges, let me begin with what I think we all know is true. The principal mission of a college or university is to provide a quality education for all students. Excessive emphasis on sports programs, however, contradicts this mission in three ways. [*COGNITIVE DISSONANCE*] First, athletic prowess, not academic ability, is often given priority by colleges. Athletes receive scholarships to attend colleges and universities, not to become great scholars or even to receive a quality education. They receive scholarships to play ball and entertain fans. Pursuing an education is often secondary at best, a time-consuming irritant that interferes with athletes' opportunity to practice their sport.

According to Murray Sperber in *Beer and Circus*, previously cited, the University of North Carolina's basketball team in 1999 averaged 905 on the SAT; regular undergraduates at UNC averaged 1220. UNC admits only 35% of its applicants. Chris Washburn, a future professional basketball player, entered North Carolina State University with an SAT score of 470. The average SAT score for the student body at NC State was 1,030 at the time. More than 100 universities offered Washburn a scholarship to play basketball. Partly as a result of this widely publicized and embarrassing example, the NCAA tightened SAT score requirements. Nevertheless, marginal student athletes continue to receive special treatment. As Professor Eitzen notes in the September 2000 *USA Today Magazine*, football and men's basketball players are six times as likely to be admitted below standard college entrance requirements as other students. SAT scores for athletes are, on average, according to Eitzen, more than 200 points lower than those of the rest of the student body, placing them in the bottom quarter of all entering students. Clearly, athletic prowess, not academic potential, is what counts.

Second, student athletes and nonathletes alike are harmed by the emphasis placed on athletic ability. [*CONTINUATION OF COGNITIVE DISSONANCE*] Admitting marginal students because of their athletic abilities prevents other more academically qualified students from gaining entrance to some of the best colleges and universities. Some of you may have been denied entrance to the college of your choice and had to settle for a second, third, or even fourth choice because athletes with far weaker academic records were granted preferential admittance. [*MILD ANGER APPEAL*] Does this seem unfair to you? I know

it does because Professor Sperber reports results of his study on college sports in *Onward to Victory*. A huge majority, 83% of undergraduate respondents to the survey, agreed with the statement "Athletic scholarship winners should meet the same college entrance requirements as regular students."

In addition, admitting marginal students with athletic ability does no favors for the student athletes. Marginal students struggle to keep up in classes, often require tutors at college expense, and many never get a degree. Journalist Linda Seebach, editorial writer for *Inside Denver*, states in her December 14, 1997, editorial, "Athletes on scholarship . . . often have wall-to-wall tutors and major in 'hideaway curriculums' designed solely for them." John Hennessy and Nannerl Keohane, presidents of Stanford and Duke Universities respectively, note in a January 14, 2003 opinion piece in the *San Jose Mercury News* that "two-thirds of male athletes in all sports have grade point averages that place them in the bottom third of their class. In general, female athletes also have poorer academic records than their non-athlete counterparts."

Third, the primary mission of colleges and universities, to educate students, is often diminished by athletic department deficits. [*CONTINUATION OF COGNITIVE DISSONANCE*] Both Andrew Zimbalist, Professor of Economics at Smith College and author of the 2001 book *Unpaid Professionals*, and Professor Sperber, in *Beer and Circus*, note that only a handful of colleges and universities make money on their big athletic programs. As Sperber notes, "The vast majority of colleges and universities do not make money in big-time intercollegiate athletics." The huge majority of NCAA schools run a debt each year, many run a very sizeable deficit. Even teams that go to big bowl games typically lose money on the game despite huge television revenues paid to the NCAA. The University of Wisconsin, for example, played in the 1999 Rose Bowl. The university, according to Sperber in *Beer and Circus*, received $1.8 million for the bowl appearance. Expenses to the university, however, totaled $2.1 million, leaving a $300,000 loss. In 2003, university presidents Hennessy and Keohane noted that college athletic programs run a billion dollar deficit annually. [*USE OF PERSUASIVE EVIDENCE; STARTLING/UNUSUAL STATISTICS*]. The NCAA deficit figures, as bad as they are, undoubtedly underestimate the problem because coaches' salaries, frequently in the half-million to million dollar range, aren't included in the athletic budgets. They're listed as faculty salaries.

What about the $6.2 billion contract with CBS referred to earlier? Won't this bail out the debt-ridden colleges and universities? According to Economist Andrew Zimbalist already cited, the "CBS contract will have precious little

Box 18-3 **Sharper Focus** (continued)

impact on the economics of college sports." A few highly successful colleges will benefit, but most other colleges won't. He concludes that only a tiny percentage of the 300-plus athletic departments operating big-time basketball programs will "generate black ink in any given year. The prudent bet is that college sports will be in the same financial mess or worse in 2003" when the CBS contract kicks in.

These huge deficits threaten academic programs. [*MILD FEAR APPEAL*] Professor Eitzen notes that in 1996 Tulane University announced a sixfold increase in the athletic department budget from $550,000 to $3.4 million. Simultaneously, Tulane hacked $8.5 million from the general budget used to support academic programs. Student tuition was raised 4%, faculty and staff salaries were frozen for a year, 50 staff positions were cut, and funding for undergraduate and graduate financial aid and stipends was reduced. Athletic department deficits siphon precious resources from academic programs, possibly academic programs central to your educational and career goals. Big-money athletic programs clearly contradict the primary mission of institutions of higher education by admitting poorly prepared and underqualified students, by valuing students for their athletic prowess and not their academic potential, and by creating huge deficits that necessitate diminished resources for academic programs.

So what should be done about this problem? Clearly, since football and basketball programs are typically the source of all these problems, we should eliminate them from all colleges and universities. [*CONTRAST EFFECT*] If we were to eliminate football and basketball, less visible and far less costly sports such as baseball, golf, gymnastics, and field hockey could provide some athletic opportunities for students. Intramural football and basketball programs, at virtually no cost to the college, could be established for those students who prefer such sports. Let's face facts—getting the money out of college sport is essential if we are going to solve the problems I've outlined.

Total elimination of football and basketball except for intramural programs solves the problems I've underscored. Perhaps, however, we don't need such a radical solution. As a sports fan and former athlete, I would be disappointed if colleges dumped their football and basketball programs entirely. [*IDENTIFICATION*] I do strongly believe, however, that the big money must be taken out of college sports.

[*SATISFACTION STEP*] My plan to do this is simple:

1. There will be no scholarships for students based on athletic ability. Scholarships and grants must be based on academic potential and financial need. This is a strong recommendation of the National Alliance for College Athletic Reform.

2. Student athletes must be admitted according to the same standards as all other students. They must maintain a minimum 2.5 GPA to participate in athletic programs.

3. Team practice sessions will be limited to no more than 10 hours per week. Economist Andrew Zimbalist in the September 2001 article in *On Campus* notes that athletes are often required to spend 40 to 60 hours per week practicing their sport. This competes with time for academic pursuits.

4. Absolutely no corporate money goes to athletic programs. No corporate logos or names should appear on any sports facilities, equipment, or apparel of any kind.

5. No money from television rights or bowl games will go to college athletic programs.

6. College coaches must be paid instructors' salaries just like any professor. This is a strong recommendation of the Knight Foundation Commission on Intercollegiate Athletics. In a highly publicized story, Steve Spurrier, football coach at the University of Florida, was given a contract averaging $2 million per year in salary, bonuses, and extras until the year 2002. Even that wasn't enough salary to keep him from jumping to the NFL. No coach should earn 10 to 20 times what the college president earns. It sends a distorted message about college priorities.

7. Football and basketball must be self-supporting. Ticket sales and sports merchandise will be primary sources of funds.

8. The NCAA will enforce all provisions, using probation, suspension of a sports program, or banishment from a league as possible penalties.

This plan will substantially reduce college athletic programs without eliminating them. I have merely taken the big money out of college sports. Leagues, championships, and bowl games can continue but without the huge financial incentives to distort the academic mission of colleges. Academic programs will no longer be threatened by huge athletic department debts. Without the big money, colleges can return to their primary mission—to provide a quality education for all students.

[*SATISFACTION STEP CONTINUED*] In case you're not completely convinced that my plan is a good idea, let me address common objections to my proposal. [*TWO-SIDED PERSUASION*] The first objection might be that disadvantaged student athletes will lose scholarships and be

Box 18-3 Sharper Focus (continued)

denied a college education. That's true. Athletic scholarships awarded each year, however, could be added to the general scholarship and grant pool at each college. The net effect on students as a group would be zero. The faces would change, but the same number of students could receive financial help. In addition, if student athletes realize that they cannot play college sports unless they qualify academically, they will have an incentive to take their studies seriously or risk ineligibility.

A second objection [TWO-SIDED PERSUASION CONTINUED] might be that many academically unprepared student athletes will lose a training ground for a career in professional sports. This may be true, but is it relevant? Should a college be a farm team for professional sports corporations? Journalist John Simons in his March 24, 1997, article in *U.S. News* notes that any high school athlete's chances of playing professional sports is remote—about 1 in 10,000. Yet according to the Northeastern University's Center for the Study of Sport in Society cited in the same article, 66% of all African American males between the ages of 13 and 18 believe they can make it to the professional ranks some day. Economics professors Frank and Cook in their 1995 book *The Winner Take-All Society*, note that 60% of NCAA Division I college basketball starters believe they will some day start for an NBA team. The actual figure is fewer than 5%. University of Chicago sports economist Allen Sanderson, quoted in the 1997 *U.S. News* article, says, "It's like pinning your hopes on the lottery."

These students are attending college to play ball as a way of auditioning for professional teams. Educational success often gets lost in the hoopla and hubbub over athletic accomplishment. Colleges should not be a party to such exploitation [COGNITIVE DISSONANCE]. As Professor Eitzen concludes, "When schools over-recruit minorities for their athletic skills and under-recruit minorities for their academic skills, they contradict the fundamental reason for their existence." As John Simons notes in his 1997 *U.S. News* article, African Americans are vastly underrepresented in such important professions as medicine, law, journalism, and engineering, to name just a few. Colleges should be working hard to prepare minority students for these and other professions because that is the colleges' primary mission. They should stop serving as farm teams for professional sports corporations interested only in profit.

Finally, won't sports fans lose a key source of entertainment if my plan is implemented? [TWO-SIDED PERSUASION CONTINUED] This is not true. Notre Dame and USC will still remain arch rivals on the football field. Bowl games will still exist. Championships will still be contested, simply in scaled-down versions as they once were in the 1950s and 1960s. The difference will be that academic programs will not be diminished because of huge deficits from athletic programs, and the academic mission of colleges will not be distorted to pay for bloated athletic programs. The scale of college athletics will be substantially reduced, but the excitement and spectacle can remain.

[VISUALIZATION STEP] Imagine what my plan will accomplish. No longer will colleges be tempted or forced to reduce or eliminate an academic program, perhaps a program in your major, to pay for deficits incurred by bloated athletic programs. Millions of dollars in scholarships and grants will be available for academically qualified and needy students. Colleges will no longer serve as farm teams for profit-motivated corporations. Colleges will no longer appear hypocritical, espousing an educational mission on one hand while undermining it on the other. Your student fees and tuition will not have to be raised to support a faltering, expensive sports program.

Imagine what will happen if this problem is ignored. Athletic budgets will continue to swell and deficits will rise. Your tuition and fees will increase, academic programs will be cut, and some programs and majors will be eliminated to cover the athletic department deficits. The quality of your education and your opportunities for academic success will be threatened. [MILD FEAR APPEAL]

[ACTION STEP] College sports have become too closely connected to corporate interests. Big money has corrupted college athletics and the primary mission of colleges and universities. I have proposed a solution that will work by taking money out of college sports. I have responded to common objections raised against my plan, and these objections have been found meritless. I ask that you support my proposal to significantly reduce college athletic programs. Stop the erosion of academic values and quality. Speak to your Student Senate officers and representatives. Discuss the issues I have raised with the college administration. This college can be a beacon of light signaling the way for other colleges to follow. Change begins with us. Sign this petition that I will circulate in a moment that asks the NCAA to change the rules and remove big money from our college sports programs. [EFFORT REQUIRED IS MINIMAL] Begin the dialogue! Stop the hypocrisy [COGNITIVE DISSONANCE].

Summary

Persuasion is the communication process of converting, modifying, or maintaining the attitudes, beliefs, and behavior of others. Changing attitudes alone may not change behavior. Personal experience, personal impact, and effort required to perform the behavior all affect how consistent attitudes and behavior will be. There are two primary paths to persuasion: peripheral and central. Uninvolved listeners are more easily influenced by peripheral factors such as the credibility of the speaker and how others react to the persuasive message. Involved listeners are more influenced by central, quality arguments and evidence. There are many persuasive strategies a speaker can use. Among these are establishing identification, building credibility, building solid arguments, inducing cognitive dissonance, making emotional appeals, using the contrast effect, and using persuasive organizational patterns. Competent public speakers will find success if they utilize some or all of these strategies to persuade others.

Quizzes Without Consequences

Go to *Quizzes Without Consequences* at the book's Online Learning Center at **www.mhhe.com/rothwell2** or access the CD-ROM for *In the Company of Others.*

www.mhhe
com/**rothwell2**

Key Terms

anchor
attitude
cognitive dissonance
competence
composure
contrast effect
counterpersuasion
credibility
door-in-the-face
dynamism
ego involvement

elaboration likelihood
  model
ethos
identification
latitude of acceptance
latitude of
  noncommitment
latitude of rejection
logos
pathos
persuasion

proposition
proposition of fact
proposition of policy
proposition of value
refutation
social judgment theory
stylistic similarity
substantive similarity
trustworthiness

See Audio Flashcards
Study Aid.

www.mhhe
com/**rothwell2**
See Crossword Puzzle
Study Aid.

Suggested Readings

Cialdini, R. (1993). *Influence: The new psychology of modern persuasion.* Glenview, IL: Scott Foresman. This is a very well-written work on common persuasion strategies used in everyday life.

Pratkanis, A., & Aronson, E. (2000). *The age of propaganda: The everyday use and abuse of persuasion.* New York: W. H. Freeman. This title says it all. This is a very readable work on common persuasion strategies.

Film School

My Cousin Vinny (1991). Comedy; R ★★★★
This is a "must see" comedy if you haven't already had the pleasure of viewing this hilarious account of a bumbling New York lawyer (Joe Pesci) attempting to free his cousin (Ralph Macchio) from a murder charge in a small town in Alabama. Analyze this film for the persuasive, and often not so persuasive, use of identification.

Primary Colors (1998). Drama; R ★★★★
There's little doubt that this film is more than loosely based on former President Bill Clinton's campaign. Examine the ethics of persuasion.

APPENDIX
Interviewing

Interviewing is a common communication event. **Interviewing** is defined as "a purposeful, planned conversation, characterized by extensive verbal interaction" (Peterson, 1997, p. 288).

In every instance, communication competence is a central element of effective job interviewing. In a study by Peterson (1997), all 253 personnel interviewers at small and large businesses agreed that communication ability during an interview has a major effect on hiring decisions. Fewer than 60%, however, believed current job applicants demonstrate even adequate communication skills.

The principal purpose of this appendix is to offer ways to improve your interviewing skills. There are two objectives:

1. to identify common mistakes made during job interviews, and
2. to present specific advice that can improve your interviewing skills.

Chapter 15 discussed the informational interview conducted for research purposes.

Job Interview Mistakes

Few events are as anxiety producing and as significant to our lives as a job interview. So much can be riding on such a brief encounter. Communicating competently during a job interview can be crucial to securing a job. In this section, common mistakes and effective communication strategies are addressed.

There probably is no such thing as a perfect interview. Communication strategies that work in one interview may not work as well in another. Nevertheless, there are some behaviors that seem destined to torpedo any chance of success in an interview for a job. Personnel executives have offered the following examples of actual communication behaviors that demolished the credibility of job applicants (as cited in Miller, 1991):

"Said if he was hired, he'd teach me ballroom dancing at no charge, and started demonstrating."

"Took three cellular phone calls. Said she had a similar business on the side."

"Applicant walked in and inquired why he was here."

"After a difficult question, she wanted to leave the room for a moment
to meditate."

"Candidate was told to take his time answering, so he began writing down
each of his answers before speaking."

"Man brought in his five children and cat."

"Wanted to borrow the fax machine to send out some personal letters."

"Brought a mini tape recorder and said he always taped his job interviews."

"Applicant handed me an employment contract and said I'd have to sign it if
he was going to be hired."

"She sat in my chair and insisted that I sit in the interviewee's chair."

These examples are clearly cases of clueless communication behavior on the
part of interviewees. Peterson (1997) identified more typical, less extreme interviewing mistakes. They include weak eye contact, irrelevant response to topic, disorganized response to questions, poor listening skills, unclear response to questions,
problems with response fluency, weak voice projection, inadequate volume control,
and lack of preparation for the interview.

In addition to making these mistakes, interviewees commonly err in general
ways during the interview. First, they approach the interview as though it were a
sales pitch and they were the product. Most people are mildly, sometimes profoundly repelled by a hard sell no matter what the product. Using a hard sell to land
a job will likely produce a similar response from an interviewer or employment
committee. Second, interviewees sometimes attempt to relate their entire life story
when answering a question. Too much detail can make interviewers weary and
cause their attention to fade. Third, interviewees sometimes try to fake their knowledge and experience by inflating the importance of relatively minor background
and accomplishments. If an interviewing committee senses that you are unreasonably padding your résumé, they may doubt your credibility across the board.
Fourth, interviewees who are obviously unprepared to answer tough questions
have little hope of being chosen for the job.

Competent Interviewing Skills

Anderson and Killenberg (1999) identify three qualities that are necessary for an interview to be a success: empathy, honesty, and respect. Empathy puts us in the position of seeing from the other person's perspective. This is a vital quality for an
interviewee. Empathy allows you to anticipate questions that will be asked and to
frame answers that will speak to the concerns of those interviewing you. Honesty is
vital, because no one is likely to hire a person he or she does not perceive to be candid and straightforward. If a person lies on his or her résumé and the lie is discovered, it can be grounds for immediate dismissal from the position. Embellishing
minor accomplishments walks close to the precipice of dishonesty. Respect, the final
quality, shows sensitivity and concern. Respect, of course, is a two-way street. Interviewers should show the applicant respect by addressing him or her in a manner
that is not demeaning. Similarly, interviewees should show respect for interviewers.
Some of the previous examples of clueless behavior during interviews show disrespect for the interviewer. Taking cell phone calls during the interview and taking the
interviewer's chair both show disrespect.

There are several ways to improve your interviewing skills. First, *be prepared*. Do research on the job you seek. Most job announcements specify what experience, skills, and knowledge are essential to the performance of the job. Be prepared to adapt your background to the specific requirements of the job. If the job calls for knowledge of specific software or computer technology, be prepared to list your experience with such software and technology. If the job announcement expressly identifies "effective interpersonal skills" as desirable in an applicant, have a list ready that speaks to this qualification directly. For example, if you have taken a college course in interpersonal communication, if communication is your college major or minor, if you have taken any workshops in conflict management or couples communication, or if you have conducted workshops or classes in interpersonal communication, list these on your résumé. Have these examples ready in case you are asked questions on such background during the interview.

Second, *rehearse for your interview*. Have a friend ask typical interview questions:

What are your strengths and weaknesses?
Why did you apply for this particular job?
Why did you leave your previous job?
Have you ever had difficulty working for a boss or supervisor?
What problems did you encounter at your last position?
Where would you like to be professionally in 5 years?
What's the worst job you've ever had?
Would you have difficulty contradicting your boss if you thought he or she
   was about to make a bad decision?
Do you work well on a team?
Have you had good or bad experiences working in groups?

Frame your answers as positive reflections of your work ethic and determination to excel. For example, the question "Have you ever had difficulty working for a boss?" could be answered this way: "Yes, and it taught me a lot about how to deal with difficult people. . . ." "Where would you like to be professionally in 5 years?" could be answered this way: "I'd like to have my work recognized and receive a promotion because of it." You certainly don't want to answer such a question by indicating that the job you are seeking is merely a stepping stone to a better position elsewhere. Honesty doesn't require an answer that wasn't sought.

Third, *look and act the part of a credible candidate for the job*. Professional jobs require professional attire. Show that you care about the position by arriving on time, appearing well-groomed and neat, and dressing in professional clothing. During the interview, speak so everyone can easily hear you. Listen carefully to all questions, and if in doubt, ask for clarification or elaboration. Answer questions directly and eliminate nervous mannerisms (tapping fingers on the table, cracking knuckles, twirling hair, tapping a pen or pencil, or biting nails). Humor is often welcomed, but avoid sarcasm or ethnic humor. Self-deprecating humor often works well as long as it doesn't diminish your qualifications for the position. Establish direct eye contact with the interviewer. If a panel conducts the interview, establish initial eye contact with the panel member who asks you the questions and then gradually direct your eyes to all panel members as you develop your answer. Do not express anger or hostility for previous bosses that have "done you wrong." Interviewers are looking for composure as an indicator of credibility. Speak fluently. Avoid long vocal pauses and disfluencies (uhm, uh, you know, like).

Don't be reticent, fail to smile, look unfriendly, or demonstrate a lack of enthusiasm for the position.

Fourth, *provide sufficient elaboration when answering questions.* Very brief answers ("Yes, I did that") with no detail provided leave interviewers guessing about your qualifications for the position. Successful applicants for jobs use focused elaboration when asked questions (Anderson & Killenberg, 1999). This means they provide considerable detail when answering questions, and the detail is always directly relevant to the questions asked. Unsuccessful applicants usually provide no elaboration, or their answers drift to irrelevant experiences, stories, or knowledge. When providing detail, look for signals from interviewers that you've answered the question sufficiently. When interviewers glaze over, fidget, glance around the room, stare at a pencil, look at the clock, or shift in their chairs, it is usually time to wrap up your answer.

Fifth, *organize your answers.* If you have prepared sufficiently for the interview, you should be able to answer most questions asked clearly and in an organized fashion. "What experience do you have working with individuals from diverse cultural backgrounds?" might be one question asked. A possible answer is "I've worked with three very diverse groups. At Datacom West, a third of the workers were Asian. When I worked at Silicon Software, several of the workers I supervised were from India and Pakistan. When I ran my own printing business, most of my workers were either African American or Jewish. As you can see, I've worked with a rich mixture of ethnic groups, and I feel such diversity has produced synergy."

Sixth, *provide sufficient evidence of your qualifications for the job.* **Behavioral interviewing** is becoming increasingly popular, especially in the business world. Behavioral interviewing involves asking interviewees for specific examples of behavior that illustrates an answer (Eng, 1997). Here are some typical behavioral interviewing questions:

Describe a time when you tried to persuade a person or group to do something they opposed.

Give an example of a time when you faced many obstacles to achieving a goal and explain how you handled the situation.

Identify a stressful experience and discuss how you dealt with it.

Describe a conflict you've had with a fellow worker.

Tell us about a time when you had to meet strict deadlines.

Provide an example of a situation in which you were forced to make an important decision without adequate information.

All of these questions seek evidence of your skills on the job. Answers to these behavioral questions reveal an applicant's knowledge of real-life situations. Be prepared to provide specific evidence of your talents and abilities. Brainstorm examples that illustrate your strengths. Use the STAR interviewing method for answering such behavioral questions. *ST* stands for *situation/task,* *A* is *action,* and *R* stands for *result.* Thus, you identify the situation or task, explain what action you took, and describe what resulted from that action.

Seventh, *be prepared to ask relevant questions of interviewers.* An interview is a conversation, not an interrogation. Unlike a witness in a court trial, you have a right to ask questions of your interviewers. Your interviewers want to know if you are right for the job, but you also want to know if the job is right for you. Use the behavioral interviewing technique when asking questions of your interviewers. Don't ask, "Do people get promoted in this company?" Instead, ask, "Can you give me an example of the last person to receive a promotion and how that person earned it?"

 Summary

Interviews are important events in our lives. An interview is a purposeful, planned conversation characterized by extensive verbal interaction. Empathy, respect, and honesty should imbue every interview. Preparation is a major element of an interview both from the standpoint of the interviewee and of the interviewer. The interview should be focused. Questions and answers should be direct, relevant, and purposeful.

GLOSSARY

Abstracting The process of selective perception whereby we formulate increasingly vague conceptions of our world by leaving out details associated with objects, events, and ideas.

Accommodating style Yielding to the needs and desires of others during a conflict.

Ad hominem fallacy A personal attack on the messenger to avoid the message.

Ad populum fallacy Basing a claim on popular opinion.

Advising response Listeners telling individuals how they should act.

Agenda-setting function The news media telling us not so much what to think but what to think about.

Alliteration The repetition of the same sound, usually a consonant sound, starting several words in a sentence.

Ambushing When we listen for weaknesses and ignore strengths of a speaker's message.

Analogy Alleges that two things that resemble each other in certain ways also resemble each other in further ways as well.

Anchor attitude A preexisting attitude on an issue that serves as a reference point for how close or distant other attitudes and positions are.

Antithesis A stylistic device that uses opposites to create impact.

Appropriateness The avoidance of violating social or interpersonal norms, rules, or expectations.

Assertiveness The ability to communicate the full range of thoughts and emotions with confidence and skill.

Assimilation The absorption of one group's culture into the dominant culture.

Attention Focused awareness on a stimulus at a given moment.

Attitude A learned predisposition to respond favorably or unfavorably toward some attitude object.

Attribution Assigning a cause, either situations or personal characteristics, to people's behavior.

Avoiding Sidestepping or ignoring conflict.

Behavioral interviewing Interviewers ask for specific examples of behavior by an applicant that illustrate an answer given to a question.

Belief What we think is true or probable.

Bilateral symmetry The right and left sides of the human body match; eyes are straight across from each, not one higher than the other, and so forth.

Brainstorming The creative problem-solving process characterized by encouragement of even zany ideas, freedom from initial evaluation of potential solutions, and energetic participation by all group members.

Breadth (of self-disclosure) The range of subjects discussed.

Burden of proof The obligation of the claimant to support a claim with evidence and reasoning; whoever makes the claim has the burden to prove it.

Central idea (of a speech) Identifies the main concept, point, issue, or conclusion that a speaker wants an audience to understand, believe, feel, or do.

Channel Medium through which a message travels, such as oral or written.

Charisma Constellation of personal attributes that people find attractive and that they accord influence to a person perceived to have such attributes.

Chilling effect A person low in power avoids discussing issues with another person higher in power from fear of an abusive response.

Claim A generalization that requires support.

Closedness An unwillingness to communicate with others.

Coalitions   Temporary alliances formed by individuals to enhance their power relative to others.

Co-culture   A group of people who live in a dominant culture yet remain connected to another cultural heritage that typically exhibits significant differences in communication patterns, perceptions, values, beliefs, and rituals from the dominant culture.

Cognitive dissonance   The unpleasant feeling produced by seemingly inconsistent thoughts.

Cohesiveness   The degree of liking we have for members of a group, and the level of commitment to the group that this liking produces.

Cohesiveness   The degree to which members identify with a group and wish to remain in the group.

Collaborating   Style of conflict management in which parties work together to maximize the attainment of goals for all involved in the conflict.

Collectivist culture   A culture that has a "we" consciousness; individuals see themselves as being closely linked to one or more groups and are primarily motivated by the norms and duties imposed by these groups.

Commitment   A conscious decision to invest time and energy in improving our communication with others.

Common couple violence   The occasional violence that arises out of strong reactions to the escalation of a particular disagreement.

Communication   A transactional process of sharing meaning with others.

Communication climate   The emotional atmosphere, the pervading or enveloping tone that we create, by the way we communicate with others.

Communication competence   Communicating effectively and appropriately in a given context.

Communication orientation   Public speakers focusing on making their message clear and interesting to listeners.

Communication skill   The successful performance of a communication behavior and the ability to repeat such a behavior.

Communication style of conflict management   A typical way an individual addresses a conflict.

Competence (of speaker)   An audience's perception of a speaker's knowledge and experience on a topic.

Competition (MEGA)   Mutually exclusive goal attainment; for you to win others must lose.

Competitive interrupting   When we dominate the conversation by seizing the floor from others who are speaking.

Composure   A speaker's emotional stability, confidence, and degree of control over himself or herself when under stress.

Comprehension   Shared meaning between and among parties in a transaction.

Compromising   Attempting to resolve a conflict by giving up something to get something in return.

Confirmation bias   The psychological tendency to look for and listen to information that supports our beliefs and values and to ignore or distort information that contradicts our beliefs and values.

Conflict   The expressed struggle of interconnected parties who perceive incompatible goals and interference from one or more parties in attaining those goals.

Conformity   The inclination of group members to think and behave in ways that are consistent with group norms.

Confrontation   A strategy of the collaborating style of conflict management in which there is an overt recognition of a conflict and a direct effort is made to find creative ways to satisfy all parties in the conflict.

Connecting bid   An attempt to engage another person in a positive transaction, sometimes at a deep and enduring level and other times at a superficial and fleeting level.

Connection-autonomy dialectic   The desire to come together with another person (connection) yet remain apart, independent, and in control of one's own life (autonomy).

Connotation   The volatile, personal, subjective meaning of words composed of three dimensions: evaluation, potency, and activity.

Consensus   A state of mutual agreement among members of a group in which all legitimate concerns of individuals have been addressed to the satisfaction of the group.

Constructive conflict   Conflict that is characterized by We-orientation, de-escalation, cooperation, and flexibility.

Content dimension (of messages)   What is actually said and done.

Content-only response   Focuses on the content of a message, but ignores the emotional side of communication.

Context   The environment in which communication occurs; the who, what, where, when, why, and how of communication.

Continuous changes   Extensions of previous decisions of a group.

Contrast effect   A persuasive strategy that begins with a large request that makes a smaller request seem more palatable.

Conventionality-uniqueness dialectic   Wanting your relationship to be perceived by others as the same yet different from other relationships.

Convergence   Similarities that connect us to others.

Conversational narcissism   The tendency of listeners to turn the topics of ordinary conversation to themselves without showing sustained interest in others' topics.

Cooperation (MIGA)   Mutually inclusive goal attainment; for you to achieve your goals others must also achieve their goals.

Cooperative argumentation   Engaging in a process of deliberation with understanding and problem solving as ultimate goals.

Correlation   A consistent relationship between two variables.

Counterpersuasion   Attacks from an opposing side on an issue of controversy.

Credibility (of evidence)   Believability of supporting materials determined by its trustworthiness and reliability.

Credibility (of speaker)   Judgments made by listeners concerning the believability of a communicator.

Critical listening   The process of evaluating the merits of claims as they are heard.

Cultural relativism   The view that cultures are merely different, not deficient, and each culture's norms and practices should be assessed only from the perspective of the culture itself, not by standards embraced by another culture.

Culture   A learned set of shared interpretations about beliefs, values, and norms, which affect the behaviors of a relatively large group of people.

Culture shock   The anxiety that comes from the unfamiliarity of new cultural surroundings, rules, norms, and practices.

Cynics   Those who unthinkingly mock, ridicule, and tear down other people and their ideas.

Dead-level abstracting   The practice of freezing on one level of abstraction (getting stuck using mostly very vague or very concrete words).

Defensiveness   A protective reaction to a perceived attack on our self-esteem and self-concept.

Defiance   Unambiguous, overt, purposeful noncompliance with the dictates of others who exercise greater power.

Demographics   Characteristic of an audience such as age, gender, culture, ethnicity, and group affiliations.

Denotation   The socially agreed upon meaning of words; it is the meaning shared by members of a speech community.

Depth (of self-disclosure)   How personal you become when discussing a particular subject that reveals something about yourself.

Description   Verbal reports that sketch what we perceive from our senses.

Descriptivists   Linguists who describe how language is used, not how it should be used, and identify rules for using a language effectively as a tool of communication.

Destructive conflict   Conflict that is characterized by escalation, retaliation, domination, competition, cross-complaining, defensiveness, and inflexibility.

Dialectics   Impulses that push and pull us in opposite directions simultaneously within our relationships with others.

Directive Style (of leadership)   Leaders tell group members what to do and they expect compliance.

Directory   An Internet tool in which humans edit indexes of Web pages that match, or link with, key words typed in a search window.

Discontinuous change decisions   Major changes that depart significantly from the direction a team is taking currently.

Displacement   The human ability to use language to talk about objects, ideas, events, and relations that don't just exist in the here and now and may not exist at all except in our minds.

Display rules   Culture-specific prescriptions that dictate appropriateness of behaviors.

Divergence   Differences that separate people.

Dogmatism   The belief in the self-evident truth of one's opinion.

Dominance   The exercise of power over others.

Door-in-the-face strategy   A version of the contrast effect.

Downward communication   Messages that flow from superordinates to subordinates in a hierarchical organization.

Dynamism   The enthusiasm and energy exhibited by a speaker.

Dysfunctional speech anxiety   When the intensity of the fight or flight response prevents an individual from performing a speech appropriately and effectively.

Effectiveness   How well an individual progresses toward the achievement of his or her goal.

Elaboration Likelihood Model (of persuasion)   Theory of how persuasion works positing two routes to persuasion—the central route that requires mindfulness and the peripheral route that is relatively mindless.

Emblem   A gesture that has a precise meaning separate from verbal communication and is usually recognized across an entire culture or co-culture, sometimes even across cultures.

Empathic listening   Requires listeners to take the perspective of the other person and to listen for what that person needs.

Empathy   Thinking and feeling what you perceive another to be thinking and feeling.

Empowerment   Power derived from enhancing the capabilities and influence of individuals and groups.

Equivocation   Using language that permits more than one plausible meaning, often as a substitute for outright lying.

Ethics (in communication)   Set of standards for judging the moral correctness of communication behavior.

Ethnocentrism   The notion that one's own culture is superior to any other. It is the idea that other cultures should be measured by the degree to which they live up to one's own cultural standards.

Ethos   Aristotle's version of credibility characterized by "good sense, good moral character, and good will" of the speaker.

Euphemism   Form of linguistic Novocain whereby word choices numb us to or camouflage unpleasant or offensive realities.

Evaluations   Value judgments made about individuals and about their performance exhibited as praise, recognition, admiration, criticism, contempt, or blame.

Evaluative response   A judgment by a listener about a person's conduct.

Explicit norms   Norms that specifically and overtly identify acceptable and unacceptable behavior in groups.

Extemporaneous speech   A speech delivered from a prepared outline or notes.

Facial feedback hypothesis   Facial expressions can influence emotions.

Fallacies   Errors in evidence and reasoning.

Feedback   The receiver's verbal and nonverbal responses to a message.

Feminine culture   A culture that exhibits stereotypic feminine traits such as affection, nurturance, sensitivity, compassion, and emotional expressiveness.

Fields of experience   Cultural background, ethnicity, geographic location, extent of travel, and general personal experiences accumulated over the course of a lifetime that influence messages.

Flaming   A cyberterm for an abusive, attacking e-mailed message.

Flooding   When you can no longer think clearly because conflict triggers intense emotional reactions.

Forgiveness   Letting go of feelings of revenge and desires to retaliate.

Formal roles   Assigned positions usually in an organizational structure.

Framing   The influence wording has on our perception of choices.

Friendship-warmth touch   Touch communication that can be ambiguous but is intended to express friendship between people.

Functional speech anxiety   When the fight or flight response is managed and stimulates an optimum speech presentation.

Functional-professional touch   Instrumental touch communication that is limited to the requirements of the situation.

Fundamental attribution error   Overemphasizing personal characteristics and underemphasizing situational causes of other people's behavior.

Gender   Socially constructed learned feminine and masculine role characteristics and behavior derived from communicating with others.

General purpose (of speech)   Identifies the overall goal of a speech (to inform, describe, explain, demonstrate, persuade, celebrate, memorialize, entertain, or eulogize).

Glazing over   When listeners' attention wanders and daydreaming or sleeping occurs.

Group   Three or more individuals, interacting for the achievement of some common purpose(s), who influence and are influenced by one another.

Groupthink   An ineffective process of group decision-making in which members excessively emphasize cohesiveness and agreement instead of skepticism and optimum decision-making.

Hasty generalization   A broad claim based on too few or unrepresentative examples.

Hearing   The physiological process of registering sound waves as they hit the eardrums.

Hierarchy   The rank ordering of members of an organization.

High power-distance cultures   Cultures with a relatively strong emphasis on maintaining power differences.

High-context communication style   Indirect verbal expression; significant information is derived from contextual cues, such as relationships, situations, setting, and time; typically found in collectivist cultures.

Hindsight bias   The tendency to look back after a fact or outcome has been revealed and say to yourself, "I knew that all along."

Horizontal communication   Messages that flow between individuals with equal power in organizations.

Hostile environment sexual harassment   Insult, ridicule, humor, or intimidation of a sexual nature that makes the work environment an unpleasant, even threatening place to remain.

Hyperbole   Exaggeration for effect that is not meant to be taken literally.

Hypercompetitiveness   The excessive emphasis on beating others to achieve one's goals.

Hypothetical examples   Instances that describe an imaginary situation, one that is concocted to make a point, illustrate an idea, or identify a general principle.

Identification (in persuasion)   The affiliation and connection between speaker and listeners.

Illustrators   Gestures that help explain what one person says to another person.

Implicit norms   Observable patterns of behavior exhibited by group members that identify acceptable and unacceptable conduct.

Impromptu speech   A speech delivered off the cuff without notes.

Inclusion-seclusion dialectic   The desire to spend time alone with one's partner and also spend time together with others outside of the relationship.

Individual achievement   The realization of personal goals without having to defeat an opponent.

Individualist culture   A culture with an "I" consciousness; individuals see themselves as loosely linked to each other and largely independent of group identification.

Inferences   Statements or generalizations about the unknown based on the known.

Inferential error   A mistaken conclusion that results from the assumption that inferences are factual descriptions of reality instead of interpretations of varying accuracy made by individuals.

Informal roles   Roles that identify functions not positions; they usually emerge naturally from group transactions.

Information bulimia   Cramming information into short-term memory.

Informational listening   Listening for comprehension of a speaker's message.

Integration   A collaborating strategy that finds alternatives that meet the goals of all parties in a conflict.

Intensity   Concentrated stimuli; an extreme degree of emotion, thought, or activity.

Interdependence   When all parties rely on each other to achieve goals.

Internal summary   Restates a key point or points of a speech in the body of the speech.

Interpersonal communication   Dyadic communication; a transaction that takes place between two people.

Interpersonal relationship   A connection two people have to each other because of an association (brother-sister), an attraction (friends), or a power distribution (boss-employee).

Interpreting response   A listener expressing what he or she thinks is the underlying meaning of a situation presented by another person.

Interrupting   When one person stops speaking when another person starts speaking.

Interviewing   A purposeful, planned conversation, characterized by extensive verbal interaction.

Intimacy   The feeling of closeness in a relationship; the degree to which a person can share feelings freely with another person.

Jargon   The specialized language of a profession, trade, or group.

Judgments   Subjective evaluations of objects, events, or ideas.

Knowledge   An understanding of what is required by a communication context to be effective and appropriate.

Language   A structured system of symbols for communicating meaning.

Latitude of acceptance   Positions a person finds acceptable or at least tolerable.

Latitude of noncommitment   Positions that provoke only a neutral or ambivalent response from individuals.

Latitude of rejection   Those positions people find objectionable because they are too far from their anchor attitude.

Leadership   A transactional influence process whose principle purpose is group goal achievement produced by competent communication.

Legitimate authority   Someone who is perceived to have a right to direct others' behavior because of his or her position, title, role, experience, or knowledge.

Lexicon   The total vocabulary of a language.

Linguistic determinism   The claim that we are prisoners of our native language, unable to think certain thoughts or perceive in certain ways because of the grammatical structure and lexicon of our language.

Linguistic relativity   The claim that the grammar and lexicon of our native language powerfully influences but does not imprison our thinking and perception.

Listening   The process of receiving, constructing and reconstructing meaning from, and responding to spoken and/or nonverbal messages.

Logos   Aristotle's conception of building arguments based on logic and evidence.

Love and intimacy touch   Touch that is reserved for a very few, special individuals, that is not sexual but does express tenderness between individuals.

Low power-distance cultures   Cultures with a relatively weak emphasis on maintaining power differences.

Low-context communication style   Verbally precise, direct, and explicit method of communicating usually found in individualistic cultures.

Manipulative communication   An attempt by one person to maneuver another toward the manipulator's goal.

Manipulators   Gestures with no particular meaning made by one part of the body, usually the hands, that rub, pick, squeeze, clean, or groom another part of the body.

Masculine culture   A culture that exhibits stereotypic masculine traits such as male dominance, ambitiousness, assertiveness, competitiveness, and drive for achievement.

Masculine-generic gender references   The use of masculine nouns and pronouns to include references to both women and men.

Meaning   The conscious pattern humans create out of their interpretation of experience; making sense of our world.

Message   Stimulus that produces meaning.

Metaphor   An implied comparison of two seemingly dissimilar things.

Metasearch engine   An Internet tool that will send your keyword request to several search engines at once.

Mindful   Thinking about our communication with others and continually working at changing what we do to become more effective.

Mindless   Not being cognizant of our communication with others and putting little or no effort into improving it.

Misattribution   An attribution about the reason for an event given by a foreigner that differs from that typically given by a member of the host culture.

Mixed messages   Inconsistencies or outright contradictions between verbal and nonverbal messages.

Mixed metaphor   The use of two or more vastly different metaphors in a single expression.

Morpheme   The smallest unit of meaning in a language.

Multiculturalism   Social-intellectual movement that promotes the value of diversity as a core principle and insists that all cultural groups be treated with respect and as equals.

Murphy's Law   The assertion that anything that can go wrong likely will go wrong.

Muscle dysmorphia   A preoccupation with one's body size and a perception that, though very muscular, one actually looks puny.

Myth   A belief that is contradicted by fact.

Negative synergy   The product of joint action of group members that produces a result worse than that expected based on perceived individual abilities and skills of members.

Negativity bias   A strong tendency to weigh negative information more heavily than positive information, especially when forming perceptions of others.

Netiquette   Etiquette (rules of proper conduct) when using the Internet.

Neutralizing   A strategy to manage dialectics in which a compromise is struck between opposing impulses by partially satisfying both impulses.

Niches   Specialized segments of an audience.

Noise   Any interference with effective transmission and reception of messages.

Nominal group technique   Creative problem-solving method in which team members work alone to generate ideas, those ideas are announced to the group, and team members' ranking of ideas result in the group's top preferences.

Nonverbal communication   Sharing meaning with others nonlinguistically.

Norms   The rules that indicate what group members have to do (obligation), should do (preference), and cannot do (prohibition) if they want to accomplish specific goals.

Onomatopoeic words   Those words that imitate sounds such as *bang* and *awchoo*.

Openness   A willingness to communicate.

Openness-closedness dialectic   The tension in relationships between accessibility and privacy.

Operational definition   Specifies measurable behaviors or experiences that indicate what a word means to the user.

Organizational culture   A particular way of doing things, certain shared values, and specific ways members talk about their organization.

Participative style (of leadership)   Leaders encourage all group members to engage meaningfully in discussions and decision-making.

Pathos   Aristotle's conception of emotional appeals used for persuasion.

Pattern recognition   The process of piecing together seemingly unrelated information into a plan, design, or whole picture.

Perception   The process of selecting, organizing, and interpreting data from our senses.

Perceptual set   A mental predisposition to perceive a stimulus in a fixed way as the result of an expectation.

Performance orientation   Public speakers focusing on the do's and don'ts of giving a speech.

Personal relationship   A close connection between two people that is characterized by strong emotional bonding and commitment.

Persuasion   A communication process of converting, modifying, or maintaining the attitudes, beliefs, or behavior of others.

Phonemes   The individual sounds that compose a specific spoken language.

Physical noise   External, environmental distractions, such as startling sounds, poorly heated rooms, and the like that divert our attention from the message sent by a source.

Physiological noise   Biological influences such as sweaty palms, pounding heart, and butterflies in the stomach induced by speech anxiety, or feeling sick or exhausted at work that interfere with sending and receiving messages.

Power   The ability to influence the attainment of goals sought by oneself or others.

Power resource   Anything that enables individuals to achieve their goals, assist others to achieve their goals, or interferes with the goal attainment of others.

Power-distance dimension   Cultural variations in the acceptability of unequal distribution of power in relationships, institutions, and organizations.

Predictability-novelty dialectic   The desire for both stability and change within a relationship.

Prescriptivism   The perspective that tells us that we should unerringly follow standardized rules for the dominant language of a culture.

Prevention   Power used to thwart the influence of others.

Primacy effect   The tendency to perceive information presented first as more important than information presented later.

Principle of least interest   The person who cares less about continuing a relationship usually has more power.

Probing response   A listener seeking more information from others by asking questions.

Productivity (in language)   The capacity of language to transform a small number of phonemes into whatever words, phrases, and sentences that we require to communicate our abundance of thoughts, ideas, and feelings.

Productivity (in groups)   The degree to which a group accomplishes its work efficiently and effectively.

Proposition   The primary overriding claim for a persuasive speech.

Proposition of fact   The primary overriding claim in a persuasive speech that alleges a truth.

Proposition of policy   The primary overriding claim in a persuasive speech that calls for a significant change from how problems are currently handled.

Proposition of value   A primary overriding claim in a persuasive speech that calls for a judgment that assesses the worth or merit of an idea, object, or practice.

Prototype   The most representative or "best" example of something.

Provisionalism   Qualifying our statements with words such as possibly, probably, perhaps, maybe, and could be, and avoiding absolutes such as always, never, must, can't and won't.

Pseudolistening   When someone pretends to listen.

Psychological noise   Preconceptions, biases, and assumptions that interfere with effective message transmission and reception.

Psychological reactance   The more someone tries to control our behavior and restrict our choices, the more we are inclined to resist such efforts, even do the opposite behavior.

Quality circles   Teams composed of employees in an organization who volunteer to work on a similar task and attempt to solve a particular problem.

Quid pro quo sexual harassment   When the more powerful person requires sexual favors usually from the less powerful individual in exchange for keeping a job, getting a high grade in a class, landing an employment promotion, and the like.

Random sample   Portion of the population chosen in such a manner that every member of the entire population has an equal chance of being selected.

Readiness   The ability of group members, their motivation, and their experience with relevant tasks that make them suitable for assuming greater responsibility for decision-making and problem solving.

Real examples   Actual occurrences used to illustrate an idea, make a point, or identify a general principle.

Re-bid   An attempt to connect with another person after an initial bid has been ignored.

Receiver   Decoder of messages.

Recency effect   The tendency to evaluate others on the basis of the most recent information or evidence available.

Referents   The objects, events, ideas, or relationships referred to by words.

Reframing (dialectics)   A strategy for managing dialectics in which two seemingly contradictory impulses are viewed from a new and different frame of reference.

Reframing (problem-solving technique)   The creative process of breaking rigid thinking by placing a problem in a different frame of reference.

Refutation   The process of answering opposing arguments in a debate or disagreement.

Relationship dimension (of messages)   How the message defines or redefines the association between individuals.

Relevance (of evidence)   Supporting evidence must relate directly to the claim made.

Resistance   Covert, ambiguous noncompliance with the dictates of more powerful individuals.

Revelation-concealment dialectic   The dilemma you face when wanting to share information about your relationship with another person with those outside the relationship yet also wanting to conceal the relationship for various reasons.

Rhetorical question   A question asked by a speaker that the audience answers mentally, but not out loud.

Role fixation   Playing a group role rigidly with little or no inclination to try other roles.

Roles   Patterns of behavior that group members are expected to exhibit.

Rule   A followable prescription that indicates what behavior is obligated, preferred, or prohibited in certain contexts.

Sapir-Whort hypothesis   A claim that we are either prisoners of our native language, unable to think certain thoughts or perceive in certain ways (linguistic determinism), or that our language powerfully influences but does not imprison our thinking and perceptions (linguistic relativity).

Schemas   Mental frameworks that create meaningful patterns from stimuli.

Script   A predictable sequence of events that indicates what we are expected to do in a given situation.

Search engine   An Internet tool that computer generates indexes of Web pages that match, or link with, key words typed in a search window.

Segmenting   A strategy to manage dialectics in which certain parts of a relationship are divided into separate domains and some of these domains are declared off limits.

Selecting   A strategy for managing dialectics in which one contradictory impulse is given attention and another is ignored.

Selective memory bias   The tendency to remember information that supports our stereotypes but to forget information that contradicts them.

Self-concept   The sum total of everything that encompasses the self-referential term "me"; your identity or self-perception.

Self-disclosure   The process of purposely revealing to others information about ourselves that they otherwise would not know.

Self-esteem   The evaluative element of self-perception; self-appraisal or your perception of self-worth, attractiveness, and social competence.

Self-managed work teams   Self-regulating groups in organizations that complete an entire task.

Self-reflexiveness   The ability to use language to talk about language.

Self-selected sample   Individuals, usually the most committed, aroused, or motivated, choose themselves to participate in a survey, poll, or study.

Self-serving bias   The tendency to attribute our successful behavior to ourselves (personal traits) but to assign external circumstances (situations) to our unsuccessful behavior.

Semantic noise   Word choice that is confusing or distracting that interferes with accurate message transmission and reception.

Semantic reaction   A delayed, thoughtful response to language that seeks to decipher the users' intended meaning of a word.

Sender   Initiator and encoder of messages.

Sensitivity   Receptive accuracy whereby we can detect, decode, and comprehend signals in our social environment.

Sensory acuity   The level of sensitivity of our senses.

Sex   Biological differences between males and females.

Sexual touch   Intimate touch between individuals.

Shift response   A competitive vying for attention and focus on self by shifting topics.

Signal reaction   An automatic, conditioned response to a symbol (usually a word).

Signposts   Organizational markers for a speech that indicate the structure of a speech and notify listeners that a particular point is about to be addressed.

Simile   An explicit comparison of two seemingly dissimilar things using the words *like* or *as*.

Skepticism   The process of listening to claims, evaluating evidence and reasoning supporting those claims, and drawing conclusions based on probabilities.

Smoothing   A collaborative strategy that attempts to calm the agitated feelings of those involved in a conflict.

Social dimension (of groups)   Relationships between group members and the impact these relationships have on the group.

Social judgment theory   A theory of persuasion that focuses on how close or distant an audience's position on a controversial issue is from its anchor attitude.

Social loafing   The tendency of individuals to reduce their work effort when they join groups.

Social-polite touch   Touch communication that occurs during initial introductions, business relationships, and formal occasions.

Spamming   Sending unsolicited e-mail, especially advertisements for products or activities.

Specific purpose statement (of speech)   A concise, precise declaration composed of simple, clear language that encompasses both the general purpose and the central idea of a speech and indicates what the speaker hopes to accomplish with the speech.

Speech anxiety   Those situations when an individual reports that he or she is afraid to deliver a speech.

Standardization   A set of formal rules dictated by a dominant culture governing how everyone, even members of co-cultures, ought to speak and write a language, especially in formal situations.

Stereotype   A generalization about a group or category of people.

Stonewalling   A form of the avoiding style of conflict management exhibited by refusing to discuss problems or by physically leaving when one person is complaining, disagreeing, or attacking the other person.

Style (of speaking)   Words chosen to express your thoughts and the ways you use language to bring your thoughts to life for an audience.

Style shifting (language)   Using language flexibly to suit the context.

Stylistic similarity   An identification strategy of persuasion in which a speaker attempts to look and act similarly to his or her audience.

Substantive similarity   An identification strategy of persuasion in which a speaker tries to establish common ground between the speaker and his or her audience.

Support response   A cooperative effort to focus attention on the other person, not oneself during conversation.

Supporting response   Acknowledges the feelings of the speaker and tries to boost the person's confidence.

Supportiveness   A confirmation of the worth and value of others and a willingness to help others be successful.

Synergy   By individuals working together as a group, the work of group members yields a greater total effect than the sum of the individual members' efforts could have produced.

Syntax   The rules that govern appropriate combinations of words into sentences.

Systematic desensitization   A technique used to control speech anxiety involving incremental exposure to increasingly threatening stimuli coupled with relaxation techniques.

Task dimension (of groups)   The work performed by a group and its impact on the group.

Team   A small number of people with complementary skills who are equally committed to a common purpose, goals, and working approach for which they hold themselves mutually accountable.

Teamwork   The process of members exercising competent communication within the framework of teams.

Technology   A tool to accomplish some purpose.

Territoriality   A predisposition to defend a fixed geographic area, or territory, as one's exclusive domain.

Traits   Relatively enduring characteristics of a person that highlight differences between people and are displayed in most situations.

Triangular Theory of Love   The interaction among three elements of love—intimacy, passion, and commitment—that determines seven different types of love between people.

True believers   Those who willingly accept claims by authorities or valued sources without question, and protect beliefs based on these claims by embracing confirmation bias.

Trustworthiness   How truthful or honest an audience perceives a speaker to be.

Turning against response   An overtly negative rejection of a connecting bid.

Turning away response   Ignoring a connecting bid or acting preoccupied when a bid is offered.

Turning points (in relationships)   Key moments that move a relationship forward, such as sharing an interest, disclosing a personal secret, or lending something important.

Turning toward response   Reacting positively to a connecting bid.

Understanding response   A listener checking his or her perceptions for comprehension of the speaker's message or paraphrasing the message to check for accuracy.

Upward communication   Messages that flow from subordinates to superordinates in an organization.

Values   The most deeply felt, generally shared views of what is deemed good, right, or worthwhile behavior or thinking.

Variable   Anything that can change.

Virtual library   An Internet search tool that combines Internet technology and standard library techniques for cataloguing and appraising information.

Vividness effect   When graphic, outrageous, shocking, controversial, and dramatic events distort our perceptions of the facts, and we listen to the dramatic example and conclude that we have problems wholly out of proportion to the facts.

Vocal fillers   The insertion of *uhm, ah, like, you know, know what I mean, whatever* and additional variants that substitute for pauses when speaking and often draw attention to themselves.

REFERENCES

Abell, G. (1981). Astrology. In G. Abell & B. Seiger (Eds.), *Science and the paranormal*. New York: Charles Scribner's Sons.

Abramson, J. (1998, November 20). Starr: A man with two missions. *San Jose Mercury News*, p. A16.

Adam, D. (2001). Lifelines: Boom and bust. Retrieved from http://www.nature.com/nsu/010118/010118-5.html.

Adams, C. C. (1992). *Boontling: An American lingo*. Philo, CA: Mountain House Press.

Adelmann, P. (1995). *Why don't men do more housework? A job characteristics exploration of gender and housework satisfaction*. Working paper, Center for Urban Affairs and Policy Research.

Adelmann, P. K., & Zajonc, R. B. (1989). Facial efference and the experience of emotion. *Annual Review of Psychology, 40*, 249–280.

Adler, J., & Springen, K. (1999, May 3). How to fight back. *Newsweek*, 36–38.

Adler, J. E. (1998, January/February). Open minds and the argument from ignorance. *Skeptical Inquirer*, 41–44.

Adler, M. J. (1983). *How to speak, how to listen*. New York: Macmillan.

Adler, R. (1977). *Confidence in communication: A guide to assertive and social skills*. New York: Holt, Rinehart & Winston.

Adler, R., & Elmhorst, J. M. (2002). *Communicating at Work: Principles and practices for business and the professions*. New York: McGraw-Hill.

Adler, R., & Towne, N. (1993 & 1999). *Looking out, looking in*. Fort Worth, TX: Harcourt Brace.

Advertising is hazardous to your health. (1986, July). *University of California, Berkeley Wellness Letter*, 1–2.

Aguayo, R. (1990). *Dr. Deming: The American who taught the Japanese about quality*. New York: Simon & Schuster.

Ahrons, C. (1994). *The good divorce: Keeping your family together when your marriage comes apart*. New York: Harper Perennial.

Akert, R. M. (1998). *Terminating romantic relationships: The role of personal responsibility and gender*. Unpublished manuscript, Wellesley College.

Allan, K., & Burridge, K. (1991). *Euphemism and dysphemism: Language used as shield and weapon*. New York: Oxford University Press.

Allen, G. (1996). Military drug testing. *Winning Orations*, 80–83.

Allen, M. (1991). Comparing the persuasiveness of one-sided and two-sided messages using meta-analysis. *Western Journal of Speech Communication, 55*, 390–404.

Allen, M. (1993). Determining the persuasiveness of one- and two-sided messages. In M. Allen & R. Preiss (Eds.), *Prospects and precautions in the use of meta-analysis*. Dubuque, IA: Brown & Benchmark.

Allen, M. (1998). Methodological considerations when examining a gendered world. In D. J. Canary & K. Dindia (Eds.), *Sex differences and similarities in communication*. Mahwah, NJ: Lawrence Erlbaum.

Alter, J. (1998, July 13). Something in the coffee. *Newsweek*, 66.

Altman, I., & Taylor, D. (1973). *Social penetration: The development of interpersonal relationships*. New York: Holt, Rinehart & Winston.

Amato, P., & Loomis, L. (1995). Parental divorce, marital conflicts, and offspring well-being during early adulthood. *Social Forces, 73*, 895–915.

American Society of Plastic Surgeons (2000). *Gender distribution 2000: Cosmetic surgery*. Retrieved from www.plasticsurgery. org.

Amoral majority "fesses up." (1991, April 19). *San Jose Mercury News*, p. A1.

Amparano, J. (1997, January 23). Taking good care of workers pays off. *The Arizona Republic*, pp. E1, E3.

An intense look at alternative medicine. (1998, November 11). *San Jose Mercury News*, p. A5.

Anatomy of a massacre. (1999, May 3). *Newsweek*, 25–31.

Andersen, P. (1999). *Nonverbal communication: Forms and functions*. Mountain View, CA: Mayfield.

Andersen, P., Murphy, M., & Wendt-Wasca, N. (1985). Teachers' reports of students' nonverbal communication in the classroom: A development study in grades K–12. *Communication Education, 34*, 292–307.

Andersen, P., Todd-Mancillas, W., & Di-Clemente, L. (1980). The effects of pupil dilation on physical, social, and task attraction. *Australian Scan: Journal of Human Communication, 7 & 8*, 89–95.

Andersen, P. A., & Guerrero, L. K. (1998). In P. A. Andersen & L. K. Guerrero (Eds.), *Handbook of communication and emotion*. New York: Academic Press.

Anderson, C. A. (1999). Attributional style, depression, and loneliness: A cross-cultural comparison of American and Chinese students. *Personality and Social Psychology Bulletin, 25*, 482–499.

Anderson, N. (1981). *Foundations of information integration theory.* New York: Academic Press.

Anderson, R., & Killenberg, G. (1999). *Interviewing: Speaking, listening, and learning for professional life.* Mountain View, CA: Mayfield.

Anderson, R., & Ross, V. (1994). *Questions on communications: A practical introduction to theory.* New York: St. Martin's Press.

Angier, N. (2002, March 5). One lifetime is not enough for a trip to distant stars. *The New York Times.* Retrieved from www.nytimes.com/2002/03/05/science/space/05TRAV.html.

Ansen, D. (1997, July 14). The all American hero: James Stewart, 1908–1997. *Newsweek*, 74–78.

Anti-sweatshop activist brings delegates to their feet. (2002, March/April). *California Teacher*, p. 4

Antonucci, M. (1998, June 6). Hope's alive and quipping. *San Jose Mercury News*, p. A1.

Antonucci, M., & Quinn, M. (1998, January 27). Media accused of reckless reporting. *San Jose Mercury News*, p. A12.

Archer, J. (2000). Sex differences in aggression between heterosexual partners: A meta-analytic review. *Psychological Bulletin, 126*, 651–680.

Armas, G. C. (2000, April 24). Women cracking the glass ceiling. *Santa Cruz Sentinel*, pp. A1, A14.

Aronson, E. (1999). *The social animal.* San Francisco: W. H. Freeman.

Aronson, E., Fried, C., & Stone, J. (1991). Overcoming denial and increasing the intentions to use condoms through the induction of hypocrisy. *American Journal of Public Health, 81*, 1636–1638.

Arrillaga, P. (2001, August 15). Trauma of 'civilizing.' *San Jose Mercury News*, p. 13A.

At the beep, USC fires Robinson. (1997, December 18). *San Jose Mercury News*, p. D2.

Atkins, L. (2001, July 26). From computer meek to geezer geek. *San Francisco Chronicle*, p. A25.

Aune, K. S., Kim, M., & Hu, A. (2000). *"Well I've been talking long enough about me. . . . What do you think of my accomplishments?": The relationship between self-construals, narcissism, compulsive talking, and bragging.* Paper presented at the meeting of the National Communication Association, Seattle, WA.

Avila, J. (2001, August 3). Women bringing home the bacon. Retrieved from www.msnbc.com/news.

Axtell, R. E. (1998). *Gestures: The do's and taboos of body language around the world.* New York: John Wiley.

Ayres, J., & Hopf, T. (1995). *Coping with speech anxiety.* Norwood, NJ: Ablex.

Bach, G., & Goldberg, H. (1972). *Creative aggression.* New York: Avon.

Bahrick, H. P. (1984). Semantic memory content in permastore: Fifty years of memory for Spanish learned in school. *Journal of Experimental Psychology, 113*, 1–35.

Bailey, B. (1996, November 2). Perot says Clinton's promises are like vows of a bank robber. *San Jose Mercury News*, p. A21.

Balgopal, P., Ephross, P., & Vassil, T. (1992). Self-help groups and professional helpers. In R. Cathcart & L. Samovar (Eds.), *Small group communication: A reader.* Dubuque, IA: Wm. C. Brown.

Baran, S. (1999). *Introduction to mass communication: Media literacy and culture.* Mountain View, CA: Mayfield.

Barker, L., Edwards, C., Davis, K., & Holly, F. (1981). An investigation of proportional time spent in various communication activities by college students. *Journal of Applied Communication Research, 8*, 101–109.

Barker, L., & Watson, K. (2000). *Listen up: How to improve relationships, reduce stress, and be more productive by using the power of listening.* New York: St. Martin's Press.

Barnard, B. (1994, August 6). Could you cheer for the Denver Darkies? *Desert News*, p. A9.

Barnes, S. B. (2001). *Online connections: Internet interpersonal relationships.* Cresskill, NJ: Hampton Press.

Barnett, T. (1996, April 19). A clean slate, a fresh start. *Santa Cruz Sentinel*, p. A2.

Baron, R. A. (1988). Negative effects of destructive criticism: Impact on conflict self-efficacy, and task performance. *Journal of Applied Psychology, 73*, 199–207.

Baron, R. A. (1990). Countering the effects of destructive criticism: The relative efficacy of four interventions. *Journal of Applied Psychology, 75*, 235–243.

Barreca, R. (1991). *They used to call me Snow White . . . but I drifted: Women's strategic use of humor.* New York: Viking Penguin.

Barry, D. (1991). *Dave Barry's guide to life.* New York: Wings Books.

Bauer, B. (1996, February 24). Undue pride tied to violence. *San Jose Mercury News*, p. A20.

Bauer, L., & Trudgill, P. (1998). *Language myths.* New York: Penguin Books.

Baumeister, R., Smart, L., & Boden, J. (1996). Relation of the threatened egotism to violence and aggressions: The dark side of high self-esteem. *Psychological Review, 103*, 5–33.

Bavelas, J., Black, N., Choil, N., & Mullett, J. (1990). *Equivocal communication.* Newbury Park, CA: Sage.

Bavley, A. (1998, October 23). Girth of a nation. *Santa Cruz Sentinel*, p. A1.

Baxter, L. (1990). Dialectical contradictions in relationship development. *Journal of Social and Personal Relationships, 7*, 69–88.

Baxter, L. (1994). A dialogic approach to relationship management. In D. Canary & L. Stafford (Eds.), *Communication and relational maintenance.* New York: Academic Press.

Baxter, L., & Montgomery, B. (1996). *Relating: Dialogues and dialect.* New York: Guilford Press.

Baxter, L. A. (1992). Forms and functions of intimate play in personal relationships. *Human Communication Research, 18*, 336–363.

Baxter, L. A., & Bullis, C. (1986). Turning points in developing romantic relationships. *Human Communication Research, 12*, 469–494.

Baxter, L. A., & Wilmot, W. W. (1984). "Secret tests": Social strategies for acquiring information about the state of the relationship. *Human Communication Research, 11*, 171–201.

Bazil, J. (1997). The ferrous wheel of death. *Winning Orations*, 118–121.

Beating the odds. (2002, August 5). *People*, pp. 78–79.

Bechler, C., & Johnson, S. (1995). Leadership and listening: A study of member perceptions. *Small Group Research, 26*, 77–85.

Bednar, A. S., & Oleny, R. J. (1987, December). Communication needs of recent graduates. *Bulletin of the Association for Business Communication*, 22–23.

Begley, S. (1998, January 19). Aping language. *Newsweek*, pp. 40–41.

Begley, S. (1998, July 13). You're OK, I'm terrific: Self-esteem backfires. *Newsweek*, 69.

Belbin, R. (1996). *Team roles at work*. London: Butterworth-Heinemann.

Bellamy, R., & Walker, J. (1996). *Television and the remote control*. New York: Guilford Press.

Bem, S. L., & Bem, D. J. (1973). Does sex-biased job advertising "aid and abet" sex discrimination? *Journal of Applied Social Psychology, 3*, 6–18.

Benedetto, R. (2000, October 10). Poll: Bush more honest, likable. *USA Today*, p. 1A.

Benne, K., & Sheats, P. (1948). Functional roles of group members. *Journal of Social Issues, 4*, 41–49.

Bennett, A. (1995, January 10). Economics meeting. *Wall Street Journal*, p. B1.

Bennis, W., & Biederman, P. (1997). *Organizing genius: The secrets of creative collaboration*. New York: Addison-Wesley.

Bennis, W., & Nanus, B. (1985). *Leaders: The strategies for taking charge*. New York: Harper & Row.

Benoit, W., & Benoit, P. (1987). Everyday argument practice of naive social actors. In J. Wenzel (Ed.), *Argument and critical practices*. Annandale, VA: Speech Communication Association.

Benton, B. (1995). Very fake badges, very real guns. *Winning Orations*, 31–33.

Berger, C. R., & Calabrese, R. J. (1975). Some explorations in initial interaction and beyond: Toward a developmental theory of interpersonal communication. *Human Communication Research, 1*, 99–112.

Berko, R. (1996, May). News and statistics in the world of education. *Spectra*, 9.

Berko, R., & Brooks, M. (1994). *Rationale kit: Information supporting the speech communication discipline and its programs*. Annandale, VA: Speech Communication Association.

Berko, R., Rosenfeld, L., & Samovar, L. (1997). *Connecting: A culture-sensitive approach to interpersonal communication competency*. Fort Worth, TX: Harcourt Brace.

Berlo, D. (1960). *The process of communication*. New York: Holt, Rinehart & Winston.

Bernieri, F. J. (2001). Toward a taxonomy of interpersonal sensitivity. In J. A. Hall & F. J. Bernieri (Eds.), *Interpersonal sensitivity: Theory and measurement*. Mahwah, NJ: Lawrence Erlbaum Associates.

Berns, N. (2001). Degendering the problem and gendering the blame: Political discourse on women and violence. *Gender & Society, 15*, 262–281.

Bernthal, J. (2001, June 15). Stuttering experiment cannot be justified. *San Jose Mercury News*, p. 11B.

Berscheid, E., Schneider, M, & Omoto, A. M. (1989). Issues in studying close relationships: Conceptualizing and measuring closeness. In C. Hendrick (Ed.), *Close relationships*. Newbury Park, CA: Sage.

Best English lesson. (1999, December 26). *Parade*, p. 8.

Biggs, C. (2001, January). Instant messaging. *Enterprise Systems Journal, 16*, 42.

Billie, K., & Chatterjee, C. (1998, September/October). The new gender gap. *Psychology Today*, 22.

Billingham, R. E., and Sack, A. R. (1986). Courtship violence and the interactive status of the relationship. *Journal of Adolescent Research, 1*, 315–325.

Bingham, S. (1991). Communication strategies for managing sexual harassment in organizations: Understanding message options and their effects. *Journal of Applied Communication Research, 19*, 88–115.

Birdwhistell, R. (1970). *Kinesis and context*. Philadelphia: University of Pennsylvania Press.

Black, K. (1990a, March). Can getting mad get the job done? *Working Women*, 86–90.

Black, K. (1990b, March). The matter of tears. *Working Women*, 88.

Black, K. (1993, October 31). Dennis: No longer a menace. *Newsday* [fanfare section], 12.

Blake, R., & Mouton, J. (1964). *The managerial grid*. Houston: Gulf Publishing.

Blakely, E., & Snyder, G. (1997). *Fortress America: Gated communities in the United States*. Washington, DC: Brookings Institute.

Blumstein, P., & Schwartz, P. (1983). *American couples: Money, work, sex*. New York: Pocket Books.

Bochner, S., & Hesketh, B. (1994). Power distance, individualism/collectiveness, and job-related attitude in a culturally diverse setting. *Journal of Cross-Cultural Psychology, 25*, 233–258.

Body builders thinking small. (1998, January 6). *San Jose Mercury News*, p. A4.

Boffey, P. (1985, May 30). Rise in science fraud is seen: Need to win cited as a cause. *The New York Times*, p. B5.

Bok, S. (1978). *Lying: Moral choice in public and private life*. New York: Random House.

Bolton, R. (1979). *People skills: How to assert yourself, listen to others, and resolve conflicts*. New York: Simon & Schuster.

Bond, M., Wan, K., Leung, K., & Giacalone, R. (1985). How are responses to verbal insults related to cultural collectivism and power distances? *Journal of Cross-Cultural Psychology, 16*, 111–127.

Booknews. (1994, January 8). *San Jose Mercury News*, p. A2.

Bookwala, J., Frieze, I. H., Smith, C., & Ryan, K. (1992). Predictors of dating violence: A multivariate analysis. *Violence and Victims, 7*, 297–311.

Bormann, E. (1990). *Small group communication: Theory and practice*. New York: Harper & Row.

Bostrom, R. (1970). Patterns of communicative interaction in small groups. *Speech Monographs, 37*, 257–263.

Bower, S., & Bower, G. (1976). *Asserting yourself*. Reading, MA: Addison-Wesley.

Boyett, J., & Boyett, J. (1998). *The guru guide*. New York: John Wiley.

Bradbury, T. N., & Fincham, F. D. (1990). Attributions in marriage: Review and critique. *Psychological Bulletin, 107*, 3–33.

Bradley, B. (1991). *Fundamentals of speech communication: The credibility of ideas*. Dubuque, IA: Wm. C. Brown.

Brehm, J. (1972). *Responses to loss of freedom: A theory of psychological resistance*. Morristown, NJ: General Learning Press.

Brembeck, W., & Howell, W. (1976). *Persuasion: A means of social influence*. Englewood Cliffs, NJ: Prentice-Hall.

Bricking, T. (1997, June 16). Internet blamed for neglect. *The Cincinnati Enquirer.* Retrieved from http://enquirer.com/editions/1997/06/16/loc_hacker.html.

Bridge, K., & Baxter, L. (1992). Blended friendships: Friends and work associates. *Western Journal of Communication, 56,* 200–225.

Brin, D. (1998). *The transparent society: Will technology force us to choose between privacy and freedom?* Reading, MA: Addison-Wesley.

Brislin, R. (1993). *Understanding culture's influences on behavior.* Fort Worth, TX: Harcourt Brace Jovanovich.

Brody, G. (1990, April). Effects of television viewing on family interactions: An observational study. *Family Relations, 29,* 216–220.

Broeder, D. (1959). The University of Chicago jury project. *Nebraska Law Review, 38,* 760–774.

Brooks, L., & Perot, A. (1991). Reporting sexual harassment: Exploring a predicted model. *Psychology of Women Quarterly, 15,* 31–47.

Bross, I., Shapiro, P., & Anderson, B. (1972). How information is carried in scientific sub-language. *Science, 176,* 1303–1309.

Brown, D. (1999, January 16). Sex survey stumbles into political fray; medical editor fired. *San Jose Mercury News,* p. A1.

Brown, R. (1970). The sentences of child and chimpanzee. In R. Brown (Ed.), *Psychology.* New York: Free Press.

Brown, R. (1986). *Social psychology.* New York: Free Press.

Browne, A. (1993). Violence against women by male partners: Prevalence, outcomes, and policy implications. *American Psychologist, 48,* 1077–1087.

Brownell, J. (1990). Perceptions of listening behavior: A management study. *Journal of Business Communication, 27,* 401–416.

Bruch, H. (1978*). The golden cage: The enigma of anorexia nervosa.* Cambridge, MA: Harvard University Press.

Bruch, H. (1980). Preconditions for the development of anorexia nervosa. *American Journal of Psychoanalysis, 40,* 169–172.

Bruck, M., Ceci, S. J., & Heinbrook, H. (1998, February). Reliability and credibility of your children's reports. *American Psychologist, 53,* 136–151.

Bruess, C. J., & Pearson, J. C. (1996). Gendered patterns in family communication. In J. Wood (Ed.), *Gendered relationships.* Newbury Park, CA: Sage.

Bryson, B. (1990). *The mother tongue: English and how it got that way.* New York: William Morrow.

Buckingham, M., & Coffman, C. (1999). *First, break all the rules: What the world's greatest managers do differently.* New York: Simon & Schuster.

Buller, D., & Aune, K. (1992). The effects of speech rate similarity on compliance: Application of communication accommodations theory. *Western Journal of Communication, 56,* 37–53.

Burgoon, J. (1985). Nonverbal signals. In M. Krapps & G. Miller (Eds.), *Handbook of interpersonal communication.* Beverly Hills, CA: Sage.

Burgoon, J., Manusou, V., Mineo, P., & Hale, J. (1985). Effects of gaze on hiring, credibility, attraction, and relational message interpretation. *Journal of Nonverbal Behavior, 9,* 133–146.

Burgoon, J. K., Buller, D. B., & Woodall, W. G. (1996). *Nonverbal communication: The unspoken dialogue.* New York: McGraw-Hill.

Burke, K. (1950). *A rhetoric of motives.* New York: Prentice-Hall.

Burns, J. (1978). *Leadership.* New York: Harper & Row.

Burpitt, W., & Bigoness, W. (1997). Leadership and innovation among teams: The impact of empowerment. *Small Group Research, 28,* 414–423.

Bush, B. (1991). Choices and changes. In O. Peterson (Ed.), *Representative American Speeches, 1990–1991.* New York: H. W. Wilson Company.

Bushman, B., & Baumeister, R. (1998). Threatened egotism, narcissism, self-esteem, and direct and displaced aggression: Does self-love or self-hate lead to violence? *Journal of Personality and Social Psychology, 75,* 219–229.

Business bulletin. (1996, July 18). *Wall Street Journal,* p. A1.

Businesspeople suffering information indigestion. (1996, October 25). *San Jose Mercury News,* p. 1C.

Buss, D. M. (1989). Sex differences in human mate preferences: Evolutionary hypotheses tested in 37 cultures. *Behavioral and Brain Sciences, 12,* 1–49.

Buss, D. M., & Schmitt, D. P. (1993). Sexual strategies theory: An evolutionary perspective on human mating. *Psychological Review, 100,* 204–232.

Cahn, D., & Lloyd, S. (1996). *Family violence from a communication perspective.* Thousand Oaks, CA: Sage.

Campbell, A. (1993). *Men, women, and aggression.* New York: Basic Books.

Campbell, K., & Jerry, E. (1987). Woman and speaker: A conflict in roles. In S. Brehn (Ed.), *Social roles and personal lives.* Westport, CT: Greenwood Press.

Campo-Flores. A. (2002, June 3). A chat-room encounter's tragic end. *Newsweek,* 30.

Canary, D., Emmers-Sommers, T. M., & Faulkner, S. (1997). *Sex and gender difference in personal relationships.* New York: Guilford Press.

Canary, D., & Stafford, L. (1994). Maintaining relationships through strategies and routine interaction. In D. Canary & L. Stafford (Eds.), *Communication and relational maintenance.* New York: Academic Press.

Canary, D. J., & Cupach, W. R. (1988). Relational and episodic characteristics associated with conflict tactics. *Journal of Social and Personal Relationships, 5,* 305–325.

Canary, D. J., Cupach, W. R., Messman, S. J. (1995). *Relationship conflict: Conflict in parent-child, friendship, and romantic relationships.* Thousand Oaks, CA: Sage.

Canary, D. J., & Hause, K. S. (1993). Is there any reason to research sex differences in communication? *Communication Quarterly, 41,* 129–144.

Canary, D. J., & Spitzberg, B. H. (1987). Appropriateness and effectiveness of perception of conflict strategies. *Human Communication Research, 14,* 96.

Canary, D. J., & Spitzberg, B. H. (1989). A model of perceived competence of conflict strategies. *Human Communication Research, 15,* 630–649.

Canfield, J., Hansen, M. V., & Kirberger, K. (1997). *Chicken soup for the teenage soul.* Deerfield Beach, FL: Health Communications.

Caplan, M., & Goldman, M. (1981). Personal space violations as a function of height. *Journal of Social Psychology, 114,* 167–171.

Carey, S. (1977). The child as a word learner. In M. Halle, J. Bresnan, & G. Miller (Eds.), *Linguistic theory and psychological reality.* Cambridge, MA: MIT Press.

Carnevale, A. (1996). *Workplace basics: The skills employers want.* Washington, DC: U.S. Department of Labor Employment and Training Administration.

Carnevale, P., & Probst, T. (1998). Social values and social conflict in creative problem solving. *Journal of Personality and Social Psychology, 74,* 1300–1309.

Carpenter, D. (2000, August 2). Americans' new hang-up: Cell phone rudeness. *Santa Cruz Sentinel,* p. D5.

Carroll, J. B. (Ed.). (1956). *Language, thought, and reality: Selected writings of Benjamin Lee Whorf.* Cambridge, MA: MIT Press.

Carroll, J. L., Volk, K. D., & Hyde, J. S. (1985). Differences between males and females in motives for engaging in sexual intercourse. *Archives of Sexual Behavior, 14,* 131–139.

Carver, T. B., & Vondra, A. A. (1994, May–June). Alternative dispute resolution: Why it doesn't work and why it does. *Harvard Business Review,* 120–130.

Celoria, J. (1997). The counterfeiting of airline safety: An examination of the dangers of bogus airline parts. *Winning Orations,* 79–81.

Charnofsky, H., Ching, R., Dufault, D., Kegley, J., & Whitney, D. (1998, December 16). Final report of Merit Pay Task Force, CSU Academic Senate. Retrieved from www.academic senate.cc.ca.us

Chatman, J., & Barsade, S. (1995). Personality, organizational culture, and cooperation: Evidence from a business simulation. *Administrative Science Quarterly, 40,* 423–443.

Chen, G. (1993). *A Chinese perspective of communication competence.* Paper presented at the annual convention of the Speech Communication Association, Miami Beach, FL.

Chen, G., & Starosta, W. (1998b). *Foundations of intercultural communications.* Boston: Allyn & Bacon.

Chen, G., & Starosta, W. J. (1998a). Chinese conflict management and resolution: Overview and implications. *Intercultural Communication Studies, 7,* 1–16.

Chiarappo, M. (1996, June). I went bald at 33. *Ladies Home Journal,* 36–40.

Childers, A. (1997). Hormone hell. In L. G. Schnoor (Ed.), *Winning Orations.* Northfield, MN: Interstate Oratorical Association.

Children labeled slow learners may be deaf instead. (1978, May 20). *Eugene Register-Guard,* p. C13.

Chmielewski, D. C. (2003, January 31). TV is "casualty" of Internet use. *San Jose Mercury News,* p. 1C, 5C.

Christensen, D., Farina, A., & Boudreau, L. (1980). Sensitivity to nonverbal cues as a function of social competence. *Journal of Nonverbal Behavior, 4,* 145–156.

Christopher, F. S., & Lloyd, S. A. (2000). Physical and sexual aggression in relationships. In C. Hendrick & S. Hendrick (Eds.), *Close relationships: A sourcebook.* Thousand Oaks, CA: Sage.

Ciach, M. (1994). Hepatitis B—What every college student doesn't know. In L. G. Schnoor (Ed.), *Winning orations.* Northfield, MN: Interstate Oratorical Association.

Cialdini, R. (1993). *Influence: Science and practice.* New York: HarperCollins.

Cialdini, R., & Trost (1998). Social influence: Social norms, conformity, and compliance. In D. T. Gilbert, S. T. Fiske, & G. Lindzey (Eds.), *Handbook of social psychology,* Vol. 2. Boston, MA: McGraw-Hill.

Clark, J., & Barber, B. (1994). Adolescents in postdivorce and always married families: Self-esteem and perceptions of father's interest. *Journal of Marriage and the Family, 56,* 608–614.

Clark, R. D., & Hatfield, E. (1989). Gender differences in receptivity to sexual offers. *Journal of Psychology and Human Sexuality, 2,* 39–55.

Clarke, C. (1995). Title unknown. In L. G. Schnoor (Ed.), *Winning orations.* Northfield, MN: Interstate Oratorical Association.

Clendenin, M. (1996, May 25). Buzz cut or bald? *San Jose Mercury News,* p. B1.

Cloven, D., & Roloff, M. (1991). Sense-making activities and interpersonal conflict: Communicative cure for the mulling blues. *Western Journal of Speech Communication, 55,* 134–158.

Coates, J. (1993). *Women, men and language.* New York: Longman.

Cohen, J. (2002, May 16). When to stop an e-mail exchange. *San Jose Mercury News,* p. 3E.

Cohen, S., & Bailey, D. (1997). What makes teams work: Group effectiveness research from the shop floor to the executive suite. *Journal of Management, 23,* 239–291.

Cole, J. I., Suman, M., Schramm, P., van Bel, D., Lunn, B., Maguire, P., Hanson, K., Singh, R., Aquino, J., & Lebo, H. (2000). The UCLA Internet Report: Surveying the digital future. Retrieved from www.ccp.ucla.edu/newsite/pages/internet-report.asp.

Coleman, D., & Straus, M. (1986). Marital power, conflict, and violence in a nationally representative sample of American couples. *Violence and Victims, 1,* 141–157.

Coleman, J. (2001, February 8). India's traditional social system is complicating distribution of relief to earthquake survivors. *San Jose Mercury News,* p. 7A.

Collins, S. (2001). Men's voices and women's choices. *Animal Behaviour, 60,* 773–780.

Colt, G. (1997, August). The magic of touch. *Life,* 53–62.

Conway, F., & Siegelman, J. (1995). *Snapping: America's epidemic of sudden personality changes.* New York: Stillpoint Press.

Coontz, S. (1997). *The way we really are: Coming to terms with America's changing families.* New York: Basic Books.

Cooper, L. (1960). *The rhetoric of Aristotle: An expanded translation with supplementary examples for students of composition and public speaking.* New York: Appleton Century Crafts.

Cooper, V. W. (1994). The disguise of self-disclosure: The relationship ruse of a Soviet spy. *Journal of Applied Communication Research, 22,* 338–347.

Costanzo, M., Archer, D., Aronson, E., & Pettigrew, T. (1986). Energy conservation behavior. *American Psychologist, 41,* 521–528.

Courtright, J. A., & Perse, E. M. (1998). *Communicating Online: A guide to the Internet.* Mountain View, CA: Mayfield.

Cox, T., Lobel, S., & McLeod, P. (1991). Effects of ethnic groups' cultural differences on cooperative and competitive behavior on a group task. *Academy of Management Journal, 34,* 827–847.

Craig, K., & Rand, K. (1998). The perceptually "privileged" group member: Consequences of solo status for African Americans and Whites in task groups. *Small Group Research, 29,* 339–358.

Cram, A. (1997). High school sex education. In L. G. Schnoor (Ed.), *Winning orations.* Northfield, MN: Interstate Oratorical Association.

Crandall, C. (1988). Social contagion of binge eating. *Journal of Personality and Social Psychology, 55*, 588–598.

Crawford, J. (1996, March 21). *Anatomy of the English-only movement: Social and ideological sources of language restrictionism in the United States.* Paper presented at a conference at University of Illinois at Urbana-Champaign, Illinois.

Crawford, W., & Gorman, M. (1996). Coping with electronic information. In J. Dock (Ed.), *The press of ideas: Readings for writers on print culture and the information age.* Boston: St. Martin's Press.

Crossen, C. (1994). *Tainted truth: The manipulation of fact in America.* New York: Simon & Schuster.

Crusco, A., & Wetzel, C. (1984). The Midas touch: The effects of interpersonal touch on restaurant tipping. *Personality and Social Psychology, 10*, 512–517.

Crystal, D. (1997). *The Cambridge encyclopedia of language.* New York: Cambridge University Press.

Cupach, W. R., & Canary, D. J. (1997). *Competence in interpersonal conflict.* Prospect Heights, IL: Waveland Press.

Cupach, W. R., & Spitzberg, B. H. (Eds.). (1994). *The dark side of interpersonal communication.* Hillsdale, NJ: Lawrence Erlbaum.

Curtis, K. (2002, March 8). Critics nip at attorney's trial tactics. *Santa Cruz Sentinel*, pp. A1, A4.

Cytowic, R. (1993). *The man who tasted shapes.* New York: Warner Books.

Dahlberg, T. (2001, June 3). Violence in youth sports reaching an ugly point. *Santa Cruz Sentinel*, pp. C1, C2.

Dale, P. (1972). *Language development: Structures and functions.* Hinsdale, IL: Dryden Press.

Damasio, A. R., & Damasio, H. (1999). Brain and language. In *The Scientific American book of the brain.* New York: Lyons Press.

Davidowitz, M., & Myricm, R. D. (1984). Responding to the bereaved: An analysis of "helping" statements. *Death Education, 8*, 1–10.

Davidson, J. (1996, June 1). The shortcomings of the information age. *Vital Speeches, 62*, 495–503.

Davis, D. (1993). *The five myths of television power, or why the medium is not the message.* New York: Simon & Schuster.

Davis, K. E., & Todd, M. J. (1985). Assessing friendship: Prototypes, paradigm cases and relationship description. In S. W. Duck & D. Perlman (Eds.), *Understanding personal relationships: An interdisciplinary approach.* London: Sage.

De Klerk, U. (1991). Expletives: Men only? *Communication Monographs, 58*, 156–169.

De Moor, A. (1996). Toward a more structured use of information technology in the research community. *American Sociologist, 27*, 91–102.

DeBono, E. (1992). *Sur/petition: Going beyond competition.* New York: HarperCollins.

DeFleur, M., & Dennis, E. (1998). *Understanding mass communication: A liberal arts perspective.* Boston: Houghton Mifflin.

Deike-Sims, C. (1999, Spring). Language war. *True North*, 36–39.

DePaulo, B., & Kasby, D. (1998). Everyday life in close and casual relationships. *Journal of Personality and Social Psychology, 74*, 63–79.

DePaulo, B., Kasby, D., Kirkendol, S., Wyer, M., & Epstein, J. (1996). Lying in everyday life. *Journal of Personal and Social Psychology, 70*, 979–995.

Derber, C. (1979). *The pursuit of attention: Power and individualism in everyday life.* New York: Oxford University Press.

Derlaga, U., & Chaikin, A. (1975). *Sharing intimacy: What we reveal to others and why.* Englewood Cliffs, NJ: Prentice-Hall.

Derlega, V. J. (1984). Self-disclosure and intimate relationships. In V. J. Derlega (Ed.), *Communication, intimacy, and close relationships.* New York: Academic Press.

Deutsch, M. (1985). *Distributive justice: A social-psychological perspective.* New Haven: Yale University Press.

DeVito, J. (1970). *The psychology of speech and language: An introduction to psycholinguistics.* New York: Random House.

DeVito, J. (1990). *Messages: Building interpersonal communication skills.* New York: Harper & Row.

DeVito, J. A. (1986). *The communication handbook: A dictionary.* New York: Harper & Row.

Dewar, H. (1997, March 23). Nominees now face "trial by fire": Senate confirmation process has evolved into political warfare. *Washington Post*, p. A10.

DeZutter, H., & MacDonald, S. (1993). *Who says a dog goes bow-wow?* New York: Bantam.

Diamond, D. (1997, January 31). Behind closed gates. *USA Weekend*, pp. 4–5.

Diamond, R. (1997, August 1). Designing and assessing course and curricula. *Chronicle of Higher Education*, B7.

Diehl, M., & Stroebe, W. (1987). Productivity loss in brainstorming groups: Toward the solution of a riddle. *Journal of Personality and Social Psychology, 53*, 497–509.

Dillard, J. (1994). Rethinking the study of fear appeals: An emotional perspective. *Communication Theory, 4*, 195–323.

Dillard, J. P., & Miller, K. I. (1988). Intimate relationships in task environments. In S. Duck (Ed.), *Handbook of personal relationships.* Sussex, UK: John Wiley.

Dindia, K. (1997, November). *Men are from North Dakota, Women are from South Dakota.* Paper presented at the Speech Communication Association Conference, Chicago, Illinois.

Dindia, K. (1998). "Going into and coming out of the closet": The dialectics of stigma disclosure. In B. M. Montgomery & L. A. Baxter (Eds.), *Dialectical approaches to studying personal relationships.* Mahwah, NJ: Lawrence Erlbaum.

Dindia, K. (2000). Sex differences in self-disclosure, reciprocity of self-disclosure, and self-disclosure and liking: Three meta-analyses reviewed. In S. Petronio (Ed.), *Balancing the secrets of private disclosures.* Mahwah, NJ: Lawrence Erlbaum.

Dindia, K., & Tieu, T. (1996, November). *Self-disclosure of homosexuality: The dialectics of "coming out."* Paper presented at the Speech Communication Association Convention, San Diego.

Dion, K. K., & Dion, K. L. (1996). Cultural perspectives on romantic love. *Personal Relationships, 3*, 5–17.

Dobash, R. P., Dobash, R. E., Wilson, M, & Daly, M. (1992). The myth of sexual symmetry in marital violence. *Social Problems, 39*, 71–91.

Domagalski, T. (1998). *Experienced and expressed anger in the workplace.* Unpublished doctoral dissertation, University of South Florida.

Donn, J. (1999, August 23). *Can't resist the online pull.* Retrieved from www.abcnews.go.com/sections/tech/Daily News/netaddiction990823.html.

Donohue, W. A., & Kolt, R. (1992). *Managing interpersonal conflict.* Newbury Park, CA: Sage.

Dorfman, P., & Howell, J. (1997). Managerial leadership in the United States and Mexico. In C. Granrose & S. Oskamp (Eds.), *Cross-cultural work groups*. Thousand Oaks, CA: Sage.

Dowd, E. T., Hughes, S., Brockbank, L., Halpain, D., Seibel, C., & Seibel, P. (1988). Compliance-based and defiance-based intervention strategies and psychological reactance in the treatment of free and unfree behavior. *Journal of Counseling Psychology, 35*, 363–369.

Downs, C., & Conrad, C. (1982). A critical incident study of effective subordinancy. *Journal of Business Communication, 19*, 27–38.

Doyle, J. A. (1995). *The male experience*. Dubuque, IA: Brown & Benchmark.

Dressler, C. (1995, December 31). Please! End this meeting madness! *Santa Cruz Sentinel*, p. D1.

Drew, E. (1994). *On the edge: The Clinton presidency*. New York: Simon & Schuster.

Drewnowski, A., & Yee, D. (1987). Men and body image: Are males satisfied with their body weight? *Psychosomatic Medicine, 49*, 626–634.

Dreyfuss, I. (1999, August 30). Sports parents need to keep cool. *Santa Cruz Sentinel*, p. A9.

Driscoll, R., Davis, K., & Lipetz, M. (1972). Parental inference and romantic love: The Romeo and Juliet effect. *Journal of Personality and Social Psychology, 24*, 1–10.

DuBois, C. (1992, September/October). Portrait of the ideal MBA. *The Penn Stater*, p. 31.

DuBrin, A. J., Ireland, R. D., & Williams, J. C. (1989). *Management & organization*. Cincinnati: Southwestern.

Duck, S. (1991). Some evident truths about conventions in everyday relationships: All communications are not created equal. *Human Communication Research, 18*, 228–269.

Duck, S. (1994a). *Meaningful relationships*. Thousand Oaks, CA: Sage.

Duck, S. (1994b). Strategems, spoils, and a serpent's tooth: On the delights and dilemmas of personal relationships. In W. R. Cupach & B. H. Spitzberg (Eds.), *The dark side of interpersonal communication*. Hillsdale, NJ: Lawrence Erlbaum.

Duck, S. W., & Allison, D. (1978). I liked you but I can't live with you: A study of lapsed friendships. *Social Behavior and Personality, 6*, 43–47.

Dunlap, A. (1997). *Mean business: How I save bad companies and make good companies great*. New York: Simon & Schuster.

Durham, G. (2001, October 16). Study finds widespread lying, cheating among teens. *Santa Cruz Sentinel*, p. A1.

Dyer, J. (2001, June 10). Ethics and orphans: The Monster Study. *San Jose Mercury News*, pp. 1A, 14A–16A.

Dziech, B. W., & Hawkins, M. W. (1998). *Sexual harassment in higher education: Reflections and new perspectives*. New York: Barland.

Eagley, A. H. (1995). The science and politics of comparing women and men. *American Psychologist, 50*, 145–158.

Eagly, A., Karau, S., & Makhijani, M. (1995). Gender and the effectiveness of leaders: A meta-analysis. *Journal of Personality and Social Psychology, 117*, 125–145.

Early, C. (1989). Social loafing and collectivism: A comparison of the United States and People's Republic of China. *Administrative Science Quarterly, 34*, 555–581.

Eclov, B. (1997). True peace of mind. In L. G. Schnoor (Ed.), *Winning orations*. Northfield, MN: Interstate Oratorical Association.

Edward, G. (1995). *Scuse me while I kiss this guy*. New York: Simon & Schuster.

Edwards, J. (2002, May 8). Songwriter Otis Blackwell, 'Don't Be Cruel' among hits. *Santa Cruz Sentinel*, p. A8.

Edwards, R. (1995, February). New tools help gauge marital success. *APA Monitor*.

Eisenhardt, K. (1989). Making fast strategic decisions in high-velocity environments. *Academy of Management Journal, 32*, 543–576.

Eitzen, S. (1996, January 1). Ethical dilemmas in American sport. *Vital Speeches of the Day*, 182–185.

Ekman, P. (1992). *Telling lies: Clues to deceit in the marketplace, politics, and marriage*. New York: W. W. Norton.

Ekman, P. (1993). Facial expression and emotion. *American Psychologist, 48*, 384–393.

Ekman, P. (1994). Strong evidence for universals in facial expressions: A reply to Russell's mistaken critique. *Psychological Bulletin, 115*, 268–287.

Ekman, P., & Friesen, W. (1969). The repertoire of nonverbal behavior: Categories, origins, usage, and coding. *Sanities, 1*, 49–98.

Ekman, P., & Friesen, W. (1987). Universal and cultural differences in the judgment of facial expressions of emotion. *Journal of Personality and Social Psychology, 53*, 712–717.

Ekman, P., Friesen, W., & Bear, J. (1984, May). The international language of gestures. *Psychology Today*, 64–69.

Eldridge, N. S., & Gilbert, L. A. (1990). Correlates of relationship satisfaction in lesbian couples. *Psychology of Women Quarterly, 14*, 43–62.

Elgin, S. H. (1989). *Success with the gentle art of verbal self-defense*. Englewood Cliffs, NJ: Prentice-Hall.

Emmert, P. (1996, Spring). President's perspective. *ILA Listening Post, 56*, 2–3.

Employee tiffs twice the hassle of decade ago. (1996, June 5). *Denver Post*, p. 2G.

Endicott, F. (1979). The Endicott Report: Trends in the employment of college and university graduates in business and industry. Evanston, IL: Placement Center, Northwestern University.

Eng, S. (1997, May 14). Cover story. *San Jose Mercury News* [Getting Ahead section], pp. 1, 8.

Eng, S. (1999, February 9). Love among the workstations. *San Jose Mercury News*, pp. C13, C14.

English find living close together can be bloody murder. (1996, April 29). *San Jose Mercury News*, p. 13A.

Erickson, P. (1985). *Reagan speaks: The making of an American myth*. New York: New York University Press.

Estrich, S. (2001, December 9). The gender gap. *San Jose Mercury News*, pp. 1D, 5D.

Etchingham, J. (2000, January 13). Welcome to the world of net racists. *The Times* (London), n.p.

Ex-pal's tapes give Lewinsky voice. (1998, December 18). *San Jose Mercury News*, p. A15.

Excerpts from the report. (2001, February 3). *Santa Cruz Sentinel*, p. A5.

Exline, J. J., & Baumeister, R. F. (2000). In M. E. McCullough, K. I. Pargament, & C. E. Thoresen (Eds.), *Forgiveness: Theory, research, and practice*. New York: Guilford Press.

Eyes wide open. (2000, October 30). *Newsweek*, 8.

Fadiman, C. (Ed.) (1985). *The Little, Brown book of anecdotes*. Boston: Little, Brown, & Company.

Fairhurst, G., & Sarr, R. (1996). *The art of framing: Managing the language of leadership*. San Francisco: Jossey-Bass.

Falling cow injures coffee house customer. (2001, July 12). *Santa Cruz Sentinel*, p. A8.

Fallon, A. E., & Rozin, P. (1985). Sex differences in perceptions of desirable body shape. *Journal of Abnormal Psychology, 94*, 102–105.

Fancher, R. T. (1995). *Cultures of healing: Correcting the image of American mental health care*. New York: Freeman.

Farina, A. (1982). The stigma of mental disorders. In A. G. Miller (Ed.), *In the eye of the beholder*. New York: Praeger.

Farmer, S., & Roth, J. (1998). Conflict-handling behavior in work groups: Effects of group structure, decision processes, and time. *Small Group Research, 29*, 669–713.

Farrell, W. (1993). *The myth of male power: Why men are the disposable sex*. New York: Simon & Schuster.

Farrell, W. (1999). *Women can't hear what men don't say: Destroying myths, creating love*. New York: Tarcher/Putnam.

Feingold, A. (1992). Good-looking people are not what we think. *Psychological Bulletin, 111*, 304–341.

Female boss, bad review. (1997, September/October). *Psychology Today*, 24.

Fenell, D. L. (1993). Characteristics of long-term first marriages. *Journal of Mental Health Counseling, 15*, 446–460.

Ferraro, G. (1992). Acceptance of the Democratic nomination for vice president. In J. Andrews & D. Zarefsky (Eds.), *Contemporary American Voices*. New York: Longman.

Festinger, L. (1957). *A theory of cognitive dissonance*. Stanford, CA: Stanford University Press.

Festinger, L. (1977). Cognitive dissonance. In E. Aronson (Ed.), *Readings about the social animal*. San Francisco: W. H. Freeman.

Fiebert, M. S., & Gonzalez, D. M. (1997). College women who initiate assaults on their male partners and the reasons offered for such behavior. *Psychological Reports, 80*, 583–590.

Fiedler, F. (1970). *Leadership*. Morristown, NJ: General Learning Press.

Fiedler, F., & House, R. (1988). Leadership theory and research: A report of progress. In C. Cooper & I. Robertson (Eds.), *International review of industrial and organizational psychology*. New York: Wiley.

Fields, G. (1998, June 16). The chain saw cuts both ways, CEO finds. *San Jose Mercury News*, p. C3.

Files, J. (2002, November 19). Female leaders make small gains. *San Jose Mercury News*, pp. 1C, 6C.

Filkins, D. (2001, November 13). Letting their hair down. *San Jose Mercury News*, p. 14A.

Final report of the California task force to promote self-esteem and personal and social responsibility. (1990). Sacramento, CA: California State Department of Education.

Fine, G. A. (1986). Friendship in the workplace. In V. J. Derlega & B. A. Winstead (Eds.), *Friendship and social interaction*. New York: Springer-Verlag.

Finkelhor, D., & Yllo, K. (1985). *License to rape: Sexual abuse of wives*. New York: Holt, Rinehart, & Winston.

Fischhoff, B. (1975). Hindsight is not equal to foresight: The effect of outcome knowledge on judgment under uncertainty. *Journal of Experimental Psychology: Human Perception and Performance, 1*, 288–299.

Fisher, M. (1994, July 21). Moon landing? Don't believe it, the newspapers say. *International Herald Tribune*, p. 1.

Fisher, R., & Brown, S. (1988). *Getting together: Building a relationship that gets to yes*. Boston: Houghton Mifflin.

Fiske, E. (1990, March 5). How to learn in college: Group study, many tests. *The New York Times*, p. A1.

Fitzhenry, R. I. (1993). *The Harper book of quotations*. New York: HarperCollins.

Fletcher, G., & Fincham, F. (1991). Attribution in close relationships. In G. Fletcher & F. Fincham (Eds.), *Cognition in close relationships*. Hillsdale, NJ: Lawrence Erlbaum.

Fletcher M. A. (1999). Study: Marriage rate is at its lowest ever. *San Jose Mercury News*, p. 25A.

Flowers, B. J., & Richardson, F. C. (1996). Why is multiculturalism good? *American Psychologist, 51*, 609–621.

Floyd, K. (1996). Meanings for closeness and intimacy in friendships. *Journal of Social and Personal Relationships, 13*, 85–107.

Foertsch, J., & Gernsbacher, M. A. (1997). In search of gender neutrality: Is singular *they* a cognitively efficient substitute for generic *he*? *Psychological Science, 8*, 106–111.

Folger, J., Poole, M., & Stutman, R. (1993). *Working through conflict: Strategies for relationships, groups, and organizations*. New York: HarperCollins.

Follingstad, D. R., Wright, S., Lloyd, S., & Sebastian, J. A. (1991). Sex differences in motivations and effects in dating violence. *Family Relations, 40*, 51–57.

Forsyth, D., Heiney, M., & Wright, S. (1997). Biases in appraisals of women leaders. *Group Dynamics: Theory, Research, and Practices, 1*, 98–103.

Foschi, M., Warriner, G., & Hart, S. (1985). Standards, expectations, and interpersonal influence. *Social Psychology Quarterly, 18*, 108–117.

Fourth-grader calls in a lawyer to fight the school cafeteria. (1999, March 13). *San Jose Mercury News*, p. A20.

Foushee, M. (1984). Dyads and triads at 35,000 feet: Factors affecting group process and aircraft performance. *American Psychologist, 39*, 885–893.

France. (1997, August). *Reader's Digest, 156*.

Frank, R., & Cook, P. (1995). *The winner-take-all society*. New York: Free Press.

Freed, A. (1992). We understand perfectly: A critique of Tannen's view. In *Locating power* [Proceedings of the 1992 Berkeley women and language conference]. Berkeley, CA: University of California.

Freeley, A. J. (1996). *Argumentation and debate: Critical thinking for reasoned decision making*. Belmont, CA: Wadsworth.

Freeman, K. (1996). Attitudes toward work in project groups as predictors of academic performance. *Small Group Research, 27*, 265–282.

French, H. W. (2001, July 15). Equality is elusive for women in Japan. *San Jose Mercury News*, p. 11A.

Frerking, B. (1995, March 15). Question authority, parents say. *San Jose Mercury News*, p. A4.

Fry, D. P., & Fry, C. B. Culture and conflict resolution models: Exploring alternatives to violence. In D. P. Fry & K. Bjorkqvist (Eds.), *Cultural variation in conflict resolution: Alternatives to violence.* Mahwah, NJ: Lawrence Erlbaum.

Frymer, M. (1996, March 16). Controversy follows Dershowitz like cash follows O. J. lawyers. *San Jose Mercury News,* p. E1.

Frymier, A., & Shulman, G. (1996). The development of a learner empowerment measure. *Communication Education, 45,* 181–199.

Fucci, D., Harris, D., Petrosino, L., & Banks, M. (1993). Effects of preference for rock music on magnitude-production scaling behavior in young adults: A validation. *Perceptual and Motor Skills, 77,* 811–815.

Fukada, H. (1986). Psychological processes mediating the persuasion inhibiting effect of forewarning in fear arousing communities. *Psychological Reports, 58,* 87–90.

Gabrenya, W. (1985). Social loafing on an optimistic task: Cross-cultural differences among Chinese and Americans. *Journal of Cross-Cultural Psychology, 16,* 223–242.

Galanter, E. (1962). Contemporary psychophysics. In R. Brown, E. Galanter, E. H. Hess, & G. Mendler (Eds.), *New directions in psychology.* New York: Holt, Rinehart & Winston.

Galanter, M. (1989). *Cults: Faith, healing, and coercion.* New York: Oxford University Press.

Gallup, G., & Gallup, A. (1989, January 29). Communicating is critical to a satisfying relationship. *San Jose Mercury News,* p. A1.

Galsner, B. (1999). *The culture of fear: Why Americans are afraid of the wrong things.* New York: Basic Books.

Game show stokes the Yanks' inferiority complex. (2001, April 29). *San Jose Mercury News,* p. 4C.

Gammon, R., & Clarke, K. (1997, November 6). Kurek gets eight years. *Santa Cruz Sentinel,* pp. A1, A4.

Garcia, E. (1996, May 30). Tattoo-removal plan for ex-gang members. *San Jose Mercury News,* p. B1.

Gardner, L., & Leak, G. (1994). Characteristics and correlates of teacher anxiety among college psychology teachers. *Teaching of Psychology, 21,* 28–32.

Gardner, M. (1981). *Science: Good, bad, and bogus.* New York: Avon Books.

Gardner, M. (1997, July/August). Heaven's gate: The UFO cult of Bo and Peep. *Skeptical Inquirer,* 15–17.

Gardner, R. A., & Gardner, B. T. (1969). Teaching sign language to a chimpanzee. *Science, 165,* 664–672.

Garfield, C. (1986). *Peak performers.* New York: Avon Books.

Garner D. M. (1997, January–February). Body image survey. *Psychology Today, 1,* 30–84.

Gass, R., & Seiter, J. (1999). *Persuasion, social influence, and compliance gaining.* Boston: Allyn & Bacon.

Gastil, J. (1990). Generic pronouns and sexist language: The oxymoronic character of masculine generics. *Sex Roles, 23,* 629–643.

Gastil, J. (1994). A meta-analytic review of the productivity and satisfaction of democratic and autocratic leadership. *Small Group Research, 25,* 384–410.

Gates, D. (1993, March 29). White male paranoia. *Newsweek,* 48–53.

Gathright, A. (1990, February 18). Shots silence wife's secret terror. *San Jose Mercury News,* p. A1.

Gayle, B. (1991). Sex equity in workplace conflict management. *Journal of Applied Communication Research, 19,* 152–169.

Gayle, B., Preiss, R., & Allen, M. (1994). Gender differences and the use of conflict strategies. In L. Turner & H. Sterk (Eds.), *Differences that make a difference: Examining the assumptions in gender research.* Westport, CT: Bergin & Garvey.

Gebhardt, L., & Meyers, R. (1995). Subgroups influence in decision-making groups: Examining consistency from a communication perspective. *Small Group Research, 26,* 147–168.

Geertz, C. (1983). *Local knowledge.* New York: Basic Books.

Geier, J. (1967). A trait approach in the study of leadership in small groups. *Journal of Communication, 17,* 316–323.

Gelles, R. (1997). *Intimate violence in families.* Thousand Oaks, CA: Sage.

Gelles, R., & Straus, M. (1988). *Intimate violence: The causes and consequences of abuse in the American family.* New York: Simon & Schuster.

George, M. J. (1994). Riding the donkey backwards: Men as the unacceptable victims of marital violence. *The Journal of Men's Studies, 3,* 137–159.

Gerow, J. (1996). *Essentials of psychology: Concepts and applications.* New York: HarperCollins.

Gerstel, N., & Gross, H. (1985). *Commuter marriage.* New York: Guilford Press.

Getlin, J. (1998, July 3). CNN, Time pull nerve-gas story. *San Jose Mercury News,* pp. A1, A10.

Getter, H., & Nowinski, I. (1981). A free response test of interpersonal effectiveness. *Journal of Personality Assessment, 45,* 301–308.

Gibb, C. (1969). Leadership. In G. Lindzey & E. Aronson (Eds.), *The handbook of social psychology (Vol. 4).* Reading, MA: Addison-Wesley.

Gibb, J. (1961). Defensive communication. *The Journal of Communication, 11,* 141–148.

Giblin, P. (1994). Marital satisfaction. *The Family Journal, 2,* 48–50.

Gilovich, T. (1991). *How we know what isn't so: The fallibility of human reason in everyday life.* New York: Free Press.

Gilovich, T. (1997, March/April). Some systematic biases of everyday judgment. *Skeptical Inquirer,* 31–35.

Ginsberg, S. (1997, May 5). So many messages and so little time. *Business Outlook,* C-1.

Girion, L. (2000, December 20). Americans losing their cool at work. *San Jose Mercury News,* p. 1C, 6C.

Girl undergoes surgery for smile. (1995, December 16). *San Jose Mercury News,* p. B3.

Give Congress some credit for trying to find harmony. (1999, March 12). *San Jose Mercury News,* p. B6.

Givens, D. (1983). *Love signals: How to attract a mate.* New York: Pinnacle Books.

Glass ceiling intact, statistics show at hearing. (1994, September 9). *San Jose Mercury News,* p. E1.

Glassman, J. K. (1998, May 29). Put shootings in proper perspective. *San Jose Mercury News,* p. B7.

Gleicher, F., & Petty, R. (1992). Expectations of reassurance influence the nature of fear-stimulated attitude change. *Journal of Experimental Social Psychology, 28,* 86–100.

Goldberg, C. (2001, June 18). Bucking tradition, single fathers are on the rise. *San Jose Mercury News,* p. 10A.

Goldberg, H. (1994, March 3). Yawning gulf of perceptions. *Sacramento Bee*, p. A12.

Goleman, D. (1991, September 17). Nonverbal cues are easy to misinterpret. *The New York Times*, p. C1.

Goleman, D. (1995). *Emotional intelligence.* New York: Bantam.

Goleman, D. (1998). *Working with emotional intelligence.* New York: Bantam.

Gomes, S. (2000). Toxic noise. In L. Schnoor & B. Wickelgren (Eds.), *Winning orations.* Mankato, MN: Interstate Oratorical Association.

Goode, E. (1999, February 23). When people see a sound and hear a color. *The New York Times*, p. D3.

Goodglass, H. (1993). *Understanding aphasia.* San Diego, CA: Academic Press.

Goodman, E. (1996, August 5). Why shave Shannon? *San Jose Mercury News*, p. B13.

Gottman, J. (1994). *What predicts divorce? The relationship between marital processes and marital outcomes.* Hillsdale, NJ: Lawrence Erlbaum.

Gottman, J. M (1979). *Marital interaction: Experimental investigations.* New York: Academic Press.

Gottman, J. M. (1994, May/June). Why marriages fail. *Family Therapy*, pp. 40–48.

Gottman, J. M., & Carrere, S. (1994).Why can't men and women get along? Developmental notes and marital inequities. In D. Canary & L. Stafford (Eds.), *Communication and relational maintenance.* New York: Academic Press.

Gottman, J. M., & DeClaire, J. (2001). *The relationship cure: A five-step guide for building better connections with family, friends, and lovers.* New York: Crown Books.

Gottman, J. M., & Silver, N. (1994). *Why marriages succeed and fail: And how you can make yours last.* New York: Simon & Schuster.

Gottman, J. M, & Silver, N. (1999). *The seven principles for making marriage work.* New York: Crown.

Gottschalk, M. (1996, May 12). Do's and don'ts of dressing down. *San Jose Mercury News*, p. A17.

Gould, S. J. (1981). *The mismeasure of man.* New York: W. W. Norton.

Grace, K. (2000). Unsanitary hotels. In L. Schnoor & B. Wickelgren (Eds.), *Winning orations.* Mankato, MN: Interstate Oratorical Association.

Graham, M. A., & LeBaron, M. J. (1994). *The horizontal revolution: Reengineering your organization through teams.* Westport, CT: Quorum Books.

Grammer, K., & Thornhill, R. (1994). Human (homo sapiens) facial attractiveness and sexual selection: The role of symmetry and averageness. *Journal of Comparative Psychology, 108,* 233–242.

Graybar, S. R., Antonuccio, D. O., Boutilier, L. R., & Varble, D. L. (1989). Psychological reactance as a factor affecting patient compliance to physician advice. *Scandinavian Journal of Behavior Therapy, 18,* 43–51.

Green, W., & Lazarus, H. (1990). Are you meeting with success? *Executive Excellence, 7,* 1–12.

Greenberg, J. (1981, June/July). An interview with David Rosenhan. *APA Monitor*, pp. 4–5.

Griffin, E. (1994; 2003). *A first look at communication theory.* New York: McGraw-Hill.

Gronbeck, B., German, K., Ehninger, D., & Monroe, A. (1998). *Principles of speech communication.* New York: Longman.

Gruber, J. (2001). Heart disease in women. In L. Schnoor & B. Wickelgren (Eds.), *Winning orations.* Mankato, MN: Interstate Oratorical Association.

Grusec, J. E., Kuczynski, L., Rushton, J. P., & Simutis, Z. M. (1978). Modeling, direct instruction, and attributions: Effects on altruism. *Developmental Psychology, 14,* 51–57.

Grusec, J. E., & Redler, E. (1980). Attribution, reinforcement, and altruism: A developmental analysis. *Developmental Psychology, 16,* 525–534.

Grusky, O., Bonacich, P., & Webster, C. (1995). The coalition structure of the four-person family. *Current Research in Social Psychology,* 16–29.

Gudykunst, W. (1991). *Bridging differences: Effective intergroup communication.* Newbury Park, CA: Sage.

Gudykunst, W. B. (1995). Anxiety/uncertainty management (AUM) theory. In R. Wiseman (Ed.), *Intercultural Communication Theory.* Thousand Oaks, CA: Sage.

Gudykunst, W. B., & Kim, Y. Y. (Eds.). (1992). *Readings on communicating with strangers.* New York: McGraw-Hill.

Gumz, J. (1997, November). Payoffs from technology in schools remain unproven. *Santa Cruz Sentinel*, p. Al.

Hackman, M., & Johnson, C. (1996). *Leadership: A communication perspective.* Prospect Heights, IL: Waveland Press.

Haefner, P. T., Notarius, C. I., & Pellegrini, D. S. (1991). Determinants of satisfaction with marital discussions: An exploration of husband-wife differences. *Behavioral Assessment, 13,* 67–82.

Hahner, J. C., Sokoloff, M. A., & Salesch, S. L. (1997). *Speaking clearly: Improving voice and diction.* New York: McGraw-Hill.

Haleta, L. L. (1996). Student perceptions of teachers' use of language: The effects of powerful and powerless language on impression formation and uncertainty. *Communication Education, 45,* 16–28.

Hall, E. (1959 & 1973). *The silent language.* New York: Doubleday.

Hall, E. (1969). *The hidden dimension.* New York: Doubleday.

Hall, E. (1981). *Beyond culture.* New York: Doubleday.

Hall, E., & Hall, M. (1987). *Understanding cultural difference.* Yarmouth, ME: Intercultural Press.

Hall, J., & Watson, W. (1970). The effects of normative intervention on group decision making. *Human Relations, 23,* 299–317.

Hall, J. A., & Bernieri, F. J. (2001). *Interpersonal sensitivity: Theory and measurement.* Mahwah, NJ: Lawrence Erlbaum Associates.

Hamachek, D. (1982). *Encounters with others: Interpersonal relationships and you.* Fort Worth, TX: Holt, Rinehart & Winston.

Hamachek, D. (1992). *Encounters with the self.* Fort Worth, TX: Harcourt Brace Jovanovich.

Hamermesh, D., & Biddle, J. E. (1994). Beauty and the labor market. *The American Economic Review, 84,* 1174–1194.

Han, S., & Shavitt, S. (1994). Persuasion and culture: Advertising appeals in individualistic and collectivistic societies. *Journal of Experimental Social Psychology, 30,* 326–350.

Hanna, M. S., & Wilson, G. L. (1998). *Communicating in business and professional settings.* New York: McGraw-Hill.

Hardin, C., & Banaji, M. R. (1993). The influence of language on thought. *Social Cognition, 11,* 277–308.

Harmon, A. (2001, September 23). The search for intelligent life on the Internet. *The New York Times.* Retrieved from http://www.nytimes.com/2001/09/23/weekinreview/.

Harrison, L. E. (2000). Introduction. In L. E. Harrison, & S. P. Huntington (Eds.), *Culture matters: How values shape human progress.* New York: Basic Books.

Harrison, L. E., & Huntington, S. P. (2000). *Culture matters: How values shape human progress.* New York: Basic Books.

Harwood, B. (Ed.). (1982). *The pursuit of the presidency, 1980.* New York: Berkeley Books.

Haslett, B. (1992). *The organization woman: Power and paradox.* Norwood, NJ: Ablex.

Hatfield, E., Sprecher, S., Pillemer, J. T., Greenberger, D., Wexler, P. (1989). Gender differences in what is desired in a sexual relationship. *Journal of Psychology and Human Sexuality, 1,* 39–52.

Hats off for bobbies in Manchester. (1996, February 7). *San Jose Mercury News,* p. A12.

Hawkins, K. (1995). Effects of gender and communication content on leadership emergence in small task-oriented groups. *Small Group Research, 26,* 234–249.

Heat's on to close wage gap. (1999, January 30). *San Jose Mercury News,* p. A1.

Hecht, M., Collier, M., & Ribeau, S. (1993). *African American communication: Ethnic identity and cultural interpretation.* Newbury Park, CA: Sage.

Hecht, M., Collier, M., & Ribeau, S. (1994). Love ways and relationship quality in heterosexual relationships. *Journal of Social and Personal Relationship, 1,* 25–44.

Hefling, S. (1997). Prison rape. In L. G. Schnoor (Ed.), *Winning orations.* Northfield, MN: Interstate Oratorical Association.

Heilman, M., & Stopeck, M. (1985). Being attractive, advantage or disadvantage? Performance-based evaluation and recommended personnel actions as a function of appearance, sex, and job type. *Organizational Behavior and Human Decision Process, 35,* 202–215.

Helfand, D. (2001, August 16). "Edspeak" is in a class by itself. *Los Angeles Times.* Retrieved from www.latimes.com/news/education/la.

Hellweg, S., Samovar, L., & Skow, L. (1994). Cultural variations in negotiation styles. In L. Samovar & R. Porter (Eds). *Intercultural communication: A reader.* Belmont, CA: Wadsworth.

Henley, N. (1995). Body politics revised: What do we know today? In P. Kalbfleisch & McCody (Eds.), *Gender, power, and communication in human relationships.* Hillsdale, NJ: Lawrence Erlbaum.

Hentoff, N. (1992). *Free speech for me, but not for thee.* New York: Harper Perennial.

Henton, J., Cate, R., Koval, J., Lloyd, S., & Christopher, S. (1983). Romance and violence in dating relationships. *Journal of Family Issues, 4,* 467–482.

Herbert, W., & Hammel, S. (1999, March 22). *U.S. News & World Report,* 57.

Herriot, J. (1973). *All things bright and beautiful.* New York: Bantam.

Hershey, P., & Blanchard, K. (1988). *Management organizational behavior: Utilizing human resources.* Englewood Cliffs, NJ: Prentice-Hall.

Heslin, R. (1974, May). *Steps toward a taxonomy of touching.* Paper presented to the annual convention of the Midwestern Psychological Association.

Hess, E., & Goodwin, E. (1974). The present state of pupilometrics. In M. Janice (Ed.), *Pupillary dynamics and behavior.* New York: Plenum Press.

Hess, E., Seltzer, A., & Schlien, J. (1965). Pupil response of hetero- and homosexual males to pictures of men and women: A pilot study. *Journal of Abnormal Psychology, 70,* 165–168.

Hetherington, E., Bridges, M., & Insabella, G. (1998, February). What matters? What does not? Five perspectives on the association between marital transitions and children's adjustment. *American Psychologist, 53,* 167–184.

Hickson, M., & Stacks, D. (1989). *Nonverbal communication: Studies and applications.* Dubuque, IA: Wm. C. Brown.

Higham, S. (1998, October 17). Ex-farmer's Senate bid resonates in Vermont. *San Jose Mercury News,* p. DD6.

Hirokawa, R. (1985). Discussion procedures and decision-making performance: A test of a functional perspective. *Human Communication Research, 12,* 203–224.

Hite, S. (1987). *Women in love.* New York: Alfred Knopf.

Hoban, P. (1998, July 11). The right direction. *TV Guide,* 41–42.

Hock, R. (1999). *The extreme searcher's guide to Web search engines: A handbook for the serious searcher.* Medford, NJ: CyberAge Books.

Hofstede, G. (1980). *Culture's consequences: International differences in work-related values.* Beverly Hills, CA: Sage.

Hofstede, G. (1991). *Cultures and organizations: Software of the mind.* New York: McGraw-Hill.

Hofstede, G. (1996). Gender stereotypes and partner preferences of Asian women in masculine and feminine cultures. *Journal of Cross-Cultural Psychology, 27,* 533–547.

Hoge, W. (2002, July 20). Doctor is Britain's worst killer. *San Jose Mercury News,* p. 11A.

Hollander, E. (1985). Leadership and power. In G. Lindzey & E. Aronson (Eds.), *Handbook of social psychology.* New York: Random House.

Hollander, E., & Offerman, L. (1990, February). Power and leadership in organizations. *American Psychologist,* 179–189.

Holmes, S. (1997, March 14). Census bureau predicts huge U.S. ethnic shift. *Sacramento Bee,* p. A1.

Holtgraves, T., & Dulin, J. (1994). The Muhammad Ali effect: Differences between African Americans and European Americans in their perceptions of a truthful braggart. *Language and Communication, 14,* 275–285.

Home chores still a battle of the sexes. (1993, February 16). *San Jose Mercury News,* p. A5.

Hoover-Dempsey, K., Plas, J., & Wallston, B. (1986). Tears and weeping among professional women: In search of new understanding. *Psychology of Women Quarterly, 10,* 19–34.

Horner, T., Guyer, M., & Kalter, N. (1993). The biases of child sexual abuse experts: Believing is seeing. *Bulletin of the American Academy of Psychiatric Law, 21,* 281–292.

National Communication Association. (1998). *How Americans communicate.* Retrieved from http//:www.natcom.org/research/Roper/how_americans-communicate.htm.

Howell, J. (1982). A laboratory study of charismatic leadership. (Working paper, University of Western Ontario.)

Hsu, F. L. K. (1981). The self in cross-cultural perspective. In A. J. Marsella, B. De Vos, & F. L. K. Hsu (Eds.), *Culture and self.* London: Tavistock. Retrieved from http://www.jonwell.org/pubs/joboutlook/want.htm.

Hughes, R. (1993). *Culture of complaint: A passionate look into the ailing heart of America.* New York: Warner Books.

Hui, C. H., & Triandis, H. C. (1986). Individualism-collectivism: A study of cross-cultural research. *Journal of Cross-Cultural Psychology, 17,* 225–248.

Hunt, M. (1982). *The universe within: New science explores the human mind.* New York: Simon & Schuster.

Huspek, M. (2000). Oppositional codes: The case of the Penitentiary of New Mexico riot. *Journal of Applied Communication Research, 28*, 91–116.

Huston, M., & Schwartz, P. (1995). Relationships of lesbians and gay men. In J. Wood & S. Duck (Eds.), *Understanding relationship processes, 6: Understudied relationships: Off the beaten track.* Thousand Oaks, CA: Sage.

Hutchinson, S. (2002, March 22). Jury's verdicts reaffirm court of public opinion. *San Jose Mercury News*, p. 9A.

Hyde, J. S., & Plant, E. A. (1995). Magnitude of psychological gender differences: Another side to the story. *American Psychologist, 50*, 159–161.

In the blink of an eye. (1996, October 21). *Newsweek*, p. 6.

Inagaki, Y. (1985). *Jiko Hyogen No Gijutsu (Skills in self-expression).* Tokyo: PHP Institute.

Inch, E., & Warnick, B. (1998). *Critical thinking and communication: The use of reason in argument.* Boston: Allyn & Bacon.

Infante, D., Chandler, T. A., & Rudd, J. E. (1989). Test of an argumentative skill deficiency model of interpersonal violence. *Communication Monographs, 56*, 163–177.

Infante, D., Rancer, A., & Womack, D. (1997). *Building communication theory.* Prospect Heights, IL: Waveland Press.

Infante, D., Riddle, B., Horvatt, C., & Tumlin, S. (1992). Verbal aggressiveness: Messages and reasons. *Communication Quarterly, 40*, 116–126.

Infante, D., Sabourin, T., Rudd, J., & Sharron, E. (1990). Verbal aggression in violent and nonviolent marital disputes. *Communication Quarterly, 4*, 361–371.

Insurance policies offered against alien impregnation. (1996, August 24). *San Jose Mercury News*, p. A4.

Irvine, M. (1998, April 6). Coming out in the classroom. *Santa Cruz Sentinel*, p. A1.

Isenhart, M. W., & Spangle, M. (2000). *Collaborative approaches to resolving conflict.* Thousand Oaks, CA: Sage.

Ishii, S., Klopf, D., & Cambra, R. (1984). The typical Japanese student as an oral communicator: A preliminary profile. *Otsuma Review, 17*, 39–63.

Ivins, M. (1992, August). The billionaire boy scout. *Time*, pp. 38–39.

Ivins, M. (2000, December 28). 2000 was a great year for comedians. *San Jose Mercury News*, p. 6B.

Jackson, D. (1997, November 24). It took way too long to lower the boom. *San Jose Mercury News*, p. B7.

Jackson, M. (1999, February 14). Office romance: More and more couples mix business, personal lives. *Santa Cruz Sentinel*, p. D2.

Jacobs, J. (1989, October 2). Designs for better education elude summiteers. *San Jose Mercury News*, p. B5.

Jacobs, J. (1996, January 4). Who will raise the children? *San Jose Mercury News*, p. 7B.

Jacobs, J. (1999a, February 1). Warning: Remove label before testing. *San Jose Mercury News*, p. B7.

Jacobs, J. (1999b, June 7). Gore's hope: Boring guys aren't losers. *San Jose Mercury News*, p. B7.

Jacobson, N., & Gottman, J. (1998, March/April). Anatomy of a violent relationship. *Psychology Today*, 61–65.

Jaffe, C. (1998). *Public speaking: Concepts and skills for a diverse society.* Belmont, CA: Wadsworth.

Jaksa, J., & Pritchard, M. (1994). *Communication ethics: Methods of analysis.* Belmont, CA: Wadsworth.

James, D., & Clarke, S. (1993). Women, men, and interruptions: A critical review. In D. Tannen (Ed.), *Gender and conversational interaction.* New York: Oxford University Press.

James, D., & Drakich, J. (1993). Understanding gender differences in amount of talk: A critical review of research. In D. Tannen (Ed.), *Gender and conversational interaction.* New York: Oxford University Press.

Jamieson, K. H. (1988). *Eloquence in an electronic age.* New York: Oxford University Press.

Jandt, F. (1995). *Intercultural communication: An introduction.* Thousand Oaks, CA: Sage.

Janis, I. (1982). *Groupthink: Psychological studies of policy decisions and fiascoes.* Boston: Houghton Mifflin.

Janis, I. (1989). *Crucial decisions: Leadership in policy-making and crisis management.* New York: Free Press.

Janofsky, M. (1995, October 23). Increasingly, political war of words is fought with Nazi imagery. *The New York Times*, p. A12.

Jascob, T. (1997). Prescription drug counseling. *Winning Orations*, 97–100.

Jay, T. (1992). *Cursing in America: A psycholinguist's study of dirty language in the courts, in the movies, in the schoolyards and on the streets.* Philadelphia: John Benjamin Publishing.

Jeffrey, R., & Pasework, R. (1983). Altering opinions about the insanity plea. *Journal of Psychiatry and Law*, 29–44.

Jelinek, P. (1998, December, 19). Korean school teaches smiling. *San Jose Mercury News*, p. A6.

Jensen-Campbell, L., Graziano, W., & West, S. (1995). Dominance, prosocial orientation, and female preferences: Do nice guys really finish last? *Journal of Personality and Social Psychology, 68*, 427–440.

Jesperson, O. (1923). *Language: Its nature, development and origins.* New York: Holt, Rinehart & Winston.

Jesperson, O. (1924). *Language: Its nature, development and origin.* New York: Henry Holt.

John J. Heldrich Center for Workforce Development (2001). Making the grade: What American workers think should be done to improve education. Retrieved from www.heldrich.rutgers.edu/worktrends.cfm.

Johnson, D. (2002, March 25). Until dust do us part. *Newsweek*, p. 41.

Johnson, D., & Johnson, R. (1989). *Cooperation and competition: Theory and research.* Edina, MN: Interaction Book Company.

Johnson, D. W., & Johnson, R. T. (1991). *Learning together and alone: Cooperative, competitive, and individualistic learning.* Englewood Cliffs, NJ: Prentice-Hall.

Johnson, G. (1995, June 6). Chimps talk debate: Is it really language? *The New York Times*, p. C1.

Johnson, J., & Szczupakiewicz, N. (1987). The public speaking course: Is it preparing students with work-related public speaking skills? *Communication Education, 36*, 131–137.

Johnson, M. P. (1995). Patriarchal terrorism and common couple violence: Two forms of violence against women. *Journal of Marriage and the Family, 57*, 283–294.

Johnson, M. P. (2001). Conflict and control: Symmetry and asymmetry in domestic violence. In A. Booth, A. C. Crouter, & M. Clements (Eds.), *Couples in conflict.* Mahwah, NJ: Lawrence Erlbaum.

Johnson, S., & Bechler, C. (1998). Examining the relationship between listening effectiveness and leadership emergence: Perceptions, behaviors, and recall. *Small Group Research, 29,* 452–471.

Johnson, W. (1946). *People in quandaries.* New York: Harper.

Johnston, L., Bachman, J., & O'Malley, P. (1992). *Monitoring the future: Questionnaire responses from the nation's high school seniors, 1989.* Ann Arbor, MI: Survey Research Center, University of Michigan.

Johnstone, C. (1981). Ethics, wisdom, and the mission of contemporary rhetoric: The realization of human being. *Central States Speech Journal, 32,* 177–188.

Jones, E. (1979). The rocky road from acts to dispositions. *American Psychologist, 34,* 107–117.

Jones, E., & Gallois, C. (1989). Spouses' impressions of rules for communication in public and private marital conflicts. *Journal of Marriage and the Family, 51,* 957–967.

Jones, S. (1994). *The right touch: Understanding and using the language of physical context.* Cresskill, NJ: Hampton Press.

Jones, S. G. (1995). *Cybersociety: Computer-mediated communication and community.* Thousand Oaks, CA: Sage.

Judge, C. (1997, November 21). Greatest victory: Saving a life. *San Jose Mercury News,* p. D7.

Judge, C. (1998, July 31). Rookie's father would be proud. *San Jose Mercury News,* p. D8.

Jurors' views differ on King beating trial. (1993, February 15). *San Jose Mercury News,* p. B3.

Kalb, C., & McCormick, J. (1998, September 21). Bellying up to the bar. *Newsweek,* 89.

Kalbfleisch, P., & Cody, M. (Eds.). (1995). *Gender, power, and communication in human relationships.* Hillsdale, NJ: Lawrence Erlbaum.

Kalof, L., Eby, K. K., Matheson, J. L., & Kroska, R. J. (2001). The influence of race and gender on student self-reports of sexual harassment by college professors. *Gender & Society, 15,* 282–302.

Kampeas, R. (2001, July 17). Government lacks diversity at decision-making levels. *Santa Cruz Sentinel,* pp. A1, A8.

Kaplan, T. (1998, November 27). Few using health plan. *San Jose Mercury News,* p. B1.

Karau, S., & Williams, K. (1993). Social loafing: A meta-analytic review and theoretical integration. *Journal of Personality and Social Psychology, 65,* 681–706.

Kassin, S. (1998). *Psychology.* Upper Saddle River, NJ: Prentice-Hall.

Katayama, H. (1982). Koto Ni Hanei Sareta Nipponjin No Gengokan: Japanese views of language as reflected in proverbs. *Kyoiku Kiyo 8-go.* Matsudo, Chiba-ken: Matsudo Dental School, Nihon University, pp. 1–11.

Kato, D. (1996, May 13). Make-over dreams. *San Jose Mercury News,* pp. C1, C8.

Katz, G. (2001, May 6). The mobile life is the only way for most of Europe. *San Jose Mercury News,* p. 9E.

Katzenbach, J., & Smith, D. (1993a). *The wisdom of teams.* Boston: Harvard Business School Press.

Katzenbach, J., & Smith, D. (1993b, March/April). The discipline of teams. *Harvard Business Review,* 111–120.

Kava, B. (1999, January 16). "Perry Mason" tops Clinton trial on TV. *San Jose Mercury News,* p. A11.

Keller, H. (1955). *Teacher: Anne Sullivan Macy.* Garden City, NY: Doubleday.

Kelley, H. (1979). *Personal relationships: Their structures and processes.* Hillsdale, NJ: Lawrence Erlbaum.

Kelley, H. (1984). Affect in interpersonal relations. *Review of Personality and Social Psychology, 5,* 89–115.

Kelsey, B. (1998). The dynamics of multicultural groups: Ethnicity as a determinant of leadership. *Small Group Research, 29,* 602–623.

Kendall, K. E. (1985). Do real people ever give speeches? *Spectra, 31,* 10.

Kershner, V. (1991, March 30). Budget "emergency" declared by governor. *Santa Cruz Sentinel,* p. A1.

Kiecolt-Glaser, J., Fisher, L., Ogrocki, P., & Stout, J. (1987). Marital quality, marital disruption and immune function. *Psychosomatic Medicine, 49,* 13–34.

Killion, A. (1996, July 5). VanDerveer ordeal proves worth it for well-drilled team. *San Jose Mercury News,* pp. D1, D3.

Killion, A. (1999, January 29). Pro football becoming a woman's game. *San Jose Mercury News,* pp. A1, A22.

Kilmann, R., & Thomas, K. (1977). Developing a force-choice measure of conflict handling behavior: The "mode" instrument. *Educational Psychological Measurement, 37,* 309–325.

Kilpatrick, W. (1975). *Identity and intimacy.* New York: Dell.

Kim, M. (1992). A comparative analysis of nonverbal expressions as portrayed by Korean and American print-media advertising. *Howard Journal of Communication, 3,* 321.

Kim, U., Triandis, H., Kagitcibasi, C., Choi, S., & Yoon, G. (1994). *Individualism and collectivism: Theory, method, and application.* Thousand Oaks, CA: Sage.

King, R. D. (1997, April). Should English be the law? *The Atlantic Monthly,* pp. 55–64.

King, S. (1995, May 1). Commentary—interpersonal cyberspace relationships. Electronic message to Interpersonal Computing and Technology Discussion List, archived at ipctl@guvm.georgetown.edu.

Kipnis, D. (1976). *The powerholder.* Chicago: University of Chicago Press.

Kirshmeyer, C., & Cohen, A. (1992). Multicultural groups: Their performance and reactions with constructive conflict. *Group and Organizational Management, 17,* 153–170.

Kirtley, K. (1997). Grave matter: The high cost of leaving. *Winning Orations,* 154–157.

Klapp, O. (1978). *Opening and closing: Strategies of information adaptation in society.* New York: Cambridge University Press.

Kleiman, C. (1991, July 28). A boost up the corporate ladder. *San Jose Mercury News,* p. PC1.

Klein, R. C. A., & Johnson, M. P. (1997). Strategies of couple conflict. In S. Duck (Ed.), *Handbook of personal relationships.* New York: Wiley.

Klein, S. (1996). Work pressure as a determinant of work group behavior. *Small Group Research, 27,* 299–315.

Klopf, D. (1998). *Intercultural encounters: The fundamentals of intercultural communication.* Englewood, CO: Morton.

Klopfenstein, B. (1997). New technology and the future of the media. In A. Wells & E. Hakanen (Eds.), *Mass media and society.* Greenwich, CT: Ablex.

Knapp, M. (1980). *Essentials of nonverbal communication.* New York: Holt, Rinehart & Winston.

Knapp, M., & Vangelisti, A. (1992). Stages of relationships. In M. Knapp & A. Vangelisti (Eds.), *Interpersonal communication and human relationships*. Needham Heights, MA: Allyn and Bacon.

Kohn, A. (1987, October). It's hard to get left out of a pair. *Psychology Today*, 53–57.

Kohn, A. (1992). *No contest: The case against competition*. Boston: Houghton Mifflin.

Kohn, A. (1993). *Punished by rewards*. New York: Houghton Mifflin.

Kohn, A. (1994, December). The truth about self-esteem. *Phi Delta Kappan*, 272–283.

Kolb, D., & Putnam, L. (1992). The multiple faces of conflict in organizations. *Journal of Organizational Behavior, 13*, 311–324.

Korzybski, A. (1958). *Science and sanity*. Lakeville, CT: International Non-Aristotelian Literary Publishing Company.

Kottke, J. L., & MacLeod, C. D. (1989). Use of profanity in the counseling interview. *Psychological Reports, 65*, 627–634.

Kouri, K., & Lasswell, M. (1993). *Black-White marriages*. Binghamton, NY: Hayworth Press.

Koury, R. (1998, June 9). Berkeley may strip down law on nudity. *San Jose Mercury News*, p. B1.

Kramer, T. J., Fleming, G. P., & Mannis, S. M. (2001). Improving face-to-face brainstorming through modeling and facilitation. *Small Group Research, 32*, 533–557.

Kraut, R., Patterson, M., Lundmark, V., Kiesler, S., Mukopadhyay, T., & Scherlis, W. (1998). Internet paradox: A social technology that reduces social involvement and psychological well-being? *American Psychologist, 53*, 1017–1031.

Kraut, R. E. (1973). Effects of social labeling on giving to charity. *Journal of Experimental Social Psychology, 9*, 551–562.

Kristof, N. (1995, December 14). Sales pitch. *San Jose Mercury News*, p. A27.

Kroll, W., & Peterson, K. (1965). Study of values test and collegiate football teams. *The Research Quarterly, 36*, 141–147.

Krucoff, C. (1998, November 11). When winning becomes the reason. *San Jose Mercury News*, p. D3.

Kubicka, T. (1995). Traitorous transplants: The enemy within. *Winning Orations*, 9–11.

Kuhl, P. K. (1994). Speech perception. In F. D. Minifie (Ed.), *Introduction to communication sciences and disorders*. San Diego, CA: Singular Publishing Group.

Kuiper, N., & Rogers, T. (1979). Encoding of personal information. *Journal of Personality and Social Psychology, 37*, 499–514.

Kunin, M. (1994). *Living a political life*. New York: Knopf.

Kunkel, A. W., & Burleson, B. R. (1998). Social support and the emotional lives of men and women: An assessment of the different cultures perspective. In D. J. Canary & K. Dindia (Eds.), *Sex differences and similarities in communication*. Mahwah, NJ: Lawrence Erlbaum.

Kurdek, L. A. (1989). Relationship quality of gay and lesbian cohabiting couples: A 1-year follow-up study. *Journal of Social and Personal Relationships, 6*, 39–59.

Kurdek, L. A. (1998). Relationship outcomes and their predictors: Longitudinal evidence from heterosexual married, gay cohabiting, and lesbian cohabiting couples. *Journal of Marriage and the Family, 60*, 553–568.

Kurklen, R., & Kassinove, H. (1991). Effects of profanity, touch, and subject's religiosity on perceptions of a psychologist and behavioral compliance. *The Journal of Social Psychology, 131*, 899–901.

Kurtz, L. (1997). *Self-help and support groups: A handbook for practitioners*. Thousand Oaks, CA: Sage.

Kushner, H. (1981). *When bad things happen to good people*. New York: Avon.

Kutner, L. (1994, February 20). Winning isn't only thing that counts. *Santa Cruz Sentinel*, p. D2.

Lacayo, R. (1995, June 12). Violent reaction. *Time*, pp. 25–39.

Lacayo, R. (2001, December 3). About face. *Newsweek*, pp. 34–49.

LaFasto, F., & Larson, C. (2001). *When teams work best: 6,000 team members and leaders tell what it takes to succeed*. Thousand Oaks, CA: Sage.

Lakoff, R. T. (2000). *The language war*. Berkeley, CA: University of California Press.

Lamberth, J. (1998, August 6). Driving while black: A statistician proves that prejudice still rules the road. *Washington Post*, p. C1.

Landers, A. (1995, February 25). Low income families need fire protection too. *Santa Cruz Sentinel*, p. D5.

Langer, E. (1989). *Mindfulness*. Reading, MA: Addison-Wesley.

Langer, E., & Abelson, R. (1974). A patient by any other name: Clinician group differences in labeling bias. *Journal of Consulting and Clinical Psychology, 42*, 4–9.

Langer, S. (1951). *Philosophy in a new key*. New York: New American Library.

Langfred, C. (1998). Is group cohesiveness a double-edged sword? An investigation of the effects of cohesiveness on performance. *Small Group Research, 29*, 124–143.

Langlois, J., Roggman, L., & Musselman, L. (1994). What is average and what is not average in attractive faces? *Psychological Science, 5*, 214–220.

Lanka, B. (1989). *I dream a world: Portraits of Black women who changed America*. New York: Stewart, Tabori, & Chang.

Lantz, D., & Stefflre, V. (1964). Language and cognition revisited. *Journal of Abnormal and Social Psychology, 49*, 454–462.

Lapakko, D. (1997). Three cheers for language: A closer examination of a widely cited study of nonverbal communication. *Communication Education, 46*, 63–69.

Lardner, G. (1997, August 25). Survey: Number of violent attacks underestimated. *San Jose Mercury News*, p. A6.

Lardner, G. (1998, July 27). Crime at work often unreported. *San Jose Mercury News*, p. A3.

Larson, C. (1992). *Persuasion: Reception and responsibility*. Belmont, CA: Wadsworth.

Larson, C., & LaFasto, M. (1989). *Teamwork: What must go right, what can go wrong*. Newbury Park, CA: Sage.

Larson, J. R. (1989). The dynamic interplay between employees' feedback-seeking strategies and supervisors' delivery of performance feedback. *Academy of Management Review, 14*, 408–422.

Last year's best. (1997, July 9). *San Jose Mercury News*, p. A4.

Latane, B., Williams, K., & Harkin, S. (1979). Many hands make light the work: The causes and consequences of social loafing. *Journal of Personality and Social Psychology, 37*, 822–832.

Lavrakas, P. J. (1975). Female preferences for male physiques. *Journal of Research in Personality, 9*, 324–333.

Lazar, J. (1991). Ensuring productive meetings. In R. Swanson & B. Knapp (Eds.), *Innovative meeting management*. Austin, TX: Minnesota Mining and Manufacturing.

Le Poire, B. A., & Yoshimura, S. M. (1999). The effects of expectancies and actual communication on nonverbal adaptation and communication outcomes: A test of interaction adaptation theory. *Communication Monographs, 66*, 1–30.

Leathers, D. (1970). The process effects of trust-destroying behaviors in the small group. *Speech Monographs, 37*, 181–187.

Leathers, D. (1976). *Nonverbal communication systems*. Boston: Allyn & Bacon.

Leathers, D. (1979). The impact of multichannel message inconsistency on verbal and nonverbal decoding behavior. *Communication Monographs, 46*, 88–100.

Leathers, D. (1986). *Successful nonverbal communication: Principles and applications*. New York: Macmillan.

Leavitt, H. (1964). *Managerial psychology*. Chicago: University of Chicago Press.

Lederer, R. (1990). *Crazy English: The ultimate joy ride through our languages*. New York: Pocket Books.

Lee, B. (1997). *The power principle: Influences with honor*. New York: Simon & Schuster.

Lee, Y., Lee, J., & McCauley, C. R. (1995). *Stereotype occurring toward appreciating group differences*. Washington, DC: American Psychological Association.

Lefton, L. (1991). *Psychology*. Boston: Allyn & Bacon.

Leland, J., & Miller, M. (1998, August 17). Can gays "connect"? *Newsweek*, 47–52.

Leonard, K. E., & Senchak, M. (1996). Prospective prediction of husband marital aggression within newlywed couples. *Journal of Abnormal Psychology, 105*, 369–380.

Letellier, P. (1994). Gay and bisexual male domestic violence victimization: Challenges to feminist theory and responses to violence. *Violence and Victims, 9*, 95–106.

Leung, K., Bond, M., Carment, D., Krishnan, L., & Liebrand, W. (1990). Effects of cultural femininity on preference for methods of conflict processing: A cross-cultural study. *Journal of Experimental Social Psychology, 26*, 373–388.

Lev, M. A. (2000, January 30). Women fight harassment. *San Jose Mercury News*, p. 6AA.

Levander, C. (1998). *Voices of the nation: Women and public speech in nineteenth-century American literature and culture*. Cambridge, UK: Cambridge University Press.

Levine, K. (2001). The dentist's dirty little secret. In L. Schnoor & B. Wickelgren (Eds.), *Winning Orations*. Mankato, MN: Interstate Oratorical Association.

Levine, M., & Shefner, J. (1991). *Fundamentals of sensation and perception*. Pacific Grove, CA: Brooks/Cole.

Levine, R. B. (1993). Is love a luxury? *American Demographics, 15*, 27–28.

Levy, S. (2002, March 25). Silicon Valley reboots. *Newsweek*, pp. 42–45.

Lewin, T. (1996, March 2). Child care in conflict with job. *The New York Times*, p. 8.

Lewis, M. H., & Reinsch, N. L. (1988). Listening in organizational environments. *Journal of Business Communication, 25*, 49–67.

Lewis, R. D. (1996). *When cultures collide: Managing successfully across cultures*. London: Nicholas Brealey.

Lieberman, M., & Snowden, L. (1993). Problems in assessing prevalence and membership characteristics of self-help group participants. *Journal of Applied Behavioral Science, 29*, 166–180.

Linder, M., & Nygaard, I. (1998). *Void where prohibited: Rest breaks and the right to urinate on company time*. Ithaca, NY: Cornell University Press.

Linville, P. W., Fischer, G. W., & Fischoff, B. (1992). Perceived risk and decision-making involving AIDS. In J. B. Pryor & G. D. Reeder (Eds.), *The social psychology of HIV infection*. Hillsdale, NJ: Erlbaum.

Lipstadt, D. (1993). *Denying the holocaust: The growing assault on truth and memory*. New York: Penguin.

Littlejohn, S. (1999). *Theories of human communication*. Belmont, CA: Wadsworth.

Littlejohn, S., & Jabusch, D. (1982). Communication competence: Model and application. *Journal of Applied Communication Research, 10*, 29–37.

Liu, M. (2001, September 22). Rumors fueling fears in already stressful times. *San Jose Mercury News*, p. 8A.

Lloyd, S., & Emery, B. (1993). Abuse in the family: An ecological life-cycle perspective. In T. Brubacker (Ed.), *Family relations: Challenges for the future*. Newbury Park, CA: Sage.

Locke, J. (1998). *The de-voicing of society. Why we don't talk to each other anymore*. New York: Simon & Schuster.

Lodge, A. (1998). Myth 4: French is a logical language. In L. Bauer & P. Trudgill (Eds.), *Language myths*. New York: Penguin Books, Inc.

Loftus, E., & Ketcham, K. (1994). *The myth of repressed memory*. New York: St. Martin's Press.

Loftus, E., & Palmer, J. (1974). Reconstruction of automobile destruction: An example of the interaction between language and memory. *Journal of Verbal Learning and Verbal Behavior, 13*, 585–589.

Loftus, E., & Zanni, G. (1975). Eyewitness testimony: The influence of the wording of a question. *Bulletin of the Psychonomic Society, 5*, 86–88.

Lohr, N. (1997, September). Dicks-R-Us. *Wired*, pp. 1–5. Retrieved from http://www.urbekah.com/housewife/dicks.html [1998, May 20].

Lott, J. R. (2001, June 17). Zero tolerance goes too far. *San Jose Mercury News*, p. 7C.

Lubman, S. (1996, September 15). Volunteers bring schools more than they bargained for. *San Jose Mercury News*, pp. A1, A21.

Lubman, S. (1998a, February 22). Asian equation troubles UC. *San Jose Mercury News*, p. A1.

Lubman, S. (1998b, February 21). Culture clash crops up within families as Asian-American students assimilate. *San Jose Mercury News*, p. A20.

Lubman, S. (1998c, January 12). Majoring in pragmatism. *San Jose Mercury News*, p. A4.

Luchins, A. (1957). Primacy-recency in impression formation. In C. Hovland (Ed.), *The order of presentation in persuasion*. New Haven, CT: Yale University Press.

Luk, H. (2001, February 23). Hong Kong considers jamming cell phone reception in public places. *Santa Cruz Sentinel*, p. A9.

Lulofs, R. (1994). *Conflict: From theory to action*. Scottsdale, AZ: Gorsuch Scarisbrick.

Lund, M. (1985). The development of investment and commitment scale for prediction continuity of personal relationships. *Journal of Social and Personal Relationships, 2*, 3–23.

Luria, A. (1968). *The mind of a mnemonist.* New York: Basic Books.

Lustig, M., & Koester, J. (1993). *Intercultural competence across cultures.* New York: HarperCollins.

Lustig, M., & Koester, J. (2003). *Intercultural competence: Interpersonal communication across cultures.* New York: Longman.

Lutz, W. (1996). *The new doublespeak: Why no one knows what anyone's saying anymore.* New York: HarperCollins.

Lying in America. (1987, February 23). *U.S. News & World Report*, pp. 54–61.

Lying is part of everyday life, research confirms. (1996). Retrieved from http://www.nando.net/newsroom/ntm/health/061096/health 16_10972.html.

Maccoby, E., & Mnookin, R. (1992). *Dividing the child: Social and legal dilemmas of custody.* Cambridge, MA: Harvard University Press.

Mainiero, L. A. (1989). *Office romance: Love, power, and sex in the workplace.* New York: Rawson.

Makau, J. M., & Marty, D. L. (2001). *Cooperative argumentation: A model for deliberative community.* Prospect Heights, IL: Waveland Press.

Mallory, J. (1999, November/December). Sexual assault in prison: The numbers are far from funny. *The Touchstone*, pp. 1–4.

Maloy, T. K. (1999). *The Internet Research Guide.* New York: Allworth Press.

Man falls into his cat's water dish and drowns. (2001, August 16). *San Jose Mercury News*, p. 15A.

Mandal, M., Bryden, M., & Bulman-Fleming, M. (1996). Similarities and variations in facial expressions of emotions: Cross-cultural evidence. *International Journal of Psychology, 31*, 49–58.

Mandelbaum, D. G. (Ed.). (1949). *Selected writings of Edward Sapir.* Los Angeles: University of California Press.

Mansfield, M. (1990). Political communication in decision-making groups. In D. Swanson & D. Nimmo (Eds.), *New directions in political communication: A resource book.* Newbury Park, CA: Sage.

Marano, H. E. (1997, November). Gottman and Gray: The two Johns. *Psychology Today*, p. 6.

Marcel, A. (1983). Conscious and unconscious perception: An approach to the relation between phenomenal experience and perceptual processes. *Cognitive Psychology, 15*, 238–300.

Marcus, D. (1999, March 22). When granny goes online. *U.S. News & World Report*, 61–62.

Mariah "quote" spreads. (1999, February 21). *San Jose Mercury News*, p. 2A.

Marks, M. L. (1986, March). The question of quality circles. *Psychology Today*, pp. 36–44.

Marshall, L. (1994). Physical and psychological abuse. In W. Cupach & B. Spitzberg (Eds.), *The dark side of interpersonal communication.* Hillsdale, NJ: Lawrence Erlbaum.

Martell, R. F., Lane, D. M., & Emrich, C. (1996). Male-female differences: A computer simulation. *American Psychologist, 51*, 157–158.

Martin, A. (1997). On teenagers and tattoos. *Journal of the American Academy of Child and Adolescent Psychiatry, 36*, 860–861.

Martin, J., & Nakayama, T. (2000). *Intercultural communication in contexts.* Mountain View, CA: Mayfield.

Martin, L. (1986). Eskimo words for snow: A case study in the genesis and decay of an anthropological example. *American Psychologist, 88*, 418–423.

Martin, M., & Porter, M. (2002). *Video movie guide 2002.* New York: Ballantine Books.

Martinez, A., & Garcia, E. (2001, March 30). With most dramatic racial mix, California is America's melting pot. *San Jose Mercury News*, pp. 1A, 21A.

Masters, B. A. (1999, April 3). Indians laud court ruling to void "Redskin" trademark. *San Jose Mercury News*, p. 13A.

Matlin, M. (1992). *Psychology.* Fort Worth, TX: Harcourt Brace Jovanovich.

Matsumoto, D. (1990). Cultural influences on facial expressions of emotion. *The Southern Communication Journal, 56*, 128–137.

Matsumoto, D. (1994). Culture and emotion. In L. Adler & U. Gielan (Eds.), *Cross-cultural topics in psychology.* Westport, CT: Praeger.

Maugh, T. H. (1998, February 21). The secret to happy marriage: "Yes, dear." *San Jose Mercury News*, p. A1.

May, P. (2002, March 22). Jury says it's murder. *San Jose Mercury News*, pp. 1A, 8A.

May, P. (2002, March 30). Dog owner explains why he showed no remorse. *San Jose Mercury News*, pp. 1A, 18A.

May, R. (1972). *Power and innocence: A search for the sources of violence.* New York: W. W. Norton.

McAleer, N. (1985). *The body almanac.* New York: Doubleday.

McCall, W. (1996, June 25). The hand that holds the remote rules the most. *San Jose Mercury News*, p. D1.

McCann, D., & Margerison, C. (1996). High-performance teams. In R. Cathcart, L. Samovar, & L. Henman (Eds.), *Small group communication: Theory and Practice.* Dubuque, IA: Brown & Benchmark.

McConnell, A. R., & Fazio, R. H. (1996). Women as men and people: Effects of gender marked language. *Personality and Social Psychology Bulletin, 22*, 1004–1013.

McCroskey, J. C., Fayer, J. M., & Richmond, V. P. (1985). Don't speak to me in English: Communication apprehension in Puerto Rico. *Communication Quarterly, 33*, 185–192.

McCrum, R., Cran, W., & MacNeil, R. (1986). *The story of English.* New York: Penguin.

McCullough, M., Rochal, K. C., & Worthington, E. L. (1997). Interpersonal forgiving in close relationships. *Journal of Personality and Social Psychology, 73*, 321–336.

McDaniel, E., & Andersen, P. (1995, May). *Intercultural variations in tactile communication: An empirical field study.* Paper presented at the International Communication Association, Albuquerque, NM.

McDaniel, E. R. (2000). In L. A. Samovar & R. E. Porter (Eds.), *Intercultural communication: A reader.* Belmont, CA: Wadsworth.

McDermott, I. E. (1998, June). Informed consent: Disease and ailment information on the Web. *Searcher*, pp. 50–55.

McDonald, M. (2001, August 13). Regimes worry about Net's reach. *San Jose Mercury News*, pp. 1E, 2E.

McDonald's Listens—Finally! (1998, March 9). *Listening Leaders.* Retrieved from http://www.listencoach.com.

McGarity, A. (1997). Big brother goes to the doctor. *Winning Orations, 127*–130.

McGinn, D. (2000, October 16). Mired in meetings. *Newsweek,* pp. 52–54.

McGirk, J. (1998, February). You're not fat, you're in the wrong country. *Marie Claire,* pp. 52–56.

McGonagle, K. A., Kessler, R. C., & Gotlif, I. H. (1993). The effects of marital disagreement style, frequency, and outcome on marital disruption. *Journal of Social and Personal Relationships, 9,* 507–524.

McGuinnies, E., & Ward, C. (1980). Better liked than right: Trustworthiness and expertise as factors in credibility. *Personality and Social Psychology Bulletin, 6,* 467–472.

McGuire, W. (1964). Inducing resistance to persuasion: Some contemporary approaches. In L. Berkowitz (Ed.), *Advances in experimental social psychology.* New York: Academic Press.

McKay, M., Rogers, P., & McKay, J. (1989). *When anger hurts: Quieting the storm within.* Oakland, CA: New Harbinger.

McLaughlin, S. (1996). The dirty truth about your kitchen: Using common sense to prevent food poisoning. In L. G. Schnoor (Ed.), *Winning Orations.* Northfield, MN: Interstate Oratorical Association.

McLuhan, M. (1964). *Understanding media: The extensions of man.* New York: McGraw-Hill.

McLuhan, M. (1967). *The medium is the massage.* New York: Random House.

McNeil, B. J., Pauker, S. G., Sox, H. C., & Tversky, A. (1982). On the elicitation of preferences for alternative therapies. *New England Journal of Medicine, 306,* 1259–1262.

McNutt, P. (1997, October/November). When strategic decisions are ignored. *Fast Company,* p. 12.

Meacham, J. (1996, July 27). Revenge of the nerd. *San Jose Mercury News,* p. DD8.

Mecca, S. J., & Rubin, L. J. (1999). Definitional research on African American students and sexual harassment. *Psychology of Women Quarterly, 23,* 813.

Meg Ryan: The new Lombard? (1993, June 27). *Akron Beacon Journal,* p. D1.

Mehrabian, A. (1981). *Silent message: Implicit communication of emotion and attitude.* Belmont, CA: Wadsworth.

Mehrabian, A., & Ferris, S. (1967). Inference of attitudes from nonverbal communication in two channels. *Journal of Consulting Psychology, 31,* 248–252.

Menzel, K. E., & Carrell, L. J. (1994). The relationship between preparation and performance in public speaking. *Communication Education, 43,* 17–26.

Mercer, G., & Benjamin, J. (1980). Spatial behavior of university undergraduates in double-occupancy residence room: An inventory of effects. *Journal of Applied Social Psychology, 10,* 32–44.

Merritt, A. (1998). *Replicating Hofstede: A study of pilots in eighteen countries.* Retrieved from http://www.psy.utexas.edu.psy. helmreich/hofrep.htm.

Message of hope. (1998, July 24). *USA Weekend,* pp. 9–10.

Metts, S., Cupach, N., & Imahori, T. (1992). Perceptions of sexual compliance resisting messages in three types of cross-sex relationships. *Western Journal of Communication, 56,* 1–17.

Meyrowitz, J. (1997). Shifting worlds of strangers: Medium theory and changes in "them" versus "us." In K. Massey (Ed.), *Readings in mass communication: Media literacy and culture.* Mountain View, CA: Mayfield.

Michael, K. (1997). Corporate welfare: A national injustice. In L. G. Schnoor (Ed.), *Winning orations.* Northfield, MN: Interstate Oratorical Association.

Mikulan, S. (2002). Downtown dog days. *LA Weekly.* Retrieved from http://www.laweekly.com/ink/02/16/ open-mikulan.shtml.

Milbank, D. (2002, April 17). Bush gaffes get an official fix up. *San Jose Mercury News,* p. 8A.

Milgram, S. (1974). *Obedience to authority.* New York: Harper & Row.

Miller, A. G. (1986). *The obedience experiments: A case study of controversy in social science.* Westport, CT: Praeger.

Miller, J. G. (1984). Culture and the development of everyday social explanation. *Journal of Personality and Social Psychology, 46,* 961–978.

Miller, K. (1996, April). Together forever. *Life,* 44–56.

Miller, K., & Monge, P. (1986). Participation, satisfaction, and productivity: A meta-analytic review. *Academy of Management Journal, 29,* 727–753.

Mills, N. (1996, July). The (almost) born-again Dennis Quaid. *Cosmopolitan, 156,* 162.

Minister accidentally kills self. (1998, October 3). *San Jose Mercury News,* p. A13.

Mintz, H. (1998, April 18). The end of a 12-year nightmare. *San Jose Mercury News,* p. A1.

Mishkind, M., & Rodin, J. (1986). Embodiment of masculinity. *American Behavioral Scientist, 29,* 545–562.

Misunderstood word costs D. C. official job in mayor's office. (1999, January 28). *San Jose Mercury News,* p. A2.

Mnookin, S. (2003, May 19). A journalist's hard fall. *Newsweek,* pp. 40–41.

Moghaddam, F., Taylor, D., & Wright, S. (1993). *Social psychology in cross-cultural perspective.* New York: W. H. Freeman.

Moghaddam, F. M. (1998). *Social psychology: Exploring universals across cultures.* New York: W. H. Freeman and Company.

Mohamed, A., & Wiebe, F. (1996). Toward a process theory of groupthink. *Small Group Research, 27,* 416–430.

Montemayor, R. (1986). Family variation in parent-adolescent storm and stress. *Journal of Adolescent Research, 1,* 15–31.

Moody, F. (1996, June/July). Wonder women in the rude boys' paradise. *Fast Company,* 12–14.

Moore, D. W. (2002, May 14). Americans more accepting of female bosses than ever. *Gallup News Service.* Retrieved from www.gallup.com/login?URL=/poll/releases/ pr970829a.asp.

More Americans "too busy" to vote. (1998, August 17). *San Jose Mercury News,* p. A7.

Morreale, S. (1999, March). Ability to communicate ranked no. 1 by employers. *Spectra, 35,* 10.

Morris, D. (1977). *Manwatching: A field guide to human behavior.* New York: Harry N. Abrams.

Morris, D. (1985). *Body watchers.* New York: Crown.

Morris, D., Collett, P., Marsh, P., & O'Shaughnessy, M. (1979). *Gestures: Their origins and distribution.* New York: Stein & Day.

Morris, T., & Gorham, J. (1996). Fashion in the classroom: Effects of attire on student perceptions of instructors in college classes. *Communication Education, 45,* 135–148.

Morse, B. J. (1995). Beyond the Conflict Tactics Scale: Assessing gender differences in partner violence. *Violence and Victims, 10,* 251–272.

Morse, S., & Gergen, K. (1970). Social comparison, self-consistency and the concept of self. *Journal of Personality and Social Psychology, 16,* 149–156.

Motley, M. T. (1995). *Overcoming your fear of public speaking: A proven method.* New York: McGraw-Hill.

Movie content. (1999, August 12). *The Gallup Poll 1999.* New York: Gallup.

Mudrack, P., & Farrell, G. (1995). An examination of functional role behavior and its consequences for individuals in group settings. *Small Group Research, 26,* 542–571.

Muehlenhard, C., Koralewski, M., Andrews, S., & Burdick, C. (1986). Verbal and nonverbal cues that convey interest in dating: Two studies. *Behavior Therapy, 17,* 404–419.

Mulac, A. (1998). The gender-linked language effect: Do language differences really make a difference? In D. J. Canary & K. Dindia (Eds.), *Sex differences and similarities in communication.* Mahwah, NJ: Lawrence Erlbaum.

Mulac, A., & Bradac, J. (1995). Women's style in problem solving interaction: Powerless, or simply feminine? In P. Kalbfleisch & M. Cody (Eds.), *Gender, power and communication in human relationships.* Hillsdale, NJ: Lawrence Erlbaum.

Mulac, A., Wiemann, J., Wideman, S., & Dibson, T. (1988). Male/female language differences and effects in same-sex and mixed-sex dyads: The gender-linked language effects. *Communication Monographs, 55,* 315–335.

Mullen, B., Anthony, T., Salas, E., & Driskill, J. (1994). Group cohesiveness and quality decision making: An integration of tests of the groupthink hypothesis. *Small Group Research, 25,* 189–204.

Mulshine, P. (1998, April 26). Statistics distort drunken-driving standards debate. *San Jose Mercury News,* p. F3.

Murphy, B., & Zorn, T. (1996). Gendered interaction in professional relationships. In J. Wood (Ed.), *Gendered relationships.* Mountain View, CA: Mayfield.

Murray, B. (1997, May). How important is teaching style to students? *APA Monitor,* 1–3.

Myers, D. G. (2001). *Psychology.* New York: Worth Publishers.

Myers, S. (1999, January 23). Military discharging more gays, but why? *San Jose Mercury News,* p. A17.

Myerson, J. (2001). *IDEO: Masters of innovation.* London: Calmann & King, Ltd.

Na, E. Y., & Loftus, E. F. (1998). Attitudes toward law and prisoners, conservative authoritarianism, attribution, and internal locus of control: Korean and American law students and undergraduates. *Journal of Cross Cultural Psychology, 29,* 595–615.

Naked came the commencement speaker. (1998, July 18). *San Jose Mercury News,* p. A3.

Nanda, S., & Warms, R. L. (1998). *Cultural anthropology.* Belmont, CA: Wadsworth.

Napolitan, D., & Goethals, G. (1979). The attribution of friendliness. *Journal of Experimental Social Psychology, 15,* 105–113.

Narcisco, J., & Burkett, T. (1975). *Declare yourself.* Englewood Cliffs, NJ: Prentice-Hall.

Nash, A. (1998, July). Marvelous Meg. *Good Housekeeping,* 96–99.

Natale, R. (1994, December). Megabucks megastar Meg Ryan. *Cosmopolitan,* 150–153.

National Archives and Records Administration. (1987). *Kennedy's inaugural address of 1961.* Washington, DC: U.S. Government Printing Office.

National Association of Colleges and Employers. (1999). *Job Outlook '99.* Retrieved from http://www.jonwell.org/pubs/joboutlook/want.htm.

Neisser, A. (1983). *The other side of silence.* New York: Knopf.

Nellermoe, D. A., Weirich, T. R., & Reinstein, A. (1999). Using practitioners' viewpoints to improve accounting students' communications skills. *Business Communication Quarterly, 62,* 41–60.

Nelson, M. (1998). *Embracing victory: Life lessons in competition and compassion.* New York: William Morrow.

Neuliep, J. W., & Ryan, D. J. (1998). The influence of intercultural communication apprehension and sociocommunicative orientation on uncertainty reduction during initial cross-cultural interaction. *Communication Quarterly, 46,* 88–99.

Neuman, S. (1991). *Literacy in the television age: The myth of the TV effect.* Norwood, NJ: Ablex.

Neumann, P. G. (1999, July). Information is a double-edged sword. *Communications of the ACM,* p. 120.

New Pentagon manual focuses on cooperation. (1991, December 19). *San Jose Mercury News,* p. A2.

Nicotera, A., & Rancer, A. (1994). The influence of sex on self-perception and social stereotyping of aggressive communication predispositions. *Western Journal of Communication, 58,* 283–307.

Nishida, T. (1991). *Sequence patterns of self-disclosure among Japanese and North American students.* Paper presented at the conference on communication in Japan and the United States, California State University, Fullerton.

Noe, R. (1988). Women and mentoring. *Academy of Management Review, 13,* 65–78.

Noller, P. (1993). Gender and emotional communication in marriage: Different cultures or differential social power? *Journal of Language and Social Psychology, 12,* 132–152.

Noonan, P. (1998). *Simply speaking: How to communicate your ideas with style, substance, and clarity.* New York: HarperCollins.

Northouse, P. (1997). *Leadership: Theory and practice.* Thousand Oaks, CA: Sage.

O'Brien, T. (1995, November 5). No jerks allowed. *West,* 8–14.

O'Keefe, D. (1990). *Persuasion: Theory and research.* Newbury Park, CA: Sage.

O'Leary, M., Curley, A., Rosenbaum, A., & Clarke, C. (1985). Assertion training for abused women: A potentially hazardous treatment. *Journal of Marital and Family Therapy, 11,* 319–322.

O'Neil, J. (2002, January 22). Patterns: Piercing's popularity, beyond the ears. *The New York Times.* Retrieved from www.nytimes.com.

Oakes, J. (1985). *Keeping track: How schools structure inequality.* New Haven, CT: Yale University Press.

Oberg, K. (1960). Cultural shock: Adjustments to new cultural environments. *Practical Anthropology, 7,* 177–182.

Offner, A. K., Kramer, T. J., & Winter, J. P. (1996). The effects of facilitation, recording and pauses upon group brainstorming. *Small Group Research, 27,* 283–298.

Ofshe, R., & Watters, E. (1994). *Making monsters: False memories, psychotherapy, and sexual hysteria.* New York: Charles Scribner's Sons.

Onishi, N. (2001, February 17). Fat is the ideal body shape in West Africa. *San Jose Mercury News*, p. 2A.

Oprah: A heavenly body? Survey finds talk-show host a celestial shoo-in. (1997, March 31). *U.S. News & World Report*, p. 18.

Orbe, M. O. (1998). *Constructing co-cultural theory: An explication of culture, power, and communication.* Thousand Oaks, CA: Sage.

Orlick, T. (1978). *Winning through cooperation: Competitive insanity, cooperative alternatives.* Washington, DC: Acropolis Books.

Ornish, D. (1990). *Dr. Dean Ornish's program for reversing heart disease.* New York: Ballantine.

Orr, D. (1968). Time compressed speech—a perspective. *Journal of Communication, 18*, 272–282.

Orwell, G. (1949). *Nineteen eighty four.* New York: New American Library.

Osborn, M., & Osborn, S. (1997). *Public speaking.* New York: Houghton Mifflin.

Osgood, C., Suci, G., & Tannenbaum, P. (1957). *The measurement of meaning.* Urbana, IL: University of Illinois Press.

Osgood, G. (1969). The nature of measurement of meaning. In J. Snider and C. Osgood (Eds.), *The semantic differential technique.* Chicago: Aldine.

Ostrom, M. (1999, March 18). Poll: Clinton disliked, but effective as ever. *San Jose Mercury News*, p. A10.

Ostrom, M. A. (2001, July 26). More Hispanics using the Internet, study finds. *San Jose Mercury News*, pp. 1C, 9C.

Ostrom, M. A., & Seipel, T. (2001, June 21). Net changing ways today's youth connect. *San Jose Mercury News*, pp. 1A, 18A.

Overholser, G. (2001, September 3). Executive pay enters the stratosphere. *San Jose Mercury News*, p. 9B.

Owen, W. F. (1987). The verbal expression of love by women and men as a critical communication event in personal relationships. *Women's Studies in Communication, 10*, 15–24.

Pacheco, T. (1995). Untitled. In L. Schoor (Ed.) *Winning Orations*, Mankato, MN: Interstate Oratorical Association, 116–117.

Paetzold, R., & O'Leary-Kelly, A. (1993). Organizational communication and the legal dimensions of hostile work environment sexual harassment. In G. Kreps (Ed.), *Sexual harassment: Communication implications.* Creskill, NJ: Hampton Press.

Page, S. (1977). Effects of the mental illness label in attempts to obtain accommodation. *Canadian Journal of Behavioral Science, 9*, 84–90.

Paivio, A. (1969). Mental imagery in associative learning and memory. *Psychological Review, 76*, 241–263.

Palmer, P. (2000, October 9). Look closely at that bill. *Newsweek*, pp. 81–82.

Park, M., & Floyd, K. (1995). Making friends in cyberspace. *Online Journal of Computer Mediated Communication, 1*, p. 4.

Parks, C., & Vu, A. (1994). Social dilemma of individuals from highly individualist and collectivist cultures. *Journal of Conflict Resolution, 3*, 708–718.

Parks, M. R., & Floyd, K. (1996). Making friends in cyberspace. *Journal of Communication, 46*, 80–97.

Pasel, J. L. (2001). Burning Issue. In L. Schnoor & B. Wickelgren (Eds.), *Winning orations.* Mankato, MN: Interstate Oratorical Association.

Passer, M. W., & Smith, R. E. (2001). *Psychology.* New York: McGraw-Hill.

Patterson, D. (1996, February 4). Public speaking skills can give job seekers an edge. *Seattle Times*, p. B1.

Patterson, F. (1978, October). Conversations with a gorilla. *National Geographic*, 438–465.

Patterson, F., & Linden, E. (1981). *The education of Koko.* New York: Holt, Rinehart & Winston.

Patterson, M., Powell, J., & Lenihan, M. (1986). Touch, compliance, and interpersonal affects. *Journal of Nonverbal Behavior, 10*, 41–50.

Paulos, J. (1994, March). Counting on Dyscalculia. *Discourse*, 30–36.

Paulos, J. A. (1988*). Innumeracy: Mathematical illiteracy and its consequences.* New York: Hill & Wang.

Pavitt, C. (1999). Theorizing about the group communication-leadership relationship: Input-process-output and functional models. In L. R. Frey, D. S. Gouran, and M. S. Poole (Eds.), *The handbook of group communication theory & research.* Thousand Oaks, CA; Sage.

Pavitt, C., & Haight, L. (1985). The "competenet communicator" as a cognitive prototype. *Human Communication Research, 12*, 225–241.

PC buyers influenced strongly by salespeople. (1996, October 21). *Investor's Business Daily*, p. A6.

Pendergrast, M. (1995). *Victims of memory: Incest accusations and shattered lives.* Hinesburg, VA: Upper Access, Inc.

Peplau, L. A., & Campbell, S. M. (1989). The balance of power in dating and marriage. In J. Freeman (Ed.), *Women: A feminist perspective.* Mountain View, CA: Mayfield.

Peplau, L. A., & Cochran, S. D. (1980, September*). Sex differences in values concerning love relationships.* Paper presented at the annual meeting of the American Psychological Association, Montreal.

Perret, G. (1994). *Classic one-liners.* New York: Sterling.

Peterson, D. (1991). Physically violent husbands of the 1980s and their resources. *Journal of Family Violence, 6*, 1–15.

Peterson, M. S. (1997). Personnel interviewers' perception of the importance and adequacy of applicants' communication skills. *Communication Education, 46*, 287–291.

Petofi, A. (1988). The graphic revolution in computers. In E. Cornish (Ed.), *Careers tomorrow: The outlook for work in a changing world.* Bethesda, MD: World Future Society.

Pettigrew, T., & Martin, J. (1987). Shaping the organizational context for Black American inclusion. *Journal of Social Issues, 43*, 41–78.

Petty, R., & Cacioppo, J. (1984). The effects of involvement on responses to argument quantity and quality: Central and peripheral routes to persuasion. *Journal of Personality and Social Psychology, 46*, 69–81.

Petty, R., & Cacioppo, J. (1986a). The elaboration likelihood model of persuasion. In L. Berkowitz (Ed.), *Advances in experimental social psychology* (Vol. 19). New York: Academic Press.

Petty, R., & Cacioppo, J. (1986b). *Communication and persuasion: Central and peripheral routes to attitude change.* New York: Springer-Verlag.

Petty, R., Kasmer, J., Haugtvedt, C., & Cacioppo, J. (1987). Source and message factors in persuasion: A reply to Stiff's critique of the elaboration likelihood model. *Communication Monographs, 54*, 233–249.

Pfau, M., & Van Bockern, S. (1994). The persistence of inoculation in conferring resistance to smoking initiation among adolescents: The second year. *Human Communication Research, 20,* 413–430.

Pfeiffer, K., Cole, B., & Dada, M. K. (1998). Attributions for youth crime among British and Nigerian primary school children. *Journal of Social Psychology, 138,* 251–253.

Phillips, E., & Cheston, R. (1979). Conflict resolution: What works? *California Management Review, 21,* 76–83.

Philpot, J. (1983). *The relative contribution to meaning of verbal and nonverbal channels of communication: A meta-analysis.* Unpublished master's thesis, University of Nebraska.

Pinker, S. (1994). *The language instinct: How the mind creates language.* New York: HarperCollins.

Pinker, S. (1997). *How the mind works.* New York: W. W. Norton & Company.

Pinker, S. (1999). *Words and rules: The ingredients of language.* New York: HarperCollins.

Pipher, M. (1994). *Reviving Ophelia: Saving the selves of adolescent girls.* New York: Ballantine.

Pipher, M. (1996). *The shelter of each other: Rebuilding our families.* New York: Ballantine.

Platt, K. (2000, July 30). Internet changing a culture. *San Jose Mercury News,* pp. 1AA, 3AA.

Plotnik, R. (1996). *Introduction to psychology.* Pacific Grove, CA: Brooks/Cole.

Pogrebin, L. C. (1987). *Among friends.* New York: McGraw-Hill.

Poll: One in three aren't convinced Holocaust occurred. (1993, April 20). *San Jose Mercury News,* p. A1.

Pollack, I., & Pickett, J. M. (1964). Intelligibility of excerpts from fluent speech: Auditory vs. structural context. *Journal of Verbal Learning and Verbal Behavior, 3,* 79–84.

Pondy, L. R. (1992). Reflections on organizational conflict. *Journal of Organizational Behavior, 13,* 257–262.

Pope, H. G., Gruber, A. J., Mangweth, B., Bureau, B., deCol, C., Jouvent, R., & Hudson, J. I. (2000). Body image perception among men in three countries. *American Journal of Psychiatry, 157,* 1297–1301.

Popenoe, D., & Whitehead, B. D. (2001, June 28). *Singles seek soul mates for marriage.* Gallup Poll News Service. Retrieved from http://www.gallup.com/Poll/releases.

Postman, N. (1985). *Amusing ourselves to death: Public discourse in the age of show business.* New York: Viking Penguin.

Postman, N. (1993). *Technopoly: The surrender of culture to technology.* New York: Knopf.

Powell, G. N., & Mainiero, L. A. (1990). What managers need to know about office romances. *Leadership and Organization Development Journal, 11,* i–iii.

Powell, J. L. (1988). A test of the knew-it-all-along efffect in the 1984 presidential and statewide elections. *Journal of Applied Social Psychology, 18,* 760–773.

Praise thy employees survey says. (1994, September 13). *San Jose Mercury News,* p. E1.

Pratkanis, A., & Aronson, E. (2001). *The age of propaganda: The everyday use and abuse of persuasion.* New York: W. H. Freeman.

Propp, K. (1995). An experimental examination of biological sex as a status cue in decision-making groups and its influence on information use. *Small Group Research, 26,* 451–474.

Provine, R. R. (2000). *Laughter: A scientific investigation.* New York: Viking.

Pruitt, D., & Rubin, J. (1986). *Social conflict: Escalation, stalemate, and settlement.* New York: Random House.

Pullum, G. K. (1991). *The great Eskimo vocabulary hoax.* Chicago: University of Chicago Press.

Purdy, M., & Borisoff, D. (1997). *Listening in everyday life.* Lanham, MD: University Press of America.

Put enjoyment ahead of achievement. (1994, February 20). *Santa Cruz Sentinel,* p. D2.

Puzzanghera, J. (1996, December 5). Drug helps high-risk patients survive surgery, study says. *San Jose Mercury News,* pp. A1, A28.

Quarttrone, G., & Jones, E. (1980). The perception of variability within in-groups and out-groups: Implications for the law of small numbers. *Journal of Personality and Social Psychology, 38,* 141–152.

Raban, J. (1997, November 24). What the nanny trial tells us about transatlantic body language. *The New York Times,* p. 55.

Rae-Dupree, J. (1997, December 30). Disk-drive leap doubles capacity. *San Jose Mercury News,* p. A1.

Rampton, S., & Stauber, J. (2001). *Trust us, we're experts: How industry manipulates science and gambles with your future.* New York: Jeremy P. Tarcher/Putnam.

Rand, H. (1998, February 15). Science, non-science and nonsense. *Vital Speeches of the Day,* 282–284.

Rathus, S. (1990). *Psychology.* Fort Worth, TX: Holt, Rinehart & Winston.

Reardon, K. (1991). *Persuasion in practice.* Newbury Park, CA: Sage.

Reason, J., & Mycielska, K. (1982). *Absent-minded? The psychology of mental lapses and everyday errors.* Englewood Cliffs, NJ: Prentice-Hall.

Reeling in the years. (1998, April 13). *Newsweek,* p. 14.

Regan, D., & Totten, J. (1975). Empathy and attribution: Turning observers into actors. *Journal of Personality and Social Psychology, 32,* 850–856.

Regan, P. C., Kocan, E. R., & Whitlock, T. (1998). Ain't love grand! A prototype analysis of the concept of romantic love. *Journal of Social and Personal Relationships, 15,* 411–420.

Reilly, M. E., & Lynch, J. M. (1990). Power-sharing in lesbian relationships. *Journal of Homosexuality, 19,* 1–30.

Reis, H. T., & Wheeler, L. (1991). Studying social interaction with the Rochester Interaction Record. In M. P. Zanna (Ed.), *Advances in experimental social psychology.* New York: Academic Press.

Remland, M., Jones, T., & Brinkman, H. (1995). Interpersonal distance, body orientation, and touch: Effects of culture, gender, and age. *The Journal of Social Psychology, 135,* 281–297.

Renzetti, C. (1991). *Violent betrayal: Partner abuse in lesbian relationships.* Newbury Park, CA: Sage.

Rethinking black leadership (2001, January 28). *Newsweek,* pp. 42–43.

Reyneri, A. (1984). The nose knows, but science doesn't. *Science, 84,* 26.

Rezendes, D. (1998, November 11). Medical information sites on the Web can be bad for your health. *San Jose Mercury News,* pp. A1, A5.

Ribeau, S. A., Baldwin, J. R., & Hecht, M. L. (2000). An African American communication perspective. In L. A. Samovar &

R. E. Porter (Eds.), *Intercultural communication: A reader.* Belmont, CA: Wadsworth.

Richmond, V., & McCroskey, J. (1989). *Communication: Apprehension, avoidance, and effectiveness.* Scottsdale, AZ: Gorsuch Scarisbrick.

Richter, P. (2001, June 2). Gay-dismissal rates in military highest since '94, Pentagon says. *San Jose Mercury News,* p. 14A.

Ricks, D. (2000, February 4). Cancer likely to become leading U.S. killer. *San Jose Mercury News,* p. 10A.

Riechmann, D. (2001, August 17). Flight safety spiels really work. *Santa Cruz Sentinel,* pp. A1, A10.

Ritts, V., & Patterson, M. (1992). Expectations, impressions, and judgments of physically attractive students: A review. *Review of Educational Research, 62,* 413–426.

Rivals blast Robertson talk about hostages. (1988, February 25). *San Jose Mercury News,* p. A8.

Robertson sets off furor on hostage. (1988, February 26). *Chicago Tribune,* p. C12.

Rodkin, P. C., Farmer, T. W., Pearl, R., & Van Acker, R. (2000). Heterogeniety of popular boys: Antisocial and prosocial configurations. *Developmental Psychology, 36,* 14–24.

Rodriguez, J. (1995). *Confounds in fear arousing persuasive messages: Do the paths less traveled make all the difference?* Unpublished doctoral dissertation, Michigan State University, East Lansing, MI.

Roediger, H., Capaldi, E., Paris, S., & Polivy, J. (1991). *Psychology.* New York: HarperCollins.

Rogers, C., & Roethlisberger, F. (1952, July/August). Barriers and gateways to communication. *Harvard Business Review,* 28–35.

Rogers, L. E., Castleton, A., & Lloyd, S. A. (1996). Relational control and physical aggression in satisfying marital relationships. In D. D. Cahn & S. A. Lloyd (Eds.), *Family violence from a communication perspective.* Thousand Oaks, CA: Sage.

Rollins, B. C., & Oheneba-Sakyi, Y. (1990). Physical violence in Utah households. *Journal of Family Violence, 5,* 301–309.

Roloff, M. E., & Cloven, D. H. (1990). The chilling effect in interpersonal relationships: The reluctance to speak one's mind. In D. Cohen (Ed.), *Intimates in conflict: A communication perspective.* Hillsdale, NJ: Lawrence Erlbaum.

Romano, D. (1988). *Intercultural marriage: Promises and pitfalls.* Yarmouth, ME: Intercultural Press.

Romig, D. (1996). *Breakthrough teamwork: Outstanding results using structured teamwork.* Chicago: Irwin Professional Publishing.

Rosch, E. (1973). On the internal structure of perceptual and semantic categories. In T. E. Moore (Ed.), *Cognitive development and the acquisition of language.* New York: Academic Press.

Rose, V. (2001). The bowels of our nation. In L. Schnoor & B. Wickelgren (Eds.), *Winning orations.* Mankato, MN: Interstate Oratorical Association.

Rosenbaum, L., & Rosenbaum, W. (1985). Morale and productivity consequences of group leadership style, stress, and type of task. *Journal of Applied Psychology, 55,* 343–358.

Rosenfeld, L. (1983). Communication climate and coping mechanisms in the college classroom. *Communication Education, 32,* 169–174.

Rosenfeld, L. B., Richman, J. M., & Bowen, G. L. (1998). Supportive communication and school outcomes from academically "at-risk" and other low income middle school students. *Communication Education, 47,* 309–325.

Rosenhan, D. (1973). On being sane in insane places. *Science, 179,* 250–258.

Rosenthal, D. B., & Hautaluoma, J. (1988). Effects of importance of issues, gender, and power of contenders on conflict management style. *Journal of Social Psychology, 128,* 699–701.

Rosenthal, N. (1997, July 15). How to prevent that "us vs. them" feeling within the family. *San Jose Mercury News,* p. E4.

Rosenthal, R. (Ed.). (1979). *Skill in nonverbal communication: Individual differences.* Cambridge, MA: Gunn & Hain.

Rosenthal, R., & Jacobson, L. (1968). *Pygmalion in the classroom: Teachers' expectations and pupils' intellectual development.* New York: Holt, Rinehart & Winston.

Roth and Strong, Inc. (1989). *Roth and Strong climate index.* Lexington, MA: Roth & Strong, Inc.

Rothwell, J. (1982). *Telling it like it isn't: Language misuse and malpractice.* Englewood Cliffs, NJ: Prentice-Hall.

Rothwell, J. (2001). *In mixed company: Small group communication.* Fort Worth, TX: Harcourt Brace.

Rottenberg, A. T. (2000). *The structure of argument.* New York: St. Martin's Press.

Rozanski, A. (1988). Mental stress and the induction of silent ischemia in patients with coronary artery disease. *New England Journal of Medicine, 318,* 1005–1012.

Ruback, B. R., & Jweng, D. (1997). Territorial defense in parking lots: Retaliation against waiting drivers. *Journal of Applied Social Psychology, 27,* 821–834.

Rubenstein, M. (1975). *Patterns of problem solving.* Englewood Cliffs, NJ: Prentice-Hall.

Rubin, A., Peplau, L. A., & Hill, C. T. (1981). Loving and leaving: Sex differences in romantic attachments. *Sex Roles, 7,* 821–835.

Rubin, D. L., Greene, K., & Schneider, D. (1994). Adopting gender-inclusive language reforms: Diachronic and synchronic variation. *Journal of Language and Social Psychology, 13,* 91–114.

Rubin, L. (1985). *Just friends: The role of friendship in our lives.* New York: Harper & Row.

Rubin, L. B. (1984). *Intimate strangers: Men and women together.* New York: Harper & Row.

Rubin, R. B., & Graham, E. E. (1988, January). Communication correlates of college success: An exploratory investigation. *Communication Education, 37,* 14.

Rubin, T. (1999, March 21). China aims to have it both ways on the Net. *San Jose Mercury News,* p. P7.

Ruch, W. (1989). *International handbook of corporate communication.* Jefferson, NC: McFarland.

Ruggeiro, V. (1988). *Teaching thinking across the curriculum.* New York: Harper & Row.

Russell, D. E. H. (1982). *Rape in marriage.* Bloomington, IN: Indiana University Press.

Russell, R. J. H., & Hulson, B. (1992). Physical and psychological abuse of heterosexual partners. *Personality and Individual Differences, 13,* 457–473.

Rusting, C. L., & Nolen-Hoeksema (1998). Regulating responses to anger: Effects of rumination and distraction on angry mood. *Journal of Personality and Social Psychology, 74,* 790–803.

Ryan, M. (1991, March 31). Another way to teach migrant students. *Los Angeles Times*, p. B20.

Rymer, R. (1993). *Genie: An abused child's flight from silence*. New York: HarperCollins.

Sabourin, T. C. (1995). The role of negative reciprocity in spouse abuse: A relational control analysis. *Journal of Applied Communication Research, 23,* 271–283.

Sabourin, T. C., & Stamp, G. H. (1995). Communication and the experience of dialectical tensions in family life: An examination of abusive and nonabusive families. *Communication Monographs, 62,* 213–242.

Sacks, O. (1990). *Seeing voices: A journey into the world of the deaf.* New York: Vintage Books.

Safire, W. (2001, September 30). Every conflict generates its own lexicon. *The New York Times.* Retrieved from http://www.nytimes.com/2001/09/30/magazine/.

Sagan, C. (1995, January/February). Wonder and skepticism. *Skeptical Inquirer,* 24–28.

Sagrestano, L. M. (1992). Power strategies in interpersonal relationships. *Psychology of Women Quarterly, 16,* 481–495.

Saint, S., & Lawson, J. (1997). *Rules for reaching consensus.* San Diego, CA: Pfeiffer.

Salazar, A. (1995). Understanding the synergistic effects of communication in small groups. *Small Group Research, 26,* 169–199.

Samovar, L., & Porter, R. (2001). *Communication between cultures.* Belmont, CA: Wadsworth.

Sapir, E. (1931). Conceptual categories in primitive languages. *Science, 74,* 572–578.

Savage-Rumbaugh, E. S. (1993). Language learnability in man, ape, and dolphin. In L. Roitblat, L. M. Herman, & P. E. Nachtigall (Eds.), *Language and communication: Comparative perspectives.* Hillsdale, NJ: Erlbaum.

Savage-Rumbaugh, E. S., & Lewin, R. (1994, September). Ape at the brink. *Discover, 15,* 91–98.

Savage-Rumbaugh, S., & Lewin, R. (1994). *Kanzi.* New York: Wiley.

Sazer, L., & Kassinove, H. (1991). Effects of counselor's profanity and subject's religiosity on tenet acquisition of a counseling lecture and behavioral compliance. *Psychological Reports, 69,* 1059–1070.

Schaef, A. (1985*). Women's reality: An emerging female system in a White male society.* New York: Harper & Row.

Schittekatte, M., & Van Hiel, A. (1996). Effects of partially shared information and awareness of unshared information on information sampling. *Small Group Research, 27,* 431–449.

Schlosser, E. (2002). *Fast food nation: The dark side of the all-American meal.* New York: Perennial.

Schlossler, E. (1997, September). A grief like no other. *The Atlantic Monthly,* 37–76.

Schmidt, S., & Kipnis, D. (1987, November). The perils of persistence. *Psychology Today,* 32–34.

Schmidt, W. (1991, October). *Oral communication across the curriculum: A critical review of literature.* Paper presented at the meeting of the Florida Communication Association Convention, Vero Beach, FL.

Schmitt, C., & Slonaker, L. (1996, January 14). High technology doesn't always equal high achievement. *San Jose Mercury News,* p. A1.

Schmitt, E. (1996, September 7). Minnesotans battle over a 5-letter word. *San Jose Mercury News,* p. A7.

Schmitt, E. (2001, April 30). Census data finds major racial shift in largest cities. *San Jose Mercury News,* p. 9A.

Schneider, K., & Levitt, S. (1996, June 3). Mission impossible. *People,* 65–74.

Schneider, K. S. (1993, August 2). Educating Meg. *People Weekly,* 68–74.

Scholar, E. (1990, April 6). Americans a threat to planet. *Charlotte Observer.*

Scholtes, P. (1990). An elaboration of Deming's teachings on performance appraisal. In G. McLean, S. Damme, & R. Swanson (Eds.), *Performance appraisal: Perspectives on a quality management approach.* Alexandria, VA: American Society for Training and Development.

Schultz, C. (1998, May 30). Message of peace from war photo. *San Jose Mercury News,* p. E3.

Schultz, E. A. (1990). *Dialogue at the margins: Whorf, Bakhtin, and linguistic relativity.* Madison, WI: University of Wisconsin Press.

Schultz, H., & Yang, D. J. (1997). *Pour your heart into it: How Starbucks built a company one cup at a time.* New York: Hyperion.

Schultz, P. W., & Oskamp, S. (2000). *Social psychology: An applied perspective.* Upper Saddle River, NJ: Prentice Hall.

Schuster, M. (1984). The Scanlon Plan: A longitudinal analysis. *Journal of Applied Behavioral Science, 20,* 23–28.

Schwartz, S. (1995). Identifying culture-specifics in the context and structure of values. *Journal of Cross-Cultural Psychology, 26,* 92–116.

Sciolino, E. (1996, November 12). Subject of famous photograph lays wreath at Vietnam Memorial. *San Jose Mercury News,* pp. A1, A14.

Sedikides, C., Campbell, W., Reeder, G., & Elliott, A. (1998). The self-serving bias in relational context. *Journal of Personality and Social Psychology, 74,* 378–386.

Seibold, D. R., & Spitzberg, B. H. (1982). Attribution theory and research: Review and implications for communication. In B. Dervin & M. J. Voight (Eds.), *Progress in communication sciences.* Norwood, NJ: Ablex.

Seipel, T. (1997, October 4). The spit felt round the world. *San Jose Mercury News,* pp. A1, A26.

Sessums, K. (1995, May). Maximum Meg. *Vanity Fair,* 104–111.

Sexton, J. (1993, September 21). Brave's second wind blows everyone away. *San Jose Mercury News,* p. C5.

Shachtman, T. (1995). *The inarticulate society: Eloquence and culture in America.* New York: Free Press.

Shackelford, S., Wood, W., & Worchel, S. (1996). Behavioral styles and the influence of women in mixed-sex groups. *Social Psychology, 59,* 284–293.

Shafir, E. (1993). Choosing versus rejecting: Why some options are both better and worse than others. *Memory and Cognition, 21,* 546–556.

Shenk, D. (1997). *Data smog: Surviving the data glut.* New York: HarperCollins.

Shenk, D. (1999). The end of patience. In D. Shenk (Ed.), *The end of patience: Cautionary notes on the information revolution.* Bloomington, IN: Indiana University press.

Shepela, S. T., & Levesque, L. L. (1998). Poisoned waters: Sexual harassment and the college climate. *Sex Roles, 38,* 589–611.

Sheridan, C., & King, R. (1972). Obedience to authority with an authentic victim. *Proceedings of the 80th Annual Convention: American Psychological Association, 7,* 165–166.

Sherif, M., Sherif, C., & Nebergall, R. (1965). *Attitude and attitude change: The social judgment-involvement approach.* Philadelphia: Saunders.

Sherman, S., & Lee, J. (1997, May 12). Levi's: As ye sew, so shall ye reap. *Fortune,* 104–111.

Shevlin, J. (1994). Wife abuse: Its magnitude and one jurisdiction's response. In A. Taylor & J. Miller (Eds.), *Conflict and gender.* Cresskill, NJ: Hampton Press.

Shimanoff, S. (1992). Group interaction via communication rules. In R. Cathcart & L. Samovar (Eds.), *Small group communication: A reader.* Dubuque, IA: Wm. C. Brown.

Shimanoff, S., & Jenkins, M. (1996). Leadership and gender: Challenging assumptions and recognizing resources. In R. Cathcart, L. Samovar, & L. Henman (Eds.), *Small group communication: Theory and practice.* Dubuque, IA: Brown & Benchmark.

Shimanoff, S. B. (1980). *Communication rule: Theory and research.* Beverly Hills, CA: Sage.

Shirley, D. (1997). *Managing creativity: Inventing, developing, and producing innovative products.* Retrieved from http://www.managingcreativity.com

Sillars, A. L., Coletti, S. G., Parry, D., & Rogers, M. A. (1982). Coding verbal conflict tactics: Nonverbal and perceptual correlates of the "avoidance-distributive-integrative" distinction. *Human Communication Research, 9,* 83–95.

Sillars, M. L., Weisberg, J., Burggraf, C. S., & Zietlow, P. H. (1990). Communication and understanding revisited: Married couples understanding and recall of conversations. *Communication Research, 17,* 500–532.

Silva, J. (1982). *The current status of applied sport psychology: A national survey.* Paper presented at the American Alliance for Health, Physical Education, Recreation, and Dance Convention, Houston, TX.

Silver, M., & Perry, J. (1999, March 22). Hooked on instant messages. *U.S. News & World Report,* 57–58.

Simons, D. J., & Levins, D. T. (1998). Failure to detect changes to people during a real-world interaction. *Psychonomic Bulletin & Review, 5,* 644–649.

Simons, L., & Zielenziger, M. (1996, March 3). Culture clash dims U.S. future in Asia. *San Jose Mercury News,* pp. A1, A22.

Singer, M. (1987). *Intercultural communication: A perceptual approach.* Englewood Cliffs, NJ: Prentice-Hall.

Singer, M. T., & Lalich, J. (1995). *Cults in our midst: The hidden menace in our everyday lives.* San Francisco: Jossey-Bass.

Singh, D. (1993). Adaptive significance of female physical attractiveness: Role of waist-to-hip ratio. *Journal of Personality and Social Psychiatry, 65,* 293–307.

Sisk, H. (1997). Dirty hands across America. In L. G. Schnoor (Ed.), *Winning orations.* Northfield, MN: Interstate Oratorical Association.

Sklaroff, S. (1999, March 22). E-mail nation. *U.S. News & World Report,* 54–55.

Sloan, A. (1998, June 6). Chainsaw massacre. *Newsweek,* p. 62.

Sloan, W., Stovall, J., & Startt, J. (1993). *Media in America: A history.* Scottsdale, AZ: Publishing Horizons.

Smedes, L. B. (1984). *Forgive and forget: Healing the hurts we don't deserve.* New York: Harper & Row.

Smith, D. (1997). Women and leadership. In P. Northouse (Ed.), *Leadership: Theory and practice.* Thousand Oaks, CA: Sage.

Smith, D., Gier, J., & Willis, F. (1982). Interpersonal touch and compliance with a marketing request. *Basic and Applied Social Psychology, 3,* 35–38.

Smith, M. J. (1982). *Persuasion and human interaction: A review and critique of social influence theories.* Belmont, CA: Wadsworth.

Smith, P., & Bond, M. (1994). *Social psychology across cultures: Analysis and perspective.* Boston: Allyn & Bacon.

Smith, P., Dugan, S., & Trompenaars, F. (1996). National culture and the values of organizational employees. *Journal of Cross-Cultural Psychology, 27,* 231–264.

Snyder, M., & Uranowitz, S. (1978). Reconstructing the past: Some cognitive consequences of person perception. *Journal of Personality and Social Psychology, 36,* 941–950.

Something about Meg. (1998, July). *Good Housekeeping,* p. 98.

Sommer, R., Barnes, C. E., & Murray, R. R. (1992). Alcohol consumption, alcohol abuse, personality and female perpetrated spouse abuse. *Journal of Personality and Individual Differences, 13,* 1315–1323.

Sorensen, S. (1981, May). *Grouphate.* Paper presented at the International Communication Association, Minneapolis, MN.

Sorenson, S. B., & Telles, C. A. (1991). Self-reports of spousal violence in a Mexican-American and Non-Hispanic White population. *Violence and Victims, 6,* 3–15.

Spencer, L., & Spencer, S. (1993). *Competence at work: Models for superior performance.* New York: Wiley.

Spencer, T. (1994). Transforming relationships through ordinary talk. In S. Duck (Ed.), *Understanding relationship processes, 4: Dynamics of relationships.* Thousand Oaks, CA: Sage.

Spitzberg, B., & Cupach, W. (1989). *Handbook of interpersonal competence research.* New York: Springer-Verlag.

Spitzberg, B., & Hecht, M. (1984). A component model of relational competence. *Human Communication Research, 10,* 575–599.

Springen, K. (1997, June 3). The biology of beauty. *Newsweek,* pp. 61–66.

Staff, N. (1988, February 15). Love in the office. *Newsweek,* pp. 48–52.

Stafford, L., & Daly, J. A. (1984). Conversational memory: The effects of recall and memory expectations on remembrances of natural conversations. *Human Communication Research, 10,* 379–402.

Stanford Institute for the Quantitative Study of Society. (2000). *SIQSS Internet Study.* Retrieved from http://www.stanford.edu/group/siqss/Press_Release/InternetStudy.html.

Starr, T. (1991). *The natural inferiority of women: Outrageous pronouncements by misguided males.* New York: Poseidon Press.

Steelman, B. (1999, September 16). The curse of free speech. *Santa Cruz Sentinel,* p. A1.

Steffins, S. (2001, May 12). Cupid in the cubicles. *San Jose Mercury News,* pp. 1F, 4F.

Steil, L. K. (1980, May 26). Secrets of being a better listener. *U.S. News & World Report,* 65.

Stephan, W. G., & Stephan, C. W. (1996). *Intergroup relations.* Boulder, CO: Westview Press.

Sternberg, R. J. (1986). A triangular theory of love. *Psychological Review, 93*, 119–135.

Sternberg, R. J. (1988). *The triangle of love.* New York: Basic Books.

Sternberg, R. J. (1997). Construct validation of a triangular love scale. *European Journal of Social Psychology, 27*, 313–335.

Stets, J. E., & Henderson, D. A. (1991). Contextual factors surrounding a conflict resolution while dating: Results from a national study. *Family Relations, 40*, 20–36.

Steward, A., & Lupfer, M. (1987). Touching as teaching: The effect of touch on students' perceptions and performing. *Journal of Applied Psychology, 17*, 800–809.

Stewart, E. C., & Bennett, M. J. (1991). *American cultural patterns: A cross-cultural perspective.* Yarmouth, ME: Intercultural Press.

Stewart, L., Cooper, P., Stewart, A., & Friedley, S. A. (1996). *Communication and gender.* Scottsdale, AZ: Gorsuch Scarisbrick.

Stewart, P. (2001, December 21). Researchers uncover world's funniest joke. *Santa Cruz Sentinel*, p. A12.

Stiff, J., Dillard, I., Somera, H., & Sleight, C. (1988). Empathy, communication, and prosocial behavior. *Communication Monographs, 55*, 198–213.

Stoll, C. (1995). *Silicon snake oil: Second thoughts on the information highway.* New York: Anchor Books.

Stone, D., Patton, B., & Heen, S. (1999). *Difficult conversations: How to discuss what matters most.* New York: Viking Press.

Stone, J., Aronson, E., Crain, A. L., Winslow, M. P., & Fried, C. B. (1994). Inducing hypocrisy as a means of encouraging young adults to use condoms. *Personality and Social Psychology Bulletin, 20*, 116–128.

Stone, J., Cooper, J., Wiegard, A. W., & Aronson, E. (1997). When exemplification fails: Hypocrisy and the motive for self-integrity. *Journal of Personality and Social Psychology, 72*, 54–65.

Strack, F., Martin, L. L., & Stepper, S. (1988). Inhibiting and facilitating conditions of facial expressions: A non-obtrusive test of the facial feedback hypothesis. *Journal of Personality & Social Psychology, 54*, 768–777.

Straus, M., & Gelles, R. (1990). *Physical violence in American families.* New Brunswick, NJ: Transaction Publishers.

Straus, M., & Kantor, G. F. (1994, July 19). *Change in spousal assault rates from 1975 to 1992: A comparison of three national surveys in the United States.* Paper presented at the Thirteenth World Congress of Sociology, Bielefeld, Germany.

Straus, M. A. (1989). *Assaults by wives on husbands: Implications for primary prevention of marital violence.* Paper presented at 1989 Meeting of the American Society of Criminology.

Straus, M. A. (1993). Husband abuse and the woman offender are important problems. In R. J. Gelles & D. Loseke (Eds.), *Current controversies in family violence.* Beverly Hills, CA: Sage.

Straus, M. A., & Sweet, S. (1992). Verbal/symbolic aggression in couples: Incidence rates and relationship to personal characteristics. *Journal of Marriage and the Family, 54*, 346–357.

Street, M. (1997). Groupthink: An examination of theoretical issues, implications, and future research suggestions. *Small Group Research, 28*, 72–93.

Strong, W., & Cook, J. (1990). *Persuasion: Strategies for speakers.* Dubuque, IA: Kendall/Hunt.

Sudweeks, S., Gudykunst, W., Ting-Toomey, S., & Nishida, T. (1990). Developmental themes in Japanese–North American relationships. *International Journal of Intercultural Relations, 14*, 207–233.

Sugarmann, J. (2001). *Every handgun is aimed at you: The case for banning handguns.* New York: The New Press.

Sulek, J. P (2000, December 3). Harris latest in hit list of women ambushed for their appearance. *San Jose Mercury News*, p. 17A.

Sunstrom, J. (1997). A child's last hope. *Winning Orations*, 151–154.

Supercomputers can perform trillions of calculations. (2001, August 16). *San Jose Mercury News*, p. 1B.

Superville, D. (2001, June 19). Many languages facing extinction. *The Herald*, pp. A1, A10.

Survey: Violence in the workplace a universal issue. (1998, July 20). *San Jose Mercury News*, p. A12.

Suter, E. A. (1994). Guns in the medical literature—a failure of peer review. *Journal of the American Medical Association.*

Sutton, R. I., & Hargadon, A. (1996). Brainstorming groups in context: Effectiveness in a product design firm. *Administrative Science Quarterly, 41*, 685–718.

Svoren, Velimir. (1998, January 11). Letters. *Time.*

Swain, S. (1989). Covert intimacy in men's friendships: Closeness in men's friendships. In B. J. Risman & P. Schwartz (Eds.), *Gender in intimate relationships: A microcultural approach.* Belmont, CA: Wadsworth.

Sypher, B., & Sypher, H. (1984). Seeing ourselves as others see us. *Communication Rewards, 11*, 97–115.

Tal, K. (1994, June 10). VWAR-L as a network community. *The Network Observer, 1*, 6.

Talbot, M. M. (1998). *Language and gender: An introduction.* Malden, MA: Blackwell.

Tamosaitis, N. (1995). *Net.sex.* Emerville, CA: Ziff-Davis Press.

Tang, J. (1997). The Model Minority thesis revisited: (Counter)evidence from the science and engineering fields. *Journal of Applied Behavioral Science, 33*, 291–314.

Tannen, D. (1979). Ethnicity as conversational style. In *Working Papers in Sociolinguistics (No. 55).* Austin, TX: Southwest Educational Development Laboratory.

Tannen, D. (1990). *You just don't understand: Women and men in conversation.* New York: Ballantine.

Tannen, D. (1994). *Talking from 9 to 5.* New York: Avon.

Tannen, D. (1998). *The argument culture: Moving from debate to dialogue.* New York: Random House.

Taps, J., & Martin, P. (1990). Gender composition, attributional accounts, and women's influence and likability in task groups. *Small Group Research, 4*, 471–491.

Taraban, C. B., Hendrick, S. S., & Hendrick, C. (1998). In P. A. Andersen & L. K. Guerrero (Eds.), *Handbook of communication and emotion,* New York: Academic Press.

Tavris, C. (1989). *Anger: The misunderstood emotion.* New York: Simon & Schuster.

Tavris, C. (1992). *The mismeasure of women.* New York: Simon & Schuster.

Taylor, A. (2000). Drowsy driving: A deadly epidemic. In L. Schnoor & B. Wickelgren (Eds.), *Winning Orations.* Mankato, MN: Interstate Oratorical Association.

Tebbel, J. (1987). *Between covers: The rise and transformation of American book publishing.* New York: Oxford University Press.

Telecommuting boosted in 1998 by Internet and economy. (1999). *Working Moms' Refuge.* Retrieved from http://www.momsrefuge.com/telecommute/survey.html.

Teubner, G. (2002, November 9). *The emergence of control in the flattened organizational structure: Toward a theory of the spiral of control following organizational change.* Paper presented at the National Communication Association Conference, Seattle, WA.

The dress-down revolution. (1996, May 12). *San Jose Mercury News,* p. A17.

The ethics of American youth. (2000, October 16). Josephson Institute of Ethics. Retrieved from http://www.Josephson institute.org.

The ethics of American youth: A warning and a call to action. (1990). Marina Del Rey, CA: The Josephson Institute of Ethics.

The gate debate: How you voted. (1997, February 28). *USA Weekend,* 19.

The perils of geek speak. (1998, December 21). *Newsweek,* p. 77.

Thomas, J. (1998, November 8). A state ready to wrestle with the future. *San Jose Mercury News,* p. P3.

Thomas, K., & Velthouse, B. (1990). Cognitive elements of empowerment: An "interpretive" model of intrinsic task motivation. *Academy of Management Review, 15,* 666–681.

Thomma, S. (1996, February 4). Nostalgia for '50s surfaces. *Philadelphia Inquirer,* p. B1.

Thompson, E. (1960). An experimental investigation of the relative effectiveness of organization structure in oral communication. *Southern Speech Journal, 26,* 59–69.

Thompson, E. H. (1991). The maleness of violence in dating relationships: An appraisal of stereotypes. *Sex Roles, 24,* 261–278.

Thompson, J. (1986, April). Larger than life: Many women see themselves as roundfaced and pudgy, even when no one else does. *Psychology Today,* 39–44.

Thourlby, W. (1978). *You are what you wear.* New York: New American Library.

Ting-Toomey, S. (1983). An analysis of verbal communication patterns in high and low marital adjustment groups. *Human Communication Research, 9,* 306–319.

Ting-Toomey, S., Gao, G., Yang, Z., Trubisky, P., Kim, H., Lin, S., & Nishida, T. (1991). Culture, face maintenance, and styles of handling interpersonal conflict: A study in five cultures. *International Journal of Conflict Management, 2,* 275–296.

Tolchin, M., & Tolchin, S. (1973). *Clout: Woman power and politics.* New York: Coward, McCann & Georghepon.

Tolhuizen, J. H. (1989). Communication strategies for intensifying dating relationships: Identification, use and structure. *Journal of Social and Personal Relationships, 6,* 413–434.

Tomb, G. (1999, August 2). Boonters losing the lingo. *San Jose Mercury News,* pp. 1A, 12A.

Torbiorn, I. (1982). *Living abroad.* New York: John Wiley.

Toulmin, S., Rieke, R., & Janik, A. (1979). An introduction to reasoning. New York: Macmillan.

Townsend, P. (1996, April 13). Face the truth. *Santa Cruz Sentinel,* p. D1.

Tran, Q. G. (2001, August 16). Black men in professions earn less than Whites. *San Jose Mercury News,* pp. 1C, 4C.

Trask, R. L. (1999). *Language: The basics.* New York: Routledge.

Trenholm, S., & Jensen, A. (1988). *Interpersonal communication.* Belmont, CA: Wadsworth.

Triandis, H. (1975). Values, attitude, and interpersonal behavior. In R. Bushlin, S. Bochnerm, & W. Lonner (Eds.), *Cross-cultural perspective on learning.* New York: Wiley.

Triandis, H. (1990). Cross-cultural studies of individualism and collectiveness. In J. Berman (Ed.), *Cross-cultural perspective.* Lincoln, NE: University of Nebraska Press.

Triandis, H. (1995). *Individualism and collectiveness.* Boulder, CO: Westview Press.

Trippett, F. (1981, July 13). Why so much is beyond words. *Time,* pp. 71–72.

Tropman, J. (1988). *Meetings: How to make them work for you.* New York: Van Nostrand Reinhold.

Tropman, J. (1996). *Making meetings work: Achieving high quality group decisions.* Thousand Oaks, CA: Sage.

Trounstine, P. (1998, November 20). Democrats, GOP battle in a tale of two inquiries. *San Jose Mercury News,* p. A1.

Tucker, P., & Aron, A. (1993). Passionate love and marital satisfaction at key transition points in the family life cycle. *Journal of Social and Clinical Psychology, 12,* 135–147.

Turow, J. (1999). *Media today: An introduction to mass communication.* Boston: Houghton Mifflin.

Tutzauer, F., & Roloff, M. (1988). Communication processes leading to integrative agreements: Three paths to joint benefits. *Communication Research, 5,* 360–380.

Tziner, A., & Eden, D. (1985). Effects of crew composition on crew performance: Does the whole equal the sum of the parts? *Journal of Applied Psychology, 70,* 85–93.

U.S. Bureau of the Census (1998). *Statistical abstract of the United States.* Washington, DC: U.S. Government Printing Office.

U.S. Department of Justice, Bureau of Justice Statistics. (1994). *Special report: Murder in families.* Washington, DC: U. S. Department of Justice.

U.S. Department of Justice, Bureau of Justice Statistics. (1998, March). Violence by intimates. Report NCJ-167237. Retrieved from http://www.ojp.usodj.gov/bjs.

U.S. Department of Labor. (1991). *Skills and the new economy.* Washington, DC: U.S. Government Printing Office.

Understanding culture: Don't stare at a Navajo. (1974, June). *Psychology Today,* 107.

Unger, R., & Crawford, M. (1992). *Women and gender: A feminist psychology.* New York: McGraw-Hill.

Unseth, A. (2001). Child warriors: Pawns in international warfare. In L. Schnoor & B. Wickelgren (Eds.), *Winning orations.* Mankato, MN: Interstate Oratorical Association.

Ury, W. (1993). *Getting past no: Negotiating your way from confrontation to cooperation.* New York: Bantam.

Van der Heijden, A. H. C. (1991). *Selective attention in vision.* New York: Routledge.

Van Oostrum, J., & Rabbie, J. (1995). Intergroup competition and cooperation within autocratic and democratic management regimes. *Small Group Research, 26,* 269–295.

Vangelisti, A., Knapp, M., & Daly, J. (1990). Conversational narcissism. *Communication Monographs, 57,* 251–274.

Veitch, M. (1997, December 8). Data overload causing addiction—Reuters. Retrieved from http://www.zdnet.co.uk/news/news1/ns-3381.html.

Ventura: Keillor book "cheating." (1999, February 6). *San Jose Mercury News,* p. A2.

Verderber, R., Elder, A., & Weiler, E. (1976). *A study of communication time usage among college students.* Unpublished manuscript, University of Cincinnati.

Vitanza, S. (1991). *The relationship of stress, cognitive appraisal and dating violence.* Unpublished master's thesis, University of North Texas, Denton, TX.

Vitanza, S., & Marshall, L. (1993). *Dimensions of dating violence, gender and personal characteristics.* Unpublished manuscript.

Vobejda, B. (1998, July 27). Habit to cohabit increasing. *San Jose Mercury News,* p. A3.

Volkema, R. J., & Bergmann, T. J. (1989). Interpersonal conflict at work: An analysis of behavioral responses. *Human Relations, 42,* 757–770.

Wachtel, P. (1983). *The poverty of affluence: A psychological portrait of the American way of life.* New York: Free Press.

Wade, C., & Tavris, C. (1990). *Psychology.* New York: HarperCollins.

Wade, C., & Tavris, C. (1999). *Invitation to psychology.* New York: Longman.

Wald, M. (1997, July 18). Highway violence surges with more traffic, fewer cops. *Santa Cruz Sentinel,* p. A1.

Waldner-Haugrud, L. K., Gratch, L. V., & Magruder, B. (1997). Victimization and perpetration rates of violence in gay and lesbian relationships: Gender issues explored. *Violence and Victims, 12,* 173–184.

Walker, L. (1999). Psychology and domestic violence around the world. *American Psychologist, 54,* 21–29.

Wallace, P. (1999). *The psychology of the Internet.* New York: Cambridge University Press.

Waller, W., & Hill, R. (1951). *The family: A dynamic interpretation.* New York: Dryden.

Wallerstein, J., & Blakeslee, S. (1995). *The good marriage: How and why love lasts.* Boston: Houghton Mifflin.

Walsh, M. W. (2000, November 27). Many workers barred from trip to bathroom. *San Jose Mercury News,* p. 6E.

Walters, E., & Kendler, K. (1995). Anorexia nervosa and anorexia-like syndromes in population-based female twin samples. *American Journal of Psychiatry, 152,* 64–71.

Walther, J. B., & Tidwell, L. C. (1995). Nonverbal cues in computer-mediated communication, and the effect of chronemics on relational communication. *Journal of Organizational Computing, 5,* 355–378.

Watzlawick P., Beavin, J., & Jackson, D. (1967). *Pragmatics of human communication.* New York: W. W. Norton.

Wayne, M. (1974). The meaning of silence in conversations in three cultures. In *Patterns of communication in and out of Japan.* Tokyo: ICU Communication Department.

WB lays down law on haircuts. (2000, June 8). *San Jose Mercury News,* p. 2A.

We met at the office. (1999, February 14). *Parade,* 25.

Webb, T. (1998, October). Obesity in kids at epidemic level. *San Jose Mercury News,* p. A11.

Weber, S. N. (1994). The need to be: The socio-cultural significance of black language. In L. A. Samovar & R. E. Porter (Eds.), *Intercultural communication: A reader.* Belmont, CA: Wadsworth.

Weber, T. (2000, September 26). E-mails too e-motional? Let the computer decide. *Santa Cruz Sentinel,* pp. A1, A5.

Webster, E. (1964). *Decision making in the employment interview.* Montreal, Canada: Industrial Relations Center, McGill University Press.

Weick, K. (1990). The vulnerable system: An analysis of the Tenerife air disaster. *Journal of Management, 16,* 571–593.

Weiner, B., Graham, S., Peter, D., & Zmuidinas, M. (1991). Public confession and forgiveness. *Journal of Personality, 59,* 281–312.

Weingarten, G. (1994, September 27). I'm absolutely sure: You need a marshmallow enema. *San Jose Mercury News,* p. B7.

Wener, R., Frazier, W., & Farberstein, J. (1987, June). Building better jails. *Psychology Today,* 40–49.

Wetzel, P. (1988). Are "powerless" communication strategies the Japanese norm? *Language in Society, 17,* 555–564.

What dictionaries say. (1999, January 30). *San Jose Mercury News,* p. A19.

White, D. (1998, December 30). Stupid things really said by famous people. *San Jose Mercury News,* p. E5.

White, J. E. (1997, May 5). I'm just who I am. *Time,* pp. 32–36.

White, M. M. (2002, September 4). Women to overtake men in management. *Santa Cruz Sentinel,* p. D5.

Whitkin, R. (1987, September 19). FAA says Delta had poor policies on crew training. *The New York Times,* p. 1.

Whorf, B. (1956). *Language, thought, and reality.* (J. B. Carroll, Ed.). Cambridge, MA: MIT Press.

Wilgoren, J. (2002, October 31). Memorial for Wellstone assumes spirit of rally. *The New York Times.* Retrieved from http://www.nytimes.com/2002/10/30/politics/30WELL.html?todaysheadlines.

Williams, E. (1995). Margarine. *Winning Orations,* 1–2.

Williams, L. (1999, January 15). Study shows rising diversity of Net users. *San Jose Mercury News,* p. A15.

Williams, R., & Williams, V. (1993). *Anger kills.* New York: Random House.

Wilmot, W. W., & Hocker, J. L. (2001). *Interpersonal conflict.* New York: McGraw-Hill.

Wilson, L. R. (1998, January 1). The new frontier: Cyberspace and the telecosm. *Vital Speeches, 64,* 182–186.

Wilson, M. (1992). Say "AHA" to virtual reality. In L. G. Schnoor (Ed.), *Winning orations.* Northfield, MN: Interstate Oratorical Association.

Winch, P. (1959). Nature and convention. *Proceedings of the Aristotelian Society, 60,* 242.

Winsor, J. L., Curtis, D. B., & Stephens, R. D. (1997). National preferences in business and communication education: An update. *Journal of the Association for Communication Administration, 3,* 170–179.

Wiseman, R., Sanders, J., Congalton, J., Gass, R., Sueda, K., & Ruiqing, D. (1995). A cross-cultural analysis of compliance gaining: China, Japan, and the United States. *Intercultural Communication Studies, 1,* 1–18.

Wiseman, R. (2003). LaughLab. Retrievel from www.laughlab.co.uk/home.html.

Witte, K. (1998). In P. A. Andersen & L. K. Guerrero (Eds.), *Handbook of communication and emotion.* New York: Academic Press.

Witte, K., & Allen, M. (1996, November). *When do scare tactics work? A meta-analysis of fear appeals.* Paper presented at the annual meeting of the Speech Communication Association, San Diego, CA.

Witteman, H. (1993). The interface between sexual harassment and organizational romance. In Kreps, G. (Ed.), *Sexual harassment: Communication implications*. Cresskill, NJ: Hampton Press.

Wolf, N. (1994). *Fire with fire: The new female power and how to use it*. New York: Fawcett Columbine.

Wolf, S. (1979). Behavioral style and group cohesiveness as sources of minority influence. *European Journal of Social Psychology, 9*, 381–395.

Wolfram, W., & Fasold, R. W. (1974). *The study of social dialects in American English*. Englewood Cliffs, NJ: Prentice-Hall.

Wolkomir, R., & Wolkomir, J. (1990, February). How to make smart choices. *Reader's Digest*, pp. 27–32.

Wolvin, A. (1984). Meeting the communication needs of the adult learners. *Communication Education, 33*, 267–271.

Wolvin, A., & Coakley, C. (1996). *Listening*. Dubuque, IA: Brown & Benchmark.

Wolvin, A., & Corley, D. (1984). The technical speech communication course: A view from the field. *Association for Communication Administration Bulletin, 49*, 83–91.

Woman angry over online time attacked computer, cops say. (1999, July 1). *San Jose Mercury News*, p. A11.

Women can be violent, too, in relationships. (1998, August 4). *San Jose Mercury News*, p. F1.

Women in the House. (1997, June 16). *Time*, p. 20.

Wood, A. F., & Smith, M. J. (2001). *Online communication: Linking technology, identity, and culture*. Mahwah, NJ: Lawrence Erlbaum.

Wood, J. (1994). *Gendered lives: Communication, gender, and culture*. Belmont, CA: Wadsworth.

Wood, J. (1996). She says/he says; communication, caring, and conflict in heterosexual relationships. In J. Wood (Ed.), *Gendered relationships*. Mountain View, CA: Mayfield.

Wood, J. (1997). *Communication theories in action: An introduction*. Belmont, CA: Wadsworth.

Wood, J. T. (2000). *Relational communication: Continuity and change in personal relationships*. Belmont, CA: Wadworth.

Wood, J. T., & Dindia, K. (1998). What's the difference? A dialogue about differences and similarities between women and men. In D. J. Canary & K. Dindia (Eds.), *Sex differences and similarities in communication*. Mahwah, NJ: Lawrence Erlbaum.

Woodman, T. (1991). *The role of forgiveness in marital adjustment*. Unpublished doctoral dissertation, Fuller Graduate School of Psychology, Pasadena, CA.

Workers lack verbal skills, survey finds. (1992, September 21). *San Jose Mercury News*, p. A2.

Wright, R. (1993, July 1). Women are taking center stage in the worldwide political arena. *San Jose Mercury News*, p. A10.

Wright, S. (2002). The Freeman Institute. Retrieved from http://www.freemaninstitute.com/Wright.html.

Wronge, Y., & Fernandez, L. (2000, December 19). Teenagers define "sex" too narrowly, study finds. *San Jose Mercury News*, pp. 1A, 14A.

Wurman, R. (1989). *Information anxiety*. New York: Doubleday.

Yaukey, J. (2000, July 4). Your e-mail can get you fired. *San Jose Mercury News*, p. 3C.

Yelsma, P., & Athappilly, K. (1988). Marital satisfaction and communication practices: Comparisons among Indian and American couples. *Journal of Comparative Family Studies, 19*, 37–54.

Yerby, J., & Buerkel-Rothfuss, N. L. (1982, November). *Communication patterns, contradictions, and family functions*. Paper presented at the meeting of the Speech Communication Association, Louisville, KY.

Yingling, J. (1994). Constituting friendships in talk and metatalk. *Journal of Social and Personal Relationships, 11*, 411–426.

Yoshitake, T. (1977). A Chinese stereotypic image of Japan and its people. *Communication, 6*, 18–28.

Young, K. S. (1996, August 10). *Pathological Internet use: The emergence of a new clinical disorder*. American Psychological Association's 104th Annual Convention, Toronto, Canada. Retrieved from http://www.pitt.edu/~ksy/Welcome.html.

Yu, X. (1997). The Chinese "nature" perspective on mao-dun (conflict) and mao-dun resolution strategies: A qualitative investigation. *Intercultural Communication Studies, 7*, 63–82.

Zakahi, W. R., & Duran, R. L. (1984). Attraction, communicative competence, and communication satisfaction. *Communication Research Reports, 1*, 54–57.

Zander, A. (1982). The psychology of removing group members and recruiting new ones. *Human Relations, 29*, 1–8.

Zillmann, D. (1993). Mental control of angry aggression. In Wegner, D., & Pennebaker, J. (Eds.), *Handbook of mental control (Vol. 5)*. Englewood Cliffs, NJ: Prentice-Hall.

Zimbardo, P. (1992). *Psychology and life*. New York: HarperCollins.

Zormeier, S. M., & Samovar, L. A. (2000). Language as a mirror of reality: Mexican American proverbs. In L. A. Samovar & R. E. Porter (Eds.), *Intercultural communication: A reader*. Belmont, CA: Wadsworth.

Zuckerman, L. (1999, April 17). Words go right to the brain, but can they stir the heart? *The New York Times*, p. 9.

Zurawik, D. (1998, August 18). On all-news cable channels, no news is bad news for the public. *San Jose Mercury News*, p. A8.

CREDITS

INDEX